A Companion to Nineteenth-Century Britain

A COMPANION TO NINETEENTH-CENTURY BRITAIN

Edited by

Chris Williams

THE
HISTORICAL
ASSOCIATION
THE VOICE FOR HISTORY

© 2004 by Blackwell Publishing Ltd

350 Main Street, Malden, MA 02148-5020, USA
108, Cowley Road, Oxford OX4 1JF, UK
550 Swanston Street, Carlton South, Melbourne, Victoria 3053, Australia

The right of Chris Williams to be identified as the Author of the Editorial Material in this Work has been asserted in accordance with the UK Copyright, Designs and Patents Act 1988.

First published 2004 by Blackwell Publishing Ltd

Library of Congress Cataloging-in-Publication Data

A companion to nineteenth-century Britain / edited by Chris Williams.
    p. cm. – (Blackwell companions to British history)
   Includes bibliographical references and index.
   ISBN 0-631-22579-X (alk. paper)
    1. Great Britain – History – 19th century – Handbooks, manuals, etc. 2. Great Britain – Civilization – 19th century – Handbooks, manuals, etc. I. Williams, Chris, 1963– II. Title.
III. Series.

DA530.C76 2004
941.081 – dc22

2003021511

A catalogue record for this title is available from the British Library.

Set in 10 on 12 pt Galliard
by SNP Best-set Typesetter Ltd., Hong Kong
Printed and bound in the United Kingdom
by TJ International Ltd, Padstow, Cornwall

For further information on
Blackwell Publishing, visit our website:
http://www.blackwellpublishing.com

BLACKWELL COMPANIONS TO BRITISH HISTORY
Published in association with The Historical Association

This series provides sophisticated and authoritative overviews of the scholarship that has shaped our current understanding of British history. Each volume comprises up to forty concise essays written by individual scholars within their area of specialization. The aim of each contribution is to synthesize the current state of scholarship from a variety of historical perspectives and to provide a statement on where the field is heading. The essays are written in a clear, provocative and lively manner, designed for an international audience of scholars, students and general readers.

The *Blackwell Companions to British History* is a cornerstone of Blackwell's overarching Companions to History series, covering European, American and World History.

Published

A Companion to Roman Britain
Edited by Malcolm Todd

A Companion to Britain in the Later Middle Ages
Edited by S. H. Rigby

A Companion to Tudor Britain
Edited by Robert Tittler and Norman Jones

A Companion to Stuart Britain
Edited by Barry Coward

A Companion to Eighteenth-Century Britain
Edited by H. T. Dickinson

A Companion to Nineteenth-Century Britain
Edited by Chris Williams

A Companion to Early Twentieth-Century Britain
Edited by Chris Wrigley

In preparation
A Companion to Britain in the Early Middle Ages
Edited by Pauline Stafford

A Companion to Contemporary Britain
Edited by Paul Addison and Harriet Jones

The **Historical Association** is the voice for history. Since 1906 it has been bringing together people who share an interest in, and love for the past. It aims to further the study of teaching of history at all levels. Membership is open to everyone: teacher and student, amateur and professional. Membership offers a range of journals, activities and other benefits. Full details are available from The Historical Association, 59a Kennington Park Road, London SE11 4JH, enquiry@history.org.uk, www.history.org.uk.

Other Blackwell History Companions include:

BLACKWELL COMPANIONS TO HISTORY
Published
A Companion to Western Historical Thought
Edited by Lloyd Kramer and Sarah Maza

A Companion to Gender History
Edited by Teresa A. Meade and Merry E. Wiesner-Hanks

BLACKWELL COMPANIONS TO EUROPEAN HISTORY
Published
A Companion to the Worlds of the Renaissance
Edited by Guido Ruggiero

A Companion to the Reformation World
Edited by R. Po-chia Hsia

In preparation
A Companion to Europe Since 1945
Edited by Klaus Larres

A Companion to Europe 1900–1945
Edited by Gordon Martel

BLACKWELL COMPANIONS TO AMERICAN HISTORY
Published
A Companion to the American Revolution
Edited by Jack P. Greene and J. R. Pole

A Companion to 19th-Century America
Edited by William L. Barney

A Companion to the American South
Edited by John B. Boles

A Companion to American Indian History
Edited by Philip J. Deloria and Neal Salisbury

A Companion to American Women's History
Edited by Nancy A. Hewitt

A Companion to Post-1945 America
Edited by Jean-Christophe Agnew and Roy Rosenzweig

A Companion to the Vietnam War
Edited by Marilyn B. Young and Robert Buzzanco

A Companion to Colonial America
Edited by Daniel Vickers

A Companion to American Foreign Relations
Edited by Robert D. Schulzinger

A Companion to 20th-Century America
Edited by Stephen J. Whitfield

A Companion to the American West
Edited by William Deverell

BLACKWELL COMPANIONS TO WORLD HISTORY
In preparation
A Companion to the History of the Middle East
Edited by Youssef M. Choueiri

Contents

Maps, Diagrams and Tables

Contributors

William J. Ashworth is Senior Lecturer in the School of History at the University of Liverpool. He is the author of *Customs and Excise: Trade, Production and Consumption in England 1640–1845* (2003).

Gregory Claeys is Professor of the History of Political Thought at Royal Holloway, University of London. His current research focuses on British utopianism, *c*.1700–1950.

Matthew Cragoe is Reader in Modern British History at the University of Hertfordshire. His publications include *An Anglican Aristocracy: The Moral Economy of the Landed Estate in Carmarthenshire, 1832–95* (1996) and (with Nigel Aston) *Anticlericalism in Britain 1500–1900* (2000).

Andy Croll is Principal Lecturer in History at the University of Glamorgan. Author of *Civilizing the Urban: Popular Culture, Class and the Urban Experience, Merthyr c.1870–1914* (2000), his research interests focus on various aspects of British urban history.

John R. Davis is Reader in Modern European History and Head of History at Kingston University. His research concerns nineteenth-century British and German history, Anglo-German and international relations. He is currently working on a monograph on the Victorians and Germany.

Shani D'Cruze is Reader in Gender and Women's History, Crewe and Alsager Faculty, Manchester Metropolitan University, and is co-editor of *Gender and History*. She lectures in cultural and gender history and the history of crime. Main publications include *Crimes of Outrage: Sex, Violence and Victorian Working Women* (1998) and *Everyday Violence in Britain, 1850–1950: Gender and Class* (edited, 2000). She is presently working on a monograph which explores gender and cultural constructions of criminality between 1918 and 1965. She also maintains an interest in gender and the history of the family since the eighteenth century and in the twentieth-century history of middle-class culture, leisure and performance.

Philip Gardner is Senior Lecturer in History of Education at the Faculty of Education of the University of Cambridge and a Fellow of St Edmund's College. He has written widely on nineteenth- and twentieth-century educational history and is the author of the prize-winning *The Lost Elementary Schools of Victorian England* (1984). His latest book, *Becoming Teachers: Texts and Testimonies 1907–50* (2003), is co-authored with Peter Cunningham.

Simon Gunn is Reader in History at Leeds Metropolitan University. He has written on the history of the English middle class and on urbanism. His publications include *The*

Public Culture of the Victorian Middle Class (2000) and (co-edited with R. J. Morris) *Identities in Space: Contested Terrains in the Western City since 1850* (2001). He is currently writing on history and cultural theory.

Lesley A. Hall is an archivist at the Wellcome Library for the History and Understanding of Medicine and an Honorary Lecturer in History of Medicine, University College London. She has written extensively on British sexual attitudes and behaviour in the nineteenth and twentieth centuries. Her publications include *Hidden Anxieties: Male Sexuality 1900–1950* (1991); (with Roy Porter) *The Facts of Life: The Creation of Sexual Knowledge in Britain, 1650–1950* (1995); *Sex, Gender and Social Change in Britain since 1880* (2000); and co-edited volumes on *Sexual Cultures in Europe* (1999) and *Venereal Diseases in European Social Context Since 1870* (2001), besides numerous articles, chapters and reviews. She has contributed to a wide variety of television and radio programmes. She is a Fellow of the Royal Historical Society.

Philip Harling is Professor of History at the University of Kentucky. His books include *The Modern British State: An Historical Introduction* (2001) and *The Waning of 'Old Corruptio': The Politics of Economical Reform in Britain, 1779–1846* (1996).

Martin Hewitt is Professor of Victorian Studies at Trinity and All Saints, University of Leeds. His publications include *The Emergence of Stability in the Industrial City: Manchester, 1832–67* (1996) and (with Robert Poole) *The Diaries of Samuel Bamford, 1858–61* (2000).

Anthony Howe is Professor of Modern History at the University of East Anglia. His publications include *The Cotton Masters, 1830–1860* (1984) and *Free Trade and Liberal England, 1846–1946* (1997). His current interests include the international history of free trade and globalization, and he is editing in several volumes *The Letters of Richard Cobden (1804–1865)*.

Jane Humphries is Reader in Economic History at All Souls College, University of Oxford. She has published extensively on gender, the family and the history of women's work. She is currently working on child labour in the British Industrial Revolution including a comparison with child labour in poor countries today.

Aled Jones is Sir John Williams Professor of Welsh History at the University of Wales, Aberystwyth, and is the author of *Press, Politics and Society: A History of Journalism in Wales* (1993); *Powers of the Press: Newspapers, Power and the Public in Nineteenth-Century England* (1996); and (with Bill Jones) *Welsh Reflections: Y Drych and America 1851–2001* (2001).

Christine Kinealy is Professor in History at the University of Central Lancashire. She has published *'This Great Calamity': The Irish Famine 1845–52* (1994), *A Disunited Kingdom? England, Ireland, Scotland and Wales, 1800–1949* (1999); *The Great Irish Famine: Impact, Ideology and Rebellion* (2002); and (both with Gerard MacAtasney) *A Death-Dealing Famine: The Great Hunger In Ireland* (1997) and *The Hidden Famine: Hunger, Poverty and Sectarianism in Belfast, 1850–50* (2000). She is currently undertaking research on the history of the Orange Order in the nineteenth century.

William M. Kuhn is Associate Professor of History at Carthage College in Kenosha, Wisconsin (USA) and is the author of *Democratic Royalism: The Transformation of the British Monarchy, 1861–1914* (1996) and *Henry and Mary Ponsonby: Life at the Court of Queen Victoria* (2002).

E. W. McFarland is Professor of Scottish History at Glasgow Caledonian University. Her publications include: *Protestants First: Orangeism in Nineteenth Century Scotland* (1990); *Ireland and Scotland in the Age of Revolution* (1994); *Scotland and the Great War* (edited with C. M. M. Macdonald, 1999); *John Ferguson 1836–1906: Irish Issues in Scottish Politics* (2003). She is currently working on a history of death, mourning and commemoration in modern Scotland.

Iwan Rhys Morus lectures in the history of science, technology and medicine at

Queen's University, Belfast. He is the author of *Frankenstein's Children* (1998) and editor of *Bodies/Machines* (2002). His current research interests focus on electricity, bodies and popular culture in the nineteenth century.

Douglas M. Peers is currently Associate Professor of History and Associate Dean of the Faculty of Social Sciences, at the University of Calgary. He is the author of *Between Mars and Mammon: Colonial Armies and the Garrison State in Early-Nineteenth-Century India* (1995); co-editor (with David Finkelstein) of *Negotiating India in the Nineteenth Century Media* (2000); co-editor (with Martin Moir and Lynn Zastoupil) of *J. S. Mill's Encounter with India* (1999); and has also published articles on the military in India and their impact on the political, social and medical policies of the Raj and their representations in contemporary print culture. He is currently completing a study of India and Victorian Britain and co-editing *India and the British Empire* with Nandini Gooptu for the Oxford History of the British Empire.

Patricia Pulham is lecturer at Queen Mary, University of London, where she teaches nineteenth-century literature and twentieth-century poetry. She has published work on the writer Vernon Lee, and has forthcoming articles in the journal *Victorian Literature and Culture*, and in the essay collections, *Victorian Women Poets* (*Essays and Studies* series) and *Feminist Forerunners: (New) Womanism and Feminism in the Early Twentieth Century*.

Sarah Richardson is lecturer in history at the University of Warwick. She has recently published (with Kathryn Gleadle) *Women in British Politics, 1760–1860: The Power of the Petticoat* (2000) and (with Anna Clark) *The History of the Suffrage, 1760–1867* (2000).

Heather Shore is lecturer in Social and Cultural History, University of Portsmouth. She is the author of *Artful Dodgers: Youth and Crime in Early Nineteenth Century London* (1999), and has co-authored two collections of essays: (with Pamela Cox) *Becoming Delinquent: European Youth,* *1650–1950* (2002) and (with Tim Hitchcock) *The Streets of London: From the Great Fire to the Great Stink* (2003). She is currently working on her second monograph, a study of the cultural and historical perspectives on the criminal underworld in London since 1700.

Mark A. Smith is lecturer in the Modern History of Christianity at King's College, London. His publications include *Religion in Industrial Society: Oldham and Saddleworth 1740–1865* (1994) and 'A foundation of influence: The Oxford Pastorate and elite recruitment in early twentieth-century Anglican Evangelicalism', in D. W. Lovegrove, ed., *The Rise of the Laity in Evangelical Protestantism* (2002).

Michael S. Smith gained his doctorate in British and European History at the University of California, Riverside. His scholarly interests include popular politics and political culture in the late Hanoverian and early Victorian periods, local, religious, and national identity in modern Britain, intellectual history and printing and culture. He has published on British politics and culture in the era of the French Revolution and has taught at the University of California, Riverside, and California State Polytechnic University, Pomona.

Edward M. Spiers is Professor of Strategic Studies at Leeds University. He has written extensively on British military history, including *Haldane: An Army Reformer* (1980); *The Army and Society, 1815–1914* (1980); *Radical General: Sir George de Lacy Evans, 1787–1870* (1983); *The Late Victorian Army, 1868–1902* (1992) and *Sudan: The Reconquest Reappraised* (edited, 1998).

Noel Thompson is Professor and Head of the Department of History at the University of Wales, Swansea. His most recent books are *The Real Rights of Man: Political Economies for the Working Class, 1775–1850* (1998) and *Left in the Wilderness: The Economics of Democratic Socialism since 1979* (2002).

Michael J. Turner is Reader in Modern British History at the University of Sunderland. His most recent books are

The Age of Unease (2000) and *Pitt the Younger* (2003). His research interests relate mainly to nineteenth-century radicalism and reform movements and he is currently completing a book entitled *Independent Radicalism in Early Victorian Britain*.

Keir Waddington is lecturer in History in the School of History and Archaeology at Cardiff University. He is co-author of *The History of Bethlem* (1997) and author of *Charity and the London Hospitals* (2000) and *Medical Education at St Bartholomew's Hospital* (2003). He is currently working on a history of bovine TB and the public's health in Victorian and Edwardian Britain.

Ian Whyte is Professor of Historical Geography at Lancaster University. He has written widely on the landscape, society and economy of Britain between the seventeenth and nineteenth centuries. He is the author of *Scotland Before the Industrial Revolution: An Economic and Social History 1050–1750* (1995) and *Migration and Society in Britain 1550–1830* (2000).

Chris Williams is Professor of History, Director of the Centre for Modern and Contemporary Wales and Co-Director of the Centre for Border Studies at the University of Glamorgan. He is the author of *Democratic Rhondda: Politics and Society, 1885–1951* (1996), *Capitalism, Community and Conflict: The South Wales Coalfield, 1898–1947* (1998), and editor (with Duncan Tanner and Deian Hopkin) of *The Labour Party in Wales, 1900–2000* (2000).

Michael Winstanley is Senior Lecturer in History at Lancaster University where he teaches modern British, Irish and regional history. He has published extensively on both retail development and rural society and has a particular interest in all aspects of the history of north-west England.

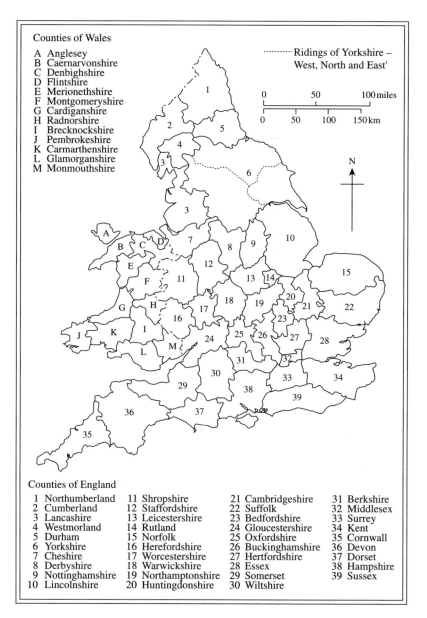

Counties of Wales

A Anglesey
B Caernarvonshire
C Denbighshire
D Flintshire
E Merionethshire
F Montgomeryshire
G Cardiganshire
H Radnorshire
I Brecknockshire
J Pembrokeshire
K Carmarthenshire
L Glamorganshire
M Monmouthshire

·········· Ridings of Yorkshire –
West, North and East'

N

Counties of England

1 Northumberland	11 Shropshire	21 Cambridgeshire	31 Berkshire
2 Cumberland	12 Staffordshire	22 Suffolk	32 Middlesex
3 Lancashire	13 Leicestershire	23 Bedfordshire	33 Surrey
4 Westmorland	14 Rutland	24 Gloucestershire	34 Kent
5 Durham	15 Norfolk	25 Oxfordshire	35 Cornwall
6 Yorkshire	16 Herefordshire	26 Buckinghamshire	36 Devon
7 Cheshire	17 Worcestershire	27 Hertfordshire	37 Dorset
8 Derbyshire	18 Warwickshire	28 Essex	38 Hampshire
9 Nottinghamshire	19 Northamptonshire	29 Somerset	39 Sussex
10 Lincolnshire	20 Huntingdonshire	30 Wiltshire	

Map 1   The counties of England and Wales in the nineteenth century

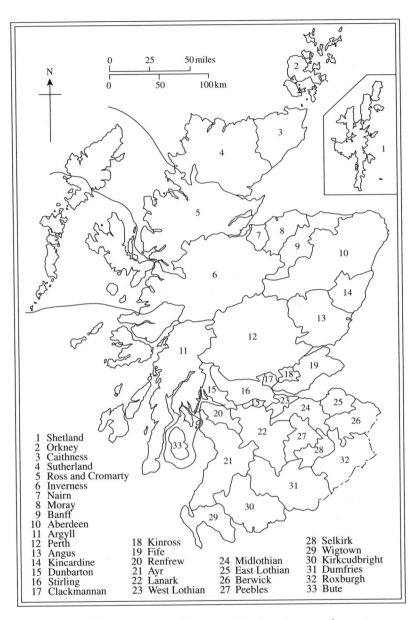

1 Shetland
2 Orkney
3 Caithness
4 Sutherland
5 Ross and Cromarty
6 Inverness
7 Nairn
8 Moray
9 Banff
10 Aberdeen
11 Argyll
12 Perth
13 Angus
14 Kincardine
15 Dunbarton
16 Stirling
17 Clackmannan

18 Kinross
19 Fife
20 Renfrew
21 Ayr
22 Lanark
23 West Lothian

24 Midlothian
25 East Lothian
26 Berwick
27 Peebles

28 Selkirk
29 Wigtown
30 Kirkcudbright
31 Dumfries
32 Roxburgh
33 Bute

Map 2   The counties of Scotland in the nineteenth century

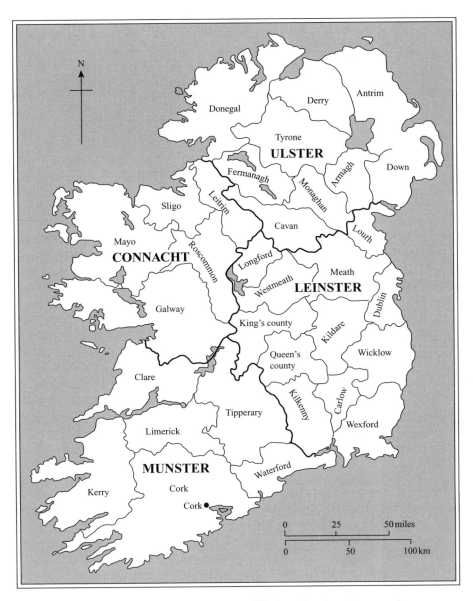

Map 3 The counties and provinces of Ireland in the nineteenth century

Introduction

CHRIS WILLIAMS

For Britain and the peoples of Britain, the nineteenth century was a century of transformation. The population of mainland Britain rose from some 10.5 million in 1801 to over 37 million in 1901 (the population of Ireland fell in the same period from 5.2 to 4.5 million). London grew from a city of 1,117,000 souls in 1801 to encompassing 6,586,000 by 1901; Glasgow from 77,000 to 762,000 and Liverpool from 82,000 to 685,000 in the same period. British troops fought wars all over the world, from Afghanistan to the Ashanti, from Cairo to the Cape of Good Hope, and from North America to New Zealand. The British empire grew to include territories on every habitable continent, and inspire a trajectory of popular heroes that began with Nelson and ended with Baden-Powell. The production of coal rose from 11 m tons in 1800 to some 225 m tons in 1900. The invention of the railway meant that there were 18,680 miles of track in Britain by 1900, carrying 1,114 million passengers in that year. In the course of the century some twenty different men served as prime minister, political parties gradually formed, split and formed again, and, by century's end, more men (though no women) were eligible to vote at parliamentary elections than ever before. This was the century of the decennial census, the civil registration of births, marriages and deaths and the Great Exhibition; of the penny post, the cigarette card, and Charles Darwin's *Origin of Species*. It was a century which witnessed the abolition of the slave trade and the coming of Catholic Emancipation. Elementary education became available to all, and the electric telegraph was invented. Women gained more legal rights to their own property and to divorce. Social protest movements such as Luddism and Chartism inspired some and frightened others. Trade unionism eventually became legal, and a system of professional policing was extended to all corners of the kingdom. Karl Marx wrote *Capital* while living in London and the *Daily Mail* became the first mass circulation newspaper. What have historians made of this eventful century? The first half of this introductory essay surveys the key paradigms and perspectives that have been applied by successive generations of scholars, from the liberal historians of the early twentieth century down to the poststructuralists of the present day. The second half of the introduction then outlines the approach, structure and contents of this volume.

One of the first major historians to attempt a history of nineteenth-century Britain was George Macaulay Trevelyan, whose *British History in the Nineteenth Century (1782–1901)* was published in 1922. Trevelyan began his century in the 1780s because he felt this allowed him to 'give a sketch of the quiet, old England of the eighteenth century before machines destroyed it, and the political scene before the French Revolution came to disturb it.'[1] To Trevelyan this was an epoch of change, 'more rapid . . . than in any previous epoch of our annals', in which economic growth 'led to social, and social to political change'. This was a period of 'new thoughts and new ideals'.[2] 'Modern history', he wrote, 'beginning from the England of 1780, is a series of dissolving views', with 'the rate of progress in man's command over nature' being 'ten times as fast [since 1780] as in the period between Caesar and Napoleon'.[3] Behind this tale of economic transformation Trevelyan perceived a moral. He argued that, initially, the Industrial Revolution had proceeded untrammelled and unhindered, and was thus more a destructive force than a constructive one. After 1832, however, (and the date is surely significant), systematic efforts were made to control industrialization in the interests of the community, thereby building 'a wholly new type of society, infinitely more complicated and interdependent in its parts, more full of potentialities for progress or disaster than anything the world has before seen.' This 'rapid and continuous reform' had been the work of 'all classes and of all parties'. Foreign influences had been limited: 'the work of reform has in our island been British, and most of its ideas and expedients have been of British origin.'[4]

In Trevelyan's formulation the essentials of what came to be known as 'the Whig interpretation' of British history may be identified: the stress on dramatic economic and social change; the priority accorded to political developments, especially those interpreted as marking the evolution of a constitutional democracy; and a dash of national pride in what had been achieved. For Trevelyan – notwithstanding the enormous upheavals of the nineteenth century – the age-old fundamentals of 'British character and temperament . . . commonsense and good nature, . . . idiosyncrasy and prejudice', remained in place.[5] Industrial progress had eventually filtered down to ordinary people and the British empire had 'spread far over the face of the globe', carrying 'justice, civilisation and prosperity'.[6]

This 'Whig interpretation' dominated most historical writing about the nineteenth century down to the Second World War. It was, of course, given more sophisticated and nuanced outings by other historians. Elie Halévy had published the first part of his *A History of the English People in the Nineteenth Century* in French before the First World War, but it was not translated into English until 1924. Halévy died before completing his massive enterprise, leaving volumes dealing with England from 1815 until the early Victorian era, and a treatment of the years 1895–1914. His most influential volume has been his first, a portrait of England in 1815, which wove together an analysis of political institutions, economic life, religion, culture and science. Halévy was essentially an anglophile, admiring of English 'freedoms', be they political, economic, religious, ethical or intellectual, and viewing England as 'essentially the country of compromise and toleration'.[7] The appearance of relevant volumes of the 'Oxford History of England' in the 1930s did not challenge the fundamentals of the Whig view: Llewellyn Woodward's 1938 volume covering the period 1815–1870 was titled *The Age of Reform* and concluded that, notwithstanding continuing social inequality, class division and other 'grave defects', '[f]or leisure or work, for getting or spending, England was a better country in 1870 than in 1815'. A 'robust belief in progress' was therefore justified.[8] Even R. C. K. Ensor, who covered England from 1870 to 1914, felt that although this period had witnessed both the rise of American and German threats to English industrial pre-eminence and the collapse of English agriculture, the bad was still outweighed by the good: the expansion of the British empire, and the dual conversion of 'English government into a democracy' and of 'the English as a whole into a school-taught and literate people'.[9]

The most influential texts of the post-war period tended to endorse the broad contours of this interpretation, albeit often in works based on much more extensive archival research and on a greater openness to social and cultural history. The prodigious enterprise of Asa Briggs brought the nineteenth century alive for a new audience, whether through his volume in the Longman History of England series (*The Age of Improvement 1783–1867*, published 1959), or through his fascinating trilogy *Victorian People, Victorian Cities* and *Victorian Things* (1954–88). Briggs's approach was perhaps more social democratic than liberal in flavour: he was a historian of Chartism and of the labour movement as well and, unlike many, he was prepared to acknowledge the artificiality of a history of 'England' in the modern era.[10] David Thomson's *England in the Nineteenth Century (1815–1914)* is a less authoritative interpretation and, given that it was published in 1950, is now heavily dated, but its status as a volume in the paperback 'Pelican History of England' means that it has been read by many who will have shied away from the task of tackling the Oxford Histories. For Thomson 'Liberalism' was the key to England's 'greatness', to its 'power, prestige and prosperity'.[11]

Progressive interpretations of Britain's nineteenth-century experience did not, however, carry all before them. Indeed, from the 1960s they began to be challenged from both Right and Left. The 'Whig interpretation' of history had of course been critiqued by Butterfield in the 1930s, and Namier's work on the political nation of the eighteenth century had suggested an alternative methodological approach to questions of power. From the 1960s a small group of right-wing sceptics grouped around Peterhouse College, Cambridge, began to publish a series of books and articles that eschewed historical interpretations based on ideas of progress, democracy or economic development, and focused instead on the thought-worlds of politicians as revealed through letters and diaries. Politicians were credited not with grand motives or ideological principles, but viewed as essentially ambitious and driven by the struggle for power. At one level, this 'high politics' school had quite an impact on historical scholarship, as revisionist accounts were produced of the Reform Acts and of other key moments in the British constitutional and political development.[12] Yet this could only ever be a partial history: a story of the governing elite not of all society. Readers will search such volumes in vain for interpretations of industrialization, urbanization, or the development of a class society, and much of the momentum behind the 'high politics' school has been lost in recent years.

More groundbreaking in reshaping the contours of historical writing on the nineteenth century was the explosion of interest in social and labour history that began in the 1960s. Here the key work was E. P. Thompson's *The Making of the English Working Class*, published in 1963, 'incontestably the single most influential work of English history of the post-war period.'[13] Thompson's call for a 'history from below', for an explicit engagement with Marxist notions of class and class consciousness, and

for a commitment by the scholar to those who so often were history's 'losers', resonated not just across Britain but around the world, and his influence can be traced
amongst historians of Latin and North America, India, South-East Asia and Africa.
With the exception of Eric Hobsbawm's economic history *Industry and Empire*, there
were to be no Marxist surveys of the nineteenth century as a whole, but monographs
examined various forms of popular struggles *à la* Thompson, before spreading out
to consider work, leisure and class formation.[14] Thompson's rhetorical and conceptual apparatuses were far from uncontroversial, even within the circles of Marxist
history. The perspective of a history 'from below' was challenged by histories 'from
above' and, in time, feminist scholarship accused the Thompsonian paradigm of being
gender-blind.[15] Eventually the broader disciplines of labour and social history were
to be troubled by these and other concerns, but by the late 1960s they were flourishing sub-disciplines whose foundational texts continue to underpin much of today's
historical debate.

The boom in social history inspired the launching of a number of series of texts
which attempted to synthesize and make sense of the mass of new scholarship.
Although only three parts of the projected seven-part series on 'The History of British
Society' appeared, nevertheless J. F. C. Harrison and Geoffrey Best between them
covered (1971–91) *Early*, *Mid* and *Late Victorian Britain*. Avoiding technical jargon
and aiming for the general reader (Best admitted he wrote social history 'of rather
an old-fashioned sort') these volumes were successful in capturing both a sense of
the fabric of individual lives across the social scale, and the 'feel' of the specific epochs
they covered. A more self-consciously ambitious project was the *Cambridge Social
History of Britain 1750–1950*, published in 1990 under the editorship of F. M. L.
Thompson. Its three volumes contain some excellent chapters on, *inter alia*, various
regions, demography, housing, food and drink, government, crime and philanthropy.
It has been seen as a non-Marxist, indeed non-Whiggish synthesis of existing scholarship that avoids both 'the language of class' (there is no chapter on social structure) and any overarching interpretative framework.

Such a refusal to engage explicitly with questions of class was perhaps indicative
of the uncertainties surrounding modernist epistemologies (including Marxism) by
the 1980s. The impact of post-modernist and post-structuralist thought on British
historical scholarship has been fragmented and partial. A sub-group of self-
consciously post-structuralist historians has emerged, remarkable both for the
ferocity of their prose and for the indifference with which they have been greeted by
most professional historians.[16] Yet although few seem willing to label themselves
'post-structuralist', there is little doubt that an interest in the questions raised by a
post-structuralist approach to language and representation and an awareness of the
fragility of modernist grand narratives have been profoundly influential in much
recent writing on nineteenth-century Britain, as is revealed by many of the essays in
this volume.

Gender history and women's history, the first particularly influenced by post-
structuralist methodology, have also challenged many of the masculinist assumptions
and exclusions of women's experiences at the heart of conventional historiography.
Whereas, in the past, women barely figured even in many ostensibly social histories
of the nineteenth century, and no explicit attention whatsoever would be paid to the
ways in which masculinity and femininity defined each other, more and more schol-

arship is at least engaging with such questions, even if an authoritative overarching interpretation is not yet available.[17]

It will have been noted that many of the texts dealing with the 'nineteenth century' interpret that century to cover different dates. Trevelyan began in 1782, Briggs in 1783, Halévy and Thomson in 1815. Trevelyan ended in 1901, Briggs in 1867, Halévy and Thomson in 1914. The Oxford History of England broke its volumes at 1815 and 1870, whereas F. M. L. Thompson chose to cover 1830–1900, and Harrison and Best together 1832–1901. However, the core of each work, even of the *Cambridge Social History*, has remained the nineteenth century, or the biggest part of it. Richard Price has recently challenged even that, with a stimulating argument that seeks to 'dissolve the common conception of the nineteenth century', linking it more closely to the eighteenth and breaking his analysis (which starts in 1680) at 1880.[18] This makes sense, it has to be said, only through a particular lens: one that privileges a deliberately undramatic account of industrialization and that stresses the continuities in the aristocratic domination of parliament and in the financial centrality of the City of London. Readers of the essays in this volume may agree that they contain sufficient evidence to suggest that such a perspective is one-eyed at best.

One final development in recent historiography that needs acknowledgement is the gradual, sometimes grudging recognition given to the 'British' dimension of nineteenth-century history. To be fair, some historians (Trevelyan was one) were prepared to engage with the experiences of England, Scotland and Wales (and maybe Ireland) rather than merely the former (and one may excuse Trevelyan's occasional use of 'England' and 'English' as synonyms for 'Britain' and 'British'). Others were less interested in what went on beyond England (for some, beyond London) and could even be 'unrepentant' about saying so.[19] Such unwarranted anglocentrism is less in evidence today. Paul Langford, general editor of the new 'Short Oxford History of the British Isles', whilst acknowledging both the problematic nature of the expression 'British Isles' and the diversity of approaches to the past that it invites, notes that even if the English had never been interested in extending their rule beyond the borders of what is now called England, 'the economic and cultural relationships between the various parts of the British Isles would still have generated many historiographical problems.'[20] It is simply unacceptable for historians of what was the United Kingdom of Great Britain and Ireland, ruled over by one monarch and by one parliament, acting in war and across its empire as one state, to pretend that somehow a narrative that focuses on England alone may suffice.

The historiography of nineteenth-century Britain is, then, in a state of continuous flux, and looks likely to remain so. Whilst Whiggish certainties about 'progress' and Marxist emphases on 'class' have progressively been undermined and questioned by repeated generations of scholarship, no other grand narrative has been generated in their place. Historians are today more alive to questions of gender, of national and regional identity, and of the instability of language and representation. Whether any of these approaches has the capacity to provide an overarching interpretation of the century looks highly doubtful, and it is regrettable that some of today's historians appear to be more concerned with methodological debates than with the recovery of traces of the past. In his *The Making of Victorian England*, George Kitson Clark wrote that photographs of street scenes offered a tantalizing glimpse of the past:

They are of things that really happened and of people who really lived and have not been recalled to a reconstructed existence with the help of the historian's ink-bottle; and therefore the result is something we cannot fully understand. The street is filled with people who were once without question there going about their business; but no one can ever recover who they all were, what they were doing before the photograph was taken or what they were going to do afterwards, still less what occupied their minds. Nor can anyone recover that sense of common reality, that natural understanding of the world in which they moved as the matter of everyday fact, which they all shared at that moment, and which disappeared for ever as soon as they retreated from life into history.[21]

Kitson Clark was, of course, right. That world is unrecoverable in the pure sense. But we lose sight of the appeal of history if we think the effort to recover that once 'natural understanding of the world' is not one worth making.

Any and every choice made by an author or an editor about chronology, structure and content reveals something about how that scholar understands the period or subject in question. Titles, dates, tables of contents, the precise ordering of chapters, the identity of contributors, all may be used to construct something of an ideological grid. This *Companion to Nineteenth-Century Britain* is no more innocent of or immune to such a mapping than any other text and, in these self-reflexive days, it is as well to be explicit about such matters.

The title and the fundamental nature of the work (a multi-authored edited text) are both givens, as this volume is part of a projected nine-volume series of *Companions* to British history running from the Romans to the present day. This British series is part of a wider enterprise embracing American, European and World history. The volume is aimed at both scholars and general readers in Britain and beyond, with expert authors drawn from universities and research institutes in Britain and North America aiming to assess the current state of historical understanding in their specialist fields, as well as contemplating the likely trajectory of future research. For some readers, well acquainted with the scholarship in question, a particular chapter may provide a refreshing perspective on the subject; for others, relatively new to the field, the same chapter may prove a reliable guide to the contours of historical interpretation, past, present and possibly future. Inevitably, some chapters are more explicitly historiographical than others, this being a choice in the hands of the individual authors and, to some extent, also being determined by the nature of the subject surveyed.

The chronological span of the volume is necessarily somewhat arbitrary. The ends and beginnings of centuries probably only have much meaning in the fields of culture and intellectual activity given the atmosphere of heady decadence (or, in earlier ages, paranoia and millennial doom) that may accompany the *fin de siècle*, or that of new opportunities or challenges that are ascribed to the birth of the next. In the *longue durées* of geology and climate, the passage from one century to another can be of no significance and, in matters of economic and social change, any such meaning that does attach itself is likely to be coincidental. Even in the world of politics centuries will regularly come and go without any transfers of power. Nevertheless, looked at in this way, one year is as good a starting point as another, and the beginning of the nineteenth century (1 January 1801 rather than 1 January 1800, to be strictly accurate) at least carries with it the virtue of having a commonly understood meaning (as opposed to the various births of 'the industrial age' or 'the century of democracy').

To choose any other date (1783? 1815? 1832?) would be explicitly to prioritize one interpretation, one way of ordering the century's multifarious experiences, over all others. Similar arguments may be applied to the terminal date of the volume, although this is confessedly open to the objection that the First World War marks a clear caesura between one sort of British experience and another. No contributor to this volume, however, has found it too difficult to bring their analyses to a close at, roughly, the end of the nineteenth century, and another editor and another *Companion* has the privilege of taking up the baton at that point. There is, in any case, a superficial neatness to the nineteenth century that makes a certain amount of sense, for it was on 1 January 1801 that the United Kingdom of Great Britain and Ireland came into being, and a century that was dominated if not by the personality of Queen Victoria then by the still contested ethos of 'Victorianism' may be considered to have ended with her death on 22 January 1901. One hundred years and three weeks may be thought a close enough approximation to the 'nineteenth century'.

As for the volume's contents and structure, these are underpinned by two broad principles. First, this is, in so far as it is possible, a truly 'British' history. Authors have, where appropriate, attempted to integrate evidence and insights drawn not just from England but from Scotland and Wales also. If drawing Irish material into the analysis makes sense (as it does in some instances) then that has also been encouraged, although it is recognized that the nature and dynamics of much of Irish society frequently render it no more assimilable to historical interpretations than it was, ultimately, to the British state. Evidently, Ireland was a special case, yet it was also a real presence in British life, not just because of the trials and tribulations of the political settlement (with the cathartic impact on the British mainland of Catholic Emancipation, for example) but also because of the economic and human connections (agriculture, famine, migration) that crossed the Irish Sea. The two chapters that have been devoted to Ireland, along with those devoted to Scotland and Wales, attempt to capture some of the 'difference' that still divided the United Kingdom in the nineteenth century.

A second requirement has been for authors to confront in their individual chapters, wherever feasible, the varying experiences of both men and women, and the ways in which constructions of gender ran through British society at all levels. Unavoidably, whereas for some topics an explicit gender history is available and thus may be addressed, for others it is more dormant and implicit. This volume is unlikely to answer all the questions that may be asked about women and gender in nineteenth-century Britain, but it will provide a guide both to further leads and to how the history of gender relations may be located within the context of political, economic, social and cultural developments as a whole.

As for the organization and contents of the volume, it is divided into five parts. Part I ('Britain and the World') engages directly with the fact that, during the nineteenth century, Britain was, parodies apart, 'top nation'. Anthony Howe, in his chapter on Britain and the world economy, assesses the extent to which such global pre-eminence was related to Britain's economic success. Britain was the pivot of the international economy and this had profound implications for its relationships with the rest of the world. John R. Davis's examination of Britain's relationship with the European continent during a largely peaceful century reveals how deeply Britain was committed to the 'European balance of power' after 1815, and how pragmatic British foreign-policy makers were in accepting the limits of their power and influence. Limits on British power in Europe seem to have been overcome on the imperial stage, as Douglas M. Peers discusses in his chapter on the British empire. But although Britain's empire was huge, it was shot through with what Peers terms 'ambivalence and anxiety', and imperial-policy makers frequently had no greater scope for decisive action than those charged with monitoring the European situation. Empire had a massive impact on British society and culture, but Peers resists wholeheartedly embracing fashionable post-colonial approaches that appear too binaristic and reductive. Implicated in both the European balance of power and empire were the armed forces, discussed by Edward M. Spiers. After the end of the French Wars the British Army, the Crimea apart, confined itself largely to imperial adventures; whilst the Royal Navy 'discharged a vast and growing array of global responsibilities.' By the end of the century the services were a more pervasive element of British popular culture than ever before, with military values seemingly appreciated, if not fully endorsed, by all levels of society.

Part II ('Politics and Government') opens with a chapter on the 'dignified' parts of the constitution, William M. Kuhn assessing the current state of writing on both the monarchy and the House of Lords. Recent scholarship in these areas has drawn on but not been enslaved by the cultural and linguistic 'turns', in the process throwing off its rather outmoded and fusty image and drawing attention to issues of political symbolism and cultural representation. Philip Harling's chapter on the state also undermines any Whiggish teleologies: the state did grow in power but there was no clear-cut, rational and progressive mid-Victorian 'revolution in government'. Even the 'explosion of government' from the 1880s onwards was not thought to be irreversible. Michael J. Turner supplies two chapters on political leadership and political parties divided in 1846 by the repeal of the Corn Laws. Turner provides a core narrative of political change that will be invaluable to those coming to the subject afresh, as well as indicating the many directions in which further reading might proceed. His chapter is complemented by Michael S. Smith's on parliamentary reform and the electorate, which explains the complexities and contexts surrounding the three Reform Acts of 1832, 1867 and 1884, traditional signposts on the way towards a twentieth-century democratic polity. Both Turner and Smith are aware of the post-structuralist challenge to what has often been a simplistic grand narrative, but they remain unconvinced that new perspectives should wholly displace a more orthodox reading of the past. Sarah Richardson's chapter on politics and gender exposes the gender-blindness of traditional readings. Fortunately, since the 1970s there has been substantial interest in both women's involvement in politics (broadly understood) and in the way in which gendered assumptions underpinned much conventional political discourse. Nonetheless, gender history and women's history remain highly contested, not least from within. As with Kuhn's chapter, a re-thought notion of the 'political' which attends to questions of cultural practice and power has the potential to generate fresh appraisals and original perspectives. Finally, Gregory Claeys explores the mental world of political thought. Instead of a narrative once dominated by Bentham and Mill we are now aware of the subtle variations and divergent inflections given to debates about liberty and equality. Radicalism, socialism, debates about evolution and New Liberalism all contributed to a shift, perceptible if no longer seen as unilinear, from individualism towards collectivism.

Nineteenth-century Britain was a society in the grip of enormous social change and Part III ('Economy and Society') considers key elements in this process. Michael Winstanley's chapter on agriculture and rural society explains how what was once a predominantly *agricultural* history has become more a history of rural societies and cultures, attentive to regional and national differences across the British Isles. Old-fashioned generalizations about the 'agricultural revolution' have lost much of their meaning in such a context, and even Marxist depictions of rural protest as essentially traditional and backward-looking have been shown to be inadequate. The rural and the urban, the agricultural and the industrial, were symbiotic rather than oppositional categories. William J. Ashworth's chapter on industry and transport eschews technical econometrics in order to capture something of the novelty and excitement of the economic change of this period. Travellers' views of British industry, and comparisons with the progress of the American economy shed valuable light on what was remarkable and what disappointing about the 'workshop of the world'. Simon Gunn's chapter on urbanization similarly reveals the dramatic quality of the growth of towns and cities: for Gunn, the city was 'on the very cutting-edge of capitalism and modernity.' Urban history is one of those specialisms which shows no sign of stagnation and which seems to encapsulate all the changing fashions of historical enquiry: it is home to Marxist and post-modern scholars, cultural and gender historians, historians of local politics and government and those concerned with the built environment and social geography of the city. Shani D'Cruze's chapter on the family discusses the impact of, *inter alia*, industrialization and urbanization on the basic unit of human community. The nineteenth century was a time of dramatic demographic growth, the experience of 'family' was often structured by class, and always by gender. 'The family' was the site for a series of organizing narratives about men, women and children and the nature of the relations between them. Ian Whyte's chapter on migration and settlement treats another striking dimension of the social history of the nineteenth century: the massive movement of people within and beyond the British Isles in response to economic and social change. The experience of migration was certainly regionally and nationally differentiated, and for the Irish especially, frequently traumatic. Jane Humphries's chapter is an authoritative examination of the 'standard of living controversy', blending econometric analysis with a keen eye for the less easily quantifiable aspects of people's experiences of change. Her conclusion that the trend in recent scholarship is towards a 'new pessimism' again undermines Whiggish assumptions about the nature of nineteenth-century progress. If Humphries makes a compelling case for the continued relevance of issues of social inequality, Martin Hewitt's discussion of the meaning of 'class' further stresses that historians should not be seduced by the temptations of post-modernism into eradicating all sense of social stratification from their analyses. Hewitt's chapter provides a clear introduction to the embattled historiographical field of modern British social history. This part of the book ends with a masterly elucidation of the recent historiography of economic thought by Noel Thompson. Political economy, though often seen as difficult and unrewarding terrain by later generations of historians, was fundamental to so much of contemporary debate that it is difficult to understate its importance and Thompson's chapter provides an excellent entrée to the literature.

Part IV ('Society and Culture') is, at the risk of sounding deterministic, concerned with those dimensions of life that were obviously affected by the transitions outlined in Part III. Mark A. Smith's discussion of religion reveals how fertile that subject has become in the last two decades as scholars have questioned hitherto dominant paradigms, whether it be through reappraising the resilience of the early nineteenth-century Church of England, or debating the timing, extent and causation of 'secularization'. Philip Gardner's chapter on education and literacy utilizes individual life-stories to assess the impact of learning on ordinary people, as well as exploring the importance of gender, regional, local and occupational distinctions in determining access to education. Aled Jones's survey of the press and publishing explains that the fourth estate frequently helped to shape popular perceptions of the world, and this has been another fruitful area for scholars interested in culture, representation and language. Heather Shore performs a Herculean task in synthesizing a welter of recent scholarship on crime, policing and punishment. Criminals were at the centre of a number of discourses which sought to understand and eliminate, to reflect and deflect, social evils and social tensions, and the study of crime reveals much about the state and those it ruled and about popular conceptions of justice and injustice. The domain of popular leisure and sport has also been the site of a number of intersecting debates about class and status, change and continuity, gender relations and national identity, as Andy Croll explores in his chapter. Once-fashionable theories of 'modernization' have yielded to more subtle appraisals of the intermingling of the traditional and the novel and 'class' remains a potent but far from unchallenged vehicle for understanding what people did in their spare time and how they understood what they did. Keir Waddington's discussion of health and medicine complements such themes with debates over professionalization and power, informed at points by Foucauldian perspectives. Whiggish stories of heroic medical endeavour have been undermined as the gendered and class-structured nature of such knowledge and skills has been revealed. The subject of sexuality, investigated by Lesley A. Hall, has equally been the site of such historiographical revisionism. Stereotypes of Victorian sexual behaviour have been qualified, challenged and replaced as innovative historical scholarship has yielded insights previously obscured by prejudice or outmoded methodologies. The talk is now of a plurality of sexualities, male and female, and an awareness of how, like crime and leisure, sexuality intersected with many other discourses about social order and social meaning. Patricia Pulham's wide-ranging discussion of artistic production is also attentive to how what have sometimes been seen as works of timeless value should actually be sited within the context of producer and consumer, supplier and market. Boundaries between high and popular culture, always negotiated and never static, became more and more permeable. Art and literature, like the press, were inevitably reflective of and, to some extent, constitutive of, social issues and controversies such as the 'Condition of England' question. And, as Iwan Rhys Morus demonstrates in his chapter on the sciences, the producers of scientific knowledge were no less immune from the social and historical context in which they operated. In the nineteenth century science was probably more central to British culture than it is today. As such it was also heavily inflected by concerns of class, gender and race. Like the history of medicine, historians today take the self-serving narratives of the profession less and less at face value, probing instead the questions of power and knowledge that structured so much of scientific activity.

Part V ('The United Kingdom') addresses the separate histories of Ireland, Scotland and Wales as well as assessing the debates about the construction of an overarching 'British' identity in this period. What emerges most strongly from these chapters is both a sense of how contested such histories are in terms of their importance to and implications for various nationalisms, and of how much more work needs to be done in certain areas in order to establish the parameters for robust historiographical debate. Christine Kinealy's two chapters on politics and on economy and society in Ireland yield some fascinating insights into the highly contested and politicized terrain of Irish historical scholarship from nationalism to revisionism and on to post-revisionism. In no other area does history matter so much in terms of its impact on contemporary political debates and popular understandings of national identity. E. W. McFarland's chapter on Scotland explores how questions of 'Scottishness', particularly as expressed through religion and politics, have moved to the forefront in work on the nineteenth century, but explains that there is much, especially in the realm of social history, that remains under-researched. Matthew Cragoe's chapter on Wales takes as its overarching theme the way in which many Welsh historians have, in their scholarly interests, tended to reproduce a partial and partisan nineteenth-century reading of what constituted the Welsh 'nation'. Only by confronting its exclusions will scholarship make room to accommodate a rather more diverse array of positions, groups and interests. Finally, my chapter introduces some of the debates that have been generated around the notion of a developing 'British' identity in the nineteenth century, and how that may have related to pre-existent identities, including that of the English themselves. It ends by making a plea for the continued study of the peoples of Britain within an all-British framework that does justice to the realities of nineteenth-century history.

Each chapter in the volume is accompanied by a guide to further reading and details of all works referenced both in the notes and in the guides will be found in the bibliography of secondary sources.

It is acknowledged that, even with thirty-three chapters and approximately 300,000 words of text, this *Companion* is necessarily selective. Readers may lament the absence, variously, of chapters on philanthropy or poverty, on demography or housing, on the labour movement and on consumerism. In some instances the volume's index may help to fill a few of these gaps, but the necessity to be selective meant that there were always going to be winners and losers. It is to be hoped that what is absent will be compensated for by what is present, and that sufficient guidance will be found in this text to enable the inquisitive scholar to obtain further enlightenment in other quarters. It is not possible for a history to be comprehensive: it is desirable, however, that it should be open-ended and fecund. If readers replace this volume on their shelves with its pages well-thumbed and even dog-eared, its job will have been done.

NOTES

1. G. M. Trevelyan, *British History in the Nineteenth Century (1782–1901)* (London, 1927), p. viii.
2. Trevelyan, *British History*, p. vii.
3. Trevelyan, *British History*, p. xiii.
4. Trevelyan, *British History*, p. xvi.

 5. Ibid.
 6. Trevelyan, *British History*, p. 424.
 7. E. Halévy, *A History of the English People in the Nineteenth Century*, [vol. 2] *The Liberal Awakening (1815–1830)* (London, 1949), p. vii.
 8. L. Woodward, *The Age of Reform 1815–1870* (Oxford, 1962), p. 629.
 9. R. C. K. Ensor, *England 1870–1914* (Oxford, 1936), pp. xix–xxii.
10. A. Briggs, *The Age of Improvement 1783–1867* (London, 1959), p. 5.
11. D. Thomson, *England in the Nineteenth Century (1815–1914)* (Harmondsworth, 1950), p. 222.
12. See the chapters in this volume by Michael J. Turner and Michael S. Smith.
13. D. Eastwood, 'History, politics and reputation: E. P. Thompson reconsidered', *History*, 85 (2000), p. 635.
14. See the chapters in this volume by Martin Hewitt and Andy Croll.
15. N. Gash, *Aristocracy and People: Britain 1815–1865* (London, 1979); J. W. Scott, *Gender and the Politics of History* (New York, 1988).
16. For a fascinating assessment of some post-structuralist scholarship by an exponent of the 'high politics' approach see M. Bentley, 'Victorian politics and the linguistic turn', *Historical Journal*, 42 (1999).
17. Even a very traditional text (dominated by a political narrative) such as W. D. Rubinstein, *Britain's Century: A Political and Social History 1815–1905* (London, 1998) includes a chapter on gender.
18. R. Price, *British Society, 1680–1880: Dynamism, Containment and Change* (Cambridge, 1999), p. 11.
19. R. K. Webb, *Modern England: From the Eighteenth Century to the Present* (London, 1980), p. xiii. See also D. Read, *England 1868–1914: The Age of Urban Democracy* (London, 1979), p. ix; and the foreword by R. Blake to R. Shannon, *The Crisis of Imperialism 1865–1915* (London, 1976), p. viii.
20. P. Langford, 'Preface', to C. Matthew, ed., *The Nineteenth Century: The British Isles: 1815–1901* (Oxford, 2000), p. v.
21. G. Kitson Clark, *The Making of Victorian England* (London, 1962), p. 275.

FURTHER READING

There are a number of useful single-volume and multi-volume histories of nineteenth-century Britain. A wide-ranging, highly readable introduction is C. Matthew, ed., *The Nineteenth Century: The British Isles: 1815–1901* (2000), while H. Cunningham, *The Challenge of Democracy: Britain 1832–1918* (2001) provides an account structured largely around politics and political change. R. Price, *British Society, 1680–1880: Dynamism, Containment and Change* (1999), a work written from a 'political economy' perspective, challenges the integrity of the nineteenth century and of 'Victorianism'. T. W. Heyck, *The Peoples of the British Isles: A New History*, vol. 2, *From 1688 to 1870*; vol. 3, *From 1870 to the Present* (both 1992) attempts to integrate the histories of England, Ireland, Scotland and Wales, and M. Bentley, *Politics Without Democracy 1815–1914: Perception and Preoccupation in British Government* (1984) provides a succinct 'high political' narrative. K. T. Hoppen, *The Mid-Victorian Generation 1846–1886* (1998) is the first volume of the 'New Oxford History of England' to cover part of the century. E. J. Evans, *The Forging of the Modern State: Early Industrial Britain 1783–1870* (1996) and K. Robbins, *The Eclipse of a Great Power: Modern Britain 1870–1975* (1994) together continue to provide students with a reliable foundation for an understanding of the period.

For explicitly 'social' histories, authoritative essays on many topics will be found in F. M. L. Thompson, ed., *The Cambridge Social History of Britain 1750–1950*, vol. 1, *Regions and communities*; vol. 2, *People and their environment*; vol. 3, *Social agencies and institutions* (all 1990). F. M. L. Thompson, *The Rise of Respectable Society: A Social History of Victorian Britain, 1830–1900* (1988) is a useful companion. J. Harris, *Private Lives, Public Spirit: Britain 1870–1914* (1993) is the only relevant volume of the 'Penguin Social History of Britain' published to date. J. F. C. Harrison, *Early Victorian Britain 1832–51* (1988), G. Best, *Mid-Victorian Britain 1851–75* (1979) and J. F. C. Harrison, *Late Victorian Britain 1875–1901* (1991) together provide an insightful account of Victorian society.

Anyone seeking to understand the development of Marxist history specifically but social and labour history more broadly needs to engage with E. P. Thompson, *The Making of the English Working Class* (1963). Gender history's foundational text for this period is L. Davidoff and C. Hall, *Family Fortunes: Men and Women of the English Middle Class 1780–1850* (2002), while post-structuralist scholarship is at its most accessible and stimulating in P. Joyce, *Visions of the People: Industrial England and the Question of Class, 1848–1914* (1991). Finally, those seeking to understand either the roots of nineteenth-century developments or their subsequent trajectories might begin with either H. T. Dickinson, ed., *A Companion to Eighteenth-Century Britain* (2002) or C. Wrigley, ed., *A Companion to Early Twentieth-Century Britain* (2003).

PART I

Britain and the World

CHAPTER ONE

Britain and the World Economy

ANTHONY HOWE

Nineteenth-century Britain was uniquely fashioned by her relationship with the world economy, although historians have been keenly divided over whether her unprecedented economic growth in this period was the cause or consequence of this relationship. Contemporaries had been likewise divided, with many ascribing Britain's emergence as the world's first industrial nation to the policies of protectionism which had been followed throughout the eighteenth century, enabling her to build up domestic industries behind tariff barriers while enjoying the benefits of trade with a growing empire. For others, such a political framework had been a straitjacket, with trade artificially restricted by a network of regulation. This view was canonically associated with Adam Smith whose *Wealth of Nations* (1776) announced free trade as the basis of optimum welfare. This message that trade was the basis of national greatness was to be echoed throughout the nineteenth century by politicians and diplomats as well as merchants, bankers and industrialists. For the most part historians have been more sceptical as to the importance of trade itself as an engine of growth, and have preferred to ascribe this to endogenous factors such as Britain's favourable factor endowment. More recently historians have been less certain in their conclusions, with some now reassessing the importance of imperial markets and transoceanic trade to economic growth.[1] Britain did not live by trade alone, as cliometric historians have been keen to point out, but the experience of the people and the nature of the state itself were hugely determined by the unprecedented extent of Britain's integration into the world economy in the nineteenth century.

War, Trade and Empire, 1801–15

Britain's global economic interests were already well established by 1800, for the loss of the American colonies had in no marked way altered the growth of her trade in the Atlantic, while it continued to find new markets in Europe and Asia. The imperial redesign necessitated by the loss of the thirteen colonies had begun at home, with Pitt and his closer colleagues focusing on the need for the consolidation of the United Kingdom as a fiscal and economic union through the inclusion of Ireland. A distant prospect in the 1780s, this goal was achieved in the Act of Union of 1800. But Pitt's vision had not been simply imperial, for the Anglo-French commercial treaty of 1786 had been promoted as part of the Enlightenment's search for a civilized consortium of nations, with the bonds of commerce replacing the sinews of war. This prospect was to be rudely ended by the outbreak of the French Revolution, followed by the wars against Revolutionary and Napoleonic France. Trade with Europe remained crucial to Britain, especially as her Industrial Revolution 'took off', producing a growing flood of goods to be disposed of abroad. But, rather than France acting as Britain's premier market, Britain now needed both to look further afield for new markets (for example, to Latin America) and also to devote much energy to evading the blockade which war itself and Napoleonic policy built up around the continental market. Despite twenty-five years of war, British trade, fuelled by industrialization, continued to grow at unprecedented rates, hampered by war in Europe but enjoying huge worldwide benefits as the continental colonial empires fragmented and as the Royal Navy established its mastery of the world seas.

War also had other profound consequences for Britain's relationship with the world economy. Firstly, with Amsterdam overrun by patriots and liberators, London now became the financial centre of the world, just as in the First World War she would lose this primacy to New York. This was in part occasioned by the need to fund Britain's allies, with huge subsidies distributed over Europe in the form of loans and advances, providing profits for enterprising financiers. At the same time, facilitated by legislation such as the Warehousing Act of 1804, London became the 'warehouse of the world' and increasingly the centre for shipping and insurance, the sources of much future national wealth. Symbolically, Hopes of Amsterdam were now replaced by Barings of London as the world's leading merchant banker. Secondly, whatever the early appeal of Smith's liberal theories, British economic policy continued to be based on a combination of expediency and neo-mercantilism, as she sought to use instruments such as the Orders in Council to restrict trade with neutral powers. This ultimately led to a damaging, if short, war with the USA in 1812 but in worldwide terms Britain now acquired parcels of territory which would provide lasting economic links, for example, Ceylon, Mauritius and the Cape of Good Hope. Thirdly, as a result of population growth and the interruption of wartime trade, the British economy had seen a tremendous explosion of agricultural production. In consequence, in a way that cut firmly across the grain of earlier liberalization, this gave new force to a strong current of protectionism and support for self-sufficiency. Many now argued that rather than exploiting her links with the world as a whole Britain should consolidate her imperial power as the basis of domestic prosperity and national security. The ascendancy of this *mentalité* led to the introduction of the Corn Law of 1815, providing protection for British agriculture in defiance of the Smithian logic of the world market.

Modifying Mercantilism, 1815–46

The victory of the 'agrarian patriots' in 1815 was primarily a reflection of the twenty-five years of warfare that Britain had experienced. But their vision of imperial self-sufficiency as a national strategy was soon undermined as industrialization intensified, population growth continued, and as the peace of 1815 proved a durable one. This generated conditions in which a fundamentally different vision of Britain's place in the world economy emerged, sustained intellectually by Ricardo's theory of comparative advantage. For Ricardo, Britain's wealth would depend on her ability to specialize in those industries in which her world lead was greatest, even if this meant divesting from industries, including agriculture, in which she may also have been the world's most efficient producer. Herein lay the fundamental understanding of Britain's position in international trade that would be continued in substance by Mill, Jevons and Marshall. Intimately related to this were 'the terms of trade', the ratio between the cost at which Britain produced goods and the price at which she imported goods. Here the first stages of the Industrial Revolution gave Britain a massive initial advantage by 1820 but thereafter, as Britain produced industrial goods at cheaper and cheaper prices, the terms of trade were unfavourable as her efficiency was not matched by that of the producers of the imports she needed. But from *c*.1860, the trend of the terms of trade turned in her favour as the import prices of grain, meat and raw materials fell with the costs of world production and transport.[2]

For Ricardo, the logic of Britain's development lay in the exploitation of her industrial advantages and the transfer of resources from the land to industry and trade, a logic resisted by the agrarian elite until the 1840s, but one which would inspire some policy-makers from the 1820s. But Ricardian ideas did not carry all before them and, in the first third of the century, those of Malthus exerted greater sway. Malthus's fear that population growth would outrun food supply dominated the world-view of Britain's leading politicians, encouraging them to think in terms of a limited engagement with the international economy, in order to sustain a balance between domestic food supply and the growth of manufacturing industry. This vision would ultimately prove unsustainable but, for three decades after 1815, Britain attempted to pursue moderate growth, maximizing her gains from trade rather than manufacturing. At the same time, the return to the gold standard in 1821 created another important prop in Britain's international position, for this would prove a long-term basis for the role of sterling as the world's premier currency. Yet money could also prove a destabilizing factor. For the 1820s were to see the first great boom in capital investment overseas, at a time when agriculturalists were reluctant to invest further in an overcapitalized industry and before industry itself demanded huge investments (as it did with railways in the 1840s). As a result, rentier funds flowed into a speculative boom in South American mines – with up to £21 m transferred abroad before the crash of 1825.[3] In this context, politicians emphasized the need for stable growth avoiding immoral speculation and sought to achieve this by lubricating the wheels of trade rather than providing artificial spurs to growth.

This motivation above all lay behind the policy of Huskisson at the Board of Trade between 1823 and 1827 as he attempted to put Smithian ideas on the international economy into practice. Firstly, he overhauled the tariff, abolishing over 1,000 customs acts, substituting moderate duties for protective ones, and lowering those on raw materials. He also sought a far more extensive breach with mercantilism and the Navigation Acts by offering equality of duties on goods and shipping to any country that agreed to grant the same to British shipping. This led to an important series of reciprocity treaties, especially with France and Prussia, while he also took steps to consolidate Britain's advance into Latin American markets. British commercial expansion was therefore facilitated by this careful diplomatic process. Imperial markets were also cautiously opened to third parties, but imperial preference was retained for example, with regard to Canadian timber and West Indian sugar. Up to the 1840s, 40 per cent of British shipping tonnage was employed in trades from which other nations were excluded by Navigation Acts. Huskisson was keen to retain the economic benefits of empire, which he still saw as an essential part of Britain's emergence as the dynamic centre of an expanding world economy.

Within this policy framework, one of modified mercantilism rather than adoption of free trade, Britain's position in the world economy was based essentially on her growing bias towards exports. This has been investigated by a number of historians, working with figures which present their own difficulties of interpretation (for example, before 1854 exports were priced at official fixed values rather than current ones) but the overall pattern is generally clear. After the rapid growth of the period 1780–1802, the rate of growth of exports slowed during the wars and did not recover much before 1826. Thereafter the growth in volume of exports was rapid, although as the price of goods fell, this was not matched by an increase in the total value of exports. This was the classic period when British trade depended on the cotton industry which contributed 46 per cent of the total growth in export values between 1814/16 and 1844/6. Geographically, European trade grew only slowly while the American market remained crucial but highly volatile. As a result, in this period Britain looked particularly to 'new' markets in Asia, Africa and Latin America. Exports to Asia and Africa accounted for 44.4 per cent of the increase in total exports 1814/18 to 1842/6. Their share of total exports rose from 7.9 to 21 per cent, just as that of northern Europe and the USA fell from 44 per cent in 1814/18 to 27 per cent in 1842/6. The simple explanation of this shift is of cheap cotton goods unloaded on unprotected, low-income markets but a more complex view suggests, as Crouzet puts it, that 'exports to those areas were the dependent variable of imports from them by Great Britain', especially demand for tropical produce.[4]

These trends provide essential clues as to the next great change in the political economy of trade, the shift to free trade in the 1840s. Part of this shift was an awareness of the stickiness of exports to Europe, the lack of return goods in payment for British exports, and even apprehension that Europe would industrialize behind tariff barriers. Part, too, came from a desire to even out the pattern of boom and slump which had become marked in the 1830s and had led, between 1837 and 1842, to the greatest depression of the nineteenth century. In this context, attention now refocused on the British Corn Laws, which many argued kept out European (and American) grain, so vitiating their comparative advantage in agriculture at the expense of Britain's lead in industrial production. At the same time, it was feared that the Corn Laws acted as a market signal that deterred European production. There remained a danger that Britain would be unable to purchase food abroad in the event of a major harvest failure at home. In addition the need for exceptional large purchases of grain also distorted the exchanges, heightening the intensity of trade cycle crises. Other vital political and social considerations entered into the debate on the Corn Laws but their repeal in 1846 set the stage for the redefinition of Britain's relationship with the world economy.

Free Trade and British Hegemony, 1846–73: 'The Workshop of the World'

Repeal has traditionally, and rightly in many ways, been hailed as sealing the victory of free trade and paving the way for the era of mid-Victorian prosperity. But rather than seeing repeal as the last step in a gradual relaxation of legislative controls, we should see it as a major discontinuity in economic policy, which opened up new dangers and new opportunities to British trade. Recently scholars have been keen to see this not so much as the victory of abstract economic truth, the logic of the market triumphing over protectionist prejudice, but as creating the foundations for British hegemony within the world system as a whole. In particular theorists of 'hegemonic stability' – with the experience of the USA after 1945 in mind – have suggested that free trade enabled Britain to restructure world trade in ways which both ensured her own prosperity and provided 'public goods' (open markets, free sea lanes, the suppression of piracy and slavery) from which the world as a whole benefited. This led therefore to a period of unprecedented trade liberalization and growth in the world economy. A less generous but not wholly dissimilar assessment of free trade and British hegemony was made in the 1840s by the patriotic German economist List, for whom free trade was merely a strategy by which Britain as the first industrial nation sought to flood markets with cheap goods, in order to delay industrialization abroad and to ensure her own dominance of the world. As one of List's followers, the German historical economist Fuchs was to put it, free trade lent 'the garb of a philanthropic cosmopolitanism' to the 'special interests of England'.[5] How far, we need to ask, did repeal of the Corn Laws pave the way for the further integration of Britain into the world economy and how far did it lay an enduring basis for British hegemony?

Initially, although the effect was much slower than many feared, Britain became increasingly dependent on imports of grain. But whereas contemporaries had looked to Russia, Poland and Prussia, the long-term sources of wheat supply, aided by the dramatic fall in transportation costs after 1870, were to be the USA and Canada. Thus, total imports grew steadily from an annual average of £19.6 m in 1855–9, to £31.9 m in the decade 1860–9, before shooting up to £52 m in 1870–9, a figure which then remained more or less stable until 1900. As a percentage of total imports grain and flour also remained more or less stationary as a percentage of the growing total of imports, running at c.12–14 per cent.[6]

Much more immediate in effect, although only a subordinate issue in political debate, was the abandonment of imperial preference. Since the seventeenth century this policy had sought to bind the British empire together, and by the 1840s resulted in more favourable access to the British market for goods such as Canadian timber and West Indian sugar. As recently as 1843 Peel had granted preference to Canadian corn, a concession startlingly reversed in 1846. For in 1846 Britain opened up her market unilaterally to the corn of the whole world and this removed the political basis of future preference; in fact on their return to power in 1846 the Whig government immediately abjured preference, although prudentially staggering its eventual disappearance. This had important implications for the restructuring of the British empire – this would now be a 'free trade empire', with colonies prohibited from offering preference to the mother country, the mother country prohibited from favouring her imperial children. The 'empire' was to be a matter of sentiment and security; but the economy was proclaimed 'international', not imperial.

Thirdly, and dramatically, Britain in 1849 abandoned her centuries-old dependence on the Navigation Acts, an exception to free trade which even Smith himself had been prepared to concede on the famous grounds that 'defence is more important than opulence'. Victorian Britain was not quite to reply that opulence was more important than defence but the Navigation Acts were now considered dispensable as a prop of the navy as well as of the economy. Despite the dire predictions of the shipping interest (and some half-pay naval officers), British shipping survived and entered into the period of its greatest relative world dominance with 50 per cent of world steam tonnage in 1880. But for her Civil War (1861–5) the USA may have proved a far more serious rival but it was only by the end of the century that foreign competition began to challenge British supremacy. Even so in 1900 she still accounted for 44.5 per cent of world steam tonnage (35.5 per cent of all tonnage).[7]

In abandoning the Corn Laws, imperial preference, and the Navigation Acts, Britain had swiftly dismantled the network of legislation that had regulated her connection with the world economy for two hundred years. Not without reason did the critics of free trade see in this an unprecedented experiment for a great power to undertake. Britain had committed herself to the self-regulating market, believing that this would best serve her own economic interests but also those of the world as a whole. But she had also abandoned efforts at reciprocal trade bargaining and effectively limited herself to the power of her own example to encourage others to follow. To some extent, this was an effective model, and already in the expectation of repeal the USA had liberalized her own tariff in 1846 and would continue broadly in that direction up until the Civil War. Nor had Britain entirely abandoned the process of commercial diplomacy and had necessarily to engage in treaty-making particularly outside Europe in order to create orderly trade relations (for example, with Morocco in 1856). However, she did now rely with regard to the major economies of Europe on the power of her own example. Its immediate impact was weakened by the 1848 revolutions but in 1851 the Great Exhibition aptly symbolized Britain's relationship with the world economy and advertised the message of free trade. It provided not only a display of the goods which she now sought to sell to the world but also the products from abroad which her growing wealth enabled her to buy. It also set out an ideal, which future exhibitions would expound, of the world as an integrated whole, with the growth of international exchange as the bond of progress and peace in a new post-feudal world order. This ideology acquired a considerable grip throughout Europe at this time – and we should see Britain not as the sole 'free trade' power but simply as the most advanced free trade power. Progress towards more liberalized European trade was to be disrupted by the Crimean War (1853–6) but thereafter the momentum picked up with the Anglo-French commercial treaty of 1860 signalling a new departure in European trade policy.

The background to this treaty lay in the growing desire of Napoleon III to integrate France into the world economy while also seeking to assuage British fears of expansionary French militarism. At the same time Britain remained anxious to diffuse the benefits of free trade. The Anglo-French commercial treaty was therefore part of a deliberate attempt to reconstruct the European economy on free trade lines. It prefigured a series of treaties by Britain (with Belgium, Italy, the *Zollverein*, and eventually Austria–Hungary) but also by France, all of which contained the most-favoured-nation clause whereby tariff reductions were generalized among the treaty powers. As a result, Europe was bound together by these mutually interlocking treaties into a low-tariff bloc, arguably the nearest she got to a common market before the 1970s. Russia still lay outside this network, but Western Europe had become an economic whole in a new way and, as in the twentieth century, much trade was between relatively advanced economies.

Such treaties should be interpreted not simply as part of a narrow process of commercial bargaining nor as an attempt at British domination of Europe by means of an *entente commerciale*. Rather they contained, and derived from, a broad ideological purpose shared by diverse groups including Cobdenites in Britain and Saint-Simonians in France. Their ideology underpinned not only moves towards free trade but also a broader pattern of internationalism. For example, this period saw the most dramatic communications revolution before the Internet with canals, railways, steamships and the telegraph dramatically altering speed, time and distance within the world market. It was by the 1840s possible to argue that railways would produce a global market in industrial goods, promoting commerce as the bond of peace between nations, a development greatly assisted by oceanic steam shipping. The telegraph was hailed as the 'nerve of international life' with communication with Australia now possible in minutes rather than months. Nor is it coincidental that this period saw the first attempt at building the Channel Tunnel, not a misguided demonstration of technological bravado but an emanation of the liberal desire to integrate nations in a peaceful world order. This ideal was also propagated by a series of international exhibitions, especially that in Paris in 1867 masterminded by liberal economist Chevalier, while this generation also envisaged tariff congresses and even a European (in effect a world) currency.

This wave of capitalist internationalism was promoted by the example of British free trade but it also had further connections with the British economy. Firstly, it was closely linked with the first sustained wave of capital exports, with over £700 m raised in the British market (but not necessarily all British) invested abroad between 1860 and 1875, the source of an immediate demand for capital goods but also a long-term source of rentier income. Income from capital assets abroad grew from an average of £16.5 m (1856–60) to some £50 m (1871–5) (see figure 1.1). Much of this capital was invested in railways and social overhead capital in the great age of the communications magnates such as Sir Edward Watkin and Sir John Pender. Britain's central position within this communications network also offered sizeable commercial advantages that helped reinforce her supremacy. Secondly, it underpinned a huge growth in British trade itself although the export of capital and that of goods cannot be precisely correlated. In absolute terms, exports grew in value by £186 m between 1844/6 and 1871/3 growing at 5.7 per cent per annum in declared values and contributing 24.7 per cent of total national product in 1871. It was at this stage that the British economy may properly be termed an 'export economy'.[8] Thirdly, alongside Britain's huge export growth, the services she provided for the world economy in terms of shipping, banking and insurance also rocketed upwards, increasing from an annual average of £29 m in 1851–5 to some £88.7 m twenty years later (see figure 1.1) It was on the back of these 'invisible' earnings that the City of London established its centrality to the world economy, financing, insuring and shipping a huge

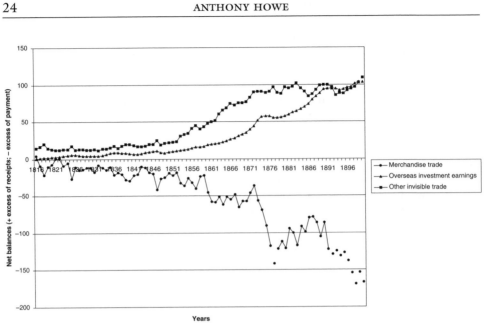

Source: B. R. Mitchell and P. Deane, *Abstract of British Historical Statistics* (London, 1962)

Figure 1.1   'Invisibles' and trade in Britain's balance of payments, 1800–1900

proportion of world trade, including a sizeable re-export trade, largely in colonial goods. Finally, in a way which is sometimes forgotten, this involved a huge outlay of human capital. Britain effectively spawned what has been termed a 'cosmopolitan bourgeoisie', a deployment of merchants, bankers, agents, traders, speculators throughout the world which in itself created an important comparative advantage within the world market.[9]

Within this pattern of a broader, deeper and 'thicker' integration of the world economy, Britain herself remained the pre-eminent power with worldwide interests. She could never be primarily a European economic power in the manner of France or Germany, although by the 1870s, as table 1.1 shows, her exports to Europe had risen as a percentage of the whole. Even so, her extra-European trade remained vital, although it was to undergo important changes in this quarter-century. Firstly, bene-fiting from earlier policies of colonization and capital investment, Australasia emerged as a significant export market for Britain, with a huge boom in 1853–4 but there-after settling down at 9–10 per cent of total exports. By comparison trade with Africa, while growing, was never to rival this throughout the century. Secondly Asia, in par-ticular India, consolidated its position as a major destination for British goods, with a significant shift upwards, despite the Indian Mutiny of 1857. India now produced a sizeable surplus of income that played a central part in Britain's worldwide network of trade and payments.[10] Thirdly, and to an extent often neglected, the relative decline in British exports lay in the Americas, with South America taking a notably smaller

Table 1.1 British exports: percentage share by destination, 1860s–1890s

Region	1866–8	1876–8	1886–8	1896–8
Europe	34	39	31	35
United States	13	8	13	8
Central and South America	10	8	9	9
Africa	5	2	2	3
Asia	5	5	5	6
Mediterranean, North Africa, Near East	4	4	3	3
Other	2	1	1	0
British settlement empire	11	17	17	18
British dependent empire	16	17	19	17
Total	100	101	100	99

Source: UK Statistical Abstracts.

percentage of goods. But most worryingly for the long term was the decline in exports to the USA as a percentage of the total, a sign that American industrialization and policies of protection were beginning to bite in a way which lent a long-term asymmetry to Anglo-American trade. For while the USA took a declining share of British exports, Britain remained crucially dependent on the USA for raw materials, especially cotton and tobacco.

Although the focus of historians has rightly been on the export economy, we should not forget the import economy. In this context, Europe was not only Britain's main export market but also her largest source of imports, with her share of the total growing from 36.2 per cent in the 1850s to 41.8 per cent in the 1870s.[11] This trade – for example, in silks and other luxury goods – was qualitatively different from the remainder of the import trade based on food and raw materials, largely from the empire and the USA. There is therefore a good deal of truth in the conventional view of Britain as the workshop of the world, importing raw materials and food and exporting a large percentage of the output of her industry. Yet 'workshop of the world' gives too limited a perspective, for Britain was also the warehouse, banking hall, shipping agency and insurance office of the world, although these services were intimately related to the growth of her trade. Trite, even fallacious though it may appear in retrospect, few contemporaries doubted the standard view of Britain's diplomats that by 1870 'trade was the basis of Britain's greatness'.

'The Gigantic Hinge': Adjusting to the Great Depression, 1873–96

The great British-led boom in the world economy between 1851 and 1873 was followed by the period, 1873–96, labelled the 'Great Depression' in which growth seems to have slowed down, unemployment grew, and an array of indices – profits, prices and rents – all fell. A voluminous governmental report left policy-makers little wiser as to the causes or reality of this 'depression' and many historians have argued that this was primarily a period of readjustment rather than of slump.[12] From Britain's point of view, three changes were marked. Firstly, the rate of growth of her trade slowed down, notably more sharply than that of other nations which were beginning a period of rapid industrialization. As a result she now encountered stiffer competition in world markets. Secondly, whether as cause or effect of her relative industrial slowdown, British capital was now exported abroad in far greater amounts, and in a way that most clearly demarcates this phase of Britain's relationship with the world economy. These two factors together gave rise to Clapham's famous metaphor of the 'Gigantic Hinge' switching the basis of economic life from the industrial North to the rentier South, from manufacturing industry to international finance. Thirdly, Britain increasingly found herself a leader without followers as a free trade power: so much for hegemony, she was even unable to enforce free trade in her own colonies. In this context, some began to question what they saw as 'one-sided free trade' and, influenced by a growing current of neo-mercantilist thought, looked to the imperial rather than the international economy as the future basis for British prosperity and power.

As a result of these changes, Britain, the first industrial nation, had in many ways become the first 'services' nation of the world economy by the 1890s. But it must be reiterated that the contribution of manufactured exports remained the central hub of the economy. Despite the long-running historical debate concerning entrepreneurial failure, Britain's share of world manufactured exports was a generous 43 per cent in 1881–5. This was however set to decline to 34.5 per cent by 1899 as other nations, especially Germany and the USA, emerged as world competitors.[13] How did this affect Britain's pattern of trade? On the export side, one marked feature was Britain's ability to supply the growing continental demand for coal. This accounted for much of the growth in exports to Europe (57 per cent of growth to France, 42 per cent to Germany, 80 per cent to Italy) but as Cain and Hopkins note 'the dependence of the world's first industrial nation upon the export of coal was a serious worry to contemporaries'.[14] At the same time, Britain's share of manufactured exports to industrial Europe fell off markedly as it did to the USA, in part a sign not so much of entrepreneurial failure as of the success of rising tariffs in keeping out British goods. This relative decline was in part compensated for by a shift to imperial markets, especially India and the settlement empire as the overall share of imperial trade rose from some 27 per cent in 1866–8 to some 35 per cent by 1896–8 (see table 1.1). Arguably this greater reliance on empire had long-term disadvantages in encouraging British industry to continue to invest in low value-added products although it was difficult to perceive this before 1914.[15] However it is not clear that this phenomenon was a matter of retreating to imperial bolt-holes, rather than relying on certain products whose main markets were in primary-producing countries, many of which were part of the British empire. But this trade would probably have taken place even had they been outside the empire. As the cliometric historians point out, British growth rates may have slowed down in an expanding world economy as the newly industrializing countries were able to occupy new niches. As they developed their own comparative advantages, often in high value-added new industries, Britain retained her market share in her traditionally strong, if low-value, areas, particularly textiles. The other marked feature of Britain's trade in this period was her continued ability to suck in imports. This worried some contemporaries, particularly as manufactured imports

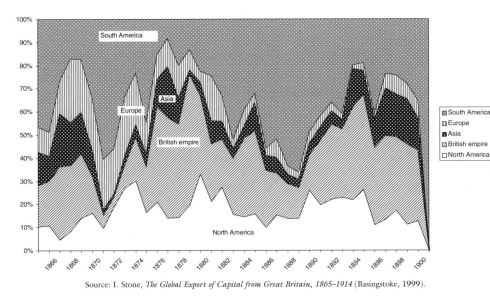

Source: I. Stone, *The Global Export of Capital from Great Britain, 1865–1914* (Basingstoke, 1999).

Figure 1.2   Geographical distribution of capital exports from Britain, 1865–1900

grew from some £5 m per annum in the years 1860–9 to £15.7 m in 1890–9. But this was only an increase from 2 per cent to 4 per cent of all imports, for many a sign of the vitality of an economy able to finance by its income from 'invisibles' a growing deficit in the balance of goods.[16]

A growing percentage of this invisible income was to derive from what many historians have identified as the most distinctive feature of the world economy in the late nineteenth century, the huge export of capital. Although historians have found it impossible exactly to quantify its extent (let alone its results), there is general agreement that the volume of British capital exported increased enormously in absolute terms and as a percentage of GNP.[17] Having totalled some £700 m in 1870, the total had climbed to *c.*£2,000 m by 1900 although this would pale by comparison with the subsequent further £1,500–2,000 m between 1900 and 1913. Growth was not continuous but normally came in 'short bursts', with peaks in the early 1870s and late 1880s. As figure 1.2 shows, export of capital to the British empire, particularly India and the settlement empire, was the most marked characteristic of the movement of capital in this period (as it was to be between 1900 and 1913). Europe itself greatly diminished its share of the market, while the USA and particularly Argentina remained important. The huge bulk of this capital represented direct portfolio investment, loans to foreign or colonial governments or (especially) to railway companies, and represented social overhead capital; only 4 per cent of the total is held to have been invested in industrial enterprises which competed with British goods. However, these figures must be treated with caution. Platt in particular highlighted serious weaknesses in the statistics used by some historians and suggests that the totals for

'British' investment include much non-British capital invested through the London money market.[18] However, we need also to allow for British capital invested through the Paris and other bourses and also for growing direct investment which became a notable feature of the world economy towards the end of the century. It is likely therefore that the estimates used by historians may be roughly correct, although our knowledge of their composition and computation have been significantly altered by recent research.

This huge outflow of capital has generated an equal outflow of historical literature concerning its causes and effects. Was it the result of the push of falling profits and surplus savings at home or the pull of greater profits abroad? Were the consequences harmful or beneficial? It has often been argued that this export of capital 'starved' British industry of the funds it needed to modernize and so slowed down the rate of economic growth at home, and held down the standard of living of the working class. Alternatively, it has been seen as a response to the declining rate of profit at home, an attempt to stave off the crisis of capitalism by shifting funds abroad.[19] Both views are too dramatic. Given the slowdown in industrial demand (through the resort to tariff protection in Europe, the Dominions and the USA), investment abroad is better seen as a logical and rational response, which in the long run would provide raw materials and cheap food for the working class. It also provided huge gains in income through the City of London, and capital export in this period represented future capital import through the interest which would accrue; between 1876 and 1900 income from abroad had grown by a further £80 m. The City's expertise in international finance arguably now gave it an institutional bias towards overseas lending and diminished its flexibility in the face of industry. But there is no convincing evidence that British industry lacked capital, and some evidence that industrialists themselves were ready to invest abroad. But the vast export of capital in this may rightly be taken as a further sign that Britain's international comparative advantage now lay in services centred on the City of London rather than in industrial production. Even so, we should be wary of seeing the City of London as semi-detached from Britain, simply an offshore island of the world economy, 'a paradise for the rentiers', for this seriously underestimates the continuing importance of London to the national economy.

If, therefore, we now turn to the best summary of Britain's overall relationship with the world economy, the balance of payments shows an intriguing story.[20] For contrary to common assumptions, but as figure 1.1 shows, Britain had had an adverse balance of commodity trade from the 1820s, even at the peak of her industrial leadership. Britain's net income therefore had depended on 'invisibles' – the income from the sale of shipping, commercial and financial services. This was a factor reinforced throughout the nineteenth century. In fact many had long argued that the adverse balance of trade did not matter and that, as the free traders had long argued, increased imports were the sign of a thriving economy. Since imports paid for themselves through further exports, imports rather than exports were the engine of growth. In effect, within the pattern of trade that had developed in the world economy by, say, 1890, Britain had become the hub of the international system of multilateral trade and payments. Her ability to settle her debts in Europe and America was based on credits earned in other parts of the world, particularly India, but this multilateral system itself helped generate and sustain the growth of world trade.

Britain's position at the centre of the world economy was further reinforced by the effective globalization of sterling as gold became the world's monetary standard. Although there had been considerable support for an international currency in the 1860s, the stability of the gold standard in Britain allowed the Bank of England and Treasury to remain deaf to this cause. After 1870 country after country joined gold, despite the strong and continuing arguments of many that the interests of Britain and the world as a whole would be better fostered by a bimetallic standard. Sterling's position had been achieved by the stability lent to the gold standard in Britain after 1821 and consolidated in the Bank Charter Act of 1844; despite the undermining of the theoretical basis of this legislation, its practical benefits soon outweighed its intellectual weaknesses. For it effectively guaranteed stable exchange rates through-out the world economy, in a way that would become the envy of inter-war financial experts. In a way too the world banking system became centred on London. Not only did it become a magnet for imperial and international banks but the Bank of England itself became the vital linchpin of the system. If the world economy had a centre this was it. For although there was no active policy of monetary management (the virtue of the gold standard was that it was self-regulating) the Bank of England in effect operated as the lender of last resort for the world as a whole.

Finally, the evolution of the world economy was vitally affected by Britain's com-mitment to free trade. Initially, as we have already seen, she encouraged the maximum diffusion of free trade within a liberal international order. But if anything marked the 'Great Depression' it was a widespread backlash against the proto-globalization of the period 1846–73. Most European countries now returned to at least moderate tariffs (for example Germany in 1879, France in 1881 and 1892) while the USA achieved new peaks of protection in the McKinley and Dingley tariffs of 1890 and 1897; even tariff wars were now played out with sharpened intensity. Virtually alone, Britain continued to adhere to free trade. The openness of the British market had several consequences. For British consumers it meant low prices and was seen as vital to the standard of living of the working classes. Even so, as Britain began to consume not only food and raw materials but also manufactured goods, some began to argue that Britain's consumers benefited at the expense of her producers. More widely, the openness of the British market ensured a free flow of goods and services from which the rest of the world benefited. From one perspective, countries such as Germany and the United States could be seen as 'free riders' within that world order – erecting their own tariff barriers while sending growing volumes of goods to Britain. Yet since the 1840s Britain had declared herself in favour of 'free imports' and this remained a paramount 'national interest' with both economic and diplomatic benefits.

Given this overriding commitment to free trade, it became increasingly difficult for Britain to respond to the growth of foreign tariff barriers as she became entwined in what has been called the 'hegemon's dilemma'. Should she, that is to say, end her policy of unilateral free trade and adopt an aggressive commercial diplomacy, involv-ing retaliatory and preferential tariffs in order to coerce other nations back to the free trade fold? Or should she retain her traditional policy, as better suited to her national interests, even if it meant 'free riders' proliferated while she increasingly faced exclusion abroad and 'unfair' competition at home. The former policy was strongly urged by the 'fair trade' movement but this never acquired a deep enough political base to topple Britain's free trade orthodoxy. In practice therefore she could only take minor steps in order to ensure that as much of the world market remained as open as possible, for example the negotiation of commercial treaties in south-eastern Europe in the late 1870s and early 1880s. She also sought to negotiate favourable treaties in Asia, for example Korea and Japan, while also seeking guarantees of the 'open door' in China. But elsewhere she remained an impotent spectator in an age of growing tariff warfare. Fear of foreign tariffs was also a contributing factor to Britain's readiness to acquire new territories abroad, particularly in Africa in the 1880s as a pre-emptive attempt to maintain a 'fair field and no favour'. Even so, Africa was only ever to provide a relatively small and poor market for British goods. Britain was also to find that her own self-governing colonies, Australia (with the major exception of New South Wales) and Canada, with much higher incomes per capita, were to erect tariff barriers. These naturally impeded British exports, although Edelstein speculates that these tariffs were lower than those which foreign-governed colonies would have imposed.[21] Against this background, an increasingly vocal body of opinion was to argue that Britain should adopt a more active imperial economic policy, seeking either to recreate a 'free trade empire' (an unlikely possibility by the 1880s) or that she should at least form an imperial *zollverein*, in which the goods of the colonies would be favoured and those of 'foreigners' discriminated against. By the early 1890s pressure groups such as the United Empire Trade League and British Empire League saw in empire the solution to the economic problems that the 'Great Depression' had posed.

Fin de Siècle, 1896–1900: How 'Weary' was the 'Titan'?

In a famous speech in 1902 Joseph Chamberlain was to lament the fate of Britain, the 'Weary Titan' staggering 'under the too vast orb of its fate'. More widely, intimations of the mortality of the British economy were rife by the late 1890s, part of a *fin de siècle* wave of pessimism and a Europe-wide intellectual preoccupation with degeneration. In particular, the growth in imported manufactured goods gave rise to series of 'scares', precipitated by Williams's polemical tract *Made in Germany* (1896), and followed by growing fear of an 'American invasion'. The Boer War (1899–1902) was vastly to extend this concern to a national obsession with deterioration, and the converse need to increase 'efficiency'. How did this bear on the relationship between Britain and the world economy? In part this was a matter of fashionable Social Darwinian imagery alone with thrusting young nations assumed to be ready to take over from the senescent and decaying, of whom Britain as the oldest industrial power was necessarily the prototype. Such rhetoric went back to the 'fair trade' movement of the 1880s and had been reinforced by opinion favouring an imperial *zollverein* but it now became part of a much more widely based appeal of 'constructive imperialism'. This would culminate in Chamberlain's tariff reform movement after 1903 but was foreshadowed by his period as colonial secretary from 1895 to 1902. For Chamberlain, the remedy for the relative decline of the British economy was to reorder Britain's relationship with the world economy – above all, to reinforce the empire as an organized economic unit. Initially this could be done only in minor ways. In the face of growing anxiety over exports, he set up in 1896 a committee into foreign competition in imperial markets, a signpost to future debate.

In 1897 Britain abrogated her commercial treaties with Germany and Belgium thereby opening up the possibility of the colonies granting preference to British goods (which Canada did in 1897). Chamberlain also took up the cause of the West Indian sugar planters by seeking to impose countervailing duties on bounty-fed sugar-beet imports, leading to the Brussels sugar convention of 1902. The Pacific Cable was also taken up as a model of imperial economic co-operation. We can see here the groundwork for the subsequent case for tariff reform, that Britain should erect tariffs against foreign countries while favouring her empire, and so reversing the course of British economic policy since 1846.

This case was necessarily based on what had been perceived as the benefits of the empire in the previous generation – tariff reformers drew attention to the export of capital to the empire and the growing percentage of trade (especially by value) with the colonies. Their arguments however have not been well supported by recent research. Sophisticated calculations as to the costs and benefits of empire suggest that empire offered little that could not be gained elsewhere and that to some extent an imperial 'cushion' was damaging to the British economy, encouraging an 'over-commitment' to staple industries. Some have suggested it distorted the educational system, generating a supply of civil servants at the expense of technically proficient entrepreneurs.

In the longer perspective, the dream of retreat within the imperial economy was to run up against the reality of a long boom in the international economy between 1890 and 1914, with rapid growth of trade, export of capital and migration of peoples. This produced the nearest the world got to a genuinely global economy before the 1990s. How foreseeable was this from the perspective of 1900? Arguably a new boom in capital exports had just begun, prompted by gold discoveries in South Africa, where the Boer War was to prove local, not global, in its ramifications. The 'Great Depression', if it had existed, was also held to have ended after 1896 with the beginnings of a new acceleration in the growth of world trade. In this context, Britain was unlikely to look inwards but was set to remain as the pivot of a period of rapid 'internationalization' within the world economy. This was famously eulogized by Keynes in his *Economic Consequences of the Peace* in 1919:

> The inhabitant of London could order by telephone, sipping his morning tea in bed, the various products of the whole earth, in such quantity as he might see fit, and rea-sonably expect their early delivery upon his doorstep; he could at the same moment and by the same means adventure his wealth in the natural resources and new enterprises of the world and share, without exertion or even trouble, in their prospective fruits and advantages; or he could decide to couple the security of his fortunes with the good faith of the townspeople of any substantial municipality in any continent that fancy or informa-tion might recommend . . . he regarded this state of affairs as normal, certain and permanent.

Keynes's *fin de siècle* 'economic Eldorado', while perhaps too comfortably bourgeois in its emphases, was nevertheless, as this chapter has attempted to show, essentially accurate in its delineation of the relationship between Britain and the world economy. For however important the empire, Britain remained pre-eminently an international economy. If the Titan was weary, the forces of recuperation were unlikely to come from the empire alone but from sustaining the open interdependent economy, the internationalization of economic and social life with which Keynes rightly associated British prosperity before 1914.

ACKNOWLEDGMENT

I am grateful to Dr Gabi Lombardi for compiling the statistical figures and tables used in this chapter.

NOTES

1. P. K. O'Brien, 'Imperialism and the rise and decline of the British economy, 1688–1989', *New Left Review*, 238 (1999), p. 62.
2. C. K. Harley, 'Foreign trade: comparative advantage and performance', in R. C. Floud and D. McCloskey, eds, *The Economic History of Britain since 1700*, vol. 1, *1700–1860* (Cambridge, 1994), p. 305.
3. L. H. Jenks, *The Migration of British Capital to 1875* (London, 1971), p. 68.
4. F. Crouzet, *Britain Ascendant: Comparative Studies in Franco-British Economic History* (Cambridge, 1990), p. 241.
5. C. J. Fuchs, *The Trade Policy of Great Britain and Her Colonies since 1860* (London, 1905), p. 18.
6. P. Mathias, *The First Industrial Nation* (London, 1969), p. 467.
7. P. Davies, 'Nineteenth-century ocean trade and transport', in P. Mathias and J. Davis, eds, *International Trade and British Economic Growth* (Oxford, 1996), p. 66.
8. Crouzet, *Britain Ascendant*, ch. 6.
9. C. A. Jones, *International Business in the Nineteenth Century: The Rise and Fall of a Cosmopolitan Bourgeoisie* (Brighton, 1987).
10. S. B. Saul, *Studies in British Overseas Trade, 1870–1914* (Liverpool, 1960).
11. W. Schlote, *British Overseas Trade from 1700 to the 1930s* (Oxford, 1939), table 18.
12. S. B. Saul, *The Myth of the Great Depression, 1873–1896* (Basingstoke, 1985), p. 55.
13. R. C. O. Matthews, C. H. Feinstein and J. C. Odling-Smee, *British Economic Growth, 1856–1914* (Oxford, 1982), p. 435, table 14.5.
14. P. J. Cain and A. G. Hopkins, *British Imperialism: Innovation and Expansion, 1688–1914* (Harlow, 1993), p. 165.
15. Harley, 'Foreign trade', p. 328.
16. Mathias, *First Industrial Nation*, p. 467.
17. Edelstein, M., 'Foreign investment and accumulation, 1860–1914', in R. C. Floud and D. McCloskey, eds, *The Economic History of Britain Since 1700*, vol. 2, *1860–1939*, (Cambridge, 1994), table 7.1.
18. D. C. M. Platt, *Mickey Mouse Numbers in World History* (Basingstoke, 1989).
19. S. Pollard, 'Capital exports, 1870–1914: harmful or beneficial?', *Economic History Review*, 38 (1985).
20. A. H. Imlah, *Economic Elements in the Pax Britannica: Studies in British Foreign Trade in the Nineteenth Century* (Cambridge, MA, 1958).
21. M. Edelstein, 'Imperialism: cost and benefit', in R. C. Floud and D. McCloskey, eds, *The Economic History of Britain since 1700*, vol. 2, *1860–1939* (Cambridge, 1994), p. 203.

FURTHER READING

Britain's position in the nineteenth-century world economy is central to A. G. Kenwood and A. L. Lougheed, *The Growth of the International Economy, 1820–2000* (1999), to K. H. O'Rourke and J. G. Williamson, *Globalization and History: The Evolution of a Nineteenth-Century Atlantic Economy* (1999), and to the interpretative essay by P. K. O'Brien, 'Imperialism and the rise and decline of the British economy, 1688–1989', *New Left Review*, 238 (1999). The chapters by C. K. Harley and M. Edelstein in R. C. Floud and D. McCloskey, eds, *The Economic History of Britain since 1700*, vols 1 and 2 (1994) provide reliable, up-to-date guides to central issues. All historians rely heavily on the statistics provided in W. Schlote, *British Overseas Trade from 1700 to the 1930s* (Oxford, 1939), B. R. Mitchell and P. Deane, *Abstract of British Historical Statistics* (1962), A. H. Imlah, *Economic Elements in the Pax Britannica: Studies in British Foreign Trade in the Nineteenth Century* (1958), and B. R. Mitchell, *British Historical Statistics* (1988), to which I. Stone, *The Global Export of Capital from Great Britain, 1865–1914* (1999) is a valuable addition. Particular issues are dealt with in F. Crouzet, *Britain Ascendant: Comparative Studies in Franco-British Economic History* (1990), P. Mathias and J. Davis, eds, *International Trade and British Economic Growth* (1996), and D. McCloskey, *Enterprise and Trade in Victorian Britain: Essays in Historical Economics* (1981). The link between trade and industrialization is explored by R. Davis, *The Industrial Revolution and British Overseas Trade* (1979), while S. B. Saul's *Studies in British Overseas Trade, 1870–1914* (1960) and *The Myth of the Great Depression, 1873–1896* (1985) remain valuable for changes in the late nineteenth century. The relationship with empire is central to P. Cain and A. G. Hopkins, *British Imperialism, 1688–2000* (2001) and there are relevant essays in A. Porter, ed., *The Oxford History of the British Empire*, vol. 3, *The Nineteenth Century* (1999). For the political economy of British trade policy, see A. Howe, *Free Trade and Liberal England, 1846–1946* (1997) and D. Winch and P. K. O'Brien, eds, *The Political Economy of British Historical Experience, 1688–1914* (2002).

CHAPTER TWO

Britain and the European Balance of Power

JOHN R. DAVIS

Introduction

The first dedicated works on British relations with Europe in the nineteenth century were produced in the inter-war period.[1] The Treaty of Versailles of 1919 and the documenting of Britain's previous involvement in Europe were their main preoccupations at the time. Historical literature on British relations with Europe in the nineteenth century has maintained this narrative and diplomatic thrust.

Radical innovation has seldom occurred. New approaches are often restricted in topic, not synthesized into the whole, or only reach that limited readership, PhD examiners. The connection of domestic and foreign policy is not a subject investigated deeply. Diplomatic historians still speak in embarrassingly generalized, personified, even gendered, terms about relations between the 'Powers'. General books on nineteenth-century Britain cover foreign relations as part of their remit, but coverage is slight and also fails to link foreign and domestic issues.

The more recent emergence of the discipline of international relations has not substantially affected things. Its findings have related to twentieth-century international history and have been heavily transatlantic. Only regarding histories of the First World War, and the Concert of Europe, has international relations peered into the nineteenth century. In both cases it has fortified prevailing diplomatic emphases, and, in the latter, has been superficial.

Economic dimensions have also been avoided. Economic historians avoid trespassing on political property; diplomatic historians feel ill-equipped for orientation on the economic side of the fence.[2] Economic statements in diplomatic histories all too often seem unsubstantiated and general.

Finally, historical literature has also characteristically been general in nature, with few studies of British relations with one country, and anglocentric in its interpretation and conclusions. A look through British history theses completed since 1901 reveals a tiny amount of focused research on British relations with Europe – probably stemming from the language barrier. Research on nineteenth-century British foreign policy is dwarfed by domestic and local history.

Of course, anglophone historians may have been right to cling to diplomacy in the face of new approaches. Britain gave its foreign secretaries a surprising degree of autonomy of action until the First World War.[3] A. J. P. Taylor's stridently diplomatic *Struggle for Mastery in Europe* is perhaps one of the finest books in any category of historical literature, and demonstrates that diplomatic history remains popular with lay readers and undergraduates.[4] The personal rivalry of grand personalities such as Canning and Metternich, the heroic but fated struggle of liberal England (not the more complex Britain) against absolutist Europe, is gripping reading. The nineteenth century is now possibly too far in the past, and gentle in comparison with more recent times, for anything but grand narratives to be of wider interest.

Furthermore, one should not generalize about diplomatic narrative. Arguably, a longstanding interest in domestic and economic factors has been expressed pragmatically and unobtrusively, rather than explicitly and in abstract. Writers like Bourne, Kennedy and Lowe have produced magisterial works providing both additional context to diplomatic decision-making, and domestic, institutional and psychological dimensions.[5] The interaction of European and imperial spheres of foreign policy has latterly attracted attention. There have been notable in-depth discussions of 'highlights' – for example, British policy during the Crimean War, Italian and German unification, the Berlin Congress and its aftermath. A more practical view of the actual limits of British power – for example in military terms – and their influence on decision-making has been undertaken. There have also been attempts to apply theories of decision-making to Britain's nineteenth-century foreign relations.

In order to demonstrate the contribution such research has made, this chapter will seek to reproduce the orthodox diplomatic narrative, highlighting areas of uncertainty or inconsistency where they still exist. Against this backdrop, the more intensive, focused revisionist studies will be introduced, and their ramifications for the history of the subject explained.

Setting the Scene: Vienna and Afterwards

One of the most signal gaps in histories of British foreign policy in the nineteenth century regards the years 1800–15. With the 1919 Versailles Treaty in mind, interwar historians invariably chose 1815 as the starting-point of their inquiries. Later historians have cast their nets further into the past to investigate the evolution of the agreements of 1815 out of events since 1789 or else to underline the novelty of the post-1815 agreements.[6] Still, this remarkable period has never adequately been covered. The complexity of shifting alliances and, between Pitt's death in 1806 and Liverpool's ministry of 1812, changing ministries has seemingly prevented this. Regrettably, 1815 is still seen as the de facto start of nineteenth-century British foreign policy by most historians.

Reinforcing a widely shared view, Schroeder argued that the Napoleonic Wars produced a transformation in the thinking of statesmen about international relations in 1815.[7] For the first time, a peace was constructed based on treaties, great power solidarity, and congress diplomacy. Certainly, more than any other subsequent foreign secretary, Castlereagh spoke convincingly of great power unity based on conservative principles. He perpetuated Pitt's argument that an important part of European peace – its 'future repose' – should be 'a general and comprehensive system of public law in Europe', and envisaged Britain participating in ongoing diplomatic co-operation.[8]

Yet this view of 1815 is contested. The hard-headed power calculations underlying British thinking have been recognized: Castlereagh was keen to link Prussia and Austria in a reformed, defensive German Confederation set up to restrict the expansion of France and Russia. A united Netherlands and an expanded Prussia would check France in the north, and keep the European coastline near Britain safe. Austria's position in Italy was supported as a barrier to any French adventures. France itself was treated leniently to underpin the Bourbon regime. The Vienna settlement gave something to all five great powers – and the consequent solidarity of conservative regimes rested on this fact. It was 'a settlement of eighteenth-century *Realpolitik*'.[9] Castlereagh spoke of it as a 'just equilibrium'.

The level of agreement between Castlereagh and Europe is questioned. European statesmen such as Hardenberg in Prussia and Metternich in Austria sought territorial expansion at the expense of weaker powers. Castlereagh's concern was the disengagement of Britain from the Continent, enabling internal and colonial consolidation.

British conservatives were possibly more pragmatic than their continental counterparts. They focused on the revolutionary threat and renewed French ambition, not on European conservative ideology. Tories found the quasi-Romantic basis of the Holy Alliance hard to understand and feared it would entangle Britain in a myriad of continental disputes. Castlereagh termed it 'sublime mysticism and nonsense'.

Liberal assessment of Castlereagh in the nineteenth century tended to be that he sacrificed small, sovereign states to the greed of large, absolutist powers. Later judgements have been more positive, however.[10] From Webster onwards, Castlereagh's 'appeasement' transmogrified into an heroic effort to make the diplomatic machinery for ensuring the permanent 'repose' of Europe work. Accordingly, it was Castlereagh's personal standing that enabled the Congresses to take place. The backdrop of the post-war British dilemma with the European Union even encouraged historians to see Castlereagh as 'the most European-minded of British ministers, perhaps until Edward Heath'.[11]

Seen in this light, Castlereagh was involved in an uphill struggle. Between 1815 and 1822, nationalist and liberal opposition to the Vienna system, fuelled by economic and social issues, became more virulent on the Continent. At Troppau (1820), Laibach (1821) and Verona (1822), France, Austria and Russia sought Congress agreement for intervention in Spain, Naples and Greece respectively. Castlereagh insisted that the treaties of 1815 were not meant for 'the Superintendence of the Internal Affairs of other States'. He believed the results of the Holy Alliance's agenda would be a massive increase in Russian influence and an early end to the balance of power just established. The centre of Europe would become a Russian preserve, France would be alienated, and Britain's access to the eastern Mediterranean and the colonies would be threatened from Spain and southern Italy.

Since the nineteenth century, and particularly after the publications of Temperley and Webster, a theme of historical enquiry has been the comparison of Castlereagh and Canning. Castlereagh's attempt to conduct European affairs through congresses contrasted with Canning's assertive unilateralism. Temperley and Penson extended this polarity to oppose the non-interventionism of Castlereagh, Aberdeen, Granville and Gladstone, to the more assertive, risky, bluffing policy of Canning, Palmerston, Disraeli and Salisbury.[12] Such sharp contrasts have, however, given way to an emphasis on the continuity of foreign policy. Notions of polarity persist, but are a function of emerging public opinion, limitations of power, and personality, rather than of overall aims.

For both Castlereagh and Canning, the starting-point was that British involvement on the Continent must be limited. However, whereas Castlereagh hoped congresses might achieve that end but was forced to accept the balance of power, Canning took a direct approach of bilateral negotiations and demonstrations of force, but ultimately also sought to preserve the balance of power underpinning the Vienna settlement.

Canning negotiated directly with France over Spain, acquired a French undertaking that intervention would be limited, and thus drew Britain and France together. He co-operated with the USA, promoting recognition of the Latin American colonies to prevent continental influence there ('called the New World into existence to redress the balance of the Old'). He exploited Austro-Russian disagreement and worked with Russia over Greece, achieving Greek separation from Turkey with Turkish suzerainty.

Canning's near-modern use of publicity has also attracted attention.[13] A public statement regarding foreign policy could send a shudder of reaction round European courts and bring about the required result. Canning's domestic support for emancipation of the Catholics alienated him from Tories. Demonstrative protests to absolutist powers brought parliamentary dividends. Canning's use of gunboat diplomacy to protect Portugal from intervention can also be seen in this light. It was cheap to undertake, but brought great rewards in terms of publicity.

Metternich saw Canning as the 'devil incarnate', and thus he remains the hero of British diplomatic narrative. By avoiding entrapment in congresses and masterfully exploiting the balance of power, Canning had discovered a way of dealing with the Continent. Still, Canning's success extended merely to damage limitation: ultimately, France did enter Spain, Austria entered Naples, and Greek separation from Turkey represented a Russian gain of some sorts. Canning made the best of a bad situation: nothing more could be done until after the French revolution of 1830.

The Palmerston Years

There have been a wide variety of descriptions of Palmerston's foreign policy. He has been described as 'opportunistic', conservative at home but liberal abroad, and aiming to overturn the agreements of 1815 and dominate Europe (an argument echoing contemporary criticism of him by foreign conservatives). Yet recent studies have played down Palmerston's revisionism towards Europe. The blend of liberalism and conservatism in Palmerston's foreign policy was a function of domestic exigencies. The evolution of his domestic position from Canningite Tory to radical Whig, and his exploitation of popular support in foreign affairs, explain how the two aspects of his activities – domestic and foreign – fitted together. The consequences of his undeniable, ebullient personality, in terms of lending a sharp edge to an otherwise relatively supine policy, have also been explored.[14] Moreover, the international environment of Palmerston's policy – in particular the revolutions of 1830 and 1848 – explain much. Palmerston enjoyed opportunities for action not open to Canning, Wellington or Aberdeen.

Palmerston's arrival at the Foreign Office in the Grey administration of 1830 marked the end of a catastrophic policy of 'drift'. Wellington had sought to revive harmony with conservative Europe. He disavowed Greek independence and apologized to the Turkish sultan for British naval pressures. In Portugal, he withdrew British naval support for the liberal regime. Foreign governments ruthlessly exploited Wellington's retraction, however. Predictably, Turkey declared war on Russia and Greece, producing even greater calamity, Russian victories and an about-turn by Britain in support of full Greek independence. In Portugal, reactionaries simply reassumed control. From Palmerston's point of view, all of this represented the loss of hard-won gains.

However, the French revolution of 1830 allowed Palmerston to act. Palmerston never thought in terms of a lasting alliance with France or, famously, with any other country. But France's revolution removed it from the influence of the Holy Alliance and made it a potential ally. This was not immediately obvious. The King of Holland's resistance to Belgian cessation tempted French intervention and expansion into Luxembourg. Palmerston was faced by pressure at home and also from the Eastern Powers to intervene. However, through dogged insistence on neutrality, timely threats of war and a Canningite offer to work with France rather than against her just sixteen years after Waterloo, Palmerston eventually secured Dutch acquiescence in Belgian independence. Uprisings in Poland and Italy in 1830 had distracted the Holy Alliance. Nevertheless, Palmerston is usually credited with bringing Belgium into existence. He had also staved off reactionary intervention, maintained peace and created a precedent for future Anglo-French co-operation.

Just as new room for manoeuvre appeared, the necessity for it became obvious: Russia seemed intent on increasing its power. Palmerston's opposition to Russia was grounded in both ideological and power-political considerations. He had publicly ignored Russian actions in Poland in 1830. Little could be done, and Poland helped distract Russia from Belgium. The Near East was a different matter. Muhammad Ali's attack on the sultan's rule in the wake of Greek autonomy brought an ominous offer of Russian support for Turkey. Palmerston's desire to counter Russian aggrandizement at this point was, however, opposed by a cabinet more concerned with the Reform Act. Palmerston was forced to watch as Russia's support for the sultan was traded for the Treaty of Unkiar Skelessi, closing off the Straits to foreign ships. Throughout the 1830s Russia exerted pressure in Afghanistan.

Palmerston's promotion of the Quadruple Alliance of 1834 (with France, Spain and Portugal) was one counterweight to Russia. When, in 1839, the sultan launched a war against Muhammad Ali and called on Russian support, Palmerston was finally able to convince the Melbourne cabinet of the Russian threat. Demonstrating the possibilities of Anglo-French co-operation, Palmerston persuaded France, which supported Ali as a way of reviving historic Napoleonic claims in Egypt, to join forces.

On the other hand, Palmerston could simultaneously, and with another Canningite flourish, argue the case for direct co-operation with the Russians in Turkey, using the threat of joint Anglo-French action: the Straits Convention of 1841 reversed

Russian gains, and effectively neutralized Turkey and the Straits.[15] French hopes that Ali's gains would be recognized were, however, dashed: Palmerston gained the support of Russia and Austria against France, ensuring that Ali's right to rule was restricted to Egypt. While he welcomed the new opportunities of working with France to uphold the balance of power, and nurtured them with a secret alliance in the wake of the Straits Convention, Palmerston was not willing to see the French usurp the place of Russia or Britain. The Vienna balance should be preserved, not overthrown.

Neither Wellington's foreign policy of 1828–30, nor Aberdeen's of 1841–6 has received much attention from historians, possibly due to their support for the idea of conservative solidarity – a policy revealingly described by Bourne as 'appeasement'.[16] Aberdeen sought to curb foreign involvement against a backdrop of anti-Corn Law and Chartist agitation and Irish problems. Concessions were made to Russia in Afghanistan. An increasingly assertive French government was accommodated on the issue of Spanish succession.

More attention has been paid to Palmerston's foreign policy after his return to office in the Russell administration in 1846; indeed, his reputation as a redoubtable opponent of foreign despotism rests on these years – though no sustained work replicates Bourne's on Palmerston's early period. Although Palmerston followed Canning's model in terms of his crowd-pleasing, an increasing moral support for nationalism and liberalism abroad from the late 1840s arguably stemmed from domestic considerations. The middle classes had become more important politically after 1832. Greater political representation and the limitation of aristocratic power domestically meant British foreign policy supporting foreign liberalization and counteracting the Holy Alliance was welcomed. Palmerston shared a widespread view that British constitutional forms were superior to those elsewhere. But his support for reforms abroad was no doubt strengthened by the fact that Russell's government after 1846 was constantly in danger of being overturned. Gaining popular approval for foreign policy was a useful weapon against Conservative opposition based on 'vested interests'. It was also useful in shoring up Palmerston's own political position as a Canningite Tory in a Whig cabinet, in the face of political competition from Russell, and, ultimately, in view of Victoria and Albert's personal and political antipathy to him. Palmerston's need for 'sound-bites' was similar to, but far greater than, Canning's.

Foreign considerations also necessitated Palmerston's promotion of nationalism and liberalism abroad. The revolutions of 1848 altered things fundamentally. Russian assistance in imposing order in Hungary and Austria, and the paranoia of reactionary regimes after 1849, made Russia the moral protector of conservative governments. To astute contemporaries, the result of the revolutions was the growth of Russian power on the Continent. Revolution in France curtailed the hostility of the Orleans regime and revived France as a potential ally.

In this situation, it was only natural that Palmerston would signal his opposition to reaction through demonstrative support for Mazzini, Kossuth or the assailants of General Haynau. It was at this point that he also made the first steps towards creating liberalism as a popular movement. Through voicing opposition to absolutism abroad, Palmerston was able to unite a broad coalition of support drawn from liberals, radicals, Peelites and moderate and patriotic conservatives.

Still, the overriding rationale for Palmerston's actions at this point was probably his concern to limit Russian power. Queen Victoria believed Palmerston's playing to the liberal gallery was a cheap affront to the Holy Alliance and undermined Austria. Victoria and Albert's position on Europe, while sympathetic to liberal reform, was always closer to that of German legitimists, who saw the Vienna agreements as defining and protecting the borders of German states. Albert remained, after all, a German prince. Victoria also, rightly, sensed that Palmerston's attempt to draw on the authority of public opinion constituted a real threat to her own right to be consulted on foreign policy – a right which seemed increasingly untenable as popular sovereignty began to replace that of the monarch.

It was ironic, and a sign of her desperation, that Victoria should finally succeed in demanding her foreign secretary's head on a platter from Russell because Palmerston had recognized the imperial regime of Napoleon III in France. Palmerston's policy was guided not by naive support for liberals, but by considerations of power, and he had pushed support for Napoleon III in order to create a basis for future co-operation. Victoria and Albert's sympathies for liberal reform had also resulted in early overtures to Napoleon, so there was no natural antipathy on that point between the queen and foreign secretary. However, Victoria's blinkered understanding of Palmerston, and the poor relations between the two, resulted in a situation greatly to Russia's advantage in Europe.

Unlike his earlier career, Aberdeen's role in the Crimean War has been thoroughly researched. His administration was possibly a contributing factor to the conflict. Aberdeen, a Peelite Conservative, sought to revive solidarity with the Eastern courts and seek understanding with Russia. The tsar had visited Britain in 1844 and got on well with Aberdeen, then foreign secretary to Peel. There had also been a Foreign Office note to Russia in 1845 foreseeing greater Anglo-Russian collaboration in the Near East. Bourne has argued these factors were misinterpreted in St Petersburg as an opening for the expansion of Russian power in Turkey.[17]

The nature of the Aberdeen cabinet also produced fits and starts in British policy in the early stages of the conflict. It was a coalition based mainly on domestic concerns about avoiding social unrest and retaining free trade. It reflected the general fluidity and fragmentation of the political spectrum and, with personnel consisting of experienced political grandees and several previous foreign secretaries, it was not surprising that foreign policy was inconsistent and slow. Political weakness in London arguably gave Stratford Canning, ambassador in Constantinople, even greater freedom than rudimentary communications normally allowed to cause friction between Turkey and Russia. Though Aberdeen was forced to accept Napoleon III's offer of an alliance against Russia, the British contribution was contradictory and halting. Russian advances were watched with growing public alarm.

The Crimean War was the first European conflict to be reported on daily in the newspapers as it progressed. Public opinion could now be harnessed to bring in a government much more intent on pushing Russian power back. Palmerston was identified by the press – and saw himself – as the man to lead such a government. When Aberdeen stood down in the face of parliamentary opposition to the conduct of the war, Palmerston replaced him. He ensured that the parliamentary enquiry into the war would go ahead, discredited Aberdeen, and set about reinstating the balance of power.

Palmerston famously considered pushing Russia completely out of Europe. The Paris Peace of 1856 that concluded the Crimean War was not so harsh – but it still represented a defeat for Russia and entailed retraction of its power from the Balkans. The problem for historians has been that while Palmerston intended restoring the European balance, rectifying a dangerous Russian preponderance and extending the Vienna settlement to the Balkans and eastern Mediterranean, the Paris Peace encouraged the reverse. The decline of Russian influence pulled the rug out from under the feet of European conservatives. In this situation, nationalist and liberal reformers scented new openings. The governments of Austria and Prussia were no longer held in check in central Europe. Most significant of all, the disappearance of effective pressure from the east, and Palmerston's increasing reliance on Anglo-French co-operation, had opened the way for Napoleon III's revisionism.

Such momentous consequences encourage cynical interpretation of Palmerston's support for national and liberal reforms abroad. Dispatches on the subject were intended to promote good government, reduce Russian influence, and thus sustain the balance of power. Yet contemporary and later observers believed Palmerston favoured wholesale change. This is seen in Palmerston's attitude towards German revolution in 1848: as foreign secretary he watched the affairs of the Frankfurt Assembly hopefully. When it became obvious that German national unity would bring war with Denmark over Schleswig-Holstein and, potentially, Russian intervention in central Europe, he had to side with reaction. Conservatives thus believed he had incited revolution. Liberals saw themselves betrayed.

It has also been too easy to judge Palmerston by later developments. Until his death in 1865, Palmerston seems to have believed he could still control the situation in Europe. He continued to view France as a vital ally in Europe at least until 1860. In 1858, Palmerston was temporarily removed from office for agreeing to French demands to control the activities of foreign revolutionaries based in Britain after an assassination attempt on Napoleon III was proved to have been arranged in London. On this occasion, Palmerston sacrificed the support of liberal opponents of foreign absolutism in London for continued Anglo-French alliance. Though seen as a milestone in British free trade policy, the commercial treaty of 1860 similarly aimed at cementing Anglo-French partnership. When Napoleon III emerged as the successful promoter of Italian unification in 1859, there was a great deal of support for his actions. It was only in 1860, when France acquired Nice and Savoy from Piedmont, that doubts about French expansionism seemed substantiated. Even then Napoleon III's intentions were hard to divine. Prussia's 'New Era' of liberal politics also promised new allies in opposing French power.

Intervention: 1860–71

Britain's failure to intervene in the 1860s against any of the major alterations made to the Vienna settlement was the subject of contemporary criticism as well as that of historians. Early historians explored it with reference to (non-)intervention, appeasement, or as a moment in British decline.[18]

More recently, however, historians have pointed to the fact that the government was facing a new situation. For the first time since 1815, Britain was unable to find a power on the Continent with which it could co-operate.[19] The quality of British information-gathering has also been called to account.[20] British diplomats failed to report on important developments of nationalism and liberalism. The Foreign Office was inadequately equipped to deal with the information it was receiving. There was also not quite as much worry about the future as was supposed with hindsight.

The tendency of the government to rely on the navy and disregard the army has also been noted.[21] The military was ill-equipped and poorly organized – as demonstrated by the Crimean War. In the 1860s, the necessity of defending Canada's border during the American Civil War left Britain with virtually no forces at all to send to Europe. In the past Britain's lack of land-based forces had not stopped it influencing events. Rhetoric and a few well-positioned 'triple-deckers' had usually sufficed, because, if push came to shove, there was always the possibility of allying with a land-based power. Now that no power was willing to support Britain in upholding the status quo, rhetoric and gunboat diplomacy seemed at best pointless, at worst suicidal.

Palmerston's European policy is often described as being one of 'bluff' by 1863. When Prussia and Russia co-operated to repress Polish dissent, Palmerston refused to turn a joint Anglo-French protest into anything resembling formal alliance, as France had demanded. Palmerston recognized the reality of Britain's position: that little could be achieved, given the geographic position of Poland, and the vital nature of the question to Prussia and Russia. Indeed, all that would result would be the alienation of Britain from Prussia – a situation which Napoleon III would be able to use for his revisionist purposes. However, when Confederate German forces marched into Schleswig-Holstein in 1863, followed by the armies of Austria and Prussia in 1864, Napoleon III used Britain's attitude towards Poland as a reason for not supporting Palmerston's calls for intervention against the German states. Napoleon III's move signalled less his commitment to Polish nationalism – which was always a ploy – and more his decision to throw in his lot with the German states and Russia and go for revisionism. The British government thus found itself powerless to intervene. Palmerston's bluff was called.

Yet the problem with arguments about military capacity and 'bluff' is that Britain's inability to act was not fully appreciated at the time, because there was no political will to get involved. Both Palmerston and Russell were more concerned about the legal precedent set by the abrogation of the London Treaty of 1852 because they knew France might follow it. But Palmerston was able to content himself with bellicose statements in parliament once he had convinced himself there was no possibility of intervening. The public was famously confused about Schleswig-Holstein, and rather alienated by this seemingly archaic struggle over succession rights. Bismarck exploited confusion by arguing that Austro-Prussian forces were simply reinstating order. Political forces seemed divided: Victoria was pro-German; Russell was pro-Danish.

The same point can be made about the Austro-Prussian war of 1866. Here, too, the Russell government – with Clarendon as foreign secretary after Palmerston's death a year before – was unable to act alone. Again, a variety of factors combined to prevent full scrutiny of Britain's foreign policy. Since 1848, many liberals in Britain had identified Prussia as the most likely vehicle for delivering greater freedom in Germany. They tended to be ill-informed about Bismarck and, hence, more tolerant of him. Bismarck, in turn, exploited British prejudices by talking constantly of

Prussia as a progressive state. Once more political affiliations were split – with Victoria showing her dynastic colours and supporting Austria and the Confederation against Prussian centralization. And many in Britain viewed the whole affair as sordid: the powers which had sought to profit by war in Schleswig-Holstein were now rioting with each other in a kind of Bacchanalian frenzy. Britain's lack of power may have been clear to the experts, and used to sober up idealists calling for intervention. But it was not the main reason for non-intervention.

After 1866 things appeared to be moving in a promising direction as seen from London. The foundation of the North German Confederation betokened moderate liberalism, with some deference to the existence of individual German states. Prussia was pushing forward commercial and economic liberalization within northern Germany. Hanover's absorption was only of concern to Queen Victoria – who was thus unable to forgive Bismarck. Most importantly, however, the Confederation appeared to offer a moderate expansion in Prussian power to check French ambitions.

A consistent feature of British foreign policy towards Europe since 1815 had been its minimalism: the Vienna settlement was supported as a way of limiting British involvement on the Continent. It had also been accepted in the past that, where Britain could not hope to intervene, there should be no foolhardy interventionist ventures. With so much support for peace from various quarters at home, with mounting criticism of Palmerstonian threats and rhetoric, and with things seemingly going Britain's way in Europe with little effort, the idea of non-intervention was becoming an article of faith: the notion that the balance of power could operate without any intervention at all, as a self-sustaining mechanism, was influential on Stanley, foreign secretary from 1866 to 1868, and on Granville, foreign secretary from 1870 to 1874.

Perhaps the most important, and underestimated, reason for British non-intervention in 1870, however, was that France was identified as the main threat: Prussia appeared as the saviour of the status quo, having delivered a change which had appeared an attractive modification of the Vienna settlement to British foreign secretaries in the past. French subversion seemed proven by Nice and Savoy, Poland, Schleswig-Holstein and, latterly, the Luxembourg crisis of 1866, a clumsy French bid for control of Belgian railways and the Benedetti affair.

Hence, when France and Prussia went to war in 1870, Gladstone, Granville and Clarendon might use Britain's lack of military strength to defend non-intervention. In reality it had more to do with the lack of clear necessity to intervene. On the contrary: many expected and feared French victories and expansion. Anti-French feeling and pro-Prussian sympathy was enough, in fact, to produce a policy of neutrality, which worked greatly to Prussia's advantage. On the other hand, Britain's continued official adherence to balance-of-power thinking meant that Anglo-French co-operation was still seen as desirable and few wished to see the destruction of French power: this would completely annihilate the status quo. It would leave Britain at the mercy possibly of an alliance of the eastern powers. It would certainly enable Russia to start expanding once more in the Near and Far East – a fact demonstrated by Russia's decision unilaterally to abrogate the Black Sea agreements of the Paris Peace in 1870. But in general the dangers of Britain's situation were not apparent.

Gladstone, Disraeli, Salisbury

There were those who watched the new type of warfare being conducted on the Continent and felt Britain was deficient in this respect. The Cardwell army reforms (1868–74) reflected this. Gladstone's attempts to assuage American grievances in 1870 and improve relations with Russia over Afghanistan were possibly motivated by a desire to maximize army strength in Europe. Disraeli and Salisbury felt Gladstone was dangerously squandering British prestige abroad. Overall, however, there was no sustained sense of urgency with regards to British security, nor necessity of questioning the methods of Britain's engagement with Europe. The principles of British foreign policy survived relatively unscathed until 1885. Indeed, the reasons for questioning them diminished.

Gladstone's government supported a return to Aberdeen's principles of co-operation with foreign powers based on arbitration for moral reasons – a forerunner of 'ethical foreign policy', as a way of making efficiency gains, and to accommodate Britain's lack of military strength. The problem for Gladstone was that in the wake of tumultuous upheaval European powers were not willing in general to sit and negotiate with each other more than they already had done. Bismarck in particular would have no reopening of the Alsace-Lorraine question, and avoided every attempt to raise the issue. There was not enough steam behind Gladstone's policy at this point. Gladstone entered office with a vast programme of domestic legislation to be passed in a reformed parliament. Domestic politics encouraged a less assertive approach to European affairs.

Things also did not seem particularly worrying abroad. Bismarck's foreign policy until his resignation in 1890 was geared towards preserving the status quo in Europe and the consolidation of the German empire. This basic commitment to peace and the balance of power meant there was a great deal of similarity between British and German priorities. While he avoided Gladstone's overtures regarding a renewal of the European Concert, Bismarck's tactic of offering his services as 'honest broker' over the Black Sea clauses in 1871 – repeated in 1878 and 1884 – was accepted rather naively as evidence of Prussian good intentions. There was little that could be done regarding Russia's actions other than give them the semblance of European legality, but Bismarck's pressure on Russia was appreciated. The Three Emperors' Alliance (1873) appeared to reduce friction in the Balkans. Until 1878, Bismarck also pursued a liberal course at home that, if it did not convince all British liberals, at least divided them.

French primacy in Europe was now at an end. France faced the huge challenges of reconstruction, reparations and the political establishment of the Third Republic. For the moment, French revisionism and ambition appeared checked. Much of it had only been possible through exploiting differences in the Near East. Russian gains in 1871 and the Three Emperors' Alliance now appeared to prevent this. Doubts about the effectiveness of the altered balance of power and Britain's attitude to Europe began to recede.

After 1875, however, things became more difficult when an uprising in Bosnia-Herzegovina threatened an Austro-Russian war in the Balkans. Taylor's account of Disraeli's handling of the Near East crisis of 1875–8 and the Berlin Congress of 1878 is still perhaps one of the most lively and multifaceted to date.[22] It is also traditional in portraying events as a major triumph for Disraeli. Like Bismarck, Disraeli recognized the potential for dispute between Austria and Russia in the Near East. But whereas Bismarck saw the dispute as vitally threatening the German empire, Disraeli identified an opening for undoing what he viewed as a revival of the Holy Alliance, and resuscitating British influence. There was probably little intention on the part of either Russia or Austria to intervene in Turkey: both of them had some interest in seeing the Ottoman empire maintained. But Disraeli, once involved, was not keen to see this agreement reached under the auspices of the Three Emperors' Alliance. The results of the Congress appeared to meet all Britain's demands. Russia was forced to reduce its gains. Disraeli appeared to have revived British prestige abroad. Simultaneously, he had restored a power balance amenable to British influence. Rhetoric and prestige were important tools to maintaining British influence.

Recent historians have, however, emphasized Disraeli's similarity to Palmerston in linking external and internal affairs.[23] In post-1867 parliaments, nationalism, imperialism and jingoism appealed to the expanded electorate, and enabled Conservative governments to survive. One symptom of this was Disraeli's imperialism. It was in this vein too that he approached events in the Near East.

Disraeli's triumphs perpetuated the notion that Britain could control Europe with minimal effort. Once again, events seemed to require nothing more than the use of naval power. Serious doubts about Britain's military capabilities would not resurface until 1898. The self-congratulation surrounding Disraeli's achievement masked the fact that it happened only because Bismarck wanted it to. Disraeli had unwittingly been performing an important task for Bismarck: by bringing Austria and Russia to the negotiating table he was defending the German empire. Bismarck had called British prestige and power back to life as a way of controlling Austria and Russia.

While the growing domestic audience meant Disraeli emulated the liberal Palmerston in foreign affairs, it paradoxically encouraged Gladstone to act like Aberdeen: Disraeli's exploitation of power and dissent among foreign countries, his rumbustious policies in the Near East, in Afghanistan and the Cape, had all repelled one large constituency just as much as it attracted another. Gladstone's Midlothian campaign – begun in 1878 – appealed to anti-interventionist liberals, Christians, commercial and industrial interests, pacifists and internationalists. His election in 1880 demonstrated that this Cobdenite constituency was still a powerful force. From 1880 to 1885 he and his foreign secretary Granville would seek with renewed vigour to apply ethics to foreign policy. Though Seton-Watson established the importance of Gladstone's Midlothian campaigns in terms of tying foreign and domestic policy together, recent research has revived interest in the traditional 'Concert' thinking of the Foreign Office.[24]

Historians have also sought to explain why, even before Gladstone's Concert policy was applied, he contradicted it in Egypt.[25] Since 1876, Britain had tried to co-operate with France to stabilize government in Egypt, both in order to secure the Suez route, and to uphold the interests of British and French investors. In 1880, however, Egyptian nationalist revolts against Turkish and Anglo-French rule began to necessitate intervention. As in Turkey in 1876, France was too worried about the threat from Germany to collaborate. In the face of pressure from their cabinet colleagues, the financial and commercial community, and perhaps Gladstone's own sense of moral and pecuniary propriety, the government decided to intervene and bomb Alexandria in 1882. This was, however, just the start of a process of increasing involvement, and for this reason it has attracted the attention of historians of British imperial policy.[26] In European terms, however, Gladstone's decision is generally seen as seriously damaging Anglo-French relations, and alienating Russia and Turkey.

Medlicott, like others, views Gladstone's notion of the European Concert as naive and self-defeating.[27] It ran directly against Bismarck's desire to maintain, and manipulate, the balance of power. With Russian power momentarily reduced at the Berlin Congress of 1878, Bismarck aimed at a renewed Three Emperors' Alliance reflecting the alterations. The danger still existed that Austria might ally itself with Britain and France and go to war with Russia – a situation undoubtedly resulting in the collapse of Germany. The San Stefano Treaty had raised Bismarck's fears of Russian expansionism, however, and underlined that German defence rested ultimately on Austria. Bismarck therefore signed the Dual Alliance with Austria first in 1879. Bismarck hoped the Dual Alliance, and the knowledge that Germany and Austria would defend each other, would help goad the Russians into a Triple Alliance. This would contain the threat of the Balkans, and strengthen Germany's hand with regard to France.

Bismarck therefore did not welcome Gladstone's approach to the European powers for harmony. His first tactic of arguing that Gladstone's Concert was simply a way of spreading revolutionary ideas on the Continent did not wash, so he changed tack. He decided to work with Gladstone, and thereby convince the Russians that, if they did not sign up, Austria might ally itself with an aggressive Britain. Conversely, he thought the Austrians might accept the Russians as partners if he could show there was a danger of an Anglo-Russian division of Turkey. This was more successful. Russia and Austria both showed interest in co-operating with Britain over the implementation of the agreements of 1878, even if it was only as a way of countering each other.

Gladstone needed little help from Bismarck to undermine his own policy. As Turkish resistance grew to the reforms demanded in 1878, he was forced, and encouraged by Bismarck, into an ever-more-interventionist policy. Together with Britain's actions in Egypt – which Bismarck likewise encouraged to cause a rift between Britain and France – Russia and Austria soon had all the evidence they needed to show that Britain was intent on an aggressive policy regarding Turkey. The Russian government recognized that co-operation with the Eastern Powers would be a better foundation for peace in the Balkans. Austria could see safety in embracing Russia before Britain. The Triple Alliance was signed in 1881. It marked the re-establishment of a balance of power in Europe more favourable to German interests. It also marked the end of any hopes of success for Gladstone's policy of the European Concert.

With the situation to the east stabilized, Bismarck now turned west. The division of Britain and France over Egypt had opened up a route to maintaining good Franco-German relations: encouraging bad Anglo-French ones. This was Bismarck's so-called *bâton egyptienne*. The idea has been picked up again as historical interest in the causes of imperialism has moved back to European-based explanations.[28] Bismarck promoted an imperialist policy, thus supporting French competition to British colonial influence. Friction suddenly appeared between Germany and Britain in Morocco, Angra Pequena, New Guinea, Togoland, the Cameroons and in the Congo. This perplexed Gladstone, who wished ultimately to reduce direct British control in the colonies, and began to irritate his imperialist political opponents and economic interests worried about reviving protectionism abroad. How far Bismarck would have gone before Britain and France came to blows is open to question: ultimately, however, he had no desire to alienate the British entirely, and Gladstone wished to maintain international harmony. The Berlin West Africa Conference of 1884 resulted in great concessions to Germany, and Bismarck could be satisfied that Anglo-French friction was perpetuated. Whether European differences brought about imperialism, or imperialism sowed dissent in Europe, by the end of Gladstone's government, British European and imperial policy had merged.

Until the end of the century, British foreign policy was increasingly concerned with the expansion of Russian power. Russia's stance over the unification of Bulgaria and eastern Rumelia in 1885 had become ever more threatening. Crucially for Britain, it was accompanied by renewed pressure on Afghanistan and India. Indeed, since 1878, Russia appeared to have been set on a much more aggressive course in Asia, possibly recognizing the effectiveness of the Berlin Treaty in closing the Black Sea for now. Yet, since 1880, the French attitude to Britain had also been hostile, and policies pursued by France in North Africa increasingly aggressive.

Bismarck's about-turn towards Britain in 1884 had much to do with German fears about Russian intentions and the rise of Boulangism in France. It had also begun to encourage closer Franco-Russian relations. The Italian government – brought into the Triple Alliance in 1882 as a bulwark against Russian advances on Austria – also sought greater support from Britain in the Mediterranean against France. Salisbury appreciated that the most natural reaction to growing Russian and French aggressiveness was to move closer to the Triple Alliance. His policy was initially hesitant: cabinet opposition from Randolph Churchill, who supported Tory democracy and reduced expenditure, prevented any movement. However, by 1887, the Bulgarian situation was so pressing that Salisbury was able to overrule Churchill.

The first Mediterranean Treaty was an important victory for Salisbury – as it reduced Russian pressure in the Near East, protected Bulgaria and Turkey, and enabled Britain to focus attention elsewhere. It was a sign of the times, in that it was made necessary because of nascent European competition to Britain's position outside Europe. The most comprehensive and multilateral study of the subject remains that of Lowe.[29]

The treaty has often been interpreted as a radical deviation from previous British policy towards Europe – in that Salisbury bound Britain into an alliance neither relating to immediate national defence nor signed by all European powers. It is viewed as a step on the road to Britain's inclusion in the alliance system of 1914. However, perhaps accommodating his rather fragmented political support in parliament, and fearing foreign entanglements when the issue of Ireland was creating discord at home, Salisbury avoided presenting the agreement as a major departure of foreign policy: he insisted that the treaty did not commit Britain to the defence of particular countries, but was simply a joint declaration of support for the status quo in the Mediterranean. Italian efforts to exploit the treaty to tie Britain into its increasingly heated altercation with France in North Africa were rejected. So, too, were Bismarck's efforts to make the treaty stipulations more binding as France and Russia moved closer together. Salisbury's starting-point was still the reduction of British involvement to the minimum necessary – and he possibly calculated that a more binding commitment to Italy would encourage further pretensions in Rome. He also recognized that the only real obstacle to better Anglo-French relations was Egypt – and when signing the Mediterranean Treaty he simultaneously approached the French for an agreement on the issue – though this was for the moment prevented by Russian pressure.

From the late 1880s the danger to Britain became a combined one of Russia and France. The French threat was momentarily the most obvious after Russia unilaterally recognized Bulgaria in 1888 (a result of the Mediterranean Treaty). There was a war scare over Italy. Salisbury shared many of the public doubts about Britain's ability to compete with France in the Mediterranean – especially given France's technically superior fleet, and its collaboration with Russia. However, he faced, on the one hand, the hesitancy of military planners at the Board of Admiralty about the best way forward and, on the other, the dangers of being forced into a closer relationship with the Triple Alliance. By 1888 Bismarck was making heavy references to a full Anglo-German alliance. In the end, Salisbury was able to play one against the other: Bismarck's concerns about the Franco-Russian threat were used to persuade public and parliament to agree to the biggest-ever increase in naval spending in peacetime. The 'two-power standard', then, was the alternative to agreeing to full-blown alliances with Italy or Germany.

Overall, the growing Franco-Russian threat forced the Triple Alliance and Britain together in the late 1880s. But there was still a factor which separated them: the Triple Alliance powers – Italy, but also Germany – were much more directly threatened by France and Russia than Britain. In consequence, though domestic, personal and party factors played a role, Salisbury only ever looked for a limited form of co-operation. The same was true of the Anglo-German agreement to exchange Heligoland for territory in East Africa in 1890, even if the German government was now already headed on a much more aggrandizing policy in Europe: after Bismarck's fall, the government of Wilhelm II made a perhaps fatal decision to push for an Anglo-German alliance, and base its security on that and its relationship with Austria. Wilhelm II hoped that Germany could now perhaps wrest itself free of conservative Russia, expand in Eastern Europe, and build up its own navy. Whereas the German government saw the Zanzibar–Heligoland negotiations as an important step towards full alliance and its own navy, however, Salisbury continued to view it as merely a way of maintaining a good relationship with Germany as long as the threat from France and Russia continued.

Until the mid-1890s, the diplomatic situation remained similar in configuration, if ever more sharply in relief: Wilhelm II's decision to scrap the Reinsurance Treaty with Russia in 1890 – signed in 1889 to try and calm nerves on both sides over the Balkans – led directly to Franco-Russian political alliance in 1891 and full military alliance in 1894. This necessitated however the von Schlieffen military plan for war on two fronts in 1892, and an even more forceful bid by Germany for Anglo-German alliance. The Siam crisis of 1893 was used to put pressure on Britain – an early indication of a recurring pattern later in the decade. The return of Gladstone in 1892, however, made alliance with Germany impossible. Gladstone's personal antipathy to empire, his increased domestic difficulties, his pacifist leanings and his desire – like Salisbury – to bridge the gap with France, worked against it. By this point, German commercial competition round the world and even on British markets was also making Germany unpopular in Britain. In many ways, it seemed continued French dreams of Egypt – culminating in the Fashoda incident of 1878 – was the only thing maintaining good Anglo-German relations.

Historians tracing Britain's traditional policy of non-intervention and inaction in the face of growing power often argued that traditional ways of thinking about Europe still survived.[30] Certainly, Salisbury's policies in the late 1880s encouraged their longevity. The Mediterranean Treaty seemed to provide some basis for believing Russian influence in Turkey was under control. The 'two-power standard' was a psychological barricade of sorts; a temporary structure supporting notions that Britain could ultimately defend itself and needed no firm alliances with foreign powers. The foundation of British foreign policy since 1815 had been an underlying sense of security against foreign threats, and a belief that the balance of power would serve to protect British interests.

Nevertheless, between 1894 and 1897, a combination of factors has been identified contributing to the demise of such ways of thinking. As Bourne and Kennedy have argued, there was the growing threat from Russia after 1894, particularly in the Far East. Franco-Russian agreement intensified between 1892 and 1895. The necessity for increased naval spending as a response to this forced Gladstone's resignation in 1894. Gladstone was opposed to the financial and moral implications of such an increase, but his departure also perhaps symbolized the weakening of policies of pacification and the onset of power politics in Europe. Gladstone's foreign secretary and successor as prime minister, Rosebery, was faced by a renewed push by Russia in Afghanistan, however. Rosebery, like Gladstone and Salisbury, continued to seek an understanding with France – but to no avail. The situation worsened for Britain as Russia's exploitation of the Trans-Siberian railway led to pressure on China for access to Mongolia in 1894–5, and a pre-emptive invasion of China in Korea by Japan. Arguably, Salisbury's Mediterranean Treaty had failed to curtail Russian expansionism, and had even distracted it further east. However, even in the eastern Mediterranean, Russian power seemed to grow again – with intervention in Armenia in 1895 causing great alarm in Britain.

By the mid-1890s, Salisbury was one of many reflecting on the incessant growth of competition to British power and the possible application of Darwinist theories to international relations. His response seems at first to have been a decision to recognize realities and consolidate and defend gains, and only then to look for an alliance based on a careful assessment of Britain's needs. Possibly, even now, he continued to believe that the onslaught on British interests was a temporary one, and, by judicious action, it might be outlived. This pragmatic and conservative approach often caused concern among critics. However, historians have interpreted this stance as constructive, not blinkered.[31] Here, perhaps, lay the germ of Grey's morally upright, but doomed, search for peace.

One of the first realities faced by Salisbury was the indefensible nature of Turkey, morally and practically. Even by the time of the Armenian crisis, however, Britain's security interests in the Mediterranean had shifted away from a concern for Turkey proper, and towards the Suez Canal. The diminishing lack of concern for Turkey and focus on Egypt explained the British push into Uganda and the Sudan in 1894. This provided the background to Anglo-French confrontation at Fashoda, and explains why Salisbury began exploring the possibilities of an arrangement with Russia to divide Turkey in 1896. This, in turn, reveals why Salisbury failed to agree with the German ambassador, Hatzfeldt, on an Anglo-German treaty over the Balkans. The German price for agreement – an alliance for defence of Germany in Europe which would have alienated Russia and possibly been a blank cheque for German aggression – now seemed far too high.

Indeed, the other major problem Britain began to face from 1896 onwards, most substantially researched by Kennedy, was the increasingly aggressive posture of the German government and its attempts to extract ever greater rewards from Britain's predicament.[32] The practice found its roots in Bismarck's foreign policy, but Wilhelm II had used it in the 1890s with increasing audacity and clumsiness. Attempts to highlight to the British government its own weakness in order to drive it into an embrace with Germany – such as the Kruger telegram in 1895 – had a certain logic, but were patently not enough to bring the agreement desired on either side. Neither could the efforts of Joseph Chamberlain to solve Britain's problems through full-blown alliance with Germany overcome the differences of interest and priority, as negotiations over China in 1898 illustrated. Salisbury was not prepared to make an arrangement which would commit Britain to the defence of Germany in Alsace-Lorraine. Germany, meanwhile, simply was not able to provide the defence Britain needed in China. The dilemma for Britain at the turn of the century, caught between Russian and German expansionism, has been impressively researched in Steiner's magisterial book on the origins of the First World War.[33]

The way out of Britain's dilemma was, perhaps paradoxically, opened up by the Fashoda incident. France's climb-down over Egypt removed one of the lasting obstacles to Anglo-French agreement. British foreign policy was beginning to turn full circle, in the sense that France was also identified in 1815 as the key to Britain's ability to maintain the balance of power in Europe. However, this way of thinking was still embryonic at the turn of the century. Fashoda possibly blew a last gasp of wind into the sails of those who thought Britain could determine its own fate – encouraging involvement in the Boer War in 1899. It was only once all permutations of alliance had been tried, and Britain was finally cast upon the assistance of Japan in the Far East, that the way to an understanding with France became possible. Even when it came in 1904 it could not muster an alliance, only an *entente*.

Conclusion

The historical literature on British foreign policy in the nineteenth century remains overwhelmingly diplomatic and narrative in character. The small amount of research benefiting from more recent lines of enquiry regarding foreign policy has so far failed to dislodge older, established, lines of enquiry. Nevertheless, incisive new approaches have been undertaken, even if limited in period or subject. There has also been a healthy pragmatism in diplomatic literature which has meant that, while questions such as structural, economic, cultural or personal factors of decision-making have not been dealt with in the abstract, they have often been woven into an integrated narrative. Particularly with regards to the latter third of the nineteenth century, a preoccupation with the origins of the First World War has led to greater interaction with decision-making approaches and awareness of the links between British and imperial policy-making.

The main preoccupation has been the issue of British willingness to intervene in Europe from 1815 onwards. A polarity has been identified between one approach favouring congresses and diplomatic co-operation between the five powers and another tending towards reliance upon the balance of power, with Britain intervening unilaterally to a greater or lesser extent to maintain equilibrium. Some literature has sought to take issue with the notion of polarity, insisting on the continuity of British foreign policy. Some recent research, however, reiterates this polarity and broadens explanations of it. Overall, however, there appears agreement that Britain was committed to the balance of power underpinning the Vienna agreements. Differences may have existed regarding how to maintain that balance. But commitment to it as a method of ensuring peace in Europe remained strong, despite the huge changes taking place on the Continent.

Another unifying theme in historical literature about British foreign policy in this period is the contrast between aims and the actual ability to achieve them. British decision-makers showed either a remarkable reluctance to accept the realities of their own power, or else a canny recognition of their own limitations and methods of overcoming them. However, towards the end of the nineteenth century, a variety of factors forced upon decision-makers in London both a realization that the balance of power of Vienna offered no further hope of peace and a recognition of Britain's limits of action. By the close of the century this way of thinking had still not become dominant in political discourse, and can be perhaps characterized as one present as yet only in the nation's subconscious.

NOTES

1. H. Temperley and L. M. Penson, *Foundations of British Foreign Policy: From Pitt (1792) to Salisbury (1902)* (Cambridge, 1938); A. Ward and G. P. Gooch, *The Cambridge History of British Foreign Policy* (Cambridge, 1923); R. W. Seton-Watson, *Britain in Europe 1789–1914* (Cambridge, 1937); C. K. Webster, *The Foreign Policy of Lord Castlereagh*, 2 vols (London, 1931 and 1934); idem, *The Congress of Vienna, 1814–1815* (London, 1934).

2. D. C. M. Platt, *Finance, Trade and Politics in British Foreign Policy 1815–1914* (Oxford, 1968), p. xiv.

3. Z. S. Steiner, *Britain and the Origins of the First World War* (Basingstoke, 1977), pp. 1–3.

4. A. J. P. Taylor, *The Struggle for Mastery in Europe, 1848–1918* (Oxford, 1954).

5. K. Bourne, *The Foreign Policy of Victorian England, 1830–1902* (Oxford, 1970); P. M. Kennedy, *The Rise of the Anglo-German Antagonism 1860–1914* (London, 1980); C. J. Lowe, *Salisbury and the Mediterranean, 1886–1896* (London, 1965).

6. M. Chamberlain, *'Pax Britannica'? British Foreign Policy, 1789–1914* (London, 1988).

7. P. W. Schroeder, *The Transformation of European Politics 1763–1848* (Oxford, 1994).

8. J. Joll, ed., *Britain and Europe: Pitt to Churchill 1793–1940* (London, 1950), pp. 48–69.

9. Chamberlain, *'Pax Britannica'?*, p. 50.

10. Chamberlain, *'Pax Britannica'?*, p. 35.

11. C. J. Bartlett, *Defence and Diplomacy: Britain and the Great Powers, 1815–1914* (Manchester, 1993), p. 28.

12. Temperley and Penson, *Foundations*.

13. Bartlett, *Defence and Diplomacy*, p. 28.

14.   D. S. Brown, 'Palmerston and the politics of foreign policy 1846–1855', PhD diss., University of Exeter, 1988; G. Billy, *Palmerston's Foreign Policy 1848* (New York, 1993).

15.   C. J. Bartlett, 'Britain and the European balance 1815–48', in A. Sked, ed., *Europe's Balance of Power* (London, 1979), pp. 152–6.

16.   Bourne, *Foreign Policy*, pp. 48–56.

17.   Bourne, *Foreign Policy*, p. 75.

18.   Temperley and Penson, *Foundations*; Joll, *Britain and Europe*; F. S. Northedge, *Foreign Policies of the Powers* (London, 1968).

19.   For example, Steiner, *Britain and the Origins*.

20.   F. L. Müller, *Britain and the German Question: Perceptions of Nationalism and Political Reform, 1830–63* (Basingstoke, 2002).

21.   J. Lowe, *Britain and Foreign Affairs, 1815–1885: Europe and Overseas* (London, 1998), p. 11.

22.   Taylor, *Struggle for Mastery*, ch. 11.

23.   Lowe, *Britain and Foreign Affairs*, pp. 74–6.

24.   Seton-Watson 'Preface', *Britain in Europe*; S. A. Odubena, 'The idea of "concert" in diplomatic practice between 1878 and 1906', PhD diss., University of London, 1995.

25.   W. N. Medlicott, *Bismarck, Gladstone, and the Concert of Europe* (New York, 1969).

26.   R. Langhorne, *The Collapse of the Concert of Europe: International Politics 1830–1914* (Basingstoke, 1981).

27.   Medlicott, *Bismarck*.

28.   J. Lowe, *The Great Powers, Imperialism and the German Problem 1865–1895* (London, 1994).

29.   Lowe, *Salisbury and the Mediterranean*, chs 1–3.

30.   Ward and Gooch, *Cambridge History*; Temperley and Penson, *Foundations*.

31.   Steiner, *Britain and the Origins*, pp. 22–8; Bourne, *Foreign Policy*, pp. 165–75.

32.   Kennedy, *Rise of the Anglo-German Antagonism*.

33.   Steiner, *Britain and the Origins*.

FURTHER READING

C. J. Bartlett, *Defence and Diplomacy: Britain and the Great Powers, 1815–1914* (1993) is a pragmatic study of British foreign policy and in particular the problems of organizing military and naval defence and the impact of these issues on decision-making. K. Bourne, *The Foreign Policy of Victorian England, 1830–1902* (1970) is still one of the richest and most detailed narratives of Victorian foreign policy, if given to diplomatic generalization in places. M. Byrne, *Britain and the European Powers 1815–65* (1998) is a recent study of British foreign policy with an approach borrowing from recent theories of decision-making. R. Langhorne, *The Collapse of the Concert of Europe: International Politics 1830–1914* (1981) is a diplomatic account of European history which charts the breakdown of the Vienna system. It is essential for the context of British decision-making. J. Lowe, *The Great Powers, Imperialism and the German Problem 1865–1985* (1994) offers a useful and thought-provoking study of the relationship between imperialism and the German problem in Europe. J. Lowe, *Britain and Foreign Affairs 1815–1885: Europe and Overseas* (1998) is a general study of British foreign affairs, but which sets its narrative in the context of evolving international systems. Z. S. Steiner, *Britain and the Origins of the First World War* (1977) is a work which is useful for the later period and is one of the most readable, realistic and fair studies of decision-makers as they faced the emerging Franco-Russian, and, subsequently, German threat.

CHAPTER THREE

Britain and Empire

DOUGLAS M. PEERS

Lord Salisbury, prime minister when Queen Victoria died, eulogized her reign by singling out the developments which best characterized the preceding sixty-three years: rising wealth, civic order, and the growth of the British Empire. Empire was also a central theme in Victoria's funeral procession which contained some 50,000 British and empire troops, a glittering spectacle intended to impress observers with Britain's global reach. In the words of the *Daily Mail*, it was 'an anthropological museum – a living gazetteer of the British Empire.' Eight years before, historian and essayist W. E. Lecky summed up this popular impression when he gushed that 'Nothing in the history of the world is more wonderful than that under the flag of these two little islands there should have grown up the greatest and most beneficent despotism in the world, comprising nearly two hundred and thirty millions of inhabitants under direct British rule, and more than fifty millions under British protectorates . . .'.[1]

The empire was one of the defining characteristics of nineteenth-century Britain. By 1914, it comprised some 88 m people – a quarter of the total population of the world – and an estimated one-fifth of the world's landmass. Add in those parts of the world where British economic, political and cultural influence had deeply penetrated (such as China and parts of Latin America), and the proportion of the world's population under British sway would exceed one-third. And the empire had not reached its greatest extent – that would come in 1918 when the colonial territories of Germany and the remnants of the Ottoman empire were distributed amongst the First World War victors. It is the difference between the size of the core and its ever-expanding periphery (which has been computed at a ratio of 125 to 1) that informed early efforts at understanding how Britain acquired such an empire, for such a disparity seemed to many to suggest some innate and unique potential on the part of the British, a potential that was the basis of much celebration and some reflection. Imperial historiography hence had, from the outset, a predisposition towards emphasizing what was unique and exceptional to Britain, often delivered in a celebratory manner.

Yet empire was not simply about pomp and ceremony: even at its height there was considerable ambivalence and noticeable anxiety. Beneath this apparent pride, even arrogance, lurked a much more complex and contested set of imperial relationships and cultures. Britain, after all, was a small island off the north coast of Europe, ruling a vast empire, and some authorities were deeply anxious about its survival. Other commentators had begun to question its value in light of the moral and political objections raised against it. The empire was growing, but the gap between Britain and its closest rivals on the Continent as well as the USA was closing at an even faster rate. To this can be added the growing challenges from within the empire – the growth of colonial nationalism as seen in the formation of the Indian National Congress in 1885, the outbreak of the South African War in 1899, and unresolved questions over Ireland, to name but a few. All of these developments helped to expose the fault-lines within the empire as well as illuminate its many paradoxes. It is the tension between pride and anxiety, between complacency and ambivalence, and between optimism and pessimism about what the future had in store for the empire, that historians have profitably begun to explore, for it opens up a wide range of possibilities for an examination of imperial and British history, not as two discrete fields as was often the case in the past but as mutually constitutive fields of enquiry.

For example, it was an empire that made frequent appeals to ideals of political and legal liberty, yet depended ultimately on coercion and the suspension of such principles.[2] This disjuncture was not lost on contemporaries. The historian Seeley, while convinced that empire was a positive force, could not help but note the paradox, querying in 1883, 'How can the same nation pursue two lines of policy so radically different without bewilderment, be despotic in Asia and democratic in Australia, be in the East at once the greatest Mussulman Power in the World . . . at the same time in the West be the foremost champion of free thought and spiritual religion.'[3] It would be too easy to dismiss this as just another example of Victorian hypocrisy. We need instead to see beyond such caricatured images. It was after all the Victorians who returned the first Asian MP to parliament. Such caveats, however, should not be overstated, as there was little fear at that time that Britain would experience the kinds of migrations that marked the post-1945 period and consequently there were fewer fears in the nineteenth century that British identity would be diluted. But as work on the 1867 Reform Bill has illustrated, race did make its presence felt in debates over citizenship as the franchise was extended in some places (Canada, Australia and Britain) while it was retracted or delayed in others (Jamaica, Natal).[4]

Another paradox is that much of the contemporary rhetoric as well as subsequent historiography has played up the interventionist character of imperial rule, implying an association between imperialism and modernization (however warped this became in practice), yet imperialism often had the opposite effect, that in fact British rule petrified if not invented outright social and political institutions that obstructed economic and social development within subject communities. Moreover, this emphasis on the capacity of the British to impose their will and in so doing remake the societies over which they had gained control (for good or ill), which has been a stock theme in much imperial historiography, has done so by playing down the resilience and initiatives of local societies as well as by exaggerating both the resources and the single-minded determination of the British to effect such changes. Again, the story is much more complex and nuanced.

More recently, attention has shifted to the pathways through which the empire left its mark on domestic society. Until recently this had been largely ignored: imperial historians were moving outwards to the periphery and losing sight of Britain in the process while domestic historians rarely looked beyond Britain, or at best they gazed briefly at the Continent, prompting Salman Rushdie to lament that 'the trouble with the English is that their history happened overseas, so they don't know what it means'.[5] No history of nineteenth-century Britain can be complete without acknowledging the impact that the empire had in fashioning political culture, informing strategic and diplomatic priorities, shaping social institutions and cultural practices, and determining, at least in part, the rate and direction of economic development. Moreover, British identity was bound up with the empire. 'In the nineteenth century the empire, both imagined and directly experienced, was a powerful part of what it meant to be English, intimately linked to what it meant to be white.'[6]

The imperial legacy does not end there, for the empire has left a very visible imprint on contemporary Britain. This can be seen in the composition of British society and the development of its national culture, all of which were affected by its adjustment to a post-imperial world. Over half of London's school-age children speak at least one of the other 250 languages in use in London: many of these languages were brought to London by immigrants from the empire. The shortlists in recent years for the Booker Prize testify to the persistence of imperial echoes in British society. The importance of the empire in fashioning modern Britain is also attested to by the results of the 2001 census which tell us that while nearly 52 million residents of Britain identify themselves as white, there are about 500,000 who trace their ancestry to the Caribbean, a further 200,000 descended from immigrants from Africa, 840,000 from India, nearly 500,000 from Pakistan, and a further 163,000 from Bangladesh. Islam is now the fastest-growing religion in Britain, and its adherents already outnumber the Methodists and Baptists combined while demographic forecasts point to Leicester being Britain's first ethnic-majority city by 2011.

It is these imperial legacies that lie behind much of the most recent and exciting work in imperial history, for they have suggested that imperialism had a deeply pervasive and sustained impact on Britain and consequently imperial history has been reinvigorated, new questions are being asked and old questions have been recast in new and innovative ways. The subsequent transformation of imperial history within the last decade has been quite remarkable. Periodic attempts at assessing the state of the field undertaken prior to this resurgence (which began in the late 1980s) generally made for depressing reading, at least for imperial historians.[7] The rise of area studies had shifted the study of particular colonies out of an imperial rubric while British historians were either turning inwards or were looking to the Continent. That this is no longer the case is evident in the publication of the *Oxford History of the British Empire* (1998–9) and the vigorous debates which followed its appearance.

But a word of caution is in order: not all dimensions of imperial history have benefited equally from this renewed engagement. The economics of empire have been curiously absent from many recent studies, and there is a clear preference for studying either the non-white parts of the empire or the metropole itself. The white settlement colonies, once the favoured subject of those who wished to highlight the evolutionary and beneficial nature of imperialism, have fallen from view and have become largely the preserve of their own national historians for whom the empire is often an anachronism, and an awkward one at that. Moreover, the current emphasis on the power/knowledge equation that underpinned imperial rule, which has emphasized the ability of imperial knowledge not only to make the empire more manageable but also to remake colonized societies in such a way as to render them vulnerable to forms of post-imperial exploitation (often referred to as neo-colonialism), has ironically led at times to a reversion to an older mode of thinking about empire, one which emphasized imperial initiative at the expense of indigenous resistance and resilience.

In addition, while much is being written on the two-way flow of ideas, institutions and people between the metropole and periphery, work needs to be done on similar currents within the periphery, since imperialism was not simply a series of bilateral relationships. Instead it was a complex matrix. We need also to bear in mind that imperialism was never a monolithic enterprise, nor was its experience the same for all. Imperialism meant and continues to mean different and sometimes opposing things to different groups. It is just as easy to exaggerate the impact of the empire on Britain as it is to overplay the role of imperialism in the lives of its subject peoples. Imperialism was often a decisive and traumatic force on people's lives, but it was not the sole process that shaped their existence and moulded their identity. We should also acknowledge that many of the lines of debate found within current imperial historiography echo earlier debates, though they are often articulated with greater sophistication today.

What is Imperial History?

Studying imperial history is much easier than defining it; unlike national histories, imperial history has no clear-cut geographical boundaries, nor do imperial historians subscribe to a common analytical framework, perspective or methodology. Furthermore, empire and imperialism conjure up such strong images of exploitation and oppression that imperial historians have had to contend with the often passionate feelings aroused by their study. The contentiousness of the topic is by no means a recent development. In fact, for much of the nineteenth century, imperialism was a term of abuse – an epithet to be hurled at the French or the Russians – for it carried with it connotations of aggressive, militaristic expansion of the kind associated with a Napoleon or a Russian tsar. The situation was not much different in 1959, when one notable imperial historian bemoaned that imperialism 'is no word for scholars . . . In our times it has become a football, a war cry, a labelled card in a sociological laboratory.'[8] Yet, in the absence of a commonly agreed-upon alternative, and confronted by the fact that the British Empire did exist, the word imperialism has remained part of our vocabulary. But what was imperialism; was it simply the power to dominate, either politically, economically or some combination of both, or was it much more of a cultural form, one in which power was ultimately about the power to represent?

The debate over which of these definitions is more appropriate shows no sign of abating. A narrow political definition can be applied, one which refers to a particular political form in which authority is vested in an emperor. While this definition would include, among others, the Roman, Mughal, Byzantine and Aztec empires, it would exclude many others, including for much of the time those of France, Holland and even Britain where Victoria's title of Empress only referred to India. Another definition of empire which has been invoked is that it refers to a geographically defined area brought under the territorial control of another state. Yet this definition, with its emphasis on formal political control over a fixed area, has also been found wanting, for it fails to address those instances where one state controls or has considerable influence over another without necessarily claiming sovereignty – such as that enjoyed by Britain in China, Siam or much of Latin America. Hence, people speak of informal imperialism and cultural imperialism, neither of which requires overt political domination. Such a definition makes allowance for the great number of avenues through which authority can be exercised, and does not require power to be politically formalized and applied to a clearly demarcated territory. Such flexibility does not come without some cost. Critics have pointed out that all types of power relationship could be included within such an elastic rubric. Their arguments have been countered by those who insist that by limiting ourselves to formally constituted empires, it becomes difficult to incorporate the perpetuation of imperial influences in nominally independent countries.[9] This struggle over mapping out the empire has a long history; as early as 1959 Curtin was complaining that empire 'is not only an ungainly beast, but one that constantly changes its size and shape with the passing of the years.'[10]

In the end, we must acknowledge that a comprehensive definition of imperialism will continue to elude us, and should do so because the definition will be determined by what is being measured, and that is notoriously difficult to pin down. Yet we can conclude that what unites imperial historians is that they study empires, and a process (or processes) which can be termed imperialism, which produces and sustains empires. It is not surprising that the current practice in defining empires and imperialism is to leave them as broad as possible at the outset, and allow them to be refined by the particular context being examined. These terms serve as umbrellas under which a variety of structures and processes can shelter. Imperialism then would refer to the control and influence exercised by a strong state over a weaker state, with such controls and influences being applied in ways different to but drawing upon those that the dominant state would employ within its own metropolitan territories.

The British Empire, 1800–1901

1800 is not a particularly significant date in imperial history for there was no particular piece of legislation or dramatic event which would have suggested to a contemporary observer that the post-1800 empire would be different from that which preceded it. It does, however, fall roughly part-way through an era (1776–1815) in which there were a number of developments that would transform the empire. The loss of the American colonies had a profound impact, as did the experience of the Revolutionary and Napoleonic Wars. Britain lost valuable territories in the New World, but wars with France accelerated expansion in India and also enabled Britain to seize territories from its French, Dutch and Spanish rivals. Britain emerged from the Napoleonic Wars as the first global superpower: politically its opponents were in disarray, Britain's economic potential had grown considerably through the war, its naval forces together with strategic annexations gave it effective command over the major seaborne lines of communication, and the war encouraged the growth of a national feeling which would strengthen and in turn be strengthened by imperial expansion.[11]

In 1792, the British Empire consisted of twenty-six colonies. In 1815 that number had grown to forty-two, following a series of conquests from France and its allies, as well as expansion from already occupied territories. While some wartime acquisitions were returned to their previous imperial rulers (Java and Surinam were relinquished to the Dutch and the French received back, among others, Martinique and Guadeloupe) many strategically valuable or economically promising conquests were retained. Cape Town and its environs and Sri Lanka were taken permanently from the Dutch who had allied themselves with the French. In India, Governor General Wellesley had taken advantage of fears of French and Russian threats to extend British authority over a number of Indian states, making the British the paramount power in the subcontinent. Efforts at forestalling French or Russian designs also embroiled the British in Central Asian affairs as alliances were pursued with Persia and Afghanistan, thus setting in motion the 'Great Game' which would lead to a series of wars, costly in men and resources, but providing plenty of dramatic episodes which fed the public taste for heroic acts. The British also established a number of beach-heads in Africa: Cape Town, kept because of its strategic location, became a spring-board for expansion into southern Africa, and Sierra Leone, initially established by a charity as a place where ex-slaves and free blacks from Nova Scotia and Britain could be repatriated, provided a base for British interests in West Africa. Tasmania was added to New South Wales as the basis for what would become Australia, and Britain's Caribbean possessions grew with the addition of Trinidad and Tobago.

Not only was the empire growing in size, its orientation and complexion were also being transformed. The empire's centre of gravity was shifting eastwards, and it was increasingly peopled by persons of non-European origins. The so-called 'Swing to the East' produced a very different empire, one which was more visible but whose overall political and economic importance had declined. In strictly economic terms, empire was more important in the eighteenth century when Atlantic trade was a vital part of the British economy. The loss of the American colonies and the declining significance of the sugar plantations to the British economy encouraged a shift eastwards. The plantation lobby in parliament began to decline, especially following abolition of the slave trade in 1807 and then emancipation of the slaves in 1833. In 1815, trade with the West Indies amounted to 17.6 per cent of Britain's total overseas trade. By the early twentieth century, it had fallen to less than 1 per cent. The British Empire of the nineteenth century was becoming much more global, extending its roots more deeply into India and entrenching itself in Africa and South-East Asia.

The political and economic institutions necessary to administer and benefit from such acquisitions also became more complex. Imperial policy in the eighteenth century did not belong to any particular department, and there was no systematic bureaucracy to administer imperial affairs with the exception of India which, until 1858, remained under the control of the East India Company, a chartered corporation though from 1774 onwards increasingly subject to government oversight. India's unique place within the empire, and the elaborate bureaucracy that had emerged to govern it, led to it being made a separate government ministry following the abolition of the East India Company in the aftermath of the Indian Rebellion of 1857–8. Elsewhere, the increasingly large and diverse empire demanded some form of administrative control and consequently the office of Secretary for War and the Colonies was established in 1801 when colonial affairs were added to the existing secretary for war's portfolio. The two were kept together until 1854 when the demands of the Crimean War led to a separate war ministry. While the position of colonial secretary (and that of secretary for India) generally lagged behind the offices of chancellor, foreign secretary and home secretary, at least as far as rank and influence were concerned, it did offer considerable scope for individuals with imperial appetites such as Joseph Chamberlain because they were subject to less public and parliamentary scrutiny, and hence could enjoy more autonomy than their colleagues elsewhere in the administration. In addition, the Foreign Office played an important role in imperial affairs, especially in those parts of the world that were not formally under British control but where the British had important interests and over which they exercised influence.

Hindsight also indicates just how much the culture of that empire was changing. It was becoming more capacious. Earlier objectives of facilitating trade and commerce were being joined by more ambitious designs such as devising systems of rule for societies that were deemed to be vastly different from those at home. This led to demands for greater knowledge about the world, as well as the means to organize and disseminate such information. Geographical, economic and ethnographic data gained in importance, and with it came new techniques of acquisition. The rise of statistical thinking was closely tied to imperial needs as evidenced in the pages of the *Journal of the Statistical Society of London*. Censuses and handbooks proliferated, and travelogues gained in popularity. The demands for expert knowledge encouraged growing professionalization which resulted in an array of specialist periodicals.

There was also a growing sense of purpose – empire was not simply about economic benefit at home; rather, empire brought with it responsibilities for the moral, economic and social improvement of the subject peoples. While such beliefs would strike us today as naive, paternalistic and frequently hypocritical (and they were often deployed to camouflage baser motives), they widened and extended the scope for imperial intervention as well as participation. As one recent assessment has put it, 'Although the immediate results of so much righteous fervour were often disappointing, its indirect and long-term consequences were considerable.'[12] The empire provided scope for groups such as missionaries and medical doctors who sought to enhance their status and confirm their professionalism. The growth in missionary activity is but one example of this – by the end of the nineteenth century it is estimated that there were approximately 10,000 British missionaries serving overseas. As many as two-thirds of these were women, who found in the imperial arena a place where they could demonstrate that they were ready for imperial citizenship.

Yet this surge in imperial activity did not necessarily draw upon any deep or sustained popular commitment to empire on the part of domestic society. Interest in imperial issues was there, and the slave trade became an especially contentious topic with its opponents mobilizing a broad swathe of opinion against it, including an especially important role for women.[13] Similarly, readers were often eager to hear about British military campaigns in far-off exotic lands. The defeat of Tipu Sultan of Mysore in 1799 was a popular subject in the press and many were eager to read of the atrocities he had inflicted upon his British prisoners. Interest was also generated by accounts of the Afghan Wars (1839–42, 1878–9), Zulu War (1879) and the campaigns of the Indian Rebellion (1857–8).[14]

But public interest in and commitment to the empire should not be assumed to exist in all situations and at all times, for attention to imperial issues remained fitful and often partisan. Empire was distant from the lives of many in Britain. This is also true for parliament where it was joked that the fastest way to clear the House of Commons was to introduce a discussion about British policy in India. Parliamentary interest in imperial topics would continue to fluctuate over the course of the nineteenth century, peaking during sensational crises like that of the Indian Rebellion or Morant Bay, or when imperial developments intersected with major domestic issues; otherwise, imperial topics tended to languish. Even the British North America Act (1867) evoked little interest and even less debate despite this legislation granting internal self-government to what would become Canada, thereby establishing a prototype for the later Commonwealth.

This sputtering interest in imperial issues is bound up with what an earlier generation of historians had argued was a declining interest in and commitment to empire in the mid-nineteenth century. The conventional periodization of the British Empire divides the nineteenth century into three broad eras: the period up to around 1820 when, as a consequence of the global wars against France and its allies, the empire was expanding, a prolonged period between 1820 and 1870 when interest in empire was either languishing or declining, and then a resurgence in imperial interest in the last three decades, symbolized by British participation in the scramble for Africa. The pace of imperial acquisitions certainly quickened after 1870, and not surprisingly this has been one of the most heavily scrutinized periods in imperial history. Ironically, though, the acquisitions of the late nineteenth century did not economically or politically benefit the British as much as earlier conquests. Much of tropical Africa, for example, yielded little by way of natural resources, and the societies found within Africa could not be easily transformed into imperial consumers. Africa, the focus for so much imperial activity, was responsible in 1900 for only about 4 per cent of Britain's overseas trade.

The mid-nineteenth century has not been so well explored of late, largely because many erroneously assumed that this period was one in which opposition to empire was in the ascendancy. Evidence for this position comes from a number of directions. For one, the first halting steps towards colonial self-government were taking place in the white settler colonies of British North America, the Cape Colony, Australia and New Zealand. Such moves were taken as proof of a drift towards imperial disengagement. Then there were a number of very vocal critics of the empire who stressed that empire was not only incompatible with British values, but was also ultimately not in Britain's interests for it would retard rather than encourage economic development at a time when liberal capitalism was already well on the way to becoming the new orthodoxy. Finally, there were those who argued that imperial expansion had little to offer as the most profitable bits had already been taken up and what remained could be secured without having recourse to conquest.

Ethical concerns about empire were also being raised during this period. This was not the first time that ethics had entered imperial debates: the attempted impeachment of Warren Hastings in the eighteenth century had brought British actions in India under intense scrutiny and Britain's dominant role in the Atlantic slave trade was the subject of an intense campaign that cut through class, regional and gender lines in its mobilization of mass support. But the mid-Victorian critique of empire drew upon a heady blend of free-market economics and liberal ideologies which were infused with the moralism of an earlier era. Imperial critics could also count upon public antipathy to shouldering the expense of imperial expansion, and hence the government consistently sought to deflect the costs of imperialism back onto colonial territories whenever possible.

But the empire did expand during this period, not as spectacularly as it had before or would later, but slowly and in the eyes of its subjects unstoppably, whether they were the Sikhs in India, the Xhosa in South Africa, the Aborigines of Australia, the Maoris in New Zealand or the Cree on the Canadian Plains. While this expansion was often done either without approval from London or even in face of its opposition – which has led some to argue for a theory of sub-imperialism in which the active agents for empire were officials and entrepreneurs on the periphery – the fact that the empire continued to push outwards should not be ignored. Moreover, while there was talk of granting more political rights to white settlers in Canada, Australia, New Zealand and South Africa, few voices were raised in favour of granting anything remotely equivalent to any of Britain's non-European subjects. Historians who subscribe to the idea that mid-Victorian Britain was essentially anti-imperial must also explain why, with few exceptions, the British did not relinquish any of their conquests and annexations – even though many proved to be of little or no economic value and ended up as a drain on imperial finances.

The revitalized interest in empire that came after 1870 and was manifested most visibly in the quickened pace of imperial expansion, especially in Africa but also in the Pacific and South-East Asia, has been the subject of considerable examination and speculation. A host of forces came into play: intensified competition with its European rivals (which has led some historians to see late-nineteenth-century imperialism as principally the outgrowth of intra-European squabbles),[15] the move away from free trade and towards imperial protection and preferences, and what historians have identified as a deeper commitment to empire on the part of the British public.[16] The empire expanded faster than it had in the past, quadrupling in size during the last thirty years of the century. Equally important is that empire came to play a larger role in the cultural life of Britain. The increasingly powerful mass media, who discovered empire could capture the public imagination, widening consumer choices that brought more imperial products into circulation, and the coupling together of nationalism and imperialism, heightened awareness of the empire, and for many instilled a sense of pride and accomplishment that contributed to a notion of Britishness which could transcend, though not without some tensions, more localized English, Scottish, Welsh and somewhat more problematically Irish identities.

The empire consisted of four major elements, First there were the white settler colonies of Australia, Canada and New Zealand. These were largely a legacy of the seventeenth and eighteenth centuries, though marked by a considerable influx of new migrants – often Irish – in the nineteenth century. Their overall weight within the imperial body politic had declined somewhat with the loss of the American colonies, yet for much of the nineteenth century they still occupied a particularly privileged place for emigrants, investors, and imperial spokesmen like Dilke who, when speaking of a Greater Britain, had these lands very much in mind. This settling with peoples from Europe also led to a form of double-colonization: the indigenous inhabitants were not only subjected to the rules and depredations of the settlers, but also to a distant imperial regime which tried, often half-heartedly and usually unsuccessfully, to mediate between the settlers and the original inhabitants.

This category of settler colonies also includes, more problematically, British territories in the West Indies and South Africa where, despite being in the minority, white settlers had managed to entrench themselves and claim the kinds of rights and privileges demanded by settlers elsewhere. The importance of the West Indies declined precipitously in the nineteenth century as the value of its sugar production declined. The emancipation of the slave workforce exacerbated political and economic conditions on these islands. Not surprisingly, freed slaves showed little inclination to work as labourers for their one-time owners and instead chose, wherever possible, to strike out on their own. The export economy suffered, and the prospect of black islanders claiming the same political and legal rights as were enjoyed by the whites further inflamed the situation and in Jamaica helped to contribute to the outbreak of the Morant Bay uprising in 1865 which was savagely put down by Governor Eyre. His decision to impose martial law, the dubious grounds upon which Paul Bogle, the leader, and at least 400 more protesters were hanged, and the destruction of over 1,000 homes, brought home to the British public the brutal nature of imperialism.[17] A number of influential Victorians aligned themselves either for or against Eyre; Thomas Carlyle and Charles Dickens were two of his defenders who believed that 'native' uprisings required drastic intervention otherwise others might join in, while John Stuart Mill and Charles Darwin were amongst those who demanded that his actions be disavowed and that he be punished in part on the grounds that the legitimacy of British law demanded that it be colour-blind in its application.

Then there was India, where British commercial activities dating back to 1600 had resulted in a territorial empire that continued to grow at a considerable rate through the first half of the nineteenth century. India played a vital role in shoring up Britain's overseas trade, since Indian opium funded the lucrative tea trade with China; it provided employment opportunities; and it put at Britain's disposal a military force which could be deployed in support of British interests elsewhere at little cost to the taxpayer. As the 'jewel in the crown' it registered deeply in British culture, though the extent of that imprint remains hotly contested.

How India came under British control, given just how outnumbered were the British, has also been one of the key testing grounds for explaining imperial conquests. Explanations that rest upon innate British superiority, while popular in the nineteenth century, have little purchase today. In their place have come a number of alternatives, including superior British organization and technology.[18] Recent scholarship has called such efforts into question: for at least the first half of the nineteenth century, Indian opponents were often armed with weapons every bit as good, and in some cases better, than those possessed by the British. Indian opponents often displayed considerable organizational innovation. Increasingly, explanations for the British conquest have come instead to emphasize the degree to which the British were able to appropriate and adapt to Indian conditions, raising armies in which most of the troops were Indian, funded with Indian revenues or loans from Indian financiers that were underwritten by Indian revenues, and reliant upon Indian allies and Indian sources of information. To this can be added the fact that the British tended to be much more single-minded and hence there was a greater degree of co-operation in pursuit of their common interests. But if technology is no longer as powerful an explanation for conquest, at least in sweeping terms, British technical excellence became one of the more common yardsticks used to differentiate between the British and their imperial subjects.

The events of 1857–8 in India, known variously as a mutiny, a revolt, a rebellion and the first war of independence (the debates over which only confirm just how contested imperial history can become), marked a major watershed not only in the history of British India but also of British imperialism as a whole. It began as a military mutiny, but soon after drew in much of the civilian population of north central India, and for a time threatened Britain's hold on India. Attempts at distinguishing between mutiny and revolt are ultimately rather futile for 'it was essentially the revolt of a peasant army breaking loose from its foreign masters.'[19] The rebels' failure to extend their revolt much beyond the Gangetic Plain allowed the British to encircle and eventually close in on them. But the rebellion proved to be deeply unsettling in Britain and elsewhere in the empire, and the atrocities committed by both sides created a spiral of violence that racialized the conflict.[20] Two of the more noticeable characteristics of the late-Victorian empire, its preoccupation with racial boundaries and its inherently cautious and conservative approach to indigenous societies, were in large part due to memories of the Indian Rebellion. The cause of the uprising was explained in terms of Indian society not being ready for rapid reform and transformation, and consequently the British concluded that they should proceed more slowly and operate through what they identified as traditional mediators, in particular native princes and large landlords, rather than the Westernizing classes to whom they had made some overtures prior to 1857.

This emphasis on working through traditional elites – which in many cases involved resurrecting or even inventing such authorities – became a marked feature of imperial rule elsewhere in the British Empire, and helps to explain the pervasive conservatism of colonial rule. Lutyens, whose imperial footprint is still visible in the buildings he designed in many cities scattered about the globe, famously declared that 'India, like Africa' left him feeling 'very Tory and pre-Tory feudal'. This conservatism, frequently tinged with a medieval nostalgia, also played itself out in such imperial events as the Delhi Durbar of 1877, held to commemorate Victoria's accession to the title of Empress of India, as well as in the emergence of a distinctive imperial Gothic style of architecture which found expression throughout the empire.[21]

The conservative ethos was also at work in the evolution of what would become one of the principal strategies of imperial authority, the use of indirect rule. In strictly legal terms, indirect rule was a system whereby the British left local rulers in place with much of their authority intact. There were some exceptions – foreign relations were usually taken out of their hands, and rulers were expected to consult regularly with British advisers who were dispatched to their courts. It was a popular technique, buttressed by pragmatic as well as ideological considerations. Some two-fifths of India came to be administered this way, with the so-called Princely States varying in size from large states like Hyderabad to states that were not much bigger than a small town. Indirect rule also proved to be very popular in West Africa and in Malaysia. But in West Africa there were occasions when rulers had to be conjured up. These so-called warrant chiefs, whose authority and status did not predate the arrival of colonial rule, satisfied what had become a fetish for indirect rule.

Indirect rule was popular for a number of reasons: it seemed to offer imperialism on the cheap, provided a convenient mask for imperial expansion by hiding the actual reach of colonial authority, and conformed to widespread beliefs about the nature of 'primitive' government. Indirect rule was also a tacit acknowledgement of the limited resources at hand. Such forms of government spared the British the expense of establishing administrative structures from scratch, especially as they had so few officials on the ground in their empire as compared with other European powers. They also conformed to the belief that local peoples were best ruled through institutions and practices with which they were already familiar. But in practice, the distinction between indirect and direct rule was often blurred. Local rulers found that they had little choice but to accept British advice; their subjects became aware of the limited authority of their rulers; and the British in many instances did not so much work through existing institutions as introduce what they later rationalized as traditional forms of governance.

The third category were the colonies acquired by conquest, most famously those obtained during the last two decades of the nineteenth century in the 'Scramble for Africa', but also including a scattering of accessions ranging from small islands intended to secure shipping routes to lands in South-East Asia and into the Pacific. The origins of the 'Scramble for Africa' have been the subject of intense historiographical debate as it involved so many participants. Much of what has been written stresses the scramble as a by-product of intra-European rivalries, though economic theories have also figured prominently.

Most of the seized territories were wrested from indigenous rulers, and the bulk of the population were easily distinguished from their rulers by race, religion, language and what for Victorians was especially important – state of civilization. Many of these territories initially appeared to offer little by way of economic opportunity, and consequently the amount of investment in terms of infrastructure or personnel was kept quite limited. But they nevertheless felt an imperial presence as authority was imposed upon them, often with brute force, along with an attempt to make such colonies pay as much of their costs as possible which necessitated their being drawn into a cash-based economy. Unlike India, where technological differentials between ruler and ruled did not play so strong a role in allowing for conquest, Britain's technological edge in Africa was often decisive. By the latter half of the nineteenth century, advances in weapon technology, and with it the degree of industrial organization necessary to produce and maintain such weapons, had created a vast gulf between what the British had and what was available to indigenous societies. Quick-firing artillery, machine-guns and breech-loading rifles ripped through African armies with deadly consequences: at Omdurman (1898), the British experienced only 140 casualties as compared with over 11,000 suffered by their opponents. This highlights the brutal nature of colonial warfare, and the willingness of imperial powers to use deadly force in pursuit of their aims. Colonial warfare operated on a different set of moral principles than did warfare in Europe. Efforts to restrict the use in Europe of such weapons as dum-dum bullets on the grounds that they were too barbaric were not carried over into the empire where it was argued that 'savage' warfare required stronger means.

Lastly, and often the most difficult to pin down, were territories within Britain's informal empire, an empire whose extent and even contents remain hotly debated by historians since Britain did not exercise the usual forms of sovereignty in such places. These include China where military and naval power was employed on several occasions to extract concessions from the Chinese that would enable British economic interests to penetrate there and Latin America where British commercial and political influences were also registered. In the case of China, economic penetration was enabled by force as British military and naval power was used to pry open Chinese markets to British imports, including opium from India. British influence in Latin America (and Siam) was considerably more subtle, and scholars have questioned whether the term informal imperialism is actually appropriate.[22]

The significance of each of these sectors to Britain varied considerably by time and also by what was being measured. The white settler territories, for example, saw their economic significance to Britain decline relative to Britain's activities elsewhere, but with an influx of British migrants, their cultural and political ties remained strong. India remained an important economic and military asset throughout this period, and increasingly the demand for certain raw materials like copper from Zambia, rubber from Malaysia and diamonds and later gold from South Africa raised the profile of some overseas territories as protectionist policies adopted in the late nineteenth century drew parts of the empire closer together. It is also important to note some differences between settler colonies and tropical colonies. In settler colonies, the permanent settler population, who often but not always outnumbered the indigenous population (who had either been killed off, pushed aside or outnumbered by the sheer force of migration), demanded and secured levels of political autonomy and representation for the white settlers that were denied to their non-white residents as well as to British subjects within the tropical colonies where much more autocratic regimes prevailed owing to the absence of a permanent European population.

The Course of Imperial Historiography

The beginnings of imperial historiography coincided with two other important developments – the rise of history as a profession and the surge of imperial expansion and its accompanying enthusiasm in the latter decades of the nineteenth century. Living in the present, yet looking to the future, historians in late-nineteenth-century Britain sought not only to account for Britain's rise to dominance, but also confirm that such greatness was not merely a fluke, but attributable to characteristics which the historians were expected to identify such that they could be nurtured and thereby ensure the continuation of Britain's unique historical role. So it comes as no surprise that well before the sun had set on the British Empire, historians were eagerly trying to illuminate the causes and consequences of British imperialism, both at home as well as abroad.

The most famous of these was Seeley who, in declaring that the British seem to 'to have conquered and peopled half the world in a fit of absence of mind', produced one of the most commonly heard statements on the empire. As many as 80,000 copies of *The Expansion of England* (1883) were sold within the first two years of its release, and it remained in print until 1956. While it attempted to bring a historical perspective to the British Empire, it was also informed by a particular vision of the future, one in which empire played a powerful and positive role. Not surprisingly, imperial enthusiasts like Joseph Chamberlain and Tennyson were both impressed by it; Gladstone less so. But it was one that too often has been yanked out of its context, and moreover it was not that original. Seeley in fact was borrowing from Carnarvon who, when colonial secretary, declared in 1870 that the British Empire was 'the child, sometimes of accident, and sometimes of mistake'. In penning these words, Seeley did not intend, as many assumed, to suggest that Britain was simply destined to acquire an empire. He was instead drawing attention to the fact that in general terms, the British had not thought deeply or systematically about their empire, either at the time of annexation or later during its consolidation. Seeley was only partially correct: while the formal study of empire was only just beginning, there were a number of historical impressions of empire in circulation. Of these, the most important was a general view of empire as a progressive force, one that promised social, political and economic benefits to ruler and ruled alike.

Many of Seeley's forecasts proved to be inaccurate. Wishful thinking led him to overplay the bonds that tied the white settler colonies to Britain, and cultural chauvinism blinded him to the dynamics as well as the resilience of non-Western societies. He failed to appreciate the distinctive identities emerging in Australia, Canada and New Zealand and underestimated the force of nationalism in places like India. He was ahead of his time in other ways, for example emphasizing the degree to which the British conquest of India was only accomplished with Indian capital and labour. But his hope that by sparking interest in the empire he could kindle an imperial federation was only partly successful. An Imperial Federation League was formed in 1884, but the ideal of a Greater Britain never took off though some might point to the Commonwealth as the heir to this tradition. The fact that neither Seeley nor Milner in subsequent decades could mobilize much support for their ambitious schemes of imperial federation suggests that there were important limits to imperial identification. Even at its height, the Victorian empire only fitfully captured the interests of the wider public.

While Seeley can be credited with establishing imperial history on a firmer footing, owing largely to the popularity of his work, the message he delivered owed much to earlier strands of historical writing. Like Macaulay, Seeley subscribed to a Whiggish teleology, one that assumed the near-inevitability of empire, and while they both decried the excesses and brutalities of colonial rule (which fortunately for them were either from an earlier era or could be dismissed as aberrations), they looked upon the introduction of Western institutions, ideologies and practices as ultimately beneficial to their subjects, while imperialism was itself central to Britain's greatness. Dilke's *Greater Britain* (1868), another work which celebrated imperialism, did so in much more racialized terms: the white settler empire was his major focus and the empire he depicted was cleaved along racial lines. This preoccupation with race reminds us of just how important race had become to a late Victorian audience. Dramatic events like the Indian Rebellion of 1857–8, frontier wars in South Africa, conflicts with the Maori in New Zealand, and the Morant Bay uprising in Jamaica were often read as racial struggles (though race itself was a highly unstable and often contentious term), and memories of these events reinforced a growing tendency to differentiate between ruler and ruled along racial lines.

The Victorian love of biography offered another critical arena for imperial historiography. The lives of important colonial officials and military officers were popular fodder for the nineteenth-century press; often intended to provide examples of exemplary figures, such didactic works together with fictional adventure stories were instrumental in investing imperialism with a higher purpose and in placing human agents at the centre of history. And with so many aimed at younger readers, imperial themes were introduced into the educational curriculum through writers such as Marryat, Henty, Kaye and Kipling.[23] But not all commentaries were so laudatory. A radical critique, often quite pointed, can be occasionally heard. Bright, Cobden, Buckingham, occasionally Gladstone, and others feared that imperialism could erode British liberties, bolster autocratic forms of government, and embroil Britain in nasty and expensive wars with other European powers. Yet even the most aggressively anti-imperial works were anchored in a common set of assumptions about the superiority of Western science and society, and more particularly that of Britain. Progress was a relatively unproblematic concept, and while the white settler colonies could be placed somewhere close to Britain, the tropical colonies were commonly depicted as languishing far behind.

An idealized view of progress, especially when defined in constitutional, political and economic terms, carried over into the twentieth century where they found a home in such epic works as the *Cambridge History of the British Empire* (1925–59). In general terms, the series reflected an optimistic perspective on empire, one which, through its focus on constitutional development, anticipated that the empire would be transformed into a tightly-knit community of states held together by a shared set of customs, beliefs and expectations. The fundamentally progressive nature of colonial rule was accepted, though these volumes were by no means uncritical of particular aspects or episodes in the unfolding imperial relationship, and continue to offer readers a wealth of detail. The first three volumes looked at imperial policy from a largely political and constitutional perspective, and were followed by individual volumes on each of the major dominions, plus two more for India. The absence of volumes on the tropical colonies reflects this preoccupation with constitutional evolution. The dominions pointed the way to the modern Commonwealth, for it was in those colonies that the narrative of progress could be most easily tracked. The importance attributed to India can be explained in terms of it being not only the jewel in the crown, but also because it too provided examples of political evolution, albeit along a more tortuous path. Noticeably absent from these volumes was sustained discussion of the economics of empire; nor did questions of culture feature.

Optimists were not the only ones writing imperial history. An earlier tradition of anti-imperialism found voice in writers such as Hobson who sought to expose the less ennobling motives underpinning imperial rule, identifying a particularly lethal combination of financial interests and popular enthusiasm at work.[24] He argued that the origins of the South African War lay in the needs of British capitalists for new and profitable places for investment, who were able to persuade the government to back up their demands. There was a seductive logic to this analysis, especially in light of the Great Depression following 1873 which had so limited domestic opportunities. In addition, government officials had discovered that imperialism had the potential to distract the wider public, and it was Hobson who popularized the term 'jingoism'. Hobson can therefore be credited with perhaps not inventing but certainly popularizing two analytical strands that continue to inform imperial historiography: economic explanations and social-cultural explanations.[25] The latter was taken up by Schumpeter, who was one of the first to identify the often atavistic nature of colonial administrators in this period, in effect giving scholarly credibility to Bright's disparaging comment that the empire was little more than a 'gigantic system of outdoor relief for the aristocracy of Britain'.[26]

By shifting attention to the political economy of imperialism, Hobson set in motion the longstanding practice of accounting for imperialism, its origins and operation, in economic terms. While many of the earlier simplistic assumptions about empire being about finding new markets or new sources of supply have been found wanting, especially when there is little evidence of either a particular incentive or the government's willingness to act on behalf of such interests, as well as growing data that shows that empire was not nearly as profitable as might otherwise be assumed, few historians are willing to jettison economic explanations entirely. Davis and Huttenback's exhaustive study of exports, imports and capital flows led them to conclude that empire overall was not a paying proposition.[27] Their work has been borne out by observations that the empire's share of Britain's overseas trade hovered around 25 per cent, peaking on a few occasions at 35 per cent. Moreover, of the ten major commodities that Britain secured from overseas in the nineteenth century, only two came from within the empire. This has bolstered the arguments of those who claim that economic calculations were relatively minor in setting imperial policy.

Others have countered by arguing that it is not necessarily aggregate data that matters, but rather the gains or expected gains of those who were able to influence policy-makers. There were some industries that were intimately bound up with empire: the soaps which came out of Port Sunlight were made from West African palm oil, Calcutta jute fed the mills of Dundee, the electrical industry as well as the bicycle and later automobile manufacturers turned to Malaya for rubber. The empire was also a crucial market for British textiles: in 1870 India took in one-fifth of British textile exports. Key elements in the service sector were also intimately bound up with empire, shipping, insurance and investment banking. So too were many of the emerging professions, perhaps no more so than army officers, for the British Army in the nineteenth century had become largely a colonial gendarmerie in which officers and soldiers were trained and organized to fight what were then called small or savage wars.

Cain and Hopkins have taken up this line of enquiry in their work which has argued that the key driving force behind imperial expansion were the so-called 'gentleman capitalists', a coalition of interests including those in the banking and trading sectors, service industries and the rising professional classes, all of whom tended to cluster around London and who aspired to a 'gentlemanly' lifestyle.[28] Their work has resulted in a very lively debate. Some critics have objected to the absence of industrialists from this mix, still others chaff at the focus on London as well as the weight assigned to metropolitan as compared to peripheral forces. Yet the emphasis placed on the importance of empire for key segments of Britain's economic, social and political elite marks a welcome acknowledgement of how central the empire was to the British economy, and by extension to Britain as a whole.

The rise of nationalism in the colonies began to produce counter-narratives. Dutt initiated a discussion of the 'drain theory' by his exposure of what he identified as the asset-stripping of India by the British. He and others have pointed to the ways through which the British, by virtue of their political power, forced India to accept British-manufactured textiles, thereby hastening the industrialization of Lancashire by destroying India's manufacturing capacity. Even more radical criticisms of the British Empire began to appear, a number of which such as those by Savarkar were censored because of what the British saw as their inflammatory nature.

Critical appreciations, with their emphasis upon economic exploitation, provided the foundation for later Marxist analyses of empire. One of the best known of these was Eric Williams's pioneering work on the slave trade. In *Capitalism and Slavery* (1944) he argued that the British decision not only to abolish the slave trade but to pressure other countries to follow suit stemmed not from humanitarian or moral reactions to the slave trade but rather from economic motives. His study triggered a debate that continues to reverberate, and while subsequent research has challenged some of the economic calculations upon which he based his conclusions, few historians are now willing to attribute abolition solely to moral or ethical pressure. Recent works have begun to identify how moral and religious objections to slavery conformed to many of the emerging economic ideologies, which in turn has revitalized studies of missions and missionaries where we again find numerous examples of how Christianity and commerce could converge in quite sophisticated combinations, thereby enabling us to go beyond simplistic and cynical assessments of missionaries and their motives.

If Marxist theories of empire differed from the Whig historians in their emphasis on the exploitative nature of colonialism, they did share an important common thread: both assumed that the West had an important and progressive role to play. Equally important is the fact that these writers were all writing from a metropolitan perspective; locating the driving force for empire in Britain, and implicitly or otherwise treating colonial territories as a *tabula rasa* upon which the British were free to inscribe whatsoever they chose.

A watershed was reached in 1953 with the publication by Robinson and Gallagher of 'The imperialism of free trade' in the *Economic History Review*. This radically changed not only the terms of the debate over the motives underlying imperialism but also the way in which empire was conceived.[29] It began by questioning the entrenched periodization of imperial history in which early-nineteenth-century enthusiasm for imperial expansion was followed by a prolonged period of anti-imperial sentiments that in turn gave way to a renewed bout of imperial conquests from about 1870 onwards. As already noted, historical orthodoxy had declared that the mid-nineteenth century was an anti-imperial age, largely because the ideals of free trade were replacing the practices of mercantilism. The repeal of the Corn Laws in 1846 and the Navigation Acts of 1849 were seen as signalling the triumph of free trade liberalism, which in turn was viewed as being incompatible with imperialism. Rather than dividing the period into eras of anti-imperialism and pro-imperialism, Robinson and Gallagher stressed continuity across the century, if not necessarily in means, certainly in motives. In their words, '[b]y informal means if possible, or by formal means when necessary, British paramountcy was steadily upheld.' They played down what they saw as the superficial changes in British imperialism of the nineteenth century, and argued for a basic continuum across the century on the grounds that, wherever possible, the British sought to protect their interests by indirect means, and only turned to outright annexation when circumstances required.

The controversies which arose were not simply about continuities versus discontinuities, for Robinson and Gallagher had introduced another key concept into imperial historiography that proved to be even more contentious – informal imperialism. If, as they argued, imperialism was about ends rather than means, then imperialism could not simply be mapped according to its political frontiers. Informal imperialism raised the possibility that British ends could be pursued indirectly; its interests did not require armies or administrators but could be secured through investments, imports and exports, and cultural ties. While this opened up new possibilities for analysis, its critics pointed out that the term was too elastic. To some, 'informal imperialism' seemed to be so capacious as to embrace all forms of political, cultural, economic and social influence emanating from Britain, which would ultimately call into question its explanatory value. And in places where Robinson and Gallagher claimed to have detected it at work, such as China or Latin America, the British were often vying with other powers, and economic influence did not necessarily lead to enhanced political or cultural sway.

Most of the contributors to the nineteenth-century volume of the recent *Oxford History of the British Empire* tend to adopt a more cautious approach to the idea of informal imperialism. Yet its value is still accepted by many. By bringing in the idea of an informal empire, Robinson and Gallagher widened the scope of imperial history and indirectly anticipated our current preoccupation with what has been called globalization and thereby suggested some fruitful links between imperial history and world history. Another important legacy of Robinson and Gallagher, and which was manifested more clearly in their *Africa and the Victorians: The Official Mind of Imperialism* (1961), was an appreciation of just how much developments along the periphery dictated not only the speed but the shape of the unfolding empire. The transition from informal to formal empire, for example, was often forced by crises on the frontier which compelled decision-makers to replace informal influences with formal annexations so as to maintain British interests at a time of flux.

This preoccupation with what was happening far from London or Manchester dovetailed with the growing authority claimed by area studies specialists. Their insistence that we cannot fully appreciate what actually happened in Europe's empires unless we cease treating the world outside Europe as an inert mass moulded by decisions taken in Europe's capitals or by Europe's capitalists gained increasing credibility. The proliferation of area studies programmes in the USA, Britain and France, accompanied by a growing recognition that African, Latin American and Asian histories were all legitimate fields of enquiry, helped forge an important alternative to metropolitan readings of imperial history. Despite the rearguard actions by some who subscribed to Hegel's bifurcation of the world into Europeans and peoples without history, there was a growing recognition of the value and vitality of African and Asian history, and historians began to concede that more attention needed to be paid to their stories and initiatives. In part this was the result of major changes within the empire, and in particular the expectation that decolonization would come sooner than had been expected. But it also came about because of changes within the historical profession. The historical horizon expanded beyond simply the political and the economic to take in social processes and eventually cultural formations. Yet its trajectory seemed at times to point to a time when the empire would become largely invisible. Such was the case with the *Cambridge Economic History of India* (1982) which placed so much stress on developments within India that some critics complained that imperialism had been effectively erased from its history. Another consequence of the rise of area studies is that the traditional emphasis on the dominions weakened and the white settler colonies largely receded from view as attention now turned to Africa and Asia.

The growing importance attached to area studies, the diminished presence of white settler colonies, and changes within domestic British history that played down imperial themes combined to produce a crisis of confidence in imperial history that was attested to in a number of articles that lamented (or celebrated) the imminent demise of imperial history. But such dire prognostications proved to be short-sighted as imperial history began to rebound in the second half of the 1980s. The reasons for this resurgence are many, but include the growing impact of cultural history which came to recognize that imperialism was as much a cultural force as it was a political state, and the popularity of what has become known as post-colonial studies. The two developments share a number of similarities, but like all broad movements, there are also a number of contentious issues that lie between and within them.

A crucial development came with the publication of Edward Said's *Orientalism* (1978). *Orientalism* was in part a fierce and sustained polemic against Western stereotypes of the Orient, which in this book was centred largely on the Muslim world, and many historians have struggled with and often objected to the polemical force of this work and its successor, *Culture and Imperialism* (1992). Yet these works were much more than simply anti-Western diatribes for Said's critique was ultimately aimed at the manner in which Western forms of knowledge not only reflected imperial power, but helped to constitute it in such a way as to suggest that the Western world is largely the product of imperial culture. Said's greatest contribution has been his demonstration that imperialism is as much about the power to represent as it is the power of political and economic domination. This raises important questions concerning the extent to which systematic representations of subject peoples strengthened imperial control and what the legacy of such representations are today.

Said made an impassioned plea for us to re-examine not only what we knew about the 'Orient', and how we knew it, but why we knew it. He coupled together the passionate anti-imperialism of Fanon, as well as Fanon's insights into the psychological trauma unleashed by colonial rule, with Foucault's emphasis on discourse as the means through which knowledge is transformed into power. Thus, Said exposed orientalism's complicity in Western domination. Orientalism had until recently been an uncontentious term: since the late eighteenth century it has been shorthand for the study of the peoples and cultures of Asia. Its practitioners were all part of a scholarly tradition which privileged textual sources and emphasized competency in oriental languages. Orientalism would eventually cut across many disciplines, including history, literature, anthropology and sociology, but nevertheless it remained anchored in philology. With iconoclastic zeal, Said attacked the canonical writings of Middle Eastern scholarship in the West. He moved well beyond illuminating the bias and stereotypes found in such works, for that was already widely known, and charged that the very act of representation, which included the reduction of non-European societies to allegedly timeless essences, lay at the heart of modern imperialism. Novels, travelogues and historical works about the lands of the 'other', and later censuses, district reports and other forms of textual information were as important, if not more so, as the Gatling gun or the steamship in accounting for European domination. Knowledge of the Orient was the same as power over the Orient, for it was Western epistemologies that shaped our impressions of non-Western peoples. European models, terminology and theories were the methods used and consequently the distinction between the European self and the conquered other was rigidly demarcated through other potent binary oppositions: masculine vs. feminine, progress vs. stagnation, adulthood vs. childhood, reason vs. superstition, and so on. Such oppositions bolstered colonial hierarchies and rationalized colonial rule. And this command over information was to persist after the formal ending of empires, ensuring the conditions necessary for what many have called neo-colonialism. From this perspective, previous historians have been charged with not only being blind to the way in which knowledge functioned, but also actively participating in its hegemonic ambitions. One of the foremost proponents of a critical re-reading of colonial texts insists that: 'The British, by contrast, had to historicize the Indian past in order to have access to it. But historicization, like the formation of the colonial state, could not be achieved except by the operation of metropolitan rules and models on native materials.'[30]

The case put forward by Said, and its later development by scholars inspired by him, has not met with universal acceptance. In fact, the polemical nature with which he delivered his arguments was met by equally heated counter-claims though, ironically, many of his harshest critics shared his belief that imperialism was a pervasive cultural force. What has been questioned though is the idea that colonial knowledge was a one-sided production, in part because to make this case would be to deny colonial subjects agency, something which historians had been emphasizing for the past several generations. So too has the idea that colonial power drew upon unvariegated, unsubstantiated and all too often hostile views of indigenous societies.

Hence, post-colonialism in its most simplistic guise runs the danger of perpetuating orientalism by reinforcing orientalism's most lasting legacy – labelling non-Western societies as static and timeless. The dynamism inherent in cross-cultural relations, even relations marked by great inequalities in the distribution of power and knowledge, has at times been ignored. Conquest did not simply occur; resistance was commonplace, there were considerable debates over whether expansion should continue, and what shape empires should take, and there were also many efforts made by indigenous actors to create their own empires. Alternative historical experiences of hegemony are evaded, and with them, non-European-generated constructs and categorizations are ignored. Europeans were not unique in establishing internalized hierarchies, and though they may have interpreted and consolidated them in their own interests, they were generally working with already existing structures. The role of native informants has been played down as have the disagreements between those tasked with collecting and analysing colonial knowledge. And the more highly imagined constructions of non-Western peoples which are taken to typify colonial knowledge were more often the exception rather than the rule. It was the absence of information, and the subsequent anxiety, rather than its abundance, which contributed most to orientalist representations.[31] Another by-product of post-colonialism has been the occasional eruption of occidentalism, or the reduction of European activity to a simple linear trajectory. If recent scholarship has begun to break down the image of a homogeneous and passive colonized 'other', the same understandings have not been employed in examining the agencies and individuals allegedly responsible for constructing orientalism.

A recent objection to Said's work was offered by Cannadine who argued against the priority assigned to race in configuring imperial relations. Cannadine suggested instead that imperialism was more about social gradations than racial divides, and hence status was of greater weight than skin colour. He declared that 'The British Empire was not primarily about race or colour, but about class and status.'[32] While a number of historians have welcomed the reintegration of questions of class and status into the imperial equation, many object to the playing down of race for there is abundant evidence to suggest just how significant race was to imperial rule. Definitions of race, and with them racial boundaries, were not necessarily stable, but they were most certainly one of the principal characteristics of nineteenth-century imperialism.

Post-colonialism also brought with it an enhanced realization of the way in which imperialism reworked domestic cultures, though by no means everyone working on this topic necessarily subscribes to the theoretical underpinnings of post-colonialism. Hitherto, it was largely assumed that, with the exception of the occasional outburst of imperial patriotism, for example during the Boer War, the working and middle classes were largely apathetic to and uninfluenced by the empire.[33] Imperialism was viewed as something confined to the rarefied circles of Britain's political, economic and military elite. However, a proliferation of studies now show how imperialism helped to configure social structures and identities, primarily in the late nineteenth and twentieth centuries. Important works have come out which detail the ways in which imperialism impinged on gender roles (mainly female, but studies of masculinity are beginning to emerge), how imperialism informed our understanding of nature and sexuality, how science was shaped by imperial ideals and prejudices, and how nationalism was intertwined with imperialism.

The very nature of Britain has been tied to empire, as an argument has been made that it was the empire which enabled the Scots, Welsh, English (and much more fitfully and problematically the Irish) to identify themselves as British. Remove the empire, or so the argument goes, and the notion of being British is emptied of its emotional and ideological appeal. While the Welsh presence in the empire is more difficult to track, the Scots and Irish figured out of proportion to their numbers. Irishmen comprised a large part of the armies used throughout the empire, and the Scots and Scots-Irish were regularly to be found in the middle and higher reaches of the colonial hierarchy. But if empire was crucial to the formation of a British identity, it needs to be noted that the end product was not necessarily a homogeneous British identity into which the Scots, Welsh and English were dissolved, for as recent developments have attested, these identities have reappeared.

Objections have also been made to the conclusion that the self–other dichotomy that lies at the heart of post-colonialism (and which was instrumental in making Britishness), could only be worked out within an extra-European empire. Internal colonization, the conquest and subordination of Britain's Celtic fringes, and relations with the Continent were also instrumental in defining what it meant to be British. As Colley has argued, the 'other' that was so crucial to forging the British character in the eighteenth and early nineteenth centuries tended to be European and Catholic, and not Indian and Hindu, or Arab and Muslim. Ultimately, it must be asked whether post-orientalism risks replacing one form of essentialism (orientalism) with another (imperialism). We must take care not to think of imperial traffic flows as simply between the periphery and the metropole: exchanges also took place along the frontier as labour was shifted about (over one million Indian and Chinese indentured labourers were taken on between 1834 and the end of the century), commodities were shipped back and forth, and ideas and officials shuttled between imperial outposts. An example of this is the importation of Anglo-Indian medical ideas and practices into Africa where they helped lay the foundations for various strategies of segregation that manifested themselves in urban planning and settlement patterns. Another example is the idea of martial races, a variant of colonial ethnology which targeted particular communities as more martial and hence more suitable for recruitment than others. Popular in India, such ideas also found fertile ground in Africa.

Conclusion

Having sketched out the broad contours of the British Empire as well as the historiographical frameworks that have been employed to make sense of it, we can now reflect more broadly on what empire meant for ruler and ruled. But before doing so, it is important to remember Marshall's cautionary injunction that 'Ambiguity of meaning and aspiration was inherent in the lack of precision in defining the British empire at any time in its existence.'[34] Also worthy of note is the fact that imperialism as represented on maps was considerably different from that experienced on the ground. Empire expressed cartographically gives an impression of omnipotence. But if we look at what actually transpired on the ground, the limited means available to the British become more apparent. There were, for example, twenty-five British officials in Uganda in the 1890s; in India in the 1820s there were no more than 30,000 Europeans, of which 20,000 were soldiers. Accordingly, imperial authority could not simply rely upon the weight of its coercive power: it required the active assistance, or at least tacit acquiescence, of key sectors of the local population. This could be achieved in a number of ways, both directly and indirectly. The small detachments of European troops dispatched to imperial outposts could always count upon locally raised troops. Indigenous elites could be co-opted, either by offering them something they wished, or by relying upon their realization that the alternatives were worse. Imperial membership had its benefit, at least for some. But it is necessary here to inject a caveat against dismissing those who worked with the British as simply collaborators. Not only is this term anachronistic, it ignores the complex reasoning behind co-operation. For some, there appeared to be little choice, while others believed that association would in the end benefit their societies by giving them access to new forms of knowledge and wealth. Nationalist movements, for example, drew heavily on Western political concepts and organizational strategies. Moreover, the consequences of co-operation would often only become apparent to later generations – at the time relatively few people had any idea of just how profoundly their worlds would be altered.

Equally importantly, imperial policy was largely focused on a limited range of priorities: maintain law and order, maximize revenues and limit costs. Imperial rhetoric did invoke notions of reform and of development, but in many instances this rhetoric never made it into practice, at least in the nineteenth century, for there were not the resources to engage in the kinds of transformation envisaged, and even if there had been, the lack of consensus as to what needed to be done and how it could best be effected frustrated decision-makers. Moreover, the institutions and policies devised by the British, often rather fitfully, were subject to a host of other constraints, often well beyond their control, including ideology, technology and the quality of their local intelligence. Communications, for example, were a major obstacle, at least until the telegraph network became more widespread. London did not have regular and reliable contact with its officials in Calcutta or Cape Town, nor were those officials in touch with their subordinates along the frontier. Hence, policy-making tended to be more reactive than active in this period, reflecting in part the inherent conservatism of colonial rule but also confirming the sheer unwieldiness of colonial machinery. This is not to say that the empire was a peaceful and harmonious place: it was all too often rocked by violent clashes, local rebellions and other acts of violence which always threatened to undermine the fragile stability.

Another common theme in the nineteenth-century empire was its strongly paternalist character, in both its authoritarian and liberal variants. In India the authoritarian–liberal tension was often presented as a struggle between orientalists and anglicists with the former seeking to graft Western ideas and values onto Indian society whereas the latter wished for a more radical policy of transplantation which offered little space for indigenous forms and customs. Few historians today would subscribe to such a stark dichotomy for in practice the two not only overlapped in places, but they both tended to share the same sense of superiority. In other words, their debates, over issues such as suttee, women's education, religious practices and so on, were more about means than ends. But the limited means at hand meant that imperial policies took time to penetrate into local societies. Even the more mundane instruments of imperial rule, such as schools and hospitals, touched comparatively few persons, for despite the rhetoric of reform and improvement, imperial authorities lacked the resources, and sometimes the will, to engage in the kinds of attempted transformations that were otherwise suggested by the ideologies they espoused. Yet imperialism indirectly touched the lives of millions upon whom it had a tremendous and often traumatic impact. Economic upheavals occasioned by, among other things, the hasty yet incomplete transformation to cash economies, for example, rendered societies much more vulnerable to famine.

The empire left an undeniable yet complex and often ambivalent impact on Britain. It contributed to the evolution of the British economy (though the consensus today tends to play down its overall significance),[35] was instrumental in giving direction to Britain's international relations, impinged on domestic political life and contributed to the shaping of social, religious, intellectual and cultural forms and practices. Empire also provided a range of even more tangible benefits to its subjects. It was a source of employment, a destination for emigrants, a market for exports, a place for patriotic outbursts and a measure of progress. As consumers, the British were surrounded with imperial commodities: Indian tea, West African palm oil, South African gold, Malaysian rubber, Australian wool, Canadian timber; but historians will continue to debate whether the consumption of such commodities awakened any sense of imperial identity amongst their consumers. Nevertheless, empire figured elsewhere in their lives and hence writing empire back into British history will enrich it by enabling us to see more clearly the complex interplay of material and discursive processes that helped to produce the United Kingdom and, as some have recently argued, now threaten to hasten its disintegration.

NOTES

1. W. E. Lecky, *The Empire: Its Value and Its Growth: An Inaugural Address* (London, 1893).

2. U. S. Mehta, *Liberalism and Empire: A Study in Nineteenth Century British Liberal Thought* (Chicago, 2000).

3. R. W. Winks, ed., *The Oxford History of the British Empire*, vol. 5, *Historiography* (Oxford, 1999), p. 10.

4. C. Hall, K. McClelland and J. Rendall, *Defining the Victorian Nation: Class, Race, Gender and the Reform Act of 1867* (Cambridge, 2000).

5. Quoted in A. Burton, 'Rules of thumb: British history and "imperial culture" in nineteenth- and twentieth-century Britain', *Women's History Review*, 3 (1994).

6. C. Hall, 'White visions, black lives: the free villages of Jamaica', *History Workshop Journal*, 36 (1993).

7. D. Fieldhouse, 'Can Humpty Dumpty be put together again? Imperial history in the 1980s', *Journal of Imperial and Commonwealth History*, 12 (1984); R. W. Winks, ed., *The Historiography of the British Empire-Commonwealth: Trends, Interpretations and Resources* (Durham, NC, 1966).

8. A. P. Thornton, *The Imperial Idea and Its Enemies: A Study in British Power* (London, 1959).

9. A. G. Frank, *ReOrient: Global Economy in the Asian Age* (Berkeley, 1998); J. M. Blaut, *The Colonizer's Model of the World: Geographical Diffusionism and Eurocentric History* (Harlow, 1994); W. Rodney, *How Europe Underdeveloped Africa* (Washington, 1981).

10. P. Curtin, 'The British Empire and Commonwealth in recent historiography', *American Historical Review*, 65 (1959), p. 51.

11. C. A. Bayly, *Imperial Meridian: The British Empire and the World 1780–1830* (London, 1989); L. Colley, *Britons: Forging the Nation 1707–1837* (New Haven, 1992).

12. A. Porter, 'Trusteeship, anti-slavery, and humanitarianism', in A. Porter, ed., *The Oxford History of the British Empire*, vol. 3, *The Nineteenth Century* (Oxford, 1999), p. 198.

13. R. Anstey, *The Atlantic Slave Trade and British Abolition, 1760–1810* (Cambridge, 1975); S. Drescher, *Capitalism and Antislavery: British Mobilization in Comparative Perspective* (New York, 1987); C. Midgley, *Women against Slavery: The British Campaigns, 1780–1870* (London, 1992); J. R. Oldfield, *Popular Politics and British Anti-Slavery: The Mobilisation of Public Opinion against the Slave Trade, 1787–1807* (Manchester, 1995).

14. D. M. Peers, '"Those noble exemplars of the true military tradition": constructions of the Indian Army in the mid-Victorian press', *Modern Asian Studies*, 31 (1997).

15. W. Baumgart, *Imperialism: The Idea and the Reality of British and French Colonial Expansion, 1880–1914* (Oxford, 1982).

16. J. M. MacKenzie, *Propaganda and Empire: The Manipulation of British Public Opinion, 1880–1960* (Manchester, 1984).

17. G. Heuman, *'The Killing Time': The Morant Bay Rebellion in Jamaica* (Knoxville, 1994); T. C. Holt, *The Problem of Freedom: Race, Labor, and Politics in Jamaica and Britain, 1832–1938* (Baltimore, 1991).

18. D. R. Headrick, *The Tools of Empire: Technology and European Imperialism in the Nineteenth Century* (Oxford, 1981).

19. E. Stokes, *The Peasant Armed: The Indian Revolt of 1857* (Oxford, 1986), p. 14.

20. B. English, 'Debate: the Kanpur massacres in India in the revolt of 1857', and R. Mukherjee, 'Reply', both *Past and Present*, 142 (1994); R. Mukherjee, *Spectre of Violence: The 1857 Kanpur Massacres* (Delhi, 1998).

21. T. R. Metcalf, *An Imperial Vision: Indian Architecture and Britain's Raj* (Berkeley, 1989).

22. A. Knight, 'Britain and Latin America', and M. Lynn, 'British policy, trade, and informal empire in the mid-nineteenth century', both in A. Porter, ed., *The Oxford History of the British Empire*, vol. 3, *The Nineteenth Century* (Oxford, 1999); D. C. M. Platt, 'Further objections to an "imperialism of free trade", 1830–1860', *Economic History Review*, 22 (1973) and 'The imperialism of free trade: some reservations', *Economic History Review*, 21 (1968).

23. J. A. Mangan, ed., *The Imperial Curriculum: Racial Images and Education in the British Colonial Experience* (London, 1993).

24. J. A. Hobson, *Imperialism: A Study* (London, 1948).

25. P. J. Cain, *Hobson and Imperialism: Radicalism, New Liberalism and Finance, 1887–1938* (Oxford, 2002).

26. J. A. Schumpeter, *Imperialism and Social Classes* (Oxford, 1951).

27. L. Davis and R. A. Huttenback, *Mammon and the Pursuit of Empire: The Economics of British Imperialism* (Cambridge, 1988).

28. P. J. Cain and A. G. Hopkins, *British Imperialism: Innovation and Expansion, 1688–1914* (Harlow, 1993).

29. W. R. Louis, ed., *Imperialism: The Robinson and Gallagher Controversy* (New York, 1975).

30. R. Guha, *An Indian Historiography of India: A Nineteenth Century Agenda and its Implications* (Calcutta, 1987), p. 12.

31. C. A. Bayly, *Empire and Information: Intelligence Gathering and Social Communication in India, 1780–1870* (Cambridge, 1996).

32. D. Cannadine, 'Ornamentalism', *History Today*, May 2001, p. 16.

33. R. Price, *An Imperial War and the British Working Class: Working-Class Attitudes and Reactions to the Boer War, 1899–1902* (London, 1977).

34. P. J. Marshall, 'Presidential address: Britain and the world in the eighteenth century: IV, The turning outwards of Britain', *Transactions of the Royal Historical Society*, 11 (2001).

35. P. K. O'Brien, 'The costs and benefits of British imperialism, 1846–1914', *Past and Present*, 120 (1988); A. Offer, 'Costs and benefits, prosperity and security, 1870–1914', in A. Porter, ed., *The Oxford History of the British Empire*, vol. 3, *The Nineteenth Century* (Oxford, 1999).

FURTHER READING

There are a number of very good surveys of the nineteenth century. R. Hyam, *Britain's Imperial Century: A Study of Empire and Expansion* (1993) is an excellent introduction to the empire as a whole though it tends to be weighted in favour of political explanations. Equally valuable – though one covers much more than the nineteenth century, and the other starts in 1850 – are P. J. Marshall, ed., *The Cambridge Illustrated History of the British Empire* (1996) and B. Porter, *The Lion's Share: A Short History of British Imperialism, 1850–1995* (1996). A provocative reassessment of imperialism that stresses metropolitan economic forces can be found in P. J. Cain and A. G. Hopkins, *British Imperialism: Innovation and Expansion, 1688–1914* (1993). Useful recent efforts at surveying the historiographical landscape are to be found in D. Kennedy, 'Imperial history and post-colonial theory', *Journal of Imperial and Commonwealth History*, 24 (1996) and P. Wolfe, 'Imperialism and history: a century of theory, from Marx to postcolonialism', *American Historical Review*, 102 (1997). A number of primers on post-colonial theory have recently appeared; of these, B. Moore-Gilbert, *Postcolonial Theory: Context, Practices, Politics* (1997) is well suited to a historical audience, though readers may also want to consult R. J. C. Young, *Postcolonialism: An Historical Introduction* (2001).

More detailed case studies of particular colonies or themes within the nineteenth century are contained in A. Porter, ed., *The Oxford History of the British Empire*, vol. 3, *The Nineteenth Century* (1999). The individual chapters are nearly all of a high standard. More troubling is the absence of any sustained engagement with questions of gender, race and imperialism. Fortunately there are a number of excellent introductions to what has become a most exciting areas; on questions of gender, readers may want to look at one of the following: A. Burton, *Burdens of History: British Feminists, Indian Women, and Imperial Culture, 1865–1915* (1994), C. Midgley, ed., *Gender and Imperialism* (1995) and M. Sinha, *Colonial Masculinity; The 'Englishman' and the 'Effeminate Bengali' in the Late Nineteenth Century* (1995). Race and the Victorian empire features in many works: good points of departure are offered in the following: C. Bolt, *Victorian Attitudes Towards Race* (1971), D. Lorimer, *Colour, Class and the Victorians* (1978) and the essays in S. West, ed., *The Victorians and Race* (1997). While not limited exclusively to the British Empire, A. L. Stoler, *Carnal Knowledge and Imperial Power: Race and the Intimate in Colonial Rule* (2002) brings together in one place a number of ideas on the interrelationship of race, class and gender which have had an important impact on the field as a whole. In addition to the titles already identified, imperialism's impact on domestic society can be tracked through a number of vectors. Literature has been one of the favoured areas of study, and good introductions to this relationship are to be found in P. Brantlinger, *Rule of Darkness: British Literature and Imperialism, 1830–1914* (1990) and D. David, *Rule Britannia: Women, Empire and Victorian Writing* (1995). Other vectors have been explored in the books which have appeared as part of Manchester University Press's 'Studies in Imperialism' series, including J. M. MacKenzie, ed., *Imperialism and Popular Culture* (1986) and J. M. MacKenzie, ed., *Imperialism and the Natural World* (1990). For science, medicine and technology, see M. Adas, *Machines as the Measure of Men: Science, Technology, and Ideologies of Western Dominance* (1989), D. Arnold, ed., *Imperial Medicine and Indigenous Societies* (1988), R. MacLeod, ed., *Nature and Empire: Science and the Colonial Enterprise* (2001) and B. R. Tomlinson, 'Empire of the dandelion: Ecological imperialism and economic expansion, 1860–1914', *Journal of Imperial and Commonwealth History*, 26 (1998).

CHAPTER FOUR

The Armed Forces

EDWARD M. SPIERS

By the onset of the nineteenth century the British armed forces had already engaged their French counterparts in seven years of warfare and, apart from a fourteen-month interlude following the Treaty of Amiens (1802), would continue to oppose Napoleonic ambitions until 1815. Faced originally with French aggression in the Low Countries, laced with an ideological challenge from Revolutionary France and later Napoleonic domination of much of the Continent, British governments not only resisted stubbornly but also enlisted the assistance of other European states, proffering them subsidies and aid to sustain the struggle. If the 1790s had demonstrated that Britain, even with allies, could not counter the vast army of France (and had to abort limited interventions in Flanders, 1793–4, and in the Helder campaign, 1799), she had successfully thwarted three invasions (one through Wales and two through Ireland) while preserving its naval predominance.

British security rested on the twin pillars of sea power and economic power. The Royal Navy blockaded enemy ports, seized colonies, and triumphed over the French, Spanish and Dutch fleets in separate encounters: the 'Glorious First of June' (1794), Cape St Vincent and Camperdown (both 1797). On 1 August 1798 a Mediterranean squadron, under Nelson's command, annihilated the French fleet at the Battle of the Nile. Whereas the number of French ships fell by more than a half between 1793 and 1803, Britain had the resources and industrial capacity to replace ship losses and build a fleet that was numerically superior in ships of the line and frigates to the combined fleets of France, Spain and Holland. Britain's naval forces, though, were dispersed across the globe and suffered far more from the sea and weather than enemy fleets secure in harbour.[1]

As an island heavily dependent on overseas trade, Britain's strategic requirements were readily determined. The Royal Navy – the first line of defence against invasion and the principal means of projecting power overseas – needed supplies of timber, iron, pitch, tar and hemp, much of which came from Scandinavia. So when Russia abandoned the allied coalition and formed a League of Armed Neutrals with other Baltic powers, Britain employed its Baltic fleet to destroy the Danish fleet in harbour at Copenhagen (1801). This audacious act, in which Nelson ignored orders to break off the attack, followed the assassination of the tsar in the previous month: both events broke the League. In the same year the navy conveyed and supported an expeditionary force of 14,000 men under Abercromby to rout the French forces in Egypt.

To meet the threat of invasion, particularly once Napoleon began to assemble his 160,000-strong 'Army of England' along the Channel coast, the Channel fleet had the support of rapidly constructed defences (the Royal Military Canal in Kent and some 100 Martello towers at strategically salient points), substantial bodies of regular soldiers, militia raised for home defence, and, by the end of 1803, around 400,000 local volunteers. By 1805, Napoleon abandoned his invasion plans to concentrate upon destroying the continental powers of the Third Coalition, but within days of crushing the Austrian forces at Ulm, French and Spanish naval forces suffered a devastating defeat at Trafalgar (21 October 1805). Although Nelson died in battle, thereby adding to his legendary heroic appeal, his victory confirmed Britain's mastery of the seas. If this command of the sea was not absolute (French squadrons from Toulon and Mauritius posed difficulties for a few more years), it was never seriously challenged by Napoleon.

Accordingly Britain used its capital ships and frigates to sustain the blockade of enemy ports, protect supplies from the Baltic, seize colonies from the French and Dutch in the West Indies, East Indies and Indian Ocean as well as the Cape of Good Hope, and retain Malta (taken in 1800 and not returned under the Treaty of Amiens). Although these operations severed the colonial resources of enemy states and gained strategically vital harbours across the globe, they required lengthy missions on the high seas, with concomitant strains on ships and crews. The navy's losses in shipwrecks were always heavier than those from naval engagements, and, in seeking to replace these losses, the naval budget soared from £15 m in 1806 to over £20 m by 1813. Similarly, the navy lost far more men from desertion than it did in action, and, despite raising its number of seamen from 100,000 in 1804 to 145,000 in 1810, the Admiralty constantly struggled to replace manpower losses during the Napoleonic Wars.[2]

Nevertheless, constant exposure to the sea enhanced the standards of British seamanship, enabling squadrons to manoeuvre more rapidly and precisely than their adversaries because of greater discipline, better signalling systems and tactical cohesion. The Royal Navy's commanders became highly professional and aggressive, ready to exploit 'gaps' in the enemy's line (at Trafalgar), to sail into shallow and unchartered waters and attack from unexpected sides (at the Nile and Copenhagen) and to close with the enemy and launch devastating broadsides from their carronades – easily manoeuvrable, quick-firing guns. The navy supported further interventions on the Continent: some were none too effective (the Walcheren operation, 1809, and the expedition of Sir John Moore which ended with his death and defeat at Corunna, 16 January 1809), but others proved more successful, notably the Peninsular campaign when commanded by Sir Arthur Wellesley (later Duke of Wellington).

The Duke of York (Commander-in-Chief, 1795–1809) had radically reformed the British army during the French wars, establishing a military college and school for cadets, improving rations, health care and barrack accommodation, standardizing tactical drill and manoeuvres, and creating permanent light infantry regiments. The army had grown prodigiously from some 40,000 men in 1793 to over 250,000 by 1813. Recruiting, though, had always proved difficult and had to replace an annual wastage of 16–24,000 casualties from wounds and illness throughout the Napoleonic Wars. Governments relied on direct recruiting, raiding the militia for trained manpower, and finding one-fifth of its strength from foreign soldiers (52,000 by 1813). However, the demands of colonial and Mediterranean garrisons, an inconclusive war with the United States (1812–14) and home defence (including internal security in Ireland and the army's role in maintaining public order, collecting taxes and combating smuggling in Britain), left Wellesley with only 32,000 men in 1810, rising to some 60,000 by 1813 (of whom only 42,700 were fit to take the field).[3]

Wellesley, nonetheless, assisted by Portuguese regulars and militia, drove the French out of Portugal, defended Lisbon behind three lines of fortifications (the Lines of Torres Vedras), and utilized Spanish armies and guerrillas to tie down some 200,000 French troops by 1813. His string of victories in Spain (Talavera, 1811; Badajoz and Salamanca, 1812; Vitoria, 1813), followed by the drive into southern France (Bidassoa, Nivelle, Orthez and Toulouse, 1814) helped to undermine the Napoleonic empire, even if the latter was primarily threatened from central Europe. Finally, Wellington thwarted Napoleon's restoration at Waterloo (18 June 1815). Commanding an Anglo-Dutch army of 68,000 men, Wellington held a compact defensive position until the Prussian army under Marshal Blücher intervened to secure a decisive victory described by the duke as 'a close run thing'.

Victory had proved both costly and conclusive, leaving Britain without any major adversary, particularly on the high seas. Liverpool's government duly slashed expenditure on the armed services and reduced their numbers drastically. The army's budget fell from £43m in 1815 to £10.7m in 1820, while the effective strength plummeted from 233,952 men in 1815 to 102,539 men in 1828, falling even further in the 1830s. Naval expenditure fell from £22.8m in 1815 to £6.4m in 1820 and to a mere £4.1m in 1836. Ships of the line were also cut from 214 in 1815 to about 80 in 1817 and to 58 in 1835.[4] Within the smaller peacetime services, officers were drawn from a narrow segment of society, notably from families with a military or naval tradition, as well as the landed aristocracy, gentry and, to a lesser extent, the country parsonage. Often younger sons with limited career prospects entered the services but family ties could stretch back over several generations and only rarely did officers transfer from one military profession to another (although Evelyn Wood would rise from the rank of midshipman to field marshal, 1852–1903). Most naval entrants came from families located in the 'sea-shires' of southern England (that is, south of the Humber or Mersey); most army entrants came from families located south of a line from the Bristol Channel to the Wash, with more prominent minorities coming from county families in Scotland or from the Anglo-Irish gentry.[5]

In 1815 the 'interest' of family or friends secured the vast majority of appointments in the Royal Navy: 97 per cent of midshipmen entered the service as captain's 'nominees' or 'servants' without any qualifying examination. Although captains retained a vestige of this prerogative throughout the century, the Admiralty steadily expanded its own source of entry, originally through the Royal Naval College at Portsmouth and then by establishing its right to approve every nominated midshipman. It examined them from 1839 onwards, regulating the number of 'nominations' in 1840 and imposing age-limits one year later. By 1870 the Admiralty required that 'nominations' should be competitive and that the number of 'nominations' should be twice the number of vacancies. Meanwhile, the Admiralty expanded its own entry and extended the remit of naval education and training. By 1830 it established HMS *Excellent* as a gunnery (and boys') training ship, so facilitating the abolition of the Portsmouth college seven years later. Training afloat now became the objective, initially in HMS *Illustrious*, moored in Portsmouth harbour in 1857, and, within two years, in HMS *Britannia* – a larger three-decker which, in September 1863, would be moored at Dartmouth where she would remain for the next fifty years. Neither these reforms nor the sequence of examinations required of *Britannia* cadets, of midshipmen after five years and of sub-lieutenants at the Royal Naval College, Greenwich (opened in 1873), nor even the response to scientific developments (including the creation of a separate torpedo school at HMS *Vernon* in 1876), diminished the force of naval tradition and the priorities accorded to basic seamanship. The navy's social intake reflected that tradition: promotion from the lower deck rarely occurred, and only two warrant officers were promoted in the second half of the century, both in Victoria's jubilee honours list of 1887.[6]

Within the army an officer-gentleman tradition, with its codes of honour, duty and accepted standards of behaviour, sustained the exclusivity of the service and buttressed its degree of regimental *esprit de corps*. Until 1871 this tradition was reinforced by the practice of purchasing commissions in the Guards, cavalry and infantry. First commissions, as set by Royal Warrant in 1821, ranged from £450 in the infantry to £1,260 in the Life Guards, and rose to become £4,500 for a lieutenant-colonelcy in the infantry or £9,000 for a lieutenant-colonelcy in the Foot Guards. Unlike the navy, where a reluctance to retire captains after the Napoleonic Wars had led to a promotions blockage for the next thirty years, promotion could be extremely rapid in the army, especially for rich officers able to afford the official and unofficial 'over-regulation' payments. In 1830, after a mere six years' service, Lord Brudenell became a lieutenant-colonel in the 15th Hussars, having paid between £35,000 and £40,000 for his lieutenant-colonelcy. Nevertheless, approximately one-quarter of the pre-Crimean army gained promotions without purchase, either by entering the non-purchase corps (the artillery and engineers) from the Royal Military Academy, Woolwich, or, after 1842, by receiving free commissions from the Royal Military College, Sandhurst, if they were the sons of impecunious officers or orphans from military families, or by succeeding to vacancies caused by deaths, full-pay retirements or promotion beyond the regiment to major-general. Free commissions, like the promotions of non-commissioned officers, multiplied rapidly during the Crimean War but the normal pattern of promotion resumed in its aftermath.[7]

Even after the abolition of purchase, the army preserved its social exclusivity by attracting the former pupils of public schools, especially those who were financially independent. Officers in the home-based army could never live on their pay (as set in 1806, the rates ranged from £95 16s 3d per annum for an ensign to £365 per annum for a lieutenant-colonel and were not raised until 1914). On entering a regiment, subalterns had to provide their own uniform, cases, furniture, mufti, servant's outfit and incoming mess contribution. By 1920 these items cost some £200 for an infantry officer and from £600 to £1,000 for a cavalry officer. Thereafter, the annual expenses of living in the mess, sport, social life, entertainment and the constant moving of army life presumed an annual income of £100 to £150 for an infantry officer and of £600 to £700 for a cavalry officer. Few non-commissioned officers, even those serving in India and the colonies where the expenses were less, could meet these costs and so relatively few sought promotion. Most of those who did settle for the posts of quartermaster or riding master: Sir Hector Macdonald and Sir William Robertson, who rose from the ranks to become major-general (1870–1900) and field marshal (1877–1920) respectively, were glittering exceptions.[8]

After the Napoleonic Wars the navy no longer impressed men for service (other than convicted smugglers) and so avoided having to take the 'sweepings of the British merchant navy and of foreign mercantile marines'.[9] It found much smaller numbers (only 23,000 in 1820) by recruiting men from the major seaports for single commissions on specific ships. These commissions often lasted for three years but sometimes for twice as long. The sailor lacked any formal terms of service and, unless re-engaging, embarked on his commission without training and had to learn his craft during his first year at sea (although specialist training was eventually provided for seamen-gunners in *Excellent* and all aspects of torpedo and mine warfare in *Vernon*). The army also found the bulk of its peacetime recruits from unskilled casual labourers. As a recruiting sergeant recalled in the 1830s, 'it was only in the haunts of dissipation or inebriation, and among the very lowest dregs of society, that I met with anything like success'.[10] In the early nineteenth century, significant numbers of men still enlisted from rural areas (about 40 per cent of all recruits from Ireland), manpower often regarded as stronger, healthier, more obedient and malleable than their slum-bred counterparts. The drift of people from the country to towns and massive emigration from Ireland following the famine of 1846 made the army increasingly dependent upon recruits from the urban industrial centres of England. Hunger, privation and want of alternative employment probably drove the vast majority to enlist in both services but some sought an escape from the law or amatory indiscretions and others joined on impulse, possibly influenced by alcohol or the promises made by recruiting staff. Yet there were certainly some, if only a small minority, who enlisted in the quest for adventure, foreign travel or to follow in parental footsteps – not least the boy soldiers from the Royal Military Asylum, Chelsea, and the Royal Hibernian School, Dublin.[11]

Both services suffered from lowly rates of pay and unattractive conditions of service. In the early-nineteenth-century navy, pay (£1 5 s 6 d per month, with another 8 s per month for an able seaman) was always months, and sometimes years, in arrears. The army's 'one shilling' a day (1 s for the infantry, 1 s 3 d for the cavalry) was never paid in full: stoppages were deducted for messing, laundry, kit replacement, hair-cutting, barrack damages and hospital treatment, if necessary. In both services, personnel endured cramped and unhealthy quarters, with sailors sleeping in hammocks eighteen inches apart. Although ships were less crowded and the voyages shorter than in Nelson's navy, many sailors, like their military counterparts, suffered from tuberculosis and other respiratory diseases aggravated by insanitary, overcrowded and poorly ventilated living conditions. Service rations, though regular, were hardly appetizing, particularly the ageing salt beef or pork, fetid drinking water and hard-tack biscuit on board ships. Many servicemen sought relief from their daily fatigues (and periods of idleness in the army) through drink, with sailors entitled to half a pint of spirits or a pint of wine, and a gallon of beer, a day. Drunkenness, fights, leave-breaking and insubordination bedevilled both services, with many men requiring treatment for venereal disease. The authorities kept order by flogging, branding (of 'bad characters' and 'deserters' in the army) and, in extreme cases, by capital punishment.[12]

In the first half of the nineteenth century Britain's naval mastery was never challenged (as the other great powers were preoccupied with internal affairs and lacked substantial fleets fit for service). In spite of parliamentary pressure to economize, the Royal Navy discharged a vast and growing array of global responsibilities. Deployed in growing numbers in the English Channel, the Atlantic, the Mediterranean, the Indian Ocean and even the Pacific, the navy relied increasingly upon minor warships, frigates, sloops and brigs (leaving the greater part of the battle fleet 'in reserve' to save money and manpower). As an instrument of government policy, the navy protected free trade on the high seas and British commercial interests by bombarding the pirates in Algiers (1816) and thwarting foreign intervention in the Latin American revolutions. It continued to annex vital harbours and strategic bases: Singapore (1819), the Falkland Islands (1833), Aden (1839) and Hong Kong (1841). It assisted the Greeks in their quest for independence by smashing the Turkish fleet at Navarino (1827), isolated the French in actions against Mehemet Ali (1840), supported the Portuguese monarchy against internal and external dangers and coerced the Chinese after two wars and numerous clashes to permit Western merchants to trade with full security.[13]

If the navy was employed primarily to defend British interests, by protecting trade and projecting influence overseas, it could also serve broader purposes. To facilitate the use of the open seas, naval survey vessels pioneered the charting of the oceans, measuring coastlines and sounding depths all over the world. To enhance the safety of maritime trade, the Royal Navy took the initiative in suppressing piracy, not only in the Mediterranean and the Aegean but also in the Orient, especially in Chinese waters. It assumed the leading role, too, in the suppression of the slave trade following Britain's abolition of the practice in 1807 and of slavery itself in most dominions in 1833. Whether undertaken by the West African squadron, which had thirty-two warships by 1847, or by the Cape and East Indies squadrons, the anti-slave trade patrols were difficult and often frustrating undertakings. When conducted off the coast of West Africa, they were also profoundly unhealthy. The introduction of steam-powered vessels briefly gave British patrols an advantage in the 1840s but the slavers soon acquired steamships, and the Atlantic slave trade would not slump into terminal decline until President Lincoln, in 1861, permitted the right to search ships flying an American flag. The export of slaves towards Arabia and Asia proved more resilient, and, despite forceful action against the Sultan of Zanzibar in 1873, persisted into the twentieth century.[14]

Unlike the Royal Navy, the army had no role to play as an instrument of foreign policy. Until 1854 there was never any desire to intervene on the Continent to uphold the balance of power. Even when home defence briefly surfaced as an issue during the invasion scares of 1844–8 and 1852–3, the naval estimates, dockyard defences and the revived militia (1852) were the prime beneficiaries, with only minimal increases in regular soldiers.[15] Manning colonial garrisons remained the main military duty, with British forces guarding disputed borders – Maine–New Brunswick (1841–2) and Oregon (1845–6); quelling local disturbances – riots in Montreal (1832, 1849 and 1853); guarding against revolts – Jamaica (1831); suppressing rebellions – Demerara (1823), Mauritius (1832), Ceylon (1848) and Cephalonia (1849); and waging wars of conquest to protect European settlers – as in New Zealand intermittently between 1845 and 1872. Military forces mounted larger campaigns, often in fractious border regions and sometimes at the behest of local officials, such as the disastrous Afghan campaign (1838–42), the conquest of Sind (1843) and the acquisition of the Punjab after two Sikh wars (1845–9). Aggressive operations were mounted on the eastern frontiers of Cape Colony (1834–5, 1846–7 and 1850–3) and Lord Elgin led two punitive expeditions against Canton and the mainland Chinese between 1857 and 1860.[16]

The army at home not only provided reliefs for units overseas but also aided the civil power. At a time when the use of petty constables, aided by part-time special constables, stood discredited, when the yeomanry's reputation had been fatally damaged after the Peterloo Massacre (1819) and when the new full-time police forces were in the process of becoming established, military units proved indispensable to the civil authorities. In coastal communities, especially Cornwall, they supported customs and excise officers in countering smuggling. In Ireland they provided escorts for excise officers, sheriffs, bailiffs and other functionaries and helped to quell local disorders. Throughout the United Kingdom they were called out whenever public affrays were likely, particularly during the Corn Law agitation, election campaigns, the Reform Bill riots (1831), rural protests and the Chartist disturbances of the 1840s. Military forces, often widely dispersed in small detachments, sometimes proved ineffective (as in 1831, when Bristol's city-centre was burnt out), but they were generally better armed and disciplined than their opposition. Frequently, the mere presence of disciplined soldiery overawed the crowd, and the army, in aiding the civil power, generally relied upon a display of arms rather than the force of arms.[17]

Both armed services would be tested by the Crimean War (1854–6) when Britain, France and Sardinia sought to check Russian territorial designs on the Ottoman empire and Russia's growing naval strength in the Black Sea. The Royal Navy proved the 'backbone of the British war effort'.[18] It supplied the army before Sevastopol, dominated the Black Sea (with the Russian fleet remaining in port), and blockaded the Russian coastline in the Baltic (threatening St Petersburg and detaining an army of 200,000 troops). After inconclusive operations in 1854 and 1855, the Admiralty planned to dispatch a substantial Baltic fleet in 1856, including some 100 gunboats and 64 mortar vessels (capable of operating in coastal waters) to attack the fortress at Kronstadt and open the passage to St Petersburg – an undertaking thwarted by Russia suing for peace in January 1856.[19]

The army sent a small expeditionary force to the Crimea (about 26,000 initially – one-third of the size of the French army). It suffered heavy casualties in the battles of the Alma, Balaclava and Inkerman (1854). Losses had already occurred from cholera and other diseases, and these would mount rapidly during the severe winter as the allies besieged Sevastopol (only taking the city in September 1855). While the army found reinforcements from various sources, including some 33,000 from the militia and another 40,000 foreign mercenaries, it incurred condemnation over its medical, supply and transport arrangements. Following the critical reports of William Howard Russell and Thomas Cherney in *The Times*, Florence Nightingale went out to head a government nursing service and parliamentary committees denounced the army mismanagement in the Crimea.[20]

The Crimean War revived interest in the reform of both services. The navy had already undertaken some reforms of the conditions and terms of service. In 1824, an attempt had been made to standardize uniforms on each ship and, in the following year, petty officers of first or second class were exempted from punishment by flogging. They were also allowed to wear badges of rank, and were to be retained as supernumeraries and given another seagoing appointment after paying off their original ship. Engineers, who had joined the service with the coming of steam and screw propulsion, were neither officers nor ratings nor warrant officers. They were only given uniforms in 1837 and commissioned rank in 1847, but they still had to mess by themselves. In July 1838 the Admiralty approved the supply of libraries to seagoing ships and, in 1825 and again in 1850, halved the daily issue of rum, abolishing the evening issue of grog (having already abolished the beer ration in 1831). How far these measures reduced drunkenness is debatable as some sailors, when granted more leave under the long-service commissions, could indulge themselves on shore and smuggle more spirits on board, but the rum reductions complemented efforts to improve the health and diet of sailors.[21]

The replacement of ship's bilges – open sewers of ballast in the hold – by iron pigs or casks removed some of the dreadful odours from ships built after 1815, and many efforts were made to improve ventilation and reduce condensation below decks. These measures had a limited effect on wooden ships, where deck-washing was an all too regular occurrence. Nevertheless, the incidence of disease fell significantly partly because the navy was recruiting more healthy seamen who were cleaner in their habits. Scurvy killed far fewer seamen not only because lemon juice was issued throughout the fleet but also because fresh vegetables were now provided and peacetime voyages were shorter. Diet was further enhanced by the provision of more wholesome water stored in iron casks in the hold, more condiments per man and, in the late 1840s, tea and sugar as an alternative to spirits as well as the issue of 'pressed beef' for the lower deck.[22]

Manning was overhauled in the 1850s, partly as a response to the more efficient use of trained manpower in the French navy. Following the recommendations of a committee of naval officers, Lord Aberdeen's government secured an Order in Council of April 1853 and parliamentary approval for the Continuous Service Act whereby all new entrants into the navy from July 1853 engaged for ten years' continuous service, starting from the age of 18. The Act was made even more attractive for peacetime service by the provision of higher rates of pay, the creation of a new rating of 'leading seaman', more opportunities for promotion to petty officer, paid leave between commissions and the opportunity to change ships. When coupled with the issue of permanent uniforms and more moderate punishments, the foundations had been laid for 'a standing force of the Crown'.[23] However, the Crimean War with its demands for manning two separate fleets had exposed the navy's lack of a wartime reserve of trained seamen. The Admiralty responded with expedients: inviting long-service men to take their discharge without payment in 1857 and, when another invasion scare erupted in 1859, employing bounties to boost recruiting (thereby attracting many deplorable recruits). Meanwhile the Royal Commission on Manning reported in 1859, advocating more training ships for boy entrants, improved victualling, enhanced pay for seamen-gunners, more free kit and free uniform for long-service sailors and the formation of a naval reserve. Parliament duly authorized the creation of the Royal Naval Reserve in August 1859, with the expectation that some 20,000 merchant seamen would be attracted by the offer of limited enlistment, twenty-eight days' training per year, naval rates of pay and a pension at 60. Few merchant sailors set aside their suspicions of the Admiralty and joined initially but an outburst of national outrage over the American stopping of the *Trent* on the high seas accelerated enrolment, producing a reserve of 17,000 by 1865.[24]

As the army had incurred even more criticism during the Crimean War, the demands for army reform seemed irresistible. Reforms of the terms and conditions of service had been mooted before the war: individuals had advocated reforms in the military press and some regiments had established libraries, savings banks and funds for widows. Howick (later Earl Grey) had also accomplished some minor reforms as secretary at war (1835–9) and as colonial secretary (1846–52), including the introduction of good-conduct pay and badges, permanent libraries in the principal barracks, the provision of more recreational facilities and a more varied diet (without a free spirit ration for soldiers overseas). He had sought improvements in overseas barracks and more self-reliance in the defence of colonies of European settlement (but both measures took many years, even decades, to accomplish). He also promoted limited-service enlistments to produce a reserve, but encountered opposition from Wellington, the Commander-in-Chief, who only supported a limited reform and insisted that old soldiers could re-enlist. After Wellington's death in 1852, his successor, Hardinge, responded to fear of a French invasion by adopting a more efficient rifle, creating the Hythe School of Musketry, promoting professional education and arranging a camp at Chobham for army exercises. Yet these measures hardly transformed the army before its test in the Crimea.[25]

The Crimean War failed to accelerate reform partly because the necessary measures were so disparate and, in the case of barrack renovation, very expensive, and partly because the army redeemed its reputation in the Indian Mutiny (1857–8). Although the Staff College was founded in 1858 and army certificates of education were introduced in 1861, fundamental reforms required the election of a strong government under Gladstone (1868–74), with a determined secretary of state for war, Cardwell, assisted by several military reformers. Colonial garrisons were reduced, the War Office reorganized, and short-service enlistments introduced, thereby forming a reserve that would number 80,000 by the end of the century. In seeking to link regular and auxiliary forces, Cardwell was prepared to abolish the purchase system by Royal Warrant (1871) and localize regular, militia and volunteer forces within sixty-six territorial districts (the permanent linking of two regular infantry battalions per district – one for home, the other for overseas service – was completed by Childers in 1881). Although these measures were intended to foster local connections and induce a better class of man to enlist, they had limited effect as successive governments failed to increase the pay of soldiers significantly. As governments also deployed more and more battalions overseas, they undermined the balance of units at home and abroad and hindered the formation of expeditionary forces from the United Kingdom.[26]

Conditions of service were improved. Discipline was eased by abolishing branding in 1871 and flogging in 1881 (while flogging was suspended in the peacetime navy in 1871 and altogether in 1879). More wholesome rations were introduced, the pay and conditions of non-commissioned officers were improved and more barrack-building begun in the 1890s (after the revelation of fever-ridden conditions in the Royal Hospital Barracks, Dublin). But the army still discouraged marriage: only 4 to 7 per cent of soldiers were allowed to marry 'on the strength', all other wives were neither allowed in barracks nor granted separation allowances nor allowed to accompany their husbands overseas. Other than some engineers, gunners and cavalrymen, soldiers left the forces without a trade and were given no assistance in finding employment as a reservist or as a pensioner. They also enjoyed few recreational facilities, and so the temptations of drink persisted. All attempts to wean men off alcohol in both services were left to temperance officers, like Lord Roberts, and religious activists, like Mrs Louisa Daniell, her daughter, Georgiana, and Elsie Sandes, who established soldiers' homes in many garrisons. Agnes Weston and her helpers in the Royal Naval Temperance Society opened the first of their Sailors' Rests in Devonport in 1876. Whether these measures transformed the image of military service is doubtful: the army struggled to attract sufficient recruits of the desired quality throughout the century.[27]

As national institutions, though, the armed services continued to flourish. The Royal Navy remained the world's dominant naval power: it had political and public support, especially the backing of a large, literate and nationalistic section of middle-class opinion, and the financial, scientific, industrial and organizational resources to respond to any challenge. Within three years of France laying down the hulls of the *Gloire* class – the first wooden, armoured steamships – Britain launched the larger and faster ironclad, HMS *Warrior* (1861). Despite the waning of Anglo-French rivalry after France's defeat by Prussia in 1871, the navy continued to receive some formidable battleships: the *Inflexible* with its 24 inches of armour, the mastless *Devastation* and the *Benbow* with its two 16.5 inch breech-loading guns. When concerns were voiced about the vulnerability of British maritime trade in the mid-1880s and the shortcomings of the navy after the 1888 manoeuvres, parliament passed the Naval Defence Act of 1889. This established a two-power standard for the navy and authorized a five-year programme to build seventy warships, costing £21.5 m. The main fleets of the Royal Navy served as Britain's ultimate deterrent, and British naval preparations had a significant effect on the French during the Fashoda incident of 1898.[28]

Meanwhile in advancing its imperial, diplomatic and maritime interests, Britain relied upon cheap, heavily armed gunboats and, increasingly from the 1870s onwards, on gunvessels which had more guns and more seaworthy hulls. Gunboats and gunvessels silenced the Peiho forts during the Third China War (1860); hunted pirates in the South China Seas (capturing forty-six vessels in the period 1861–6); helped to suppress the Jamaican rebellion (1865); deterred Fenians from crossing the Great Lakes into Canada (1866–7); showed the flag and mounted punitive riverine expeditions in West Africa (1869 and 1875); punished slavers off Mombasa (1875); and supported various military operations, most notably in the Sudan (1898) when ten gunboats – one of which sank – provided reconnaissance, mobile firepower, transportation and the means of exploiting the victory after Omdurman, not least in confronting the French at Fashoda. Naval support was not only vital offshore and onshore (in various naval brigades) but it also enabled future naval leaders to gain their baptisms of fire – Fisher in China (1859), Beresford and Jellicoe in the shelling of Alexandria (1882) and Beatty in the Sudan (1898) and two years later in the relief of the Peking legation.[29]

The army was the principal instrument of imperial policy, guarding the North-West Frontier against the possibility of Russian encroachment, mounting campaigns of conquest or annexation, suppressing lawlessness and undertaking punitive expeditions to avenge a wrong, wipe out an insult or overthrow a dangerous enemy.

It met adversaries like the Maoris, Ashanti, Xhosa, Afghans, Zulus, Boers and Mahdists, who differed greatly in their tactics, weaponry and fighting qualities. British forces not only had to adapt to these challenges but often had to move over immense distances across arduous terrain and in debilitating climates. As these natural obstacles frequently posed significant threats to the health and manoeuvrability of expeditionary forces, Victorian commanders such as Roberts, Wood, Herbert Kitchener and Sir Garnet (later Viscount) Wolseley and their staffs became adept at calculating their supply, transport and support arrangements. Although British forces suffered notable defeats at Isandhlwana (1879), Maiwand (1880) and Majuba Hill (1881), and failed to relieve Khartoum before Major-General Gordon was slain (1885), they often triumphed in colonial campaigns, employing disciplined firepower at Ulundi (1879) and Omdurman (1898), the bayonet in the famous charge of the Highland Brigade at Tel-el-Kebir (1882), and the cavalry wielding the *arme blanche* at Kassassin (1882).[30]

None of these successes prepared the army for confrontation with the Boers in the South African War (1899–1902). For the first time British forces experienced the difficulties of crossing battlefields swept by smokeless, magazine rifles. After humiliating defeats at Stormberg, Magersfontein and Colenso – the 'Black Week' of 10–15 December 1899 – British forces overwhelmed the Boers at Paardeberg (February 1900), relieved the beleaguered towns of Ladysmith, Kimberley and Mafeking, and captured the Boer capitals. Thereafter the resourceful and highly mobile Boers waged a protracted guerrilla war, prompting Roberts and Kitchener to burn farms, kill livestock and detain the families of commandos in concentration camps – tactics denounced as 'methods of barbarism' by the Liberal leader Campbell Bannerman. Eventually these tactics and Kitchener's use of blockhouses, barbed wire and drives by mounted infantry undermined the Boer will to resist, and a peace was signed (Vereeniging, 1902). The war had proved unexpectedly costly and unpopular, requiring the services of 448,435 British and imperial troops, costing £201 m, and resulting in the deaths of 5,774 men in action and another 16,168 from disease or wounds. It fuelled demands for the further reform of the War Office and the army.[31]

Both services, nonetheless, had experienced a surge of popularity in the late nineteenth century. The exploits of soldiers and sailors were graphically recounted by war correspondents who, like their fellow war illustrators and the battle painters, concentrated upon the heroism, drama and glory of warfare. Military writing in biographies, campaign histories and fiction, including invasion fantasies, proved highly popular. Juvenile fiction catered for a widespread interest in war and militarism, whether in journals such as the *Boy's Own Paper* which had sales in excess of one million by the mid-1880s or in the adventure stories of Ballantyne, Rider Haggard and Henty. War literature was avidly read in the 1880s and 1890s, particularly the works of Kipling when he began to write extensively about the private soldier and describe army life in India with a stark realism. The adventures of soldiers and sailors were celebrated in poems, popular songs, plays and melodramas, and in cine-film during the Boer War. The armed services featured prominently in large-scale exhibitions, and the Royal Navy and Military Tournament became a popular annual attraction from 1893 onwards.

Military values and notions of service pervaded the ethos, texts, lectures and iconography of public schools (quite apart from the army classes in some schools). Paramilitarism was equally apparent in the newly formed cadet corps and various youth movements (the Boys' Brigade and similar Anglican, Jewish, Catholic and non-denominational bodies such as the Lads' Drill Association). Military imagery reinforced these perceptions, with pictures of military heroes, frontier warfare, and ordinary soldiers and sailors adorning advertisements, postcards, cigarette cards and commemorative memorabilia. The huge military displays during Victoria's two jubilees, 1887 and 1897, underlined the royal and imperial connections of both services, with the Spithead Review of 1897, involving over 165 warships including twenty-one first-class battleships and fifty-four cruisers, confirming Britain's maritime dominance at the end of the century.[32]

This veneration of the services contrasted with the limited appeal of service life and the shunning of soldiers at home (with some barred from saloons, public auditoriums and omnibuses). In certain localities the army's image may have suffered from its continuing involvement in aiding the civil power. Although police forces were more self-sufficient in the late nineteenth century, military units were called out in disparate parts of the country (Lancashire, the Western Isles, North Wales and Trafalgar Square during the 1880s), and, in the Featherstone riot of 1893, soldiers accidentally killed two people. Military literature possibly reinforced traditional attitudes towards service life – that it was poorly paid, lacked status and had limited prospects. Moreover, the reporting and illustrating of wars in remote, exotic locations probably confirmed the impression that this lifestyle and warrior ethos were utterly remote from civilian trades and professions. Many people distinguished between the services as national institutions, with laudable imperial missions, and the services as a potential career for themselves or their children.

NOTES

1. P. M. Kennedy, *The Rise and Fall of British Naval Mastery* (London, 1976), p. 126.
2. D. Gates, *The Napoleonic Wars, 1803–1815* (London, 1997), pp. 40–1.
3. D. G. Chandler and I. F. W. Beckett, eds, *The Oxford Illustrated History of the British Army* (Oxford, 1994), pp. 133, 137, 147; R. Muir, *Britain and the Defeat of Napoleon 1807–1815* (New Haven, CT, and London, 1996), pp. 14–15, 129, 276.
4. Chandler and Beckett, eds, *History of the British Army*, p. 164; Kennedy, *Rise and Fall*, p. 156.
5. M. Lewis, *The Navy in Transition 1814–1864: A Social History* (London, 1965), pp. 26, 30, 37–8; E. M. Spiers, *The Army and Society, 1815–1914* (London, 1980), pp. 8–11, 297.
6. Lewis, *Navy in Transition*, pp. 93, 102–3, 108–9, 112; J. R. Hill, ed., *The Oxford Illustrated History of the Royal Navy* (Oxford, 1995), pp. 251–2, 256–9, 265–9, 272–3.
7. Spiers, *Army and Society*, pp. 10–12, 16–17.
8. Ibid., pp. 2–4, 14, 24–5; G. Harries-Jenkins, *The Army in Victorian Society* (London, 1977), p. 86.
9. Lewis, *Navy in Transition*, p. 251.
10. Spiers, *Army and Society*, p. 41.
11. J. Winton, *Hurrah for the Life of a Sailor! Life on the Lower-deck of the Victorian Navy* (London, 1977), pp. 14, 57–60, 261; A. R. Skelley, *The Victorian Army at Home: The Recruitment and Terms and Conditions of the British Regular, 1859–1899* (London, 1977), pp. 247–9; Spiers, *Army and Society*, pp. 44–8.

12. Lewis, *Navy in Transition*, p. 268; Winton, *Hurrah for the Life*, pp. 14, 90; Skelley, *Victorian Army at Home*, pp. 25–31, 63–6, 130, 147–9; Spiers, *Army and Society*, p. 53.

13. Kennedy, *Rise and Fall*, pp. 155–7, 167–71; C. J. Bartlett, *Great Britain and Sea Power 1815–1853* (Oxford, 1963); pp. 53, 61, 67; A. Preston and J. Major, *Send a Gunboat! A Study of the Gunboat and its Role in British Policy, 1854–1904* (London, 1967), p. 6.

14. Kennedy, *Rise and Fall*, pp. 162–6; Winton, *Hurrah for the Life*, pp. 241–6.

15. M. S. Partridge, *Military Planning for the Defense of the United Kingdom, 1814–1870* (Westport, CT, 1989), pp. 24, 70–1, 101–6, 127–34.

16. Chandler and Beckett, *History of the British Army*, pp. 160–3.

17. Spiers, *Army and Society*, pp. 76–84.

18. W. Baumgart, *The Crimean War 1853–1856* (London, 1999), p. 84.

19. A. D. Lambert, *The Crimean War: British Grand Strategy, 1853–56* (Manchester, 1990), pp. xvii and 304.

20. Baumgart, *Crimean War*, pp. 78–81.

21. Lewis, *Navy in Transition*, p. 269; Winton, *Hurrah for the Life*, p. 24.

22. Lewis, *Navy in Transition*, pp. 251–3, 266–7; Winton, *Hurrah for the Life*, p. 91.

23. R. Taylor, 'Manning the Royal Navy: the reform of the recruiting system, 1852–1862', *Mariner's Mirror*, 44 (1958), p. 309.

24. Ibid., pp. 49–56; Hill, *History of the Royal Navy*, pp. 260–4.

25. Strachan, *Wellington's Legacy: The Reform of the British Army 1830–54* (Manchester, 1984), pp. 20–6, 70–4, 157–8, 167–72, 190–6; *Oxford Illustrated History of the British Army*, pp. 169–78.

26. E. M. Spiers, *The Late Victorian Army 1868–1902* (Manchester, 1992), pp. 1–24, 126–7, 274.

27. Skelley, *Victorian Army at Home*, pp. 38–41, 164–5, 210–18, 257–61.

28. C. I. Hamilton, *Anglo-French Naval Rivalry 1840–1870* (Oxford, 1993), pp. 273, 278–80; Hill, *History of the Royal Navy*, pp. 195, 211–12, 215–20; B. Ranft, ed., *Technical Change and British Naval Policy 1860–1939* (London, 1977), p. 7; A. J. Marder, *The Anatomy of British Sea Power: A History of British Naval Policy in the Pre-Dreadnought Era, 1880–1905* (Hamden, CT, 1964), chs. 8, 15.

29. Preston and Major, *Send a Gunboat!*, pp. 51–3, 69, 76–81, 84, 122, 124, 130, 158–9; Kennedy, *Rise and Fall*, p. 180.

30. Chandler and Beckett, *History of the British Army*, pp. 199–203; Spiers, *Late Victorian Army*, ch. 10.

31. T. Pakenham, *The Boer War* (London, 1979), pp. 504, 572.

32. Kennedy, *Rise and Fall*, p. 205; Spiers, *Late Victorian Army*, pp. 186–203.

FURTHER READING

Contemporary writing on British military history has moved beyond the highly specialized studies characterized by the seven-volume history of the Royal Navy by Sir W. L. Clowes, *The Royal Navy: A History from the Earliest Times to the Present* (1897–1903) and the thirteen-volume *A History of the British Army* by Hon. Sir J. W. Fortescue (1897–1930). It has brought military history within the mainstream of writing on social, economic, technological and administrative change in the nineteenth century and tied it more closely to the burgeoning literature on international relations and imperialism. Both services now have major social studies – M. Lewis, *The Navy in Transition 1814–1864: A Social History* (1965), J. Winton, *Hurrah for the Life of a Sailor! Life on the Lower-deck of the Victorian Navy* (1977), A. R. Skelley, *The Victorian Army at Home: The Recruitment and Terms and Conditions of the British*

Regular, 1859–1899 (1977), E. M. Spiers, *The Army and Society, 1815–1914* (1980) and G. Harries-Jenkins, *The Army in Victorian Society* (1977) – while P. M. Kennedy, *The Rise and Fall of British Naval Mastery* (1976) is a masterly account of naval affairs within a larger political, military and economic context. Administrative reform is particularly well covered in the army with H. Strachan, 'The early Victorian army and the nineteenth-century revolution in government', *English Historical Review*, 85 (1980) serving as a prelude to his revisionist writing on *Wellington's Legacy: The Reform of the British Army 1830–54* (1984). W. S. Hamer, *British Army: Civil–Military Relations, 1885–1905* (1970) fills a major gap. The navy's role as an instrument of state policy is admirably reviewed by C. J. Bartlett, *Great Britain and Sea Power 1815–1853* (1963) and naval rivalry with France is covered by C. I. Hamilton, *Anglo-French Naval Rivalry 1840–1870* (1993). All the major wars have substantial single-volume studies based on recent research (D. Gates, *The Napoleonic Wars, 1803–1815* (1997), W. Baumgart, *The Crimean War 1853–1856* (1999), A. D. Lambert, *The Crimean War: British Grand Strategy, 1853–56* (1990) and T. Pakenham, *The Boer War* (1979)) and several minor wars are examined in B. Bond, ed., *Victorian Military Campaigns* (1967). Naval support of the army during these wars has been analysed perceptively by R. Brooks, *The Long Arm of Empire: Naval Brigades from the Crimea to the Boxer Rebellion* (1999). Both D. G. Chandler and I. F. W. Beckett, eds, *The Oxford Illustrated History of the British Army* (1994) and J. R. Hill, ed., *The Oxford Illustrated History of the Royal Navy* (1995) contain several chapters that provide excellent overviews of writing on the armed services in the nineteenth century.

PART II

Politics and Government

CHAPTER FIVE

The Monarchy and the House of Lords: The 'Dignified' Parts of the Constitution

WILLIAM M. KUHN

His family owned a bank in Somerset. His father, a strict Nonconformist, insisted that his son attend the new and non-denominational University of London. At a young age he began to find his vocation as a writer. He fell into an influential position editing a weekly financial newspaper by marrying the daughter of the publisher. He loved to write essays on Horace and Shakespeare, but he grew to be an expert on banking and currency. He tried several times to get into parliament and failed. He divided his time between London and Somerset, with his wife choosing often to remain in the country, as she was frequently ill and suffered from headaches. They had no children. After he had just turned 40, political agitation for a second reform bill developed. He agreed to publish a series of articles on the way the constitution worked and the likely constitutional impact of a further expansion of the electoral register. He wrote these articles for a new highbrow journal called the *Fortnightly Review*. They appeared two years later as a book, in the same year (1867) as the passage of the Second Reform Act. When he wrote that the English constitution was divided into dignified and efficient parts, he forever changed the way people thought and wrote about government in Britain. His name was Walter Bagehot.

Nearly all important accounts of the constitution since Bagehot's have either sought to show his genius, to criticize him or to elaborate on his ideas. Marxist and social historians have attacked Bagehot for calling the average English worker dull and stupid. The Tory ex-minister who is Bagehot's most authoritative editor has praised him for his style. Royal tutors and secretaries anxious to impress them with the limits of their powers have made every sovereign since George V read and summarize Bagehot. Those who have held high office, or historians with the benefit of hindsight, often begin their commentaries on him, 'What Bagehot did not and could not know is that . . .' The point is that all study of the constitution starts with him.

So important a figure is Bagehot that anyone interested in the nineteenth-century constitution as a whole, or especially in its dignified parts, the monarchy and the House of Lords, had still better start with *The English Constitution*. Start there, however, knowing that Bagehot is both a reasonable guide to the Victorian constitution, and someone whose text, soon after his death in 1877, began to shape the way the constitution was written about and discussed. So Bagehot is a source in the historiography of the constitution, while at the same time his book was an event in its development. The book influenced the direction of writing on the constitution and shaped the way the constitution is conceived by the wider world even today. Although he cannot be held responsible, there have been several overarching trends in the recent historiography of the constitution that are foreshadowed, hinted at or outlined in his book.

Bagehot believed that, although the dignified parts of the constitution still ranked high, they were more important for their psychological hold on the people than for their contribution to the framing of policy. Policy was mainly the business of the efficient House of Commons and the cabinet. The importance of the dignified parts lay in the deference they commanded, the assent they attracted from the governed. Their historical and hereditary associations guaranteed quiet and stable government by the elective and non-hereditary parts of the constitution. For nearly a hundred years after Bagehot's death, this gave commentators and historians licence to ignore the dignified parts of the constitution and to dwell on the efficient parts where the real power, as they understood it, lay.

In the last twenty years, there has been a shift. Writers have dwelled more on the symbolic, imaginative and linguistic appeals of the dignified parts; they have been ignoring the efficient parts in droves. It is as if historians have at last come to appreciate and to want to analyse further the intangible, theatrical and mythical dimensions of power at the expense of legislation, poll books and political biography that were once considered sources for the brute facts of English constitutional and political history.

Three trends in recent historiography appear to be influencing this shift in interest toward the dignified parts of the constitution at the expense of the efficient parts. The shift has had more to do with cultural anthropology than with Bagehot, although its effect was to highlight dimensions of power to which Bagehot had been uniquely sensitive. In 1973 Geertz argued in playful, accessible language, and taking his examples from opera and literature as well as from fieldwork in Indonesia, that cultural artefacts could be read as 'texts' in order to understand the way a culture saw itself and the world around it.[1] He drew attention to the symbolic dimensions of power, to ritual and processions, cock fights and marriage contracts. He emphasized the meaningful quality of 'mere' forms as a way to understanding what makes a society work. This book had a huge impact on the humanities. Whether consciously imitating Geertz, or merely flowing with the tide, historians and literary critics began to take 'culture' as their fundamental unit of analysis.

The second trend follows from the first but is different in character. In the last decade or so, 'cultural studies', including feminist, non-Western and queer critiques of modern and historical inequalities, overtook the original anthropological impulse of this research. Geertz was never a critic of capitalist, or white, or Western, or heterosexual, or male culture in the way the new proponents of cultural studies are. In the 1960s and 1970s historians writing against what they perceived to be the dominant powers in historical studies had often been inspired by Marx. As Marxism and social history waned in popularity, scholars began to take up the tools of anthropological analysis, that is an interest in cultural meanings, in language, in symbols and in other forms of representation. They used these tools in an oppositional way, often in an uneasy amalgam of Geertz and Marx. An influential segment of the new generation of historians in the 1980s and 1990s wanted to show how the old stories of how nations and their institutions operated oppressed or silenced under-privileged groups, sometimes called 'others'. People working in 'cultural studies' have affected the writing of British history and work on the constitution, though perhaps because of the hard-headed empiricism in the field, their influence here has been less than in literature, art history or study of the cinema.

The last broad influence over the historiography of the constitution might be labelled 'contemporary political events of the 1980s and 1990s'. This was a period in which Britain continued to cope with the after-effects of having once had a colonial empire. These after-effects included a large population of recently arrived immigrants from former colonies and heightened racial tensions in Britain. It was a period in which, perhaps owing to the dominance of large media organizations in American politics, people became more sensitized to the influence of the media and the manipulation of images in British politics. These were decades in which the monarchy experienced both a boom and bust of popularity related to the marriage and divorce of the heir to the throne. Finally, questions about the political future of the House of Lords attended the ejection by Tony Blair's government of a majority of the hereditary peers from the upper house. These contemporary events then, like the shift in emphasis from efficient to dignified, and the new interest in cultural studies, had an effect on writing about the constitution as a whole, about the monarchy and about the House of Lords. We can follow these large trends in greater detail by turning to each of these three topics in turn.

The Constitution

Some of the most useful commentaries on the constitution as a whole emerge from commentaries on Bagehot. They are useful because they show the precise political and intellectual context in which he wrote his scene-shifting work. Norman St John-Stevas edited the definitive text of *The English Constitution* and also grouped together several of the most interesting introductions to Bagehot over the years as well as a large selection of Bagehot's lesser-known journalism which sheds useful light on the better-known books.[2] It should be remembered that St John-Stevas was a Tory, completing an act of *pietas* that was subsidized in part by Bagehot's old newspaper, the *Economist*. If he erred, it was on the side of sometimes being too admiring and uncritical of Bagehot. Nevertheless, these volumes are the best and most complete resources for finding Bagehot's text and for seeing how it compares to his other work.

John Burrow has been most expert at setting Bagehot in his intellectual context.[3] He has shown that Bagehot was not a man writing a timeless account of the constitution, but a man of his times, affected by the intellectual cross-currents of the mid-Victorian era. From Burrow we learn how Bagehot was situated in English political thought and specifically in debates about the competing claims of liberty and equality. Burrow also traces elements of Bagehot's work back through Coleridge to Burke. Seen in this light, Bagehot appears as one who valued history, tradition and precedent, as someone who was sceptical of the results of French revolutionary change and its consequent political instability across the Channel during the nineteenth century. Bagehot was not quite as cynical about the stupidity of the common man as Burrow and some others tend to imply. He believed there was irrationality in the political decisions even of educated men. Nevertheless, for seeing the ways in which Victorian ideas about psychology, geology, anthropology and political 'science' informed Bagehot, Burrow is unsurpassed.

Brian Harrison is the most recent commentator on Bagehot to merit attention.[4] In general essays setting out broad developments in British politics over the last century and a half, Harrison has acute things to say about what Bagehot did and did not know about the workings of the English constitution both in his own time and afterwards. Harrison highlights Bagehot's love of paradox. Bagehot said no daylight should be let in on the magic monarchy at the same time as he was doing just that. Harrison also shows how Bagehot has grown into the only text that resembles a rationale *for* the monarchy. He reviews the different critiques of the monarchy and concludes with the somehow unsatisfactory conclusion that the monarchy simply is and this is its best defence.

Critics of Bagehot saw right away that his work was essentially a pro-monarchical defence of the status quo, and of the constitution's ability to achieve gradual reform from within rather than more radical change by popular or external demand. Frederic Harrison responded to Bagehot by making the case for a republic in 1872.[5] He wanted the monarchy abolished and the electoral franchise widened further still. Commentators who align themselves with the political Left since Frederic Harrison's time have often identified themselves as republicans. Their work on the constitution usually stresses the preponderance of conservative or traditionalist elements in the constitution whether it be, for example, the survival of the monarchy and House of Lords, or the disproportionate numbers of public-school and Oxbridge-educated personnel in parliament and the civil service.

Tom Nairn is one of the most vivid, colourful and angry of these republican critics of the constitution, and of the monarchy in particular.[6] He believes that British people live in a fantasy world and see all their dreams of themselves in the mirror of the monarchy. As a result they live not in the UK but Ukania, a dangerously mythic place obsessed with the past. Like other republican writers on the constitution, Nairn sees this as preventing Britain from fully embracing modernity.

Other republican critics of the constitution have pressed for a written document that spells out the rights of British citizens. Charter 88 argued that the 300th anniversary of the Glorious Revolution in 1988 was the right time for parliament to adopt a written constitution. Charter 88 was also prominent in organizing attacks on the monarchy, which it saw as one of the central obstacles in the way of a thorough and progressive reform of the constitution. They took advantage of the monarchy's unpopularity in the 1980s and 1990s to organize a conference and a volume of essays about it.[7]

Frank Prochaska has made one of the most interesting and authoritative interventions in this debate, arguing that English writers working on political ideas since the Renaissance were aware that it was not necessary to abolish the monarchy to have a republican constitution.[8] Rather, the necessities for a republic were participation by citizens in government decision-making, elections and representative bodies carrying out their work in a public setting. By those criteria Bagehot's point that Britain had long ago inserted a republic beneath the folds of monarchical drapery was valid.

Prochaska himself, though critical of the ways royal servants schemed to prop up the throne, was in favour of retaining the monarchy. He was an example of someone whose sympathies were generally with the political Left, who was *both* a royalist and a republican.

Writing on the constitution has also been affected by scholars variously labelling themselves as 'postmodern' or influenced by the 'linguistic turn' in scholarship in the humanities. This group has read widely among continental theorists and has often adopted ideas taken from Habermas or Foucault in order to approach the historical record from a new angle. They are concerned that historians should be more self-conscious about what they are doing, more aware of the snares, traps and myths attending an attempt to record objectively what the truth was. They are concerned with language, with the ways it frames, makes possible and limits the choices of historical actors as well as those who would record those actions. Usually their sympathies are with groups, for example women rather than men, the Scots, Irish and Welsh rather than the English, who have often been excluded from historical accounts. Their repeated phrases are 'unstable meanings', 'contested spheres', 'oppressed' or 'silenced others', and 'teleological' or 'triumphalist narratives'. By these they mean that British history has been written with inadequate attention to the ways that different words could be used by different people. For example, 'liberty' might mean one thing to an aristocratic Whig, but his definition was likely to have been too restrictive to suit a signatory of the People's Charter in the 1840s. This group of scholars wants to emphasize the extent that fighting was going on amongst ideologically, ethnically and socially opposed groups. Victory for one meant suffering for another. Any story that stresses the freedoms enjoyed by Englishmen has missed the extent to which women, blacks and those living outside England were not free.

James Vernon provides an example of work in this vein. The result of his engagement with postmodern theory and the linguistic turn is his argument that liberty and freedom were not expanding during the nineteenth century with each successive expansion of the electoral franchise. Instead, he wishes to 'subvert' this narrative by showing that as the century wore on, the two political parties increasingly mobilized the channels for political participation and political dissent that had previously been more anarchic and free of form. This shut down a radical and libertarian tradition which offered more multiple opportunities for criticism of the status quo.[9] He sees the constitution as a 'discursive system', or a series of discussions, conversations, arguments taking place in print and public oratory and in symbols. He emphasizes the 'fluidity, fragility and discordances of constitutional discourse and the subjects they imagined'. His 'focus is on the representation of politics and its technologies and metaphors. In common with much of the linguistic turn in modern British history, the predominant concern is with the metaphor of language or the means of representation.'[10]

Vernon and his fellows have honourable motives but they indict themselves with the very language they wish to emphasize in their analysis. They belong to a long tradition in British political thought. Like Paine in the eighteenth century, or the Puritans in the seventeenth century, Vernon is dissatisfied with things as they are. He is more intent upon showing the past inequalities in the British political system, which were certainly there, than with celebrating the relative freedom, equality and stability in British politics that made it more desirable than many of its continental counterparts. If he valued clarity in his own language he would make a stronger case for clarity and openness in British political forms.

Ronald Quinault is one writer on the constitution as a whole who, like Vernon, is more interested in political culture, meaning the symbolic frame in which political action as traditionally conceived took place. He has written in an engaging and pellucid style about the rebuilding of the Houses of Parliament in the 1840s.[11] He shows how the architecture, with all its heraldic display and the prominence of the sovereign's throne in the House of Lords, was a setting for *ancien régime* ideas. The building and its decorative ornamentation communicated ideas about hierarchy and deference to ancient precedents. It was not a forward-looking building anxious to show its egalitarian or popular credentials. There was even a special dock on the river for elite legislators to escape out of the back in a hurry if there were a hostile crowd at the front door. Quinault shows how it is possible to revise or question traditional stories about the increasing expansion of British political freedom during the course of the nineteenth century without calling too much attention to the brave new world of discourse and symbolic representation that make such questioning possible. What is as clear for Vernon as for Quinault, however, is that the attention has shifted away in broad constitutional history from the laws and debates of the House of Commons. Rather it is the dignified parts of the constitution, and their capacity to attract, to represent and to put on theatrical shows that are now proving more attractive to scholars.

The Monarchy

For a long time no historian paid much attention to the nineteenth-century monarchy. Those on the Right were more interested in a traditional notion of politics where what counted took place in politicians' letters, parliamentary debates or national elections. For them the monarchy was irrelevant. They accepted Gladstone's idea that the nineteenth century had witnessed the substitution of influence for power in the monarchy. On the whole they concluded that this influence was waning. There were one or two who were still impressed with the political influence of individual sovereigns, or with the way Victoria intervened in a crisis to make peace between the political parties, for example in the negotiations over the Third Reform Bill in 1884–5.

For those on the Left who were interested in the working classes, or in a cost–benefit analysis of the Industrial Revolution, the monarchy was at best a symbol of the old order that was quickly being replaced by a new world. That new world was progressive, urban and looking towards the welfare-state reforms of the coming century. At worst the monarchy was an obstacle to the arrival of that new world. Or it was an embarrassment, the centrepiece of big celebrations especially at the time of the jubilees of 1887 and 1897 that the urban working classes, contrary to their political interests, stubbornly seemed to enjoy.

What historical writing there was on the monarchy appeared in the shape of biography. This was a genre that many historians viewed with contempt. There was a large popular audience for biography and this rendered it suspect in their eyes. It tended to focus on narrative and chronology rather than on analysis and thematic organization. For these reasons professional historians regarded it as less scholarly, less scientific, less apt to grasp the broad underlying trends in British history. Biography placed too much emphasis on the power of individuals and employed the 'great man' theory of history at a time when most historians were interested in slow-moving structural forces of change in the economy and society.

Nevertheless, over the last quarter-century there has been a movement by scholarly historians to join popular writers in the field of royal biography. Both sorts of historian have produced work of lasting value. George III, George IV, William IV and Victoria are all the subjects of newer critical biographies. The overall conclusion is that sovereigns had considerable power in the worlds of art patronage, military affairs, architecture, science and technology, as well as in the political sphere. They also had more influence upon middle-class mores than has usually been thought. John Brooke on George III, E. A. Smith on George IV and Philip Ziegler on William IV are all readable, dispassionate and authoritative on their subjects.[12]

There are enough biographies of Victoria to fill an entire bookshelf. Those produced in her own lifetime were written in the context of her enormous popularity toward the end of the nineteenth century. They were hagiographies and adopted a sycophantic attitude. They were often inaccurate. She read several of them herself and enjoyed writing indignantly in the margins, 'a complete invention' or 'I never did'. However, she commissioned and was deeply involved in the writing of T. Martin's three-volume biography of her late husband.[13] She also published two excerpts from a journal she kept of travel in Scotland.[14] These published journals were unprecedented as sovereigns had never before published their private reflections, or authorized public glimpses into their private holidays. Indeed, an authority on the Tudor monarchy has argued that nothing equivalent to a private sphere existed for the early modern monarchy. Privacy was a recent acquisition and a completely new concept in the context of the Victorian monarchy.[15]

The biography of the prince consort along with the *Leaves* from the queen's journals published in her lifetime and nine volumes of her correspondence published after her death remain important and under-used primary sources for the study of her life. The editors of the *Letters of Queen Victoria* made their selections from a mass of material with the deliberate intention of making the queen appear a useful and influential adjunct to the framing of ministerial policy.[16] Much was left out. The *Letters* show the queen deeply interested in a wide range of both domestic and foreign affairs, as well as able to command authentic reports from ministers, army officers, senior diplomats and churchmen. What they do not show is how often her complaints were ignored or her demands were successfully refused.

Of recent biographies, the most important remains Elizabeth Longford's.[17] She went through all the important primary sources, both published, as well as those in manuscript at Windsor and in Germany. Longford remains the best place to go to locate the queen in relation to the most important episodes and personalities of her reign. After nearly forty years the book is still the first resource for information on the queen's life and the affairs of the Victorian monarchy.

There have been half a dozen biographies since that have added here and there to Longford's achievement, though they all stand on her shoulders. The most interesting specialized biographies of late are those that focus on the queen's gender. Dorothy Thompson and Lynne Vallone are both interested in the ways the queen's role as a woman contrasted with the usual confinement of Victorian women to the domestic sphere. Thompson approaches this from the angle of a labour historian and her knowledge of Chartism.[18] It is interesting to see the way she struggles with the question of whether economic status or gender was more important in shaping the major contests of the reign. Vallone, a literary critic who knows the literature on girlhood in the eighteenth and nineteenth centuries, dwells on the early years of Victoria's life and her education prior to becoming sovereign.[19] Both Thompson and Vallone give important new attention to the contributions of gender to the way Victorians looked at the world and understood the personality of the woman who was queen.

Less successful in this regard is the work of Adrienne Munich and Margaret Homans.[20] They are interested in whether or not Victorian women had 'agency'. By this they mean power, or the ability to control their own lives, despite being limited to a subordinate, domestic sphere by contemporary ideas about the proper relations of men and women. They wish to recast the traditional narrative whereby the monarchy's political power was declining over the course of the century. Rather, the monarchy as they see it had immense symbolic power over the ways men and women, Englishmen and colonial 'others', conceived of and imagined their lives. Homans and Munich are feminists and literary critics. They bring sensitivity to language, knowledge of literature and determination to write powerful women back into the historical record to their task. They are imaginative and comprehensive in the sources they use. To the traditional texts in political thought, or political history usually consulted when examining the monarchy, they have added poetry, popular songs, portraiture, novels and images taken from advertising. They are interested in undermining a traditional historiography that centred on upper-class men in London, and replacing it with something that is more popular, attentive to the ways power was exercised against the Celtic periphery, women and the empire. Ultimately their conclusions are that the symbolism of the monarchy was so powerful and multi-dimensional that it could be read in many different ways. The fact that there was a woman on the throne had both positive and negative consequences for Victorian women. It opened up possibilities for them in going against the orthodoxy that women had no political abilities; but it also reinforced prevailing gender stereotypes, as when, for example, Victoria had herself represented in portraiture as submissive and deferential to her husband.

Sometimes these critics grotesquely exaggerate or distort the elements of truth that they have discerned. For example, were the rock piles or cairns that the queen and her husband liked to build on mountains in Scotland really symbols of English sovereignty over the oppressed Scots? When they dressed up in Plantagenet costume for a fancy dress party in the 1840s were they really trying to clothe themselves in legitimacy and hide the German elements in their family background? These are two examples where Munich sees the royal couple exerting their power over others that are at odds with how people at the time might have understood what they were doing. For Munich this does not matter. In her world, where truth is in the eye of the beholder, what the critic makes of the historical record is as valid as the way historical actors would have themselves described their world. In the absence of contemporaries describing their understanding of events, the critic's theorizing about the meaning of these events will do. If the critic's interpretation is at odds with what contemporaries said, it is because contemporaries were out to disguise the power relations that oppressed women, non-whites and non-Englishmen. Homans and Munich are to be praised for their attempts to bring women back into the historical picture from which they have been too long excluded. However, their project is too confusingly worded, too doubtful of ever finding objective and verifiable evidence about the past to be lasting.

Two other scholars have produced clear and accessible work that will probably have more long-term impact. They share an unspoken confidence that intelligent readers, independently examining the evidence they present, would reach similar conclusions. Vernon Bogdanor provides an account of the sovereign's political interventions in the twentieth century, uncovering their Victorian precedents.[21] His is the most thorough examination of the question of whether the monarchy has any remaining political influence and whether that influence has been useful or harmful. His answer is that the monarchy's influence has not been negligible and that it has assisted rather than thwarted discussion, liberty and democracy in Britain.

Prochaska, like Bogdanor, reached conclusions about the Victorian monarchy that supported or defended the monarchy's continued existence in the latter half of the twentieth century.[22] Prochaska's work is more surprising than Bogdanor's, however, and makes a dramatic link to the world of philanthropy. His success came from 'thinking outside the box' of biography and high politics. His argument is that as the monarchy lost ground with politicians, it gained ground in the world of charitable giving. Victoria gave to a wide variety of worthy causes including hospitals, societies to promote the employment of women and needy individuals. Albert was interested in building model dwellings for the working classes and improving urban sanitation. In this they gave a lead to private enterprise devoted to the public good. They found a new area in which the monarchy could be influential at a time when ministers and party organizations were overtaking the functions once exercised by kings and queens. Prochaska believes that in cultivating local and provincial committees that were devoted to improving the lives of the sick, the ill or the underprivileged, the monarchy was fostering the civic altruism that is the bedrock of a democratic political system. In this work and in his subsequent work on republicanism, Prochaska has established himself as *the* expert on the modern monarchy – on its contributions to political culture as much as its remaining presence in high politics.

His only rival is David Cannadine. Cannadine attracted attention after suggesting that anything that appeared ancient about the monarchy was in fact false or 'invented tradition'.[23] He focused on royal ceremonial over the period 1820 to 1977 to show how the most ancient-seeming parts of royal ritual had served as bread and circuses to keep the working classes happy and loyal. This appealed tremendously to people on the Left who saw the monarchy as a hated and powerful tool of the political Right in Britain. They were satisfied that Cannadine had unmasked the monarchy. He was like Dorothy's little dog Toto who pulled away the curtain and revealed the wizard in *The Wizard of Oz* as nothing more than a funny old man behind a curtain making booming noises on a machine.

Subsequent research found Cannadine's account a little too conflict-oriented to explain the survival and popularity of ceremonial in Britain.[24] The expanding ceremonial role of the monarchy and its popularity cannot be explained away as a confidence trick that one class succeeded in pulling over another. Moreover, the politicians, clergymen and other organizers of royal ceremonial were more often concerned with preserving or reviving precedents, with making tradition intelligible to a new working-class electorate, with rendering the middle and upper classes humble, than they were with inventing tradition to swindle the poor.

The latest development in scholarship on the monarchy emphasizes its amusement or its entertainment value. Henry Ponsonby was for twenty-five years the most import-ant official in Victoria's household. He managed correspondence with ministers as her private secretary and latterly her finances as keeper of the privy purse. Ponsonby's wife, Mary, was a former maid of honour to the queen, who remained her friend and helped to advise her husband in his work. The Ponsonbys' private correspond-ence offers two new insights on the later Victorian monarchy.[25]

The monarchy experienced a republican crisis in the 1870s, the queen having become unpopular though her seclusion after the death of her husband in 1861. Henry Ponsonby wrote to his wife that he had no definite pro-monarchical argu-ment to use in answer to republican critics of the throne. There would be plenty of people to fight on his side and to defend the queen, but they would do so more from instinct, chivalry and sentiment than from logical reasons as to why a monar-chical form of government was best suited for Britain or most conducive to freedom. It is surprising when the queen's foremost official admits that he has no defence to put up for his chief. Yet, when the correspondence between husband and wife is examined, it is clear that there was a stimulus to his loyalty and a compensation for his hard work on behalf of the queen. This could best be summarized as enjoyment, amusement, a sort of aesthetic and satirical pleasure the Ponsonbys both derived from the queen's performance of her routine duties. They enjoyed the way she crossed a drawing-room. They laughed at the Lord Mayor dressing up in robes and chain in order to be presented to her. They made fun of the pomposities of her princely chil-dren and took pleasure from the simple, modest way she underlined her position by refusing to participate in overly formal occasions.

The Ponsonbys suggest one dimension of the Victorian monarchy's appeal that has not so far been covered in biography, political history, the history of republican-ism or the history of philanthropy, in social history or in postmodernist criticism. The monarchy survived the loss of its political powers because people found it appealing, pleasurable, amusing. This cannot be defended or explained in a utilitarian argument any more than the pleasurable taste of potatoes or the wearing of red shirts, or looking up at cathedral ceilings can be defended. They are aesthetic pleasures and they are not best understood though cost–benefit analyses. Further, the Ponsonbys' irrever-ence about the monarchy, their refusal to take it seriously, anticipated the amusement that Bloomsbury was soon to have at the Victorian era's expense. It seems right that this combination of loyalty and laughter is nowhere more clearly articulated than in the letters of Victoria's private secretary to his wife.

The House of Lords

As with the monarchy, there was always greater popular interest in the aristocracy than scholarly enquiry. Academics were not interested in the Lords because theirs was a time that had passed. The traditional narrative about the role of the House of

Lords ran parallel to that of the monarchy. As the commercial and industrial portions of the economy gained strength, agriculture declined in importance. With the exception of a few of the richest peers, who diversified their holdings, most of the aristocracy suffered from the declining economic importance of farming from which most of their fortunes derived. In addition, three successive reform bills widened the electoral franchise. This curtailed the ability of rich peers to put their nominees into the House of Commons and the Commons itself, as the more popular body, increasingly gained power and initiative at the expense of the House of Lords over the course of the century.

This is how the old story went. It omitted to account for the fact that all cabinets formed during the nineteenth century had significant aristocratic elements. It also did not account for the fact that, though the House of Lords seldom asserted its right to reject legislation brought forward by the Commons, there were still disproportionately high numbers of MPs who had aristocratic connections. Even at the end of the century, Salisbury, one of the era's most powerful prime ministers, was leading the government from his place in the House of Lords.

Recent scholarship on the power and social position of the Victorian aristocracy has tended to divide between those who are impressed with its decline and those impressed with its survival. For most of these people, the real decline, or the most interesting evidence of survival, takes places beyond the nineteenth century. It is usually located at the time of the First World War. A large sale of landed estates took place in several years just after the close of the war. Both sides in the debate, however, trace the causes of this back into the nineteenth century.

Cannadine's account of aristocratic decline has been the most charismatic. He writes in a bold, lush manner that is appealing to the general reader. His origins in social and urban history lead him on the whole to be critical of hereditary peers and the arrogant power they wielded over the common man. However, the opulence of his prose and his eye for the telling detail suggest that, like many of his readers, he has a sneaking kindness for a lord. In two important books Cannadine has laid out the case for the decline of aristocratic power and influence. In an early case history of two aristocratic families and their relationship to urban development, he found that as aristocratic power ebbed away they became more congenial to urban authorities as lord mayors, university chancellors and in other largely symbolic or formal posts. As their power declined, their prestige increased. This model runs directly parallel to what had always been said about the Victorian monarchy, but Cannadine was the first to apply it to the aristocracy.[26]

Cannadine's *Decline and Fall*, with its title suggestive of both Gibbon and Waugh, is a big book that charts aristocratic decline in political power, economic power, leadership in the towns and in the arts.[27] Wherever he looks, he sees the landowning order in retreat and defeat. He makes a slightly different case in his recent book on the British Empire. There he sees social hierarchy, and especially appreciation for the style and pageantry of an aristocratic order, as the most important organizing category of the British approach to the Victorian empire.[28] He is combating the notion that race was the most important category in the way the British conceived of the Indian empire. He believes the British ruling classes were ready to meet rajahs and other high-caste Indians as the equivalents of lords and therefore equals. Class, he is arguing, meant more to British imperialists than race. It is his response to what he regards as an overemphasis on racial difference and an over-reliance on works like Said's *Orientalism* that put race before class as a way of understanding interaction between colonizers and colonized in Victorian England. What holds the earlier and the later Cannadine together is a general satisfaction with the passing of the aristocracy and the end of their caste-based empire. Like a Paine who has incorporated elements of Burke into his argument, he is able to appreciate the plumage whilst at the same time rejoicing that the bird has finally died.

No one on the other side of the debate has put his case as sweepingly or engagingly as Cannadine. Yet all of them are more impressed with aristocratic survival than with aristocratic decline. They do not dispute that the landed nobility was losing ground during the nineteenth century. Their surprise and the point of their work is to show how much the landed nobility retained long after commentators had pronounced them on the way out if not already dead. Peter Mandler has shown how, after 1832, Whig aristocratic politics enjoyed a resurgence rather than heading into decline.[29] In the 1830s and 1840s there was a renewed will to govern among reform-minded nobles. Their power base was in their country houses and they successfully played a large role in politics by taking over key posts in the cabinet.

The last two decades of the century also show effective aristocratic political manoeuvre. Lord Salisbury, three times prime minister between 1885 and 1902, developed a theory to justify renewed activity in the House of Lords. His 'referendal theory' justified the Lords' rejection of legislation sent up to it by the House of Commons on which the public had not yet been consulted or was undecided. This was an attempt to show that the Lords could be an active, democratic force just as much as the Commons. There were inevitably issues that might come up during a legislative session which had not been placed before the electorate at the most recent poll. The Lords might reject legislation sent up to it by the Commons and hence provoke an election whereby the public could issue its referendum on the matter. Salisbury was able to use the Lords on several occasions during the end of the century to thwart a Liberal majority in the lower house seeking to pass electoral reform or legislation on Ireland. Essentially this was an attempt to defend the use of the peerage in a democratic system at a time when large landed estates were increasingly coming under radical attack. By showing that the Lords was an active, working part of the constitution, he was attacking the widespread stereotype that the peers were a leisured class broadly opposed to democratic reform of the constitution.[30]

There are two broader surveys of the strength of aristocratic influence up until 1914 and beyond. John Beckett's work covers more than two centuries and is concerned to show how comprehensive was aristocratic power and how long it survived.[31] F. M. L. Thompson's work reaches similar conclusions and is based upon his earlier book that covered English landed society in the nineteenth century.[32] Neither is likely to have the long-term impact of Cannadine's because they are addressed to a more scholarly audience and make a case that runs contrary to our understanding of Britain as a modern society. How could an industrial nation, with perhaps the most vibrant democracy anywhere in Europe, have allowed hereditary peers, whose titles derived from wars, confiscations and political deals long forgotten, to play such an active role its affairs? The overwhelming evidence is that, nevertheless, they did play an active part through the century and even beyond the First World War.

Conclusion

It is hard not to feel that Bagehot was extremely perceptive in placing the emphasis he did on the importance of the dignified elements of the constitution. It is the symbolic or theatrical role of the monarchy that has most interested historians in the last years of the twentieth century. The survival of what seems to be ancient and outmoded has also been a theme, whether we look at scholarship on the constitution as a whole, on the monarchy, or on the House of Lords. All this has resulted from the meaning of 'politics' being vastly expanded in the last several decades. The term was once confined to what men discussed in cabinet and the Commons. Now, sensitized as we are to the power of the media, to the demands of former colonies to be repaid for injustices committed more than a century ago by colonizers, to expanding our democratic system to include voices that were never heard before – of women, of blacks, of gay men and lesbians – our understanding of power has grown. We now think of power as the ability to disseminate images, like the picture of the queen, to sponsor national ceremonies, like the jubilees, to decorate important buildings, like the Palace of Westminster in the 1840s. All this is reflected in a new literature that treats questions of power as questions really of political culture, by which is meant the language, image-making and physical surroundings of the constitution as well as its personnel and the legislation that it produced.

The late twentieth century was a time when many on both the Left and Right felt that a corruption or a vulgarization of British politics was taking place. Many attributed this to British political parties adopting what they thought was an American style of media manipulation or 'spin'. Academics on the whole have embraced this fascination with the media as something that has helpfully expanded their understandings of the way Victorian society operated. Two other features of Britain in the 1990s may be acting as stimulants to further research. The unpopularity of the monarchy through much of the decade and the ejection of the majority of the hereditary peers from the House of Lords have led to curiosity about the recent past of these institutions. Postmodernism is probably a fad. Young people who heed the needs of decision-makers for more accurate and substantial historical information on topics of current interest will avoid fashion and write their work in accessible prose if they hope to attract a broad audience. It is not a bad idea to be interested in race and class and gender. Historical works on these areas can improve knowledge of the past and make it more comprehensive, as well as leading to more positive and enlightened attitudes in the present. But we are storytellers not scientists. Excessively self-conscious theorizing is a way to speak to one another, but also to shut us off from the larger world that looks to us to tell them what happened.

NOTES

1. C. Geertz, *The Interpretation of Cultures* (New York, 1973).
2. W. Bagehot, *The Collected Works of Walter Bagehot*, ed. N. St John-Stevas, 15 vols (London, 1965–86).
3. J. Burrow, *A Liberal Descent: Victorian Historians and the English Past* (Cambridge, 1981), and 'Sense and circumstances: Bagehot and the nature of political understanding',

in S. Collini, D. Winch and J. Burrow, eds, *That Noble Science of Politics: A Study in Nineteenth-Century Intellectual History* (Cambridge, 1983).

4.   B. Harrison, *The Transformation of British Politics, 1860–1995* (Oxford, 1996); see also M. Taylor, 'Introduction', to W. Bagehot, *The Victorian Constitution* (Oxford, 2001).

5.   F. Harrison, *Order and Progress*, ed. M. Vogeler (Brighton, 1975).

6.   T. Nairn, *The Enchanted Glass: Britain and its Monarchy* (London, 1988).

7.   A. Barnett, ed., *Power and the Throne* (London, 1994).

8.   F. K. Prochaska, *The Republic of Britain, 1760–2000* (London, 2000).

9.   J. Vernon, *Politics and the People: A Study in English Political Culture, c.1815–67* (Cambridge, 1993), p. 7.

10. J. Vernon, ed., *Re-Reading the Constitution: New Narratives in the Political History of England's Long Nineteenth Century* (Cambridge, 1996), pp. 9, 19.

11. R. Quinault, 'Westminster and the Victorian constitution', *Transactions of the Royal Historical Society*, 2 (1992).

12. J. Brooke, *King George III* (London, 1972); E. A. Smith, *George IV* (New Haven, CT, 1999); P. Ziegler, *King William IV* (London, 1971).

13. T. Martin, *The Life of His Royal Highness the Prince Consort*, 5 vols (New York, 1875).

14. Victoria, Queen of Great Britain and Ireland, *Leaves from the Journal of Our Life in the Highlands, from 1848 to 1861*, ed. A. Helps (New York, 1868), and *More Leaves from the Journal of a Life in the Highlands, from 1862 to 1882* (New York, 1884).

15. D. Starkey, 'The modern monarchy: rituals of privacy and their subversion', in R. Smith and J. S. Moore, eds, *The Monarchy: Fifteen Hundred Years of British Tradition* (London, 1998).

16. Victoria, Queen of Great Britain and Ireland, *The Letters of Queen Victoria, 1837–61*, ed. A. C. Benson and Viscount Esher, 3 vols (London, 1907); *1862–85*, ed. G. E. Buckle, 3 vols (London, 1926–8); *1886–1901*, ed. G. E. Buckle, 3 vols (London, 1930–2).

17. E. Longford, *Queen Victoria* (New York, 1965).

18. D. Thompson, *Queen Victoria: Gender and Power* (New York, 1990).

19. L. Vallone, *Becoming Victoria* (New Haven, CT, 2001).

20. A. Munich, *Queen Victoria's Secrets* (New York, 1996); M. Homans, *Royal Representations: Queen Victoria and British Culture, 1837–76* (Chicago, 1998).

21. V. Bogdanor, *The Monarchy and the Constitution* (Oxford, 1995).

22. Prochaska, *Republic of Britain*, and *Royal Bounty: The Making of a Welfare Monarchy* (New Haven, 1995).

23. D. Cannadine, 'The context, performance and meaning of ritual: the British monarchy and the "invention of tradition", c.1820–1977', in E. Hobsbawm and T. Ranger, eds, *The Invention of Tradition* (Cambridge, 1983).

24. W. M. Kuhn, *Democratic Royalism: The Transformation of the British Monarchy, 1861–1914* (Basingstoke, 1996).

25. W. M. Kuhn, *Henry and Mary Ponsonby: Life at the Court of Queen Victoria* (London, 2002).

26. D. Cannadine, *Lords and Landlords: The Aristocracy and the Towns 1774–1967* (Leicester, 1980).

27. D. Cannadine, *The Decline and Fall of the British Aristocracy* (New Haven, CT, 1990).

28. D. Cannadine, *Ornamentalism: How the British Saw Their Empire* (London, 2001).

29. P. Mandler, *Aristocratic Government in the Age of Reform* (Oxford, 1990).

30. C. C. Weston, *The House of Lords and Ideological Politics: Lord Salisbury's Referendal Theory and the Conservative Party, 1846–1922* (Philadelphia, 1995).

31. J. V. Beckett, *The Aristocracy in England, 1660–1914* (Oxford, 1986).

32. F. M. L. Thompson: 'Presidential address: English landed society in the twentieth century: I, prosperity, collapse and survival', *Transactions of the Royal Historical Society*

(TRHS), 5th ser., 40 (1990); 'II, new poor, new rich', *TRHS,* 6th ser., 1 (1991); 'III, self-help and outdoor relief', *TRHS,* 6th ser., 2 (1992); 'IV, prestige without power?', *TRHS,* 6th ser., 3 (1993); and *English Landed Society in the Nineteenth Century* (London, 1963).

FURTHER READING

On the constitution a good place to start is P. Smith, ed., *Bagehot: The English Constitution* (2001). J. Burrow, 'Sense and circumstances: Bagehot and the nature of political understanding', in S. Collini, D. Winch and J. Burrow, eds, *That Noble Science of Politics: A Study in Nineteenth-Century Intellectual History* (1983) is the best source on the political thought that leads up to and informs Bagehot. R. Quinault, 'Westminster and the Victorian constitution', *Transactions of the Royal Historical Society,* 6th ser., 2 (1992) fuses architectural history with constitutional history while J. Vernon, ed., *Re-Reading the Constitution: New Narratives in the Political History of England's Long Nineteenth Century* (1996) makes the argument that historians should pay more attention to theory.

For analysis of the Victorian monarchy from a postmodernist and feminist perspective M. Homans, *Royal Representations: Queen Victoria and British Culture, 1837–76* (1998) and A. Munich, *Queen Victoria's Secrets* (1996) are the places to look. L. Vallone, *Becoming Victoria* (2001) is written from a similar perspective, but is much more readable. V. Bogdanor, *The Monarchy and the Constitution* (1995) sketches in the Victorian precedents for the continuing political involvement of English sovereigns during the twentieth century. F. K. Prochaska, *Royal Bounty: The Making of a Welfare Monarchy* (1995) has broken new ground in studying how the court expanded its influence in the philanthropic world and thereby cultivated a degree of civic altruism that sustained republican values in Britain. D. Starkey, 'The modern monarchy: rituals of privacy and their subversion', in R. Smith and J. S. Moore, eds, *The Monarchy: Fifteen Hundred Years of British Tradition* (1998) has fascinating things to say about the Victorian monarchy and its search for privacy. I have suggested one dimension of the Victorian monarchy's appeal – its entertainment or amusement value – by looking at the lives of two Victorian courtiers, in *Henry and Mary Ponsonby: Life at the Court of Queen Victoria* (2002).

On the aristocracy and the Lords, the main book is D. Cannadine, *Decline and Fall of the British Aristocracy* (1990). A number of people have suggested that Cannadine's pronouncements about the death of the aristocracy are premature. The most authoritative of these is F. M. L. Thompson, 'Presidential address: English landed society in the twentieth century', *Transactions of the Royal Historical Society,* 5th series, 40 and 6th series 1, 2 and 3 (1990–3).

CHAPTER SIX

The State

PHILIP HARLING

The Victorian state was a much more perceptible force in the lives of Britons than its late-Georgian predecessor had been. While in 1800 the central government still assumed few responsibilities beyond the defence of the realm, by 1900 it was (among many other things) obliging parents to send their children to elementary school, limiting the hours of women and child labourers, and sending inspectors out to monitor working and sanitary conditions. At first glance, this broadening of the responsibilities of the state seems like a logical response to the needs of a rapidly growing, urbanizing and industrializing population. So, to a considerable extent, it was – and was routinely treated as such by historians writing in the 1950s and 1960s.[1] But just as scholars now question whether an era marked by uneven and often slow rates of growth and fitful technological innovation deserves to be called an era of 'Industrial Revolution', so too do they question the notion of a 'Victorian revolution' in government. By 1880, Britons entrusted the state with more responsibilities than they had ever done before. But the historiography now stresses that they did so haltingly and grudgingly, and could console themselves with the thought that the government cost them less than it had their grandparents, sent few of them to war, and indeed rarely presented itself to their eyes in any shape other than that of the postman.

The recent literature pertaining to nineteenth-century state development is extensive but diffuse – perhaps inevitably so, given the breadth of the subject. Such a fragmented body of scholarship is difficult to summarize, particularly since it has not developed into rival schools of interpretation. So the most efficient way of proceeding is not through a serial analysis of particularly noteworthy works, but through a brief exploration of a series of propositions that historians now generally endorse. The first is that the state was relatively cheap – by no means the hugely expensive military juggernaut that its Georgian predecessor had been. The second point is that it was relatively neutral, inasmuch as its patrician stewards were fairly successful in convincing the enfranchised and unenfranchised alike that the state was not a thoroughly corrupt broker of special privileges. The third point is that the commitment to negative liberty enshrined in the state's minimal economic and social agenda did not prevent it from acting as a stern moral authoritarian that meted out discipline to the ostensibly feckless poor. The fourth point is that the Victorian state's very efforts to inflict market discipline on the poor prompted it to make fitful interventions in the market itself in order to make the living and working conditions of the poor more tolerable. There was no doctrinaire line drawn between laissez-faire and state intervention, because it quickly became obvious to most Victorians that strict laissez-faire was both unjust and unwise. The final point is that until the closing decades of the century, most Victorians felt they had good reasons to keep state intervention the exception rather than the rule: their loathing of higher taxes; the adverse effect that social reform was bound to have on 'respectable' propertied interests; an abiding fear of central dictation and bureaucratic corruption; and a marked preference for local autonomy. The perceived imperial and social crises of the *fin de siècle* challenged these assumptions and enhanced the responsibilities and fiscal capacities of the state to an extent that would have been scarcely conceivable a few decades earlier.

Cheap Government

In one respect, the mid-Victorian state was much less perceptible to Britons than its late-Georgian predecessor had been. Chronic warfare on an ever greater scale was a hallmark of the Georgian era, and it led to the emergence of what Brewer has memorably called a 'fiscal-military' state that was more successful than any of its European counterparts in extracting revenue from its subjects and devoting it to the purposes of war-making.[2] While it was still widely believed after Waterloo that the defence of the realm was the most important duty of the central government, it was a far cheaper one than it had been hitherto. Retrenchment cut public spending by 25 per cent over the two decades after 1815, and relative peace and quiet in Europe, interrupted only by the Crimean War (1854–6), enabled British governments to contain military spending thereafter. The civil costs of central government rose as the state assumed new domestic responsibilities. But these duties remained modest compared with the traditional ones of maintaining the army and navy and paying the interest on a massive national debt that had grown as a consequence of the chronic war-making of the recent past. Thus, while the mid-Victorian state was beginning to intrude in the lives of its citizens in ways that it had never done before, it required far less of them in the shape of taxation and military service than had the Hanoverian state.

There were three main reasons why the mid-Victorian state was comparatively inexpensive. The first was one it shared with its Continental counterparts: a lower level of military spending. Preserving the overwhelming superiority of the British navy and extending the empire to include about a quarter of the earth's surface meant that military spending remained the central government's highest priority. But in many ways this was an empire on the cheap. As late as the 1880s, for instance, it was managed by less than 6,000 officials, while the overwhelming technical superiority of British military forces usually meant that their indigenous foes suffered far higher battlefield casualties than they did. Meanwhile, the decisive diplomatic settlement forged at the Congress of Vienna as well as the military and economic disarray in which the Napoleonic Wars had left virtually all of Britain's Continental rivals helped to keep the peace in (and British forces out of) Europe until the 1850s. Although the Crimean War was expensive while it lasted, by Georgian standards it ended in a hurry.

The second reason why the Victorian central government remained relatively cheap was the slowness with which it took up additional non-military responsibilities. While it devoted considerably more tax money to education, public health, regulation of workplace conditions and the like at the end of Victoria's reign than it had done at its beginning, there was no sudden or dramatic reallocation of the state's spending priorities. Per capita spending on civil government was exactly the same in 1841 as it had been on the eve of the French Revolutionary War fifty years earlier. While civil-government spending as a percentage of total spending grew over the next several decades, it did so at a fairly deliberate pace, from an average of 10 per cent for 1846–50 (still well within Georgian-era parameters), to 17 per cent for 1861–5, to 22 per cent for 1876–80. As late as 1880, military spending and the debt service for which it was largely responsible still accounted for 65 per cent of central expenditure. Thus, in fiscal terms, the mid-Victorian shift in the state's priorities was gradual and limited. Taxpayers who were now paying substantially less for the defence of the realm did not suddenly find themselves spending a vast amount more on social services.

The third reason why the mid-Victorian state was relatively light on its subjects' pocketbooks was that there was considerably more money in most of them than there had ever been before. Britain was the world's undisputed industrial, financial and commercial champion in the mid-nineteenth century. While the roughly 10 per cent of Europe's population that lived within the British Isles at mid-century were still heavily taxed in comparison with their neighbours on the Continent, Britons' control of 60 per cent of Europe's industrial capacity and their supremacy in trade and finance generated a level of affluence that made their central government comparatively affordable.

The gradual dismantling of the fiscal-military state in the decades after Waterloo was accompanied by an incremental reform of the central bureaucracy that made it more recognizably 'modern' and less obviously 'corrupt' than its Georgian predecessor. By the mid-1830s all sinecures had been slated for abolition, the practice of granting reversions had long since fallen into disuse, and the pension money in the hands of the crown and its ministers had been dramatically reduced and brought under parliamentary supervision. These reforms marked the gradual acceptance of the notion that public office was not the private property of the office-holder, but a public trust that should be carried out in person, compensated by strict salary, and superannuated according to an authorized scale of retirement provisions. By 1850, virtually every centrally appointed office was subject to strict terms of service and payment. The only 'rational' bureaucratic principle that was not yet generally accepted by 1850 was recruitment by competition. While the much-vaunted Northcote–Trevelyan Report of 1853 recommended a limited form of open competition based on examinations that privileged the best and brightest from the elite public schools, it took several more decades for uniform standards of competitive recruitment to be established throughout the civil service. But even though nepotism in appointments remained a noticeable feature of the Victorian administrative system, that system was much more closely bound by strict rules of service and of compensation, and thus much better insulated against charges of 'extravagance' and 'corruption', than its Georgian predecessor had been.

A Relatively Neutral State

This comparatively inexpensive state was still controlled by a narrow political elite. But while the persistence of landed domination within both Houses of Parliament throughout the nineteenth century is a noteworthy fact, its importance is easily exaggerated. Commercial and financial wealth was already well represented in the Georgian-era Commons, and even the industrialists who remained under-represented there over the Victorian decades 'saw nothing much wrong in leaving the details of government in aristocratic hands, provided that the government created a suitable framework for the promotion of economic growth and pursued congenial economic policies'.[3] By the 1850s, there were few measures raised in either House that starkly opposed the interests of one group of property-holders to those of others. 'Respectable' opinion felt that all of them were pretty well represented at Westminster, and that the influence of the Lords helped to ensure that parliament would continue to fulfil its functions in a cautious and dignified manner. The passage of legislation was only one of those functions, as Bagehot and many other commentators pointed out; its deliberative proceedings were also designed simultaneously to express the considered opinions of and to provide learned instruction to the nation. The nation, in turn, paid remarkably close attention to those proceedings. During the parliamentary session, debates in the Commons and the Lords dominated the pages of virtually every newspaper. In sum, parliament, which now convened in Barry's magnificent Palace of Westminster, with its famous clock tower and its 940-foot expanse along the Thames, was probably held in broader esteem by the mid-Victorian generation than by any other one before or since.[4]

One of the chief reasons why this was so was that the politicians who sat there shared with most of their constituents the belief that the central government's main obligation was to permit people to look after themselves. Statesmen sought 'to create a neutral, passive, almost apolitical state, standing above and apart from the fast-moving, chaotic, and open-ended evolution of mid-Victorian society'.[5] 'Disinterestedness' was perhaps the most highly prized public virtue within elite political circles by the middle decades of the century. Most of the reforming legislation of this era sought to convince an ever more diverse body of social interests that the state was no longer in the business of privileging some of them at the expense of others. Even the relatively activist Whig coalition governments of the 1830s were strongly interested in the promotion of a negative social fairness that sought to remove the state from social disputes by cutting down on contentious political privileges. But at the same time, their constitutional reforms encouraged under-privileged groups – Catholics, Dissenters, and the plebeian radicals of the enormous Chartist movement – to call upon the state to play a more active role in the amelioration of their grievances. 'Respectable' opinion ultimately concluded that Whig activism, rather than legitimating the patrician state, had only exposed it to dangerous popular clamour. Thus, in 1841, the Conservatives under Peel's leadership won a landslide parliamentary victory, and for the next forty years it was the chief aim of virtually all governments, regardless of their party complexion, to cultivate the neutrality of the state – and public trust in its motives – by ostentatiously dissociating it from social disputes.

Conservative and Liberal governments sought to secure the neutrality of the state through the same repertoire of means. One of them was adherence to public service.

Even if mid-Victorian politicians had wanted to gorge themselves on the fruits of office, the decline of patronage gave them few chances to do so. But few of them would have wanted to, anyway. For over the first decades of the nineteenth century, most politicians had come to believe that it was their responsibility to pay closer attention to the duties than to the emoluments of office. There are several explanations for the development of this self-denying notion of public service, and the growth of evangelical religion and the exacting standard of Victorian 'respectability' that partly stemmed from it are prominent among them. But it also stemmed in part from the conviction that one means of demonstrating the political elite's fitness to govern was to show that it did not subordinate public interest to private profit.

A second means of securing the neutrality of the state was to absolve it of virtually all responsibility for the direction of the economy. Mid-Victorian governments accepted cycles of boom and bust as inevitable facts of life, and did virtually nothing to mitigate their impact. The state, moreover, almost completely removed itself from the monetary system through the Bank Charter Act (1844), which strictly linked banknote issues to the gold supply. From then on, it only occasionally intervened in monetary arrangements in order to help smooth over major liquidity crises. If the gilt-edged security of sterling benefited the exporters of financial services more than it did anybody else, none of the major players in the booming mid-century economy felt that it was doing them serious harm.

Much the same can be said of free trade, which by the 1860s was an even more popular shibboleth than sound currency. Rhetorically speaking, free trade had started life as a critique of the allegedly unfair protection that the government had granted to the landed interest by means of the protective Corn Laws of 1815. Northern manufacturers came to see them as a blatant piece of agricultural favouritism, and united under the banner of one of the most formidable extra-parliamentary pressure groups of the century, the Anti-Corn Law League, to do away with the so-called 'bread tax'. In 1846, Peel split with the protectionist majority in the Conservative party in committing himself to the repeal of the Corn Laws, sacrificing his own political career in order to do away with them. He did so for several reasons, but prominent among them was his belief that one of the most effective ways for the ruling elite to legitimate its power was to renounce its most glaring fiscal privileges. There is little doubt that free trade did indeed become the potent legitimating device that Peel had envisioned. The popularity of free trade helps to account for the virtual hegemony of the Liberal party in the 1850s and 1860s as the party of fiscal fairness, as against the protectionist Conservatives, who were widely stigmatized as the party of landed monopoly.

The minimalist neutrality of the state thus became an especially prominent political theme in the third quarter of the century, and it was a Peelite, Gladstone, who virtually came to personify it as chancellor of the exchequer and later as prime minister. The influence of his policies helped to ensure that, with the notable exception of gilded-age America, 'no industrial economy can have existed in which the State played a smaller role than that of the United Kingdom in the 1860s'. By the end of that decade, it had rid itself of all protective tariffs; its direct involvement in labour relations was restricted to management of the royal dockyards and the inspection of factories; its responsibility for education extended merely to the rather modest subsidies which it gave to the denominational schools; and its very limited intervention in the areas of public health and the poor laws left a great deal of discretionary power in local hands.[6] While Disraeli was as flamboyant and pragmatic as Gladstone was sober-sided and moralistic, these adversaries in the great two-party rivalry shared the same predisposition for a minimalist state that generally let society take care of itself. The much-vaunted Disraelian 'paternalism' did not entail a much more noticeably interventionist role for the state. Indeed, the most significant legislation pushed through by his 1874–80 government was an act of disengagement. The reform of trade union law, by protecting unions' right to engage in peaceful picketing, turned the state's role in labour relations into that of a strictly neutral referee. Thus, however wide the personal and tactical differences between their two great leaders may have been, neither the Liberal nor the Conservative parties envisioned an expansive role for the state at the height of the Victorian era.

Nor was there any longer significant 'pressure from below' to enhance the powers of the central government as a means of redressing social grievances. Such pressure had been powerful indeed in the 1830s and 1840s, when the widespread plebeian anger provoked by the limited extension of the franchise in 1832, by the disciplinary rigour of the New Poor Law, and by the narrow limits of factory reform gave birth to Chartism, the most formidable working-class political movement in British history. One of several reasons why the Chartist movement went into precipitous decline after the House of Commons rejected the third and final Chartist petition in 1848 was the relative neutrality of the state. Free trade, the reduction of indirect taxes, recent factory and public-health legislation – all of these measures helped to signal that the political elite was perhaps not as *utterly* corrupt as the radicals of the Napoleonic era had assumed. Criticism of elite parasitism remained a prominent radical theme throughout the mid-Victorian era. Nevertheless, after 1848 there developed among many radicals a conviction that it was now possible to work within the political system to enforce economy and to promote greater religious liberty. Gladstone and other elite politicians, for their part, were more inclined than their predecessors to entrust at least the upper ranks of the working classes with the vote. The Reform Act of 1867 was partly the result of a series of impressive demonstrations on behalf of the right to vote that had been sponsored by the Reform League and other working-class organizations. But it was at least as much an elite declaration of faith that the 'respectable' artisans at the top of the working-class hierarchy would not use their new power to vote in parliamentary elections to try to force the state into interventionist adventures. As it happened, their faith was well founded. In the short term, at least, new voters showed little interest in broadening the social agenda of the state, which most of them, like their 'betters', preferred to keep as inexpensive and unobtrusive as possible.

The State as Social Disciplinarian

It is easy to exaggerate that unobtrusiveness, however. For despite its minimal framework, historians have recently stressed that the Victorian state could be quite intrusive in its attempts to regulate the behaviour of its most impoverished subjects. The point behind this intrusiveness was to discipline the down-and-out into a standard of personal conduct in line with the cherished social virtues of the day: self-reliance, sobriety, orderliness and sexual decency. It is due in large part to the enormous influence of Foucault that historians now devote far more attention than they did thirty years ago to the ways that the institutions of the Victorian state sought to regulate social conduct.[7] Foucault has been justly criticized for minimizing human agency and exaggerating the power of the state to 'police' social behaviour. There were distinct limits to the disciplinary activities of the Victorian state, because it lacked the administrative resources to engage in anything like a systematic policing of public morals, and because civil libertarianism remained a deeply entrenched social value. Still, it had no qualms about regulating the behaviour of marginal but numerically substantial groups of poor people, most notably paupers, prostitutes and prisoners, and making sense of its efforts to do so is now a well-established scholarly preoccupation.

The Poor Law Amendment Act of 1834, which sought to make poor relief less attractive or 'less eligible' to the able-bodied by tying it to the performance of a variety of irksome tasks to be carried out within workhouses, provides the most important case in point. Scholars now generally agree that the New Poor Law was considerably more revolutionary on paper than it was in practice. A great many paupers continued to be aided outside workhouse doors, not least because seasonal and cyclical fluctuations in the demand for labour made it impossible for guardians to effect an absolute divorce between wages and poor relief.[8] Thus in many respects 1834 did not mark a radical turning-point in the administration of poor relief.

In other respects, however, it clearly did. Most guardians were virtually excluding male 'breadwinners' from outdoor relief by the mid-1850s. The rough estimates available, moreover, suggest that as late as the 1870s, Britain had not yet returned to Napoleonic-era levels of poor relief expenditure in *absolute* terms, even without taking into account the buoyant population growth of the intervening decades. Finally, even workhouses where decent conditions prevailed were essentially penal institutions that obliged inmates to give up their freedom and their individuality in exchange for relief. Thus upon entry paupers had all their personal belongings taken from them, were strictly segregated according to sex and age, were 'disinfected', given standard haircuts, and obliged to exchange their own clothing for dingy and ill-fitting uniforms. Families were broken up in order to promote a Malthusian sort of population control. Paupers were set to humiliating tasks, often of little economic value, such as the picking of oakum, the grinding of corn, the digging of ditches, and the crushing of bones. A strict uniformity was imposed on their diet as well as their hours of work and sleep. Guardians devised elaborate penalties for those who swore, refused to work, or 'malingered'.

It is possible to exaggerate the repressiveness of the workhouse system. Most workhouses were anything but 'total institutions' because Poor Law guardians were unwilling or unable to hire enough competent workhouse officers to police the activities of the paupers. Certainly, many of the wilder rumours concerning the workhouse 'bastilles' were false: that workhouse bread was deliberately poisoned, for instance, or that workhouse children were killed and then ground into pie-filling. The workhouse system was not intended to kill paupers. But it certainly was intended to shame them into independence. That much said, it was nevertheless true that the urban working classes, at least, took a fairly cynical and utilitarian view of the workhouse, and indeed felt little shame in falling back on it when they felt they were left with no choice but to do so. Only late in the century did pauperism become stigmatized in urban working-class neighbourhoods, when spreading prosperity made it easier for the 'respectable' poor to avoid the workhouse altogether.[9] In any case, there can be little question that the workhouse system taught the poor to identify the Victorian state as a disciplinary agent that sought to humiliate them into self-sufficiency, even at times when the vagaries of the market system made self-sufficiency an unattainable goal for a good many of them.

The down-and-out who managed to avoid the workhouse, moreover, stood a growing chance of encountering some other disciplinary agency of the state beyond its walls. The most formidable of them was the police. It was not until the 1850s that police forces were made compulsory in all boroughs and counties, and as late as 1881 there were thirty-one such 'forces' composed of fewer than six men. Still, the 32,000 policemen employed in England and Wales in that year constituted a far more formidable law-enforcement mechanism than the watchmen and parish constables of the late-Georgian era.[10] The rise of the police reflected and reinforced a decline in social permissiveness. By the last quarter of the century, it was far more likely than hitherto that vagrants, drunkards and prostitutes would be arrested and sentenced to short terms in gaol. The corollary to the growth of police forces in this era was a growth in the prison population. There is no greater testament to the moral author-itarianism of the Victorian state than the increasingly centralized prison system over which it presided, which sought simultaneously to discipline and to redeem the convict through an increasingly elaborate set of punishments directed more at the mind than at the body. 'Separate confinement' and the 'silent system' were taken to extremes in the centrally administered Pentonville prison that opened in 1842 as a sort of national monument to the new carceral regime; within a few years prison authorities there were obliged to cut in half the standard eighteen-month sentence because so many inmates were developing symptoms of madness.[11] Few other early-Victorian gaols were this rigorous, not least because few of them could afford to hire enough guards to enforce such comprehensive penal measures. The separate and silent systems, moreover, were gradually supplanted by the so-called 'stages system', by which prisoners could expect to receive a growing variety of privileges according to their good behaviour. But the prison system, finally centralized under the Home Office in 1877, was still predicated on a harsh 'reformatory' regimen that provided vivid testimony to the moral and physical force with which the ostensibly minimal Victorian state could intrude in the lives of its most wayward subjects.

That state's most notorious attempt at moral regulation outside the walls of the penitentiary took shape in the Contagious Diseases Acts of the 1860s, which were intended to reduce the incidence of venereal disease among soldiers and naval ratings by forcing suspected prostitutes to submit to vaginal examination. Those found to be suffering from either syphilis or gonorrhea could be interned in venereal wards of certified 'lock hospitals' for up to nine months at a time. As a consequence of the Acts, many working-class women (by no means all of them prostitutes) were sub-jected to an extremely humiliating form of state compulsion, and those who were consigned to venereal wards were thus incarcerated solely because of their physical state.[12] Pressure groups managed to get the Acts repealed in 1886, but their appear-ance on the statute books and sporadic enforcement over the course of two decades provide especially vivid testimony to the moral interventionism of the Victorian state.

The Contagious Diseases Acts simply provide the most glaring example of the legal double standard that it was the state's responsibility to enforce. It is true that the legal 'coverture' of women was more obvious on paper than in practice. Wives' legal disability to contract and to litigate debts, for instance, was frequently ignored or mitigated in practice, and women did meet with some success in obtaining judicial separations and protection orders from the divorce courts, even though the Matrimonial Causes Act (1857) made it considerably easier for a husband to divorce his wife than the other way round. The double standard was glaringly obvious. The mid-Victorian 'protective' measures that reduced the hours of factory work, moreover, helped to construct a 'male breadwinner' ideology of labour, because they were predicated on two interrelated patriarchal assumptions: that working-class men were free agents whose conditions of employment should not be tampered with, and that women's conditions of employment could be tampered with because they were *not* free agents.[13] The notion that men were solely responsible for the economic well-being of their families was deeply embedded in Victorian social policy. It not only helped to deny wages to women, but to complicate their ability to obtain poor relief under the terms of the New Poor Law, which was so preoccupied with able-bodied men that it scarcely took the needs of women into account.

The assumption that working-class men were economic free agents, however, did not prevent the state from imposing constraints on their ability to gain workplace concessions through collective action. For it presided over a framework of labour law that in many ways favoured employers over their workers. The Master and Servant laws, which defined the legal relationship between employers and workers for much of the era, were deeply biased in favour of the former, stipulating, for instance, that a workman found in breach of contract could be liable to up to three months' imprisonment, while an employer found in breach of contract could only be sued in a civil action. The law of liability was similarly biased, so that a worker who was injured on the job had virtually no legal remedy. Only in 1875 were unions given the right to engage in free collective bargaining, and a series of legal decisions thereafter threatened that right until the passage of the Trades Disputes Act of 1906. Trade unionists thus had good reason to mistrust the Victorian state. They had to fight hard simply to win its neutrality in industrial disputes, and they were not inclined to think that a central government that had so long begrudged them the opportunity to compete on anything like even terms with their employers could be relied on to intervene in their behalf.[14]

The Limits of Laissez-Faire

The Victorian state occasionally intruded in the lives of its humbler subjects in more positive ways, however. While most Victorians felt that the state's intervention in social and economic relationships should be strictly limited, the urban squalor, disease and overcrowding that accompanied rapid industrialization obliged virtually every observer to admit that the central government had *some* responsibility to curb its worst excesses, not least because the 'great unwashed' might rise up in revolt if it did not. As Polanyi long ago pointed out, the 'great transformation' from heavily regulated to self-regulating markets towards the end of the eighteenth century that christened laissez-faire as the great organizing principle of economic life inevitably led to repeated violations of that very principle, because untrammelled laissez-faire would have quickly 'destroyed the very organization of production that the market had called into being'.[15]

Nevertheless, it would be short-sighted to suggest that interventionism was an *inevitable* response to the social problems arising from the urban explosion of the first half of the century. Contrary to what some historians used to suggest, social reform was not always prompted by a widespread humanitarian notion that a particular evil had simply become generally recognized *as* an evil and deemed 'intolerable'.[16] Reform itself, moreover, by no means always took the commonsensical form of a series of rational bureaucratic measures that gradually closed the loopholes to be found in pioneering legislation. Many of the social debates of the early and mid-Victorian decades were highly contentious and sometimes highly principled, pitting powerful interests and ideologies against each other. Much of the legislation that stemmed from them remained ineffective for long periods of time, because opponents tried to neuter it and because the state lacked the means and often the will to enforce it.[17]

Factory reform provides a telling case in point. Only after twenty years of lobbying and agitation did parliament come to accept the principle of the ten-hour day for women and children workers in 1847, and it took another twenty years for this principle to be extended to most non-textile factories and workshops. Even then, there was as yet no legal acknowledgement that the state had any business interfering with the hours of adult male workers. Moreover, while factory inspectors had access to virtually all non-domestic industrial establishments by the 1870s, they generally lacked effective means of compelling widespread compliance with the law, and in any case most infractions went unnoticed because there were not enough inspectors to detect them. It is true that inspectors' recommendations sometimes prompted the drafting of more effective legislation, which in turn granted them more extensive powers of inspection. It is also true that Britain was more amply endowed with inspectorates than the major Continental states, which were only just beginning to appoint them at mid-century. But the point here is simply that the growth of effective mechanisms of enforcement was a slow and painstaking process.

That process would have been even slower had it not been for the activist civil servants who took advantage of the principles of official inquiry and inspection to influence the development of Poor Law, police, factory and public-health reform. Several of these officials were indeed self-conscious followers of the utilitarian philosopher Bentham, and a good many more went along with the notion that a good government was one that sought to secure the greatest happiness for the greatest number of people, and that the effort to secure it sometimes justified closer government intervention in the workings of society and economy. Just as often, however, they felt that the utility principle justified government efforts to withdraw itself from the market. Thus Edwin Chadwick, the most influential administrative Benthamite of them all, conceived of the New Poor Law that he had helped to mastermind as a means of helping the poor to help themselves by weaning them from parochial relief, and he persisted in viewing it in that way.

One of Chadwick's particular obsessions, sanitary reform, ended up being just as contentious and almost as gradual a process as factory reform. Amendments turned the landmark Public Health Act of 1848 into a largely permissive one, and ratepayers who feared the expense of sanitary reform were slow to petition for the establishment of local boards of health. Only in the 1870s do we see the establishment of compulsory sanitary machinery for the entire country and the codification of the (now fairly extensive) powers of local public-health authorities. There were four main reasons why sanitary reform was such a halting and fractious process.[18] The first one was technical controversy and ignorance. The second was political: the creation of a local sanitary authority financed through the rates and backed by legal statute posed a potentially grave threat to a number of formidable propertied interests. The third was financial: the installation of sewers was an expensive and unglamorous business, and ratepayers across the political spectrum were often loath to pay for it. A final and particularly important reason for resistance to the 'sanitary idea' was the Victorian faith in the superiority of local government. Small landlords tended to be particularly resentful of local sanitary measures, for they paid a disproportionate share of the rates and feared that local boards of health would condemn their slum properties. A great many ratepayers suspected that local sanitary regulation was simply the thin end of a centralizing wedge, and they shared the attitude that Dickens famously satirized in the shape of Mr Podsnap of *Our Mutual Friend*: 'Centralization. No. Never with my consent. Not English.' Many advocates of local autonomy, whether Conservative or radical, truly believed that the interventionist schemes of Whig-Liberal governments and their Benthamite associates were but so many attempts to amass patronage whilst destroying local self-government.

The prevalence of this sentiment ensured that most government growth for non-military purposes would take place at the local level. By 1886, local authorities in England and Wales spent well over twice as much as the central government did on civil services. Thus, if there was a Victorian 'revolution in government' it took place at the local level. But even this local 'revolution' is easily exaggerated. It is true that by the 1870s the functions of civil government had broadened to include newer ones such as education, professional police forces and water supply along with more traditional ones such as poor relief, and the cost of civil government had grown a great deal in consequence. But broadening the scope of government was as piecemeal and contentious a process at the local as it was at the national level. Virtually all of the new rating powers granted to local government by parliament in this era were permissive rather than compulsory. Take, for instance, the landmark Education Act of 1870, by which the state sanctioned the immediate establishment of some 2,000 elected school boards in order to furnish a sound, non-denominational drilling to the million-plus working-class children who had not been provided for by the voluntary schools. There is no question that this Act marked a dramatic extension of government involvement in the lives of a great many of the common people. But it left the setting of rates and school fees entirely to the discretion of the new school boards that were elected by the ratepayers. Thus in the short term, at least, the localities enjoyed immense discretionary power in the performance of their new role of schoolmaster. While some of them took to the task with zeal, others showed themselves more interested in saving the ratepayers' money than in providing decent facilities and instruction to their pupils.

Education was by no means the only sphere in which local discretion guaranteed uneven improvement. The growth of the municipal electorate, for instance, was just as much a bane as it was a boon to the accumulation of broader and more expensive borough responsibilities. We have already seen that petty tradesmen and small landlords were well aware that they bore a disproportionate share of the burden of local rates, and were often loath to see them grow heavier. But while it would be a mistake to assume that humble 'rateocrats' always stood in the way of urban improvements, so too would it be to assume that the more well-to-do businessmen who sometimes dominated town councils always sought to facilitate them. The same northern textile masters who looked upon the building of monumental town halls as a rate-worthy badge of civic honour sometimes put off the laying of sewers as a costly and unglamorous enterprise. The city fathers of Birmingham were far more aggressive in the promotion of public health and the provision of services then, say, their counterparts in Bradford. But it was only in the 1870s, during Joseph Chamberlain's famous mayoralty, that the 'civic gospel' bore fruit in Birmingham with the municipalization of the gas and water supplies and the installation of a new sanitary regime. Municipal leaders elsewhere did not immediately follow Birmingham's example.[19] Until the 1880s, 'cheap government' and laissez-faire were still ruling principles, even if they were frequently honoured in the breach. Most mid-Victorians, while willing to admit that urban and industrial expansion required new forms of intervention, still wished to preserve a governing structure that left them to shift more or less for themselves. Generally speaking, they got what they wanted.

By the time Victoria died in 1901, in contrast, state intervention was a principle that was readily accepted, and one that was seen to be advancing along a broad front. What accounted for this transformation? The list of the usual suspects is a long one: an emerging environmental critique of poverty that was noticeable, for instance, in the journalistic exposés of slum life in the 1880s, the social investigations of Booth and Rowntree, and the academic assault on the tenets of classical political economy; the municipalization of 'natural' monopolies such as gas and water supply, and the extension of the municipal franchise to working-class voters who were predisposed to entrust the local council with more responsibilities than they were a national government they continued to mistrust; and the growing (and largely inaccurate) assumption of elite politicians that the mass electorate created by the constitutional reforms of the mid-1880s would use their power to promote 'class legislation' unless they were fobbed off with piecemeal social reforms.

The perceived imperial crisis of the turn of the century provides the rest of the usual suspects: a vast increase in military spending, much of it related to the Boer War, which combined with rising Exchequer subsidies to hard-pressed local authorities to *double* central expenditure between 1894 and 1902; and a growing preoccupation with the need to promote 'national efficiency' through a more vigorous set of policies to reverse the (widespread if exaggerated) perception of terminal industrial decline, a tightening up of imperial connections, and even state policing of the gene pool, as suggested by the popular science of eugenics. Indeed, the 'degeneration' of the urban 'residuum' became something of a national obsession, and the harsh measures that many social reformers advocated to discipline the ostensibly feckless poor, most notably the confinement of habitual 'loafers' in penal colonies, indicate that there was no seamless transition from a predominantly moral to a predominantly environmental critique of poverty at the *fin de siècle*.

Fortunately, the Edwardian state never resorted to extensive coercion in order to promote national efficiency. Vagrants were never deposited in forced-labour camps, nor were the physically or mentally 'unfit' ever legally sterilized, as many were in

California and other American states. It is nevertheless worth stressing (in accordance with recent scholarly trends) that a broad range of legislation, often championed by formidable moral pressure groups, helped to narrow the definition of permissible behaviour in this era and led to the criminalization of drunkenness, soliciting for or into prostitution, cruelty to animals, cruelty to children, failure to send one's children to school, and even 'failing to maintain one's family'.[20] Other new statutes substantially narrowed the limits of appropriate sexual conduct, raising the age of consent for girls to 16 and turning all forms of male homosexual activity into misdemeanours that were punishable by up to two years' hard labour. At the same time, petty offenders were being incarcerated in droves. A quarter of all young men between 16 and 21 who were imprisoned in metropolitan London in 1912–13 served seven-day sentences for offences such as public drunkenness, obscene language, gaming, sleeping rough or 'playing games in the street'.[21] Thus it is small wonder that the police were still widely detested in working-class neighbourhoods. In conclusion, then, it is worth stressing that while the Edwardian state sought to liberate human potential through interventionist measures that would have been anathema to the mid-Victorian generation, that state was perhaps even more intrusive than its predecessor had been in its policing of 'deviant' behaviour. One need not subscribe to a crude notion of 'social control', nor to a Foucauldian notion of historical anti-progress, to acknowledge that the agents of the Edwardian state promoted 'positive liberty' in ways that were sometimes disquietingly authoritarian.

Having examined some of the more salient themes in the recent literature on the nineteenth-century state, it is appropriate to close with a brief identification of some other themes that will almost certainly receive closer scrutiny from the rising generation of historians. One is the shifting balance of power between central and local authority. It is now a truism that the 'explosion of government' first noticeable in the 1880s marked the beginning of a century-long trend away from local discretion and towards central control over an increasingly broad range of public services. This was a trend that late Victorians readily identified. But by no means all of them assumed it was permanent, and historians who wish to resist the Whiggish assumption that centralization was an inevitable corollary of 'modernity' would do well to explore the central–local relationship in greater detail. A second theme deserving closer analysis is the nature of parliamentary supremacy. Everyone agrees that the 'Westminster model' of constitutional development, so widely criticized today, was broadly and deeply revered in the mid-Victorian era. But why was this so, and for what reasons did this consensus seem considerably less obvious at the end of the century than it had done three-quarters of the way through it? A final theme that deserves and will undoubtedly receive closer attention is the connection of the state of the United Kingdom to the four distinct nations over which it exercised sovereignty. It has recently been pointed out that the 'Unionist State was formally a union of multiple identities which made precisely limited demands on British subjects', such as 'loyalty to the Crown, obedience to Parliament, tolerance of Church establishment, and acceptance of English as the primary public language'.[22] The stability of that state clearly had much to do with the modesty of those demands, just as the weakening of its grip on Ireland had much to do with the perception among Irish Catholics that it was unwilling to grant them the fairly broad measure of cultural and institutional autonomy that it readily granted to the other peoples of the British Isles.

A fuller reckoning of the relative success or failure of the unionist state awaits a fuller understanding of its complicated relationships with all of those peoples.

ACKNOWLEDGEMENT

This article is based on material from chapters three and four of Philip Harling, *The Modern British State: An Historical Introduction* (Cambridge, 2001). The author wishes to thank the Rights Controller at Blackwell Publishing/Polity Press for permission to adapt these chapters for this purpose.

NOTES

1. O. MacDonagh, 'The nineteenth-century revolution in government: a reappraisal', *Historical Journal*, 1 (1958); D. Roberts, *Victorian Origins of the British Welfare State* (New Haven, CT, 1960).
2. J. Brewer, *The Sinews of Power: War, Money and the English State, 1688–1783* (London, 1989), p. xviii.
3. G. R. Searle, *Entrepreneurial Politics in Mid-Victorian Britain* (Oxford, 1993), p. 294.
4. J. Parry, *The Rise and Fall of Liberal Government in Victorian Britain* (London, 1993), pp. 8–9.
5. J. Harris, *Private Lives, Public Spirit: Britain 1870–1914* (London, 1993), p. 184.
6. H. C. G. Matthew, *Gladstone: 1809–1874* (Oxford, 1986), pp. 168–9.
7. M. Foucault, *Discipline and Punish: The Birth of the Prison* (London, 1977).
8. A. Digby, *Pauper Palaces* (London, 1978).
9. L. H. Lees, *The Solidarities of Strangers: The English Poor Laws and the People, 1700–1948* (Cambridge, 1998), ch. 5.
10. V. A. C. Gatrell, 'Crime, authority and the policeman-state', in F. M. L. Thompson, ed., *The Cambridge Social History of Britain 1750–1950*, vol. 3, *Social Agencies and Institutions* (Cambridge, 1990).
11. M. Ignatieff, *A Just Measure of Pain: The Penitentiary in the Industrial Revolution, 1750–1850* (London, 1978), ch. 7.
12. J. R. Walkowitz, *Prostitution and Victorian Society: Women, Class, and the State* (Cambridge, 1980).
13. W. Seccombe, 'Patriarchy stabilised: the construction of the male breadwinner model in nineteenth-century Britain', *Social History*, 11 (1986).
14. J. E. Cronin, *The Politics of State Expansion: War, State and Society in Twentieth-Century Britain* (London, 1991), p. 24.
15. K. Polanyi, *The Great Transformation: The Political and Economic Origins of Our Time* (New York, 1944), p. 141.
16. MacDonagh, 'Nineteenth-century revolution'.
17. J. Hart, 'Nineteenth-century social reform: a Tory interpretation of history', *Past and Present*, 31 (1965).
18. D. Fraser, *The Evolution of the British Welfare State* (London, 1973), pp. 60–4.
19. F. M. L. Thompson, 'Town and city', in F. M. L. Thompson, ed., *The Cambridge Social History of Britain 1750–1950*, vol. 1, *Regions and Communities* (Cambridge, 1990), pp. 64–71.
20. M. J. Wiener, *Reconstructing the Criminal: Culture, Law and Policy in England, 1830–1914* (Cambridge, 1990), pp. 259–62.

21. Harris, *Private Lives*, pp. 208–10.
22. D. Eastwood, L. Brockliss and M. John, 'Conclusion: from dynastic union to unitary state: the European experience', in L. Brockliss and D. Eastwood, eds, *A Union of Multiple Identities: The British Isles, c.1750–c.1850* (Manchester, 1997), pp. 194–5.

FURTHER READING

The best introduction to the intellectual framework for nineteenth-century state development is W. H. Greenleaf, *The British Political Tradition*, vol. 2, *The Ideological Heritage* (1983). Equally good on developments in social administration is U. R. Q. Henriques, *Before the Welfare State: Social Administration in Early Industrial Britain* (1979). On the dismantling of the 'fiscal-military' state, see P. Harling and P. Mandler, 'From "fiscal-military" state to *laissez-faire* state, 1760–1850', *Journal of British Studies*, 32 (1993). P. Harling, *The Waning of 'Old Corruption': The Politics of Economical Reform in Britain, 1779–1846* (1996) provides the most up-to-date account of the politics of administrative reform in the first half of the century. For a sensible treatment of the balance between laissez-faire and interventionism, see H. Perkin, 'Individualism versus collectivism in nineteenth-century Britain: a false dichotomy', *Journal of British Studies*, 17 (1977). A classic that remains the best study of Benthamite influence in administrative practice is S. E. Finer, *The Life and Times of Sir Edwin Chadwick* (1952). C. Hamlin, *Public Health and Social Justice in the Age of Chadwick: Britain, 1800–1854* (1998) is a provocative Foucauldian reassessment of Chadwick's contribution to the public-health debate. Particularly insightful on the state's efforts to regulate sexuality is J. Weeks, *Sex, Politics and Society: The Regulation of Sexuality since 1800* (1981). On the gendered dimensions of other forms of regulatory activity, see S. Rose, *Limited Livelihoods: Gender and Class in Nineteenth-Century England* (1991), and P. Thane, 'Women and the Poor Law in Victorian and Edwardian England', *History Workshop Journal*, 6 (1978). An excellent introduction to the broadening reach of the state in the late-Victorian and Edwardian eras is P. Thane, *Foundations of the Welfare State* (1982).

CHAPTER SEVEN

Political Leadership and Political Parties, 1800–46

Michael J. Turner

Introduction

During the nineteenth century British politics changed considerably as crown, ministers, parliament and public responded to new events, needs, pressures and opportunities. Initially the main preoccupations related to the war against France, the Catholic question, and the problem of how to protect the established social and political order in times of unrest. Increasingly, attention was taken by the question of how best (or whether or not) to reform the established order. There was also an abiding controversy about royal power. For more than a generation political leaders had ranged themselves on either side of this issue, some maintaining that the crown should have a say in appointments and policies, others arguing that the crown must be prevented from interfering in what were really parliament's spheres of influence. At times there was ministerial instability, marked by rapid changes of government (especially between 1801–12 and 1827–30). Even so, the cabinet system and office of prime minister continued steadily to evolve during the early nineteenth century. Related phenomena included the rise of recognizable parties, with their differing goals and commitments, and the more widespread use of party labels in political contention. Many of these developments were confirmed and extended as the Great Reform Act of 1832 increased the importance of elections and reinforced the power of the House of Commons (which had long been the dominant branch of the legislature). During the period under review, therefore, particular constitutional conventions, new practices, organizational and ideological aspects, a sense of pragmatic necessity, clearly defined positions on key issues, individual talent, collective 'party' effort and the growth of popular influence all became essential features of the British political system.

Politics in Wartime

By 1800 the war against Revolutionary France had entered its seventh year. The government of Pitt the Younger, prime minister since 1783, had seemed secure for so

long, notwithstanding the domestic and external pressures of war, that it was hard
to imagine a change. Several developments combined, however, to prompt Pitt's
resignation early in 1801. There were cabinet divisions on war strategy and the pros
and cons of suing for peace, and Pitt was unable to impose unity. George III was
dissatisfied with the conduct of the war and, at a time when royal approval was still
essential for a government's survival, he was losing confidence in the chief ministers
Pitt, Grenville (foreign secretary) and Dundas (war secretary). The king also knew
that some of the cabinet would carry on under a new leader, and that Addington,
the respected Speaker of the Commons, was willing to take the premiership. The
main issue over which Pitt resigned was the Catholic question. Pitt effected the legislative union of Britain and Ireland for security reasons and in order to ensure that
Britain and Ireland would henceforth pursue common policies. He had intended the
Union to be accompanied by Catholic emancipation. Freeing Irish Catholics from
outdated penal laws, Pitt thought, would encourage them to support the Union,
assist in the settlement of outstanding Anglo-Irish disagreements, and facilitate
administrative efficiency and social peace in Ireland. But the king refused to accept
Pitt's analysis, not least because his coronation oath bound him to defend the established church (which he and many contemporaries believed would be threatened if
Catholics were granted more civil rights). Pitt deemed this a resignation matter, and
also a matter of constitutional propriety: George III was taking advice from persons
other than the prime minister.

Addington's administration lasted for a little over three years. It attracted wide
support by concluding peace with France and lowering taxation, and it was assured
of royal approval because the king valued Addington as a barrier against Catholic
emancipation and opposition politicians (especially reform-minded Whigs Fox and
Grey, whose political priorities were quite unlike those of George III). Addington's
position was weakened, however, when the war resumed in May 1803. Taxation had
to be increased and there were loud complaints about Britain's lack of military preparedness. Addington's opponents temporarily combined in spring 1804 to bring
him down. Realizing that he had no reliable parliamentary majority, he resigned and
Pitt returned as prime minister.

Pitt had some sympathy with Grenville's argument that an effective war effort
required the formation of a broad coalition ministry bringing together the leaders of
the main parliamentary groupings. Yet Pitt and Fox had long been rivals, and Fox's
record of opposition to royal influence meant that George III would not admit him
to the cabinet. This proscription pushed Grenville and Fox closer together. Both were
committed to Catholic emancipation, both had condemned Addington's administration, and Grenville decided not to join his former colleague Pitt in office in 1804.
Pitt's second administration was seriously weakened as a result. He still had a considerable personal following in parliament, and the king respected him highly (Pitt's
relations with George III recovered after 1801, and Pitt had agreed that Catholic
relief should not be taken up as a government policy). But Pitt was not the energetic
and resolute leader he had been in the past, and he found it impossible to restore
political stability, strengthen his cabinet or make a decisive breakthrough in the war
against France. His health gave way and he died in January 1806.

The king had to call upon Grenville to form an administration; none of Pitt's
closest associates yet had the talent or influence to carry on in office without him.

This also meant that George III had to accept Fox. In fact, Fox did his best not to alienate the king and the new 'Ministry of All the Talents' might have lasted had Fox survived, but he died in September 1806. The government, led by Grenville and Fox's deputy Grey, was then forced to resign in March 1807 after clumsily proposing a measure of Catholic relief. By this time Portland, Hawkesbury and Eldon, all of whom had previously served under Pitt and Addington, were ready to take office and shield the king from objectionable men and measures. Grenville and Grey repeated the now-familiar opposition Whig arguments about improper royal influence, but the Talents administration had been weak and divided from the outset. Though it secured the abolition of the British slave trade, it failed to live up to its reformist credentials in other respects, did little to improve Britain's defences, and pursued no coherent war strategy. In consequence the Talents had rapidly forfeited parliamentary and public support.

From 1807, appointment to ministerial office was conditional upon respect for the king's position on the Catholic question (as well as a determination vigorously to prosecute the war against France). Cabinets might include supporters of emancipation, but it could not be taken up as government policy. It remained an 'open' question. The prime minister had to be a known opponent of concessions to Catholics: Portland was premier from 1807 to 1809, Spencer Perceval from 1809 to 1812 and Liverpool (formerly Hawkesbury) from 1812 to 1827. This context for appointments and policies continued despite George III's final collapse into mental instability in 1811. He had suffered periodic bouts of madness but always recovered in the past. This time his condition did not improve. Regency powers were granted to George, Prince of Wales, who would succeed as George IV in 1820. Although the prince regent had previously associated with Fox and other opposition Whigs, once he assumed executive authority he accepted his father's ministers and ruled out Catholic emancipation. But he was never the political force his father had been. He was inattentive to government business and too lazy and temperamental to get his way on important matters of state. The initiative increasingly lay with ministers who could command a majority in parliament. Royal support, though still important, was a declining asset for them relative to other political advantages, and the administrative and financial reforms of preceding decades meant that government policy and personnel had passed beyond the crown's direct control. Most of these developments were apparent before the death of George III.

Dealing with the court from a position of strength, securing its majority in parliament and bringing the war to a successful conclusion, Liverpool's government appeared competent and confident as Britain began to adapt to peace after 1815. Peace brought new problems, however, such as balancing the budget at a time of growing pressure for retrenchment, and dealing with popular protest and disorder. During the final years of the war shortages, heavy taxes and general economic dislocation had taken their toll, and ministers had been hard pressed to restore order as Luddism, strikes and reform protests broke out. The adjustment to peace was not easy. There was no rapid return to prosperity and plenty. Reformers took advantage of the discontent to attract mass support for meetings, petitions and radical organizations, and distressed working people were taught to trace their miseries to the 'rotten' system of government. The difficult post-war years posed a severe test for ministers and undermined respect for aristocratic institutions. Having restored some stability at the centre of power after rapid changes of ministry between 1801 and 1812, and having won the most expensive and exhausting war ever known in the nation's history, Liverpool and his colleagues had now to convince the British people that order and prosperity could best be promoted within the established constitutional framework.

Tories and Whigs

The party labels 'Tory' and 'Whig' arose during the political and religious controversies of the seventeenth century, and were originally terms of abuse. Their purchase and meaning changed during the course of the eighteenth century. By the beginning of the nineteenth century they were beginning to enjoy wider currency and their significance was more generally understood. At the 1807 general election 'Tories' were defenders of court, church and established institutions, and 'Whigs' were advocates of greater civil and religious liberty. This distinction indicated a polarization of opinion on the main issues of the day, particularly Catholic emancipation, parliamentary reform, retrenchment (or 'economical reform'), the royal prerogative, ministerial conduct and public order. The fact that Tories were in power for most of this period, and Whigs in opposition, added to the rivalry and shaped the development of party ideology, goals and methods.

Pitt had managed to forge a conservative coalition during the 1790s, mainly in response to the French Revolution and the domestic political consequences of war. This coalition broke up after 1801. Though Pittites and Addingtonians were later reconciled, the alliance between Grenville and Fox laid the foundations for opposition Whig revival. Thereafter the party led by Grenville and Grey was known as 'Whig'. Pitt's former associates and followers went on to lead the Tory governments of 1807–27, and the Grenvillites' return to the government fold in 1821 restored the old Pittite coalition. Grey and the Foxites were left as the core of the Whig opposition (Grenville and Grey separated in 1817, when they disagreed about government repression of popular agitation, but it was four years before Liverpool secured the Grenvillites' formal adhesion to his administration).

During the 1820s ministerial ascendancy still depended on successful management of parliament, especially the House of Commons. This task was becoming more difficult because of continuing efforts to reduce the cost and raise the efficiency of government. Executive patronage, exercised more by ministers than the crown, had long been in decline. Eager to improve the reputation of the political elite, Pitt and his successors had no choice but to respond to attacks on official corruption and extravagance. Sinecures, parliamentary seats, offices, contracts, pensions and other elements of government largesse were all affected, and this interfered with ministers' ability to control parliament. Liverpool's cabinet was sometimes forced to retreat when a majority of MPs made plain their hostility to a particular measure (retention of income tax, for example, in 1816). Party discipline and cohesion took time to develop, therefore, and the independence of MPs proved a resilient, if decreasingly important, feature of parliamentary life. Meanwhile, the strengths and longevity of Liverpool's administration ensured that the cabinet system, collective responsibility and role of the prime minister continued to develop along the lines first seen under Pitt. In 1823 Liverpool wrote that his colleagues would all resign if he was dismissed by the king, and it would soon be an agreed convention that the forced departure of a prime minister – the main channel of advice from cabinet to monarch – must result in a change of government. Collective responsibility meant that individual ministers were not expected to repudiate an agreed policy. It is significant that Liverpool preserved Catholic emancipation as an 'open' question, on which the government was to remain neutral, despite the demand from some of his most influential colleagues that this policy should be changed.

Liverpool's government weathered the storms of the post-war years, most notably the upsurge in popular radicalism between 1815 and 1821, and the controversy surrounding George IV's attempt to divorce his wife Caroline. This royal marriage had been disastrous, and, after separating (1796), both the Prince and Princess of Wales had plumbed the depths of scandal and debauchery. On succeeding to the throne in 1820 George IV ordered his ministers to secure a divorce, which necessitated an embarrassing and controversial 'trial' before the House of Lords. Reluctant though they were, Liverpool and his colleagues carried forward this tawdry proceeding, but the attempt to secure a divorce was abandoned when it became obvious that the Commons would not give its approval. Though the furious king threatened to remove his ministers, he could find no suitable replacements. Whig leaders were unwilling to take office under these circumstances, and they knew that their own policy initiatives would not receive royal backing. The Whigs also lacked unity and sufficient numbers in the Commons, and Grey in particular had no desire to serve such a difficult, self-indulgent master as George IV.

Leader of the opposition after the Grenvillite defection of 1817, Grey did his best to keep the Whig party intact. Having been elevated to the Lords in 1807, however, he found it difficult to impose unity and discipline on opposition MPs in the Commons, where progressive and conservative groups within the Whig connection struggled to control the party's agenda. There were frequent quarrels, and Grey's usual answer was to instruct his followers not to become too active: unity would be even more elusive, he thought, if the opposition tried to do too much. Lack of effective leadership in the Commons became a major problem. Tierney was accepted as chief spokesman there in 1817, but he resigned in 1821 because of the party's internal divisions. The Whigs had no recognized leader in the Commons until Althorp assumed the responsibility in 1830. During the 1820s prominent Whigs tended to concentrate on three main goals: public retrenchment, a non-interventionist foreign policy and Catholic emancipation. Privately Grey also favoured moderate parliamentary reform, but this was a divisive issue and, for the sake of unity, he insisted that it should not become party policy. Any Whig who wished to propose parliamentary reform had to do so as an individual, without committing a future Whig administration to anything specific. Russell and Lambton emerged as the most forceful advocates of parliamentary reform on the Whig side, while all the leading Whigs repeatedly spoke up for concessions to Catholics and pressed (sometimes successfully) for economical reforms designed to lower taxation, reduce government expenditure and 'purify' administrative and constitutional practices.

There were important ministerial changes in 1822 and 1823, with new cabinet appointments for Canning (foreign secretary), Peel (home secretary), Robinson (chancellor of the exchequer) and Huskisson (president of the board of trade). Liverpool oversaw these changes with his usual tact, and continued to guide general

policy as a highly respected chairman of the cabinet, uniting talented but very different personalities into an effective team. Disagreements did occur, but collective
responsibility was observed and, for the most part, ministers worked well together.
The new appointments of the early 1820s created for the government a reputation
for progressivism and efficiency. Now that post-war difficulties were receding (with
economic recovery and the decline of popular unrest), a more flexible approach to
political, social and economic problems was possible. Though there was no sharp
break with the past, the new mood and the new men brought about a period of
'liberal' Toryism. As a governing creed Toryism lost some of its former conservative,
managerial rigidity, and there was a more obvious commitment to economic progress,
social improvement and administrative expertise. This accorded with the views of the
dominant ministers, and with changing times: policies could now be framed in a
context of relative prosperity and social peace. On the other hand, there was no
seismic ideological shift. Indeed, the change in personnel was necessitated primarily
by immediate political difficulties. Liverpool had to strengthen the government's
position in the Commons in order to attract more support there (the government
had suffered a number of defeats during 1821), to prevent the king from finding an
alternative administration, and to improve the ministry's reputation after the divorce
controversy.

Backed by Liverpool, the 'liberal' Tories Canning, Peel, Robinson and Huskisson
came to have increasing influence over government policy. The movement towards
freer trade was accelerated. Prisons and the penal code were reformed. The banking
system was reorganized and efforts were made to stabilize the currency. In foreign
affairs Britain became avowedly more favourable to liberal, constitutionalist regimes
and reassessed old friendships with reactionary and despotic ones. On the most pressing and complex issues of the 1820s, however, Liverpool's remodelled government
could make little progress. A division developed between the Tory party's progressive leadership and its more conservative parliamentary and extra-parliamentary supporters. In particular, the Tory rank and file stood for agricultural protection and the
Protestant constitution while some ministers began to favour relaxation of the 1815
Corn Law, and decided that the time had come to emancipate the Catholics (not
least because of violence and mass agitation in Ireland). Corn and Catholics seemed
to Liverpool to pose intractable problems, and the prime minister preferred to tem-
porize. Agricultural protection was increasingly difficult to justify, however, at a time
when commercial freedom was being extended and landowners were the only major
interest still enjoying preferential treatment from parliament. The cabinet therefore
agreed to replace the Corn Law of 1815 with a sliding scale of duties. Meanwhile
the Commons had passed bills for Catholic emancipation in 1821, 1822 and 1825.
Though these were defeated in the Lords, it was clear to Liverpool and to the Protestant 'champion' Peel that concessions could not be withheld indefinitely. This situation was further complicated by the fact that Canning, leader of the House of
Commons, had long been a forceful advocate of emancipation (he was persuaded to
treat it as an 'open' question in cabinet).

Liverpool suffered a serious stroke on 27 February 1827, shortly before key
debates were due to begin in parliament on corn and Catholics. Toryism splintered.
The cabinet broke up and the party divided between those who supported the liberal-
minded Canning, Liverpool's successor as premier, and those who followed former

ministers Peel, Eldon and Wellington into opposition. Party identities were further muddled as Canning, seeking replacements for those Tories unwilling to serve under him, made overtures to the Whigs. Three Whigs (Tierney, Carlisle and Lansdowne) agreed to serve in Canning's coalition ministry. This divided the Whig party, for Grey distrusted Canning and was outraged to find that some of his friends were willing to support Canning in office.

Canning never had the chance to establish himself in power, for he died unexpectedly only four months after becoming prime minister. His successor Goderich was too weak to keep Canning's coalition together. He soon resigned, increasing the sense of crisis and confusion of parties. George IV had favoured Canning, who flattered him and made him feel important, and wanted the malleable Goderich as prime minister because he saw an opportunity to gain more influence (and bigger grants for the court). Goderich's departure, and the obvious need for a restoration of firm government and political order, forced George to invite Wellington and Peel to form an administration (despite his continuing resentment at their decision not to serve under Canning). The corn and Catholic questions awaited further attention, the economic situation deteriorated, popular pressure for parliamentary reform was beginning to revive, and intra-party divisions threatened to prolong the instability at the centre of power.

Wellington became prime minister in January 1828. A new Corn Law was passed, but as well as offending reformers and free traders, because they found it too moderate, it also annoyed landowners and farmers who regarded its sliding scale of duties as an injurious departure from the protective policy of 1815. Pressure from the Commons forced the government to accept repeal of the Test and Corporation Acts, an important constitutional change that extended civil rights to Protestant Dissenters and thereby undermined the exclusively Anglican basis for public life. Though Dissenters had, in practice, long enjoyed religious and political freedom, the *principle* of equal rights had now been recognized, with obvious implications for the Catholic question. This change alienated some of Wellington's hard-line conservative supporters. He also angered 'liberal' Tories by ruling out even a moderate measure of parliamentary reform (demonstrating his insensitivity to extra-parliamentary opinion) and so mismanaging relations with the Canningites in his cabinet (Canning's former allies Huskisson, Palmerston, Grant and Dudley had all accepted office under Wellington) that they resigned. Peel had hoped that Wellington would reunite the Tory party forged under Liverpool, but personal and political differences made this impossible. Then, when the situation in Ireland and the government's vulnerable position in the Commons prompted Wellington and Peel to overcome the king's objections and take up Catholic emancipation as a government measure, 'ultra' Tory MPs and peers revolted. The measure was passed in the spring of 1829 with the support of Canningites, Whigs (now drawing together after the splits of 1827) and the government's loyal Tory supporters. But a core of 'ultra' Tories turned against the ministry and began to demand parliamentary reform on the grounds that a more representative legislature would never have allowed such an assault upon the established constitution in church and state.

The government's opponents voted together in November 1830 to force its resignation. For the first time in over twenty years the Whigs were now able to take office as a party. Though the administration formed by Grey was a coalition that included Canningites and one 'ultra' Tory, in leadership, identity and parliamentary support this was substantially a Whig government. Having placed themselves at the head of the burgeoning reform movement in the country, Whigs were committed to introducing a parliamentary reform bill. Ministers disagreed about the details of the measure, and about the wisdom of persevering with it during the 'reform crisis' of spring 1831 to summer 1832, but a combination of popular approval, Tory disarray and Whig opportunism helped to secure the passing of the Great Reform Act in June 1832. Voting rights were extended, parliamentary seats were redistributed, and the nature of representation was irreversibly altered to provide broader opportunities for political participation. After this period of unprecedented excitement the Tories adapted themselves to new political realities and began to co-operate more as a party under Peel (though there was still some lack of understanding between the progressive leadership and conservative rank and file). The Whigs in office carried several important measures before losing direction and energy. Their parliamentary majority shrank and their alliance with non-Tory groups all but collapsed in an atmosphere of recrimination and disappointed expectations.

Government and Reform

Grey's government responded to the mood of reform in parliament and out of doors by setting up inquiries, gathering expert advice and backing legislative proposals on such topics as the legal system and criminal code, slavery, factory regulation, municipal government, trade and the Poor Laws. These were controversial issues, however, and conflicts of opinion within the cabinet and the government coalition encouraged a Tory recovery. Many Whigs were, in any case, reluctant reformers. They hoped for a period of respite after the 'reform crisis' of 1831 and 1832; instead they were pressed to follow up parliamentary reform with further changes. This made them uncomfortable, as did the need to rely in some Commons divisions on a bloc of radical MPs and the Irish members led by O'Connell. O'Connell had helped to secure Catholic emancipation in 1829 and was now calling for Irish reforms as a prelude to repeal of the Union. In the Lords, meanwhile, the Tories had a commanding majority and could amend or block those measures that appeared not to serve the public good (as they understood it).

Ireland was the source of mounting difficulties. Some ministers, notably Russell and Durham, were sympathetic to Ireland's political and economic grievances and advocated a policy of concession. Stanley, the Irish chief secretary, preferred a coercive approach, believing that reforms should not be granted while violence and disorder persisted. Initially the cabinet reached a compromise. Reforms began (the Irish church was reorganized and education promoted), but a Coercion Act was also passed in February 1833, to last for one year. Cabinet disputes soon prompted Durham's resignation, however, and Stanley was moved to another post. In 1834, when ministers came to discuss renewal of the Coercion Act, several argued strongly for its relaxation. The latter group included Althorp, chancellor of the exchequer and leader of the House of Commons. Grey sided with Stanley and threatened to resign unless the measure was renewed in its entirety. By May 1834 the ministry was in crisis. When Russell told the Commons that some of the revenues of the Church of Ireland should be appropriated for other purposes, Stanley (colonial secretary), Graham (first lord of the admiralty), Ripon (lord privy seal), and Richmond (paymaster general) all resigned from Grey's government. Their conservative-minded group subsequently moved closer to the Tory party.

After a ministerial reshuffle Grey also decided to resign (9 July 1834). He was frustrated by recent developments, and angered to find that some of his colleagues had plotted behind the scenes to weaken coercion in Ireland. The new prime minister was Melbourne, formerly Grey's home secretary. Althorp wished to retire from politics but was persuaded to stay on.

Melbourne was an easygoing chairman rather than active director of the cabinet, and generally believed in letting things alone. He disliked the radicals and the broad social and economic changes that, he thought, were making the responsibilities of parliament more complicated. Having accepted the office of prime minister, however, he did his best to revive Whig fortunes and unite his ministerial team. Much depended on retaining Althorp as the government's chief spokesman in the Commons, but in November 1834 Althorp was elevated to the Lords as Earl Spencer. Melbourne wanted Russell to replace Althorp, but King William IV (who had succeeded his brother in 1830) disliked Russell's reformist predilections and, in any case, had lost confidence in the Whigs. The king complained about their Irish policy, their constant disagreements with each other, and their tendency to seek radical and popular support by making intemperate remarks in public. Since Melbourne appeared reluctant to carry on, William IV took advantage of this new cabinet crisis to dismiss the ministry.

The Whigs' dismissal, and the appointment of a minority Tory government under Peel, prompted animated debates about the constitutional propriety of the king's conduct. In fact this was the last time in British history that a monarch dismissed a government. The time when the crown could make and unmake ministries had passed; even George III had been forced to accept this. In the reformed system after 1832, moreover, the importance of elections, party organization and Commons majorities was greatly increased, and the significance of royal preferences faded still further. Though the Tories made a substantial gain at the general election of January 1835, Peel won no majority and Whig–Irish co-operation in the Commons (Russell and O'Connell formed the Lichfield House Compact in February 1835) forced his resignation in April. The king had no choice but to recall Melbourne and the Whigs.

Born in controversy, Melbourne's second ministry experienced difficulties throughout its six-year existence. As home secretary (later colonial secretary) and leader of the Commons, Russell spoke for those ministers who wished to continue with useful reforms. The prime minister was less convinced of the need for active government, but on certain matters he and his more conservative colleagues agreed that it would be impolitic for the ministry to be seen as timid or indecisive. The terms of the 1834 Poor Law Amendment Act were implemented, local government was reorganized by the Municipal Corporations Act of 1835, and the complaints of many Dissenters were addressed with measures affecting tithes, marriages and the character of the established church. But the ministry was attacked on both sides, by radicals who demanded more thorough reforms and by Tories who accused the Whigs of going too far too quickly.

In June 1837 William IV died and was succeeded by Princess Victoria. Melbourne became her chief confidant, which he found far more agreeable than tackling the government's problems. At the general election of August 1837 the Tories made further gains, reducing the ministers' Commons majority to about thirty. Peel's influence increased, and it became clear that the fate of government measures depended largely on his conduct as leader of the opposition. Popular pressure for more parliamentary reform revived in the shape of Chartism, the economy went into recession, budget deficits confirmed the Whigs' reputation for financial mismanagement, and the government lacked the boldness and ability to recapture the political initiative. The Tories secured a majority of over seventy at the general election of July 1841. Melbourne and Russell decided to meet the new parliament before resigning, mainly in order to bring up the question of tariff reform and provide the Whigs with a rallying point for the future. They also hoped to create difficulties for Peel by forcing apart the 'liberal' and protectionist wings of the Tory party.

Peel succeeded Melbourne as prime minister on 30 August 1841. This was a vital constitutional landmark, for 1841 offers the first example of an organized opposition replacing an administration in office as the direct result of victory in a general election. Peel made full use of his personal influence and parliamentary majority. His logical mind, talent for statecraft and political prudence made him one of the most intelligent debaters and administrators of the day. Deep reflection and previous ministerial experience led Peel to conclude that governors should govern, and that a party must provide the parliamentary support necessary for vigorous, efficient administration (without making improper demands on leaders who, when in office, had to place the national good before sectional interests). In accordance with his conservative predilections, Peel sought ways of protecting church and constitution by showing their worth and weakening complaints against them. He also saw that financial probity and commercial reforms would help to restore prosperity and social peace, promote political stability and win approval for his brand of constructive Toryism. Though his general approach was non-interventionist, Peel was prepared to involve the government in certain aspects of social and economic regulation in order to achieve these goals. He sometimes justified specific reforms with reference to his favourite dogmas: that direct taxation was preferable to indirect, for example, and that freer trade would mean more revenue for the government as well as a better deal for businesses and consumers.

To protect the church Peel responded to some of the Dissenters' grievances and provided the statutory means by which the Anglican hierarchy could begin a process of self-reform, thereby discrediting accusations about the church's excessive wealth, abuse of privileges and inattention to the needs of the people. To undermine Chartism Peel addressed some of the social and economic problems *behind* the demand for parliamentary reform. His 1842 budget, for example, was designed to foster an economic recovery in the benefits of which the working classes could share. Prices began to fall as duties on many articles were reduced or removed, and Peel made up for the loss of revenue by reintroducing income tax (from which low earners were exempt). The Factory Act of 1844 also demonstrated that the state would protect vulnerable workers. The message was clear: there was no need for parliamentary reform when legislators could be relied upon to improve living and working conditions and provide for the well-being of the whole community rather than just the elite.

With respect to Ireland Peel adopted similar tactics, offering moderate reforms in order to weaken the demand for (and so postpone) fundamental change. There was no question of repealing the Union or endangering the Irish church, but Peel sought to mollify Irish Catholics and especially the moderates in O'Connell's movement by strengthening the rights of Irish tenants, facilitating gifts to the Catholic church, and extending educational provisions. Some government proposals were blocked, however, and in Ireland there were complaints that Peel was no more responsive to Irish grievances than his predecessors. Indeed, if Irish policy had fatally divided the Grey ministry in 1834, Peel's cabinet suffered the same fate in 1845. By this time some ministers, and many Tory MPs and voters, had become alarmed by Peel's apparent lack of respect for two of their fondest prejudices, protectionism and Protestantism. In April 1845 Peel's proposal to increase the public grant to Maynooth College, a training seminary for Catholic priests, only passed the Commons with Whig support, for the Tory party split almost exactly in half.

Despite this rupture, and the likelihood of resignations from the cabinet, Peel and his closest allies (Graham at the home office, chancellor of the exchequer Goulburn, foreign secretary Aberdeen, and Wellington as leader of the House of Lords) decided to repeal the Corn Laws. In 1842 Peel had relaxed the sliding scale of 1828, and the trend of his commercial and financial reforms since then pointed to another amendment when circumstances permitted. Tariff reductions, income tax and the Bank Charter Act of 1844 (which stabilized the currency) made possible further experimentation, and Peel had long been of the opinion that agricultural interests should improve farming techniques and land management if they wanted to prosper, rather than rely on protective duties. Though pressure from the Anti-Corn Law League (established in 1839) was growing, the threat of famine in Ireland after the failure of the potato crop there in 1845 probably forced Peel to act sooner than he intended. The political, economic, social and humanitarian arguments for Corn Law repeal did not convince the protectionists in his own party, however, and the split over Maynooth became permanent in 1846 as Peel proceeded with repeal. On 29 June 1846, just days after the Lords had passed the government's corn bill, ministers were defeated in the Commons on a coercion bill for Ireland. Peel resigned, hoping to be judged by posterity on his record not as a party leader but as a public servant whose inclusive agenda for prosperity, order, justice and opportunity suited a changing society far more than the outdated obsessions of traditional Toryism.

Historiographical Survey

The recent historiography of political leadership and parties during the first half of the nineteenth century exhibits significant new approaches, one of which is a growing interest in what is called the 'fiscal-military state'. This concept was adopted by J. Brewer in his work on eighteenth-century Britain. He suggested that the system of government changed in response to frequent wars: specifically, Britain's increasing military commitments promoted heavier taxation, a rise in public borrowing to fund the national debt, and the growth of a central administration capable of managing the fiscal and military activities of the state. In view of the great war of 1793–1815, Brewer's findings may have some validity for the nineteenth century as well as the eighteenth, but there have been disagreements about the real cause of government growth and its impact upon the distribution of political power. P. J. Jupp argues that government expanded in order to deal with social and economic problems associated with the Industrial Revolution, especially poverty, factory conditions, health and trade. Furthermore, though the landed elite retained its control over decision-making, there was increasing reliance on non-landed 'experts' whose administrative talents and practical information gave them a unique importance as advisers and bureaucrats. Jupp also remarks that the number of MPs from non-landed backgrounds rose considerably during the first half of the nineteenth century. A rather different set of conclusions has been advanced by P. Harling and Peter Mandler. They attribute government growth, as Brewer did, to the administrative and financial demands imposed by the need to win wars, not to social and economic developments. They also view the greater professionalism and efficiency in government after 1815 as reactions against growth, not its result. According to Harling and Mandler, government growth was halted to create the Victorian 'minimal' state: politicians and public alike wanted to dismantle the 'fiscal-military' state because they came to regard it as expensive, wasteful and unnecessary. As for the agents of this change, Harling and Mandler argue that the ruling elite never lost its authority and that non-landed 'experts' and MPs from commercial backgrounds did not gain much influence over policy.

This debate about government growth and the nature of political authority will no doubt continue, and any comprehensive explanation will have to borrow from both the political-administrative and social-economic interpretations. It is interesting, though, that an analytical approach employed by Brewer to investigate eighteenth-century Britain has been found so useful to historians of the nineteenth century. A similar trend is developing with respect to the electoral system. Both F. O'Gorman (1989) and J. Phillips (1982) have indicated that the pre-1832 system was not as closed, corrupt and easily manipulated as has often been assumed. They point to high levels of politicization, participation and partisanship, varying degrees of voter independence and a continual process of negotiation between patrons and dependants. Of course electoral behaviour varied from place to place, and it should be noted that the work of O'Gorman and Phillips is based only on particular *samples* of constituencies (mostly English boroughs), but their findings have certainly intrigued other historians concerned with voter preferences and the consequences of the 1832 Reform Act. D. Eastwood (1997) has argued that a 'politics of participation' prevailed in some counties before as well as after 1832, and that the deference and clientage normally associated with rural electorates do not tell the whole story. M. Taylor, focusing on urban areas, adds a note of caution about individual voter choice. The reformed system after 1832, he contends, was not designed to enhance individual choice but to represent interests, and this was how contemporaries understood the act of voting. They voted as members of a group or community.

The Reform Act itself has continued to arouse controversy among historians. Older accounts treated it as a timely concession to popular pressure and a Whig party manoeuvre designed to weaken the Tories, but since the 1960s there have been many alternative interpretations. One of the most notable is that of D. C. Moore, who argues that the Reform Act was designed to revive electoral deference. This was achieved, Moore claims, by depriving the unpropertied of voting rights, clearly distinguishing county from borough constituencies, excluding middle-class influence from counties, and reinforcing landed influence by giving the counties more parliamentary seats. Moore's interpretation has been questioned on a number of points. Eastwood's conclusions (cited above) suggest that rural voters were less pliant, and county politics more complex, than Moore appreciates, and Parry has pointed out that counties continued to have large urban electorates after 1832. F. O'Gorman (1984) questions Moore's assumptions about deference, and N. McCord suggests that even if the government did have clear goals (which were, in his view, to remove anomalies and bring into the 'political nation' worthy sections of the middle classes), ministers did not have the time, knowledge or expertise needed to draft legislation that would give effect to these intentions. It appears, therefore, that there was no master plan, and the fact that neither Grey's cabinet nor the Whig party was really united on reform also tells against Moore's thesis.

D. Beales has argued that redistribution of seats was far more important to the framers of the Reform Act than expansion of the electorate. L. Mitchell's interpretation of reform underlines this point. For Mitchell reform was part of the old struggle against the crown. Senior Whigs believed that liberty and property were inseparable and that more influence for property would impede executive tyranny. Hence their main purpose in 1832 was to increase the political power of property by redistributing seats, disfranchising 'rotten' boroughs and revising borough voting rights. Meanwhile James Vernon asserts that reform enabled the elite narrowly to define 'the people' as propertied men and thereby contributed to a political closure. He points to 'democratic losses' experienced after 1832, though these should be balanced against the undoubted gains (especially in terms of political influence for non-elite interests).

Phillips (1992) has examined the importance of 1832 in promoting new types of political organization, registration drives, party cohesion, the rise of urban and industrial influence, and a higher number of electoral contests (with persistent partisan voting). The Great Reform Act clearly had dynamic as well as conservative aspects. In the 1830s and 1840s there were constructive economic and social policies, and parliament was able to regain lost stature and command wider approval. This ties in with the thesis of Peter Mandler about the reassertion of an aristocratic governing style, and with Parry's idea of vigorous 'liberal government' (characterized by a more interventionist approach). The Reform Act was significant not only for what it did, suggests R. W. Davis, but for what politicians *thought* it did, and reform prompted a notable change of attitudes, especially among Tories who accepted Peel as their leader. After 1832 Peel was reconciled to institutional change, and he saw clearly that the Reform Act made the influence of electors rather more significant than it had formerly been.

In some respects Peel's career after 1832, and especially his government of 1841–6, represents a culmination of many of the developments seen since the heyday of Pitt. From 1841 Peel led a conservative administration that was willing to reform. It owed its place to a general election victory and attempted to demonstrate the continuing relevance and worth of elite rule. In N. Gash's favourable assessment of Peel's character, policies and principles, we find a great man let down by the less intelligent, less public-spirited bulk of the Tory party. I. Newbould prefers to dwell on Peel's shortcomings, particularly his inability after 1832 to persuade the party to adopt his flexible style of Toryism. Newbould's Peel is a weak leader who has to compromise; he tries to impose himself, but often backs down rather than confront the Tory rank and file. Peel did not 'make' the party, Newbould remarks, though he certainly broke it. According to Eastwood (1992) Peel failed to appreciate that party organization was becoming essential for strong government. He deliberately isolated himself, and his view of the relationship between a leader and his party did not suit prevalent political circumstances. Too many observers, moreover, have allowed Peel's opinion of *himself* (the principled statesman who put national welfare before the interests of party) to determine their own assessments of his career.

Many historians have re-examined the wider political and social contexts within which parties and leaders had to act. Much of this work focuses upon agency and participation, rejects strict socio-economic determinism, and emphasizes the political and constitutional background to events, ideas and behaviour. The political importance of 'class' and the significance of extra-parliamentary radicalism have been hotly debated, most notably in connection with E. P. Thompson, *The Making of the English Working Class*, and the so-called 'linguistic turn' of the 1980s and 1990s. While Thompson linked plebeian radicalism with class-consciousness, the 'linguistic turn' attempts to recreate the intellectual framework behind political programmes and vocabulary, and maintains that identities *other* than 'class' must take precedence. Vernon endorses this claim, as does G. Stedman Jones in his work on Chartism. To Stedman Jones, Chartist language was not a 'class' language reflecting workers' experience of the Industrial Revolution, but a language of political exclusion. The primacy of *political* as opposed to other identities has also been asserted in D. Wahrman's study of the meaning of the term 'middle class'. J. Epstein combines the political with the socio-economic. He recognizes the importance of political language, symbol, behaviour and identity without discounting the importance of class-consciousness. These various approaches promise to promote a better understanding of public responses to contentious legislation, the popular (and electoral) appeal of specific politicians and the nature of party and growth of political consciousness. Crucially, they can also elucidate points of contact between parliament and people, rulers and ruled, elite preferences and 'public opinion'. During the first half of the nineteenth century the whole system of governance came under critical gaze. In this 'age of unease', those inside the formal political nation had to find ways of managing, communicating with and sometimes conciliating those outside, who pressed for access to rights and influence. This was one of the fundamental problems inherited by political leaders who rose to prominence after 1846.

BIBLIOGRAPHY AND FURTHER READING

D. Beales, 'The electorate before and after 1832: the right to vote, and the opportunity', *Parliamentary History*, 11 (1992).

J. Brewer, *The Sinews of Power: War, Money and the English State, 1688–1783* (London, 1989).

R. W. Davis, 'Toryism to Tamworth: the triumph of reform, 1827–35', *Albion*, 12 (1980).

D. Eastwood, 'Peel: a reassessment', *History Today*, 42 (1992).

D. Eastwood, 'Contesting the politics of deference: the rural electorate, 1820–60', in J. Lawrence and M. Taylor, eds, *Party, State and Society: Electoral Behaviour in Britain since 1820* (Aldershot, 1997).

J. Epstein, *Radical Expression: Political Language, Ritual and Symbol in England, 1790–1850* (Oxford, 1994).

N. Gash, *Peel* (London, 1976).

P. Harling and P. Mandler, 'From "fiscal-military" state to *laissez-faire* state, 1760–1850', *Journal of British Studies*, 32 (1993).

P. J. Jupp, 'The landed elite and political authority in Britain, 1760–1850', *Journal of British Studies*, 29 (1990).

P. Mandler, *Aristocratic Government in the Age of Reform* (Oxford, 1990).

N. McCord, 'Some difficulties of parliamentary reform', *Historical Journal*, 10 (1967).

L. Mitchell, 'Foxite politics and the Great Reform Bill', *English Historical Review*, 108 (1993)

D. C. Moore, 'Concession or cure: the sociological premises of the First Reform Act', *Historical Journal*, 9 (1966).

D. C. Moore, *The Politics of Deference* (Hassocks, 1976).

I. Newbould, 'Peel and the Conservative party 1832–41: a study in failure', *English Historical Review*, 98 (1983).

F. O'Gorman, 'Electoral deference in unreformed England, 1760–1832', *Journal of Modern History*, 56 (1984).

F. O'Gorman, *Voters, Patrons, and Parties: The Unreformed Electoral System of Hanoverian England, 1734–1832* (Oxford, 1989).

J. Parry, *The Rise and Fall of Liberal Government in Victorian England* (New Haven, CT, 1993)

J. Phillips, *Electoral Behavior in Unreformed England: Plumpers, Splitters, and Straights* (Princeton, 1982).

J. Phillips, *The Great Reform Bill in the Boroughs: English Electoral Behaviour 1818–1841* (Oxford, 1992).

G. Stedman Jones, *Languages of Class: Studies in English Working-Class History, 1832–1982* (Cambridge, 1983).

M. Taylor, 'Interests, parties and the state: the urban electorate in England, 1820–72', in J. Lawrence and M. Taylor, eds, *Party, State and Society: Electoral Behaviour in Britain since 1820* (Aldershot, 1997).

E. P. Thompson, *The Making of the English Working Class* (London, 1963).

J. Vernon, *Politics and the People: A Study in English Political Culture, c.1815–67* (Cambridge, 1993).

D. Wahrman, *Imagining the Middle Class: The Political Representation of Class in Britain, c.1780–1840* (Cambridge, 1994).

CHAPTER EIGHT

Political Leadership and Political Parties, 1846–1900

MICHAEL J. TURNER

Politics in the Mid-Nineteenth Century

After the fall of Peel in June 1846, Russell became prime minister at the head of a Whig administration that (though it survived for over five years) offered few decisive policy initiatives and rarely seemed capable of controlling parliament. These short-comings were partly attributable to the party confusion that followed the Whigs' difficulties in office during the 1830s and the Tory schisms of 1845 and 1846. Party unity had faded, and Russell's government had to rely on an unwieldy coalition of Whigs, Irish, moderate reformers and radicals. The 1847 general election did not give ministers a secure Commons majority, despite the continuing division between Peelite and Protectionist sections of the former Tory party. Before long the Protectionists were calling themselves the Conservative party, in defiance of Peel, to whom the label 'Conservative' (rather than the more traditional and inflexible 'Tory') had previously been applied. The Conservatives were the largest single group in the Commons, with 243 MPs returned in 1847. Nevertheless, they were incapable of forming a viable administration. The Peelites numbered 89; they refused to join any other group, though their hostility to the Conservatives made them anxious to prevent the collapse of Russell's ministry. The government coalition consisted of about 324 MPs, but this was no united voting bloc. Dependent on their allies, the Whigs had to govern as best they could in a period of disorganized parties, executive weakness, cross-voting and general indiscipline in the Commons.

It proved impossible to predict parliament's mood on any given question. Peelite voting patterns were inconsistent, while radicals argued among themselves on education, finance, factory reform and foreign policy. There was also unease among the Conservatives. Party leader Lord Stanley (subsequently Earl of Derby) tried several times to persuade individual Peelites to join him, but personal and political differences ruled this out. Stanley retained protection as party policy. He knew that most of his followers were still committed to protection and that it was fundamental to the Conservatives' identity and extra-parliamentary appeal. From September 1848, however, the party's main spokesman in the Commons was Disraeli, and he decided that protection should be abandoned on the grounds that the Conservatives would never win a majority unless they unequivocally accepted repeal of the Corn Laws. Disraeli tried to convince his colleagues that, instead of trying to restore the Corn Laws, it would be better to gain compensation for agriculture by such means as tax reform.

The Russell administration had modest success in continuing the movement towards free trade, revising sugar duties and repealing the Navigation Acts (which had already been relaxed during the 1820s). Though these measures were controversial they won the approval of most government supporters, but sectarian rivalries made grants for education rather more divisive. The 'Great Famine' in Ireland, moreover, prompted disagreements about the propriety of government intervention, and the high cost of famine relief upset the budget plans of chancellor of the exchequer Wood, perpetuating the Whigs' reputation for financial ineptitude. Disraeli's influence in the Commons grew, ministers suffered embarrassing defeats on minor questions and Russell's colleagues began openly to disagree with each other. One of them, foreign secretary Palmerston, often acted without first consulting the cabinet, and offended Victoria by ignoring her wish to be kept informed of his policies. Russell decided that some bold initiative was required to restore the government's fortunes. An opportunity presented itself when the pope restored the Roman Catholic hierarchy in England in 1850. Russell joined in an anti-Catholic reaction by publicly condemning 'Papal aggression', and the government passed the Ecclesiastical Titles Act in 1851 to prohibit the assumption of certain territorial titles. This measure did not improve the ministry's parliamentary position. Peelites voted against it, while many Irish Catholic MPs abandoned the government completely.

Russell had another idea. He proposed a moderate extension to the parliamentary franchise, hoping to unite the Whigs and their allies behind a useful reform. To round off the work begun in 1832, he thought, would also be to enhance his own reputation. Some of his colleagues objected to franchise reform, however, and when Russell refused to give it up his support dwindled and a Commons defeat on 22 February 1851 prompted his resignation. Stanley was unable to construct an administration and Russell returned as prime minister in March. His relations with Palmerston finally reached breaking point in December 1851 after the foreign secretary again flouted conventions relating to collective responsibility. Without consulting cabinet colleagues Palmerston congratulated Louis Napoleon on the *coup d'état* by which he proclaimed himself French emperor. Palmerston was dismissed, but had his revenge in February 1852 when he carried an amendment against a government bill in the Commons. Weary of office, bereft of ideas and now completely discredited, Russell and his cabinet resigned.

There followed a short-lived minority Conservative administration led by Derby. Disraeli was chancellor of the exchequer in this 'Who? Who?' ministry, so named because it consisted of relatively unknown figures. Though the government made gains at the general election of July 1852, it did not secure a Commons majority. Derby hoped that the experience of office would be a building block for the Conservatives' future, however, and Disraeli continued his efforts to persuade the landed interests (still the party's backbone) to press for preferential taxation rather than a return to the electorally damaging platform of agricultural protection. Disraeli's budget of December 1852 was organized around this principle, but it was savaged by the leading Peelite, Gladstone, and Peelite, Whig, radical and Irish MPs voted together to reject it. Derby's government fell and was succeeded by Aberdeen's coalition ministry.

Aberdeen had previously served as foreign secretary under Wellington and Peel. He was highly respected, enjoyed royal confidence, and secured the appointment of six Peelites (including himself as premier and Gladstone as chancellor of the exchequer) to the cabinet of thirteen. There was one radical minister, Molesworth, and the remaining six places were taken by Whigs (including Russell, Palmerston and Wood). Aberdeen and Gladstone had agreed that Peelite membership of a 'mixed' government was justifiable in view of serious problems at home (especially financial) and abroad (particularly mounting tension in the Near East). But the Whigs were not easy to deal with. Russell was touchy about his status and annoyed not to have been invited to head the new government. Peelites had insisted that they would not serve under him, and Palmerston (whose experience and popularity made his adherence essential) said the same thing. Palmerston became home secretary. It was eventually agreed that Russell should be foreign secretary and leader of the House of Commons. Russell appears to have believed that temporary objections (as he saw them) to his return to the premiership would soon disappear, and that Aberdeen would stand aside.

This coalition offered the best hope for a restoration of ministerial stability. No single parliamentary group could command a majority, the Whigs had not been able to govern successfully alone, and the only other possible combination, of Peelites and Conservatives, looked increasingly unlikely. Though protection was no longer an avowed Conservative policy, and though Derby still favoured reunion, Disraeli was unwilling to defer to his rival Gladstone and most Conservative MPs and supporters were not prepared to work with what they saw as a small knot of ambitious politicians who had no sense of loyalty. For their part, Peelites had no qualms about forcing Derby out of office in December 1852, and they knew that very few Conservatives shared their financial and economic preferences.

Aberdeen's ministry carried notable reforms on pollution and colonial government, and Gladstone's budget of 1853 laid the foundations for Victorian financial orthodoxy. Gladstone continued reducing duties and, unlike Disraeli in 1852, made no distinction for tax purposes between income from land and income from trade and industry. The prime minister proved to be an able conciliator in cabinet, gratified Victoria and Albert by keeping them informed of the government's plans, and benefited from rifts within the Conservative opposition. But the outbreak of the Crimean War in March 1854 led to the government's downfall. Arguments between the anti-Russian Whigs and more pacific Peelites hampered collective effort, while strategic blunders and the failure adequately to supply British forces provoked a public outcry. Much of this was beyond the cabinet's direct control, but parliamentary pressure grew and, instead of helping to defend the government's record, Russell decided to resign (24 January 1855). Radical MP Roebuck then carried his motion for a committee of inquiry. Aberdeen gave up the premiership and was succeeded by Palmerston, whose assertive patriotism as foreign secretary under Grey, Melbourne and Russell prompted parliament and people (though not the court, where Palmerston was unpopular) to consider him the natural choice as war leader.

Initially it seemed that Palmerston would keep the Aberdeen coalition together, but the Peelites soon resigned over nominations to the committee of inquiry (there was also an obvious lack of trust between Gladstone and Palmerston). The government therefore became more Whiggish in character. It managed to bring the Crimean War to a successful conclusion in February 1856. Attention then continued to focus on foreign affairs, not least because they were Palmerston's main interest and he could gloss over problems at home by pointing to problems abroad. Palmerston was not much of a reformer. Various plans for extending the franchise and improving the civil service made little progress. Instead, Palmerston pursued an aggressive policy in China and, in March 1857, the Commons narrowly passed a motion condemning this. Palmerston called a general election and extended his mandate by securing a large majority.

His ability to satisfy Conservatives as well as Whigs, his reliance on patriotic sentiment, skilful manipulation of the press and willingness to *discuss* (though not implement) reforms in order to assuage radical opposition meant that Palmerston became the dominant political figure of the 1850s and early 1860s. Parties were still disorganized and Palmerston's broad appeal was therefore an essential asset, though it did not always guarantee success. In February 1858 his majority was shown to be unsafe when an amendment was carried against a government bill. Derby again took office at the head of a minority Conservative administration. The Conservatives made gains at the general election of April 1859, but a vote of no confidence was carried on 11 June. Despite Victoria's wish for a different outcome, Palmerston was the strongest candidate for the premiership among non-Conservative leaders and, crucially, Gladstone and the Peelites agreed to serve with him.

Palmerston's second ministry lasted from June 1859 to his death in October 1865. Once again foreign affairs commanded much attention, but Palmerston and Russell (foreign secretary) seemed increasingly out of touch as Britain's international influence declined. On the domestic front ministers made moderate improvements in factory regulation and public health. As chancellor of the exchequer Gladstone continued the reduction and removal of duties, altered the level of income tax as the government's revenue needs changed, facilitated savings and investment, lowered the cost of living and strengthened public confidence in the nation's economic future. In addition, he began to see the need for institutional change and was irritated by Palmerston's objections. Reviving interest in representation and voting rights encouraged Gladstone to take up parliamentary reform.

Liberals and Conservatives

Party coherence and ministerial stability began to increase during Palmerston's second administration. The Peelite–Whig co-operation seen under Aberdeen was restored, and the fusion of non-Conservative groups was furthered as radicals fell in behind Gladstone's reformism. Peelites and Conservatives were now so far apart that Derby had to abandon all hope of rapprochement. Gladstone took the decisive step in 1859 when he agreed to serve as Palmerston's chancellor. Four other Peelites joined him in the cabinet (Argyll, Herbert, Cardwell and Newcastle). The Palmerstonian coalition secured a majority of about fifty-eight over the Conservatives at the

July 1865 general election. This unmistakable electoral verdict, more so than that of 1857, appeared to clarify the party composition of the Commons, yet there was still a degree of fluidity. Indeed, parliament rejected the 'winners' of both the 1857 and 1865 elections before the next dissolution occurred.

Whigs, Peelites and radicals did not agree on everything, of course, and in this sense Derby's smaller and more homogeneous Conservative party may have found adaptation to new political conditions easier. The foundation of the Liberal party is traditionally traced to a meeting of Whigs, Peelites, moderate reformers and radicals on 6 June 1859. The various factions agreed to combine against Derby's minority government, and Peelite membership of Palmerston's second ministry was a consequence. But the Liberal party only really became a recognizable unit under Gladstone's leadership after the Second Reform Act of 1867 (and even then it remained a broad alliance that would eventually fall apart).

During the mid-nineteenth century the cabinet system and position of the prime minister became more firmly established and the political influence of the crown continued to decline. The three basic requirements for cabinet government were now in place: political agreement, common responsibility to parliament and acceptance of an undisputed leader. While party was weak, and in view of the previous erosion of executive patronage, ministers could not easily control parliament. Indeed, the minority status of all parliamentary groups after 1846 meant that ministers who alienated even a small number of MPs were vulnerable. Hence the practice of introducing preliminary resolutions by which a government could test Commons opinion before proceeding with significant measures. By now the wishes of the crown mattered far less than the complexion of the Commons. There may have been more scope for royal influence when no single party commanded a majority, but if most politicians of ministerial calibre agreed about the composition of a new cabinet, the crown's role was merely formal. Though she constantly made suggestions about appointments and policies, and demanded to be kept informed of cabinet deliberations, in practice Victoria's power was limited. After 1867 the direct connection between winning a majority at a general election and the royal request to form a government became even clearer than it had been in 1841. The most important decisions were made in cabinet. Rather than something to be taken or rejected as the sovereign wished, 'advice' was a decision agreed upon by ministers and for which they were accountable to parliament. By the mid-nineteenth century the principle of collective responsibility was strictly observed. Palmerston was dismissed from the Foreign Office in 1851 primarily because he contravened this principle, and in 1858, when Disraeli tried to amend resolutions (on India) formulated by the government of which he was a member, Derby angrily reminded him that changes could not be made without the cabinet's consent.

In several respects 1867 was a watershed. After the Second Reform Act the Liberal and Conservative parties became more organized, coherent and distinctive, two charismatic party leaders emerged to vie for the premiership, electoral verdicts became clearer and governments were better able to get their measures through parliament. The passing of this act was a muddled affair. Russell succeeded Palmerston as prime minister in 1865 and named Gladstone as leader of the House of Commons (from July 1861 Russell sat in the Lords as Earl Russell). Gladstone had already made clear his belief in the need for moderate parliamentary reform, and Russell saw an opportunity to round his own career off in positive fashion by passing a measure to complement that of 1832. In March 1866 Gladstone introduced a bill to lower the property qualification for voters. Some government supporters (especially conservative-minded Whigs) disliked the measure, however, and voted against it. The ministry resigned in June 1866. Derby became prime minister for the third time, with Disraeli as chancellor of the exchequer and leader of the House of Commons. The Conservatives were still in a minority in the Commons, and much depended on Disraeli's ability to keep the Liberal coalition divided. Derby's cabinet agreed to introduce its own reform bill. This would be milder than the Russell–Gladstone measure, but could conceivably accommodate respectable opinion out of doors (pressure for reform was growing) and sow further dissension among the Whigs. Disraeli also saw the chance to discredit Gladstone, seize the political initiative and consolidate his own position within the Conservative party. The new reform bill was eventually passed in August 1867, but only after a period of popular unrest, more open division on the Liberal side, resignations from Derby's administration, and amendments that rendered the measure rather more thorough than Disraeli originally intended. Indeed, in the end he was most concerned about pushing the bill through rather than closely policing each of its constituent parts and, amidst the confusion, few observers could predict how the political system would be changed by the Second Reform Act.

Disraeli had established himself as Derby's most likely successor as Conservative leader. Though some of his colleagues would never entirely trust him, and regretted that he had taken up parliamentary reform, they realized that they would now have to split the party (again) in order to get rid of him. Most Conservatives followed Disraeli in 1866 and 1867 for party advantage and because they viewed the Second Reform Act as essentially moderate. About one million adult male workers were enfranchised in 1867, but this increase was mostly confined to the boroughs. Constituency boundaries were altered, and a number of parliamentary seats redistributed, in order to reinforce Conservative dominance in the counties.

Derby resigned through ill-health in February 1868 and Disraeli became prime minister, but at the general election of November 1868 the Liberals won a majority of over 100. Those enfranchised in 1867, it appeared, were more grateful to Gladstone than to the Conservatives. Issues were important too, especially Gladstone's demand for the disestablishment of the Irish church. He appealed to the electors' sense of justice, telling them that they were capable of sound judgement and worthy of registering their opinion. This issue united the Liberal party, moreover, in the manner of a righteous crusade. It also hampered the Conservatives, for the wealth and privileges of the Irish church were difficult to defend. The Irish church served only a small proportion of the Irish people, most of whom were Catholics, yet was endowed as if it was the national church. Disraeli gave up the premiership before the new parliament assembled. Gladstone's first ministry lasted from December 1868 to February 1874.

In opposition Disraeli had to be careful and patient. Still unpopular with sections of the party, he knew that to antagonize them would be to jeopardize his own position as leader. At times he was accused of irresolution and inactivity, but the size of the Liberals' Commons majority would probably have made more vigorous opposition counter-productive. Disraeli chose to wait for the government to make mistakes.

He also encouraged the development of party organizations, and made well-publicized speeches to rally Conservatives in readiness for the next election. Two of his most important speeches were given at the Manchester Free Trade Hall in April 1872, and at London's Crystal Palace in June 1872. These were primarily attacks on the Gladstone government, but they also contained general statements about what Conservatism stood for, most notably national prestige, preservation of the empire, social reform and the protection of established institutions. By the time of the January 1874 general election, the Conservative party appeared strong and united and was able to take advantage of the Liberals' perceived shortcomings (cabinet divisions, loss of direction, a weak foreign policy, the tendency to attempt too much through legislation). The Conservatives won an overall majority of fifty and Disraeli returned to the premiership.

The Disraeli government of 1874 to 1880 passed moderate reforms affecting the licensing laws, factory regulation and industrial relations, the criminal code, public health, merchant shipping and education. Most measures were permissive in nature; often they merely codified existing regulations or set general standards. This government, therefore, was not an advanced reforming administration. Disraeli, who took little interest in the details of legislation, preferred to do nothing rather than risk creating difficulties by trying to do too much (as the Liberals had done). Most attention was devoted to foreign affairs. Disraeli succeeded in restoring British influence abroad, his greatest achievement coming at the Berlin Congress of June 1878, when he and foreign secretary Salisbury promoted a peace settlement for the unstable Near East. The British Empire was also extended in this period, though wars in South Africa and Afghanistan necessitated higher taxation at home. This was politically damaging, as were an economic recession and growing complaints about the Conservatives' unwillingness to introduce more social legislation. Opinion turned against Disraeli's government and the resurgent Liberals secured a large majority at the general election of March 1880 (the Liberals won 352 seats, the Conservatives 237, with 63 others). Disraeli died in April 1881.

Gladstone's second administration of 1880 to 1885 did not prove to be as strong or successful as the first administration of 1868 to 1874. Before it became tired and disunited in 1873 (its decline typified by defeat on the Irish Universities Bill in March of that year), the first government had done much to improve Victorian society and modernize institutions. Gladstone's main interest was Ireland, and measures were passed to disestablish the Irish church and reform the system of land tenure in Ireland. The universities bill was a failure, however, and the land reform proved to be too mild to satisfy tenants, its intended beneficiaries. Irish complaints were not silenced, indeed, and pressure for repeal of the Union rapidly increased. Gladstone had made much of his intention to solve Irish problems, and by disappointing expectations he may have made matters worse. Meanwhile, this ministry also introduced reforms affecting education, the army, civil service, local government, judicial system, criminal law and trade unions, and the Ballot Act of 1872 was designed to protect voters from undue pressure at election time.

The considerable achievements of 1868 to 1874 were not matched between 1880 and 1885. The Liberal party became more obviously divided as radicals competed with Whigs for control over policy, and both sides longed for Gladstone to retire.

The radical Joseph Chamberlain wanted to take a more progressive path, while the Whigs pressed for Hartington to be Gladstone's successor. There was mounting controversy over imperial matters, as ministers found it impossible to withdraw from Disraeli's extended commitments, and parliamentary business was obstructed by the growing faction of Irish Home Rulers. Victoria, who had much preferred Disraeli to Gladstone, also proved unco-operative. Gladstone, preoccupied with financial policy and Ireland, left other members of the cabinet to deal with their own departments as they wished, which did not make for coherence in government. These problems were compounded by intellectual disarray. Some Liberals wanted a more active state. Others preferred liberalization to regulation, yet there were also doubts about free trade and laissez-faire at a time when 'liberal economics' no longer seemed to guarantee Britain's economic supremacy. Among the measures passed by Gladstone's second government was the Second Irish Land Act (1881), which again failed to satisfy Irish tenants. It also offended some Whigs who, as landowners, objected to the principle of land reform. The Corrupt Practices Act (1883) promoted greater electoral purity, and the Third Reform Act (1884), followed by a redistribution of seats (1885), addressed some of the anomalies created in 1867. The parliamentary franchise was extended to rural workers and constituency boundaries were again revised. But these and the government's other measures failed to improve its position. In June 1885 Conservative and Irish MPs voted together to defeat the government's budget. Gladstone resigned.

Though allegiances changed and there could still be intra-party divisions, the era of Gladstone and Disraeli was notable for improvements in party discipline and organization. The new electoral conditions created in 1867 forced the parties to seek votes actively, and they needed new methods and machinery to do this. On the Liberal side party membership at grassroots level became more active and participatory. Local organizations were joined together in the National Liberal Federation, established in 1877. The Conservative National Union had been established ten years earlier, though this was controlled from the top down rather than built up from below. Conservative leaders were worried that too strong an organization would attempt to dictate to the parliamentary party. They made sure that power remained with the party hierarchy and whips. Disraeli saw the need for a more developed Conservative machine but left most of the work to others, especially the national party agent Gorst. Head of the Central Office, created in 1870, and secretary of the National Union from 1871, Gorst helped to establish and extend Conservative associations all over the country. The benefits were seen at the 1874 general election. Gorst wanted to make Conservatism popular and inclusive, but he could not persuade the party's parliamentary leaders to surrender any authority. Eventually Gorst resigned. The electoral defeat in 1880 prompted party chiefs to bring him back and there was talk of another thorough reorganization, but from about 1885 it was clear that real control belonged to the party leader, Salisbury. He dominated Central Office and allowed the National Union no influence over policy, while the whips and party agents were all loyal to him. Gladstone's attitude towards the Liberal machine was similarly ambivalent, in that he saw how important local, regional and national organizations were for electoral success, but did not want the National Liberal Federation (NLF) to control the parliamentary party. Indeed, the radicals dominated the

NLF and wished to use it in their struggle to overcome the Whigs and turn the Liberal party to their own purposes. One of the reasons why Gladstone remained in politics for so long was his concern to prevent this.

Despite the largely undemocratic nature of Victorian parties, this was the first age of genuinely 'popular' politics. The extension of the franchise in 1867 and 1884, comprehensive party organizations, the influence of the press, lively election campaigns, and the advent of major political crusades meant that the days of narrow and self-referential elite rule were over. Party leaders now had no choice but to take account of public opinion. Disraeli's Crystal Palace speech of 1872 was in part a public relations exercise. It was Gladstone, however, who more eagerly adapted his political style and language to suit changing circumstances. He realized that his position within the Liberal party, and his authority as prime minister, depended heavily upon his status as a national figure. Gladstone established a remarkable rapport with the common people, regularly addressing meetings and reaching an ever wider audience through newspaper reports of his speeches. From 1876 his attacks on Disraeli's foreign policy, which he condemned as aggressive, expensive and immoral, attracted enormous public interest, and his 'Midlothian Campaigns' of 1879 and 1880 (during which he spoke to many thousands) virtually ensured his return to the premiership. The devoutly religious Gladstone trusted that the people, if properly guided, could be made to see the moral as well as political necessity of policies to which he was attached. At the general elections of 1868 and 1880 this approach appears to have served him (and the Liberal party) particularly well.

Late-Victorian Politics

In the late-Victorian period the course of British politics was shaped principally by Gladstone's growing obsession with Ireland. The Irish reforms of his first and second governments failed to pacify Ireland as intended. Gladstone had been unable to render the Union less objectionable to those who supported Home Rule leader Parnell, or those who engaged in agrarian outrages sponsored by the Land League. His concern to treat Ireland justly, his sense of responsibility to right the wrongs of the past, and his (quintessentially Liberal) belief that a great end of government was to facilitate the development of individuals and peoples towards self-determination, finally led him to regard Home Rule as the solution. There was also cold political calculation behind this decision. To Gladstone, Home Rule represented the 'great cause' he needed to galvanize his followers, re-impose his personal authority over the Liberal party and regain political power. His decision to press for Home Rule seems to have been made during Salisbury's brief tenure as prime minister from June 1885 to January 1886. At the general election of November 1885 the Irish Home Rulers won 86 seats. They held the balance between the Liberals, with 335, and the Conservatives with 249 seats. Salisbury needed the Irish if his ministry was to maintain a Commons majority, but Parnell realized that he would get more from a bargain with Gladstone. The Irish allied themselves with the Liberal opposition, therefore, and Salisbury was forced to resign. Gladstone became prime minister for the third time on 1 February 1886.

Gladstone's commitment to Home Rule split his party, for the policy met with implacable objections from both radicals and Whigs. To the personal ambitions of

Chamberlain and Hartington were added public grounds for 'Liberal Unionist' defection: allowing the Irish their own parliament would threaten the integrity of the United Kingdom and empire, it was argued, and violence in Ireland proved that its people were not ready to govern themselves. Gladstone's Home Rule Bill was defeated in the Commons in June 1886. He secured a dissolution and appealed to the electorate, but the Conservatives and Liberal Unionists (who eventually joined the Conservative party) won a large majority. Gladstone resigned. Salisbury's second administration lasted from July 1886 to August 1892. In order to preserve the Union the government adopted the tactic of 'killing home rule with kindness', and alongside coercion there was further land reform.

Ireland continued to provoke unprecedented party rancour and public controversy, and after the general election of July 1892 the Liberals were able to command a Commons majority by relying on the Irish. Gladstone became prime minister for the fourth time. He guided a second Home Rule Bill through the Commons, but it was rejected by the Lords. This time the cabinet resisted Gladstone's call for another election. Increasingly isolated, Gladstone resigned on 2 March 1894. He was succeeded as premier by his foreign secretary Rosebery, who had never shared his commitment to Home Rule. The Liberal cabinet, exhausted and divided after recent struggles, soon collapsed.

As well as proscribing Home Rule, Salisbury's governments of 1886 to 1892 and 1895 to 1902 pursued a vigorous imperial policy and passed a number of important domestic reforms. The Local Government Act of 1888 established a system of elected county councils, the Education Act of 1891 abolished most fees for elementary education and the Workmen's Compensation Act of 1897 made employers liable for accidents at work. Much more comfortable dealing with international affairs, the arch-patrician Salisbury disliked reform and left administrative details to cabinet colleagues and government advisers. Yet he also presided over a party that had no choice but to adapt to the coming of democracy. Conservative leaders at national and local level successfully built up the party's popular base, though Salisbury imposed unity from above and disruptive elements were not permitted to thrive. The party did well at general elections, winning large majorities in 1886, 1895 and 1900. One of the Conservatives' main achievements in this respect was their capture of English middle-class suburbs, made possible by the revision of constituency boundaries and the phenomenon of 'villa Toryism'. Respectable and relatively well-off voters realized that they could trust Conservative governments to safeguard property and institutions against Gladstonian interference and assertive labour activism.

Historiographical Survey

Among the most important new interpretations of early Victorian politics is Peter Mandler's *Aristocratic Government in the Age of Reform*. Mandler sees in Whiggism after 1830 a reassertion of aristocratic power and the rise of an interventionist and populist governing style. Whig leaders acted on their sense of aristocratic duty to govern for the people, responding to national needs and demonstrating the merits of elite rule. But conditions changed during the 1840s and Whiggism began to disintegrate under Russell. As Whig reforms satisfied influential groups, there no longer seemed to be any need for government to act on the people's behalf. Reform

agitation dwindled, opinion turned against state intervention, individualistic principles came to the fore, and older notions of aristocratic responsibility and active government proved increasingly irrelevant and politically objectionable. Though Mandler
presents a strong case, he identifies Whiggism with reform and intervention, and it
was probably more complicated than this. Some Whigs resisted particular reforms
and, in any case, the Whigs' weaknesses as a party inevitably imposed limits on what
they tried to do and what they actually achieved in office (so did the Conservatives'
majority in the Lords). It is difficult to detect in Whiggism a distinctive and unifying reform philosophy, and Whig leaders were not as purposeful as Mandler suggests.
Indeed, they were rarely able to control parliamentary or public opinion and often
seemed the victims of circumstance.

   A. Sykes has stressed the bankruptcy of 'Whig centrism' under Russell: it impeded
the formation of a new Liberal party and alienated potential allies, failing to mitigate
either Peelite hostility towards Palmerston's foreign policy and Russell's Ecclesiastical Titles Act or the radicals' desire for more parliamentary reform. Sykes points out
that Peelites and most radicals wanted the same thing, cheaper and more efficient
government, which in turn necessitated a cautious foreign policy. The Russell administration of 1846 to 1852 provided neither. Yet the disarray and collapse of Whiggism should not be exaggerated. K. T. Hoppen argues that the reforms of the Russell
era helped to undermine Chartism and safeguard the constitution. Russell's government also played a key role in extending free trade after 1846. A. Howe points to
the long-term importance of Whig economic measures in this context. T. A. Jenkins
contends that free-trade policies indicate a creditable Whig approach to problems
posed by industrialization and urban growth. These policies were also politically
shrewd, for they identified Whiggism with the ascendant ideology of free trade. On
this point Hoppen holds a different opinion. He thinks that the victory of free trade
and 'the principles of 1846' owed more to the Irish famine than to Whig political
talent or vision. The famine stimulated a stronger preference for non-intervention,
Hoppen explains, because of heavy relief expenditure and general resentment against
those who were relieved (that is, the Irish).

   If the Whigs' commitment to free trade demonstrated their continuing political
relevance in changing times, it is also clear that protectionism proved remarkably
resilient. Many contemporaries considered protection a viable option, and offered
logical and principled arguments in its favour. The work of A. Gambles and
A. Macintyre shows that the victory of free trade was no foregone conclusion. The
struggle continued, even after protection was formally dropped by the Conservatives
following the 1852 general election. Most Conservatives were still intellectually,
emotionally and economically attached to the goals protection was supposed to
achieve; hence Disraeli's alternative strategy of winning tax concessions for landowners. Nevertheless, political, economic and social contexts were changing, and parties
had to change too. As N. Gash has argued, national parties could not operate effectively or win power unless they diversified. A narrowly protectionist Conservative
party would have had as limited an appeal as a narrowly aristocratic Liberal party.
Parties had to represent a range of different interests: resourceful party leaders seem
to have recognized this more clearly and more rapidly than did their supporters
(outside as well as inside parliament).

J. Parry views Whig and Liberal ministries of the Victorian era as exemplars of 'liberal government', that is, government designed to harmonize different interests in British society, strengthen the people's attachment to the state and the law and shape individual character 'constructively'. According to Parry, 'liberal government' collapsed during the 1880s because of Gladstone's populism and his failure to conduct an Irish policy in keeping with constitutional, economic and political harmony. Gladstone, indeed, did not really belong to the 'liberal' tradition as Parry understands it, and became a destructive force with his dictatorial leadership, popular appeals, narrow theology, crusading zeal and willingness to treat Ireland as a special case. One obvious problem with Parry's analysis is that 'liberal government' cannot have existed in a vacuum; yet he pays little attention to rival political persuasions (Conservative and radical) or to the role of public opinion, constituency support and grassroots Liberalism. In addition, it is more than likely that some Whigs and Liberals had other priorities than those prescribed in Parry's definition of 'liberal government'. As for the criticism of Gladstone, it could be argued that Gladstone's talents and leadership were crucial to Victorian Liberalism and that his popular appeals proved very useful in electoral terms. Parry suggests that the Liberal party was no longer 'liberal' after the split of 1886, but *some* Liberal peers, MPs, party workers and voters may have continued to pursue what Parry defines as 'liberal' goals.

There have been interesting reassessments of the most prominent political leaders after 1846. In explaining the mid-century ascendancy of Palmerston, for instance, R. Blake (1970) and J. B. Conacher both emphasize his cross-party appeal. At different times, it appears, Palmerston offered something to Whigs, Conservatives, moderates, radicals and Peelites, and he could not have risen to power or governed successfully had party identities been more rigid. Hoppen agrees that party was weak, but suggests that the key to Palmerston's longevity in high office was his ability to avoid controversy; though he made enemies, he never made the mistake of offending them all at the same time. E. D. Steele argues that Palmerston's political successes are best explained with reference to his skilful leadership rather than any distinctive policies or principles. Palmerston was the prominent Whig who had been a Canningite Tory. He could mollify radicals while also marginalizing them, and promised Conservatives stronger government than seemed possible under Derby. On these points Steele's interpretation accords with those already mentioned, but he also goes beyond them by suggesting that Palmerston was a genuine progressive who created a more open political system, and that Palmerston, not Gladstone, was the founder of Liberalism. This is a highly contentious argument and commentators will no doubt continue to interpret Palmerston's language, leadership and political style in a variety of ways.

The same is true of Gladstone. While Hoppen contends that Gladstone was less progressive and dynamic than his rhetoric suggested, E. F. Biagini considers Gladstone the architect of a 'liberal consensus' that rested upon free trade and the expansion of political participation. According to Biagini, Gladstone's career is best understood in the context of a changing relationship between rulers and ruled, key aspects of which included mass parties, charismatic leadership and a well-informed and influential press. If Biagini's treatment of Gladstone is highly complimentary, R. Shannon (1999) sees Gladstone as ambitious and manipulative. On this reading, Gladstone's respect for party and public mattered far less than his belief that God had called him to assume national responsibilities; nothing could be allowed to sway him from divinely appointed duty. To Shannon, this was a self-serving delusion. Certainly it ensured that Gladstone would become an unequivocally authoritarian type of Peelite, one who held that party, parliament and public opinion should be the tools of a strong executive.

There have been conflicting interpretations of Gladstone's commitment to Home Rule for Ireland. J. L. Hammond and Philip Magnus regard Gladstone's Home Rule project as a heroic struggle for justice and freedom led by a 'great man' who was unfortunately obstructed by selfish and factious lesser men. H. C. G. Matthew avoids such flattery, but nevertheless sees Gladstone's Irish policy as the result of deep contemplation and honest conviction (not some sudden conversion). Other historians treat Gladstone as a calculating politician rather than a disinterested moral hero. D. A. Hamer focuses on Gladstone's need to find a major issue that would enable him to restructure the Liberal party and restore order to parliamentary politics, while A. B. Cooke and J. Vincent deny that Gladstone had a clear plan or even a genuine desire to settle the Irish question. What he really wanted, they claim, was to defeat his political rivals and cling to office; Home Rule offered the best available opportunity. Shannon also focuses on the 'high political' aspects of the Irish question. He condemns Gladstone's Irish policy before 1886, especially the land reforms. Rather than oblige landlords to concede tenant right, argues Shannon, Gladstone should have facilitated the purchase of land by tenants. And when he did opt for Home Rule, he should not have adhered rigidly to his own proposals. This inflexibility, and an unwillingness to listen to others who might have come up with a more acceptable Home Rule Bill, polarized opinion and strengthened Gladstone's opponents.

Biagini denies that Gladstone's approach to Ireland was harmful or misconceived. The land reforms, he suggests, helped to combat violence in Ireland, made Parnell more co-operative and (along with the inclusion of Ireland in the parliamentary reforms of 1884–5) promised to reorganize Irish politics along English lines. If Gladstone really adopted Home Rule in order to regain power and dominate the Liberal party, adds Biagini, he must have chosen the right issue, for he achieved these ends. But Biagini detects more than merely selfish ambition in Gladstone's conversion to Home Rule. Like Matthew, he regards the Home Rule policy as an enlightened and constructive attempt, shaped by laudable public as well as personal motives, to solve the most intractable problem of the age.

Disraeli's career has also been thoroughly re-examined. Discussing the period from the late 1840s to the late 1850s, when reunion with the Peelites still seemed possible, I. Machin suggests that Disraeli strongly favoured a reconciliation and placed the needs of the Conservative party before his own ambitions (realizing that he would no longer be accepted as opposition leader in the Commons if Peelites rejoined the party). R. Blake (1998) offers a different verdict, maintaining that Disraeli obstructed reunion for personal reasons. Whatever the case, Disraeli's freedom of manoeuvre was undoubtedly restricted. His position in the party was not really secure until 1874, and until 1868 he had to follow Derby's lead. There were serious disagreements between the two men. Initially they argued about when and whether or not to abandon protection; then Disraeli's longing for office jarred with Derby's more cautious strategy. Hoppen notes that Derby preferred to have the Whigs in power, where he could restrain them with careful opposition, rather than adopt a more confrontational style that would inevitably invite an anti-Conservative backlash.

Disraeli's performance as premier between 1874 and 1880, and the nature of Disraelian Conservatism, have given rise to several different verdicts. J. T. Ward claims that Disraeli established 'One Nation Conservatism', a distinctive, consistent and principled political position to which can be credited real achievements. It taught the aristocracy and gentry to adapt to change, and showed that institutions could be better defended if a Conservative ministry offered social reforms, accepted the extension of the parliamentary franchise, and linked the party with national pride and an assertive foreign policy. P. Smith and B. Coleman are both sceptical about this. Disraeli's social reforms never lived up to the rhetoric, they insist, and he offered no creative or dynamic leadership. There was no new departure; in composition and instinct the Conservative party remained unchanged. Hoppen argues that Disraeli lacked clear policies, and R. Shannon (1992) regards 'Disraelian Conservatism' as a myth. There was nothing to it, he thinks, beyond a general desire to protect aristocratic government (which Disraeli thought could best be done if he ruled out the interventionism associated with Gladstone). On the other hand, Shannon's inattention to the roots of the Conservative party's electoral strength limits the scope of his interpretation. Though the party machine was denied influence over Conservative governments' policies and appointments, it had some importance at constituency level. Shannon is not interested in the 'popular' side of Conservatism under Disraeli and Salisbury, and hence offers little discussion of local associations, press support or the determinants of voter preference.

In Shannon's *The Age of Salisbury* Salisbury does not emerge as the astute architect of 'villa Toryism' or author of late-Victorian Conservative electoral dominance, but as a backward-looking elitist who misinterpreted contemporary political developments. Salisbury believed that the Conservative party was naturally a minority party, and he eschewed bold policies and assertive appeals to the nation. Reluctant to accept that Conservatism could in fact command majority support, he was unprepared for general election victories. This meant that he did not take full advantage of the Conservatives' mandate. Shannon suggests that Salisbury could have done more to find a workable solution to the Irish question. He might also have elevated younger men of talent and fresh ideas within his party, to consolidate its position in a time of political, social and economic change. Instead, he relied upon aristocrats and members of his own family. This image of Salisbury, as a blinkered and cautious leader perplexed by the coming of democracy, finds little substantiation in the work of C. C. Weston. According to her, Salisbury evolved the 'referendal theory' to justify partisan use of the Lords' veto in the age of popular politics. In other words, he understood the implications of democracy and turned the growth of political participation to his party's advantage. The 'referendal theory' presented the House of Lords as the true guardian of the national interests. If the Commons passed measures that were likely to harm those interests (which it often did, thought Salisbury, when the Liberals were in office), the Lords had a duty to block these measures and refer them back to the electorate.

Was there indeed a movement towards 'democracy' after 1846? James Vernon thinks not. His thesis is that politics became *less* participatory. Makeshift banners were replaced by more expensive and durable models, for example, which could no longer be constructed quickly by amateurs. Newspapers became cheaper and more widely available, so that communal reading and discussion were superseded by home-based, privatized reading. The Ballot Act of 1872 privatized the act of voting. Provision of more polling booths at election time reduced the influence of crowds at the hustings, and canvassing by post also excluded non-voters and prevented them from posing questions to candidates at election meetings. Political assemblies moved indoors and admittance was restricted to those with entry tickets. All this, Vernon concludes, amounted to a political 'closure'. Yet Vernon offers too static a vision of Victorian politics, with little appreciation of change and diversity. There were gains as well as losses for participatory politics: expansion of the electorate, opportunities for non-elite interests to shape policy, direct representation for large towns which had only been represented as part of their respective counties before 1832, and the continued ability of non-voters to be politically active in extra-parliamentary associations and, at election time, to influence outcomes through such means as exclusive dealing. Despite these developments, however, it should be recognized that in some respects political transformation proceeded very slowly. Hoppen finds that parliamentary reform had no significant impact on British politics until after 1884–5. Until then, elections carried on much as before. Local issues often predominated, candidates and their backers still had to spend a lot of money to win contests, and in many places elections continued to give rise to customary rowdiness and violence.

Historians disagree about the speed and nature of such changes as the formation of organized national parties and rise of 'class'-based politics. Biagini (1992) indic-ates that the Liberal party won popular support because it provided many workers with a more meaningful collective consciousness than that provided by 'class'. The Gladstonian programme of 'liberty, retrenchment and reform' accorded with workers' traditions, political awareness, social aspirations and economic condition. They did not think of themselves as a clearly defined 'class', argues Biagini. Rather, they were 'the people', and it was to this active and participatory public that Gladstone offered dignity and opportunity.

J. Lawrence has drawn attention to the relationship between political parties and those they claimed to represent. 'Representation' involved constant negotiation between leaders and led, and according to Lawrence parties did not make 'class' appeals. Their methods and language were far more inclusive than this, and the 'rise of class' paradigm is not the one to employ with respect to late-Victorian politics. Nor is the 'rise of party'. National parties were not yet able to control and discipline popular politics. Indeed, the increasing centralization of party machinery may have stimulated an anti-party spirit. For Lawrence it is 'place' rather than 'class' or 'party' that holds the key. People were most likely to be satisfied with their 'representation', he argues, when their would-be leaders and party activists lived in the local com-munity. Such representatives could not understand local needs, it was thought, if they lived elsewhere. Defining 'class' and 'place', however, is no easy task for the histor-ian, especially since the 'linguistic turn' of the 1980s. Lawrence's approach com-bines an examination of 'class' and 'place' as material realities with the recognition that they could also be discursive creations shaped by political argument and conduct. Devotees of the 'linguistic turn' would deny the usefulness (and even possibility) of this combination, preferring to emphasize the 'constructed' nature of social and polit-ical identities at the expense of their material contexts.

BIBLIOGRAPHY AND FURTHER READING

E. F. Biagini, *Liberty, Retrenchment and Reform: Popular Liberalism in the Age of Gladstone 1860–1880* (Cambridge, 1992).

E. F. Biagini, *Gladstone* (Basingstoke, 2000).

R. Blake, *The Conservative Party from Peel to Churchill* (London, 1970).

R. Blake, *Disraeli* (London, 1998).

B. Coleman, *Conservatism and the Conservative Party in the Nineteenth Century* (London, 1988).

J. B. Conacher, 'Party politics in the age of Palmerston', in P. Appleman et al., eds, *1859: Entering an Age of Crisis* (Bloomington, 1959).

A. B. Cooke and J. Vincent, *The Governing Passion: Cabinet Government and Party Politics in Britain, 1885–86* (Brighton, 1974).

A. Gambles, 'Rethinking the politics of protection: Conservatism and the Corn Laws, 1830–52', *English Historical Review*, 113 (1998).

N. Gash, *Reaction and Reconstruction in English Politics, 1832–52* (Oxford, 1965).

D. A. Hamer, *Liberal Politics in the Age of Gladstone and Rosebery* (Oxford, 1972).

J. L. Hammond, *Gladstone and the Irish Nation* (London, 1964).

K. T. Hoppen, *The Mid-Victorian Generation, 1846–86* (Oxford, 1998).

A. Howe, *Free Trade and Liberal England, 1846–1946* (Oxford, 1997).

T. A. Jenkins, *The Liberal Ascendancy, 1830–1886* (Basingstoke, 1994).

J. Lawrence, *Speaking for the People: Party, Language and Popular Politics in England, 1867–1914* (Cambridge, 1998).

I. Machin, *Disraeli* (London, 1995).

A. Macintyre, 'Lord George Bentinck and the Protectionists: a lost cause?', *Transactions of the Royal Historical Society*, 5th ser., 39 (1989).

P. Magnus, *Gladstone* (London, 1954).

P. Mandler, *Aristocratic Government in the Age of Reform* (Oxford, 1990).

H. C. G. Matthew, *Gladstone 1875–1898* (Oxford, 1995).

J. Parry, *The Rise and Fall of Liberal Government in Victorian Britain* (New Haven, CT, 1993).

R. Shannon, *The Age of Disraeli, 1868–81: The Rise of Tory Democracy* (London, 1992).

R. Shannon, *The Age of Salisbury, 1881–1902: Unionism and Empire* (London, 1996).

R. Shannon, *Gladstone: Heroic Minister, 1865–98* (London, 1999).

P. Smith, *Disraelian Conservatism and Social Reform* (London, 1967).

E. D. Steele, *Palmerston and Liberalism, 1856–65* (Cambridge, 1991).

A. Sykes, *The Rise and Fall of British Liberalism, 1766–1988* (London, 1997).

J. Vernon, *Politics and the People: A Study in English Political Culture, c.1815–67* (Cambridge, 1993).

J. T. Ward, *The Conservative Leadership* (London, 1974).

C. C. Weston, *The House of Lords and Ideological Politics: Lord Salisbury's Referendal Theory and the Conservative Party, 1846–1922* (Philadelphia, 1995).

CHAPTER NINE

Parliamentary Reform and the Electorate

MICHAEL S. SMITH

The Question of Parliamentary Reform

The crisis that enveloped Britain in 1831 over parliamentary reform was of monumental proportions. While the Whigs worked on a bill that would alleviate some of the problems of the system of representation, placate radicals and be amenable to both Houses of parliament, popular agitation smouldered across the country. Much public anger was directed at the House of Lords, which rejected Russell's second bill in October 1831. Reform riots took place in Bristol, London, Worcester, Nottingham, Derby and Bath. The proponents and opponents of reform were equally matched in their vehemence regarding the issue because it involved not only the electoral system, but the balance of the constitution, the status of property and the future of the state. When parliament finally passed the Great Reform Act in 1832, after Grey had endured the perilous 'Days of May', it altered a system of representation that had been in place since the days of Edward I. The crisis seemed to have erupted relatively quickly; just two years before, the question of reform had barely surfaced outside a small group of reformers. But this did not mean that reform did not have a history. parliamentary reformers traced their ancestors back to Lilburne and the Levellers in the seventeenth century. The reform question became more pressing in times of crisis, whether it was the Wilkes affair in the 1760s, which raised serious questions about parliamentary representation and the power of the executive, or the war with America, which quickly illustrated how an imperial disaster could precipitate powerful constitutional questions at home. Wyvill's Yorkshire Association in 1779 blamed the troubles with America on corruption and the persistence of aristocratic and royal influence in government, and the mass petitioning movement it inspired had as its goal a House of Commons that was independent and members who were accountable to voters. In 1780 Cartwright formed the Sheffield Society for Constitutional Information, which emphasized more radical goals: universal male suffrage, annual parliaments, equal member constituencies and the secret ballot.

More than anything, the outbreak of the French Revolution gave the reform question overwhelming purchase. In the events of 1789, Britons saw the reflection of the ills of their own political system and consequently cried for change, ushering in an unprecedented era of popular political participation and agitation. Those who raised the reform question the loudest this time were not landed gentry, liberal-minded MPs or other members of the establishment, but rather the middle and working classes who rallied together in clubs, associations and societies. The most famous of them all was Thomas Hardy, whose radical London Corresponding Society brought the platform of radical politics to the general, non-voting public, precipitated a crisis that lasted for over a decade and manifested itself in numerous popular associations, public meetings, petition movements and riots. When Thomas Paine joined the fray with the publication of part two of his *Rights of Man* in 1792, the attack on the constitution, hereditary property and the government had overwhelming popular appeal, especially because Paine's book was made available in a cheap sixpenny edition.

There were certain ironies about the French Revolution's impact on Britain. When reform finally came in 1832, it was brought about by the efforts of Whig aristocrats, not working-class radicals, although it is true that popular pressure greased the wheels. What is more, the French Revolution and the war with France were the very events that actually pushed reformers into the wilderness for more than thirty years. Anti-reformers in Westminster and loyalists across the country painted reform with the broad brush of revolution, and the Whigs, with the exception of the Foxites whose numbers had greatly dwindled by 1795, abandoned the issue. Pitt, who had proposed reform in 1783 and 1785, now associated reform with constitutional destruction. The cause itself was not entirely dead, and it resurfaced, as did more extreme forms of radicalism, in the early nineteenth century. Cobbett's *Political Register*, Hunt's *Examiner*, and Wooler's *Black Dwarf*, among other periodicals, reintroduced political and social questions to the public, while Cartwright continued to press for universal male suffrage through the Hampden Club, and Burdett, the radical MP for Westminster, continuously pledged major changes in the franchise.

So reform certainly had a tradition, and the Great Reform Act of 1832 was its end result, although one must keep in mind that the Act was by no means inevitable and was more in line with the vision of aristocratic reformers than it was with the dreams of radicals. Reform was not a single ideology by any means. There were those, like Grey, who proposed a moderate alteration of the electoral system which would involve an increase in county seats, the abolition of 'rotten boroughs', and the establishment of a standard property qualification. Whig reformers did not desire democracy: a political system in which everyone could vote secretly and without a property qualification was inconceivable to them. There were others who had a more radical vision including universal male suffrage, annual parliaments, the secret ballot and payment of MPs. If reformers had anything in common, however, it was the belief that patronage, aristocratic and royal influence, and corruption had to be reduced or rooted out. Influence and corruption had been seen, since at least the eighteenth century, as the ultimate sources of Britain's political and social problems. Rooting them out would require amending the system of representation.

Given the nature of the unreformed electoral system, altering it would be no easy task. Each county sent two members to parliament, and the county franchise rested on freehold land or property valued at 40 shillings or more. The main problem was that the county representation was not linked to population size, so even though roughly 55 per cent of all English voters resided in counties, only 16 per cent of parliamentary seats were in fact county seats. The other type of seat, the borough, was equally rife with problems. Some of the largest boroughs happened to be significant commercial and industrial centres, including Bristol, London, Liverpool, Coventry, Manchester, Birmingham, Sheffield and Leeds. Some, however, did not return any members to parliament, including Manchester and Birmingham. The problem was all the more glaring in light of the fact that boroughs with smaller populations returned members to parliament. The Cornish coastal towns of Camelford, East and West Looe, Newport, St Germans and St Mawes, for example, taken together had a total population of less than 1,000, but sent no fewer than twelve members to the Commons. One of the most notorious of all was Old Sarum in Wiltshire. It was nothing more than a small, green mound with no houses, but it had seven electors. Boroughs also had a wide variety of franchise qualifications, ranging from corporation membership to poor-rate payment, from six-month residency to simple inheritance of a franchise. By far the most problematic, however, were the nomination, or pocket, boroughs, those which were the property of a local landowner, a member of government or the crown. Candidates were simply nominated by the landowner, contested elections were rare, and voters were often bound by allegiance or by financial incentive to approve the nominated candidate. The inherent problems of the system of representation were not helped by the high cost of electioneering, one of the reasons, among many, why so few MPs were of middle-class origin, either before or after 1832. Elections could cost thousands of pounds, not only due to campaigning, but because candidates often had to pay for the voters' food, entertainment, beer and costs of travel. In 1807 Earl Fitzwilliam spent £97,000 on the Yorkshire election. If the candidates themselves did not come up with the funds, local party clubs or individual supporters would. Edward Protheroe, a Whig MP who aspired to root out corruption in government, ran for Bristol in 1826 refusing to spend any money on his campaign, and, even though his supporters raised £7,000 on their own, his austerity cost him the election.[1]

The unreformed electoral system had its defenders, and in certain ways it worked quite well. Both Tory and Whig anti-reformers argued that 'virtual representation' mitigated the need for a larger electorate because MPs represented not individual voters but communities, and the interests of non-voters as well as towns without seats were in fact represented in parliament. As Langford has noted, 'there were few constituencies so closed that an MP could afford to ignore the requests of his constituents for assistance with legislation', and 'much legislation was promoted by places which lacked seats in the House of Commons' including Manchester and Birmingham.[2] What is more, citizens who lacked the vote were not necessarily left out of the political process or denied a political voice. Elections were an integral part of the life of local communities. Election rituals, which entailed dining, drinking, entertainment, public meetings and celebrations, involved the participation of large numbers of people, and were essentially opportunities for voters and non-voters to express their opinions publicly. Given the communal nature of elections, candidates and election managers had to aim their political 'theatre' at electors and non-electors, and the participation of both groups occurred in counties and boroughs, no matter the nature of the franchise or the politics of the local patron.[3] In fact, the unreformed electorate exercised a significant amount of freedom and participation in certain constituencies, even in places controlled by local landowners or the government. Phillips has argued that active and regular participation in elections increased as the nineteenth century approached. Ninety per cent of Maidstone's electors turned out in 1790, 95 per cent of Lewes's in 1796.[4] Those who did not qualify for the vote were not left out of the process entirely. The act of petitioning national authorities on weighty political subjects became one of the most commonly used methods of participation before 1832, and, in certain boroughs, close to half of the citizens signing petitions to the government were non-voters.[5]

All of this meant that the operative element in national politics on the eve of the Great Reform Act was public opinion. If the unreformed electorate was active and participatory, the newspapers, pamphlets, handbills, advertisements, broadsides, caricatures and other political material that flooded local communities during elections and periods of crises increased awareness, facilitated participation and heightened the public influence on national politics. In many ways, the relationship between public opinion, politics and legislation was the continuing theme of the nineteenth century, and this relationship tightened in the decades after 1832. Parliament passed the Great Reform Act in part because 'public opinion made reform necessary'.[6]

The Great Reform Act of 1832 was the culmination of several significant elements, the first of which was a climate of change in early-nineteenth-century Britain. The abolition of the slave trade in 1807, by the short-lived 'Ministry of All the Talents', the resignation of the Duke of York in 1809, a Toleration Act benefiting Unitarians in 1813 and the continuing practice in the 1820s of economic reform in which useless offices were abolished meant that the public expected moral and pragmatic legislation and that the government increasingly understood its need to act responsibly. And if Wellington's government doomed itself over the questions of parliamentary and religious reform, it managed to pass two profoundly significant pieces of legislation: the Repeal of the Test and Corporation Acts in 1828, which ended seventeenth-century legislation barring Dissenters from government office, and Catholic emancipation in 1829, which granted civil and political rights to Catholics. Wellington was, in his heart and politics, anti-repeal, but the government had to be responsive to public campaigns for change and to public expectations of liberal legislation. These Acts proved to ultra-Tories that Wellington could no longer be trusted, and this realization split his party and doomed the government. The Acts also proved that public pressure worked. The Whigs learned this lesson to their great advantage.

This climate of change corresponded with the second element that resulted in the 1832 Reform Act: a series of political crises from 1829 to 1832. Bad harvests, high prices and unemployment created massive social unrest in 1829, including significant strikes in the textile industry in Manchester and Oldham and agricultural riots in Norwich, as well as mass petitioning by citizens in Spitalfields, Manchester, Stockport and Coventry. This activity was followed the next year by the formation of Attwood's economic- and political-reformist political union in Birmingham. From the perspective of Westminster, however, the major crises were the 1830 revolutions in France and Belgium, the end of Wellington's administration and the death of George IV. The events in Paris and Brussels brought old fears about domestic radicalism and revolution to the surface, and both Whigs and Tories understood the need to protect the economic and political interests of the establishment. However, for the Tories themselves, it was too late; the party was too divided after Wellington's volte-face, and while William IV might not have been a friend to reform, he was far more of a friend to the Whigs than George IV had been. So when Grey was called to form a government in 1830, he knew that reform was a necessity.

Yet Grey wanted reform not simply because he feared revolution, but because he genuinely believed in its purpose. The Act, after all, was devised by 'Whigs whose interest in the question was not sudden and tactical, but genuine and long-standing'.[7] This ideological commitment to reform was the third element in its fruition. Grey had been a reformer since the late eighteenth century, and he typically refused to serve in governments that were not friendly to the issue. Russell was cut from the same cloth, firmly believing in the principles of government for the people, in progress and in individual liberty, and he remained committed to reform, issuing bills in 1821 and 1822, and later advocating reform in the 1850s and 1860s at a time when the issue was unpopular. Althorp, like Grey and Russell, not to mention Duncannon, Durham and Graham (all who were on Grey's reform committee in 1831), held firmly to the idea that excessive executive power, heavy government, heavy taxation, and influence and corruption were unhealthy to the polity. Of course, their pursuit of reform was also self-serving; if they could pass a bill that would increase the number of Whig seats and secure Whig rule, so much the better. The tactic worked. The Whigs dominated government until 1841.

The Great Reform Act was 'great' because of the crisis surrounding its passing and its overall significance. It made major changes to the electoral system even while it retained many anomalies. The framers of the Act wanted to eliminate some of the abuses of the unreformed system without undermining the central role of property, to balance the composition of the House of Commons, and to integrate public opinion under propertied leadership. The Act enfranchised sixty-five new counties and split twenty-six into two divisions with each division returning two members. The Act also disenfranchised fifty-six boroughs, while thirty boroughs lost one seat. The householder franchise in the boroughs was standardized at £10 per annum. In the counties, the qualification was set for property worth at least 40 shillings, copyholds worth at least £10, and leased or rented property at £50 per annum. Scotland received eight new seats; Ireland received five. The borough and county franchises for both countries was set at £10 (for property-holders and leaseholders). Overall, the Act also restricted the polling period from fifteen days to two and required registration of voters in all constituencies. While the increase of county seats had long been the goal of reformers, even more important was the reduction of influence and corruption; therefore, by establishing a standard householder franchise that required residency of a minimum of one year, the Act's framers hoped to weed out non-resident voters, limit influence and establish a respectable voting force that would be resistant to bribery.

The electorate in England and Wales increased from approximately 449,000 to 656,000, or by roughly 45 per cent. One in five adult males now had the right to vote. This was a remarkable change, although anti-reformers at the time, and historians since, have argued that the Reform Act left much unchanged. Grey had never intended the Act to solve every problem in the electoral system. The size of constituencies still varied a great deal, with some boroughs having electorates of less than 300 and some towns remaining unrepresented, despite their growth in population.

The Whigs introduced the standard householder franchise, but ignored the fact that regional variation in property values would qualify some householders but disqualify others. Most important, great landowners continued to exert influence over who was returned to parliament, just as those who sat in the House of Commons were similar to those who sat before 1832. Close to 80 per cent of MPs had landed backgrounds. The politics of influence remained important in many places, assisted by the fact that seventy-three boroughs had electorates of less than 500, making them more susceptible to landed influence.

Expecting the Great Reform Act to have abolished all anomalies and to have introduced democracy would have been expecting the impossible. The Whigs had every intention of maintaining the system of virtual representation and aristocratic rule while increasing the franchise to portions of the middle classes. Virtually no one, with the exception of some radicals, wanted universal suffrage, and those who did want it did not believe in extending it to women. 'The framers and supporters of the bill of 1832 were more inclined to emphasize redistribution of seats, especially the abolition of tiny boroughs. This was partly because they thought less in terms of individuals and more in terms of interests than we do, and considered the representative system a means to achieve balanced rather than democratic government'.[8] Reform was never conceived as a complete alteration of the constitution and electoral system. Both reformers and their opponents agreed on the necessity of property ownership, just as both could not envisage a world without it.

Despite the continuities between the unreformed and reformed electoral system, the Great Reform Act was, in the larger scheme of things, monumentally important and transformative, particularly in three areas: partisanship, participation and public opinion. If the unreformed electorate was more active and partisan than previous historians have believed, the reformed electorate was even more so, as partisanship increased greatly as a result of the 1832 Act. Because electors had two votes, they could cast both of them for one party (straight voting), cast one vote for one party and the other vote for another party (split voting), or cast one vote and throw away the other (plump voting). The splitting of votes declined over the course of the late eighteenth and early nineteenth centuries, but its decline accelerated after 1832. In Bristol, for example, 51 per cent of all votes were split in 1832, but only 7 per cent in 1835, 11 per cent in 1837 and 13 per cent in 1841.[9] This meant the vast majority of votes were strictly partisan. Similar patterns of a decline in split voting and an increase in straight voting could also be found in boroughs such as Shrewsbury, Northampton, Maidstone and Lewes. Granted, boroughs by their very nature tended to have more political activity and partisanship, but the overall increase in partisanship as a result of reform is telling, particularly because partisan voting attained a high level of consistency in certain areas. Increased partisanship coincided with increased political participation. The presence and influence of local political clubs and a partisan provincial press only increased in the years around reform and, owing to the requirement to register voters, the increase of county seats, the enfranchisement of new towns and the increasing political awareness of the electorate, political parties had to organize and work more efficiently in their constituencies than ever before. Local party agents became increasingly busy and important, and the use of party labels, colours and partisan terminology went hand in hand with national political issues. The Tory victory in the 1841 election owed much to efficient party organization in various constituencies. Partisanship, party politics, popular participation and campaigning became more important than ever in post-reform Britain.

Public opinion also became more significant, asserting an influence over nineteenth-century British politics that made the polity fundamentally 'modern'. The Reform Act of 1832 marked a point of no return. It proved the necessity of listening to popular opinion, made parliament understand that it had to be aware of social and political tensions and respond accordingly, and opened the doors to further reform. Most of all, the electorate had an undeniable role in the political life of the country, and the House of Commons exerted an influence over the Upper House and the monarchy that made it the most powerful branch of government in nineteenth-century Britain.

An Incomplete Reform: Towards the Reform Act of 1867

Grey, Russell, Althorp and other reformers might not have intended it, but the Reform Act of 1832 inaugurated an era of general political and social reform, and the British government became more responsive (and legislated) more than ever before. The reasons for this phenomenon are complex, involving not simply the local and national political changes brought about by reform, but also those of changing demographics, population growth, the rising influence of commercial and industrial centres, urbanization and urban politics, working- and middle-class pressure, increasing political awareness and activity in local constituencies. Most of all, the prime mover was public opinion. William MacKinnon published an historical treatment of the development of public opinion in 1828 and predicted that 'the consequence will be, that the watchfulness of public opinion, not being occupied by foreign hostilities, is directed with greater attention to the internal state of the country, to an acute and jealous investigation of every occurrence at home connected with the public service'.[10] His prescience was confirmed by the efforts of Whigs and, later, Liberals to create a more responsible government. The abolition of slavery, factory legislation, the Poor Law Amendment Act and the Tithe Commutation Act were the hallmarks of Whig attempts at progressive legislative change, while the 1835 Municipal Corporations Act was designed to transform the structure of local government by reforming close to 200 town corporations. The Act replaced municipal corporations with town councils that were chosen by new municipal electorates, required annual elections for the councils (although one-third of the council would be replaced each year), and created registered lists of municipal voters. Even though the Act has always been under the shadow of the Great Reform Bill, its significance is difficult to overstate. The commission on municipal reform, which had been formed by Grey, desired to make local town government more accountable and more effective, particularly in regard to legal issues, and replacing the old corporations with fully elected councils seemed to be the solution. When the Act was passed, it created a more open, responsive political system. Its consequences, however, went even further than the Act's supporters had intended. Like the 1832 Reform Act, the Municipal Corporations Act fostered higher rates of partisanship in those towns affected by it, feeding the activity of local party machines and also accelerating the presence of national political issues in the localities.[11]

The increase in 'progressive' legislation was only one side of the coin. The other was the desire of Whigs, Liberals and some Liberal Tories to fashion a more stream-lined, efficient, balanced and virtuous government that would rectify the authority of the propertied elite while simultaneously reforming local and national government to make it more responsive to all of Britain's social classes. Part of the effort lay in economical reform and ridding the nation of 'old corruption', trimming the excesses of government, reducing waste and abolishing parasitism, including sinecures, offices and patronage. The other involved opening the nation to freer trade. Peel's decisions in the 1840s to reduce tariffs, abolish export duties and, most famously, to repeal the Corn Laws were all meant to make government more efficient and to bring social and economic benefits to the nation as a whole. Peel's efforts and vision notwith-standing, the call for free trade and for repeal was sounded beyond the confines of elite political clubs and the national parliament. Repeal had become an unavoidable issue because of the increasingly volatile nature of class politics, as well as the pos-sibility of famine in Ireland. Cobden and Bright's Anti-Corn Law League became the coherent voice for the popular free trade movement, receiving some working-class support as it orchestrated local campaigns, published its own free trade news-papers and held public meetings. Howe has argued that the League's aim to create a national community that could respond to popular economic grievances was real-ized by its success in turning 'free trade into a popular moral crusade'. By 1846, free trade had replaced the Corn Laws 'as a symbol of Britishness'.[12]

The League, established in 1838, was essentially a middle- and upper-class pres-sure group, but its politically oriented, working-class counterpart, Chartism, was not. The Chartists were a natural revival of working-class radicalism, the type which had been represented by the London Working Men's Association. The Chartists believed that not only had the 1832 Reform Act not gone far enough, but it was a betrayal of the British working classes. The People's Charter which gave the movement its name in 1838 sought to reverse this betrayal with six main goals that were far more radical than any envisaged by the framers of the 1832 Act: universal manhood suf-frage, annual parliaments, equal-sized constituencies, payment of MPs, no property qualifications and vote by ballot. The Chartists were not to be ignored. Their tech-niques, mostly legal, included meetings, rallies, a National Convention in 1839, a National Charter Association that could claim a membership of close to 50,000, newspapers and large-scale petitions, including one in 1839 with 1.3 million. sig-natures, and another in 1842 with almost three times as many. But, for all of its strength and its success, the Chartist movement was on the decline within a few years, largely owing to circumstances beyond its control. The fact that the European rev-olutions of 1848 fostered no similar conflagrations in Britain was one factor, but equally important was the return to prosperity in the 1850s and the fact that main-stream reformers had far less radical political goals. Nevertheless, the movement's sig-nificance is undeniable: it accelerated the political education of the working classes and made the public, and therefore Westminster, aware that although the 1832 Reform Act was necessary and important, it was only the beginning.

Yet, between the mid-1830s and the mid-1860s, few were confident that the beginning would ever find its end. One major commonplace of the historical schol-arship of the Victorian era is that reform was unimportant because no one seemed to want it. After the collapse of Chartism there was no effective reform movement.

The nation eased into a general political calm, and the debate on reform became largely academic. In the years just prior to the Second Reform Act of 1867, extra-parliamentary pressure and popular agitation for reform seemed non-existent. More pressing issues, such as the Crimean War, diverted attention. And, perhaps most important, many Victorians, generally speaking, accepted the reformed electoral system as it had been settled in 1832. They desired efficient, balanced government, not democracy, and most scoffed at the notion that the franchise should be based on an individual's rights or that anyone who depended directly on the state for sustenance (as opposed to attaining independence through property) should be allowed to vote. The time-worn idea that communal representation of interests was preferable to individual representation prevailed. Influence, too, remained integral to the electoral system, even though it was not as prevalent as it had been prior to 1832, not only because the Reform Act had had some success in rooting it out, but also because demographic changes in local communities had rendered influence less important. So when Russell submitted several reform bills in the 1850s, his efforts were unsuccessful.

To a certain extent, however, historians have exaggerated the feebleness of the reform movement in the 1850s and early 1860s. For one, the call for reform was not as loud as it had been in 1831, but there is no reason why it should have been. With the prosperity of the 1850s and the growing efficiency and accountability of government, the need for electoral modification seemed far less important. In addition, the movement for reform continued to exert pressure. Even if Victorian popular politics was not successful in causing immediate change, the radical critique of government and the franchise was an integral part of popular political ideology from the 1840s to the early days of the labour movement. In addition, a reform party in parliament promoted constitutionalism, anti-executive politics, economic and moral reform, and the utmost sovereignty of the House of Commons. The parliamentary reform party of the mid-Victorian era was a motley crew of philosophic radicals, independent Liberals, radicals and members of the 'Manchester School' such as Cobden and Bright, and their specific goals varied, ranging from public education to religious toleration, from retrenchment to non-intervention in foreign affairs. As a body, these men kept alive the traditional reformist argument that interest and corruption plagued the electoral system and that only a further extension of the franchise could provide an adequate remedy. Their electors agreed with them. As Taylor has argued, the independent MPs of the reform party in parliament were elected 'mainly because their self-professed parliamentary independence accorded with the aspirations of constituencies desiring emancipation from aristocratic influence and closed corporation politics'.[13] Their constituents might have stressed retrenchment as a primary issue, but reform was a parallel concern.

The ideological commitment to reform was as crucial in the mid-Victorian era as it had been in the 1820s and 1830s. John Stuart Mill explored the question in 1858 with his *Thoughts on Parliamentary Reform*, which coincided nicely with Grey's *Parliamentary Government*. But the torch-bearer of reform in the middle of the century was Russell. He earnestly tried to keep the dream of reform alive at a time even when he believed that few in the nation were wholeheartedly attached to it. Russell was ageing, of course, and as the Great Reform Act retreated further into the past, he become more convinced of its shortcomings. He wanted, once again, to attain the image of a great reformer and to find a single issue around which the Liberal party could rally, thereby demonstrating their concern for the middle and working classes. By 1850, Russell's premiership had already been under incredible strain, most notably from the Irish famine which killed approximately one million people. The crisis prompted the Franchise Extension Act, a necessary piece of legislation in the face of such a massive blow to the Irish population and electorate, as well as an experimental one; it introduced an occupation franchise in the country which would later serve as the basis of the 1867 Reform Act. Russell then miscalculated; his belief in the necessity of reform, no matter how right he felt about the matter, gained few adherents and instead alienated many, particularly in the Liberal party. When he introduced a reform bill in 1852 to extend the franchise to £20 householders in the counties and £5 householders in the towns, he offended fellow Whigs who saw no need for reform. He offended Palmerston most of all. As a leading Liberal, Palmerston would eventually prove to be the major hurdle to the pursuit of reform, forming an alliance with Derby and other Conservatives to oppose the issue at all costs. When Palmerston died in 1865, the door to reform opened, and Russell stepped through it, forming a ministry and pledging that reform would finally be realized.

Palmerston's death was crucial, but Gladstone's conversion to reform was even more important, for he brought the issue to the national and local public, the franchised and the unenfranchised. Like Russell, he believed that an efficient, balanced, responsible government required a larger electorate, and even though his Peelite nature told him that franchise extension was unnecessary and dangerous, he came to understand that it was a necessary tool in reducing government expenditure. Giving the vote to artisans and members of the working class would force the House of Commons to pursue cheap government. Gladstone's rise as the 'People's William' in the early 1860s put reform on the national agenda, as the speeches he gave on extensive tours were often reprinted verbatim in national and local newspapers. And then, in 1864, Gladstone made what would become one of the most famous statements of the entire Victorian era, the declaration that every man 'who is not presumably incapacitated by some consideration of personal unfitness or of political danger, is morally entitled to come within the pale of the constitution'.[14] It was a powerful statement which reverberated throughout the nation. Gladstone's evolution as a popular leader proved how the longstanding issue of fiscal reform, which was his chief concern, was inextricably tied to the question of parliamentary reform; it also proved how well public opinion responded to his overtures, and how Westminster had to respond to public opinion. Of course, Gladstone, as well as Russell, did not stand alone. A group of former Chartists formed the Reform League in 1864, reviving some of their old arguments for manhood suffrage and the ballot. The National Reform Union, formed by merchants and manufacturers in Lancashire, promoted triennial parliaments, the ballot and a ratepayer franchise, and in no time they had branches across the country. Underlying their cause, as well as the concerns of Gladstone and Russell, was the incredible 'progress' of the working classes. Economic and demographic change and the evolution of the 'labour aristocracy' had enhanced the political viability of the working classes; middle-class reformers and radicals now saw them as an important ally in the struggle against the traditional aristocracy. Gladstone moralized about them while Russell understood their political weight. Both believed it was time to integrate the working classes into the electorate.

So reform was more than just a stale academic debate. By the 1860s, it had become an unavoidable political issue, even if it had a very different temper than it had in the 1830s. But in politics the oddest things can happen, and the 1867 Reform Act was passed by Derby's Conservative minority government, not by Russell's Liberal administration. Russell and Gladstone fashioned a reform bill in 1866 that would bring far more male citizens into the pale of the constitution while preserving the political basis and pre-eminence of property. They proposed a £14 householder franchise in the counties, a £7 householder franchise in the boroughs, and a £10 lodger franchise, as well as the vote for those with at least £50 in savings, and the disenfranchisement of forty-nine boroughs. Conservative MPs realized the Liberal bill was self-serving because it was tailored to strengthen Liberal support in the counties, but the bill's failure, and the resignation of Russell's government, was rather the result of Liberal disunity. Lowe and his group of a dozen Liberal detractors, collectively known as the Cave of Adullamites, were uneasy; they would not countenance the extension of the franchise to workers and believed that further reform would weaken, not strengthen, the British polity. The Adullamites, along with a group of anti-reform Liberal MPs, refused to give Russell and Gladstone support, helped destroy the government and unintentionally opened the door to Conservative victory. Disraeli was content simply to sit back and let Lowe and his followers undermine the Liberal party. He and Derby seized the reform initiative, realizing that if their minority government was going to survive, they would have to pass a bill. Whether or not Disraeli genuinely believed in the principle of reform or was in reality a political opportunist is a debate that has long attracted historians, but it is clear that his main goals were to protect the landed interest and, most of all, to revive the Tory party, which he had argued was the true 'national party'. Disraeli believed that the real mistake of 1832 was 'the manner in which Parliament abolished the relations between the labouring classes and the constitution of this country'.[15] That might have been true, but Disraeli and Derby were in reality not prepared to extend the franchise in 1867 any further down the social ladder than it had to go. Originally, the entire Conservative bill rested upon household suffrage and plural voting, which provided certain electors with more than one vote based on their financial, propertied and educational standing. In addition, the Conservatives needed a bill that would increase the number of county seats, given that their electoral strongholds were still in the counties. And they also hoped to exclude compounders, those poorer voters who could not afford to pay their rates but compounded with their landlords to vote. The Tories, along with Liberal anti-reformers, wanted only those who paid their rates directly and had resided in the same place for three years to vote.

Disraeli's 'leap in the dark', as he put it, was the Second Reform Act, passed in August 1867 after numerous, complicated amendments, extensions and revisions. It was not quite the Act that Disraeli had wanted, but its existence improved the reputation of his party amongst the electorate and expanded the existing system without creating a new, democratic one. The problem of redistribution remained, and the Act's 'conservative' nature was evident in the disenfranchisement and transfer of only fifty-two seats, twenty-five going to English counties, nineteen to towns such as Manchester, Leeds, Liverpool and Birmingham, seven to Scotland, and one to London University. The county occupation franchise was reduced to £12 per annum, and, in the boroughs, the household suffrage required a residence of one year. The

Act also introduced a lodger franchise set at £10 per annum with a residency require-ment of one year. Hodgkinson's amendment, which Derby and Disraeli surprisingly accepted in the late summer of 1867, abolished compounding altogether, effectively enfranchising former compounders and increasing the electorate more than the Con-servatives had originally intended. The overall size of the electorate in England and Wales increased from roughly 1.3 million to just over 2 million. Whereas one in five adult males had the franchise, by 1868 one in three did.

As important as the 1867 Reform Act was in enlarging the size of the electorate, it was something of a mixed bag. The Conservatives did not benefit from it as much as they had expected. Disraeli's skills with the electorate, especially the newly enfran-chised working classes, whom he assumed were Conservative, were inferior to Gladstone's, and even the formation of the National Union of Conservative and Con-stitutional Associations in late 1867, a body that would facilitate working-class Con-servatism in the localities, was not used effectively. The Conservatives might have had a notable record on social reform legislation in 1867 and 1868, but their critics charged they were simply hanging on to Liberal coat-tails. The electorate's view of the Conservative party was not much better. In the 1868 general election, the Con-servatives won 271 seats, but the Liberals stormed away with 387. The predom-inance of the Liberal party, which Derby and Disraeli had so desperately tried to curtail with the Reform Act, continued. In many ways, continuity marked the rep-resentative system as a whole. The majority of counties and rural towns returned Tory or Conservative members. Constituencies ran the gamut from relatively free elec-torates to those still weighed down by influence, patronage and deference. In many places, voters continued to cast their ballots based on immediate needs and concerns, on local professional, cultural or familial ties, rather than on national issues. Tradi-tional electoral practices continued in a number of constituencies, as candidates treated, bribed and entertained the electors while the electors themselves remained susceptible to drinking and violence. Most important, the costs of electioneering were still high, and the same types of members made their way to parliament; no working man was elected for any constituency in the aftermath of 1867. The electorate itself remained exclusively 'masculine' even though female suffragists advocated giving women the vote. They argued that the propertied basis of the franchise should be preserved, and that basing a 'gender-neutral' franchise on property and rate-paying that would allow women to qualify would not undermine the constitution.[16]

Set in perspective, however, the Second Reform Act was significant. Neither the Conservatives who created, nor the Liberals who wanted, nor even many of the Radicals in parliament who supported it for years, had envisaged a popular demo-cracy. The British electoral system was still based on community interest, not indi-vidual politics, and the notion that a man had to be independent of the state in order to exercise good political judgement remained paramount. But, much like its prede-cessor, the Second Reform Act had a significant impact upon the political nation as a whole, and that included the unenfranchised as well as the franchised. The polit-ical weight of the electorate increased greatly as a result of Disraeli's bill, as the future of ministries now would be determined as much by the behaviour of electors as by political events in Westminster. The major parties understood these developments and responded accordingly. The Conservatives already had their National Union, and Joseph Chamberlain followed suit by forming the National Liberal Federation in

1877. Local political organization became deeply important to success at the polls; as a result, the local party agent found himself more important than ever. This increase in local political temperature could also be gauged by the rise of party-sponsored political clubs and formal constituency associations, which often had memberships running into the thousands, as well as by the increased presence of trade unions and trades councils, skilled workers' associations and temperance societies, which involved the activity of non-voters. While these developments might have happened without the Second Reform Act (owing to demographic and socio-economic change), they were exacerbated by the extension of the franchise; with so many new voters, many of them among the working classes, parties had to become more active in constituencies, had to be even more responsive to public opinion, and had to have a majority in parliament in order for their ministries to survive.

Representing the People: Parliamentary Reform in the 1880s

The third reform of the franchise in the nineteenth century did not make Britain a pure democracy in our sense of the term, but the nation had finally made the electoral system equitable, consistent, and wide enough to include agricultural labourers and two out of every three adult males. Britain was closer than ever to Joseph Chamberlain's dream of 'government of the people by the people'. If the early 1830s and the mid-1860s were significant periods, the 1880s, in terms of Britain's political structure, marked the real watershed. The electoral system created by the series of acts collectively known as the 'Third Reform Act' virtually sounded the death knell for an old order dominated by the aristocracy. To a great extent, change was already under way. In 1872, Gladstone's government had granted the secret ballot, fulfilling the longstanding dreams of radicals and reformers. Its rationale was that only a secret ballot could ensure the purity of elections and protect voters against corruption, bribery and the intimidation of elites, landowners, local party associations, trade unions and other sources of pressure. That same year, the Agricultural Labourers' Union came into existence, and Chamberlain, who would win a seat for Birmingham in 1873, began promoting ideas that would later serve as the bedrock for his famous 'radical programme' of the 1880s: land reform, free education and tax relief for the poor, among other issues. Liberals and radicals were not the only ones who realized that change was necessary; the Conservatives took up the mantle of 'Tory Democracy', as specious as it might have sounded, first in the 1870s under Disraeli's leadership, followed in the 1880s by Lord Randolph Churchill's plea to listen to and trust the people. Late-nineteenth-century Conservatism was something of a conundrum, a modern traditionalism that struggled against the tide for decades, only to be cast into the forefront of politics after the Home Rule crisis of 1886. For all its attachments to the establishment, on occasion it appeared even more progressive than the Liberal party; the Primrose League, created to organize local Conservatism, was important in involving middle- and working-class women in urban Toryism.

The Gladstonian Liberal party realized the need for further franchise reform because the political landscape had changed drastically in the twenty years since the Second Reform Act. The social composition of the House of Commons, for example, drifted away from traditional landed members to those with professional and commercial backgrounds. In 1874, 209 MPs were of landed background, but there were only 125 of them by 1880. Conversely, 314 MPs in 1874 had professional, commercial and industrial occupations, and in 1880 the number rose to 426. The social background of Liberal MPs had a similar trajectory. In 1859, 54 per cent were landed gentry or had peerage connections, contrasted with 28 per cent who were merchants, manufacturers, bankers and lawyers. Ten years later, these percentages were virtually the same, but by 1874, 40 per cent were landed gentry or had peerage connections while 45 per cent were merchants, manufacturers, bankers and lawyers. By 1886, the landed amounted to one-fifth while the professional made up half of all Liberal MPs.[17] But the most significant factors were demographic and socio-economic change and working-class pressure, largely in the form of trade unions. Boroughs and counties, once distinct communities with separate economic and political interests, had become too similar by the 1880s; it became increasingly difficult for traditionalists to defend distinct borough and county franchises. Landownership, local patronage, the dependency of rural families on local aristocrats and the power of great estates had all declined to such an extent that a high county franchise no longer seemed logical. Gladstone came to believe that if the urban working classes were 'respectable' enough to have the franchise, so too were agricultural and rural workers, and because the Second Reform Act had enfranchised urban householders, it only seemed logical to enfranchise rural householders. But socio-economic and demographic change necessitated more than just franchise extension. The social composition of the two main parties might have been changing, but middle-class and working-class candidates were greatly deterred from seeking office by the high costs of electioneering. Gladstone's party wanted to redress this issue as well. With their pledge of major reform, something Gladstone had believed was unavoidable as early as 1873, the Liberals were effectively fomenting what Chamberlain called a 'revolution'.

The assault on election expenses came with the Corrupt and Illegal Practices Act of 1883. This Act codified rules for electoral conduct, making corruption, bribery and treating punishable by imprisonment and limiting election expenses to roughly £1,000 for every 5,000 voters. The Act also provided for public inspections of candidates' accounts to ensure adherence to the law. The assault on the traditional constitution came with the Representation of the People Act of 1884 and the Redistribution of Seats Act of 1885, introduced and passed separately because of political wrangling in Westminster between Gladstone, Liberals and both Houses. The Liberals knew that an equal franchise in boroughs and counties was necessary, but they also knew they would have to offer a wide-scale redistribution of parliamentary seats to solve problems created by the growth of the county electorate and by the continued under-representation of large towns. Proportional representation was one alternative, albeit a radical one, but Liberals and Conservatives alike believed it would strike at efficient, effective government. Enfranchising women was another alternative, as some suffragists argued that giving the vote to women property-holders would buttress the propertied interests of the country against working-class radicalism. But even such a careful argument fell on deaf Liberal ears. Female suffrage was dashed as quickly as it was raised; the franchise bill would not have lasted long in the Lords had it contained a provision for women's suffrage.

The most significant feature of the 1884 and 1885 Acts was the creation of a uniform franchise in boroughs and counties, giving the vote to all male householders who paid their rates and were in residence for at least twelve months. The Franchise Act removed the traditional distinctions between the towns and the counties. It also contained a lodger franchise set at £10 with twelve months' residency and an occupation franchise with lands or tenements worth £10 per annum. The other highly significant features included the redistribution of 142 seats and the creation of single-seat constituencies. Boroughs with populations under 15,000 were disenfranchised while those under 50,000 could return only one member; some seventy-nine English and Welsh boroughs were merged with county seats (two Scottish and twenty-two Irish boroughs were also merged with counties). Thirty-nine available seats went to London, fourteen to Scotland, twenty-five to Ireland, with the remainder going to various English and Welsh counties and boroughs. Both Acts were predicated upon notions of equity, proportion and consistency, with an attempt to relate representation to population size, as well as to create an equal number of electoral districts, something radical reformers had been seeking since the 1830s.

While the percentage increase in the number of voters was less in 1884–5 than it had been in 1867, partly because the number of electors had increased since then, the sheer increase in pure numbers was larger. The electorate of Great Britain grew from roughly 2.6 million in 1883 to 4.4 million in 1886. More than 60 per cent of all adult males now had the right to vote. Britain was not a pure democracy; the franchise was still based on a connection to property, not all working-class males qualified, and anomalies remained. But the significance of the Third Reform Act is difficult to overstate. The First and Second Reform Acts were necessary, but in the long run both kept the traditional representative system largely intact. The Third Act precipitated the dismantling of that system. William Harcourt confessed in 1884 that the Franchise Act was a 'frightfully democratic measure which I confess appals me'.[18] Essentially, he was correct. Before 1884, the electoral system of Great Britain, even in the aftermath of 1832 and 1867, was one largely dominated, like most of the country, by landowners, patrons and aristocrats. After 1884, that same system was dominated by city and suburban electorates and most of all by the working classes, a phenomenon greatly welcomed by the Act's framers, notably Dilke and Chamberlain. Before the close of the nineteenth century, close to two-thirds of electors were of working-class origin, and Britain's movement towards modern democracy was confirmed. The Third Reform Act was certainly not the only factor in this development; agitations for land reform, the development of a coherent working-class political movement, accelerating urbanization and other factors were also important. But in terms of closing the door on the traditional political system and opening the door for mass politics, the Third Reform Act went further than the 1832 and 1867 Reform Acts ever did.

The changes effected by the Third Reform Act, of course, did not occur overnight. More than 30 per cent of all adult males could not vote, and women had to wait until 1918 to enjoy the franchise – and even then, those women had to be ratepayers of at least 30 years of age. Ten years after that, all women over 21 had the franchise on the same basis as men. Even for those 4.4 million men who could vote after 1884, there was no guarantee their voices would be heard. The House of Lords, the pre-eminent symbol of the old order and predominantly Conservative down to the First World War, stood in the way. Nineteenth-century reformers had finally completed altering the House of Commons; the House of Lords was next on the chopping block. In the years of the Third Reform Act, anti-Lords agitations were common across the country, organized by the branches of the People's League for the Abolition of the Hereditary Legislature. The League's efforts were not immediately effective, but the House of Lords eventually ruined itself by blocking Lloyd George's People's Budget in 1909; the Parliament Act two years later curtailed its power. By 1930, nearly one hundred years after Grey passed the first, the 'great', Reform Act, the enfranchising goals of reformers, radicals and Chartists were fully realized.

In assessing parliamentary reform in the nineteenth century, historians must be careful not to interpret the issue from the perspective of a post-industrial democracy. With the exception of some radical reformers, few advocated universal male (or female) suffrage as a viable political option in the nineteenth century. The political system, based on traditional relationships between electors and elected, on communities and interests, could not have absorbed a democratic suffrage without a massive alteration of electoral structures and practices. True, the nineteenth-century electoral system was beset by numerous problems, including widely varied constituencies, heavily under-represented regions, corruption and influence. But on the other hand the British parliament did pass not one, but three, reform bills over the course of the century, a continuum, perhaps, in a 'master narrative' of constitutionalism that dominated the era.[19] These bills were the result of reformist efforts to create a more efficient, progressive, responsive government, malleable enough to accommodate a changing, growing population and electorate. These bills were also the result of the steadily increasing influence of public opinion, which the government could not avoid. In 1831, Peel justified his opposition to reform by stating that he did not want to open a door 'which I saw no prospect of being able to close.' Once the door to reform was opened in 1832, Great Britain was set on the path towards parliamentary democracy.

NOTES

1. J. Phillips, *The Great Reform Bill in the Boroughs: English Electoral Behaviour 1818–1841* (Oxford, 1992), pp. 81–3.
2. P. Langford, *A Polite and Commercial People: England 1727–1783* (Oxford, 1983), p. 711.
3. F. O'Gorman, 'Campaign rituals and ceremonies: the social meaning of elections in England 1780–1860', *Past and Present*, 135 (1994).
4. J. Phillips, *Electoral Behavior in Unreformed England: Plumpers, Splitters, and Straights* (Princeton, 1982).
5. J. Phillips, 'Popular politics in unreformed England', *Journal of Modern History*, 52 (1980).
6. I. Newbould, *Whiggery and Reform: The Politics of Government, 1830–41* (Stanford, 1990), p. 56.
7. J. Parry, *The Rise and Fall of Liberal Government in Victorian Britain* (New Haven, 1993), p. 72.

8. D. Beales, 'The electorate before and after 1832: the right to vote, and the opportunity', *Parliamentary History*, 11 (1992), p. 150.
9. Phillips, *Great Reform Bill*, p. 96.
10. W. MacKinnon, *On the Rise, Progress, and Present State of Public Opinion* (London, 1828), p. 127.
11. J. Phillips, 'Unintended consequences: parliamentary blueprints in the hands of provincial builders', in D. Dean and C. Jones, eds, *Parliament and Locality 1660–1939* (Edinburgh, 1998).
12. A. Howe, *Free Trade and Liberal England, 1846–1946* (Oxford, 1997), p. 36.
13. M. Taylor, *The Decline of British Radicalism 1847–1860* (Oxford, 1995), p. 62.
14. H. C. G. Matthew, *Gladstone: 1809–1898* (Oxford, 1997), p. 139.
15. T. E. Kebbel, *Selected Speeches of the Late Right Honourable the Earl of Beaconsfield* (London, 1882), p. 477.
16. A. Clark, 'Gender, class, and the constitution: franchise reform in England, 1832–1928', in J. Vernon, ed., *Re-Reading the Constitution: New Narratives in the Political History of England's Long Nineteenth Century* (Cambridge, 1996), p. 244.
17. T. A. Jenkins, *The Liberal Ascendancy, 1830–1886* (Basingstoke, 1994), pp. 105, 127, 146, 198.
18. Parry, *Rise and Fall*, p. 287.
19. J. Vernon, ed., *Re-Reading the Constitution: New Narratives in the Political History of England's Long Nineteenth Century* (Cambridge, 1996).

FURTHER READING

The literature on parliamentary reform is voluminous, especially on the 1832 Reform Act. For the reform movement up to 1832 J. Cannon, *Parliamentary Reform 1640–1832* (1972) is quite useful. The most thorough study of the unreformed electorate is F. O'Gorman, *Voters, Patrons, and Parties: The Unreformed Electoral System of Hanoverian England, 1734–1832* (1989), while J. Phillips offers a fine study in *Electoral Behavior in Unreformed England: Plumpers, Splitters, and Straights* (1982). For the 1832 Reform Act itself: M. Brock, *The Great Reform Act* (1973); I. Newbould, *Whiggery and Reform: The Politics of Government, 1830–41* (1990) and J. Phillips, *The Great Reform Bill in the Boroughs: English Electoral Behaviour, 1818–1841* (1992). An important debate on the electorate took place between D. Beales, 'The electorate before and after 1832: the right to vote, and the opportunity', *Parliamentary History*, 11 (1992) and F. O'Gorman, 'The electorate before and after 1832', *Parliamentary History*, 12 (1993).

The Second and Third Reform Acts have received less historiographical attention, but there are several important works. M. Cowling, *1867: Disraeli, Gladstone, and Revolution* (1967) privileges high politics, but is essential, as is F. B. Smith, *The Making of the Second Reform Bill* (1966). For the Third Reform Act, see A. Jones, *The Politics of Reform 1884* (1972) and W. A. Hayes, *The Background and Passage of the Third Reform Act* (1982). J. Vincent provided an interesting study of electoral behaviour in his *Pollbooks: How Victorians Voted* (1967); and his *The Formation of the Liberal Party* (1965) continues to provoke debate. Also useful are H. J. Hanham, *Elections and Party Management: Politics in the Time of Disraeli and Gladstone* (1959) and C. Seymour, *Electoral Reform in England and Wales* (1915).

If most of the major studies of reform in 1867 and 1884 were published decades ago, there has been much stimulating work in recent years on the middle and later Victorian period, especially E. F. Biagini, *Liberty, Retrenchment, and Reform: Popular Liberalism in the Age of Gladstone 1860–1880* (1992), K. T. Hoppen, 'The franchise and electoral politics in England and

Ireland 1832–1885', *History*, 70 (1985), T. A. Jenkins, *The Liberal Ascendancy, 1830–1886* (1994), J. Lawrence and M. Taylor, eds, *Party, State and Society: Electoral Behaviour in Britain Since* 1820 (1997), M. Pugh, *The Making of Modern British Politics 1867–1945* (2002) and J. Vernon, *Politics and the People: A Study in English Political Culture c.1815–1867* (1993). J. Parry, *The Rise and Fall of Liberal Government in Victorian Britain* (1993) is absolutely essential. J. Vernon, ed., *Re-Reading the Constitution: New Narratives in the Political History of England's Long Nineteenth Century* (1996) contains invigorating research and raises important issues.

CHAPTER TEN

Politics and Gender

SARAH RICHARDSON

Gender, Class and Politics

The traditional political historiography of the nineteenth century found no place for women's or gender history. Concentrating on the development of political institutions and on male politicians it was generally assumed that the politics of the nation in the nineteenth century owed little to women – apart from a few atypical, exceptional examples. However, assessments of nineteenth-century gender and politics have undergone a series of paradigm shifts since the 1970s and the subject is now characterized by a series of conflicting narratives about the role of women in public life during the period. Interestingly, this has led to corresponding discussions about men, politics and identity, an area that had hitherto been viewed as unproblematic. The effect of these theoretical debates has been to construct a far more nuanced vision, both of the lives of nineteenth-century women and men and of the whole panorama of nineteenth-century political history.

The development of social history in the 1960s initially did little to counteract the assumption that political history could be written without reference to women or gender. The focus remained on political institutions and male political actors, albeit centred in working-class rather than elite communities. It was the rise of women's history in the 1970s – characterized by Rowbotham's *Hidden from History* – that did much to foreground women's role in the politics of the nation.[1] Although pioneer women's historians had diverse objectives, there was an underlying feminist agenda that distinguished their work as they searched both to uncover the roots of the ideology of patriarchal oppression and to trace the origins of women's political action as a means of explaining the contemporary struggle for women's liberation. Ironically, this led to a search to recover past heroines of women's movements that mimicked the 'great men' approach of many traditional political historians. There was also a concentration on the early-twentieth-century campaigns of female suffrage campaigners that focused on women's struggle to obtain the franchise and centred on women's penetration of the high political sphere. A corollary of this research was that many of these early writers assumed there was little female political agency either outside the campaign for the suffrage or for much of the nineteenth century.

A second theoretical current emerged in the 1970s and 1980s, influenced by the application of social scientific, literary and cultural methodologies to history. This considered the categories of gender, race and class as central to any social structure. The most influential and innovative example of this conceptual development was Davidoff and Hall's path-breaking *Family Fortunes*. They outlined their intentions thus: 'In particular, our concern has been to give the neglected dimension of gender its full weight and complexity in the shaping and structuring of middle-class social life in this period.'[2] In a thesis that has not been unchallenged, they attempted to demonstrate the crucial impact of changing gender roles on the formation of a distinct middle-class identity in the late eighteenth and early nineteenth centuries. In so doing, they acknowledged the important nineteenth-century rhetoric of 'separate spheres' in establishing boundaries between the public and private worlds of the English middle class. While public life was increasingly seen as an exclusively male domain characterized by the manly virtues of action, determination and resolution, the domestic setting was where women's moral virtues of gentleness, tenderness, piety and faith could and should most fully be developed. These ideals were originally expressed in England by a small group of evangelicals and, it is argued, were so suited to the values of the emerging middle class that they became central to the bourgeois identity of the nineteenth century, absorbed by government policy-makers and social commentators alike.

The use of 'separate spheres' ideologies to characterize gender relations specifically in this period has been contested by historians who have argued that the discourse of domesticity was neither novel to the nineteenth century nor restricted to a single social class.[3] There was separation of responsibilities, especially among the middle class but these did not necessarily take place along public/private boundaries and were continually negotiated. In certain fields, notably philanthropy, the boundaries between the public and private spheres intersected. Historians have continued to consider the use of the language of separate spheres. A recent contributor to the debate has argued that 'several spheres' is a more adequate term to describe the ways in which middle-class women interpreted their public and political identity and that it is difficult to establish a single definition of such a complex term.[4] It has become clear that these multiple, sometimes contradictory, interpretations of 'separate spheres' reflect the attitudes of nineteenth-century commentators themselves. Whilst many conduct manuals and social-policy makers extolled the virtues of the bourgeois culture of domesticity, some radicals and early feminists embraced the idea of the home as an enabling site for specifically female political agency. Thus the notion of public and private were ideological constructs utilized in different ways rather than fixed, unchanging entities.

Davidoff and Hall contributed to a chronology of women and politics that had been established by the early women's historians. The early nineteenth century was viewed as a period of closure, excluding both women and the working class from certain types of political activity. The rise of the bourgeoisie, the ideology of domesticity and economic trends separating the home from the workplace, confirmed the political arena as a middle-class masculine world from which women and the poor were largely excluded. This world, it is argued, was only penetrated by women in the second half of the century when new opportunities for participation were opened in the emergent sphere of local government and extra-governmental organizations such as school boards. This Whiggish interpretation therefore considered the 1860s and 1870s as the cradle of campaigns for women's civil and political rights. More recently this chronology has been challenged by a range of historians, who have stressed the richness of women's political culture earlier in the century and have argued for a more complex assessment of nineteenth-century politics which does not necessarily privilege women's campaigns for the vote over other areas of political engagement.

Davidoff and Hall's work represented one theoretical approach to the focus on gender and its use as a category of historical analysis. A second response emerged in the 1980s from historians influenced by French post-structuralism. Scott argued for the primary role of language in the construction of gendered identity.[5] Gender should therefore be used as an analytical category for historical investigation recognizing its shifting and unstable nature. Many feminist historians had used the terms 'gender' and 'woman' as interchangeable but Scott wanted to move away from the identification with the biological categories of male and female and explore the cultural meanings of masculinity and femininity. Scott's reasoning was summarized by Bock: 'Gender is a "category", not in the sense of a universal statement but . . . in the sense of public objection and indictment, of debate, protest, process and trial.'[6] For 'gender historians' it was considered that such theoretical methods would initiate new areas of historical enquiry, particularly in the area of political history where power relations between and within the sexes were continually 'contested and in flux'. Scott's contribution was subject to bitter challenge from women's historians who considered that they had been responsive to issues concerning women's multiple cultural identities and argued that her approach would lead to the experiences of women in the past being reduced to mere 'subjective stories'.[7] The discussions were interwoven with the wider debate in the historical profession about the contribution of postmodernism and its concentration on the construction of meaning through language.

The emphasis on contested gender identities and a more cultural approach to political history has led women's historians to revise their focus. Discussions on the endurance, or otherwise, of the patriarchal framework have moved on to a consideration of the extent of women's political agency within cultural, societal and economic constraints. The emphasis is on the diversity of women's experiences within the rich and complex political culture of the nineteenth century. Recent work has concentrated on the diversity of women's political practice and the continually shifting contexts in which they operated. Ironically, this has led to a revival of interest in elites – the traditional field of study by political historians – in order to uncover some of the methods by which women subverted institutional, legal and political constraints on their civic role, their property rights and their interaction with the wider political nation.

A further consequence of the debate between gender and women's historians has been burgeoning new research on competing versions of masculinity in the nineteenth century and the implications for political activity. Men and power have so long been seen as synonymous that these explorations offer exciting new avenues for interpretations and explanations of political activity. Notions of nineteenth-century masculinity are beginning to be problematized as historians consider that the contested versions of manhood symbolize wider debates about the structure of power. Clark considers the clash between working-class, bourgeois and aristocratic concepts of masculinity in its domestic context and gender relations within the industrial and manufacturing communities.[8] She takes a similar approach to revisionist women's historians viewing the family as a site for public debate, rather than as a private, de-politicized space. She argues that Chartists, for example, used the rhetoric of domesticity for multiple, often contradictory, purposes: to uphold manhood, to appeal to women, and to extract concessions from the state. For working-class men, struggling to come to terms with the demands of industrialization, a feminized work-force, and bourgeois notions of respectability and the patriarchal family, comman-deering the concept of domesticity allowed them to reassert their control. Whilst some Chartists argued for a more egalitarian family structure, others used the language of domesticity to justify their superiority over working-class women, arguing that they wished to protect and support them.

This confused picture of gender tensions within political movements in the nine-teenth century has been supported by studies of varied political campaigns including the anti-slavery movement, the Anti-Corn Law League, the demand for female suf-frage and the campaign against the Contagious Diseases Acts. At times, the objec-tives of male and female campaigners led to confrontation. For example, many activists for an extension of the franchise deliberately excluded a demand for female suffrage from their campaigns, in order, they argued, to secure the vote for working men. There were also bitter gender conflicts in the trade-union movement. The concept of the 'family wage' for example, furthered the adoption of gender-specific restrictive practices and the increasing prevalence of the male-provider system. Trade unions adopted the language of the bourgeois family model in the struggle over male wages. Male-dominated trade unions prioritized rights for men, pressed for the cur-tailment or outright ban on (especially married) female employees and continuously reiterated the aim of creating circumstances in which women could fulfil their duties as wife and mother. However, the model of gender and class conflict could be more complicated. Elite socialist women, for example, campaigned for the extension of the franchise to *all* adults, not just women. An important collection of essays has out-lined the 'connections between the exercise of power and the construction of mas-culinities' recovering the neglected contribution of men to the suffrage campaigns.[9] It discusses how men with radically different agendas and from a wide range of polit-ical, economic and social backgrounds were able to contribute to the women's suf-frage movement in Britain. The gender roles within the trade-union movement were not always characterized by male domination and much depended upon the social context of individual trade unions. In some textile districts, for example, the organ-ization of the workforce continued to be based upon kinship networks well into the nineteenth century. In these circumstances trade-union politics were marked by far more gender collaboration. There can therefore be no straightforward account of men and politics and recent work has complicated the traditional story of men's dom-inance of the public sphere. The contested nature of masculinity and men's diverse experiences means that direct connections between men and power are untenable.

As the historiography of political engagement in the nineteenth century has become more diverse, historians have reconsidered the sources available to recover the multifaceted nature of public participation. One example of this is an examina-tion of the representation of women and politics in the rich political culture of the period. The female body was a long-established symbol used in political prints, pamph-lets, paintings, cartoons, ballads, newspapers, poetry and literature and physically on the streets, in political meetings and as a campaigning strategy. Representations were frequently positive. For example, the nation was habitually characterized as female, in the figure of Britannia. Theatricality remained a significant component of political expression throughout the century and female politicians were particularly effective at utilizing this method of campaigning and activism. Rogers has drawn attention to the example of Eliza Sharples, an early feminist and supporter of Richard Carlile who, in her public lectures, appeared as a series of female figures to signify the different aspects of her public duties and political theology. She spoke as Isis, the Egyptian goddess of fertility and wisdom standing on a floor of white thorn and laurel; as Eve; as Liberty, the symbol of republican tradition; and as Hypatia, to highlight the personal sacrifices demanded by her mission.[10] At the end of the century the ideals of the women's suffrage movement were dramatized in demonstrations and meetings, songs, plays, poems, novels, pageants, tableaux, banners and paintings. The movement relied heavily on processions and printed material to convey its message. The white, purple and green colours of the Women's Social and Political Union adorned flags, rosettes, ribbons and hats mimicking strategies used in electoral politics from the eighteenth century. Banners were used extensively, they were embroidered, stencilled or appliquéd and were created from within the movement. Women's traditional needlework skills were therefore employed in a collective and creative endeavour. The designs were heavily influenced by the arts and crafts movement and often projected simple and powerful images of women in the public and domestic sphere. However, the female political figure could also have more negative connotations. The figure of the dissolute or debauched woman often symbolized political corruption. The notion of 'petticoat government' implied unnatural or illicit female influence in public affairs or the domestic setting and was frequently associated with royal women who were viewed as interfering in politics. The Queen Caroline affair, Queen Adelaide's alleged interventions in the reform crisis and the accession of Victoria all resulted in a flurry of popular pamphlets, ballads, images and effigies of the queens utilizing the symbolism of petticoat government. However, even these images were not straightforwardly negative regarding women's involvement in politics. There was a tacit acknowledgement of female political power within the home, community and in the realm and these images demonstrate how such characterizations could be read and interpreted in multiple ways.

Women and Parliamentary Politics

Women had little formal engagement in 'high politics' for much of the nineteenth century. Some women – usually ratepayers and/or women of property – achieved the municipal vote from 1869 and were able to stand as candidates in parish and district councils from 1894. However, the opportunities for women's official participation in national politics have been characterized by many historians as being located in the 'political background'.[11] This interpretation is gradually being challenged as the extent and variety of women's activities in political parties, in elections, in parliament and in the political and diplomatic affairs of the wider world is being uncovered by new research.

The historiography of the Conservative party has traditionally neglected the role of women. Paradoxically, however, most general histories have acknowledged the essential and extensive contributions of 'Conservative women' to the party behind the scenes as organizers, motivators, administrators, moralizers and canvassers. Jarvis has lamented this lack of focus, arguing that there has been little systematic evaluation or quantification of the involvement of women in the party and this has therefore resulted in a definition of politics which views women's role as ancillary and supportive rather than dynamic and proactive.[12] Perhaps the most obvious manifestation of Conservative women 'behind the scenes' in the nineteenth century lay in their membership of the Primrose League, an organization founded in 1883 to broaden the support of the party following defeat in the 1880 general election. Membership of the League was open to 'all classes and creeds' and significantly it was the first major political organization to admit women members. Robb has claimed that women were central to the movement, establishing large numbers of habitations or branches.[13] Female membership increased from 1,300 in 1885 to over 48,000 in 1890 although it has been claimed that half a million Primrose Dames were involved in canvassing voters for the Tory cause.[14] There is dispute about the use the party made of this massive mobilization of women from all classes. Most historians have concentrated on the activities of the aristocratic women who organized local habitations rather than the contributions of the ordinary women members, many of whom were probably attracted to the associational and social activities of the League rather than viewing it as a conduit of political influence. Although some historians have asserted that the success of the League and its model of active citizenship enabled the Conservative party to incorporate women with ease after their enfranchisement in 1918, other commentators have seen the female members as rarely going beyond the boundaries of women's informal and indirect influence in politics. Even women's extensive role as canvassers during elections, especially in rural areas, is usually connected to the already extensive philanthropic activities of these aristocratic women.

Accounts of the Liberal party in the nineteenth century have paid even less regard to the contribution of women than those of the Conservatives, and Liberal women's organizations await a monograph devoted to their own history. This is in spite of the fact that female activists in local government, school boards and Poor Law boards were overwhelmingly Liberal in their political sympathies. The Women's Liberal Federation (WLF) established in 1887 from seventeen local women's associations which had been formed to assist the party at the general election of 1886. Hirshfield has contrasted the Liberal women's determination to establish a separate female association with the Conservative women's willingness to join a mixed sex enterprise, arguing that the Liberal women were keen to establish autonomy and were less likely to consider themselves auxiliaries.[15] Certainly the WLF took a proactive stance on issues such as the suffrage, Irish Home Rule, education, the Boer War and social activism. Current research has tended to focus on the elite women who headed the WLF including the Countess of Carlisle, who herself founded forty local women's Liberal associations in the northern counties and engineered the WLF's commitment to the cause of women's suffrage. There is less information on the mass of WLF members who undertook the mundane tasks of canvassing and spreading the Liberal message at a local level. Although the national leadership of the WLF favoured the agenda of the Radical wing of the party, there was a significant core of women who adopted a more traditionally Liberal programme. These tensions led to a split in the WLF in 1890 when Howard led a challenge to Gladstone's insistence that the extension of the suffrage should be postponed until the Home Rule Bill had been passed. Although Howard achieved her objective, the issue caused a schism resulting in the departure of fifty-six local associations and 10,000 members who eventually formed the rival Women's National Liberal Association. The split, which lasted until 1919, demonstrated the two routes open to women wishing to assume a dynamic role in nineteenth-century political parties. The WLF condemned the WNLA members as 'only appendages to men' and as 'mere servants of the Liberal Party' and remained independent from the parliamentary party including the adoption of a resolution in 1902 withdrawing support from anti-suffrage Liberal candidates.[16] The WNLA retained the more traditional approach of supporting the main, male, political party by social and organizational initiatives although they too showed themselves able to take independent perspectives on some policy matters such as the conduct of the war against the Boers and social reform issues.

The Independent Labour Party (ILP) was the only nineteenth-century political party to admit women on the same terms as men and the historiography of the emerging socialist and labour movements acknowledges the significant role women played in left-wing politics. Although the ILP welcomed women into its ranks it has been dismissed as a small regional organization dominated by intellectuals who intimidated many working-class women. However, work on the ILP in the West Riding has countered this impression, demonstrating the broad base of the movement and its role in the political education of young working-class girls.[17] Perhaps the best expression of the ILP's educative potential is the Socialist Sunday School movement in which women played a prominent role. Women were also active in other left-wing political groups of the late nineteenth century including the Social Democratic Federation and the Fabian Society. However, all of these organizations were overwhelmingly male in leadership and attitudes to female activists were ambiguous and sometimes hostile. Women, therefore, turned to their own organizations and both the Women's Labour League and the Women's Co-operative Guild provided political experience for socialist and feminist working-class women. Historians have emphasized how both associations were rooted in traditional assumptions about women's role in the traditional spheres of the home and the family. League and Guild policies focused on 'women-centred' social reforms including maternity benefits and the health and welfare of children. However, both organizations were committed to women's suffrage and working women made a significant political contribution at the local and neighbourhood level even though family and work commitments meant they were often unable to stand for formal office.[18]

Increasing attention has been paid in recent research to women's role in elections and electoral management. For aristocratic women who inherited estates or controlled them on behalf of a minor, the management of electoral interests was one manifestation of their social, economic and political role. Chalus has argued that elite women's role in elections was a natural one emanating from what she terms 'their traditional female roles and their place in a fluid and flexible political world'. Thus women were active in social politics (she defines this as the management of people and social activities for political ends): canvassing, managing campaigns, employing patronage and controlling family interests.[19] Women employed a range of strategies to exercise power including direct intervention. For example, in 1832 Ripon was contested for the first time for over one hundred years. Expectations were high that proprietorial influence could be thrown off and that the election would launch a new era of democratic politics. The opposition Liberal candidates centred their campaign on the unnatural and illegal influence of Elizabeth Lawrence, owner of the Studley Royal estate and proprietor of many burgage plots in Ripon. Although the Liberals went on to win the election, Lawrence succeeded in unseating them on petition and ruthlessly evicted many of her tenants who had voted against her candidates. Ripon was not contested again in her lifetime and although the estate and the borough had been managed by a single woman for over forty years the Tory interest was passed on intact. Women who owned land on a lesser scale were also able to influence their tenants to vote on their behalf and women owners of burgage plots were able to appoint male proxies to vote on their behalf. Women played a crucial role in canvassing.[20] The wives and kin of candidates and later the women of formal political party organizations undertook much of the drudgery of election campaigns. For example, Frances Smith managed the London campaign for her husband William who was standing as a candidate for Norwich in 1801. This involved canvassing those Norwich voters resident in London and the south-east and organizing their transport to the poll. Women lower down the social scale were also active in elections. Evidence from controverted election cases has uncovered women involved in electoral violence, in bribery and corruption and active as canvassers. The evidence of female witnesses into inquiries into corrupt practices in elections has led Chalus to term women the 'repositories of electoral memory'. Evidence has also been found that women of lower social groups often viewed the vote as a piece of family property and insisted on being canvassed by candidates for their political views during election times.[21]

Women's experience as voters before 1918 has tended to be overlooked by the prevailing historiography. As Clark commented, 'masculinity was the fundamental basis for citizenship'.[22] However, Hollis has highlighted the extent of women's voting at the local level in the nineteenth century.[23] Female ratepayers – by very definition single women householders, as married women could not legally own property – were able to vote in Poor Law unions after 1834 and received the municipal franchise in 1869, forming about 17 per cent of the electorate overall. The richness of women's experience as voters and later as candidates for all areas of local government needs to be explored further. Women's experience as party activists on school boards, as Poor Law guardians and in local government was mixed. For example, there were 128 women elected to English and Welsh school boards between 1892 and 1895. Many of those who stood for election were active feminists and concerned chiefly with the field of education. Emily Davies and Elizabeth Garrett were the first two women to sit on the London School Board and remained the only two until their resignation in 1873. However, the women on school boards were commonly assigned to committees concerned to further the domestic skills of girls and many were sidelined by their male colleagues. Such offices were dominated by middle-class, 'semi-professional' women who had gained experience through philanthropic work or social reform. Some recent work has considered the participation by working-class women in local politics. These female working-class activists tended to be concentrated in a few working-class boroughs, from well-off artisan or shopkeeping families. They were often married and encouraged to enter politics by already active husbands or relatives. Beginning as canvassers and fund-raisers for local political parties, women activists graduated to service on boards of guardians and vestries, and occasionally to positions on borough councils. Poorer women tended to be discouraged from political activity by burdensome living conditions and lack of opportunity.[24]

Women could, however, hold the highest political office, that of monarch. The accession of Victoria was a moment of great expectation and anxiety in Britain. Her age and gender contrasted with the behaviour of her dissolute predecessors and there was hope that she symbolized a regeneration of British politics. Her early interventions in politics culminating with the 'Bedchamber Crisis' in 1841 appeared to confirm the misgivings of the male establishment. Although historians have emphasized Victoria's conventional representation within the 'domestic family circle', recent research has demonstrated her continuing interventions in the political affairs of the nation. Indeed, when she emerged from her seclusion following the death of Albert in the late 1870s her ministers were careful to keep her involvement in politics from their more radical cabinet colleagues. When the extent of her increasingly conservative approach to politics was revealed to the public by the publication of her letters in the early twentieth century, it caused shock and indignation.[25] The queen was therefore able to hide her political engagement behind her apparent adherence to the ideology of domesticity.

Victoria had a particular interest in imperial affairs and women's involvement in international politics is an emerging research area for many historians. The challenges of empire attracted female missionaries, moralists and philanthropists. For example, women were active in the campaigns to end suttee and to repeal the Contagious Diseases Acts in India. However, the European political stage also interested women activists in the nineteenth century who were keen to export the 'English' attributes of liberalism, freedom, democracy and national self-determination to the beleaguered continent. Recent work on female support for Mazzini's campaign for Italian emancipation has illustrated that women's direct interventions included raising money to arm the Italian patriots. The further investigation of women's role in foreign affairs promises to lead to a reconsideration of nineteenth-century diplomacy and international relations.

Women and Pressure-Group Politics

Whilst women's contribution to parliamentary politics has only recently been acknowledged, their participation in the proliferation of pressure groups that were established from the late eighteenth century has received more recognition. The prevailing rhetoric of 'woman's mission' enabled middle-class women to partake in pressure group politics by portraying their work as an extension of philanthropic and humanitarian activities.[26] This was particularly apparent in women's participation in the anti-slavery movement, where there was a close relationship between the cause and evangelical religious groups, all participants sharing a strong evangelical and philanthropic commitment.[27] The women's anti-slavery movement did allow a distinctive political voice to emerge: women's groups were particularly committed to the immediate abolition of slavery in contrast to the more cautious male leadership who favoured a gradualist approach. Women participated in a robust petitioning movement and led a campaign for morally informed consumption persuading neighbours and kin to boycott slave-grown cotton and sugar. They also articulated their abhorrence of slavery through poetry, didactic novels and moral tales as well as more overtly political pamphlets. The movement was overwhelmingly middle-class and although there were attempts to mobilize working-class women, they were not regarded as equal participants. Large numbers of working women signed petitions but they could also react with some hostility to attempts by middle-class ladies to persuade them to abstain from purchasing cheap slave-grown produce. The anti-slavery movement provides an arena to trace the connections that women themselves made between the social relations of race, class and gender.[28]

The early-nineteenth-century fascination with political economy informed both the anti-slavery movement and the Anti-Corn Law League, another pressure group noted for an extensive female following. Harriet Martineau put the case for the abolition of slavery on economic grounds: that free waged labour would be more productive and profitable than slave labour. Simon Morgan has asserted that the League also 'politicised women's role in the household' linking the household economy to economic policy.[29] The women of the League employed specifically female modes of campaigning and fund-raising, notably charity bazaars, and Morgan has argued that these created a 'national community of women' working for a common cause. In both movements the politicization of the household and family economy brought political activism into the middle-class home.

Working-class politics in the 1830s and 1840s was characterized by campaigns against the 1834 Poor Law which ushered in the despised workhouse system. This agitation fed directly into Chartism. There remains considerable debate about the participation of women in the Chartist movement. Early historians of Chartism underplayed the role of women in part because of the desire to represent the movement as a serious political organization situating working-class politics within a modern, rational context. The contribution of female Chartists and the feminine modes of campaigning which centred around social occasions and ritualistic processions and parades were viewed as belonging to an older political tradition. Historians agree that the formal organization Chartism adopted after 1840 encouraged the retreat of women from politics back into domesticity. Chartist meetings took place in the masculine world of the pub and the increasingly militant confrontations also discouraged women's participation. The rhetoric of domesticity infused the movement and promoted the view of the home-centred, family-oriented woman.[30] However, that this emphasis on the home and family necessarily represented a retreat from politics has been challenged by the view that the prominence of domestic rhetoric in the Chartist movement signalled women's active participation in and formation of a new moral world. The family was therefore seen as arena of struggle in which women took a primary political role. Chartist women used a variety of languages to represent themselves in the public domain and not all reflect a straightforward acceptance of a subordinate role. It is also clear that women continued campaigning beyond the 1840s using a range of strategies including direct militant action, education and an emphasis on improved social conditions.[31] A clear expression of Chartist women's concern with advancing their family's quality of life is the growth of self-education movements and the rise of female Chartist temperance organizations after 1840. There was a close connection between these movements and Nonconformist religious groups but working-class women were also concerned to ensure family resources were not spent overwhelmingly on alcohol and tobacco.

For a large number of 'moral reformers' in the nineteenth century, the enhanced education of the masses held the key both to self-improvement and the quality of the nation's citizens. For female reformers there was a variety of reasons why the education of girls and women should be attended to. These included enlightenment ideas connecting education with the growth of civic virtue; the importance of educating girls as they would in turn, as mothers, cultivate the minds and manners of the future citizens of the nation; and the importance of educating women for future employment. Reformers were careful that to stress that the education of women and girls should not be seen as a threat or as damaging to the feminine character. Mary Wollstonecraft, for example, stressed that appropriate education, bringing with it the right association of ideas, could transform the female character. Martineau argued that to maintain a proper household women needed the best possible education, for ignorant women were the worst housekeepers. Further, every girl's potential should be fully exploited since not every woman would be supported by a husband or father. Towards the mid-century educational reform was associated more closely with the feminist movement, and education was connected with women's rights. In 1858, the *English Woman's Journal* promoted female education to widen women's employment opportunities and increase their independence. Although progress was made in the education of especially middle-class girls, over the course of the nineteenth century, such advances need to be considered alongside the perpetuation of gender stereotypes and emphasis on the traditional domestic qualities of women.[32]

The link between pressure-group politics and the rise of feminism has been noted by a range of writers. Kathryn Gleadle's work on radical Unitarians has demonstrated how their campaigns for legal reform, sexual reform and female education were increasingly linked with calls for female emancipation.[33] Like other early-nineteenth-century radical groups, the Unitarians were influenced by the French socialists Saint-Simon and Fourier. British utopian movements, such as Owenism, also had links with the radical Unitarians. Barbara Taylor, in her exploration of Owenism and early feminism, outlines the theoretical and practical contributions the movement made to contemporary debates about women's rights.[34] Owenism promised a 'new moral world' conditioned by the correct environment and was instrumental in the establishment of the early co-operative movement. Although women were attracted to Owenite associations many were critical of the movement's libertarian views on marriage. Women's disillusionment with the realities of communitarian life, which left them with the lion's share of domestic tasks, was a factor in the failure of the seven pioneering communities that had been established in the early nineteenth century. The failure of these early experiments in feminism and socialism did not prevent the emergence by the middle of the century of a thriving feminist sub-culture which fed into movements for sexual purity, moral reform and increasingly the suffrage.[35]

Feminists' concerns with the sexual oppression of women were expressed most vociferously during the campaigns against the Contagious Diseases Acts from the 1860s onwards. These Acts enabled magistrates to detain women suspected of prostitution for compulsory examinations and treatment. The Ladies National Association, led by Josephine Butler, frequently presented the Acts as a 'slave code' imposed on women, drawing attention to the limited rights of all women, not just prostitutes. The theme of male oppression was highlighted by campaigners as they became aware that the Acts set up new structures of male authority ensuring men's unimpeded access to women's bodies. Walkowitz has explored the gender tensions in the campaign between the female campaigners and male activists who discouraged the active participation of women, especially with regard to policy formation and public appearances.[36]

The recent historiography of the women's suffrage movement has sought to give a picture of a movement supported by a diverse range of social groups, widely dispersed throughout the British Isles, drawing upon broad cultural contexts and religious traditions. The research of Liddington and Norris on the contribution of working-class women led historians to challenge the dominant position of the Pankhursts and the Women's Social and Political Union in the history of the suffrage movement.[37] The role men played in mixed-sex suffrage groups and in male-only societies has challenged the traditional view of a movement organized solely by upper-middle-class, metropolitan women. The ideology of the movement has also been reconstructed. Holton has argued that the suffragists sought to use the vote to redefine the male polity rather than as an end in itself, creating a feminized democracy.[38] Attention has also been drawn to the connections made between socialism and feminism by those women who campaigned for adult as opposed to female suffrage. Rather than interpreting the women's suffrage movement as a brief middle-class flirtation with political activism, this broader history has helped to incorporate the struggle for the franchise into the history of women's pressure-group politics in the nineteenth century.

Gender and Community Politics

A significant focus of political activity for men and women in the nineteenth century was at the family, community and neighbourhood level. It has been argued that this 'informal' politics was on the wane in the nineteenth century but this argument has obscured the importance of the home, street-corner and public house as sites for political action. For women, social activities were often the main focus of their political activities. Organizing charity bazaars for the Anti-Corn Law League, managing Chartist tea-parties, attending lectures and debates, purchasing non-slave-grown goods or canvassing within the home at elections are all examples of how women's sociability was central to their political engagement. These casual circles of friends and relations replaced the increasingly formal political institutions which men used to extend their political influence. Recent work has uncovered the world of the political salon. Aristocratic political hostesses worked in 'active partnership' alongside their husbands bestowing patronage and political advantage.[39] The middle-class political salons were 'female-*managed* spaces' and straddled the private, semi-private and public realms.[40] For literate women, correspondence networks were an essential method of exchanging political news and views and also provided an acceptable route for lobbying male politicians. For working-class women doorstep gossip could lead to direct community action. Throughout the period women were prepared to protest against community or individual injustices, for example against high bread prices or questionable evictions. During elections the practice of 'exclusive dealing' was employed by working-class women who withdrew their custom from shopkeepers who would not support the popular candidate. Occasionally this consumer action could become more violent with personal assaults or attacks on property.

A clear illustration of how informal activities could be linked to political engagement is in the example of benevolent and charitable activities which occupied the lives of a wide range of women throughout the century. It has been claimed that women, excluded from all other areas of public and political life, colonized charities, organized missionary and evangelical campaigns and adopted moral causes as an alternative or as a distraction from their otherwise domestic lives.[41] However more nuanced approaches to the motives for women's philanthropic work have recently emerged, recognizing that many women's attitudes to benevolence was of a more political character than has been admitted by the established literature.[42] Women's justifications for their charitable endeavours were influenced by a wide and often conflicting range of ideological, theoretical and theological imperatives and thus there was no simple and straightforward link between domesticity and philanthropy.

This chapter has acknowledged the rich diversity of women's and men's participation in politics in the nineteenth century which is increasingly being recognized by historians. Researchers are rethinking their notion of 'the political' and in so doing are recovering a vibrant political culture in which the story of women's supposed exclusion from public life is being reassessed. At the same time, studies of masculinity are reflecting upon the role of men in politics and established models of gender and power relations are being reconstructed in the process.

NOTES

1.   S. Rowbotham, *Hidden from History* (London, 1973).
2.   L. Davidoff and C. Hall, *Family Fortunes: Men and Women of the English Middle Class 1780–1850* (London, 2002), p. 29.
3.   L. Kerber, 'Separate spheres, female worlds, woman's place: the rhetoric of women's history', *Journal of American History*, 75 (1988); A. Vickery, 'Golden age to separate spheres? A review of the categories and chronology of English women's history', *Historical Journal*, 36 (1993).
4.   K. Gleadle, ' "Our several spheres": middle-class women and the feminisms of early Victorian radical politics', in K. Gleadle and S. Richardson, eds, *Women in British Politics, 1760–1860: The Power of the Petticoat* (Basingstoke, 2000).
5.   J. W. Scott, 'Gender: a useful category of historical analysis', *American Historical Review*, 91 (1986).
6.   G. Bock, 'Women's history and gender history: aspects of an international debate', *Gender and History*, 1 (1989), p. 10.
7.   J. Hoff, 'Gender as a postmodern category of paralysis', *Women's History Review*, 3 (1994).
8.   A. Clark, *The Struggle for the Breeches: Gender and the Making of the British Working Class* (London, 1995).
9.   A. V. John and C. Eustance, eds, *The Men's Share? Masculinities, Male Support and Women's Suffrage in Britain* (London, 1997).
10. H. Rogers, ' "The prayer, the passion, and the reason" of Eliza Sharples: free-thought, women's rights and republicanism, 1835–52', in E. Yeo, ed., *Radical Femininity: Women's Self-Representation in the Public Sphere* (Manchester, 1998).
11. G. E. Maguire, *Conservative Women: A History of Women and the Conservative Party, 1874–1997* (Basingstoke, 1998), p. 5.

12. D. Jarvis, ' "Behind every great party": women and Conservatism in twentieth century Britain', in A. Vickery, ed., *Women, Privilege and Power: British Politics, 1750 to the Present* (Stanford, 2001), p. 291.

13. J. Robb, *The Primrose League, 1883–1906* (New York, 1942).

14. P. Jalland, *Women, Marriage and Politics, 1860–1914* (Oxford, 1986), pp. 215–16.

15. C. Hirshfield, 'Fractured faith: Liberal Party women and the suffrage issue in Britain, 1892–1914', *Gender and History*, 2 (1990).

16. C. Hirshfield, 'Liberal women's organizations and the war against the Boers, 1899–1902', *Albion*, 14 (1982), p. 34.

17. J. Hannam, 'In the comradeship of the sexes lies the hope of progress and social regeneration": women in the West Riding Independent Labour Party, c.1890–1914', in J. Rendall, ed., *Equal or Different: Women's Politics, 1800–1914* (Oxford, 1987).

18. P. Graves, *Labour Women: Women in British Working-Class Politics, 1918–1939* (Cambridge, 1994); P. Thane, 'Women in the British Labour Party and the construction of state welfare, 1906–1939', in S. Koven and S. Michel, eds, *Mothers of a New World: Maternalist Politics and the Origins of Welfare States* (London, 1993).

19. E. Chalus, ' "That epidemical madness": women and electoral politics in the late eighteenth century', in H. Barker and E. Chalus, eds, *Gender in Eighteenth-Century England: Roles, Representations and Responsibilties* (London, 1997).

20. E. Chalus, 'Women, electoral privilege and practice in the eighteenth century', in K. Gleadle and S. Richardson, eds, *Women in British Politics, 1760–1860: The Power of the Petticoat* (Basingstoke, 2000).

21. M. Cragoe, ' "Jenny rules the roost": women and electoral politics, 1832–68', in K. Gleadle and S. Richardson, eds, *Women in British Politics, 1760–1860: The Power of the Petticoat* (Basingstoke, 2000).

22. A. Clark, 'Gender, class and the constitution: franchise reform in England, 1832–1928', in J. Vernon, ed., *Re-Reading the Constitution: New Narratives in the Political History of England's Long Nineteenth Century* (Cambridge, 1996).

23. P. Hollis, *Ladies Elect: Women in English Local Government, 1865–1918* (Oxford, 1987).

24. K. Y. Stenberg, 'Working-class women in London local politics, 1894–1914', *Twentieth Century British History*, 9 (1998).

25. K. D. Reynolds, *Aristocratic Women and Political Society in Victorian Britain* (Oxford, 1998), p. 214.

26. A. Tyrrell, ' "Woman's mission" and pressure group politics (1825–1860)', *Bulletin of the John Rylands Library*, 63 (1980).

27. C. Midgley, *Women Against Slavery: The British Campaigns, 1780–1870* (London, 1992).

28. V. Ware, *Beyond the Pale: White Women, Racism and History* (London, 1992).

29. S. Morgan, 'Domestic economy and political agitation: women and the Anti-Corn Law League, 1839–46', in K. Gleadle and S. Richardson, eds, *Women in British Politics, 1760–1860: The Power of the Petticoat* (Basingstoke, 2000), p. 116.

30. J. Schwarzkopf, *Women in the Chartist Movement* (Basingstoke, 1991).

31. M. de Larrabeiti, 'Conspicuous before the world: the political rhetoric of Chartist women', in E. Yeo, ed., *Radical Femininity: Women's Self-Representation in the Public Sphere* (Manchester, 1998).

32. S. Delamont, 'The contradictions in ladies' education', in S. Delamont and L. Duffin, eds, *Nineteenth Century Woman: Her Cultural and Physical World* (London, 1978).

33. K. Gleadle, *The Early Feminists: Radical Unitarians and the Emergence of the Women's Rights Movement, 1831–51* (Basingstoke, 1995).

34. B. Taylor, *Eve and the New Jerusalem: Socialism and Feminism in the Nineteenth Century* (London, 1983).

35. P. Levine, *Feminist Lives in Victorian England: Private Roles and Public Commitment* (Oxford, 1990).

36. J. R. Walkowitz, *City of Dreadful Delight: Narratives of Sexual Danger in Late-Victorian London* (London, 1992).

37. J. Liddington and J. Norris, *One Hand Tied Behind Us: The Rise of the Women's Suffrage Movement* (London, 1978).

38. S. S. Holton, *Feminism and Democracy: Women's Suffrage and Reform Politics in Britain, 1900–1918* (Cambridge, 1986).

39. Reynolds, *Aristocratic Women*.

40. S. Richardson, ' "Well-neighboured houses": the political networks of elite women, 1780–1860', in K. Gleadle and S. Richardson, eds, *Women in British Politics, 1760–1860: The Power of the Petticoat* (Basingstoke, 2000).

41. F. K. Prochaska, *Women and Philanthrophy in Nineteenth-Century England* (Oxford, 1980).

42. K. Sutherland, 'Hannah More's counter-revolutionary feminism', in K. Everest, ed., *Revolution in Writing: British Literary Responses to the French Revolution* (Milton Keynes, 1991).

FURTHER READING

The best examinations of women and politics are to be found in recent collections of essays including: K. Gleadle and S. Richardson, eds, *Women in British Politics, 1760–1860: The Power of the Petticoat* (2000); J. Rendall, ed., *Equal or Different: Women's Politics, 1800–1914* (1987); A. Vickery, ed., *Women, Privilege and Power: British Politics, 1750 to the Present* (2001); and E. Yeo, ed., *Radical Femininity: Women's Self-Representation in the Public Sphere* (1998). For the contribution of men and the idea of manliness in politics see: A. V. John and C. Eustance, eds, *The Men's Share? Masculinities, Male Support and Women's Suffrage in Britain* (1997); L. Davidoff and C. Hall, *Family Fortunes: Men and Women of the English Middle Class, 1780–1850* (2002); and A. Clark, *The Struggle for the Breeches: Gender and the Making of the British Working Class* (1995). For varied interpretations of feminism and women's rights in the nineteenth century consider: K. Gleadle, *The Early Feminists: Radical Unitarians and the Emergence of the Women's Rights Movement, 1831–51* (1995); J. Rendall, *The Origins of Modern Feminism: Women in Britain, France and the United States, 1780–1860* (1985); O. Banks, *Faces of Feminism: A Study of Feminism as a Social Movement* (1981); P. Levine, *Feminist Lives in Victorian England: Private Roles and Public Commitment* (1990); and S. S. Holton, *Feminism and Democracy: Women's Suffrage and Reform Politics in Britain, 1900–1918* (1986). The activities of elite women have been thoroughly explored by K. D. Reynolds, *Aristocratic Women and Political Society in Victorian Britain* (1998), and the most comprehensive account of women and local government is supplied by P. Hollis, *Ladies Elect: Women in English Local Government, 1865–1918* (1987). Provocative studies of women and radical politics include: H. Rogers, *Women and the People: Authority, Authorship and the Radical Tradition in Nineteenth Century England* (2000); J. Schwarzkopf, *Women in the Chartist Movement* (1991); and B. Taylor, *Eve and the New Jerusalem: Socialism and Feminism in the Nineteenth Century* (1983). A pioneering contribution to the history of the suffrage movement was J. Liddington and J. Norris, *One Hand Tied Behind Us: The Rise of the Women's Suffrage Movement* (1978) which appraised the role of working women. For recent new approaches to the study of women's suffrage see M. Joannou and J. Purvis, eds, *The Women's Suffrage Movement: New Feminist Perspectives* (1998).

CHAPTER ELEVEN

Political Thought

GREGORY CLAEYS

Nineteenth-century British political thought is dominated by a series of variations on one leading theme: the advent, either as threat or promise, of democracy. Prior to 1789 Britons had prided themselves on a constitutional settlement which notionally divided power between the three great estates as represented by the monarch, Lords and Commons, which secured a greater measure of political and civil freedom than continental nations possessed, and encouraged entrepreneurial activity so far that Britain had become the wealthiest society in the world by the late eighteenth century. The unchangeable nature of this constitutional settlement was challenged first by the American, then the French, Revolutions. Thereafter throughout the following century there was constant pressure from without to reform parliament, and in particular to extend the franchise, resulting in the Reform Acts of 1832, 1867 and 1884. These were accompanied by conservative resistance to sharp or dramatic political change, and a championing of the stabilizing and creative role played by political and intellectual elites. They were also paralleled by reform proposals which emphasized that the problems created by commercial society, and even more industrialization, especially poverty and large-scale unemployment, were not susceptible to political solutions as such, but required new schemes of economic organization. This perspective was shared by certain types of conservative thinker as well as most socialists, and in the last quarter of the nineteenth century pressure towards collectivism, towards state interference in the name of social and economic improvement and protection, and towards a more positive image of the state, came widely to displace the older 'negative' image of the state and of liberty as freedom from state interference. 'Political' thought, which cannot arbitrarily be separated from 'social' thought and intellectual history more generally, came increasingly to be determined by conceptions of the ideal society and economic organization in the last decades of the century. The key concept which had dominated political thinking from the revolutionary era onwards – *liberty* – thus by the 1880s came to be modified under the impact of an altered climate of social and economic expectation, in which there was a greater emphasis upon *equality*, and utilizing public resources to improve public well-being. This in turn engendered both attempts to redefine liberty as a cardinal political concept, and demands for its reduction or realignment in status to account for the popularity of competing principles.

The French Revolution and its Aftermath

The debate in Britain about the nature and meaning of the principles inspired and popularized by the French Revolution commenced with the publication of Edmund Burke's *Reflections on the Revolution in France* in November 1790. Writing against the radical philosopher Richard Price, Burke emphasized three main themes: that the principles of the Revolution had arisen out of the 'nakedness and solitude of metaphysical abstraction'; that while the 'real rights of man' did exist, it was only meaningful to discuss civil, rather than any pre-existing natural, rights; and that the British constitution rested on prescriptive right, which included a binding constitutional settlement agreed in 1688 and not alterable thereafter, with public order resting upon the twin pillars of the 'Corinthian capital of polished society', the aristocracy and the established church. In addition, Burke gave stress to the importance of local attachment, the primacy of national identity compared to cosmopolitanism, and the desirability of gradual, organic social and political evolution.

Against this view Thomas Paine's *Rights of Man* (1791–2) provided the main radical response. Against Burke Paine offered six leading points:

(1) The settlement of 1688 was not binding as such if contemporaries sought to alter it, for no generation could tyrannize over another.
(2) Natural rights did exist which were founded in God's granting of the world to mankind, as described in Genesis, which account established 'one point, the unity of man; by which I mean that men are all of one degree, & consequently that all men are born equal, and with equal natural rights'.
(3) Only a republic, with an elected executive, would recognize and could secure the translation of these rights into civil rights.
(4) Only a written constitution, proposed by a constitutional assembly and ratified by the population at large, could provide the basis for the effective exercise of a democratic franchise.
(5) The free commercial intercourse of nations was compatible with democracy, and posed no threat to republican virtue.
(6) The extension of such a system of commerce, coupled with the abolition of monarchy, might eliminate existing conflicts between nation-states and secure universal peace.

The debate over these fundamental principles grew extremely heated in 1791–3, and was only curtailed after war with France broke out in early 1793, and government repression curtailed freedom of the press and assembly in 1794–5, quashing a substantial popular reform movement. The publication of Malthus's *Essay on Population* in 1798 both indicated the closing shots of late-eighteenth-century political debate and heralded the reshaping of assumptions in the nineteenth century. Malthus's chief British target was William Godwin, whose *Enquiry concerning Political Justice* (1793) had suggested that indefinite moral improvement might take place if individuality and universal benevolence were given central stress in an agrarian republic in which commercial exchange had been largely abolished in favour of distribution according to need, parish organization had replaced national government, marriage had been superseded and the powers of mind given scope to rein in the lower passions. Malthus's famous ratios – of population developing geometrically, and food production arithmetically – were intended to suggest that wherever free rein was given to sexual passions, population growth would accelerate dramatically. Chiefly the 'positive' checks of famine, war and disease inhibited population, though 'preventive' checks, particularly foresight in commencing and adding to a family, might operate conjointly. Malthus thus made two substantial points for contemporaries: (a) that changes in constitution or institution would not address the fundamental cause of social disorder, poverty, which resulted from over-population; and (b) that human beings were essentially driven by passion rather than reason, and their behaviour was thus not modifiable to a substantial degree. Malthus did much both to instigate a more punitive attitude towards poverty, resulting in the Poor Law Amendment Act of 1834, and to popularize an image of society as a competition for survival among economically viable units, which would underpin the Darwinian world-view during the last third of the century.

The Development of Liberalism and Radicalism

Philosophic Radicalism

By the 1820s Whiggism was increasingly giving way to the growing predominance of laissez-faire liberalism, on the one hand, and plebeian radicalism, on the other. The utilitarian liberals, led by Jeremy Bentham (1748–1832) and James Mill (1773–1836), added to a hedonistic psychology the moral and political duty to uphold the 'greatest happiness of the greatest number', whose achievement was the means by which actions were to be judged. In his *Essay on Government* (1819) Mill upheld the extension of the franchise, the secret ballot and more frequent elections, and rejected the argument that popular representative institutions could only flourish in a balanced constitution. Mill's hostility to the aristocracy took the form of the charge that their 'sinister interests', defended by powerful oligarchies when in power, undermined the capacity of government to serve the interests of the majority. (The stabilizing role of traditional political elites was in turn defended against Mill by the historian Macaulay in an influential article in the *Edinburgh Review* in 1829.)

A far more influential utilitarian was James Mill's son John Stuart Mill (1806–74), who became the leading political economist (*Principles of Political Economy*, 1848), social and political theorist (*On Liberty*, 1858; *Considerations on Representative Government*, 1863) and philosopher (*System of Logic*, 1843; *Utilitarianism*, 1861) of his generation. Central to J. S. Mill's political thought was the belief, much influenced by Tocqueville's *Democracy in America* (1836, 1840), not only that American-style democracy would inevitably be achieved in Britain, but that its realization constituted a threat to individual liberty, through the 'tyranny of the majority' over public opinion in particular. Moreover, Mill believed that the onward progressive development of society required the protection of intellectual elites, and their willingness in turn to defy customary and traditional mores. These themes were detailed in the chapter on 'Individuality' in *On Liberty*, which is more generally concerned with delineating the justifiable sphere of social and political interference in individual conduct, according to whether one's own conduct actually harms others. *On Liberty* is famously concerned to shield eccentricity, particularly of opinion, and notably of religious heterodoxy, from over-zealous bigots. Its essentially secular orientation is a useful indicator of the importance of religion and religious controversy, and especially the growing power of Nonconformity, to ideas of the state throughout this period. Its defence of the leading role of a 'clerisy' is shared by thinkers such as Coleridge and Matthew Arnold (in *Culture and Anarchy*, 1869); its targeting of evangelical Christians as the up-and-coming zealots is shared by Arnold, among others. Most of the works of Mill's maturity represent variations thereon: *Representative Government*, for instance, centrally argues for a scheme of proportional representation, as well as other mechanisms such as plural voting and examinations of electors, for giving greater political influence to minorities; while *Utilitarianism* principally defends the 'higher' pleasures of the intellect and imagination against those of the body, as a means of defending the cultural influence of intellectual elites. Yet Mill, much influenced by Saint-Simonian historicism, was also willing to concede that the existing state of society did not represent the final stage of human progress, and even suggested in later editions of the *Principles of Political Economy* that the future might witness a 'stationary state' in which population would stabilize, greater priority would be given to individual development over wealth-acquisition, and various forms of communitarian socialist experimentation (particularly of the Fourierist type) might point the way to more advantageous social relationships. (He pointedly, if somewhat ambiguously, styled himself a 'Socialist' in his *Autobiography*, 1874.) Mill was also unusual in arguing, against his father's view in the *Essay on Government*, for the extension of the franchise and other rights to women, the case for which he presented in *The Subjection of Women* (1869).

Plebeian and middle-class radicalism

Following its suppression in the mid-1790s plebeian radicalism was rapidly revived after 1816, and before 1832 was dominated by the writings of William Cobbett (1763–1835), whose virulent opposition to placemen, parliamentary corruption, paper money and financiers, cotton lords and middlemen, the deleterious influence of the 'great wen', London, and exorbitant taxation inspired a generation of activists. Central to Cobbett's vision of England is an image of rural Britain, detailed in *Rural Rides* (1831), in which the yeoman class of small farmers co-exist harmoniously with humane landlords, pre-Malthusian parsons and benign governors. An anti-industrial, anti-commercial bias predominates in Cobbett's writings, though other radicals of the period, such as Francis Place, who was close to James Mill, were pro-Malthusian and willing to accept large parts of the Ricardian canon respecting the essential nature and operations of the economy. This division over economic principles continued to be of central importance during the Chartist period (1836–58), for many Chartists urged some form of protection for domestic, and particularly factory, labour, and found little sympathy from the most important middle-class reform movement of the period, the Anti-Corn Law League. Though Chartist leaders like O'Connor, Lovett and Bronterre O'Brien were agreed on the six-point programme of annual parliaments, universal male suffrage, equal electoral districts, payment of, and the abolition of property qualifications for, MPs, and the secret ballot, they disagreed over much else. Notable areas of disagreement were the issue of whether violence was required to achieve such reforms or whether 'moral force' alone was either permissible or feasible; and whether the unemployed poor should be returned to 'colonies' on the land, or whether socialistic planks might be added to the platform, as they commonly were during and after 1848. Though there were linkages to mid-seventeenth-century republicanism, moreover, few plebeian radicals in this period espoused republican ideals, and hostility to the aristocracy by and large remained stronger among working-class activists than antagonism to the monarchy per se, particularly under Victoria.

Plebeian and middle-class radicalism began to merge in the decades after 1867 as the franchise was widened, and large parts of *The Radical Programme* (1885), with its plea for state intervention to assist industry, education and social welfare, and its emphasis upon a four-fold programme of popular local government, free education, agricultural smallholdings and graduated taxation, would have found enthusiastic support amongst Chartists of an earlier generation. Mid-Victorian radicalism was dominated by two figures, Richard Cobden (1804–65) and John Bright (1811–89), the pioneers of the Anti-Corn Law agitation, who opposed pleas for intervention, and concentrated instead on popularizing the principles of free trade and hostility to empire, the extension of which they saw as the chief cause of European wars in the preceding 150 years, and which was captured in Bright's celebrated phrase, 'force is no remedy'.

Another strand in mid- and late-Victorian radicalism was the individualist liberalism of Herbert Spencer (1820–1903), which emanated not only from a commitment to laissez-faire, but also from an evolutionary stress on the survival of the fittest, which meant for Spencer that efforts to relieve poverty interfered with the natural process of separating out the fit from the unfit. Commencing with *Social Statics* (1850), Spencer sought across a wide range of works to offer a scientific grounding for morality and obligation, governed increasingly by evolutionary principles, which led him to rescind earlier support for both the much wider extension for the franchise and land nationalization, though his hostility to the state remained undiminished, and opposition to state intervention, collectivism and socialism of all types remains the hallmark of his political thought. Eventually appearing collected in ten volumes as the 'Synthetic Philosophy', Spencer's works tirelessly championed the idea that social progress from militarism and barbarism to civilization and industrialization relied upon individual effort and initiative and the curtailment of idleness, weakness and inefficiency, and his growing embrace of evolution displaced many of his earlier radical ideals.

A further form of radicalism, in the sense of the extension of the language of rights, was feminism, which developed substantially from the late 1860s onwards in the form of demands for equal educational opportunity for women as well as the vote. Commencing from the foundations laid in Mary Wollstonecraft's *Vindication of the Rights of Woman* (1792), assisted by the socialist William Thompson's *Appeal on Behalf of One-Half the Human Race, Women* (1824), the modern feminist movement proper emerged from the late 1860s onwards and published a variety of works on the extension of the franchise and related themes, notably by Harriet Taylor, Helen Mill, Millicent Garrett Fawcett and others. By the late 1880s feminist argument had broadened considerably as the effects of both social liberalization and Social Darwinism and eugenics made discussion of birth control publicly possible, and engendered a wide-ranging, sometimes acrimonious, debate about the relationship between sexual and marital choice, the family and child-rearing, and their implications for the theory of the state.

Non-Radical and Tory Critics of Liberalism

The early decades of the century witnessed a Romantic conservative reaction to the expansion of commercial and industrial society, of which Samuel Taylor Coleridge (1772–1834) and Robert Southey (1774–1843) were the most important representatives. In his *Lay Sermon* (1817) Coleridge emphasized the need to counterbalance the effects of a rampant 'spirit of commerce' by a landed class committed to treating landed property as stewards of the common good, and willing to educate, instruct and assist the lower orders, and to ensure the regulation of conditions in manufacturing industries. *On the Constitution of Church and State* (1829) gave greater stress to the need for a guiding role to be played by an intellectual elite, the 'clerisy', which would counteract the effects of commerce by instilling intellectual and religious values which stressed a greater respect for humanity and for national rather than merely class interests. Like Coleridge, and also Wordsworth, Southey gave priority to protecting the established Anglican church as the moral foundation of the constitution, but he was more willing to flirt with socialistic solutions to the problem of poverty.

By far the most influential of the early critics of Benthamism was Thomas Carlyle (1795–1881). His rigid puritan upbringing battered by religious doubt, Carlyle by the late 1820s found solace in German idealism, which he used to stress the need for religious vitality and the reformation of manners instead of the extension of the franchise; and a guarantee of the right to work for the lower orders, in exchange for their obedience to a ruling group possessed of a strong sense of social duty, whose position was not to be challenged by democratic reforms. The religious ideals were first explored in *Sartor Resartus* (1834), but Carlyle's main social and economic themes were first outlined in the essays, 'Characteristics' (1831), 'The Sign of the Times' (1829) and 'Chartism' (1839), and fully explored in *Heroes and Hero-Worship* (1840) and *Past and Present* (1843). One central theme unifies Carlyle's social and political thought: the need to settle the issues of poverty and unemployment by offering a guaranteed lifetime of employment to the labouring classes, in return for their unstinting loyalty to a virtuous class of supervisor-governors. Partly influenced by the Saint-Simonian socialists, Carlyle proposed a guaranteed right of employment as early as 1831, but offered a fully-fledged scheme only in *Past and Present*. Like the Saint-Simonians, he envisioned the new governing class being drawn principally from the industrial elite, 'a corporation of the best and the bravest', not the old landed aristocracy. 'Democracy', the Chartist goal, he rejected as only a corollary of 'anarchic' individualist laissez-faire, and as a plea for mere institutional, 'mechanical' reform which needed to be supplanted by an emphasis upon moral and particularly religious reformation. But the Chartist claim for 'a fair day's wages for a fair day's work', the heart of the 'condition of England problem', Carlyle did concede. In *Heroes and Hero-Worship* he outlined a theory of the role exercised by authority over opinion, stressing the religious core of true leadership. In *Past and Present* he clothed his reform ideals in medieval dress, urging that a feudal conception of honour, rather than the mere 'cash-nexus' of commercial society, serve to bind leader and led in the new moral order, and arguing that a religious devotion to work alone could provide sufficient motivation from below to ensure the successful working of the 'organisation of labour.' The dominating principle of the new economic order was to be regulation, in the shape of factory, mine, sanitary and other legislation, free emigration, and the formation of regimented industrial armies guided by a chivalric ethos, with workers guaranteed a permanent labour contract, though shirkers would be punished.

A writer much influenced by Carlyle, John Ruskin (1819–1900) would extend these ideals to a later generation, linking a Carlylean interventionist agenda with an aesthetic critique of modernity and in the process becoming the most influential single thinker on the generation which founded the Labour party. Ruskin's initial critique of commercial society focused on the effects of a narrow division of labour, and demanded, in the famous chapter in *The Stones of Venice* (1851) entitled 'The Nature of Gothic', the freeing up of the creative powers of the individual worker, and a reduction of mechanical, routinized production. In *Unto This Last* (1862), however, Ruskin turned to the critique of political economy as such, and attempted to redefine key terms, particularly 'wealth', in an effort to prove that that the acquisition of wealth was 'finally possible only under certain moral conditions of society'. Practically, *Unto This Last* called for government-run training schools; the establishment of some state-funded manufactories producing chiefly unadulterated foodstuffs; training for the unemployed; and old-age pensions. Like Carlyle, Ruskin agreed that permanent employment contracts were desirable, in the manner of the clergy, army or navy, and wages should be regulated rather than rising or falling according to market fluctuation. Like the Owenite socialists, he urged that the exchange of produce take place according to an equivalency of the value of labour and raw materials in the articles exchanged.

Later Conservatism

'Toryism' gave way to 'Conservatism' in the 1820s and 1830s. Thereafter British Conservatism underwent two substantial changes during this period: the embracing of free trade under Peel in 1846, resulting in the repeal of the Corn Laws; and an increasing commitment to democracy, particularly under Disraeli, which ensured the electoral viability of a Conservative agenda which remained surprisingly resilient even in the twentieth century. By this means Conservatism ceased to be the philosophical defence of the landed aristocracy, and while remaining committed to ideals of order, both secular and religious, became associated with an expanding imperialist agenda and strengthened monarchy in the 1870s and later. This success emanated in part from associating Whiggism and Liberalism with a more punitive approach to poverty and a less sympathetic view of the working classes generally. In his *Vindication of the English Constitution* (1835), for instance, Disraeli attacked the Whigs and Utilitarians as slavishly devoted to an industrial oligarchy, and described the Tories as the only 'really democratic party of England', devoted to the interests of the whole people. These ideals found widespread acceptance in three popular novels: *Coningsby* (1844), *Sybil* (1845) and *Tancred* (1847). This emphasis on virtue and status rather than the ties of the 'cash nexus' also coincided with a persistence in social deference noted by writers like Walter Bagehot (*The English Constitution*, 1867), for whom it represented the key element in explaining British constitutional stability and the special path of peaceful political development throughout the period.

Conservative elitism in the late-Victorian period had to respond to a variety of developments, including the extension of the franchise in 1867 and 1884, the growing appeal of the American model, and the 'lessons' of imperial expansion. Many later Conservatives, such as Henry Maine (1822–88) (*Popular Government*, 1886), who led Tory intellectual resistance to Gladstonian Liberalism after the 1884 Reform Act, remained opposed to universal suffrage, drawing upon studies of both the supposedly deleterious effects (corruption, electoral manipulation) of American democracy, and the experience of colonial rule, notably in India. Maine, the Irish historian W. E. H. Lecky (*Democracy and Liberty*, 1896) and W. H. Mallock (*The New Republic*, 1877), in particular, stressed the need for intelligence and ability in government (bolstered by Darwinian arguments from the 1870s onwards), the centrality of private property and the importance (*pace* Burke) of the maintenance of custom and tradition. Faced with the evident retreat of aristocracy in the late Victorian epoch, Conservatives turned to a vindication of inequality *per se* as providing incentives to labour, and a robust defence of individualism against the growing collectivism of the era. These themes were increasingly linked from the 1870s to the acquisition of empire and the renewed importance of monarchy in an imperial constitution. Notably in Bagehot's *The English Constitution* (1867), the distinctiveness of Britain's successful emergence into modernity with its aristocracy and monarchy intact was identified with both the naturally deferential character of the populace towards traditional forms of authority, and demurral before the visible pomp and circumstance of monarchical government. As Disraelian Conservatism reached its zenith in the 1880s, works like Sir John Seeley's *The Expansion of England* (1883) offered a justification for the extension of what was increasingly understood as racial Anglo-Saxondom throughout the globe.

The Origins and Development of Socialism

British socialist thought in the nineteenth century can be divided into two main phases: the early writers, notably Robert Owen, whose influence was greatest between 1820 and 1845; and later agitators such as William Morris and H. M. Hyndman, who were leading propagandists during the 'socialist revival' of the 1880s and 1890s, and whose principal competitors were the anti-revolutionary socialists of the Fabian Society.

Robert Owen (1771–1858) was a wealthy cotton-spinner interested in educational and factory reform. Finding his efforts frustrated, he began around 1816 to propose rehousing the unemployed poor (and eventually the entire population) in large estates in the countryside, containing around 2,000 inhabitants, where labour would alternate between agricultural and industrial activities, and property and profits would be shared in common. This communitarian ideal, proposed in its most elaborate form in *The Book of the New Moral World* (1836–44), eventually included a scheme for the complete reorganization of society according to the principle of age, with all inhabitants passing through a regime of work, supervising others and governing their community, thus obviating any need for elections to office, while encompassing what Owen regarded as the essence of democratic practice, the right of all to rule. This scheme was never implemented, and most of Owen's followers wished to link more traditional ideas of democracy to socialist economic organization.

The 'socialist revival' of the 1880s was a response to agricultural and industrial depression as well as the growing popularity of Marxian socialism on the Continent. Amongst the leading socialist propagandists, William Morris (1834–96) achieved the greatest popularity. Converted in part by a reading of J. S. Mill's unfinished 'Chapters on Socialism' (*Fortnightly Review*, 1879), Morris embarked on a series of lecture tours in the mid-1880s to publicize his embracing of the principles of 'association' against those of 'competition', and published his most extensive programme in the utopian romance, *News from Nowhere* (1890). Morris's lectures wedded Ruskinian aesthetic themes to a revolutionary socialist programme. Art in the future order was to be central to human experience, and all construction and labour governed according to principles of artistic creativity. A philo-medievalist like Ruskin, Morris harkened back to a time when 'all men were more or less artists', and the instinct for beauty was socially ingrained in all. His own practical efforts at wood-carving, stained-glass production, furniture construction and other crafts were dominated by medieval motifs, and were sold through his own company. Like Owen and other early socialists, Morris was strongly anti-urban. Twenty-first-century London is the setting for *News from Nowhere*, but the city has shrunk considerably, and the population is rehoused more equitably across the country, such that villages have been expanded to a more optimal size. The theoretical aspects of the text focus on two key problems: the organization of the economy; and politics. Exchange as such has been abolished, and commodities are produced in plenty, subject to customary or local regulation, but without any means of enforcement. There are different standards of goods produced, though it is unclear why the less good would be preferred. Politically, Morris describes crime and most sources of social disorder as having disappeared with the supersession of private property. Local 'Mote' meetings take key decisions, but attempt to avoid any tyranny of the majority over the minority. Individuality of taste in dress, food and so on is encouraged. Machinery is in use wherever it serves to alleviate labour. What is distinctive in Morris's socialism is thus both the much greater attention given to the aesthetic than most schools of socialism, and a quasi-anarchist plea for the rights of minorities against the dangers of majoritarianism. A similar stress on liberty is evident in the works of Edward Carpenter (1844–1929).

To a much greater extent than Morris, H. M. Hyndman (1842–1922) (*England For All*, 1881), was indebted to Marx for his socialist theory, and offered a more orthodox rendition of the culmination of the revolutionary process in the establishment of a dictatorship of the proletariat, and the nationalization and centralization of the land, the means of credit, transportation and industry. On the philosophical side Ernest Belfort Bax produced a range of texts explaining the materialist conception of history and the Marxist programme. More influential, however, was Fabianism. The Fabian Socialists (*Fabian Essays*, 1889) gave stress to a gradualist, bureaucratic, elitist and reformist agenda. Founded in 1884, the Fabian Society took its name from a Roman general reputed to have worn his enemies down by steady and determined resistance rather than large-scale battles. Comprising leading intellectuals like Beatrice and Sydney Webb, and novelists like H. G. Wells and George Bernard Shaw, it placed great stress on the future role of a trained managerial class of experts dedicated to bureaucratic efficiency, recruited meritocratically, introducing reforms gradually and by rational argument, and supportive of democracy in the workplace as well as in politics. Though some Fabians placed greater stress on the role to be played by a guiding elite, all agreed that the state under socialism would embody the collective wisdom and organization of society dedicated to serving the general good. Fabianism thus retained a substantial *political* emphasis in contrast to a markedly anti-partisan and anti-political emphasis in many other forms of nineteenth-century socialism.

The Impact of Evolution

There was no single 'Social Darwinist' politics which adopted evolutionary premises to support one set of political conclusions, notably, as is often assumed, an extreme form of competitive laissez-faire and non-interventionism. Instead, the theory of natural selection was used by writers across the political spectrum to bolster concepts of both competitive individualism, where the idea of the 'survival of the fittest' in animal life seemed applicable to economic efficiency, and socialist ideals of a higher ethical community in which humanity proved its superiority to the lower forms of life. Most prominently among the individualist liberals, Spencer contended that the state's alleviation of poverty would curtail the natural process of weeding out the 'fit' from the 'unfit,' which could alone secure the future evolutionary development of the human species. But although this militant anti-interventionism is often falsely identified with 'Social Darwinism' as such, many other deductions from evolutionary premises were offered by other writers. Liberals like Bagehot (*Physics and Politics*, 1872) argued that the freedoms supported by liberal democracy were most conducive to the flourishing of evolutionary variety and thus higher development, with competition in the world of ideas engendering a similar conceptual evolution. New Liberals like David Ritchie described the interventionist state as an institution fostering evolutionary growth by freeing individuals from a crude struggle for existence, while Benjamin Kidd (*Social Evolution*, 1894) described humanity's goals in terms of the supersession of self-interested behaviour and its replacement by altruism. Socialists like Alfred Russel Wallace similarly contended that a collectivist social and economic agenda followed logically from Darwinian premises. Some writers, notably Karl Pearson, also wedded socialist to eugenic principles from the 1870s onwards, with the founder of eugenics, Francis Galton, also presuming that the conscious control of biological evolution implied a greatly expanded role for the state.

From Liberalism to New Liberalism

The most substantial transformation in liberal thought to occur in the late nineteenth century involved a reassessment of the central concept of the ideology, liberty. Traditionally defined negatively as freedom *from* the interference of the state, liberty after 1880 was increasingly seen in a more positive sense as the freedom *to* develop human capacities and attributes. The most important corollary of this idea was that the state could act as an agency of positive social good, as the guardian of a common good or higher ethical community not sought by particular classes or interests, but discernible and defensible in terms of the wider, long-term, organic and evolutionary interests of the entire society. Individual liberty thus might be viewed not as contradictory to the existence of the state, but, as the philosopher Thomas Hill Green (1836–82) emphasized, as being realized within it. When the term 'New Liberalism' was coined in the *Progressive Review* by Herbert Samuel, in addition, it was assumed to give greater stress to 'the need for important economic reforms, aiming to give a positive significance to the "'equality'" which figures in the democratic triad of liberty, equality, fraternity.'

Amongst the New Liberal writers, who included the sociologist Leonard Hobhouse and the economist J. A. Hobson, there was widespread agreement that an evolutionary approach to social development required the recognition that society ought to aim at a higher ethical development, and in so doing ought to address 'the social problem' by increasing state intervention towards the satisfaction of aggregate social utilities. The exact scope or sphere of state responsibility was however a matter of some dispute among New Liberal writers. Green preferred that old age and unemployment insurance be provided by intermediary organizations such as trade unions and co-operatives. Hobson, who extended Ruskinian humanist themes in an evolutionary direction, stressed the value of community as a liberal ideal, and came after 1914 to see the state as the best agency for providing the services of health, education, insurance and pensions.

During the same period a number of writers, commonly described as 'Idealist', attempted to recraft a number of key intellectual themes by departing from the mainstream empiricist tradition and, often with the assistance of Plato or Hegel, offering a more metaphysical foundation for political thought. Idealist philosophy gave particular stress to the realization of human potential within the community rather than in isolation from it, and to the growth of rationality through history. This involved the increasing embrace of a mutually agreed conception of the social good which would instil a duty-bound sacrifice of individual interest to the community, rather than capitulation to the sordid interests of an egoistically driven civil society. Green, the leading Idealist writer, attacked the dominant Millite orthodoxy of laissez-faire, utilitarianism and empiricism by positing the existence of an eternal subject which formed the basis of all thought and the ground of will and choice. Individuals are considered in the richness of their social relations, instead of merely atomically juxtaposed. The ground of action is not, as for the utilitarians, merely desire for pleasure, but a desire for self-realization in the context of community, which thus acknowledges the primacy of social duties over individual desires and interests. In *Lectures on the Principles of Political Obligation* (1879–80) Green assumed that a society was to be judged (as Mill had increasingly conceded) by the type of character it engendered, and argued that only a reinforcement of obligation, rather than the more traditional language of natural rights, could foster such an end. While he preferred action by voluntary organizations, Green's thought encouraged a more positive idea of state interference on the basis of the fact that society collectively could assist in promoting moral life, and was developed by writers such as Bernard Bosanquet (1848–1923). This trend towards both collectivism and state interference was thus shared by socialists and New Liberals, as well as many types of Social Darwinists.

Conclusion: Leading Themes and Problems in the Interpretation of Nineteenth-Century British Political Thought

The principal transformations in nineteenth-century British political thought were once conceived of as having stemmed chiefly from the interaction of the Benthamite school with various streams of philanthropic and other idealism which pushed incrementally, via factory, labour and humanitarian reforms of various kinds, towards the vision of a collectivist state by the end of the century. This hypothesis, outlined in A. V. Dicey's *Lectures on the Relation between Law and Public Opinion in the Nineteenth Century* (1905), plots the succession of 'old Toryism' to 'Benthamism or Individualism' to 'Collectivism'. According to Dicey, the last phase commenced around 1860, and was defined in terms of a greater commitment to equality of opportunity as well as 'faith in the benefit to be derived by the mass of the people from the action or intervention of the State even in matters which might be, and often are, left to the uncontrolled management of the persons concerned'. This crucial shift – from a suspicion of the state as essentially the agency of corrupt aristocratic government to a concept of it acting as a moral and economic arbiter among, and promoter of the welfare of, all classes, but especially the majority – remains the key shift in the period as a whole. The broad thrust of this analysis, as well as its assumptions regarding the 'special' British path of non-violent, gradual constitutional reform by contrast to the revolutionary patterns of continental politics, can stand as a starting-point for further investigation. A more refined interpretation of the Diceyan view, however, would give greater heed to the influence of both socialism and Idealism in this shift, as well as the vitality of a persistent obsession with both 'character', particularly as the basis of the responsible exercise of the franchise, and 'efficiency', which helped to facilitate a more interventionist ideal of the state. A widespread perception as to the disjuncture between the enormous productive capacity and grievous social inequality of late-nineteenth-century Britain clearly also cannot be underestimated. A sense of competition amongst potential models of democracy – American, Anglo-Saxon, mixed constitutional, French republican, Greek, Roman and so on – is useful in charting debates during eras of reform in particular, particularly when linked to historical controversies (from the late Scottish Enlightenment through Macaulay to Martineau, Buckle, Lecky and Freeman) and, after 1870, the debate over imperial expansion and the impact of Darwinism. The effects of Irish, Indian and African colonial rule in promoting conservatism, rather than mere elite antagonism to American-style democracy, remain to be adequately explored, as do the interaction of socialist, liberal and New Liberal ideas from the 1880s onwards, the pressure of Christian Socialist campaigns, the recrafting of feminism after the late 1860s (perhaps most ignored in the existing 'standard' secondary literature) and the impact of Social Darwinism, which remains surprisingly misunderstood and under-explored. Finally, an appreciation of the relations between social thought, the history of ideas, or intellectual history, and 'political thought' narrowly rendered, would introduce wider debates in such areas as animal rights, racialism and concepts of gender, which have often been neglected in the study of political thought as such.

FURTHER READING

P. Adelman, *Victorian Radicalism: The Middle-Class Experience 1830–1914* (London, 1984).

R. C. Bannister, *Social Darwinism, Science and Myth in Anglo-American Social Thought* (Philadelphia, 1979).

E. Barker, *Political Thought in England 1848 to 1914* (Oxford, 1918).

R. Bellamy, ed., *Victorian Liberalism* (London, 1990).

M. Bentley, *The Climax of Liberal Politics: British Liberalism in Theory and Practice, 1868–1918* (London, 1987).

J. Bowle, *Politics and Opinion in the Nineteenth Century: An Historical Introduction* (London, 1963).

C. Brinton, *English Political Thought in the Nineteenth Century* (London, 1949).

C. Brinton, *The Political Ideas of the English Romanticists* (Ann Arbor, 1966).

J. Burrow, *Evolution and Society: A Study in Victorian Social Theory* (Cambridge, 1966).

J. Burrow, *A Liberal Descent: Victorian Historians and the English Past* (Cambridge, 1981).

J. Burrow, *Whigs and Liberals: Continuity and Change in English Political Thought* (Oxford, 1988).

A. C. Chitnis, *The Scottish Enlightenment and Early Victorian Society* (London, 1986).

G. Claeys, *Machinery, Money and the Millennium: From Moral Economy to Socialism, 1815–60* (Cambridge, 1987).

G. Claeys, *Citizens and Saints: Politics and Anti-Politics in Early British Socialism* (Cambridge, 1989).

S. Collini, *Liberalism and Sociology: L. T. Hobhouse and Political Argument in England, 1880–1914* (Cambridge, 1979).

S. Collini, *Public Moralists: Political Thought and Intellectual Life in Britain, 1850–1930* (Oxford, 1991).

S. Collini, D. Winch and J. Burrow, *That Noble Science of Politics. A Study in Nineteenth Century Intellectual History* (Cambridge, 1983).

S. den Otter, *British Idealism and Social Explanation: A Study in Late Victorian Thought* (Oxford, 1996).

M. Fforde, *Conservatism and Collectivism 1886–1914* (Edinburgh, 1990).

M. Francis and J. Morrow, *A History of English Political Thought in the Nineteenth Century* (London, 1995).

M. Freeden, *The New Liberalism: An Ideology of Social Reform* (Oxford, 1978).

W. H. Greenleaf, *The British Political Tradition*, vol. 2, *The Ideological Heritage* (London, 1983).

E. Halévy, *The Growth of Philosophic Radicalism* (London, 1952).

C. Harvie, *The Lights of Liberalism: University Liberals and the Challenge of Democracy, 1860–86* (London, 1976).

F. J. C. Hearnshaw, *The Social and Political Ideas of Some Representative Thinkers of the Victorian Age* (London, 1933).

B. Hilton, *The Age of Atonement: The Influence of Evangelicalism on Social and Economic Thought, 1795–1865* (Oxford, 1988).

G. Jones, *Social Darwinism and English Thought: The Interaction between Biological and Social Theory* (Brighton, 1980).

H. S. Jones, *Victorian Political Thought* (Basingstoke, 2000).

C. Kent, *Brains and Numbers: Elitism, Comtism, and Democracy in Mid-Victorian England* (Toronto, 1978).

B. Knights, *The Idea of the Clerisy in the Nineteenth Century* (Cambridge, 1978).

A. M. MacBriar, *Fabian Socialism and English Politics, 1884–1918* (Cambridge, 1962).

J. Meadowcroft, *Conceptualizing the State: Innovation and Dispute in British Political Thought, 1880–1914* (Oxford, 1995).

J. Mendilow, *The Romantic Tradition in British Political Thought* (London, 1986).

R. H. Murray, *Studies in the English Social and Political Thinkers of the Nineteenth Century* (Cambridge, 1929).

P. Nicholson, *The Political Philosophy of the British Idealists: Selected Studies* (Cambridge, 1990).

R. Pearson and G. Williams, *Political Thought and Public Policy in the Nineteenth Century: An Introduction* (London, 1984).

S. Pierson, *Marxism and the Origins of British Socialism: The Struggle for a New Consciousness* (Ithaca, 1973).

M. Richter, *The Politics of Conscience: T. H. Green and His Age* (London, 1964).

J. Robson, *The Improvement of Mankind: The Social and Political Thought of John Stuart Mill* (Toronto, 1968).

J. Roper, *Democracy and Its Critics: Anglo-American Democratic Thought in the Nineteenth Century* (London, 1989).

D. C. Somervell, *English Thought in the Nineteenth Century* (London, 1929).

L. Stephen, *The English Utilitarians* (London, 1900).

M. W. Taylor, *Men versus the State: Herbert Spencer and Late Victorian Individualism* (Oxford, 1992).

W. Thomas, *The Philosophic Radicals: Nine Studies in Theory and Practice, 1817–1841* (Oxford, 1979).

D. F. Thompson, *John Stuart Mill and Representative Government* (Princeton, 1976).

A. Vincent and R. Plant, *Philosophy, Politics and Citizenship: The Life and Thought of British Idealists* (Oxford, 1984).

G. Watson, *The English Ideology: Studies in the Language of Victorian Politics* (London, 1973).

T. W. Wright, *The Religion of Humanity: The Impact of Comtean Positivism on Victorian Britain* (Cambridge, 1986).

PART III

Economy and Society

CHAPTER TWELVE

Agriculture and Rural Society

MICHAEL WINSTANLEY

The expanding agenda of rural history in Britain since the early 1950s, when the Agricultural History Society and its journal, *Agricultural History Review* (1953), were established, has been reflected in the appearance of new journals such as *Landscape History* (1979), *Rural History* (1990) and *Environment and History* (1995). The most dominant strand, however, remains an interest in the technical and economic aspects of agriculture. This reflects a longstanding concern with the productivity and profitability of British farming. Prior to the 1960s, this was largely studied as a sub-discipline of economic history, concerned with structure, technology, profitability and productivity. Its development has paralleled debates about the causes and nature of British industrial performance. Was there an 'agricultural revolution'? If so, when and where? How well did British agriculture fare in the face of overseas competition in the late nineteenth century?

The emergence of social history as a separate discipline in the 1960s reawakened interest in the lifestyles and values of those who owned, rented and worked the land. These studies find an earlier resonance in the growing sympathy for the labourer and the 'peasant' which developed during the 1880s, when the poverty and apparent hopelessness of those who worked the land was no longer linked, as it had been in the 1830s, with over-population and the indolence of the poor. Initially concerned with class relations, and particularly with wage labour, rural social history has now broadened its scope to encompass studies of gender, culture and family.

In the last two decades, as agriculture's importance within the rural economy has declined still further, a third area of study has emerged, as historians have begun to explore the origins of new concerns which have come to dominate debates about land use and representation: conservation, environmental sustainability, access identity. Much of this literature concentrates on the growing importance of these issues in the twentieth century, but the cultural, economic and political dominance of urban Britain over what is now increasingly referred to as 'the countryside' can clearly be discerned in the late nineteenth century. Some of this was fuelled by nostalgia and idealism; a desire to recreate or preserve a rural idyll which was increasingly seen as under threat. Other elements were concerned with more modern concepts of planning and regulation, prompted by the varied non-agricultural demands which were being made on the land for resources and leisure.

Over the same period, historians have also become more attuned to the regional diversity which existed, and continues to exist, *within* the countries of the United Kingdom. What they have rarely done, however, is to make overt comparisons and links *between* those countries. The protracted debate about the concept of an 'agricultural revolution', for example, has been almost entirely anglocentric in orientation. Historians of Wales, Ireland and Scotland have rarely strayed over their borders and have often adopted different agendas. This insular compartmentalization makes an overview of the entire country problematic.

Agricultural Change

Much of the English historiography still addresses the agenda laid out in Lord Ernle's pioneering study first published in 1912.[1] In this he argued that an 'astonishing' increase in both production and productivity occurred between 1760 and 1830 which enabled farmers to feed 'the vast centres of commercial industry which sprang up, as if by magic, at a time when food supplies could not have been provided by another country'. His rapidly became the accepted interpretation of what became known as the Agricultural Revolution, a necessary corollary of Britain's equally dramatic Industrial Revolution. In line with the emphasis on great men of industry, Ernle also singled out the role of a few innovators and propagandists: Tull, Coke, Townshend, Young and Bakewell. He credited them with pioneering new crops, notably turnips and clover within new rotational systems, introducing new machinery and improving livestock breeding. He also stressed the importance of enclosure, particularly parliamentary enclosure, the process by which common rights over open fields, commons and wastes were converted into individual property holdings, since he felt that this created the necessary preconditions for the implementation of changes to the layout and size of farms and fields.

By the time the sixth edition of Ernle was published in 1961, however, doubts were being expressed about virtually every aspect of his analysis. These gathered increasing credibility over the next three decades so that by 1990 John Beckett could comment that '[l]ittle now remains of Ernle's views, and the old certainties about the Agricultural Revolution seem misplaced.'[2] Some historians have pushed the significant period of change back to the early eighteenth, late seventeenth or even the mid-sixteenth century. Others have brought it forward to the mid-nineteenth century. Within this context, the significance of parliamentary enclosure as a primary agent of landscape and agricultural change has been challenged. Both Robert Allen and J. M. Neeson have recently emphasized the viability and adaptability of 'pre-enclosure', 'peasant' or 'yeomen' communal forms of agriculture and argued that such farming was capable of achieving significant increases in productivity.[3] A fuller appreciation of the regional diversity of British agriculture and the limited extent of parliamentary enclosure of open fields outside the English Midlands has also undermined its central importance. The extent to which innovations were taken up has been questioned. Reviewing the extensive literature in 1986, Gordon Mingay pondered that '[p]erhaps, however, the whole idea of "agricultural revolution" is inadmissible in a branch of the economy noted neither for the speed nor for the completeness of change in the past'.[4]

The 1990s witnessed the beginnings of a reaction to this view, in much the same way as historians have begun to reassert the validity of the Industrial Revolution. Mark Overton constructed a quantitative case for an *agrarian* revolution' which largely corresponded to the period identified by Ernle. 'Although change was under way by the mid-seventeenth century, it was not until after 1750 that decisive break-throughs took place', with the half-century after 1800 in particularly witnessing 'an unprecedented increase in the output of English agriculture that was associated with an increase in the efficiency of production as measured by land and labour productivity'.[5] Without it, England would have starved. Others have emphasized that it was unreasonable to expect one model of change, largely developed in relation to studies of the English Midlands, to apply across the whole country. As in industry, the period witnessed increasing regional specialization as farmers responded to widening national market opportunities and competition from new sources of supply by concentrating on what their land and local climate allowed them to do best. These 'agricultural regions' were never fixed, and often remain loosely defined even in modern literature (Wales, for example, is often treated as one region despite its diversity), and they displayed significant differences between localities, but there is still some justification for accepting the broad distinction drawn by Caird, who drew a line on the map down the country in 1850. 'All to the East of the black line, running from North to South, may be regarded as the chief Corn Districts of England . . . the counties to the West of the same line, [which] are the principal Grazing, Green Crop, and Diary districts.'[6] Like Caird and Ernle, most historians have focused on the English Midlands and on the arable counties to the east, rather than on the development and introduction of new breeds of sheep and cattle for specific purposes and the extension and improvement of grazing land, which were more important in raising production in the pastoral districts. Equally neglected has been the potential importance of new crops such as the potato. Although the potato was widely despised over much of arable England, it was extensively grown further west and was capable of feeding many more people per acre than corn crops.

Whatever the achievements of English agriculture, however, it was incapable, from as early as the late eighteenth century, of feeding the English population without imports from other parts of the United Kingdom. Ireland's contribution to feeding the growing English population in this period has largely been overlooked by British historians, mainly because of its reputation for agricultural backwardness. Yet, as English farmers ceased to export produce overseas in the late eighteenth century, Irish farmers (and cottiers) managed not only to feed their own population, which more than doubled between the 1780s and 1840s, but to export an increasing amount of food, particularly to mainland Britain. Ireland had begun to export increasing quantities of grain as the acreage under the plough – and frequently spade – increased considerably from the 1780s. The Irish parliament's Corn Law of 1784 deliberately sought to encourage this by penalizing the import of grain into Ireland and subsidizing its export. This Act lapsed with the Union, but from 1806 Irish grain was freely admitted into Britain to supplement domestic production and the Corn Laws of 1815, which limited the importation of foreign corn into Britain, produced what Ó Gráda has called 'hothouse conditions for corn cultivation' in Ireland. Whereas in the 1790s Ireland had accounted for just 16.5 per cent of Britain's corn imports, mainly oats and wheat, by the mid-1830s the figure had risen to over 80 per cent – and the volume had also risen considerably. Irish farmers also sent increasing quantities of cattle, pigs and dairy produce, particularly to the industrial towns and cities of the North-West, as steamships facilitated transportation across the Irish Sea. By the early 1840s possibly 25 per cent of its grain was being exported, together with about half of its livestock production, and according to one estimate these amounted to at least one-sixth of the food supply of England, capable of feeding over two million people. These bald facts point to the need to consider a different perspective to the usual picture of a country racked by subsistence crises and rushing headlong towards famine. Indeed, Cormac Ó Gráda has suggested that, had land been of the same quality as England, levels of total productivity would not have been dissimilar. As it was productivity per acre was much the same as England, largely because more labour was used, the workers being largely fed on the potato, which was also an excellent soil-cleansing crop.[7]

Scottish historians have been more confident than their English counterparts in identifying the late eighteenth century and early nineteenth century as the critical period for wholesale agrarian transformation, respectively described as 'improvement' or 'clearances' by its proponents and critics. Scottish landowners were not constrained by customary or manorial rights. Consequently, when they wished to enclose or re-organize settlements on their land they were not obliged to undertake complicated legal procedures such as parliamentary enclosure. Although smaller farms retained their importance in western dairying counties like Argyll, and the cattle districts of the north-east, over much of the Scottish Lowlands what Tom Devine has described as a 'structural change, not simply a perpetuation and intensification of existing trends' occurred which 'produced a dramatic increase in crop yields, allowing Scottish cultivators to catch up on English levels of output within a few decades'.[8] In the Lothians and Borders, landlords resorted to the physical clearance, migration and resettlement of the existing populations with their various forms of archaic, communal agriculture, and created large commercially oriented holdings. Described unsympathetically by Cobbett in 1830 as 'factories for making corn and meat', these were more frequently admired as the apogee of capitalist farming by continental visitors who flocked there in preference to the English granary districts of East Anglia. Historians' attention, however, has been largely concentrated on the Scottish Highlands, particularly the Hebrides, areas of poor-quality land which were also disadvantaged by their distance from markets, where the 'clearances' involved the resettlement of people to promote commercial pastoralism in the form of large sheep farms. From the late eighteenth century both people and the indigenous black or St Kilda sheep and long-horned cattle were all ousted by new sheep breeds from the south such as the Cheviot and the Blackface. In the county of Sutherland alone, sheep numbers increased from approximately 15,000 in 1811 to 130,000 just nine years later as an estimated 8,000 to 9,000 people were moved from the interior to new fishing and quasi-industrial villages on the coast. Because these events loom large in the recent revival of interest in Scottish, and particularly Gaelic, culture, historiography of the 'clearances' has tended to focus on their social consequences and on the potential culpability of landowners for the poverty which ensued. As Richards has argued, without in any way underestimating the significance of such debates, these privilege the particularities of the region at the expense of an appreciation of the fact that 'the story of the Highlands was part of the British and European experience' in which market forces prompted changes in land use, settlement and tenures.[9]

In many respects, therefore, despite acknowledging the widespread existence of earlier changes, British, if not English, historians now increasingly accept that the late eighteenth century and the first half of the nineteenth century constituted a, if not the, critical period of structural change, regional specialization, commercialization and productivity gains in agriculture which enabled a much larger urban population to be fed, albeit sometimes at the expense of the rural poor.

Their verdict on the subsequent performance of Victorian farming is rather more ambivalent. The market in which farmers operated changed dramatically from the 1850s as rising living standards encouraged a shift towards a more varied diet, away from corn towards meat and dairy produce. Railways further opened up the domestic market, accelerating regional specialization. However, mainland British arable farmers were faced with new competition from overseas, particularly from the 1870s. Whereas they produced approximately 80 per cent of the country's staple foodstuffs in 1860s, by 1913 the figure had dropped to 45 per cent as grain, meat, wool and dairy produce flooded in. The opening up of the American prairies from the 1870s by improved railroads and steamship technology, and the subsequent tapping of supplies in Russia and India, led to a fourfold increase in wheat imports, which were more suited to bread-making than the softer British grain. Refrigeration and subsequently deep freezing allowed North American and then South American beef producers to export meat to Britain, and Australian and New Zealand farmers to supply mutton. From the 1880s they also shipped wool, and by the 1890s Canadian cheddar and Danish butter were also making inroads into the British market. The effect of all of this was a marked deterioration in the prices which farmers received for many of their products. Wheat prices were halved between the 1870s and 1890s, and wool prices fell by 40 per cent, while butter and cheese prices dropped 25 per cent in the 1880s and 1890s. Only from the late 1890s did prices stabilize.

Central to studies of this period, therefore, have been two related questions. How well did British farming respond to these changes and to what extent is it appropriate to refer to the late nineteenth century as a period of 'agricultural depression'?

There is plenty of evidence to suggest that farmers throughout the United Kingdom responded rationally to changing price differentials. The collection of agricultural statistics from as early as 1847 in Ireland shows that farmers there were particularly quick to respond to the repeal of the Corn Laws, ceasing to be major suppliers of grain to the rest of Britain by the 1850s while exporting cattle and dairy produce in increasing quantities.[10] Trends are more difficult to discern in England and Wales before 1866 when the government finally introduced the systematic collection of annual statistics, but it is likely that livestock farming was gaining ground relative to corn, especially in Caird's pastoral districts. What is clear is that relative price changes led to marked changes in the late nineteenth century. Wheat acreage halved in England between 1869 and 1914 from over 3.4 m. to just 1.7 m. acres, and dropped significantly more in percentage terms in Wales. Barley production also declined from the 1870s in response to falling demand, while oats and root crops, which could be fed to animals and were less affected by price falls or imports, remained buoyant. The land most likely to be taken out of wheat production was that least suited to it. In most cases it was converted to permanent pasture for hay or grazing, the acreage rising particularly in England from less than 10 m acres in the early 1870s to over 14 m by 1914 and from 1.5 m to 2.0 m in Wales. Livestock numbers, particularly cattle, rose significantly over the period.

The fact that British agriculture responded to changing market conditions, therefore, is not in dispute. What is less clear is how well farmers and landlords performed in comparison to earlier periods or potential competitors when measured in terms of productivity. Could they, in short, have done better? Here verdicts have been less favourable, particularly for English farmers. 'High Farming', which characterized the mid-century decades, had been championed as the epitome of progressive scientific farming which would secure Britain's future in the face of anticipated foreign imports. Its enthusiasts, particularly the Royal Agriculture Society (1838), recommended the adoption of new drainage technology, the application of steam, particularly to threshing, the construction of 'model' farms, use of mass-produced machinery and the liberal application of new manures. English growth rates during the period, however, are now estimated to have been substantially lower than in the previous half-century, and much of the expensive investment yielded little if any financial return for its promoters. The sector's performance in the late nineteenth century is also considered to be mediocre. Ó Gráda concludes that agriculture exhibited 'relatively sluggish productivity growth' and 'did not perform famously in the face of foreign competition.'[11] Quite why this should have been the case is not clear. Some have suggested that the 'failure of agrarian capitalism' was particularly acute in England during this period because of the higher incidence of large-scale farmers during a period when market conditions were favouring the smaller family farm.[12] Institutional factors, notably the structural and social inefficiencies of the estate system have also been blamed. Ireland's superior productivity record for most of the late nineteenth century where farms were smaller and the powers of the landowners were curtailed from the 1880s, would seem to support this hypothesis, but ironically it is livestock farming, including dairying – dominated in the main by smaller farmers – which is blamed for depressing productivity gains in England: labour productivity in the contracting arable sector would appear to have been substantially improved by mechanization, particularly of the harvest. Scottish farming, although less subjected to detailed scrutiny, is considered to have performed better and may help to account for Michael Turner's recent more optimistic assessment of productivity for British agriculture as a whole.[13] Whatever the overall verdict on Britain's agriculturalists, it is generally accepted that their productivity record compared favourably with much of manufacturing, mining and service industries during the period.

Ernle's assessment of the effect of overseas competition on the profitability of English farming is frequently cited. 'Since 1862 the tide of agricultural prosperity had ceased to flow; after 1874 it turned and rapidly ebbed. A period of depression began which, with some fluctuations in severity, continued throughout the rest of the reign of Queen Victoria, and beyond.' In fact his assessment was more nuanced than his critics suggest. He acknowledged that problems were particularly pronounced in the corn-growing districts; that many small farmers in the North and West not only survived but may have prospered; that new sectors such as market-gardening, fruit-growing, poultry-keeping and particularly milk production and retailing (which were to form the basis of twentieth-century farming) expanded, particularly from the 1890s; and that by 1912 the industry was generally 'sound and prosperous' and less obsessed with corn.

Since the 1960s these qualifications have been extended and developed by historians, some of whom now prefer to refer to the period as one of 'adjustment'. T. W. Fletcher disputed the notion of depression by pointing to the 'thousands of live-stock farmers', who increased their output with the aid of the cheap, imported cereals and who exploited the railway network or their proximity to urban areas to supply good quality meat and liquid milk.[14] The regional incidence of depression is also confirmed by Perry's spatial analysis of bankruptcy records and by F. M. L. Thompson's meticulous exploration of landlords' rentals and farm outputs which concludes that there was 'no general or chronic depression in English agriculture throughout this period'.[15] Rents in the corn heartlands of Norfolk and Suffolk may have been virtually halved between 1873 and 1911, but those in pastoral Cheshire remained unchanged. Gross farm output also increased in almost every county during the 'depression' and particularly so after 1894, but again there were regional variations, with the North and West experiencing the most dramatic increases.

Life on the Land: Social Relations

The transformation of Britain's economy during the nineteenth century had profound implications for those who lived in rural areas. Arguably, however, the most significant changes were those associated not with agriculture, but with the manufacturing sector. Whereas by 1914 'agricultural' could be seen as synonymous with 'rural', in much the same way as 'urban' and 'industrial' were bracketed together, a century earlier the parallel had not been so clear. Many rural families had not been totally, or even primarily, dependent on farming for their income. Craftsmen who serviced local agriculture frequently held smallholdings. Other workers produced consumer goods for regional, national or even international markets including shoes, metalwares, hats and lace. Textile outwork was particularly varied and widespread. Irish smallholders grew and processed flax for linen for export; upland farmers in the Yorkshire dales, Westmorland and Wales were supported by woollen knitting; small farmers in Lancashire undertook handloom weaving of fustians and later cotton; serge and gloves were made in the West Country. As late as 1850 Caird remarked on the 'clothiers' of the West Riding 'who hold a considerable portion of the land within several miles of the manufacturing towns; they have looms in their houses, and unite the business of weavers and farmers.'[16] Scottish landowners from the late eighteenth century were particularly active in seeking to expand such employment, primarily to provide work for families displaced by their agrarian reforms. In the Highlands, assisted by the North British Fisheries Society, they promoted fishing communities, while in many parts of central and Lowland Scotland they built handloom-weaving settlements such as Newcastleton and Langholm. Small upland farmers in the Pennines and Wales also combined agriculture with lead- or coal-mining and quarrying; elsewhere, others engaged in woodland industries.

The de-industrialization of rural areas during the nineteenth century was a protracted affair because each of these industries and trades experienced different fortunes. The dramatic collapse of many of the domestic textile trades in the second quarter of the century in the face of competition from steam-powered mills, particularly in Lancashire and Yorkshire, was a major cause of the social dislocation, poverty and rural depopulation which characterized some parts of the country, especially those with inadequate or non-existent poor relief. But 'it was in general only in the last years before 1914 that many traditional industries were forced into full retreat'.[17] Straw-plaiting, lace-making and glove-making survived as important regional industries, albeit in straitened circumstances, into the twentieth century. There were also government, philanthropic and commercial attempts to revive rural manufacturing from the 1880s. These met with mixed success. In contrast to the more utilitarian emphasis of many earlier industries, those initiatives that succeeded tended to cater for wealthier consumers who could indulge their artistic taste for authentic 'handicrafts'. Harris-tweed production supported crofting populations on the Outer Hebrides and the Congested Districts Board had some success in introducing textile manufacture into the west of Ireland. Elsewhere, however, in places like the Lake District, many of the revived handicrafts were more likely to be promoted and practised by middle-class incomers. The only major industries to expand significantly were extractive rather than manufacturing in nature, 'the great industrial "cuckoos"' such as mining or quarrying.[18] Even these became more concentrated over time, and their workforces tended to remain physically and culturally distinct from the surrounding farming communities, especially in more isolated areas such as Cumberland which relied on long-distance migrants, many of them from Ireland and Scotland.

Until recently, the agricultural workforce was usually conceived of and studied as a three-tier class society in which inequality was all-pervasive. Individuals' relationships with the land were the determining factor: a small group of affluent landowners provided the land and fixed capital and relied for their income on rent paid by tenant farmers. These in turn provided the managerial input and working capital and retained any profits from the business. They also employed a landless wage-dependent labouring class. For some observers, like Marx, the emergence of this class structure was the natural working-out of developing capitalist relations. Back in 1911, the Hammonds portrayed this as a relatively recent development, dating back only to the late eighteenth century, and associated it with landowners' policies of enclosure and clearance which extinguished 'the old village life and all the relationships and interests attached to it with an unsparing and unhesitating hand', undermining the 'the small farmer, the cottager, and the squatter'.[19] Recent studies, however, have tended to qualify this picture, emphasizing the persistence of marked regional and local variations in social structures and relations and the continued importance of family labour and farm service.[20]

The survival of landowners' papers have ensured that they have been the most amenable social class to study.[21] A small group of inter-related families, the wealthiest aristocrats, operated on a national, even international scale, with estates in several parts of the country. Many were necessarily absentees, permanently or seasonally, who employed agents or factors to manage their affairs. Below them were the regional gentry, the squires and the Scottish lairds who still owned several thousands of acres and who were, on balance, more likely to be resident on their estates. In some parts of the country, particularly the Lake District, there were also substantial numbers of smaller 'statesmen' or 'yeomen'.[22] It is usually assumed that, a few exceptions apart, the industrial and commercial *nouveaux riches* neither wished, nor were able, to buy themselves into the ranks of the more substantial country landowners, and that at the end of the century, when this became more possible as land prices fell, declining rental income from land made purchase less desirable. The new plutocracy did not desire or need to acquire the responsibility of running a struggling estate to proclaim their status; where they did acquire land, their purpose was not to develop farming. Most sought primarily to possess a fashionable house in the country or to enjoy new 'country pursuits'. Few tenants purchased their farms from their landlords until after 1918. Consequently, the distribution of landownership would appear to have changed little in England and Wales before the First World War. In other parts of the United Kingdom, however, there were more marked changes. The Irish Encumbered Estates Act of 1849, for example, facilitated the sale of 25 per cent of the country, much of it to newly rich Catholic trading families. Two-thirds of estates in the western Highlands of Scotland also changed hands between the 1810s and 1860s, as bankrupt lairds sold out to men who had made their fortunes in more favourable economic climates.[23] A wholesale transfer of land to the tenants in Ireland was also enabled by a series of land-purchase acts between the Irish Land Act of 1881 and the Wyndham Act of 1903, which offered increasingly attractive financial incentives. While the Crofters' Act of 1886 offered secure tenure and controlled rents, however, Scottish crofters were offered no such inducements to buy.

In contrast to landowners, many of whom left extensive papers and engaged in high-profile public activity, tenant farmers have been less easy to study. They were also socially and regionally diverse. Large farms, whether defined in terms of turnover, acreage or employment, were predominantly a characteristic of Caird's 'corn growing districts'. They were particularly concentrated in the recently enclosed counties of the Midlands, East Anglia and the Anglo-Scottish borders.[24] Sheep farms in the Scottish Highlands and Borders and, later, cattle ranches in the west of Ireland also operated on a large scale, although they employed significantly fewer people. However, over most of Wales, the dairying and cattle-rearing districts of south-west and north-east Scotland, and throughout the largely pastoral counties of western and northern England, farm sizes remained significantly smaller and displayed little evidence of amalgamation or expansion. Many were like 'the Welsh farmer' observed by Sir Thomas Phillips in the 1840s, who 'occupies a small farm, employs an inconsiderable amount of capital, and is but little removed, either in his mode of life, his laborious occupation, his dwelling or his habits, from the day-labourers by whom he is surrounded.'[25] Over much of the stock-rearing and dairying districts of Ireland, it was the small- to medium-sized family farmer who dominated the rural economy. As we have seen, despite the criticisms levelled at them throughout the century, such farmers were remarkably resilient, and were the chief beneficiaries of the widening differential between falling cereal prices and stable or rising beef, milk, poultry and vegetable prices in the late nineteenth century.

Labourers are even more difficult to classify or count, the numbers recorded in decennial censuses after 1841 being serious underestimates.[26] Three categories of labour in particularly were likely to have been omitted from the returns. First, there were members of farmers' families, particularly children and women, who remained crucially important to the viability of smaller farms. After 1871 both 'farmer's wife' and 'female relative' were reclassified in the census as non-occupied, although the latter was reinstated as an agricultural category in 1901. The 1911 census in particular revealed their continued importance in the north and west of England, and in some counties of west Wales, their numbers increased as male members of farming families were tempted off the land into the expanding mining and heavy industry. Second, female servants on farms were often returned as 'general' servants and were classified, therefore, as 'domestic', but it is clear from other sources that they combined their work in the house with food-processing, particularly dairying and poultry-keeping, or even field work. Third, seasonal labour, male and female, was also under-recorded. Although the decline of arable acreage, the replacement of the sickle by the scythe and the mechanization of hay- and corn-cutting from the 1870s, particularly the introduction of the reaper and reaper binder, reduced labour demands in the late nineteenth century, haymaking, harvesting, fruit- and hop-picking and potato-lifting still remained labour-intensive processes which relied on drawing in additional workers. In the early nineteenth century industrial outworkers supplemented the labour force in some parts of the country. Members of local farming and non-farming families were drafted in, and the importance of female and child labour is reflected in the ways in which many rural schools' holidays were scheduled to fit around hay, corn or potato harvests. In arable areas, especially those from Lincolnshire northwards with low population densities, much of the harvesting and labour-intensive work at other times of the year was undertaken by migrant labourers. Highland crofting and Irish peasant households relied heavily on family members' earnings from seasonal work in England and Lowland Scotland, particularly before the 1860s.[27] Elsewhere, in parts of Norfolk and Cambridgeshire, gangs of women were hired by 'gang masters', who effectively contracted with farmers for specific jobs and paid the workers. Well into the twentieth century, families from the East End of London provided the bulk of Kent's hop-pickers, while miners' wives and families from the pit villages of the North-East helped out in the corn harvest.

The composition and lifestyle of what might be called the 'regular' agricultural labourer largely reflected regional variations in farm size, specializations and fortunes, as well as the availability of employment in industry or mining. Casually employed labourers, primarily a feature of the larger farms in the arable counties of southern England and the Midlands, have been the most extensively studied. These farm-workers are usually portrayed as poor, vulnerable, exploited, landless males casually hired on a weekly basis and dependent on poor relief, charity, pilfering or poaching to see them and their families through the winter. The majority lived in low-quality accommodation rented from smaller landlords in nucleated villages and market towns, whose penury and misery were vividly evoked by Disraeli's fictional portrayal of the wretched rural town of 'Marney' in his 1845 novel *Sybil*. The plight of this group was particularly evident in the three decades from the 1820s as farmers sought to increase productivity and reduce wages in response to lower price levels. Conditions were made worse by chronic structural employment exacerbated by the demise of rural industries which had provided supplementary forms of family income, by the loss of access to common grazing through enclosure in some areas, and by an increasingly harsh system of poor relief, symbolized, but not initiated, by the Poor Law Amendment Act of 1834. Although Fox in his survey of agricultural wages in 1903 was able to demonstrate that pay and conditions improved in the second half of the century, there is little doubt that this numerous group of workers remained amongst the poorest paid and worst housed in the country.[28] Casual labourers, however, comprised a declining proportion of the labour force from the 1870s as manual jobs were taken over by horses and machinery, both of which were looked after by workers such as waggoners or ploughmen on longer-term contracts. The shift from arable to pasture also significantly reduced labour demands. In Ireland casual labourers virtually disappeared as family-run farms came to dominate the landscape.[29]

Elsewhere in Britain, apart from a few localities, those who were engaged for wages generally came under a very different hiring practice: farm service. This was characterized by longer terms of engagement, six or twelve months depending on local farming specialities, and the provision of accommodation and, in most cases, food, as part payment of wages. Recent studies of this have disputed that it was an archaic 'survival' of pre-capitalist farming by demonstrating the marked regional differences in practice. What Alun Howkins has characterized as the 'pure living-in' system, was most likely to be found on the smaller family farms in Wales, Lancashire north of the Ribble, Cumbria, and south-west and north-east Scotland.[30] This involved 'an exchange of households among equals as part of the life cycle' in which younger members of farm families effectively served periods of training or apprenticeship on farms of similar size and status. Ian Carter has similarly described how the hired farm servants who worked on the stock-rearing farms of Aberdeenshire were from peasant farms which were in a labour-abundant phase of the family farm life cycle. In Aberdeenshire farm service was not proletarianized: it was not a career in itself, but a stage in a career that began in peasant farming then moved through wage work and back to peasant farming.[31] The extent to which this idealized picture of a 'farming ladder' was realized is debatable. Not all servants were able to climb it since many were obliged to leave the land when they reached adulthood or wished to marry, and not all servants were treated as 'equals' by their employers. It was not uncommon for young men to be lodged with other farm workers on long-term contracts, as a ploughman or stockman, or to sleep in adjacent lofts or adapted shelters. The extent to which farm service was a 'traditional' practice is also unclear; it may well have been encouraged by the shift from arable to pasture during the century and by the concomitant decline and shortage of locally available waged labour. Farmers in Lancashire from the 1870s were adamant that they would have preferred to hire day-labour had it been available and complained that a shortage of workers increased farm servants' bargaining power at the hiring market.

On the large arable farms of the Scottish Lowlands and north-east England, however, very different and unquestionably new forms of 'proletarianized' farm service developed as an integral part of agricultural modernization and the creation of large holdings. Here the social gulf between employer and labourer was as large as it was in the cornlands of southern England. In grain districts of the East Riding horses were managed by teams of 'farm lads', young single men who often resided in communal lodgings.[32] On either side of the Scottish border family groups were preferred. Here, a male 'hind' or annually hired worker, could expect a better standard accommodation, usually a purpose-built cottage with adjacent garden, but his wife and other members of his family were also expected to work as required on the farm as part of the bargain. If unmarried he was expected to engage, accommodate and pay a female 'bondager', sometimes a relative, to fulfil his contractual obligation. The reasons for the different hiring practices partly relate to the nature of the farming, but also reflect the shortage of sources of casual labour in the region on which farmers could draw.

These different rural social structures, and the fortunes of the farming associated with them, spawned very different patterns of social relations. Although rural society has a popular reputation as a deferential and close-knit community with low levels of conflict, crime and violence, there was an undercurrent of alienation which occasionally generated incidents of protest and rejection. When social historians in the 1960s first turned their attention to the potential for conflict they focused on the oppressed and inarticulate southern English agricultural labourers, and on incidents of mass mobilization as vehicles for exploring their values. Eric Hobsbawm and George Rudé offered a major reappraisal of the Hammonds' Last Labourers' Revolt of 1830–1. In contrast to the increasingly organized and ideological movements which were emerging in urban Britain, they characterized this as the last and greatest of the 'improvised, archaic, spontaneous movements of resistance to the full triumph of rural capitalism'.[33] It was improvised because it resorted not to collective association and organized revolt but to whatever weapons were available locally: incendiarism; machine-breaking; anonymous threatening letters. It was spontaneous because it relied on local initiatives, not on a plan of campaign orchestrated by a clearly identified leadership. It was archaic because it utilized the 'traditional collective practices of the village' and accepted 'ancient symbols of ancient ideals of stable hierarchy'; it did not represent 'a new consciousness among the labourers' or a 'new political or social ideology'. It did not call for land redistribution and it was not apparently linked to the widespread urban protest of the time which demanded political reform. Despite the support it received from village artisans and small farmers, it was essentially a labourers' movement with economic aims: better wages; a reduction of tithes; more humane and generous poor relief; more regular employment.

Hobsbawm and Rudé's conclusions about the insularity and localism of rural society have not gone unchallenged. Despite the apparently diverse local demands and methods of the protesters, they are now increasingly seen as possessing a wider awareness of social and political issues. Historical geographers have challenged the apparent inchoate nature of the outbreaks by mapping them spatially in relation to the London highways and temporally to the ebb and flow of political crises surrounding parliamentary reform in the capital.[34] Cobbett, the champion of the rural poor, itinerant lecturer, author and proprietor of the unstamped newspaper the *Political Register*, is also increasingly credited with raising the labourers' political consciousness.[35] Above all, historians have stressed that Swing should not be seen as an aberrant, exceptional behaviour. It was rather an 'overt' manifestation of a deep and longer-lasting sense of class alienation on the part of the labourer, a refusal to acknowledge the rights of property or the inevitability of the poor's lot which was mirrored in recourse to more endemic forms of 'covert' protest, ranging from game-poaching to incendiarism, especially in the bleak 1840s, to express personal hostility towards individual farmers or Poor Law overseers who were viewed as oppressors.[36] More open respectable dissent also emerged during the mid-century in labourers' adherence to Nonconformity, especially Methodism or Primitive Methodism, which came to symbolize rejection of established, hierarchical value systems and provided them with both the moral justification for organized secular protest and the means to express it.

Viewed from this perspective 'The Revolt of the Field' which erupted in the early 1870s is now viewed as less of an aberration in an otherwise deferential society than was once thought. Taking advantage of an improving labour market, labourers throughout the corn districts of southern England formed themselves into organized trade unions, of which the most famous, Arch's National Agricultural Labourers' Union, was just one. These temporarily succeeded in wresting the initiative from their employers and obtaining substantial wage increases.[37] The success was short-lived, however. The reasons for the movement's demise were partly rooted in the varied nature of rural society, the diversity of regional and local farming, and the relative poverty of the labourers; it was difficult to mount effective action when the work-force was scattered and relatively poor and the industry so diverse. The fall in corn prices after 1873 and the decline in labour requirements that the reduction in grain acreage and the increasing mechanization of farm processes ushered in, dealt a mortal blow to labourers' hopes of effective trade unionism. Its leaders increasingly recommended migration, or emigration, to reduce the labour supply, or placed their hopes in political solutions to the 'land question' and the 'rural exodus' offered by the Liberal party from the mid-1880s which included promises of 'three acres and a cow' or the extension of smallholdings or allotments, effectively diluted versions of land reform packages being offered to Scottish crofters and Irish peasants at the time.

The origins, nature and purpose of rural protest in other parts of the country were very different. Although there was a sustained attempt in the 1870s by unmarried 'hinds' in the North-East and Scottish Borders to end the 'bondager' system, most districts characterized by farm service remained relatively untouched by any overt forms of protest throughout the nineteenth century. Whether this was due to the cordial relations between employer and employee, however, is less clear. On the one hand it has been suggested that the relative shortage of labour in such regions meant that farm servants were able to exercise considerable bargaining power at the regular hiring fairs, a power that contributed to the higher wage levels in these areas. On the other hand, collective action was undoubtedly more difficult to mount when small groups of live-in servants were not only isolated from each other for long periods, but dependent on their employers for board and accommodation. Those who were dissatisfied with the conditions on the land usually preferred the option of leaving.

In those parts of Ireland, Wales, the Scottish Highlands and parts of north-west England dominated by family farmers and smallholders, the concern was not with wages and conditions but the terms on which tenants held their land. In the first half of the century, their protest had largely been a reaction to the perceived threats posed by agricultural modernization, especially farm consolidation, the creation of labour-extensive pastoral holdings and population resettlement. On mainland Britain, physical attempts to preserve what were viewed as 'traditional' rights and customs were particularly evident in south-west Wales, a region which also witnessed the Rebecca riots in 1839 and 1843–4. Neither the agricultural transformation of the Scottish Lowlands, nor the remarkable social engineering undertaken by Highland landlords, provoked much in the way of sustained resistance despite the undoubted unpopularity of the clearances. In Ireland, however, attempts by landlords to install new tenants or introduce new farming practices on reorganized holdings often led to outbreaks of covert violence and intimidating threats from the smallholders and cottiers who felt most threatened.[38] There has been no sustained comparative spatial analysis which has sought to account for these regional variations. The reasons are likely to have included the nature of previous tenurial arrangements and, in particular, the relative strengths of customary and legal rights; the availability or otherwise of alternative employments or poor-relief measures to sustain those displaced from the land (there was no poor-relief system in Ireland until after 1838); and the extent to which landlords and tenants shared similar cultural backgrounds. Unlike Swing, there has been no suggestion that these disparate and diverse outbreaks represented a broader social or political consciousness.

By the end of the century, however, these localized, desperate reactions to increasing immiseration had been superseded by what historians now argue were organized regional and national movements with proactive political agendas, symptomatic of a growing self-confidence, and sense of collective identity and prosperity. In Ireland, a 'revolution of rising expectations', born out of several decades of modest prosperity, lay behind the formation of the Irish Land League in 1879 which campaigned for legislative redress of grievances over rents and security of tenure.[39] Similar conditions in Scotland underpinned what Hunter has called 'the making of the crofting community', the emergence of the Highland Land War in 1881 and the formation of the Highland Land Law Reform Association in 1883.[40] In Wales, the 1880s witnessed the emergence of various organizations dedicated to land reform, particularly the payment of tithes to the Anglican church. Whereas small farmers had once been viewed as obstacles to agricultural progress, they now attracted widespread sympathy and active support among significant sections of urban population, particularly radical Liberals, socialists and Celtic nationalists. These increasingly viewed the landowning class, once the undisputed leaders of rural society, as parasitic and counter-productive, and held them responsible both for the failure of agriculture and the declining viability of rural society. Consequently, small farmers' movements achieved some significant political successes. The Irish Land Act of 1881 and the Crofters' Act of 1886 guaranteed farmers security of tenure and introduced judicially determined rents while Wyndham's Land Act of 1903 offered favourable financial terms for Irish farmers wishing to purchase their holdings. An Act of 1890 provided that tithes should be paid by the owner, rather than the occupier, of land.

Back to the Land? Urban Demands on the 'Countryside'

By 1914, however, Britain was unquestionably an urban, industrial society. The relative economic importance of agriculture had declined from about 33 per cent of GNP in 1800 to less than 10 per cent, a fall which was mirrored in the proportion of the population employed on the land. Paradoxically, however, this marginalization of agriculture was paralleled in the three decades prior to the First World War by an unprecedented explosion of interest in the fortunes, face and fate of rural Britain and its inhabitants. The 'Rural Exodus' of the period threatened to undermine the nation and downtrodden 'Hodge's' ability to remain on the land and procreate was believed to be crucial to the perpetuation of the race since town-dwellers were seen as being progressively demoralized and incapacitated by conditions of urban living.

This urban interest in the 'land question' in the late nineteenth century went beyond philanthropic and economic concerns for the welfare of rural inhabitants or the prosperity of farming. It embraced agriculturists, academics, politicians, economists, artists, composers, novelists, poets, planners and conservationists. 'Beyond its life-giving role as a place of food production, the same land-space had come to assume a much wider role in terms of enhancing what, for most people, had become an urban way of life.'[41] Others now staked what Harvey Taylor has called in his history of the outdoor movement, 'a claim on the countryside'.[42] No longer was the land viewed primarily as a physical asset to be exploited by man for food and sustenance. There was increasingly a potential conflict between what Smout has called 'use' and 'delight'.[43] It was increasingly valued as a 'national' asset, a canvas on to which those who did not depend upon it for their livelihood could project their values, fears and aspirations, and an arena in which they could engage in new pursuits. Instead of being 'the pleasure ground of the few', as one critic put it, there were demands for the land to be the 'treasure trove of the many'. Although the precursors of the countryside's new roles can be identified in earlier periods, most notably the discovery of the 'picturesque' and 'sublime' in the late eighteenth century, and although most historical studies concentrate on the developments in the twentieth century, it is increasingly accepted that the half-century before 1914 was a critical transition period.

This transformation of interest in rural Britain had diverse roots and took many forms. Novels, poetry, photography (including the new picture postcard), art and architecture reflected the extraordinary extent to which an idealized 'countryside' had come to embody the qualities, virtues and attractions of the nation, by seeking to recreate rural landscapes and lifestyles, past and present, real and imagined. Yet it was more than simply an escapist 'back to the land' reaction against industrialism, a nostalgic yearning for a more fulfilling, natural way of life and a return to an unspoilt landscape and habitat. It embraced new and forward-looking concepts of outdoor leisure – particularly walking and cycling – and what A. D. Hall in 1913 called the 'residential and holiday making element that colonizes the countryside'. It fed into Arts and Crafts architecture and inspired urban planning, most obviously through 'garden cities' which sought to merge country and town in a new planned environment. Politically it embraced all shades of opinion.

Not surprisingly, this was not a coherent or united mass 'movement' with clearly defined aims, membership and shared ideological perspective. Rather there was a proliferation of organizations, each operating independently of each other, but often with a core of overlapping membership.[44] Those like the Commons Preservation Society (1865), National Footpaths Preservation Society (1884), Society for Checking the Abuses of Public Advertising (1893) and the National Trust for Places of Historic Interest and Natural Beauty (1894) sought variously to preserve or enhance the land's amenity value by promoting wider public access for leisure and recreation or preserving landscapes once dismissed as unproductive commons or 'wastes' for public enjoyment. Others, like the Selbourne Society for the Protection of Birds, Plants and Pleasant Places (1885), Society for the Protection of Birds (1889) and Society for the Promotion of Nature Reserves (1912), sought to preserve plants and wildlife. Yet others, like the Folk Song Society and the Folk Dance Society, sought to record and, where possible, revive what were seen as quaint, traditional pastimes, customs, folklore, dialect and music, while the Peasant Arts Fellowship, Art Workers' Guild and Guild of Handicraft sought to revive rural 'crafts' which were once viewed with disdain as anachronistic but which were now cherished in preference to what

George Bourne dismissed in *Change in the Village* (1912) as 'nasty machine-made stuff'. These developments were not unique to England, although they are often studied as if they were. Indeed, they took on additional significance in parts of Wales, the Scottish Highlands and Ireland where the language, lifestyle and landscape of the smallholding peasant farmer and crofter came to symbolize a revived Gaelic or Celtic identity. It is no coincidence that creation of the first Gaelic Chair at Edinburgh University and the publication of the first popular *History of the Highland Clearances* by Alexander Mackenzie both happened at the height of the Crofters' Land War in 1883, and that Ireland in the 1880s witnessed the emergence of societies dedicated to the revival of Gaelic languages, culture and sports.

The contemporary significance and success of these campaigns and developments need to be kept in perspective. They influenced government policy in some areas before 1914, but not decisively so. Nor were they yet mass movements. Their very existence reflected the fact that there were powerful countervailing imperatives within urban Britain that threatened what they held dear and fought to preserve. There were still strong countervailing economic and physical imperatives which required that the countryside continued to be exploited for food, water, fuel and housing, while improved communications and literacy threatened to undermine the distinctiveness of 'rural' ways of life. Nevertheless, they symbolized an important transition. Over the next century, not only did 'rural' and 'agricultural' become increasingly distinct, but the very purpose of rural Britain was to be questioned. The values and organizations which emerged then have increasingly influenced attitudes and policies towards the land and appear set to do so even more in the future.

NOTES

1. Lord Ernle, *English Farming Past and Present* (London, 1961).
2. J. V. Beckett, *The Agricultural Revolution* (Oxford, 1990), p. 68.
3. R. C. Allen, *Enclosure and the Yeoman: The Agricultural Development of the South Midlands, 1450–1850* (Oxford, 1992); J. M. Neeson, *Commoners: Common Right, Enclosure and Social Change in England, 1700–1820* (Cambridge, 1993).
4. G. E. Mingay, ed., *The Agrarian History of England and Wales*, vol. 6, *1750–1850* (Cambridge, 1989), p. 1.
5. M. Overton, *Agricultural Revolution in England: The Transformation of the Agrarian Economy, 1500–1850* (Cambridge, 1996), p. 206.
6. J. Caird, *English Agriculture in 1850–51* (London, 1968, originally published 1851), frontispiece.
7. C. Ó Gráda, *Ireland Before and After the Famine: Explorations in Economic History, 1808–1925* (Manchester, 1993), pp. 54, 120.
8. T. M. Devine, *The Transformation of Rural Scotland: Social Change and the Agrarian Economy, 1660–1815* (Edinburgh, 1994), p. 164.
9. E. Richards, *A History of the Highland Clearances*, vol. 1, *Agrarian Transformation and the Evictions, 1746–1886* (London, 1982), p. 8.
10. M. E. Turner, *After the Famine: Irish Agriculture 1850–1914* (Cambridge, 1996).
11. C. Ó Gráda, 'British agriculture, 1860–1914', in R. Floud and D. McCloskey, eds, *The Economic History of Britain since 1700*, vol. 2, *1860–1939* (Cambridge, 1994).
12. N. Koning, *The Failure of Agrarian Capitalism: Agrarian Politics in the United Kingdom, Germany, the Netherlands and the USA, 1846–1919* (London, 1994); J. van

Zanden, 'The first "green revolution": the growth of production and productivity in European agriculture, 1870–1914', *Economic History Review*, 44 (1991).

13. M. E. Turner, 'Agricultural output, income and productivity', in E. J. T. Collins, ed., *The Agrarian History of England and Wales*, vol. 7, *1850–1914* (Cambridge, 2000).

14. T. W. Fletcher, 'The great depression of English agriculture, 1873–1896', *Economic History Review*, 13 (1960–1).

15. P. J. Perry, *British Farming in the Great Depression 1870–1914: An Historical Geography* (Newton Abbot, 1974); F. M. L. Thompson, 'An anatomy of English agriculture, 1870–1914', in B. A. Holderness and M. E. Turner, eds, *Land, Labour and Agriculture, 1700–1920: Essays for Gordon Mingay* (London, 1991).

16. Caird, *English Agriculture*, p. 287.

17. J. Chartres, 'Rural industry and manufacturing' in E. J. T. Collins, ed., *The Agrarian History of England and Wales*, vol. 7, *1850–1914* (Cambridge, 2000), p. 1149.

18. Chartres, 'Rural industry', p. 1148.

19. J. L. Hammond and B. Hammond, *The Village Labourer* (London, 1978), p. 58.

20. A. Howkins, 'Peasants, servants and labourers: the marginal workforce in British agriculture, c.1870–1914', *Agricultural History Review*, 42 (1994).

21. F. M. L. Thompson, *English Landed Society in the Nineteenth Century* (London, 1963); D. Cannadine, *The Decline and Fall of the British Aristocracy* (New Haven, CT, 1990).

22. J. V. Beckett, 'The decline of the small landowner in eighteenth and nineteenth-century England: some regional considerations', *Agricultural History Review*, 30 (1981).

23. T. M. Devine, *Clanship to Crofters' War: The Social Transformation of the Scottish Highlands* (Manchester, 1994).

24. D. Grigg, 'Farm size in England and Wales, from Victorian times to the present', *Agricultural History Review*, 35 (1987).

25. D. W. Howell, *Land and People in Nineteenth-Century Wales* (London, 1977), p. 24.

26. E. Higgs, 'Occupational censuses and the agricultural workforce in Victorian England and Wales', *Economic History Review*, 48 (1995).

27. A. O'Dowd, *Spalpeens and Tattie Hokers: History and Folklore of the Irish Migratory Worker in Ireland and Britain* (Dublin, 1991).

28. A. W. Fox, 'Agricultural wages in England and Wales during the last fifty years', in W. E. Minchinton, ed., *Essays in Agrarian History* (Newton Abbot, 1968).

29. D. Fitzpatrick, 'The disappearance of the Irish agricultural labourer, 1841–1912', *Irish Economic and Social History*, 7 (1980).

30. A. Howkins, 'The English farm labourer in the nineteenth century: farm, family and community', in B. Short, ed., *The English Rural Community: Image and Analysis* (Cambridge, 1992).

31. I. Carter, *Farm Life in Northeast Scotland 1840–1914: The Poor Man's Country* (Edinburgh, 1997).

32. S. Caunce, *Among Farm Horses: The Horselads of East Yorkshire* (Stroud, 1991).

33. E. J. Hobsbawm and G. Rudé, *Captain Swing* (London, 1970).

34. A. Charlesworth, *Social Protest in a Rural Society: The Spatial Diffusion of the Captain Swing Disturbances of 1830–31* (Norwich, 1978).

35. I. Dyck, *William Cobbett and Rural Popular Culture* (Cambridge, 1992).

36. M. Reed and R. A. E. Wells, eds, *Class, Conflict and Protest in the English Countryside, 1700–1880* (London, 1990).

37. J. P. D. Dunbabin, *Rural Discontent in Nineteenth Century Britain* (London, 1974).

38. M. R. Beames, *Peasants and Power: The Whiteboy Movements and their Control in Pre-Famine Ireland* (Brighton, 1982).

39. S. Clark, *The Social Origins of the Irish Land War* (Princeton, NJ, 1979).

40. J. Hunter, *The Making of the Crofting Community* (Edinburgh, 1976).

41. E. J. T. Collins, ed., *The Agrarian History of England and Wales*, vol. 7, *1850–1914* (Cambridge, 2000), p. 2157.

42. H. Taylor, *A Claim on the Countryside: A History of the British Outdoor Movement* (Edinburgh, 1997).

43. T. C. Smout, *Nature Contested: Environmental History in Scotland and Northern England since 1600* (Edinburgh, 2000).

44. J. Ranlett, ' "Checking nature's desecration": late-Victorian environmental organisation', *Victorian Studies*, 26 (1983).

FURTHER READING

Essential, comprehensive surveys of England and Wales come in two volumes in a series: G. E. Mingay, ed., *The Agrarian History of England and Wales*, vol. 6, *1750–1850* (1989) and E. J. T. Collins, ed., *The Agrarian History of England and Wales*, vol. 7, *1850–1914* (2000). Both contain extensive statistical appendices and bibliographies. An earlier illustrated collection is G. E. Mingay, ed., *The Victorian Countryside* (1981). The most recent and convincing contribution to debates about the nature and time of the Agricultural Revolution is M. Overton, *Agricultural Revolution in England: The Transformation of the Agrarian Economy, 1500–1850* (1996). R. Perren, *Agriculture in Depression, 1870–1940* (1995) provides a useful summary of the later period. D. Grigg, *English Agriculture: An Historical Perspective* (1989) is both readable and wide-ranging. The workforce and social relations in the second half of the century have been explored by A. Howkins in a number of publications: 'Peasants, servants and labourers: the marginal workforce in British agriculture, c.1870–1914', *Agricultural History Review*, 42 (1994); 'The English farm labourer in the nineteenth century: farm, family and community', in B. Short, ed., *The English Rural Community: Image and Analysis* (1992); and *Reshaping Rural England: A Social History 1850–1925* (1991). It is still difficult to better D. W. Howell, *Land and People in Nineteenth-Century Wales* (1977). T. M. Devine has published extensively on Scotland: T. M. Devine, ed., *Farm Servants and Labour in Lowland Scotland, 1770–1914* (1984); *Clanship to Crofters' War: The Social Transformation of the Scottish Highlands* (1994); *The Transformation of Rural Scotland: Social Change and the Agrarian Economy, 1660–1815* (1994). A comprehensive survey is E. Richards, *A History of the Highland Clearances* (1982, 1985). The debates surrounding Irish farming can be sampled from C. Ó Gráda, *Ireland Before and After the Famine: Explorations in Economic History, 1808–1925* (1993) and M. E. Turner, *After the Famine: Irish Agriculture 1850–1914* (1996). S. Clark, *Social Origins of the Irish Land War* (1979) provides an intelligible interpretation of Irish social development before the 1880s. T. W. Guinnane, *The Vanishing Irish: Households, Migration, and the Rural Economy in Ireland, 1850–1914* (1997) deals with an agenda which is almost totally absent from studies of rural England.

CHAPTER THIRTEEN

Industry and Transport

WILLIAM J. ASHWORTH

Introduction

In 1851 Britain celebrated its status as the workshop of the world by displaying the fruits of its industry and placing the commodity at the heart of Victorian culture. 'The Great Exhibition of the Works and Industry of All Nations' was housed in an impressive iron frame covered in huge panes of glass, appearing like a huge 'modern shopping mall'.[1] On display were manufactured articles from around the world, all carefully arranged to a taxonomy informed by the imperatives of a maturing British political economy.

Although international, the focus of the exhibition was predominantly domestic with half of its display devoted to British industry. This spectacle also signalled the arrival of another significant development, namely tourism. The Great Exhibition was erected just as rail travel was taking off amongst the masses. This powerful combination provided a potential means of allaying the discontent of workers fed on a diet of industrial conflict, Chartism and economic fears. Prince Albert, for one, was keen that 'millions of workers' visit the exhibition to subdue, at least momentarily, their concerns, and perhaps even take pride in the results of their labours. Consequently 'Shilling Days' were started, making admission to the exhibition affordable to a significant proportion of the working population. The prophet of industrial doom, Thomas Carlyle, grit his teeth and quipped: 'All the loose population of London pours itself every holiday into Hyde Park round this strange edifice.' Not surprisingly, as Carlyle's contemporary Mayhew observed: 'the chief centres of curiosity are the power looms, and in front of these are gathered small groups of artisans, and labourers, and young men whose course red hands tell you they do something for their living, all eagerly listening to the attendant, as he explains the operations, after stopping the loom'. Here the masses were being taught to look at this symbol of industrial change in wonder and not in horror.[2]

What was not on display at the 'Crystal Palace', as it was dubbed, was the actual social labour, factories and dour workshops that created this magical spectacle. This was a celebration of the commodity and not of labour. The first sections of this chapter focus on the geography of industry throughout Britain, taking particular care to illuminate some of the less visible aspects of manufacturing and the sources of energy that powered it. The final section surveys both the dramatic developments in transport and the impact they had on everyday social life and on the movement of goods.

The Industrial Revolution and the View from Abroad

The once dominant perspective that Britain was a land ravaged by factories and machines during the early nineteenth century has in recent years been severely eroded. New macro-economic studies have provided seemingly incontrovertible evidence that national economic growth between 1780 and 1820 was actually much slower than once thought.[3] In other words, the view that the period associated with the Industrial Revolution marked a major economic discontinuity has been fundamentally challenged. This, in turn, has bolstered historians who stress continuity in both the social and political worlds during this era.[4]

Similarly, some imperial historians have challenged the view that the bourgeoisie rose to become the dominant political force during the nineteenth century. Adopting the rather woolly but evocative term of 'gentlemanly capitalism', they have stressed the durability and adaptability of the aristocracy within Britain's power base. In particular, it is argued that a powerful alliance was forged between the landed gentry and the financial sector, based around the City of London. Within this context the industrial bourgeoisie remained relatively powerless and subordinate to land and the City.[5] Finally, another group of historians has underlined the futility of any account of the Industrial Revolution. They claim that all interpretations are relative, since they are all inevitably tied to the prevailing socio-economic concerns within which the historian is writing.[6]

It is true that past exponents of the Industrial Revolution tended to generalize the impact of industrialization and the irresistible march of the machine; however, recent historians have once again added life to the besieged notion of a revolution. Empirical studies have shown that some regions experienced rapid industrialization, while other parts were actually characterized by de-industrialization.[7] Further, macro-economic perspectives have been shown to exclude a substantial proportion of the industrial sector from their figures.[8] Likewise, the bourgeoisie were clearly a powerful and dominant force outside Westminster, particularly in the expanding industrial centres that mattered most to their interests. The City of London was far from holding a coherent set of interests and was never as dominated by the aristocracy and their system of values as some commentators have implied.[9] In addition, if we move beyond manufactures into other cultural areas, the real and imagined impact of industrialization and the machine made profound imprints on the nature of knowledge, forging the discipline of political economy, informing Christian evangelical beliefs and moulding economic policy.[10] The Industrial Revolution should not be confined simply to the realm of material production. The imagined or very real impact of industrialization penetrated a whole array of both material and cultural forms.

While the Enlightenment has traditionally been predominantly associated with France, the French themselves viewed Britain as the place actually to view radical change. The result was a flood into Britain during the late eighteenth and early nineteenth centuries of French savants, industrial spies and curious politicians.[11] These numerous commentators were in no doubt that far-reaching industrial changes had ripped through parts of the British landscape. Whatever present-day historians may say, for contemporaries at least Britain had experienced and was clearly still experiencing what the French dubbed in the 1820s an 'industrial revolution'.

The Geography of British Industry

By the close of the eighteenth century London had become the world's largest entrepôt and financial centre, and the heart of the world's shipping and marine insurance. It was also the most important industrial centre in Britain. The huge pool of wealth gathered within its borders fuelled the production of luxury products, from furniture and clothes to carriages and children's toys. It was the core city for precision scientific instruments and the manufacturing of printing presses. Its huge population also made it the largest producer and consumer of basic items such as cheap clothing, shoes, beer, soap and other necessities. Moving northwards from London, a whole array of counties and cities had established distinctive specialized industries. For example, Birmingham and the West Midlands were known for their small metal trades; Manchester and Lancashire for cotton, Sheffield and Yorkshire for cutlery, and Leeds for wool; Newcastle and its surrounding areas for coal and heavy engineering, Leicester and Nottingham for hosiery, and Northampton for shoes. In addition, towns and villages within these regions had evolved to become responsible for a specific stage within the production of each area's particular specialities.

Spearheading industrial change was the factory system with cotton leading the way. Early factories tended to locate near water in rural areas where the environment was frequently bleak and demographically sparse. The prototype factory model was Richard Arkwright's cotton mill, situated in the appropriately wet and barren area of Cromford in Derbyshire. By 1835 there were 1,113 cotton mills and 1,333 woollen and worsted mills mainly in the north of England. The mechanics lecturer and factory propagandist Andrew Ure rejoiced at what he believed such factories embodied and represented. A cotton mill, he claimed, captured 'the perfection of automatic industry . . . it is there that the elemental powers have been made to animate millions of complex organs, infusing into forms of wood, iron, and base an intelligent agency'.[12] The notion that human intelligence operated to the dictates of a form of industrial reason also inspired a number of contemporary men of science.

It was the imperative of saving time rather than capital that fuelled this form of organization. The rather scattered process of production could be speeded up through greater centralization. Within the various factory forms of organized labour a distinct culture of time-discipline came to replace task-discipline. Here the old flexibility of working to one's own rhythm was surgically removed. The days where a domestic outworker was free to stop and start work when he or she wished were gone. Social labour now had to be trained to work to the dictates of the factory bell, and in some instances, the rhythm of a machine. Above all it enabled the master manufacturer to have greater control over the labour force. Further proof of the imperative of time came in 1847 when factory legislation reduced the legal working day from anything up to sixteen hours to ten. The result was a distinct switch to ways of intensifying the labour output within those ten hours. Consequently there was a profound increase in the adoption of machines, together with innovations in the high-pressure steam engine.

A fundamental factor in the staggering rise of the British cotton industry was the massive increase in raw cotton production in the United States: from 2 m lbs in 1791 to 182 m lbs in 1821. Its price also began continuously to decline from 1800, further aiding Britain's cotton manufacturers. By this point, too, cotton had supplanted wool as the nation's most profitable export – constituting something like 40 per cent of all profit from Britain's exports. However, exports to the United States and Europe thereafter declined, primarily owing to the erection of tariff barriers and a huge reduction in the importation of raw cotton in the 1860s during the American Civil War. Despite this, substitute markets were found elsewhere, most importantly in India, China, South America and West Africa.

Changes in the production of textiles took complicated and varying pathways. In 1803 William Horrocks patented the first powered loom, but it was not until the 1820s that the growth in number of these looms really accelerated, reaching 100,000 by 1833. By this point, too, many handloom weavers were unable to compete with mechanized weaving. As a result they were either compelled to work in the cotton factories or doomed to life-long unemployment. It is also the case that the numerous small operators that characterized much of the industry until this juncture started to fall by the way. The shift towards power looms came later in the wool industry with 46,984 powered looms by 1867. The primary reason for the divergence in the time-scale between the two textiles is the different qualities of the materials. Woollen yarn, for example, was far more vulnerable to damage, and the necessary technology capable of working good-quality wool at a decent pace did not arise until the 1850s and 1860s. Generally the size, organization and degree of concentration of textile manufacturers were a product of the local environment, and especially the history of the local workforce.[13]

In 1830 the Scottish engineer Richard Roberts designed a fully mechanized or 'self-acting' mule on behalf of certain mill-owners. It was developed as a deliberate attempt to break the entrenched power of the so-called 'minders', the chief spinning operatives, who were sub-contracted in factories to help control labour. This powerful section of the workforce had instigated a series of damaging strikes during the late 1820s. Ure could barely restrain his enthusiasm for Roberts's machine and saw it as a stark warning to unruly workers:

> Thus, the *Iron Man*, as the operators call it, sprung out of the hands of our modern Prometheus at the bidding of Minerva – a creation destined to restore order among the industrious classes, and to confirm to Great Britain the empire of art. The news of this Herculean prodigy spread dismay through the Union, and even long before it left its cradle, so to speak, it strangled the Hydra of misrule.[14]

As we shall see Ure's optimistic hyperbole was a little misplaced.

The 'iron man' allowed one person assisted by two or three boys or girls to operate 1,600 spindles as comfortably as that person had done previously for only 300 spindles. Where they were installed, the owners of the mills had to double the size of the plant in order to accommodate them. However, although women could now use the self-acting mule, as they were doing in Scotland, there was reluctance to adopt it in Lancashire. This was partly due to the recent severing of skills in the female work-force owing to the domination of men operating semi-powered mules. But it was much more the result of an economic decision by the mill-owners who, after weigh-ing up the situation, decided that the long-term perks of replacing the prevailing system with cheaply paid women and a much more hierarchical system, were out-weighed by short-term losses in production and productivity. The result was the retention of minders with a standardized wage, relative control over their work, and the creation of a strong union.

Another factor directing centralized power-driven factory production was the cost of steam power. Up until the close of the 1820s water-wheels had dominated the cotton industry. It was not until the 1830s and 1840s that the price of steam power allowed a decisive shift to factory production in textiles. Until this point domestic and factory production worked together, with just the spinning and weaving of cotton and wool becoming centralized via water-powered factories. It should be emphasized that human, animal, water and wind sources of power were still a more important source of energy than steam right up until the mid-nineteenth century.[15]

The adoption of steam-powered machines depended on the balance between the cost of fixed capital and the savings in fuel. One horsepower consumed too much coal to make it worth using until the price of coal rapidly fell in the 1840s. It was at this moment that there was a significant shift toward the use of coal in the cotton and (slightly later) wool factories. This switch was further aided by an economic depression in the late 1830s and early 1840s, and by a reduction of the working day to ten hours. This provided the incentive to increase the spread of machinery and attempt to make labour more efficient. The latter had become much more of an imperative, as the key area of cheap labour, primarily female and child, was being rapidly reduced.

Leading the labour force of the new high-productivity industries associated with the Industrial Revolution had been women and not men. As a cheap and abundant source of labour, women and children were the obvious resort for those establishing industries in the countryside during the eighteenth century. Women were concen-trated in the putting-out industries such as wool and silk, they were found in the potteries and to a certain extent in metal goods. Above all they were crucial to the cotton industry. For example, in 1818 women accounted for over half the cotton workforce with the rest composed of men and a substantial proportion of children.[16] The percentage of children employed in the textile industries depended on the region. In some places it actually constituted over half the workforce in particular mills. Before the Factory Act of 1847 children worked, on average, twelve to thirteen hours a day, six days a week, often in temperatures as high as 80°F (27°C) within en-vironments that were damp and thick with cotton dust.[17] It is the relatively sudden growth in importance of women and children in British industry between 1770 and 1830 that represents one striking reason to see the period as a major discontinuity.[18]

However, during the course of the nineteenth century the position of women in the workplace was gradually eroded. A combination of male pressure and the estab-lishment of male-based trade unions pushed females out during the transition to 'doubled' hand mules. By the Victorian period there was strong cultural opposition towards women in the workplace, and an ideal of domesticity emerged with the role of women placed firmly back in the home. The sensibilities of a growing middle class spearheaded the view that women were best suited to reproductive and nurturing activities. This, in turn, was enforced by protective legislation that served to bolster the idea of a male breadwinner and, indirectly, reinforced contemporary gendered notions of intelligence.[19]

Coal, Iron and Steel

Britain was in the vanguard of the world in developing an integrated economy during the eighteenth century. It was also the first nation to switch to mineral-based fuels during the nineteenth century. One ton of coal produced about the same energy as the output of one acre of wood from land. Already by 1800 Britain used up to five times as much coal as the rest of Europe. Wrigley sees this as the crucial difference in Britain's economy compared with the rest of Europe. It allowed the country to release itself from the restraints of an organic economy, which also further freed up valuable land for agriculture. While the Dutch, for example, continued to rely on peat, British consumption of coal grew from roughly 2.5 to 3 m tons of coal in 1700 to approximately 15 m tons in 1800. This figure then doubled to 30 m tons by 1830 and reached an impressive 70 m tons by the early 1850s. The utilization of coal was the primary factor that enabled industrialization to enter a new phase. It had already been used for some time in the production of salt, sugar, glass, beer, bread, brass, copper and bricks. However, it was cotton followed by iron – and later steel – that became the prime user of coal- and steam-powered machinery. 'On the basis of mineral wealth it proved possible to construct an industrial society with a capacity to produce material goods of use to man on a scale that dwarfed such production in any earlier period.'[20]

The impact of coal also had a significant role in redefining the location of certain industries. For example, the eighteenth-century iron industry along the river Severn quickly diminished during the early nineteenth century as cheap coal in South Wales, Staffordshire and Scotland transformed these regions into the hub of the iron industry. From producing around 40 per cent of all British iron during the 1770s Shropshire's percentage of production shrank to 12.5 by 1815. It was during this era that South Wales and Staffordshire's share dramatically increased to approximately two-thirds of total iron production. Scottish output greatly expanded during the latter half of the 1820s after hot-blast technology was pioneered and introduced. Likewise, the initial heart of the cotton industry was the Derbyshire Peak District and Staffordshire with its large abundance of water power. However, by the end of the eighteenth century and into the nineteenth steam power enabled the industry to shift to Lancashire.

It was not until furnaces and forges utilized coal that Britain started to compete in the iron market with Sweden and Russia. The application of coke to smelting iron only really took off in the second half of the eighteenth century. Before this charcoal furnaces had dominated the iron industry. Building upon the techniques of former iron makers, Henry Cort patented a rolling process during the 1780s that turned iron into bars. In a later patent, he combined this procedure with a puddling stage. Here the molten iron was first stirred until it formed an iron ball. It was then taken to the forge where it was flattened by hammers before being taken to be rolled. By this time both the hammering and the rolling were powered by steam, which meant producers were less reliant on locating near water.

The production of iron was further improved in 1828 when the Scottish engineer James Neilson patented the hot-blast system. This enabled the furnace to reach much higher temperatures by heating the air blown into it, refuting the former view that cold air was more effective. The process speeded up output, reduced fuel consumption, and helped to improve the quality of the metal. The result was a huge expansion of the Scottish iron industry. The process eventually spread to England and Wales after the patent ran out in 1842. As the price of pig iron fell it was increasingly used instead of wood, stone, brass and other metals. Peak demand for pig iron for domestic railways came during the late 1840s, accounting for 30 to 40 per cent of domestic iron production. Thereafter exports became the primary factor fuelling the iron industry with sales abroad growing by a factor of nine between 1830 and 1870, eventually taking 50 per cent of all home-produced pig iron.[21]

Steel, before its huge expansion in the late nineteenth century, had been prized as the best material for quality cutting tools, creating precision watch parts and metalworking tools for the engineering industry. In addition, it was valued for domestic items such as cutlery and razors, and agricultural tools like scythes. In short, it was a vital component in developments made in the important arena of hand tools.[22] The availability of steel radically increased after Bessemer devised a process of turning pig iron into a particular form of steel in 1856. It was cheaper than wrought iron and a great deal more resistant to corrosion. During the following decade the establishment of the Siemens–Martin open-hearth furnace further aided steel-making. Initially, British railways and shipbuilders were wary of adopting steel and continued to use traditional wrought iron. Nonetheless, between the 1870s and 1890s steel production greatly increased, with Scotland, Cumberland and the North-East all expanding in importance as iron and steel producers, primarily at the expense of South Wales.

Despite the increasing use of coal-powered steam machines, much of Britain's industry still relied on water, animal and human power. Water power especially remained a dominant source of energy well into the nineteenth century. Even during the 'steam revolution' in mid-century, water power only declined by 9 per cent within the textile industry and 14 per cent nationally. Thereafter, however, coal soon accelerated to become the most important source of energy. Accompanying this rise was the emergence of a science of energy from the 1860s with a concern for 'heat engines', and attempts to establish accurate measurements on the relationship between the mechanical equivalent of heat. Much of this work in Britain was carried out by scientists and engineers working in the great northern industrial cities of Glasgow and Manchester.

The Property of Skill and the Machinery Question: The Engineering Industry

The machinery question had a profound impact on the character of British industry, and was a dominant theme for the whole of the nineteenth century, with numerous trades resisting its implementation. In a sense the phrase 'machinery question' conceals more than it reveals: the question was about the ownership of skills and control over work. As J. Rule comments: 'General Ludd was not opposing the introduction of new machinery, but the employment of less-skilled labour on the knitting frames to turn out inferior stockings at lower wages'.[23] A skilled labourer's identity and power was embedded in the skills he – I use the gendered term deliberately – owned, and the emerging form of industrial relations centred upon this issue. The machine simply represented the most visible symbol of this seeming imperative. Resistance to the implementation of machinery was regional and cultural.[24]

Understanding the specific reaction to the machine, and the form of society that adopted it, is to realize the peculiar shape of manufactures and industrial relations in Britain. The machine certainly represented the pinnacle of industrial capitalist production, but it by no means signified the actual state of prevailing modes of production. 'What was striking in nineteenth-century Britain was not the power of the machine in displacing labour, but the dependence of most work processes on more and more labour.'[25] This was clear mid-century through the items put on display at the Great Exhibition. There was a diverse set of products made both using intensive skilled hand labour and by machine.

Indeed, it was not the British but the North American exhibits that were the most mechanized. Take, for example, Samuel Colt's repeating pistols which so aroused the curiosity of British manufacturers. At an invited address to the Institute of Civil Engineers, he told them that approximately 80 per cent of the whole cost in producing the guns was accounted for by machinery. His motives for this investment were simple, 'by finding that with hand labour it was not possible to obtain that amount of uniformity, or accuracy in the several parts, which is so desirable, and also because he could not otherwise get the number of arms made, at anything like the same cost, as by machinery'. After viewing a small-arms factory set up by Colt in Pimlico during the early 1850s, the successful British engineer James Nasymyth claimed that he had witnessed 'perfection and economy such as I have never seen before'. He also highlighted the 'traditional notions and attachment to old systems' in England as compared with the USA. The English lock-maker and lock-picker Alfred C. Hobbs similarly claimed the reason automated mechanization had not taken off to such a degree as was clearly the case in America was the very different nature of the British workforce. His concern had inspired him to cross the Atlantic and view American industry. He came back and warned the readers of the *Journal of the Society of Arts*, in 1857, that in introducing any new machinery into any part of manufacturing, 'they should endeavour to reform the minds of the workmen before they began'. Deep-seated suspicion of machines had become ingrained in the consciousness of the British workforce. Just as Americans, French and other continental Europeans had come to view British industry over the past hundred or so years, British observers were now going to North America. New developments in the world's industry were fast moving across the Atlantic and to parts of continental Europe, most notably Germany. Indeed, by 1876 the German engineering professor Franz Reuleaux recognized the switch: 'Now the entirely new ideas of American machinery have tossed the English out of the satchel, and we must without hesitation attach ourselves to the new system if we do not want to fall behind.'[26]

The emphasis across the whole of British industry concerning heavy machinery was generalist rather than specialist. The British Victorian engineer was still predominantly an artisan or a mechanic, rather than an operative or hand. Precision was more important than speed. He was still, to a certain extent, in control of his own movements and pace of work. As such he was certainly not receptive to production-control techniques like the standard design drawings used increasingly by American manufacturers. At the Great Western Railway factory in Swindon, the concentration on hand work continued right down to the outbreak of the First World War. As one contemporary wrote: 'very little is left to the chance work of the machine, which is often faulty and unreliable. Rivets put in by hand are far more trustworthy'.[27]

In contrast to Britain's engineering industry, the USA had by the 1850s already adopted specific machines, jigs, fixtures and gauges to manufacture interchangeable parts. By the end of the century significant parts of the global market had become penetrated by large volumes of American-manufactured standardized equipment. This was in stark contrast to the craft and customized products being manufactured in Britain. These contrasting pathways were forged by the differing social and cultural contexts of the two countries. It was not as if Britain had not, at one time, been at the vanguard of standardization and automation. Take, for example, the woodblock-making machinery introduced at Portsmouth in 1802, which produced interchangeable parts and significantly reduced the need for human labour. Consider too the development of steam-powered mechanized biscuit-making also at Portsmouth in 1833, 'possibly the first assembly line in the food industries'.[28] It is also the case that early British machine manufacturers developed numerous self-acting machine tools and precision instruments. Such tools, in turn, made an important impact on the division of labour on the shop floor, creating the employment of non-apprenticed workers on machinery, and other cost-saving policies such as piecework and systematic overtime. However, all of this was aggressively opposed by the early societies of journeymen engineers. Despite the defeat of the Amalgamated Society of Engineers by the London and Lancashire masters in the 1852 lockout, the reliance on the engineer's craft skills remained deeply embedded.

With the important exception of the standard machinery built for the British textile industry, the local environment and cultural conditions were not congruent with a move towards mass production of heavy engineering in the same way as the USA. There, a lack of skilled labour was mixed with a supply of unskilled immigrant labour, there was a domestic market with different demands, there were no guilds to prevent changes in production, and, perhaps most importantly, there were fewer culturally ingrained suspicions toward the possibilities of technology. Arguably, all of these combined to create an economy conducive to mass production in the modern sense. This is not to say there was no resistance in the USA to the introduction of machines, far from it, but it was not as widespread, entrenched or developed as in Britain.[29]

In addition, for much of British industry, textiles aside, the standardization of its products was not compatible with the demands of its markets. Thus it was by no means clear that investment in machinery was the correct policy for engineering. Demand was not regular, and to be cost-effective machines often needed to be run all day. As we have seen, British engineering industries tended to build to order, to meet various customer requirements. This made the industries more flexible, but less competitive in a global market that was becoming more standardized. Within this context British capitalists invested far more in capital-saving rather than labour-saving techniques. Conversely, the USA was very much under-populated, particularly in skilled workers, and thus labour-saving technology was crucial to its capitalist growth. Consequently, there was far more reason, points out Brown, for American machine-makers 'to take over planning and resourcefulness as managerial functions exerted through working drawings'.[30]

The development of engineering drawings directing production was crucial in the pathway of American industrial engineering. The use of working drawings by owner-managers was adopted to ensure managerial control over production. Brown claims they 'represented a substantial managerial incursion into craft workers' autonomy, suggesting a de-skilling motive'.[31] This is not to say it was possible to mechanize fully or standardize the products where this approach was applied. Rather, it simply increased the control of the managers and reduced the independence of the craft workers. By contrast, despite two major managerial victories over workers in the nineteenth century (1852 and 1897–8), British employers concentrated on labour investment and, indeed, increased their dependence on craft labour.

Transport

Transport in the nineteenth century is typically remembered for the arrival of steam-powered locomotives. However, the switch to transporting goods by rail was a much slower process in comparison with its almost instant success in the movement of people. Perhaps this was partly because of the effective transport system that was already in existence. By the nineteenth century a clear structure and network had already emerged with much of industry having adapted around particular modes of transportation. As a result the vital infrastructure – such as warehouses and loading equipment – was already situated by roads, outports and especially canals. Indeed, for one recent commentator, the combination of improvements to roads and the development of waterways and canals was the primary factor that separated Britain from the rest of Europe and was the crucial factor enabling the Industrial Revolution.[32]

Perhaps the most spectacular development in British transportation during the eighteenth century was the building of the Bridgwater canal under the Acts of 1759 and 1760. After this the building and use of canals quickly expanded as their economic potential was realized. Bagwell's estimate of total tonnage carried on canals by the early 1840s is between 30 m and 35 m tons. The movement of coal was a particularly popular commodity on canals with, for example, 270,753 tons out of a total 584,950 tons of coal used in Liverpool transported this way by 1833. By the mid-nineteenth century 25,000 barges were being used, with 50,000 or more persons at any one time living on board.

Road transport during the eighteenth century was generally unreliable owing to the appalling condition of roads and their vulnerability to the notoriously wet British weather. Road maintenance was a major difficulty. Owing to an old Act of 1555 all road repairs were left to unpaid farmers and local labourers, which meant they generally remained neglected. As long as inter-regional commerce was small the problem was bearable. However, as the trading importance of these roads grew it became clear that something had to be done to improve the situation. This state of affairs finally came to an end in the early 1830s, when it became the duty of parishes to levy a highway rate to finance the necessary labour for repairs.

Manufacturers and merchants had already tried to improve the state of roads during the eighteenth century with the creation of turnpike trusts. These schemes had rapidly increased in the second half of the century and especially during the nine-teenth century. By the 1830s there were approximately 22,000 miles of turnpike roads and 104,770 miles of parish highways throughout England and Wales. It was the creation of these roads that triggered new and superior approaches to road-building. Engineers such as Telford and McAdam devised new surfaces, foundations and systems of drainage. To begin with, the local nature of turnpike trusts caused road improvement to be carried out piecemeal and not regularized across the country. However, through lobbying and select committee investigations, something like a national network of roads started to emerge during the 1820s. By the 1830s the journey times between the main cities had been reduced by four-fifths when com-pared with times taken in the 1750s. Particularly impressive were the huge increases in stagecoach services and the number of passengers riding per coach. By this point the main competition for passenger travel came from steam-powered packet vessels, particularly those operating along the east coast. Both forms of customer transport, however, were eclipsed in the following two decades by the development of railways. The increase in the carriage of goods by road was not so dramatic, although it did expand significantly between 1790 and 1830.[33]

The length of coastlines around the British Isles in relation to its land size makes them ideally suited to coastal shipping. Where this mode of transport could be used there were great savings to be made. Its dominant cargo during the eighteenth century was coal followed by corn. It was ideal for goods with a low value in rela-tion to their bulk. During the days of sail its role as a carrier of people was popular, although it tended to be confined to the months between April and October owing to the risk of storms. Indeed, until the arrival of steam-powered vessels it was the weather, along with tides, which in general hampered the use of this mode of transport.

Wooden railways were established in the early seventeenth century in an attempt to move coal over land during the wet winter months. It was not until the con-struction of iron rails in the late eighteenth and early nineteenth century that these became more durable and popular. However, the development of steam-powered, as opposed to horse-pulled railways, was a slower process. By 1823 there were only twenty-eight steam engines in existence, and most of them were not much better than horse traction. All this was to change with the opening of the Liverpool and Manchester railway in 1830. It was the first line to be operated entirely by steam locomotive power and at a much faster speed. Stephenson's 'Rocket' during the Rain-hill Trials managed to reach a rate of 30 mph. The railway was operated by one company and was responsible for all the arrangements for both passengers and goods.[34]

By the 1830s faith in steam locomotives coupled with an economy that was experiencing good financial conditions helped increase the rate of railway projects. As a result forty-four additional railway acts were passed between 1836 and 1837, with expenditure increasing from £1 m in 1834 to £9 m in 1839. This represented the first railway boom. This was soon followed by an even greater railway mania between 1844 and 1847. The latter marked the height of investment with nearly 7 per cent of national income being drawn in. Indeed, such was the level of in-vestment, it required a restructuring of the British capital market. The London Stock Exchange both greatly expanded and moved towards company securities. In addition, a number of provincial stock exchanges were established such as those at Liverpool, Manchester, Leeds, Glasgow and Edinburgh.[35] During the construction of these railways a new class of labourer was born – the so-called 'navigators' or 'navvies'. Gourvish estimates that between 1831 and 1870 an average of 60,000 men were employed in the building of railways – at its peak the figure was nearly three times higher.[36] Prior to 1914 all British railways were erected via private investors with the government at no stage called in to help raise capital. By contrast, in Europe the state played a dominant role at all stages in the building and planning of a rail network.

Since each railway line was built and run by an independent company, through trips across the various lines was at first not possible. This changed, however, in 1842 when Glyn and George Stephenson set up the Railway Clearing House. The original members represented nine lines running from London to York and Leeds. This expanded to forty-five lines by 1849. By this stage only the Great Western remained outside the system. Particularly problematic was standardizing the rail gauge, since the Great Western insisted on keeping its wider track and only conformed to the more narrow gauge in the 1870s.

The Annihilation of Space through Time

The visual and audible effect of the steam train, like the machine, was awesome to the senses and the imagination. For the highly taxed masses new machinery was also making an impact on their pocket through unfair competition. The advent of untaxed steam-powered looms was having a devastating impact on the livelihood of thousands of weavers. As the harbingers of the New World gleefully celebrated its latest and most spectacular offering, steam-powered rail travel, the victims of the machine age gave their verdict at the opening of the Liverpool and Manchester railway.

Celebrities from all walks of life gathered to experience the new sensation of rail travel. The famous actress Fanny Kemble caught the mixed mood in her description of the vast crowds that gathered to watch the train: 'The most intense curiosity and excitement prevailed, and though the weather was uncertain, enormous masses of densely packed people lined the road, shouting and waving hats and handkerchiefs as we flew by.' However, on nearing Britain's industrial capital, Manchester, the mood soured. The 'sky grew cloudy and dark, and it began to rain', while the composition of the crowd changed to 'the lowest order of mechanics and artisans'. Rising 'above the grim and grimy crowd of scowling faces a loom had been erected, at which sat a tattered, starved-looking weaver, evidently set there as a representative man, to protest against the triumph of machinery and the gain and glory which the wealthy Liverpool and Manchester men were likely to derive from it'.[37]

The arrival of the steam locomotive, like the impact of the machine in general, may have made fewer inroads into industry than was once thought. However, its sculpturing of the way the world was perceived and actually experienced was, like the machine, deeply powerful. The most obvious and talked-about shock of rail travel was its reduction of space through its speed of movement. Contemporaries frequently compared the locomotive to a bullet, and used the phrase 'Annihilation of time and space' to capture the new sensation offered by this form of transport.[38]

The steam train also appeared novel because it seemed to be in unity with the railway track. In other words, it was not being propelled by an extraneous power but, rather, running by itself. In addition, the actual laying of the railway track made a fundamental imprint on the landscape. To reduce friction the track should ideally be flat, with the result that much of the earth and rock that got in the way was removed in order to level the terrain. Tunnels were bored through mountains and viaducts built over valleys. Woodland and high ground was cut and embankments were built on low ground to elevate the track. This had the effect of alienating the passenger from the landscape. As an anonymous commentator wrote in 1844: 'in travelling on most of the railways the face of nature, the beautiful prospects of hill and dale, are lost or distorted to our view'.[39] In connecting previously inaccessible places the railroad also destroyed the space between the two junctures. As a result, the annihilation of space through time had the affect of eroding local identities and speeding up the standardization of time around the country. So long as travel was slow, the varying local times throughout the nation were not a problem. However, the shrinking of distance between places and the running of a strict timetable forced the situation to become regularized – and Greenwich Time became established on all the various lines, and eventually throughout England. The factory bell had reached personal travel.

NOTES

1. T. Richards, *The Commodity Culture of Victorian England: Advertising and Spectacle, 1851–1914* (London, 1991), p. 4.
2. R. Brain, *Going to the Fair: Readings in the Culture of Nineteenth-Century Exhibitions* (Cambridge, 1993), pp. 24–7, 102.
3. N. F. R. Crafts, *British Economic Growth During the Industrial Revolution* (Oxford, 1985).
4. J. C. D. Clark, *English Society 1688–1832: Ideology, Social Structure and Political Practice during the Ancien Regime* (Cambridge, 1985).
5. P. J. Cain and A. G. Hopkins, *British Imperialism: Innovation and Expansion, 1688–1914* (Harlow, 1993).
6. D. Cannadine, 'The present and the past in the industrial revolution', *Past and Present*, 103 (1983).
7. M. Berg and P. Hudson, 'Rehabilitating the industrial revolution', *Economic History Review*, 45 (1992); P. Hudson, *The Industrial Revolution* (London, 1992).
8. J. Hoppitt, 'Counting the industrial revolution', *Economic History Review*, 43 (1990).
9. M. J. Daunton, ' "Gentlemanly capitalism" and British industry 1820–1914', *Past and Present*, 122 (1989).
10. S. Schaffer, 'Babbage's intelligence: calculating engines and the factory system', *Critical Inquiry*, 21 (1994).
11. J. R. Harris, *Industrial Espionage and Technology Transfer: Britain and France in the Eighteenth Century* (Aldershot, 1998).
12. A. Ure, *The Philosophy of Manufactures or an Exposition of the Scientific, Moral and Commercial Economy of the Factory System of Great Britain* (London, 1835), p. 2.
13. S. D. Chapman, *The Cotton Industry in the Industrial Revolution* (London, 1972), pp. 33–4, 43–5, 52, 66; M. Berg, 'Factories, workshops and industrial organisation', in R. Floud and D. McCloskey, eds, *The Economic History of Britain Since 1700*, vol. 1, *1700–1860* (Cambridge, 1994), pp. 134–5.
14. Ure, *Philosophy of Manufactures*, p. 367.

15. Chapman, *Cotton Industry*, pp. 18, 68; G. N. Von Tunzelmann, *Steam Power and British Industrialization to 1860* (Oxford, 1978).

16. M. Berg, 'Women's work, mechanization and the early phases of industrialisation in England', in P. Joyce, ed., *The Historical Meanings of Work* (Cambridge, 1987).

17. C. Tuttle, 'A revival of the pessimist view: child labour and the industrial revolution', *Research in Economic History*, 18 (1998).

18. Berg and Hudson, 'Rehabilitating the industrial revolution'.

19. Hudson, *Industrial Revolution*, pp. 229–32; Berg, 'Women's work', p. 69; S. Horrell and J. Humphries, 'Women's labour force participation and the transition to the male-breadwinner family, 1790–1865', *Economic History Review*, 48 (1995).

20. E. A. Wrigley, *Continuity, Chance and Change: The Character of the Industrial Revolution in England* (Cambridge, 1990), pp. 4–5.

21. J. R. Harris, *The British Iron Industry 1700–1850* (Basingstoke, 1988), pp. 34–40, 54–5, 60–4; K. Morgan, *The Birth of Industrial Britain: Economic Change 1750–1850* (London, 1999), pp. 51–6.

22. R. Samuel, 'The workshop of the world: steam-power and hand technology in mid-Victorian Britain', *History Workshop Journal*, 3 (1977).

23. J. Rule, 'The property of skill in the period of manufacture', in P. Joyce, *The Historical Meanings of Work* (Cambridge, 1987), p. 101.

24. A. Randall, *Before the Luddites: Custom, Community and Machinery in the English Woollen Industry, 1776–1809* (Cambridge, 1991).

25. M. Berg, *The Age of Manufactures 1700–1820: Industry, Innovation and Work in Britain* (London, 1994), p. 185.

26. Brain, *Going to the Fair*, pp. 103–6; A. E. Musson, 'James Nasymyth and the early growth of mechanical engineering', *Economic History Review*, 10 (1957), p. 126.

27. J. Zeitlin, 'Between flexibility and mass production: strategic ambiguity and selective adaptation in the British engineering industry, 1830–1914', in C. F. Sabel and J. Zeitlin, eds, *World of Possibilities: Flexibility and Mass Production in Western Industrialization* (Cambridge, 1997), pp. 249, 259–60, 265–7; J. K. Brown, 'Design plans, working drawings, national styles: engineering practice in Great Britain and the United States, 1775–1945', *Technology and Culture*, 41 (2000), pp. 220–2; Samuel, 'Workshop of the world', pp. 41–2.

28. S. Giedion, *Mechanization Takes Command: A Contribution to Anonymous History* (New York, 1969), pp. 89–90.

29. C. F. Sabel and J. Zeitlin, 'Stories, strategies, structures: rethinking historical alternatives to mass production', in C. F. Sabel and J. Zeitlin, eds, *World of Possibilities: Flexibility and Mass Production in Western Industrialization* (Cambridge, 1997), pp. 8–12.

30. Brown, 'Design plans', p. 226.

31. Ibid.

32. R. Szostak, *The Role of Transportation in the Industrial Revolution: A Comparison of England and France* (Montreal, 1991).

33. P. S. Bagwell, *The Transport Revolution* (London, 1988), pp. 4–13, 21, 24–31, 40–7, 64–5; T. R. Gourvish, *Railways and the British Economy* (London, 1980).

34. Bagwell, *Transport Revolution*, pp. 49–52, 76–80.

35. T. L. Alborn, *Conceiving Companies: Joint Stock Politics in Victorian England* (London, 1998), pp. 176–80.

36. Gourvish, *Railways*, p. 20.

37. S. Dugan and D. Dugan, *The Day the World Took Off: The Roots of the Industrial Revolution* (London, 2000), p. 35.

38. W. Schivelbusch, *The Railway Journey: The Industrialization of Time and Space in the Nineteenth Century* (Leamington Spa, 1986).

39. Ibid., pp. 19–23, 54.

FURTHER READING

By far the best starting point is M. J. Daunton, *Progress and Poverty: An Economic and Social History of Britain 1700–1850* (1995). This is much more than a textbook and provides both an historical background and insightful analysis of industrial developments during the first half of the nineteenth century. Accessible overviews of the second half of the century are not as well covered, but C. More, *The Industrial Age: Economy and Society in Britain 1750–1995* (1997) provides a useful summary of many of the main themes. The best survey of labour is still R. Samuel, 'The workshop of the world: steam-power and hand technology in mid-Victorian Britain', *History Workshop Journal*, 3 (1977), while E. A. Wrigley, *Continuity, Chance and Change: The Character of the Industrial Revolution* (1990) emphasizes the importance of Britain switching from an organic to a mineral-based economy. J. Zeitlin, 'Between flexibility and mass production: strategic ambiguity and selective adaptation in the British engineering industry, 1830–1914', in C. F. Sabel and J. Zeitlin, eds, *World of Possibilities: Flexibility and Mass Production in Western Industrialization* (1997) compares the contrasting trajectories of the engineering industry in Britain and the USA. For a synthesis of developments in transport during the nineteenth century see P. S. Bagwell *The Transport Revolution* (1988), while the social impact of rail travel is wonderfully described by W. Schivelbusch, *The Railway Journey: The Industrialization of Time and Space in the Nineteenth Century* (1986).

CHAPTER FOURTEEN

Urbanization

SIMON GUNN

Urbanization is one of the traditional 'grand narratives' of nineteenth-century British history, conventionally taught in tandem with, and viewed as a product of, the Industrial Revolution. It is a narrative that describes, in essence, the transformation of Britain from a predominantly rural and agricultural society to one that was largely town- or city-based and industrial. As such, its outline can be traced through a series of exemplary nineteenth-century texts, from William Cobbett's *Rural Rides* (1816) to the fictional Coketown of Charles Dickens's *Hard Times* (1854) and the metropolitan slums of Andrew Mearns's *The Bitter Cry of Outcast London* (1883). Yet as twin leitmotifs of the history of nineteenth-century Britain, industrialization and urbanization have been viewed very differently in historiography since the 1980s. For while economic historians have depicted industrialization as a less radical process than the term Industrial Revolution suggested, occurring gradually over several centuries, recent social and cultural historians have tended to portray urbanization as, if anything, *more* sudden and dramatic in its consequences than had previously been assumed. The city was the fulcrum for the major changes overtaking British society in the nineteenth century; it was on the very cutting-edge of capitalism and modernity.

Urban Britain has not remained immune from repeated shifts in historical interpretation; the growth of Victorian towns and cities and the manner in which they were experienced have been viewed in successively different ways over the last forty years. In the 1960s urban history took root and began to flourish in Britain, most famously under the inspiration of H. J. Dyos at Leicester University. Studying the built form and social ecology of towns and cities became an important project in its own right, as in Dyos's pioneering study of Camberwell.[1] It also attracted social historians and historical geographers interested in specific urban locales, like Oldham and East London, as case studies for hypotheses about patterns of social and spatial formation in the past. These various studies appeared at the time to be sharply divided by their commitment or opposition to forms of Marxism. But many features also united the first wave of urban history. Studies focused largely (though not exclusively) on the nineteenth century, and especially the Victorian, town or city.

Methodologically, they were predominantly empirical in approach, with an increasing sophistication of statistical techniques; and they tended to rely on models of class and social conflict to explain historical change. Overall, the first wave of studies gave rise to a rich and variegated urban historiography whose most eloquent testament was *The Victorian City: Images and Realities*.[2] In the later 1980s and early 1990s, however, a broad conceptual shift was observable in studies of nineteenth-century urban life. Class, capitalism and socio-economic structures were increasingly replaced in analysis by other categories such as identity, representation and experience. The newer, culturally inflected urban histories posed a different set of questions from their predecessors. Historians began to ask how social identities were formed through contemporary discourses about urban life and to investigate the differing ways individuals, and groups such as women and migrants, experienced towns and cities.[3] Above all, as part of the 'linguistic' or 'cultural turn', which influenced historical studies in general from the later 1980s onwards, the urban environment was construed as a text that could be deciphered or 'read'. Since the late 1990s there have been signs of a further shift, this time away from the 'cultural turn' towards an interest in the material fabric of the city, urban space and the techniques of 'rule' or governance.

These phases and trends in historiography were not insulated from each other. Although helpful in identifying major changes in interpretation, they can obscure the complexity of influences on particular histories of urbanization and the theoretical and methodological heterogeneity of such histories at any given time. Moreover, all histories have confronted similar problems of conceptualizing the urban. With its functionalist overtones, 'urbanization' itself can be an unhelpful term, suggesting a single, linear and uniform process rather than reflecting the diverse rates and patterns of development among towns. The notion of the urban reifies its object by attempting to unify under a single heading what were widely different types of settlement and processes of change. There is, indeed, no common consensus about what counts as 'urban'. Size of population is one measure, but it is unclear where the cut-off line is between towns and smaller communities or between urban and rural. As the General Report of the Population Census of England and Wales in 1891 acknowledged, 'the terms urban and rural are habitually used without any such precise meaning as would enable a clear line of demarcation to be drawn between the two'. Not only is any dividing line arbitrary, it is also historically and culturally specific. What counted as a 'town' in eighteenth-century England might only count as a village 150 years later. Clearly, other qualitative factors such as the concentration of administrative functions, markets and cultural institutions are relevant. The distinction between 'town' and 'city' is likewise problematic, particularly in a period of rapid growth in urban scale and population when legal definitions of city status lagged behind demographic reality. Towns and cities, of course, were not merely aggregates of population but also centres of government, of economic and social exchange, and of 'civilization'. They were nodes in local, national and international flows of people, goods and information. All these characteristics are bound up in the definition of the town or city, but they are also, inevitably, hard to quantify.

That such conceptual problems have practical implications becomes apparent as soon as we attempt to analyse the scale and composition of urban growth. It is a commonplace of nineteenth-century history that, in terms of population, Britain became a predominantly urban society for the first time in 1851. But this, of course, depends on the definition of 'urban' employed. If the minimal level of population to qualify as a 'town' is set at 10,000 rather than 2,500, as in 1851, then Britain could not be described as predominantly urban before 1871.[4] Moreover, many small towns merged into the surrounding countryside and were hardly distinguishable from it. The 1891 Census of Population commented that 'a very considerable number of districts that are, technically speaking, urban, are in reality of thoroughly rural character'. Nevertheless, contemporaries did register an important experiential division between urban and rural from the beginning of the nineteenth century, if not earlier, especially where this concerned London. In Book Seven of *The Prelude*, his epic poem completed in 1805, William Wordsworth recalled his first visit to London, travelling from the 'pastoral hills' to the great metropolis, where even next-door neighbours were 'strangers, each not knowing the other's name' and 'public vice', in the form of prostitutes, paraded in 'open shame'. City and countryside in Wordsworth's account stood not simply for different but incommensurate forms of human experience.

London, of course, was exceptional even by international standards. With a population of just under one million in 1801 it dwarfed its nearest rivals, Bristol, Norwich and Liverpool, which were each less than a tenth of its size. Yet one of the key features of urbanization in the nineteenth century was the growth of new provincial cities, which themselves represented regional capitals – Birmingham, Manchester, Glasgow – to go alongside the older-established centres, such as Edinburgh and Liverpool. All these new cities had populations of over 100,000 by the 1820s and, with the exception of Edinburgh, continued to grow throughout the century to 500,000 and more. They were joined in the ranks of large urban centres after 1850 by places like Bristol, Newcastle, Leeds and Sheffield. The identity of such cities was closely linked to specific industries – the metal trades in the case of Birmingham, the cutlery trades in Sheffield and so on. But it is also important to recognize the diversified economic character of the so-called industrial cities. They were centres of distribution, exchange and administration as well as manufacturing, of culture and pleasure as well as industry. Manchester was 'an axis, a metropolis; it had provinces', as W. H. Mills, editor of the *Manchester Guardian* put it, and other provincial cities could also claim metropolitan status in relation to the satellite towns and region which surrounded them.

Urban growth was not synonymous with industrialism in the nineteenth century in any simple or direct manner. The fastest-growing towns of the first half of the nineteenth century in terms of population were seaside resorts; in the 1820s Brighton matched the exponential growth rates even of industrial boomtowns like Bradford.[5] Industry itself was widespread, impacting on towns not conventionally deemed industrial, even in the south of England which is often taken to have undergone an effective 'de-industrialization' during the nineteenth century. Colchester, for example, was a centre for the woollen industry in the early 1700s. By the late eighteenth century the woollen industry had declined and the town became known principally as a centre for fashionable society. From the 1820s, however, silk manufacturing developed and Colchester 're-industrialized'. Similarly, Barnstaple, a small market town in Devon, had its own industries in the later Victorian period, including the Raleigh Cabinet Works, a glove factory and iron foundry, employing in total some thousand people. County towns, too, often flourished during the nineteenth century, though they have attracted less attention from urban historians. Lincoln, Shrewsbury, Worcester, Perth and Cambridge, for example, all remained the largest towns within their respective counties and maintained significant professional populations related to their status variously as administrative, legal, academic and ecclesiastical centres. They are examples of the numerous types of town that were part of the broad process of 'urbanization' in nineteenth-century Britain.

Population growth in the largest cities reached its peak in the 1820s, but its cumulative effects were in many cases registered most powerfully after 1850. In the major provincial cities of Birmingham, Glasgow, Leeds, Liverpool and Manchester the effective doubling of population between 1850 and 1900 confirmed their status as regional capitals, the centre of extended 'conurbations' (a term coined by the planner Patrick Geddes in 1915). Elsewhere, the most rapid rates of population growth after 1850 were to be found in towns based on the new boom industries, like Middlesbrough (iron and steel) and Swindon (railways), in satellites of existing cities, such as Croydon, south of London, or Wallasey, near Liverpool, and in the seaside resorts such as Blackpool and Bournemouth.[6] Aggregate figures for growth, however, conceal the equally important increase in population *within* towns and cities, in particular districts or neighbourhoods. In the central areas of the major cities the populations of certain parishes doubled every decade between the 1820s and 1840s, creating the teeming, insanitary 'slums' for which Victorian Britain was notorious. Manchester's Angel Meadow, Liverpool's Little Scotland, Blackfriars in Glasgow – every major town and city had one or more districts which were a byword, locally and sometimes nationally, for overcrowded and degraded habitations, 'dens' and 'rookeries' described in lurid detail in the Victorian press. Up to the 1840s immigration played a significant part in the explosion of urban populations. Between 1841 and 1851 a third of a million people migrated to London, and the same decade saw an unprecedented influx of Irish men and women fleeing the effects of famine. Nevertheless, demographic historians have seriously qualified the traditional picture of urbanization as fuelled by migration from the countryside. After the 1840s the natural increase of the urban population was more important than migration in accounting for overall growth rates.

Those who lived in nineteenth-century towns and cities did not inhabit an ordered urban environment. According to Girouard, the principle that lay behind the Georgian town was consensus; it was this ideal that governed social relations as well as architectural taste. By contrast, the Victorian town was a 'battlefield', a place where individuals and groups were in constant competition and conflict with each other.[7] One corollary of this was that urban development in Victorian Britain was not 'planned' in a modern sense. In the eighteenth and early nineteenth centuries certain towns, or parts of them, like Bath, Edinburgh New Town and London's West End, were made the object of conscious design. But this tended to be limited to places identified with polite society. From the 1840s even this spasmodic tradition ceased and, with the exception of small numbers of 'model communities', like that at Saltaire, near Bradford, urban planning was not revived until the early twentieth century. In this context it is anachronistic to argue that the state, in the form of central government or local authorities, should have intervened to provide housing for migrants, workers and the poor. There was no precedent for state intervention on this scale, locally or nationally, and housing, like the building process generally, was deemed to be the responsibility of private enterprise. Some towns, like Liverpool, Leeds and Burnley, began to introduce local building regulations in the 1840s, and after 1858 towns in England and Wales were encouraged to implement model by-laws (in parts of urban Scotland they were already in operation). But the existence of regulations did not mean that they were enforced; in any case, they applied in the first instance only to new buildings. Regulations only gradually came to have a significant impact on the quality of housing in the later nineteenth century.

House-building was part of capitalist development, not understood as a response to social need. The leading role in housing was taken by a myriad of small, speculative builders.[8] In some cases, gentry and aristocratic families exerted considerable influence over urban development and housing, especially where they leased the land and retained a substantial interest in it, as with the Calthorpes, who oversaw the creation of the select suburb of Edgbaston in Birmingham, or the Devonshires at Eastbourne.[9] But whoever carried out development, urban property remained overwhelmingly in private hands. Although housing for workers and the poor became the object of increasing philanthropic initiatives from the 1860s and local authorities were active in slum clearance after 1868, a major drive to provide public or 'council' housing was not to occur until after the First World War. One result was that towns were characterized by distinctive housing types – Sunderland's 'cottages', Leeds' back-to-backs, the tenements of Edinburgh and Glasgow – which became part of their urban identity in much the same way as the leading industries and prominent public landmarks.

The lack of planning in the nineteenth century, however, did not mean that urban form was merely haphazard. In the 1920s the 'Chicago School' of sociologists identified a model of the modern city based on a series of concentric rings leading out from the central business district to factories and workers' housing with a further band of suburbs extending out into the countryside beyond. The result was a marked degree of functional and social segregation compared with the 'pre-modern' town in which the majority of urban activities were clustered in the central area and rich and poor continued to live in close proximity to each other. The Chicago School model was itself based on the perceived development of nineteenth-century British industrial cities like Birmingham, Sheffield and, above all, Manchester, which Friedrich Engels had described in equivalent terms in *The Condition of the Working Class in England in 1844* (1845). The model was elegant in its simplicity and pinpointed certain key features of urban form, notably the centrifugal tendency among urban populations and the increased zoning of particular functions and activities. But it did not correspond with any precision to the pattern of change in many places, including industrial centres. In Nottingham, for example, much of the lace industry remained concentrated in the centre of the town in the 1860s and beyond, whereas hosiery, the other local industry, was dispersed across town and region. In Huddersfield, many major employers remained resident in the town centre up to the 1890s, long after they might have been expected to move to mansions and villas in the suburbs. More generally, the model of concentric rings can be unhelpful in describing residential patterns in certain important cases. In London, the principal division lay between East End and West End, the wealthy continuing to live in fashionable areas of the city, but separate from industry, the port and the main working-class districts as well as the financial and commercial centre, the City. Like London,

Leeds had its East End and West End in the first half of the nineteenth century, but thereafter the principal division was between a prosperous suburban north, comprising suburbs like Headingley and Roundhay, and the industrial and proletarian districts like Holbeck and Hunslet south of the river Aire.

The principal factor which historians have seen as shaping the social configuration and the built form of the city was the steady outflow of population to the suburbs during the course of the nineteenth century. Suburbanization was not a sudden or once-and-for-all development; it was a continuous process by which households moved successively to communities at an increasing distance from the old centre. Urban merchants had long been in the habit of removing their families to mansions in the nearby countryside for the summer months. But suburbanization only seems to have become a deliberate and sustained movement from the late eighteenth century. The first purpose-built suburb is generally considered to have been the Eyre estate at St John's Wood, London, started in 1794. Thereafter, the most conspicuous suburban developments were in the provincial cities, such as Everton in Liverpool and Edgbaston in Birmingham, which became fashionable residential areas for merchant, manufacturing and professional families in the 1820s. By the 1840s suburban villages were beginning to take root further afield, often superimposed on existing rural communities, as at Bowdon in Cheshire, some twelve miles south of Manchester but home to some of that city's wealthiest clans, and at Roundhay to the northeast of Leeds. The main impetus to suburbanization in the first half of the nineteenth century was not improved transport. Links by tram, stagecoach or railway tended to follow suburbanization rather than to precede it. Bowdon was only connected to Manchester by railway in the 1850s; at Roundhay a regular coach service to Leeds was not provided until 1853. For the well-to-do, private carriages remained important, not only as a closeted means of travel, but also as a public statement of success symbolized by the display of horses, footmen and equipage.

As with transport, social snobbery and a desire to emulate landed lifestyles are inadequate as explanations of the exodus of the well-to-do from the centre of towns and cities between the 1820s and the 1870s. Other factors were more important: the relative cheapness of building land on the urban fringe and its rapidly rising value in central areas; concerns about pollution and public health in the wake of the typhus and cholera outbreaks; and the cult of domesticity in the middle classes, together with a stress on privacy and individualism which merits further research in relation to housing design, gardens and the layout of suburbia.[10] From the 1870s, more social groups were engaged in the outward movement from the old centre into the inner suburbs, which the better-off were simultaneously vacating. They included an emergent 'lower middle class' of white-collar workers and the best-paid sections of the manual workforce. Both groups were aided in this case by improved transport facilities, such as omnibuses and affordable trains under the Cheap Fares Act of 1883. In London, especially, commuting became a way of life for large sections of the population by the late nineteenth century. This was a highly mobile society in residential terms. In Liverpool half of the population moved house every two years in the mid-Victorian decades, while landlords calculated the length of an average tenancy in Glasgow in 1900 at five to six months.

How far these trends encouraged the social segregation of the urban population has been debated. Nineteenth-century commentators certainly believed that they did, ritually lamenting the distance between rich and poor, middle and working classes.

But this needs to be seen in the context of the widespread belief, at least among the educated, that regular contact between different social groups would automatically diminish social conflict and lead to the moral reconciliation of classes. Some critics have argued that residential segregation only applied to the extremes of wealth and poverty; the majority of the population lived in close proximity to those of other social and ethnic groups, even if their own street or immediate neighbourhood could be defined as socially homogeneous.[11] What 'segregation' means is also difficult to define with any precision. Even in the most exclusive 'middle-class' suburbs, domestic servants, gardeners and tradespeople would more than outnumber the residents of the big houses. At the other end of the social spectrum, 'slums' were themselves the ideological construct of outsiders like journalists, sanitary inspectors and philanthropic visitors – there is no evidence that inhabitants of poor neighbourhoods ever considered that they lived in a 'slum'. In the language of the period, they were alien territories to be 'penetrated', their obscurity to be illuminated by the gaze of authority.[12] 'Slum' and suburb were connected, not only in the binary opposition that structured the discourse of spatial relationships, but also in the circuits of capital that ensured that the same group of people who decried the housing conditions of the poor from the comfort of suburbia profited, directly or indirectly, from the very conditions they so deplored.

The less-noted obverse of suburbanization was the reconstruction of the urban centre in the decades between 1840 and 1880. Whereas the suburbs were conceived in the image of the picturesque, the city centre evoked the sublime with its looming warehouses, domed exchanges and railway stations and, towering over all others, the monumental town halls. The remaking of town and city centres was a major capitalist project in its own right, part of 'industrialization' as much as a product of it, financed primarily from private capital with ratepayers subsidizing some civic buildings and municipal works. Its effects were multiple. Firstly, it literally opened up London and the major provincial cities to view, removing or screening off the dwellings of the poor and creating vistas of wide streets, squares, statues and grandiose buildings. In smaller towns, too, like Oldham and Boston, the 1850s and 1860s were years of civic expansionism, of the opening of town halls, monuments and parks.[13] Secondly, the make-over of the central area created new and differentiated urban spaces, a distinct business district, streets designed for display and consumption, and civic places defined by the visual rhetoric of municipal authority. Towns and cities became zoned in ways that were normative as well as functional: the division between home and workplace, city centre and suburbs, came to be seen as part of the 'rational' organization of modern urban life.

In the later eighteenth century British towns gained the institutional accoutrements of polite culture in the form of assembly rooms, literary and philosophical societies and subscription libraries. In the course of the nineteenth they became still more emphatically the locus of 'civility', places where the advances and rewards of 'civilization' were visible in their purest and most concentrated form. For the dissenting minister Robert Vaughan, writing in the 1840s, the city was the site of knowledge, cultivation and progress. To mid- and later Victorian observers, the range of institutions established in the town centre – libraries, art galleries, concert halls, museums, exhibitions – epitomized progress and 'improvement'. The result was a multiplication and sophistication of ways of inculcating civility, from exposure to the elevating effects of art to the subjecting of bodies to the disciplinary gaze of others.[14] Such institutions were characterized by a regime that encouraged passive contemplation and silence as a norm; they symbolized order against the noise and complexity of the urban world outside. But the urban was also the locus of pleasure in other forms. London had always represented vicarious enjoyment and escape from the workaday world, and it led the way in the later Victorian period with the creation of a distinct, commercialized theatre and music-hall district in the West End. Yet from the 1870s all the major cities saw the creation zones of pleasure to go alongside the institutions of civility and 'self-improvement', comprising variously gentlemen's clubs, music halls and shopping arcades. Popular seaside towns, like Blackpool and Southend, meanwhile, became resorts wholly committed to the business of pleasure.

In particular, the centre of towns and cities came to embody the modern in the decades after 1840. Modernity was incarnated in both material and symbolic forms, above all in the big cities. It was manifested in the monumental scale and extent of buildings, cities being described as 'Amazonian jungles' of brick or as latter-day 'labyrinths'. Modernity was also identified with the invention of materials that allowed for new kinds of experience: the introduction of plate glass, for instance, enabled shops to offer panoramic window displays, while glass roofs astounded with their immensity and light. Modern technologies such as electric lighting, the telegraph and the hydraulic lift were first visible in the city centre, offering individuals, literally, new ways of seeing, communicating and moving. The spread of street- and shop-lighting, first with gas in the early 1800s and then with electricity from the 1880s, opened up the city for walking in comparative safety at night. This in turn created the possibility of a regular urban 'night-life'. By the 1870s the illumination of the city and the existence of a night-time world were an essential part of urban modernity and of cities' claim to metropolitan status.[15] So too was the prospect of wide new boulevards with department stores, comfortable hotels and restaurants, and the latest styles of architecture and interior decor. Birmingham typified this trend in the second half of the nineteenth century. According to the city's visionary leader, Joseph Chamberlain, the centrepiece of the Birmingham improvement scheme, started in 1875, was the building of Corporation Street, which he acclaimed as a 'Parisian boulevard' that would confirm the city as 'the Metropolis of the Midland Counties'.

All these aspects of form and environment shaped the way the urban was experienced in the nineteenth century. Historians have emphasized the proximity of the countryside to most urban dwellers and the fact that even cities as large as Leeds or Newcastle could be easily crossed on foot before 1850. Yet urban growth meant that it became increasingly difficult for any individual to grasp the town imaginatively as a totality. This was the case in London from the very early nineteenth century and partly accounts for the popularity of panoramas and 'bird's-eye' views of the city, such as that displayed in the London Colosseum in the 1820s, or of prospects of the town from afar. Growth in the scale and extent of cities, and the facts of migration, heightened the experience of anonymity, which could be both frightening and liberating. The solitary stranger is a stock figure of nineteenth-century literature, from the literary *flâneur* and the beggar of poetic imagining to the 'urban rambler' of the newspaper press. Who others were – their origins, character, motives and status – were all matters of intense preoccupation. Identity might be read in the first instance from appearance; the most popular science of the nineteenth century, phrenology, was based on the idea that character was inscribed in physical features, such as the shape of the head. In the urban press identities were ritually attached to social groups by means of certain specific markers or tropes. The presence of carriages 'announced' the appearance of the wealthy on the urban stage; a reference to the barrel organ and street music connoted 'the foreign element'; the presence of a crowd invariably indicated workers, and so on.

Urban experience itself tended to be registered in visual terms; during the nineteenth century vision was prioritized over other senses, such as smell and touch. Press descriptions of urban street life and the reorganization of urban space to accentuate the vista indicate the ways in which the city came to be understood as a spectacle and the archetypal (male) citizen as an observer or spectator. Urban spectatorship was not neutral but positioned and positioning. Nineteenth-century towns and cities were, in most cases, the theatres of male members of the middle classes; it was only in the twentieth century that workers moved out from neighbourhood networks and local attachments to 'take over' the city as a whole. During the later Victorian period, nevertheless, groups beyond the male middle classes, like women suffragettes and male trade unionists, laid claim to recognition within urban society by occupying the main streets and civic places in marches and processions. Power and identity were dependent on visibility; those groups, like the Irish and the poor, 'hidden' from view in 'slums' were denied representation within the urban community. Similarly, urban reportage presented the local population to itself as well as to outsiders by the identification of social 'types', a genre early exemplified by Pierce Egan's *Life in London* (1821) and taken up by provincial satirical journals after 1850. These stereotypes encompassed 'high' and 'low' society, fashionable 'shopping ladies' as well as slumland figures such as the landlord, the child and the municipal inspector. Their effect was to stabilize the play of identities by making the strange familiar and by linking people (or 'types') with place and environment. In this way, the city itself was rendered knowable, composed of a series of recognizable social and geographical milieux.[16]

The classification of spaces and places directly affected the ways in which groups experienced the urban environment. It was the privilege of the male *flâneur* to be able to move across different locales with relative ease; this was an essential precondition of the panoptic view and the proclivity towards seeing urban life as spectacle. The casual contemplation of the *flâneur* was out of the question for women. Anything construed as 'loitering' was likely to mark a woman (at least in male eyes) as a prostitute. There was no type of the female *flâneuse*.[17] For much of the nineteenth century, indeed, women's appearance in public was inherently problematic. Certain institutions like the gentlemen's club, the improvement society and the exchange were barred to women and other sites, such as pubs and bars, were potentially injurious to feminine respectability. The streets themselves were perceived, especially by middle-class women, to be a haven for 'pests' and 'nuisances' in the form of beggars, drunks and 'mashers', jumped-up dandies posing as would-be 'gentlemen'. Yet as women sought increased access to the city from the 1870s and became more important to shops and department stores as consumers, so town and city streets became subject to increasing regulation. New construction techniques made streets less noisy and pavements cleaner for walking. Formal policing was directed increasingly at clearing undesirable elements from the central area by prosecuting street offences. The local press often joined in this campaign by 'naming and shaming' institutions and individuals identified with anti-social behaviour. This form of surveillance could prove an especially effective method of regulation in small towns, such as Merthyr Tydfil, where places and people were likely to be well-known locally.[18]

Questions of regulation point towards wider issues of power and politics. How was 'urbanization' itself regulated politically? By what means were towns and cities governed in nineteenth-century Britain? Here again it is important to register the changes in interpretation which have occurred over the last twenty years or so. In the nineteenth century histories of the town were often told through the development of what were seen as its representative institutions: vestry, Poor Law administration, improvement commission and, above all, town council. This tradition continued in increasingly sophisticated form for much of the twentieth. The history of the town was recorded not only through the development of its government and administration, but also as a narrative of increasing political autonomy and municipal responsibility. According to this narrative, towns and cities freed themselves from the shackles of unrepresentative and sometimes aristocratic tutelage following the Municipal Corporations Act of 1835. Power passed to the middle classes who instituted a tradition of municipal self-government. From the 1880s representatives of labour and the working class began to play a growing part, finally eclipsing the old middle-class order after 1918, while municipal authority was itself steadily extended to ever wider areas of urban life, from housing and utilities to popular leisure and culture. Interwoven with this institutional and class-based history was a related narrative of public health and social policy. This took the form of a romance of urban 'improvement', characterized by increasing intervention to curb the malign effects of urbanization and industrialism, which was ultimately to find its apotheosis in the foundation of the welfare state after 1945.

Recent accounts of power and politics in urban contexts have sought to question and undermine many of these assumptions on which earlier accounts were based. In the first place, power is seen as dispersed rather than embedded in particular urban institutions: the street could be as important a site of power relations as the council chamber. Secondly, policies to do with public health and welfare are not understood simply as responses to an objective social need or seen as inevitably following a path of growing state intervention, itself equated with self-evident progress. In this sense, newer histories question the Whiggish ideas implicit in the whole concept of 'urbanization'. They ask, for instance, how and why public health was constituted as a 'problem' in the first place during the era of Chadwickian reform.[19] More generally, drawing on Foucault's theory of 'governmentality', recent accounts have begun to enquire how the city was constituted as an object of 'rule' – that is, the conditions of knowledge and power that made possible the expansion of municipal administration and government from the 1830s onwards.[20] These conditions, in turn, were predicated on the substantially decentralized character of state power in Victorian Britain, which gave considerable freedom and responsibility to urban authorities.

According to Foucault, the period from the later eighteenth century saw the elaboration of a science of 'population' that lay behind the generation of new types of knowledge, including political economy. Developing this argument, historians have begun to view the early-nineteenth-century city as a laboratory for testing novel forms of bureaucratic and professional knowledge.[21] Such a project was dependent on a fundamental re-visioning of the city, the transformation of the specific urban place into abstract urban space. Space came to be conceived as empty, always the same and open to construction in grid-form. In abstract space people were no longer disparate individuals but were seen as aggregated units, as 'populations' or 'masses'. In this way, the town or city was re-conceptualized as a bounded space, amenable to curative interventions from above carried out in the name of rationality and reform. Urban space could be mapped, as it was by private cartographers and by the early Ordnance Survey; the particularity of place was rendered comprehensible by its reduction into a visual plan. Similarly, abstraction facilitated the growth of statistics as a way of knowing the city. The statistical societies of the 1830s paved the way for the host of urban surveys, from Chadwick's report on the health of the towns in the 1840s to the studies of poverty carried out by Booth and Rowntree in the last decades of the century. Here were the tools for the definition and analysis of the emergent 'social', a domain of specialized knowledge and expert intervention.

Public health is an especially important example of this type of intervention from above, since health was connected to many other domains of urban policy and social action in the nineteenth century. The city itself was considered to be a natural or organic system, akin to the human body.[22] It required parks to act as 'lungs'; it had 'veins' and 'arteries' which enabled the circulation of people and goods in and around the city.[23] Consequently, urban reformers often thought of intervention in anatomical terms, as surgical incisions that would remove the sources of infection from the social body. Slum clearance, for example, was justified in terms of removing the breeding-places of disease and vice, of 'ventilating' the crowded central areas and of opening up occluded places to public view. The health of the town was also seen to depend on circulation, not only of traffic but also of air and water. Chadwick was a 'hydraulic thinker, imagining a constant flow of water sweeping rapidly and continuously through towns, cleaning everything, carrying all wastes to be used for beneficent purposes in the countryside'.[24] Miasmatic or air-borne theories of disease, which remained predominant in medical circles till the 1870s, likewise encouraged emphasis to be placed on ventilation and linked disease with overcrowded and badly constructed housing as well as with the more general configuration of urban space. Indeed, for sanitary reformers like Chadwick, as for radicals like Engels, the poor were indivisible from their environment; they were 'slum dwellers', natives of the 'dens and rookeries of vice', depicted as a mass, not as individuals, their identity wholly subsumed by their physical location.

The concept of governmentality aims to highlight the conjuncture of power and knowledge necessary to render the urban fabric and population amenable to rule. It partially overlaps with a further concept that has come to be used by urban historians to analyse power and politics, that of 'governance'.[25] As with governmentality, the idea of urban governance refers to more than merely the institutions and processes of municipal government. It is concerned with the 'ordering of order' – the fundamental ways in which power and authority are organized, legitimized and put into effect in urban contexts. Governance is not just a matter of the state, but also involves the institutions of civil society. In establishing order and authority in early-nineteenth-century towns, for instance, the network of voluntary societies were no less important than the formal agencies of local government such as the court leet or parish vestry. Power was effective precisely because it was diffuse and multiple, devolved through numerous philanthropic, political and cultural associations, rather than centralized or concentrated. Equally, the concept of governance emphasizes the inter-relationship of diverse institutions and activities rather than their separate operation. The elaborate civic ceremonial of the mid-Victorian decades, marked by ritualized gatherings and processions, for example, was not merely a frivolous adjunct to the serious business of governing the urban but an essential means by which municipal authority was unified and sanctioned. For its full realization, power required to be made visible, to be given public and symbolic form. Similarly, it is important to see how the industrial regulation of the workplace in the 1850s and 1860s intersected with the wider project of urban 'improvement' and social reform, enabling large employers in towns like Nottingham to position themselves as civic as well as industrial leaders.[26]

The creation of a civic culture and identity was indeed a major feature of urban governance in the second half of the nineteenth century. Its periodization differed across urban locations: in the provincial cities the efflorescence of the civic occurred in the mid-Victorian decades, whereas in many other smaller towns it only reached its zenith around the turn of the twentieth century.[27] In the majority of boroughs civic improvement was implemented under the auspices of urban Liberalism, though this was not invariably the case: predominantly Conservative Liverpool was no less active in promoting municipal projects than predominantly Liberal Manchester. Of more significance than the politics of party in determining the pace and scope of civic improvements was the conflict between an expansionist element, which tended to favour ambitious large-scale projects, such as town halls and waterworks, and a self-defined 'ratepayer' interest concerned to limit costs. But wherever it occurred the creation of a civic culture took similar forms. Its best-known and most striking manifestation was the building of new town halls in classical or Gothic style, which dominated the town. Many town halls had been built in the later eighteenth or early nineteenth century, but these were usually on a modest scale and were superseded by new creations from the 1850s onwards. Burslem in the Potteries had a small town hall, which included a market, built in 1761 for £500; in the 1850s it was replaced by a more ambitious construction, costing £10,000; finally, a further town hall was built in 1911, with an auditorium seating 2,000 people, at a cost of £35,000. This escalation of ambition and cost was not untypical, often driven by rivalry with nearby towns. But town halls were only part of a larger project to build distinct 'civic-cultural complexes' in the later nineteenth century involving a range of public institutions and facilities. Birmingham's Chamberlain Square was perhaps the most prominent example, including the town hall, Council House, art gallery and Mason College together with monuments and statuary celebrating local worthies. Smaller towns followed suit. Preston had its town hall, built in the 1860s, to which was added the Harris Free Public Library, museum and art gallery. This creation of distinctive buildings and public spaces was accompanied by a civic rhetoric that sought to locate towns and cities within an historical tradition of urban culture, from the city-states of ancient Greece and Renaissance Italy to the merchant communities of the Low Countries.[28]

Under the auspices of the civic, municipal authorities engaged in the wholesale renovation of the urban fabric. New streets were built and old ones widened; 'slums' were cleared; drains and sewers were laid; and private utilities, such as gas and water, were taken into municipal hands. Birmingham Corporation under the leadership of

Joseph Chamberlain in the 1870s and 1880s liked to project itself as the leading exponent of the 'municipal gospel', but in fact Birmingham was only one instance of a nationwide impulse to urban improvement. After 1850 Glasgow rapidly created an infrastructure of municipal services alongside parks, museums, a gallery and a dignified civic centre in George Square. Other towns and cities likewise spent hitherto unprecedented sums on urban infrastructure and facilities, raised from the rates and from loans. Between 1860 and 1900 Bradford corporation expended £1.5 m on street widening, £300,000 on drainage and sewerage and £3 m on water supply. One consequence was that municipal corporations became major employers in their own right during the late nineteenth century – Glasgow, for example, employed 10,000 full-time staff by the 1890s. Towns and cities were dependent on armies of workers – lamplighters, sanitary engineers, electricians – whose purpose was to maintain the infrastructure of urban modernity. They were, as Walter Benjamin observed, 'stage extras' in the drama of modern city life, unnoticed yet indispensable. The construction of the civic, in its multiple dimensions, was the exemplar and the apogee of nineteenth-century urban governance.

The recent historiography of urbanization in Britain, therefore, has tended to accentuate the novelty and importance of that process. While life in smaller market towns may have continued much as it had in the eighteenth century, the larger, more bustling urban centres were identified with civilization and progress, and celebrated as such. This was partly a product of the spread of urbanism itself. In the nineteenth century the numbers and scale of towns in Britain expanded dramatically and the hold of London on the nation as a whole was consequently weakened, at least for a time. In 1871 Liverpool, Birmingham and Manchester were lauded in the British Parliamentary Papers as 'almost metropolitan in wealth and population', while smaller towns were likewise the object of urban pride and municipal endeavour. London no longer dwarfed the rest of urban Britain in the way it had in the eighteenth century, nor was it the cynosure of business, politics and pleasure that it was to become during the twentieth. More generally, the urban was the focus of the far-reaching changes discussed in this chapter: of industrialism, bureaucracy, sanitary reform and the recreation of the civic as ideal and practice. As current historical research begins to investigate more deeply the material culture of the Victorian city – bricks and mortar, asphalt and macadam, gas and electricity – so its strangeness and singularity are thrown into relief. If the urban was the locus of modernity in the nineteenth century, then it is a modernity that appears simultaneously familiar and alien, like a distorting mirror of our own urban preoccupations.

NOTES

1. H. J. Dyos, *Victorian Suburb: A Study of the Growth of Camberwell* (Leicester, 1961).
2. H. J. Dyos and M. Wolff, eds, *The Victorian City: Images and Realities* (London, 1973).
3. D. Feldman and G. Stedman Jones, eds, *Metropolis London: Histories and Representations since 1800* (London, 1989); J. R. Walkowitz, *City of Dreadful Delight: Narratives of Sexual Danger in Late Victorian London* (London, 1992).
4. F. M. L. Thompson, 'Town and city', in F. M. L. Thompson, ed., *The Cambridge Social History of Britain 1750–1950*, vol. I, *Regions and Communities* (Cambridge, 1990), p. 13.

5. J. K. Walton, *The English Seaside Resort: A Social History, 1750–1914* (Leicester, 1983).
6. P. J. Waller, *Town, City, and Nation: England 1850–1914* (Oxford, 1983), pp. 2–3.
7. M. Girouard, *The English Town* (New Haven, 1990), p. 190.
8. R. Rodger, *Housing in Urban Britain, 1780–1914* (Cambridge, 1995), pp. 20–2.
9. D. Cannadine, *Lords and Landlords: The Aristocracy and the Towns 1774–1967* (Leicester, 1980).
10. F. M. L. Thompson, ed., *The Rise of Suburbia* (Leicester, 1982).
11. D. Ward, 'Environs and neighbours in the "two nations": residential differentiation in mid-nineteenth-century Leeds', *Journal of Historical Geography*, 6 (1980).
12. A. Mayne, *The Imagined Slum: Newspaper Representation in Three Cities, 1870–1914* (Leicester, 1993).
13. J. Vernon, *Politics and the People: A Study in English Political Culture, c.1815–1867* (Cambridge, 1993).
14. T. Bennett, *The Birth of the Museum: History, Theory, Politics* (London, 1995).
15. J. Schlör, *Nights in the Big City: Paris, Berlin, London 1840–1930* (London, 1998).
16. S. Gunn, *The Public Culture of the Victorian Middle Class: Ritual and Authority in the English Industrial City, 1840–1914* (Manchester, 2000).
17. D. E. Nord, *Walking the Victorian Streets: Women, Representation and the City* (Ithaca, NY, 1995).
18. A. Croll, 'Street disorder, surveillance and shame: regulating behaviour in the public spaces of the late Victorian British town', *Social History*, 24 (1999).
19. C. Hamlin, *Public Health and Social Justice in the Age of Chadwick: Britain, 1800–1854* (Cambridge, 1998).
20. C. Otter, 'Making liberalism durable: vision and civility in the late Victorian city', *Social History*, 27 (2002).
21. M. Poovey, *Making a Social Body: British Cultural Formation 1830–1864* (Chicago, 1995).
22. G. Davison, 'The city as a natural system: theories of urban society in early-nineteenth-century Britain', in D. Fraser and A. Sutcliffe, eds, *The Pursuit of Urban History* (London, 1983).
23. R. Sennett, *Flesh and Stone: The Body and the City in Western Civilization* (London, 1994).
24. Hamlin, *Public Health*, p. 3.
25. R. J. Morris and R. H. Trainor, eds, *Urban Governance: Britain and Beyond since 1750* (Aldershot, 2000).
26. R. Gray and D. Loftus, 'Industrial regulation, urban space and the boundaries of the workplace: mid-Victorian Nottingham', *Urban History*, 26 (1999).
27. J. Garrard, 'Urban elites, 1850–1914: the rule and decline of a new squirearchy?', *Albion*, 27 (1995).
28. K. Hill, ' "Thoroughly embued with the spirit of ancient Greece": symbolism and space in Victorian civic culture', in A. Kidd and D. Nicholls, eds, *Gender, Civic Culture and Consumerism: Middle-Class Identity in Britain 1800–1940* (Manchester, 1999).

FURTHER READING

The starting-point for any student of Victorian towns and cities must be the essays contained in M. J. Daunton, ed., *The Cambridge Urban History of Britain*, vol. 3, *1840–1950* (2000). H. J. Dyos and M. Wolff, eds, *The Victorian City: Images and Realities* (1973) remains a pioneering and wide-ranging collection. For accessible introductions to the history of urban form see M. Girouard, *The English Town* (1990) and P. J. Waller, ed., *The English Urban Landscape*

(2000). The subject of nineteenth-century suburbia warrants fresh attention from historians; F. M. L. Thompson, ed., *The Rise of Suburbia* (1982) remains the standard work on the subject. On housing the most authoritative single study is R. Rodger, *Housing in Urban Britain, 1780–1914: Class, Capitalism and Construction* (1995). The subject of the nineteenth-century slum has been critically reinterpreted by A. Mayne, *The Imagined Slum: Newspaper Representation in Three Cities, 1870–1914* (1993). There is a voluminous literature on urban social identities, mainly focused on class. A key work in opening up new perspectives was J. R. Walkowitz, *City of Dreadful Delight: Narratives of Sexual Danger in Late Victorian London* (1992). For recent studies see D. E. Nord, *Walking the Victorian Streets: Women, Representation and the City* (1995) and S. Gunn, *The Public Culture of the Victorian Middle Class: Ritual and Authority in the English Industrial City, 1840–1914* (2000). The best analysis of urban politics in its various dimensions remains D. Fraser, *Urban Politics in Victorian England* (1976); there are important essays on Scottish cities in T. M. Devine, ed., *Scottish Elites* (1994). For new approaches on governmentality and governance see P. Joyce, *The Rule of Freedom* (2003) and R. J. Morris and R. H. Trainor, eds, *Urban Governance: Britain and Beyond Since 1750* (2000).

CHAPTER FIFTEEN

The Family

SHANI D'CRUZE

You were a pretty while in writing, Master Tom, after you left me in the dismals – three whole weeks. . . . If Mrs W, thinks an absence of three or four days so much, who has children, a mother, and sisters to chear her whilst you are away, how must I endure the deprivation of your society for three times that number of years? who have neither mother, sisters, husband, nor children. All my affections are centred in you. . . . You have *many* to shew kindness to you, and always about you, I have but one, whom I seldom see – consider this, and make some allowance for me.

Ellen Weeton to Thomas Weeton, 16 March 1809.[1]

March – I now began to feel the cares of family affairs to to [sic] press hard upon me for I had two daughters one 14 the other 16 to take care of and they were a an age the [sic] is as unmanageable as at any time of life . . . they had all to learn &c and they learn slowly mary the older kept the House & agness went to work – November this month I was off my work a month poorly . . . in this last year I have lost 42 Day work &c this has been a troublesome year to me having no wife to care for the concerns of the House nor any Company or any to care for me &c –

Benjamin Shaw, Family Records, 1828.[2]

These two quotations illustrate the importance of family to two very different early-nineteenth-century people. Ellen Weeton was writing to her married brother, a Warrington attorney. Her journal and letters tell of her own sacrifices, keeping a school and forgoing her share of their small inheritance to support Tom through his apprenticeship after the death of their parents. He married early and, according to Ellen, unwisely. His wife was very much a creature of the parlour. His marriage ended Ellen's cherished dream of keeping house with Tom once he had established himself professionally. Ellen was left with comparatively little to live on. In her twenties and thirties she took up positions as governess or companion, or lived in frugal lodgings. She inhabited an uncomfortable liminal space between classes and away from friends and kin. Although clearly subscribing to codes of middle-class gentility, she could still share scatological jokes of her own invention with Tom. A poor relation, and it seems a temperamental one, she could not find a permanent home with either Tom or her Aunt Barton. She married briefly at her brother's behest to a widowed cotton spinner who in her own account was abusive and violent. Her separation from him was achieved only at the price of parting from her young daughter and her small financial independence. Not until her daughter was married could Ellen share a home with her again. Family was crucial to Ellen Weeton, materially, socially and emotionally. Ellen's unhappiness at her exclusion from a happy family is the leitmotif of the two volumes of her surviving letters and journals.

Benjamin Shaw was in some ways the quintessential 'independent artisan' of the early textile industrial revolution. His family came from the Vale of Dent in Cumbria, and supported itself through his father's clock-making, put-out woollen work for mother and children, and a smallholding. Their combination of mechanical and textile skills made them attractive to entrepreneurs setting up a water-powered woollen mill near Lancaster, though the move proved difficult for the Shaws; illness, death, industrial accident and irregular work broke up the family. By 1798, teenage Ben was left alone serving out his mechanic's apprenticeship, with his family in Preston, twenty miles away. Ben fell in love, and married his sweetheart Betty with no money and a baby on the way, in part, he claimed, against his better judgement. Once out of his apprenticeship they moved into a couple of rooms in Dale St, Preston, where Ben could generally command good wages in this rapidly growing textile town and Betty could do put-out textile work. Their story, as related by Ben, was not a happy one, marked by repeated pregnancies and Betty's reluctance to be the thrifty and prudent housewife that Ben wanted. Eight offspring survived to adulthood and all of these conceived children outside or before marriage. The family was repeatedly stricken with illness and disease. Sons and daughters went to work in the mills early, several died as children or young adults, lacking medical care and nursed by their parents. A chronic thrombosis in his leg meant that for long periods Ben could not work, until he had the leg amputated. Recurrent poverty and uncertainty were the hallmarks of their life together.

In 1826, as Betty was becoming increasingly ill with consumption (tuberculosis), Ben Shaw began writing the history of himself, their lives together, and their extended families. As his future became uncertain Ben consciously set about rooting his identity in the gathered stories of his kin and his family history. He may have complained roundly about his wife and children, but when he chose to write about himself, exercising the skills of literacy that he had so painstakingly acquired, it was as a family man that he chose to represent himself. We learn little from Ben Shaw about work processes or organization in Preston textile mills. The quotations here come from the period immediately following Betty's death in February 1828. Despite their differences, it is clear how much he missed her. Betty had been a key part of his life, not only because of the housekeeping that his daughter Mary was not interested in doing, nor because he was ill that winter, getting older, repeatedly out of work and therefore poor, but above all because without Betty, Ben had 'no Company or any to care for me &c'.

Although the grander assumptions about an 'industrial revolution' have been modified, the social change fostered by industrialization and urbanization certainly bought opportunities and uncertainties. Both Ellen Weeton and Ben Shaw invested emotionally, socially and materially in their family; and where family failed to repay those investments they were lost and insecure. For so many people 'family' was a key resource in managing the effects of social and economic change.

Continuity or Change?

In many ways the history of the nineteenth-century family is best understood within a rather longer chronology. Some historians have used qualitative sources to explore the cultural, social and psychological meanings of family for past populations, others have concentrated on a more quantitative, demographic approach. A third direction has been to look at families and households both as flexible and effective units of consumption (and often of production) and as key loci of socialization and acculturation of individuals. The consensus of the current scholarship is that, in terms of its size and morphology, the family remained broadly stable until the later eighteenth century. From that period to the present the family is represented as changing from a pre-modern, extended form to the modern, urbanized, nuclear family, and, while not preventing change, at least buffering it and acting as an agent for social stability. Modern families were seen as more privatized, and welfare in a modern state was provided by legal, contractual and state-based institutions, in parallel with economic changes that privileged a cash wage as the means of subsistence in a capitalist and industrial economy. Thus, the nineteenth century figures as a key period where changes which had begun in the eighteenth century were realized and generalized more widely. Demographers and social historians have shown, firstly, the regional variations that existed in family forms and, secondly, the fact that English households had not for centuries followed the more extended and complex forms more typical of some mainland European peasant societies. Quantitative data from parish registers and censuses has been painstakingly aggregated to discover the size and composition of households, marriage age, family size, birth spacing and mortality rates. Wrigley and Schofield's benchmark of 4.75 individuals per household for the early modern period remains instructive. In this model, the early modern English family already contained the key features that it used to combat the historical changes of the nineteenth century.[3]

This stress on continuity should not however marginalize the importance of the nineteenth-century changes. The 8.5 million population of England and Wales recorded in the 1801 census had grown to 32.5 million by 1901. Fast-growing industrial towns came to dwarf the older urban centres. In 1901 more than 70 towns had populations over 50,000 and Greater London contained 6.5 million people. The urban population expanded by a factor of more than nine, with attendant consequences in the cost and availability of housing, overcrowding and poor sanitation.[4] The causes of population growth are not fully understood, but studies show that in parishes with significant increases in population, women were bearing their first children a year or two younger than had previously been the case. Although there was some rise in illegitimacy, overall these changes in patterns of childbearing were associated with earlier marriage. Gillis relates this pattern to industrial work paid on piece rates, done at home or in small workshops typical of textiles, nail- and chain-making in the early stages of industrialization.[5] 'Put-out' work occupied both women and children and couples could marry younger on the strength of expectations of future earnings. There was less incentive to avoid conception when children would be contributing to their keep even before adolescence. However, the 'putting-out' system cannot fully account for all the population growth through earlier first pregnancies. The causes of these behavioural changes were both complex and localized, but do seem to be associated with the changing resources available for young people to set up a marital home. Overall, where women had greater economic autonomy they married later.[6] But what is very unclear is exactly how these kinds of economic calculations were made and how they intersected with young adults' cultures of leisure, courtship and sexuality. Some young women were willing and able to support themselves and their illegitimate children from their earnings in textile work, living in their parents' home and avoiding marriage altogether.[7]

A further major demographic shift occurred, detectable from the 1871 census. The rate of population growth slowed, and it did so because married women were having fewer babies. In the 1870s there were over 295 legitimate live births per 1,000 married women between 15 and 44 years of age. In 1901–11 this figure had declined to 222 per 1,000 and to 111 per 1,000 by the 1930s. The rate of illegitimate conception was also declining. This was an uneven change that only slowly came to be the norm – in the first decade of the twentieth century, 25 per cent of women still had more than five children and 55 per cent had more than three.[8] Professional, middle-class couples led the trend. Dependent on male professional incomes to underpin a middle-class, servant-keeping lifestyle, these families did not necessarily have substantial accumulated capital. If the family was to continue to prosper into the next generation, sons had to be supported through a lengthy period of education and professional training. Daughters required marriage portions. Consequently, fewer children represented a more effective strategy for the family as a whole. However, restricting marital fertility was not something that simply 'trickled down' from the middle to the working classes. Textile workers were quick to restrict the size of their families once cloth production had moved largely into mills. Labour-protection legislation had cut back on children's earning capacity but there was paid work for women in weaving. In mining communities, however, there was scant work for women of any kind after the labour legislation of the 1840s, and families remained large. Teenage adult sons went down the pit and daughters moved away into domestic service. In arable agricultural communities women's and children's work was a highly casualized adjunct of the labour services of married farm workers. Marital fertility remained comparatively high, but children moved away in search of work and farming communities grew smaller, particularly after the agricultural depression of the mid-1870s.[9] Women had long used abortifacients to limit fertility, but this period saw an 'underlying shift in the family economy, inducing a convergence in the reproductive interests of men and women'.[10] People's expectations that their children would live to adulthood improved at the same time as the changing industrial economy and the legal requirements for elementary schooling increased the costs of child-rearing. The fertility decline, incremental improvements to mothers' health and reductions in infant mortality were all closely linked.[11] Childless couples, or those with few children, could still be pitied or frowned upon; children were evidence of a father's manliness and a successful marriage. Family limitation called for complex decision-making processes within families and households about their most intimate experience – about sex, babies, parenting and about each individual's obligations to contribute to family subsistence, about who would stay home and who would move away.

Quantitative studies have set valuable parameters for our understanding of the history of the family. However, there are limitations to the kinds of insights that such work offers. There is much that historical demography has not yet discovered; research is of necessity driven by the availability and legibility of sources. The preferred methodology of the local study has revealed the diversity of household and community structures and such diversity itself militates against historical generalization. Change occurred, but it did so unevenly and practices of family formation and familial relationships are generally best understood as being closely related to local conditions, in particular labour markets. Highly localized differentiations were made between what was men's and what was women's work, and gender relations helped shape both the material and the familial aspects of life.

Demographic historians look at household structure, often defining families and households as the same thing and their studies often use surname linkage and trace the patrimonial line. Their sources, especially census and parish registers, are themselves structured by gendered assumptions.[12] Such research often imposes on the demographic structures of the past cultural meanings more suitable to particular readings of the present. It often ignores the uses of family that extended outside the household as well as 'household relationships of service, apprenticeship and visiting'.[13] The greater complexity of household forms under early industrialization were a response to stresses in economic subsistence. In fact, nineteenth-century working-class household structure was not based on the strictly nuclear family household and extended family households were common, if not statistically dominant, by the mid-nineteenth century.[14] A more nuanced account of the cultural meaning of household structures, kinship and familial relations, affect and social support is required. If the family was remarkable in surviving the nineteenth century as unscathed as it did, it achieved this by adapting its reproductive strategies, but without abandoning either the ideals or the templates of the family itself; in Gillis's terms, the family people lived *by* was as or more important than the family they lived *in*.[15]

Historical explanations which ignore gender relations and view 'the Family' as a private, unified entity see women primarily as a function of their reproductive capacities. Such theoretical perspectives remain unable either to break into the 'private' space of 'the Family' or to look across boundaries to see the ways the familial extended into kinship, neighbourhood and friendship relations. Work for example on violence, on bigamy and cohabitation or on child abuse has examined the arguments, explanations and claims made when 'family' seemed to be going wrong and thus can discern something of people's cultural expectations of how family *ought* to be as well as how families and individuals coped when there were difficulties. Examining the ragged edges of family not only reveals the productive and powerful nexus of ideologies at work but also can draw attention to the power relations involved, particularly by age and gender. As well as the relationships between paid and unpaid work within the household the gendered cultural labour, particularly that of women, in maintaining social connections and the status and respectability of families in class-specific ways are revealed, from the power of gossip at a working-class street corner to the 'energy, aggression and skill' of Mayfair dowagers in maintaining their family's status in the battle grounds of high society.[16]

Industrialization and the Working-Class Family

Women's historians have outlined how women's consistently lower pay and the worse conditions attracted by 'women's' than 'men's' paid work, were directly related both to gendered conceptions of family roles and to women's actual unpaid work in supporting domestic economies.[17] Tilly and Scott argued that working families in the nineteenth century adapted to the stresses of industrialization by changing the ways that they organized resource generation through production and labour as well as through consumption.[18] They outlined a three-stage transition across the nineteenth century from a 'family economy', through a 'family wage economy' to a 'family consumer economy'. In the 'family economy', household members were collaborative producers and consumers who pooled both labour and resources; household survival took precedence over the interests of individuals. The balance of labour between paid and unpaid work was more evenly divided by gender than it later became. The transition from household and small workshop production to that in mills and factories accompanied an equivalent transition in family form to a 'family wage economy'. The family/household remained a collaborative unit of consumption and commanded the labour and activities of its members. However, with paid labour moving from work within the home to that in the factory it was more difficult for married women with children to combine wage-earning with household duties. The capitalist and patriarchal logic of the labour market that allocated better-paid work to men, also meant that it made more sense for married women to withdraw from waged work. Their contribution to the survival of the household was greater the more attention they devoted to the unpaid work of household management and childcare. From a feminist perspective, these changes in household working patterns necessarily also changed the dynamics of gender relations between men and women in the family.

Seccombe's Marxist account of the proletarian nineteenth-century family offers a two-stage model, revolving around the change from the early industrial economy (equating broadly with Tilly and Scott's 'family wage economy') and the later-nineteenth-century period of slowing population growth (which according to Tilly and Scott saw a change to the 'family consumer economy'). Seccombe views the nineteenth-century 'proletarian' family as the site of production of labour power that was to be consumed in the industrial workplace. He argues that industrialization in the mid-nineteenth century depended on the over-exploitation of labour power; workers had to exhaust themselves to the extent that working families were unable to maintain a productive workforce, neither in the medium term (paying the price in ill-health and shortened lives) nor by being able to reproduce the succeeding generation of fit and productive workers. In 1880 a cohort of British 13-year-old upper-class boys were on average 4.2 inches taller than a comparable working-class cohort. Upper-class girls were 5.5 inches taller than working-class girls. Glasgow's crude death rate was 24.8 in 1821–4 but 39.8 in 1845–9. Death rates in the Liverpool slums in 1841 were 54 per cent higher than those in more affluent districts. In Sheffield, Manchester and Leeds in 1840 around half of all infants died before their fifth birthday, some 10 per cent more than for poor London parishes 200 years previously.[19] Protective labour legislation restricted the paid work of children and adult women, though within these restrictions families sought to maximize their number of wage-earners; the 'breadwinner' wage which enabled a married man to support wife and children was an aspiration not the norm.[20]

Small but incremental improvements in living standards for working people arrived later in the nineteenth century through the greater stabilization of the industrial capitalist economy, and meant that many working families could acquire domestic commodities which improved the material quality of life at home. It was within this context that the limitation of fertility came to seem both possible and reasonable. Mortality amongst British working men paying into Friendly Societies decreased and their greater economic security is demonstrated by fewer incidents of illness but longer periods of sick leave.[21] Gender differentials in wages became entrenched and men retained the use of the lion's share of household resources. Although wage distribution within families varied, men could be expected to keep between a half and a third of their wage for their own use, with lower-paid workers keeping a higher proportion. Nevertheless, working-class incomes were often inadequate and uncertain. Much paid work remained seasonal. Illness, accident or other misfortune could still cause major problems for household budgeting. The often unacknowledged skills of household managers in organizing consumption were vital. Careful shopping, making do and mending, paying into clubs at a farthing ($\frac{1}{4}$d) per week to save for Christmas, and for some the judicious use of the pawn shop, all helped make ends meet. Local moneylenders were a strategy of last resort, and could charge exorbitant interest rates. The strategies were endless, each saving tiny amounts that added up to the difference between a hot meal on the table every day, or not. Sunday dinners were particularly important, not only to people's nutrition but to their sense of self-respect. Networks of mutual support between households, borrowing and lending, exchanging child-minding for other services or sometimes for cash, were based on a strictly accounted reciprocity and policed by gossip.[22] It was vital to keep up with the rent. Food was the first item to be cut in times of hardship. People's diet was dull and high in carbohydrate: bread was the chief staple, and formed a much higher proportion of children's and women's diet than it did of men's. Men, the major wage-earners, were entitled to their 'relishes': a kipper or a chop. Mothers' priorities were first to feed their husbands and then their children. If necessary they went without food themselves. Hard physical labour, an inadequate diet and lack of (expensive) medical care affected women disproportionately, particularly when they experienced repeated pregnancies. Women commonly worked even harder during pregnancy to save for the new baby.[23] Of course, mothers gained considerable economic power and influence as managers of household resources, but achieved this at the price of heavy and sustained self-exploitation. Well into the twentieth century working-class women suffered chronic and extensive health problems.[24] If the physical costs of the supply of labour power were at first paid by working families as a whole, then working women paid this price over a longer chronology than working men.

Subsequent research has also shown that many married women worked for wages much later in the nineteenth century than Tilly and Scott had assumed and has demonstrated the very slight statistical basis for the argument that married women left the workforce before mid-century. Unpaid household labour was always prioritized but wage-earning remained part of a wife's responsibilities to the household.[25] However, Tilly and Scott did much to establish a productive theoretical and historical framework for understanding how domestic economies may have adapted to unevenly shifting labour markets and also for making sense of working-class familial forms that became established as 'traditional' by the inter-war period. Although he has different theoretical concerns, Seccombe also looks within the 'closed box' of the working-class family and analyses power dynamics operating within it. Both these approaches critique the broad 'continuity' thesis, since they suggest ways in which, even if the constitution of households remained broadly similar, the meanings of relations within them shifted in key ways between men and women, between parents and children and also between siblings.

Calculation or Affect?

Michael Anderson has argued, based on census data from mid-nineteenth-century Preston (Lancashire), that relationships between kin became more 'calculative'.[26] Wage-earning teenagers could live in lodgings away from their natal families. Recent research on migration has however shown that this was only part of a more complex story.[27] Although people used their power within families (parents controlling the labour of children, men commanding the greater share of food or comfort) or married earlier and moved away from their natal families when the opportunity arose, there is also evidence of people's attachment to their families, and their distress when expectations of emotionally close domestic and family relationships were frustrated. The London housewife who said, 'My young man's that good ter me I feel as if somethink nice 'ad 'appened every time 'e comes in' was unusual in her expressiveness but perhaps not unique in her sentiments, though as Ross has commented, working-class marriage was a contract that was primarily about reciprocal material obligation than about emotional intimacy.[28] Relationships between husbands and wives were at one level structured by the institutionalized privileges of patriarchy, reinforced by women's comparative lack of economic independence. The plentiful evidence of marital discord and of domestic violence makes this plain enough. At another level, the importance of the family at all social levels, combined with the common if often unspoken acknowledgement of the importance of both women's and men's contributions to family survival, could at best generate close relations, though probably more often led to a stoical commitment to kin.

Late-nineteenth-century working-class parenting styles could be undemonstrative, particularly with older children, without signifying a lack of emotional commitment. Parents' main concern was for the material well-being and good health of their children. Motherhood meant hard and unstinting work for one's children, particularly during their early years, which one expected to be repaid in turn. Where relations were good, children contributed both paid and unpaid work to the household: shopping, scavenging and child-minding as well as contributing whatever money they earned. The social and material necessities of working-class life could make for very deep if often unspoken bonds amongst family members, which continued across the life course. Many young married adults lived near to their kin and social and material support networks extended between households amongst family and neighbours.[29]

Levine-Clarke's investigation of the records of insane asylums in the West Riding demonstrates how often the causes of women's confinement could be traced to poverty and insecurity in the economically troubled 1840s. Husbands' infidelity, sexual problems, domestic violence and indeed the whole nexus of bad providing and abuse, bereavement, quarrels or distancing from adult children, were represented amongst the precipitants of mental ill-health. Working-class women became ill because they could not achieve normative domesticity through poverty, constrained opportunities or difficult and unsuccessful emotional relationships. But sources also reveal successful and valued family ties and affection and support by family members.[30] While the remedy was available in the church courts before 1855, working- and (lower-)middle-class people brought actions for sexual slander. People initiated troublesome and potentially expensive court cases because they had been accused of having illegitimate children, of being cuckolded, of living together unmarried or of engaging in other kinds of sexual irregularities. One woman brought an action because somebody had said that her husband 'is so fat he cannot do it for her and it is a deed of charity for some one to do something for the woman'. Another man came to court because he had been told: 'You have no need to be so fond of that child, for it is not yours.'[31] Such insults had real social consequences. A poor sexual reputation (particularly for women) and the resultant gossip damaged neighbourhood relations, not to mention business and employment prospects. Furthermore, people were emotionally hurt by such allegations, which could break marriage engagements, distress family members and cause quarrels and unhappiness between husband and wife. Frost's work on bigamy and cohabitation also shows the investment working people made in marital relationships and the general willingness of neighbours, friends, kin and even the magistrates' court to countenance bigamous marriages as long as these were entered into openly and obligations to previous as well as current spouses and children were honoured.[32] From a range of sources, therefore, it is clear that although some Victorians had very unhappy family lives, for many other people in all classes family was important not only as a way of organizing material subsistence, but because it provided the context of people's closest (and most complicated) emotional relationships, and was valued on that account.

The Middle-Class Family

The Victorian middle classes, with their greater literacy, left plentiful evidence of the importance of family ties. Because people were close, and felt that they ought to be, as well as being mutually dependent on the family enterprise, there was plenty of scope for conflict. When an Ipswich baker's teenage son stayed out all night, there was a row, 'the worst we ever had', though a few weeks later father and son were living and working together in apparent harmony. A Birmingham banker reported to his wife who was away from home in 1824 about talks with his son and the chattering of his young daughter. 'We are all very good too,' he wrote, 'I have been to church with Bosco, and after that I have gathered acorns with Rosabel. So there is nothing among us but love and health and happiness and peace.'[33] Offspring brought joy and grief both in childhood and when they were grown. Childhood was seen as a distinctive life-cycle stage marked by innocence and requiring careful and affectionate guidance. Children's health could never be guaranteed and their illness and death were a traumatic emotional experience. Their moral and spiritual well-being were another source of anxiety: what to tell a son about the moral snares of the world when he left home for the first time? Siblings also forged close emotional bonds and adults remained very much attached to their parents.

The brother/sister relationship provided great scope for close and affective relations normatively untainted by the complications of sexuality. Our opening quotation by Ellen Weeton demonstrates the depths of attachment possible for just one sister for her brother, and the bitterness that could be caused. The better-known example of William and Dorothy Wordsworth, at around the same period, illustrates Dorothy's domestic, affective, emotional and intellectual labour in the service of her brother and the Wordsworth household. Unmarried sisters lived or stayed with married sisters, creating a second, junior 'angel' in the house. Relationships between sisters and brothers-in-law could prove close and indeed complicated, as the house-hold of novelist Charles Dickens exemplifies. The possibilities of illicit sexual attrac-tion could make this dangerous ground, and the decades-long controversy over whether a man might marry his deceased wife's sister proves how far-reaching were the cultural (and political) sensitivities involved.

Commercial, manufacturing and professional families, particularly in the first half of the nineteenth century and before the advent of limited liability under the Act of 1851, had little protection from the vagaries of the early industrial economy. They depended very heavily on family property to secure not only their own material comfort but also their social standing and the future of the succeeding generation. Middle-class women might act as housekeepers or general servants in the households of their kin. These were not necessarily poor women; the 'servant' role could easily be aligned with the subordinate kinship role of such women. It was a costly strategy for middle-class families to maintain adult women outside commercial or professional wage-earning, and it was one undertaken not only in the service of gendered and classed ideals, deliberately distinctive from working-class and upper-class norms, but also in order to conserve family property within the circle of close kin through the maintenance of partible inheritance and socially embedded property rights. Families organized property ownership to make welfare provision for family members across the life course. Both women and men incurred obligations to family welfare when they controlled or owned family property, though women were more commonly denied absolute ownership and held only life interests. Nevertheless, men too had gendered obligations as protectors and providers to look to the welfare needs of family, particularly wives and children. The middle-class family enterprise was under-pinned by a network linked by kinship and social connection. This was not bounded by the walls of the household, though its key nodes were households formed by marriage. It is a significant indicator of their different access to and organization of resources, as well of different patterns of family relationships, that whilst both middle- and working-class households became more complex during the early stages of industrialization, working-class households were more commonly 'stem' house-holds supporting grandchildren or grandparents, whereas middle-class households tended to be 'horizontal', taking in additional members of the same generation to optimize the use of family capital.[34]

If the Victorian middle classes were anxious to distinguish their own family forms and practices from those of working people (even while their philanthropic endeav-ours often sought to inculcate aspects of their own domestic mores into the recipi-ents of charity and welfare) they could be equally critical of upper-class family patterns. Family privacy was a prerequisite for domesticity, so the visiting and enter-taining necessary to preserve family status were carefully hedged about with ritual and formality. The upper classes used hospitality and conspicuous consumption as a means of status display and the furtherance of dynastic and political concerns, and lacked the privacy of the middle-class home. Though it was by no means universal across the upper classes, some 'sets' had a decidedly more relaxed sexual culture after first marriage than accorded with middle-class mores. Once married, it was possible for upper-class women and men to have extra marital affairs as long as absolute discretion was maintained. The upper-class practice of primogeniture gave eldest sons a precedence over and independence of their siblings far greater than was available for the middle classes.

By the later years of the century the growth of the service sector had proliferated white-collar and commercial employment and trade, and distinctive lower-middle-class family patterns had emerged. They were unable to afford live-in servants, but keen to distinguish themselves from the working class by placing a high value on domestic privacy, making sure married women ceased earning, maintaining men's commitment to domesticity and practising family limitation based on 'carefulness' in sexual life. Decency in demeanour, lifestyle and appearance were key to maintaining employability and status. Even more than the middle classes, lower-middle-class families had scant property reserves and their incomes were not necessarily greater than those of the working class and not always secure. The loss of a job, or a breadwinner's death or long-term illness could rapidly erode the comparatively small resource margins upon which their distinction from unskilled labouring families depended. Small wonder that lower-middle-class culture placed such an investment in domestic decency, in carefulness and restraint, and used clear gender distinctions to reinforce the boundaries between themselves and the labouring poor.

Domesticity

It was above all through their domestic culture that the nineteenth-century middle class established shared interests across great diversity in occupation, politics, religion and income levels. Middle-class domesticity had at its core the perceived need to maintain a domain differentiated from the insecurities of business, commerce and politics in which the family could be nurtured in an environment, certainly of material comfort but even more importantly of moral probity, religion and affection. Particularly in the first half of the century 'serious religion' (of whatever denomination) was important to middle-class home culture. Appropriate, ordered and hierarchical relationships amongst people and things structured these domestic worlds. Middle-class women were subordinated to male kin, but had considerable authority over working-class men and women and over children. Middle-class children negotiated authority and subordination with the (often) female working-class servants who cared for their physical and emotional needs. Above all such dispositions were organized around and symbolized by gender.

Women's contribution to both home and family enterprise was important, though increasingly this was behind the scenes (keeping the books, for example). They helped maintain the family's social and commercial credit through demonstrating the status of the family by their display and demeanour in social life, in orchestrating appropriate marriages for sons and daughters, as well as in bringing up children and managing an appropriately genteel servant-keeping household. The assumption that Victorian codes of middle-class domesticity required women to be merely ornamental and confined to the parlour has now been effectively undermined. Certainly some articulate women found Victorian domesticity constraining and longed for the professional, political or entrepreneurial opportunities and challenges open to their menfolk. Many others found the combination of family responsibilities, household management and the obligations to religion, philanthropy and public action that were key indicators of middle-class culture, a rounded basis for a lifestyle. The women's movement from the mid-century frequently based its claims for public and political identities for women on maternalist formulations of their particular aptitude in key areas of public life and social welfare.

Victorian women's roles and preoccupations prioritized family not just as a reaction to their exclusion from the public, but because (in private and in public) 'family' was an important way in which women and men of this class position organized their identities and activities, particularly in the High Victorian period. Women were above all, in class- and status-differentiated ways, responsible for the material and cultural reproduction of domesticity, from the bearing and rearing of children to the management of cleanliness, food production and household chores. Moreover, women's 'physical, intellectual, even emotional work' helped produce 'the public and intellectual self realisation of higher status men'.[35] Distinctions drawn between public and private spheres did not preclude women's public activity as long as they preserved both their femininity and class status, nor did it marginalize men from the domestic sphere which, certainly for the first two-thirds of the nineteenth century, was a key site for the construction of respectable middle-class masculinities.

Business and professional men adopted masculine roles of protector, father and provider, which rejected eighteenth-century libertinism but admitted both romantic sensibilities and affection as well as evangelical commitment; the complement of genteel, domestic femininity. His duty was to provide, yet his masculine privileges made these duties difficult for economically dependent women to enforce, where the gentleman proved wanting. The frock-coated, chivalric masculinity of mid-century, marked by responsibility, restraint and domestic commitment, was only one of a diversity of masculinities which historians are now beginning to recognize and periodize. After 1870, with the development both of empire and of the social and cultural infrastructure of commercial, industrial, urbanized society new terrains for the expression of masculinity opened up – both the metropolitan 'gentleman's club', a domesticized yet masculine space, and the potentially more exciting colonial territories.[36] Men married later or sometimes not at all. A new and energetic 'manliness' was marked by physicality, exertion and the rejection of domestic comforts. Within marriage, the dominance of the paterfamilias had been modified, not by undermining patriarchy but through its adaptation to changing middle-class gender roles which had to accommodate, for example, the possibilities of limited economic independence for the 'new woman'. Given that it was achieved without the widespread use of barrier contraception, across classes the fertility decline meant not only that women were less willing to see yet another pregnancy as inevitable, but that husbands were necessarily also more willing to be 'careful'. The elite 'flight from domesticity', was, however, only one of a number of respectable masculinities in circulation in the later nineteenth century. The hard-drinking, hard-working and not infrequently violent physicality that characterized some variants of working-class masculinity did not go unchallenged. 'Independent artisans', too, were increasingly being judged (and judging themselves) on their fitness for public citizenship by their abilities to maintain a more or less respectable and restrained demeanour and an ability to support a wife and children.[37]

Servants, Housework and Household Management

Although dependent on a 'character' from their last employer, it was comparatively easy for female domestic servants to change their 'place', particularly in the larger towns and cities. This was a frequent response to the heavy labour and extensive control of their free time and social life that live-in domestic service imposed. Of course by no means all domestic servants lived in, and most worked in one-servant households. Conditions of work were of course highly gendered: the few live-in male domestic servants tended to have higher status and better wages. Both the comforts of the middle- and upper-class home as well as the hard-won and limited material underpinnings of working-class domesticity depended on the physical labour of women. Domestic technologies shifted only slowly since domestic labour, both paid and unpaid, was in plentiful supply. As a workplace, the Victorian house was far from labour-saving. Although the country houses of the rich might have the benefits of indoor plumbing, central heating and electric light by the Edwardian period, the technological and mechanical ingenuity of Victorian industrialization was little applied to the domestic sphere. Fetching and shifting water, particularly from an outside tap, was both arduous and time-consuming. The weekly laundry could take up to two long days of heavy work. Although by 1876, 80 per cent of Manchester's 70,366 houses had internal water supplies other towns were less well provided and 62 per cent of rural homes in England still lacked piped water in 1913.[38] Gas for domestic lighting and cooking had been in use by more affluent households from mid-century. Slot meters and free installation by gas companies eager to gain more customers made gas a cheap and practical fuel in many working-class homes from the 1880s. The widespread use of electricity arrived only during the inter-war period. Improvements to working-class housing came slowly, impeded by the lack of town planning and by cost-conscious ratepayer interests in local government. However, although by the later nineteenth century the moral as well as the civic implications of the sanitary argument were broadly established, widespread improvements in working-class housing were delayed into the twentieth century.

By the nineteenth century cleaning had become a central part of household chores. The employment of domestic servants ensured that middle-class women's relationship to this task was highly status-differentiated from that of working-class women whose physical labour 'absorbed dirt and lowliness into their own bodies'.[39] The management of dirt and the maintenance of cleanliness meant the establishment of clear boundaries, norms and status distinctions. Domestic hygiene had both moral and sanitary implications. In the closing decades of the century, the industrial production of household soaps, detergents, linoleum and wall paper did make the labour of housework a little easier, but at the same time raised standards and increased the amount of housework considered necessary. More affluent Victorian households had long been given to a proliferation of ornamentation (which needed cleaning) and even in poorer households cheap prints and ornaments were valued appurtenances of domestic life. Clean white nets and a black-leaded grate were crucial markers of respectability for 'working people, whose rented accommodation was probably poorly maintained, with rooms beset by bedbugs; moreover they often had to share an outside tap and privy with others, who may have lacked their standards . . .'. The segregation and demarcation of domestic space by function, but also by gender, class and age, had long been a feature of upper-class domestic space, and with its own particular inflections was a principle adopted in the middle-class Victorian home. Servants' quarters were high in the (uncomfortable and unheated) attics and their specialized work spaces in the cellars or back parts of the house. Children had nurseries and only joined adults, sometimes quite briefly, at certain times of the day. The study or, in more affluent houses, the smoking-room or the gun room were masculine territory. Amongst the lower middle class, smaller families made a separate bedroom for each child a realizable aspiration. In working-class households, even when living space was scarce and it was common for family members to share bedrooms and often beds, the setting aside of a parlour for 'best' may have baffled observers, but was vital to household dignity. Even where living quarters were so cramped as to make this impossible, other kinds of demarcations were made. Children might eat their meals standing, rather than sitting, or after the adult men. 'Father' often had a particular chair reserved for his use alone.

As household size declined somewhat later in the nineteenth century, working people who could afford it put a greater premium on domestic privacy. This also meant withdrawal, at least in part, from the gregarious sociability of the streets and likewise from the social support networks which depended on neighbourhood mutuality; privacy, self-sufficiency or independence were associated and 'keeping ourselves to ourselves' became a clearer marker of respectability.

Conflict and Violence within Families

Family mutuality, shared interests and often close emotional relationships existed within the nexus of power relations by age and gender. Family cohesion was necessarily achieved at the cost of individual interests; and the dynamics of power, subordination and resistance could give rise to unhappiness and conflict. The full extent of physical, emotional and sexual abuse is undiscoverable and although there is certainly evidence of it amongst the more affluent, the Victorian public gaze was focused on the disorder of working-class homes.

The sexual abuse of children was not by any means unknown, though it was far more common for cases involving working people to come to court. Informal detection mechanisms amongst neighbourhood networks operated particularly in urban areas where people's proximity to each other brought abuse to light, and the impression given is that cases came to the attention of the courts and the police only where informal neighbourhood sanctions were ineffective. Cases involving lodgers, neighbours or shopkeepers as well as fathers whose generally drunken and abusive behaviour made them visible were more likely to enter the historical record. Children, considered contaminated or 'fallen' through the experience of abuse, could be held to be unreliable witnesses in court. The public abhorrence of child sexual abuse, even more so than in the sexual assault of adults, made it difficult to imagine an otherwise respectable man as guilty. Court decisions turned often on judgements about character, and many trials ended in acquittal.[40]

Though by no means all working men were violent, the stresses of domestic economies made physical abuse of wives and sometimes children not uncommon. Much of this violence arose out of contests over resources; many women were beaten in the kitchen because they refused their husband's drink-money or because they had not provided a meal to his liking. However, a range of other causes could also intervene. Tensions over sex, where wives were reluctant to have another pregnancy, quarrels about the 'interference' of kin or neighbours, or rows when one of the couple was unfaithful might also result in serious physical assault. Some women suffered terrible and prolonged abuse for decades. It was these women above all, the victims of 'wife torture', who focused the attention of activists such as Frances Power Cobbe. Her campaigning contributed to the passage of the 1878 Matrimonial Causes Act, which enabled abused wives to apply for a legal separation in the magistrates' court. Not all wives were passive recipients of violence, however. Some fought back hard and most mothers used physical violence to control their children. Although the numbers of cases of domestic violence recorded by the courts tended to decline towards the end of the century, this may be in part an effect of magistrates' increased tendencies towards mediation and also of the greater regard for domestic privacy amongst the respectable working classes.[41]

Marital Breakdown and Divorce

Marriage was generally an economic necessity for women as well as being the cultural norm and between 1871 and 1951 at least 60 per cent of all adult females either were or had been married.[42] Husbands' legal privileges and ability to control their wives' property and persons were not a nineteenth-century invention. Their authority in the home, their rights of sexual access and of physical 'correction' of their wives had a far longer history, though not all the rights commonly claimed were actually enshrined in legal precedent or statute. Where husbands abused these privileges, wives in the early nineteenth century were left with very little in the way of legal remedy.

Until 1857 full, legal divorce was only possible by an extensive, lengthy and public process of securing a private Act of Parliament. This was generally preceded by obtaining a separation *in mensa et thoro* (of bed and board) under ecclesiastical law as well as by an action for 'criminal conversation' brought by the husband against his wife's lover. This was a civil action for damages for the husband's loss of access to his wife's sexual and other services. Adultery by the wife, because it raised doubts about the legitimacy of children and the security of inheritance, provided the sole grounds for divorce. Unsurprisingly, comparatively few full divorce cases were brought and those that were involved members of the upper classes for whom legitimate succession to aristocratic privilege and landholding outweighed both the expense and the public scrutiny of their private lives. Husbands had complete rights of the guardianship of children over 7 (and, before the 1839 Infants Custody Act, of all children) and over any property that their wives had brought to the marriage. They could compel unhappy wives to remain in the family home and continue to allow them sexual access, virtually irrespective of their own behaviour. Adultery by a husband was no offence and physical cruelty and abuse had to be of the most extreme kind before it gave wives any cause or grievance that a court of law would pay attention to. Certain unhappy wives such as Caroline Norton in the 1830s or Georgina Weldon in the 1880s fought back fiercely and campaigned publicly against husbands who refused them a separation and used the law against them to deny them contact with their children or indeed to have them confined in an asylum on the grounds that wishing to end an unhappy marriage must necessarily evidence a wife's mental instability.[43]

However, there were other partial solutions for those so unhappily married that, despite the scandal, they were determined to end the relationship. For the more affluent, marriage settlements could preserve some sort of income or a wife's continued access to her own property and deeds of separation made possible separate households, though of course did not allow remarriage by either party. For working people (or others less concerned for their reputations and possessing the mobility to start over in a different place) simple desertion or, as we have seen, bigamy solved the most intractable marital problems. Early in the century, the customary 'wife sale' was still a possible means of regularizing second 'marriages' in rare cases. Of course the Poor Law authorities, particularly in their more stringent phases in the late 1830s and again in the 1870s, frowned upon husbands' desertion as a likely charge on the poor rate. Working-class communities could however be more tolerant of couples 'living tally', though cohabitation, illegitimate children and other familial irregularities were more disapproved of by the early twentieth century.

The key legislative change came in 1857 when, for the first time, the Matrimonial Causes Act made available final and absolute divorce in the civil courts. Although still not a cheap option on working-class budgets and difficult of access for people living away from London where the court was established, the 1857 Act did make it possible for middle- and a minority of working-class couples to separate finally and absolutely. Grounds for divorce were still unequal by gender; husband's adultery was still excluded. However, divorce following (extreme, physical) cruelty was now a possibility. Frequently, divorce cases and the associated journalism revolved around debates about the appropriate gender roles within a marriage, the limits of patriarchal authority, powers of 'correction' within the home and often supported wives' claims to the right to fulfil their obligations to home and family without undue hindrance from their husbands.[44] Married Women's Property Acts in 1870 and 1882 extended separated wives' control over their earnings and property, though these measures of course benefited middle- more than working-class women. Working-class wives and some husbands with difficult marriages generally resorted to the magistrates' courts. Their options were to bring actions for physical assault against abusive partners and from 1878 seriously physically abused wives could apply for maintenance and separation from husbands. From 1886 magistrates could act where husbands had deserted their families and 'persistent cruelty' as well as serious assault were admitted as grounds for separation and maintenance orders from 1895, though of course maintenance payments were often difficult to collect. The emphasis on remedies for a husband's physical violence, meant that there was little legal way out of marriages that were unsuccessful for other reasons.

The Family in Public

This discussion has emphasized the importance of family in people's lives and also its flexibility and adaptability in response to changing social and economic circumstances and in servicing class interests. Family roles were highly gendered as well as class-specific. The stakes of what happened to and in families also had far wider public and political currency. Dominant cultures in the nineteenth century saw the family as an important guarantor of social stability. Although particular anxieties focused on perceptions of the working-class family, divorce and inheritance were also areas relevant to middle- and upper-class families. Especially after 1850, the state overcame its earlier reluctance and was repeatedly willing to use family law to mitigate husbands' and fathers' authority over their wives, children and family property in order to defend normative ideals of gendered obligations as well as rights in the 'private sphere'. Doctrines of laissez-faire and the freedom of the market may have been prominent in economic thinking, particularly in the first half of the century, but the view was increasingly taken that direct legislative and philanthropic interventions in the 'private' sphere were necessary for its smooth operation. The tremendous energy with which the Victorian middle classes pursued philanthropic agendas depended on the identification of deserving recipients of aid. If the market required the labouring poor to labour, they would be better inclined to do so if they could be persuaded or coerced to values of sobriety, thrift and diligence through an interest in the material and moral well-being of family dependants. Protective labour legislation, such as the 1842 Mines Act and the 1844 Factory Act restricted children's and adult women's access to the industrial workforce, prioritizing husbands' and fathers' role as wage-earner. Early-nineteenth-century suspicions of an over-strong state were set aside at first over the Poor Law and policing. The 1834 Poor Law with its principle of 'less eligibility' and the practice of splitting up families seeking relief in the workhouse was deeply resented by many working people, and set a legislative precedent for the separation of families, continued into the twentieth century. The New Poor Law was predicated on categorizations of men and women informed by highly gendered assumptions of their familial roles. Victorian state and philanthropic welfare agencies saw themselves as a corrective to the inadequacies of impoverished families. The eventual working-class adoption of a breadwinner ideal was essentially a product of the nineteenth-century politics of work and welfare.[45]

From the point of view of those welfare recipients, on the one hand the acceptance of charity was demeaning, on the other certain kinds of welfare provided practical help and acted as yet another source of resources that could be juggled to manage precarious household economies. Families used one large asylum for 'idiot' children to provide a period of a few years' care. Little was achieved in the way of cure, but especially for poorer families the asylum relieved strains on the households where there was uncertain income, or a large number of younger children.[46] Outside agencies increasingly competed directly with parents for the control of and authority over children and established particular benchmarks for respectable parenting; boots and clean pinafores were prerequisites for school attendance which could make significant demands on household budgets. As household managers, working women commonly dealt with philanthropic agencies, with the 'school board man' and where necessary with the police and courts. These interactions called for skills of negotiation, sometimes confrontation and not infrequently an adoption of apparent passivity in the face of the large helpings of 'good advice' that were commonly the price for practical assistance. Nevertheless, the charitable relationship was a reciprocal one, requiring certain kinds of performance on each side.[47] The relationship was articulated across boundaries of class but also of gender; appropriate recipients of charity generally could demonstrate a family background that was congruent with dominant norms.

By the late nineteenth century more 'scientific' approaches to philanthropy and social work being spearheaded by the Charity Organisation Society and the settlement movement set the stage for the welfare legislation of the early twentieth century and intensified the scrutiny of the working-class family that was increasingly focused on the child. As Mahood puts it, 'since the late nineteenth century public interest in children has been the wedge used to prise open families.'[48] Developing discourses of eugenics, of the risk of racial 'degeneration', replaced earlier religiously inspired formulations and enabled new kinds of interventions in family life. The receipt of welfare jeopardized people's status as citizens; men on Poor Law benefit were excluded from the franchise.[49] Eugenics also gave new impetus to the argument that women's welfare work in the public sphere was legitimated by their maternalist concerns and aptitudes. Women's (as well as men's) philanthropic endeavours legitimated their 'active citizenship' in public life, in missionary societies, on school boards or boards of guardians, and as charitable visitors. As the early-twentieth-century collectivist state developed, 'family' became a terrain where notions of citizenship were worked out; these concerns were hardly private or peripheral but were at the heart of public and political conceptions of the modern state.

NOTES

1. *Miss Weeton's Journal of a Governess*, intro. J. J. Bagley, vol. 1 (Newton Abbot, 1969), pp. 152–3.
2. A. G. Crosby, ed., *The Family Records of Benjamin Shaw, Mechanic of Dent, Dolphinholme and Preston, 1772–1841* (Lancashire and Cheshire, 1991), pp. 102, 103–4. Betty Shaw died in February 1828.
3. P. Laslett, *The World We Have Lost: Further Explored* (London, 1983); E. A. Wrigley and R. S. Schofield, *The Population History of England, 1541–1871: A Reconstruction* (London, 1981).
4. M. Abbott, *Family Ties: English Families 1540–1920* (London, 1993), p. 4; W. Seccombe, *Weathering the Storm: Working-Class Families from the Industrial Revolution to the Fertility Decline* (London, 1993), pp. 30–1.
5. J. Gillis, *For Better, For Worse: British Marriages, 1600 to the Present* (Oxford, 1985).
6. B. Hill, 'The marriage age of women and the demographers', *History Workshop Journal*, 28 (1989), pp. 138–9.
7. G. N. Gandy, 'Illegitimacy in a handloom weaving community: fertility patterns in Culceth, Lancaster, 1781–1860', D.Phil. diss., University of Oxford, 1978.
8. J. Lewis, *Women in England 1870–1950: Sexual Divisions and Social Change* (Brighton, 1984), pp. 5–6.
9. R. Milward and F. Bell, 'Infant mortality in Victorian Britain: the mother as medium', *Economic History Review*, 4 (2001), p. 728.
10. Seccombe, *Weathering*, p. 37.
11. J. Schellekens, 'Wages, secondary workers, and fertility: a working-class perspective of the fertility transition in England and Wales', *Journal of Family History*, 18 (1993).
12. B. Hill, 'Women, work and the census – a problem for historians of women', *History Workshop Journal*, 35 (1993).

13. M. Doolittle, 'Close relations? Bringing together gender and family in English history', *Gender and History*, 11 (1999), p. 547.

14. E. Gordon and G. Nair, 'Middle class family structure in nineteenth century Glasgow', *Journal of Family History*, 24 (1999).

15. L. Davidoff, *Worlds Between: Historical Perspectives on Gender and Class* (Cambridge, 1995), p. 9; J. Gillis, *A World of Their Own Making: Myth, Ritual, and the Quest for Family Values* (New York, 1996).

16. Davidoff, *Worlds Between*, p. 10.

17. D. Simonton, *A History of European Women's Work: 1700 to the Present* (London, 1998).

18. L. A. Tilly and J. W. Scott, *Women, Work and Family* (New York, 1978).

19. Seccombe, *Weathering*, pp. 5–7, 18–19.

20. A. Clark, 'The New Poor Law and the breadwinner wage: contrasting assumptions', *Journal of Social History*, 34 (2000).

21. J. C. Riley, *Sick not Dead: The Health of British Workingmen during the Mortality Decline* (Baltimore, 1997).

22. E. Ross, 'Survival networks: women's neighbourhood sharing in London before World War 1', *History Workshop Journal*, 15 (1993).

23. E. Ross, *Love and Toil: Motherhood in Outcast London, 1870–1918* (Oxford, 1993), p. 109.

24. C. Chinn, *They Worked All Their Lives: Women of the Urban Poor in England, 1880–1939* (Manchester, 1998), p. 133.

25. J. Humphries, 'Women and paid work', in J. Purvis, ed., *Women's History: Britain, 1850–1945* (London, 1995); A. August, 'How separate a sphere? Poor women and paid work in late-Victorian London', *Journal of Family History*, 19 (1994); S. Horrell and J. Humphries, 'Women's labour force participation and the transition to the male-breadwinner family, 1790–1865', *Economic History Review*, 48 (1995).

26. M. Anderson, *Family Structure in Nineteenth Century Lancashire* (Cambridge, 1971).

27. J. Turnbull and C. G. Pooley, 'Leaving home: the experience of migration from the parental home in Britain since c.1770', *Journal of Family History*, 22 (1997).

28. M. Pember Reeves, *Round About a Pound a Week* (New York and London, [repub.] 1980), p. 16; E. Ross, '"Fierce questions and taunts": married life in working-class London, 1870–1914', *Feminist Studies*, 8 (1982).

29. T. Thompson, *Edwardian Childhoods* (London, 1981), pp. 71–2.

30. D. Levine-Clarke, 'Dysfunctional domesticity: female insanity and family relationships among the West Riding poor in the mid-nineteenth century', *Journal of Family History*, 26 (2000).

31. S. M. Waddams, *Sexual Slander in Nineteenth-Century England: Defamation in the Ecclesiastical Courts, 1815–1855* (Toronto, 2000), pp. 134, 139–155.

32. G. Frost, 'Bigamy and cohabitation in Victorian England', *Journal of Family History*, 22 (1997).

33. L. Davidoff and C. Hall, *Family Fortunes: Men and Women of the English Middle Class 1780–1850* (London, 2002), pp. 332, 330.

34. Gordon and Nair, 'Middle-class family structure', p. 476.

35. Davidoff, *Worlds Between*, pp. 7–8.

36. J. Tosh, *A Man's Place: Masculinity and the Middle-Class Home in Victorian England* (London, 1999), ch. 8.

37. K. McClelland, 'Masculinity and the "representative artisan" in Britain, 1850–80', in M. Roper and J. Tosh, eds, *Manful Assertions: Masculinities in Britain since 1800* (London, 1991); C. Hall, K. McClelland and J. Rendall, *Defining the Victorian Nation: Class, Race, Gender and the Reform Act of 1867* (Cambridge, 2000), pp. 71–118.

38. C. Davidson, *A Woman's Work is Never Done: A History of Housework in the British Isles 1650–1950* (London, 1982), pp. 31, 32.
39. Davidoff, *Worlds Between*, pp. 4, 5.
40. L. A. Jackson, *Child Sexual Abuse in Victorian England* (London, 2000).
41. E. Ross, 'Fierce questions'; S. D'Cruze, *Crimes of Outrage: Sex, Violence and Victorian Working Women* (London, 1998), ch. 4; A. J. Hammerton, *Cruelty and Companionship: Conflict in Nineteenth-Century Married Life* (London, 1992).
42. Lewis, *Women in England*, p. 3.
43. J. R. Walkowitz, *City of Dreadful Delight: Narratives of Sexual Danger in Late-Victorian London* (London, 1992); A. Acland, *Caroline Norton* (London, 1948).
44. Hammerton, *Cruelty and Companionship*.
45. A. Clark, *The Struggle for the Breeches: Gender and the Making of the British Working Class* (London, 1995); Clark, 'The New Poor Law'; L. H. Lees, *The Solidarities of Strangers: The History of the Poor Laws and the People, 1700–1948* (Cambridge, 1998), p. 144.
46. D. Wright, 'Family strategies and the institutional confinement of "idiot" children in Victorian England', *Journal of Family History*, 23 (1998).
47. J. Long, *Conversations in Cold Rooms: Women, Work and Poverty in Nineteenth Century Northumberland* (Woodbridge, 1999), p. 167.
48. L. Mahood, *Policing Gender, Class and Family: Britain 1850–1940* (London, 1995), pp. 2, 10.
49. S. D'Cruze, 'Unguarded passions: violence, history and the everyday', in S. D'Cruze, ed., *Everyday Violence in Britain, 1850–1950: Gender and Class* (Harlow, 2000), p. 10.

FURTHER READING

A useful recent introductory history to the nineteenth-century family is L. Davidoff, M. Doolittle, J. Fink and K. Holden, *The Family Story: Blood, Contract and Intimacy, 1830–1960* (1999). L. Davidoff and C. Hall, *Family Fortunes: Men and Women of the English Middle Class, 1780–1850* (2002) has made a major contribution to perceptions of the middle-class family. J. Tosh, *A Man's Place: Masculinity and the Middle-Class Home in Victorian England* (1999) develops an analysis of middle-class masculinity. M. Roper and J. Tosh, eds, *Manful Assertions: Masculinities in Britain since 1800* (1991) is a useful collection and contains an examination of codes of respectable masculinities for working men. A. Clark, *The Struggle for the Breeches: Gender and the Making of the British Working Class* (1995) contributes to historical debates about class and culture by taking gender identities and the family into account. E. Ross, *Love and Toil: Motherhood in Outcast London, 1870–1918* (1993) and M. Tebbutt, *Women's Talk? A Social History of 'Gossip' in Working-Class Neighbourhoods, 1880–1960* (1995) are imaginative studies of working-class neighbourhood, family and respectability. J. Long, *Conversations in Cold Rooms: Women, Work and Poverty in Nineteenth Century Northumberland* (1999) is an insightful study of the relationships of work, family and identity for nineteenth-century working women. Studies discussing the family through examining violence, abuse or irregularities include L. A. Jackson, *Child Sexual Abuse in Victorian England* (2000); S. D'Cruze, *Crimes of Outrage: Sex, Violence and Victorian Working Women* (1998); A. J. Hammerton, *Cruelty and Companionship: Conflict in Nineteenth-Century Married Life* (1992); and G. Frost, 'Bigamy and cohabitation in Victorian England', *Journal of Family History*, 22 (1997). A growing amount of recent work using demographic material to inform family history includes A. Owens, 'Property, gender and the life course: inheritance and family welfare provision in early-nineteenth-century England', *Social History*, 26 (2001). E. A. Wrigley and R. S. Schofield, *The Population History of England, 1541–1871: A Reconstruction* (1981) continues to provide an important quantitative framework for demographic analysis.

CHAPTER SIXTEEN

Migration and Settlement

IAN WHYTE

Introduction

Migration can be defined as a residential change of a permanent or semi-permanent nature operating at a variety of scales ranging from movement within an urban street to transatlantic emigration. In this chapter migration is also taken to include seasonal movements of labour such as those of harvest workers and farm servants. Of the three basic demographic variables – fertility, mortality and migration – it is the hardest to measure as it was not a finite event and is often poorly documented.

In nineteenth-century Britain, as today, migration was an important demographic, social, economic and cultural process linking communities, regions and nations. Migration had profound impacts on the lives of individuals, affecting everyone, regardless of whether they were movers or stayers, by helping to influence the social and demographic structures of the communities in which they lived through the addition or subtraction of people. This was particularly evident where the net flow of migrants was strongly outwards or inwards, and when the cultural characteristics of those who moved were different from those of the populations of the areas to which they moved, as with rural, Gaelic-speaking Highlanders or Irish moving to British industrial cities. Every community was affected by migration and modest net inward or outward movements could conceal large gross flows of people. Migration influenced many features of society such as the housing market, welfare and labour conditions. The volume and patterns of migration were important indicators of change in the maturing industrial society and economy of nineteenth-century Britain. The influences which prompted people to move could be negative ones driving them out of an area or positive ones pulling them towards particular destinations. Migration was frequently a modernizing element in social and economic change, but it could sometimes be undertaken reluctantly or be conservative in character, helping to shore up traditional economies, as with seasonal migration from Ireland to help with the British harvest.

Most research on migration in nineteenth-century Britain has been empirical in character with a lack of theoretical perspectives. An important exception was E. G.

Ravenstein whose pioneer work on the published censuses of 1871 and 1881 generated his 'laws' of migration – really a series of hypotheses based on empirical data
– which have cast a long shadow over subsequent studies of population movement
in nineteenth-century Britain. Ravenstein suggested that:

- Most migration occurred over short distances.
- Migration proceeded step by step.
- Migrants going long distances tended to go to one of the great centres of com-
  merce or industry.
- Each current of migration produced a compensating counter-current.
- The natives of towns were less migratory than those of rural areas.
- Females were more migratory than males within their county of birth but males
  more frequently migrated longer distances.
- Large towns grew more by migration than by natural increase.
- The major direction of migration was from agricultural areas to centres of indus-
  try and commerce.
- The major causes of migration were economic.[1]

Ravenstein's approach was a broad one based on data with severe limitations which
emphasized the economic causes of migration rather than social and cultural influences. The scale of his approach and the sources that he used inevitably led to an
underestimation of the amount of short-distance population movement within rather
than between counties but his work still has value as a set of ideas to be questioned,
challenged and in some cases supported. Some modern research has followed Ravenstein in utilizing large data-sets to produce aggregative, quantitative studies of migration. Such approaches, however, tend to dehumanize the process of migration by
looking at flows rather than people, patterns rather than individual decisions to move
or to stay put. More recently humanistic, biographical approaches have been developed, focusing on the migration experiences of particular families and looking in
detail at the decision-making processes involved.[2]

　　Until relatively recently it was widely believed by historians that industrialization
was associated with major changes in the volume and character of migration. It was
considered that pre-industrial societies in Britain had been relatively immobile and
that industrialization greatly increased the amount of population movement, particularly from agriculture to industry and from the countryside to the towns and cities.
These concepts were summarized by Zelinsky in his model of the mobility transition.[3] He suggested that the volume of migration increased markedly during the
change to an industrialized economy. During the same period he considered that
there were also major changes in the types of movement and an increase in the average
distance travelled by migrants. More recent research has indicated that Zelinsky's
model is seriously flawed and that the amount of population mobility in pre-
industrial society was far greater than had previously been believed. Studies spanning
the early phases of industrialization in the eighteenth and early nineteenth centuries
and the mature phase of industrialization in the mid/late nineteenth century, have
demonstrated that there was no marked increase in the volume of movement nor any
major changes in the overall patterns of mobility.[4]

Sources of Data on Migration

Even for the nineteenth century, so rich in documentation compared with earlier periods, the questions which can be asked about migration are severely limited by the nature of the surviving source material. An ever-increasing range of sources has been exploited to shed light on different groups of migrants and different facets of migration. But prior to detailed official census records in the mid-nineteenth century the social, spatial and temporal coverage of all sources is partial and often quite limited. Sources from earlier periods shedding light on migration, such as marriage registers and settlement records, continue to provide some information for the nineteenth century and new sources such as trade-union records of payments to itinerant journeyman craftsmen become available. Developments in data-handling, especially computer database systems, have greatly assisted the analysis of such information. Nevertheless, the type of information contained in such sources still dictates the kinds of migration problems which can be studied and the ways in which they are approached.

The published census returns allow large-scale, comparative studies using big datasets. The census enumerators' books from 1841 onwards provide detailed information on lifetime migration between place of birth and current residence, with some information on the intermediate moves of families being obtainable from the birthplaces of children. The migration histories of individuals can be charted in more detail by linking entries in census enumerators' books for successive censuses but the number of definite linkages that can be established tends to be small in relation to the amount of effort involved. Despite decades of use, the full potential of census enumerators' books is only starting to be realized as a result of computer analysis, yet at the same time the tendency to focus on published and unpublished census data has led to the neglect of other sources and approaches. Many official and unofficial sources, such as parliamentary reports or the New Statistical Account for Scotland, may provide specific information on migration as well as the social and economic contexts in which it operated. Settlement and vagrancy records provide more detailed, though not always easily interpreted, information on the movements of some of the poorest elements in society. Passenger lists from emigrant ships, and the records of transported criminals, provide details of the migration of specific groups of people. In most sources, however, the motives which led people to migrate are rarely stated and must be inferred. Detailed migration biographies extracted from diaries, memoirs, and genealogical research, though relatively rare and not necessarily representative, give migration a more human dimension by providing information on the reasons behind particular movements made by individuals and families.[5]

Spatial and Temporal Patterns of Migration

Longitudinal studies have shown that there was an underlying continuity in patterns of migration between the late eighteenth and early twentieth centuries.[6] Migration was ubiquitous within British society, though individual experiences varied greatly. The significance of movement from rural areas declined through the nineteenth century as a result of rural depopulation and movements within and between towns and cities became more and more common. However, the proportion of people moving over long distances rose only marginally before the end of the nineteenth century. The real rise in mobility did not occur until the very end of the century, and was due not so much to improved transport with the spread of the railway network, but to the advent of cheaper fares making mass transportation a reality. Throughout the nineteenth century the majority of moves were made over short distances, within rather than between settlements and localities. The broad patterns of migration, at a regional level, were remarkably similar throughout Britain, with movements into and out of most regions being fairly evenly balanced. Movement within rather than between regions accounted for the bulk of migration and net regional inflows and outflows were generally quite small, though some areas, such as rural Wales and the Scottish Highlands, did experience more persistent losses of population. The limited possessions owned by most people, and the predominance of rented accommodation in the housing market, greatly facilitated mobility. Many groups of workers, including agricultural and domestic servants, apprentices and some industrial and agricultural workers, received accommodation with their jobs.

Mobility Within the Countryside

Despite the importance of migration to towns and cities, much mobility within nineteenth-century Britain occurred within the countryside. As in the eighteenth century, comparisons of population listings, whether private ones made by local clergymen or landowners, or in the form of census enumerators' books, generally indicate a high rate of turnover of population within most communities that have been studied, with people moving in as well as out due to marriage, the movement of agricultural workers, vagrancy and other influences. Marriage distances – the distances between the places of residence of couples at the time of their marriage – have been widely studied, partly because of the easy accessibility of marriage registers. However, the information contained in marriage registers may be less straightforward than it seems at first sight. The assumption that people whose origins were not given were living in the parish of registration at the time of their marriage, or that the parishes in which couples were married were necessarily the ones in which they intended to live afterwards, is potentially fallacious. The proportion of exogamous marriages, involving one partner from outside the parish in which marriage took place, and the average distances over which contacts leading to such marriages were maintained, has been assumed to summarize the distances over which everyday social interactions, including courtship, were maintained. Wealthier people, such as landowners, professional men and more prosperous farmers, tended to marry brides from greater distances than did labourers and tradesmen. This was partly because of the much smaller pool of suitable partners living locally who were of the right age and social background. In the nineteenth century, as today, average marriage distances were short. There was, however, a tendency for them to increase during the later nineteenth century, possibly as a result of the increasing availability of cheaper transport. Perry's study of marriage migration in twenty-seven Dorset parishes in the late nineteenth and early twentieth centuries found little change in rural isolation until the end of the nineteenth century.[7] The achievement of virtually universal literacy, shorter working hours, higher wages and the increasing mobility provided by the bicycle were thought to have been significant in widening social contacts. Marriage contacts were also influenced by geography, being more extended along major routeways, and were constricted by topographic barriers such as hills and major rivers.

The movement of living-in agricultural servants between employers at the end of six-month or annual contracts, which accounted for so much local mobility in the seventeenth and eighteenth centuries, diminished in the nineteenth century in southern and eastern England as, with a glut of population after 1815, long-hire labour systems gave way to the cheaper practice of employing day labourers. Numbers of living-in servants had increased during the Napoleonic Wars due to a shortage of workers but they declined steadily thereafter. There was also increasing reluctance to employ servants on annual contracts in order to prevent them from gaining settlements. In parts of northern and western England where smaller, more pastoral farms were common, numbers of living-in agricultural servants remained high for much of the nineteenth century. In Lowland Scotland, long-hire systems of agricultural labour with their associated mobility persisted throughout the nineteenth century. In Scotland population growth was more sluggish than in England, workers were more willing to move to the towns, and there was strong competition for labour from industry. All these influences encouraged the retention of the system of farm servants, as did the system of farming; cereal production was less dominant than in England and mixed farming with the cultivation of root crops and sown grasses spread the demand for labour more evenly throughout the year, so that farms needed to ensure a regular labour supply. The contribution of the mobility of agricultural servants to the general circulation of population within the countryside of Lowland Scotland was a major one.[8]

Whether day labourers or living-in servants provided the normal agricultural workforce for arable farms, there was always a need for extra labour at harvest time. Formerly this had been provided locally and in the early decades of the Industrial Revolution it was common for workers from the towns to move to the countryside to act as harvest workers. But by the early nineteenth century, with the spread of factory production, urban-based industrial workers had less and less opportunity to absent themselves in this way. The result was a rise in the use of seasonal migrant harvest labour drawn from much longer distances, particularly from the Scottish Highlands and from Ireland. By the end of the eighteenth century contemporaries were suggesting that half the young women in the southern Highlands went to help with the Lothian harvest. In the early nineteenth century migrant harvest labour was increasingly drawn from more remote northern and western areas of the Highlands while labour migration to other seasonal work such as gutting herring in east-coast Scottish ports and on the Clyde also developed. The post-1815 economic recession encouraged such temporary migration, the earnings from which were used to shore up a tottering traditional economy at home. Temporary harvest migration by both men and women spread knowledge of English and an appreciation of opportunities outside the Highlands, often precipitating permanent out-migration.

The largest population flow from the periphery of the British Isles to the agricultural core during the first half of the nineteenth century was undoubtedly from Ireland. By 1841 there were nearly 58,000 Irish seasonal agricultural workers in Britain, mostly men. They gradually ousted Welsh and Scottish labour in England and even supplanted Highlanders in parts of the Scottish Lowlands. As with seasonal movement from the Highlands this flow was conservative in outlook, representing a continuation of traditional movements within Ireland from the rugged west to the lowlands of the south and east, helping to maintain a traditional peasant economy.

There has been a good deal of debate concerning the influence on local movements of labour in the English countryside of 'open' and 'close' parishes. In economic terms, close parishes were those in which a major landowner was able to control and restrict the settlement of incomers. Open parishes, by contrast, were ones where settlement was easy for immigrants owing to a lack of landlord control and the availability of cottages for rent. In close parishes all but a bare minimum of wage-earning labourers were excluded from residence and much of the workforce on local farms had to be imported daily from surrounding open parishes which had surpluses of labour to export. The distinction between these two types of community has been defined in different ways in terms of labour supply and landownership, but the impact of such differences on labour mobility may be harder to identify in practice.[9]

There has also been disagreement over the extent to which parliamentary enclosure displaced the rural population, particularly squatters, cottagers and smallholders who lost valuable common rights and either gained no land at all or received only small plots in lieu. It has been suggested that the creation of the new landscape of enclosure required a good deal of additional labour, as did the improved farming systems which were frequently adopted once open fields had been eliminated. On this basis enclosure should have increased the demand for labour and attracted workers into newly enclosed parishes. However, the work of making new boundaries, roads and farmsteads was often done by itinerant gangs of workers and where former open-field arable land was converted to pasture after enclosure, as happened in many parts of the Midlands, the result might well have been to cut the amount of labour required and displace people to nearby villages or further afield.[10]

A distinctive form of rural population displacement emerged in Scotland from the later eighteenth century as the Highland Clearances, which were caused by the spread into the region of commercial sheep farming. Large-scale sheep farming could not co-exist with traditional small-scale Highland mixed peasant agriculture. Landlords amalgamated smallholdings into larger units, leasing them to Lowland graziers and moved their tenants out of the interior glens which were best suited to sheep farming. In the southern and eastern Highlands such changes, during the later eighteenth century, were more gradual with enough alternative employment opportunities locally, or in nearby lowland towns, to prevent large-scale concern over depopulation. The rapid spread of commercial sheep farming into the far northern and western Highlands in the early decades of the nineteenth century brought more drastic changes, however. The cultivated land on the valley floors was required for wintering the sheep and the existing population was cleared out, sometimes in thousands, as in the notorious example of the Sutherland estates. The aim was not to remove people from the estates entirely but to relocate them in new planned coastal settlements where, it was hoped, the expansion of the fishing industry and a range of manufactures, combined with smallholding agriculture, would provide them with a better living and the estate with a greater income. Well intentioned but insensitive and ill executed, and blighted by the post-1815 economic depression, the Sutherland clearances uprooted thousands of families and failed to provide many of them with the wherewithal to start new lives. Inevitably many drifted away from the estates and eventually from the Highlands altogether, moving to Lowland towns or emigrating to Canada. Later in the nineteenth century the clearance of islands like Rhum was undertaken by agreement between landlord and tenant, the proprietor financing the emigration of unwanted families.[11]

Migration, Industrialization and Urbanization

As has already been mentioned, industrialization did not lead to great changes in patterns of migration. Most movement continued to be over short distances despite the spread of turnpikes, canals and then the railways. The example of Benjamin Shaw and his family is an instructive one. Shaw, a mill-worker, was born in 1772 and wrote his autobiography in 1826. His father, Joseph, was born in Garsdale, West Yorkshire, in 1748. He lived and worked in and around the village of Dent for much of his early life. After his marriage, Joseph made several short-distance moves in the Dent area to obtain more suitable accommodation for his growing family. In 1791, however, the whole family, including Benjamin, moved 50 km south to the factory village of Dolphinholme near Lancaster. The move was not a success for Joseph soon quarrelled with his new employer and returned to Dent but the children, who had been taken on as apprentices, stayed. In less than two years the mill began laying off workers. Three of the Shaw children died in 1792–3 and most of the surviving family returned to Dent but Benjamin, who had married, moved to the industrial town of Preston in 1795. His parents followed soon after. The example of Benjamin Shaw and his family highlights some key features of migration in the early phases of industrialization. Migration at this time was predominantly over short distances, involving families as well as individuals. Rural factory villages like Dolphinholme were important stepping stones in the transition from a proto-industrial rural setting to an urban industrial one.[12] Factory owners sometimes went on recruiting drives in suitable areas to attract workers to their new factory communities. This was how the Shaw family were persuaded to move from Dent to Dolphinholme. Pauper children from larger towns such as London and Edinburgh provided another source of labour for the factories at Styall, near Manchester, and New Lanark.

By the middle of the nineteenth century over half of Britain's population lived in towns and movements within the urban hierarchy had become increasingly significant. In 1851 London had the greatest number of people born in a different county (38.3 per cent) but northern industrial towns had greater proportions of long-distance migrants (Glasgow 55.9 per cent, Liverpool 57.5 per cent, Manchester 54.6 per cent). Migration from the countryside to the towns and, within the urban hierarchy, from smaller to larger centres has tended to attract the attention of both contemporary writers and historians but in fact such trends were often balanced by counter-flows from large settlements to smaller and town to country so that net inflows to large cities were often relatively small. It has been too easily assumed that migration between the countryside and the towns operated only in one direction and involved the permanent separation of rural dwellers from their agrarian roots. The significance of reverse movements from town to country is brought out by the autobiography of Alexander Somerville, born in 1811 in the village of Oldhamstocks in East Lothian. Starting his working life as a farm labourer, he moved around East Lothian as a woodsman, a worker at a lime kiln, a harvester, a sheepshearer and a drain-digger. He then moved to Edinburgh as a sawyer but a trade depression forced him back to the countryside as a hay-mower, fence-maker and general labourer. He returned to Edinburgh as a market-gardener but went back to the countryside as a sheepshearer and harvester before enlisting as a soldier and eventually emigrating to Canada. His movements suggest that occupational as well as geographical mobility was common and also that the distinction between 'temporary' and 'permanent' migration, however sharply drawn in theory, may be difficult to distinguish in practice.

Migration from the countryside to the towns in the nineteenth century was also predominantly regional in character. There is little evidence, for example, of any significant long-distance migration from poor, over-populated rural areas in southern England to the industrial towns of the north. Withers's study of migration from the Scottish Highlands to Stirling, Perth and Dundee has demonstrated that each town recruited migrants from distinct, though overlapping, hinterlands.[13] Long-distance migration did occur but it often involved particular groups of workers with specialist skills such as the migration of Welsh ironworkers to Middlesbrough, Scottish engineers and machine makers to Manchester and Scottish glassmakers to St Helens. A high proportion of migrants to large industrial centres were skilled workers.

Mobility within towns was also a prominent feature of nineteenth-century society owing to the high proportion of property for rent. Much of the movement was highly localized within streets or districts but there were also movements from inner urban areas towards higher-status residential areas in the growing suburbs. The fact that most people had to live within walking distance of their work meant that many moves within towns were job-related. Female domestic servants, whose numbers peaked at over 1.5 million in 1891, were one of the most mobile occupational groups within the urban population.

The Settlement Laws and Migration

A hotly debated aspect of nineteenth-century population movement has been the impact on mobility of the Settlement Laws. Seventeenth-century statutes established the principle that everyone should have a single parish of legal settlement in which they were entitled to receive poor relief. Settlement rights could be established on the basis of birth, marriage and, in the nineteenth century, from a father's or even grandfather's parish of settlement. Other mechanisms, such as renting property worth £10 per annum, a year's agricultural service, completing an apprenticeship, paying taxes or serving in a parish office for a year were also grounds for gaining a settlement. People who required poor relief and were living in a parish which was not their parish of settlement could be removed there or, less commonly, be provided with out-relief. It was widely believed by contemporaries that the Settlement Laws were oppressive, restricting the movement of labour, but it is difficult to generalize about a system, the effects of which depended so much on local practices. There has been acrimonious disagreement regarding how the Settlement Laws were used and to whom they were applied at local and regional levels. Snell believes that migrants were only examined when they became destitute.[14] Landau has argued for a much higher proportion of the population being monitored.[15] The documentation generated by settlement examinations and removals is rich in detail but, because of its emphasis on the poorest and least fortunate sections of society, it is far from being representative, particularly because of the varying rates of survival of such sources from one area to another.

With the decline of agricultural service during the nineteenth century as a way of gaining a settlement an increasing proportion of people in southern and eastern England took their fathers' or even their grandfathers' settlement. This may well have reduced population mobility in southern England. By the early nineteenth century it was becoming harder for sojourners (people living out of their parish of settlement) to acquire further settlements as various loopholes in the law were closed. Parish officials grew increasingly efficient in ensuring that migrants were not allowed to fulfil the criteria that would give them a settlement in a new parish.

Emigration

Emigration was an important feature of British society in the nineteenth century. Between 1815 and 1930 around 11.4 million people emigrated from Britain and 7.3 million from Ireland. In terms of migrants per head of population, Ireland had the highest migration rate reaching 14.6 per thousand per year between 1860 and 1870. Scotland's maximum, in the 1880s, was 7.1 per thousand; England and Wales's rate was only 5.6 in the same decade.[16] Motives for emigration are difficult to establish; in most cases both push and pull factors were probably involved. There was a great deal of regional variation in rates of emigration some of which, as with the Scottish Highlands, may have been chain migration encouraged by early emigrants sending back information regarding opportunities. Information was passed on not just by emigrant letters but also by returned migrants who may have made up as much as 40 per cent of those who emigrated. Long-term fluctuations in levels of emigration clearly related to economic cycles and the demand for labour in destination countries as well as conditions at home. In the early nineteenth century the typical emigrant to America moved as part of a family and went into agriculture. In the later part of the century, due partly to the lower cost and greater speed and safety of passages, emigrants were more commonly young single men.

Because the sources relating to emigration are often different from, and better than, those providing information on migration within Britain, it has sometimes been assumed that emigration was a distinctly different process from internal migration. However, it seems more likely that emigration was often a direct continuation of internal movements. It has been debated whether emigration from nineteenth-century Britain provided a means of off-loading the 'losers' of the Industrial Revolution. The 1820s and 1830s were certainly decades of rapid social change and mounting concern over the state of British society. Erickson, however, has challenged the view that emigrants at this time were necessarily the casualties of cyclical and structural changes in the British economy, suggesting that they were drawn disproportionately from high-wage industrial areas rather than from the poorest social groups.[17] Positive motives for emigration were still clearly important despite the push factors.

By the early nineteenth century mass migration to North America was well established. There were considerable short-term variations in the social background of the emigrant stream between years of peaks and troughs. It has sometimes been assumed that English emigrants in the earlier nineteenth century came predominantly from agricultural and rural craft backgrounds, driven out by enclosure and, after 1815, by agricultural depression, in contrast to the later nineteenth century when emigrants were overwhelmingly urban in origin. However, Erickson has shown that most labourers and weavers were too poor to afford to emigrate in the early decades of the nineteenth century and that they were outnumbered among emigrants by crafts-men in traditional trades whose skills had not changed much from pre-industrial times. Half the men emigrating to America in 1831 from England and Wales were in craft or industrial rather than agricultural occupations. In 1827 39 per cent of emi-grants came from the larger towns at a time when these only accounted for 28 per cent of the population; emigration at this time involved a substantial proportion of workers from new industries owing to a depression in the cotton industry. In 1831 emigrants from the most rapidly changing and expanding industries, including textiles, metalwork and engineering, were over-represented. Emigration seems then not to have acted as a major safety valve. In 1827–31 only 21 per cent of English emigrants came from agricultural low-wage counties against 55 per cent from industrial high-wage ones.

Australasia and South Africa developed during the nineteenth century as alternat-ive emigration venues to North America. Australia was settled as a penal colony from 1788, when the 'First Fleet' anchored in Botany Bay. In the early nineteenth century the colony grew slowly with around five vessels a year bringing up to 1,000 convicts. From a population of about 7,500 in 1800 the colony had grown to 36,598 at the time of the first census in 1828. Free migrants were not encouraged before the late 1820s. In 1828 there were only around 4,500 free immigrants in Australia: the passage cost far more than the voyage to America. From 1831 the colony began using money from land sales to subsidize the passage of selected migrants chosen for their skills. Mass emigration to Australia began in the 1830s and increased rapidly in the mid-nineteenth century. As emigration to Australia was always expensive compared with North America, government assistance was always needed. The unfavourable convict image also had to be overcome by positive publicity. As a result of the short-age of labour in Australia, particularly after gold had been discovered, migrants found Australian society much more open and less stratified with more scope for social mobility than in Britain.[18]

Migration to South Africa began even more slowly; the settlement at the Cape, captured from the Dutch in 1795, returned to them in 1803 and recaptured in 1806, was a mere staging post on the route to India until after 1815. Post-war depression and rising unemployment in Britain led to various schemes to aid the emigration of British settlers to South Africa. In 1820 some 5,000 people arrived in this way, many of them from urban and industrial backgrounds without the skills needed to break in new land for agriculture. The limited success of the scheme did not encourage an immediate follow-up. New Zealand was settled even later. In 1843 the European population was only 11,500 but by 1900 it had risen to 770,000.

Immigration

Immigration to nineteenth-century Britain has received much less attention than emigration as the net flow of population was markedly outwards for much of the nineteenth century, and the quality of the sources for British immigration is poorer than for immigration to America. It has indeed been suggested that Britain did not have a tradition of immigration but Holmes has argued that immigration was continual rather than episodic for much of the century; there were no controls over entry to Britain until 1905.[19] The Irish were by far the largest single group of arrivals. It is debatable whether they should really be counted as internal migrants rather than immigrants. However, as they tend to be treated in this way even by Irish historians they will be considered in this section. Numbers of Irish-born in the census rose from 289,404 in England and Wales in 1841 to a peak of 601,634 on 1861 when they formed over 2.5 per cent of the population. In Scotland there were 126,321 in 1841 rising to 207,770 in 1871, 6.2 per cent of the population.

The impact of large-scale emigration on Irish society has been given less consideration than its effects on destination areas. The outflow should, in theory, have improved conditions in the labour market at home for those who remained, but as so much of the emigration came from the more prosperous areas of Ulster and Leinster it did not relieve population pressure where it was most severe, in the west. The unskilled, illiterate character of most Irish emigrants suggests that they were not very different from the populations they left, but the preponderance of young, economically active men and women among the migrants may have increased the dependency ratio in the remaining Irish population.

Irish emigration to Britain occurred in a series of definite streams linking particular source areas and destinations; from the south-west, especially Cork and Limerick, to Bristol, South Wales and London, from Dublin to Liverpool, and from Ulster to Glasgow. Movement was facilitated by the development of regular steamship services across the Irish Sea. Competition brought fares down drastically in the 1820s and 1830s. So much emphasis has been placed on the factors that drove people out of Ireland that it is easy to overlook the influences which attracted them to Britain: the relatively high wages in industrial areas, the availability of work like handloom-weaving and labouring which was similar to what they were used to in Ireland, the increasing knowledge of the English language generated by seasonal harvest migration, and the existence of Irish communities in all the main British towns.

The Irish chose, overwhelmingly, to settle in urban environments. South-western Scotland was one of the few areas in which substantial numbers of Irish migrants settled as permanent agricultural workers. By 1841 nearly half the Irish-born in Britain were concentrated in London (17.6 per cent), Liverpool (11.9 per cent), Glasgow (10.7 per cent) and Manchester (8.3 per cent). Regionally, the main foci outside London were Lancashire and west-central Scotland. A problem in studying Irish communities in Britain during the early nineteenth century is the lack of quantitative information about them, especially on occupation, residence and family structure. From the mid-century the position improves with the details from the 1841 census and census-enumerators' books. Irish communities were rapidly augmented by children born in England but it is difficult to be sure to what extent second and third generations acknowledged themselves as Irish.

The Irish have been portrayed as the outcasts of nineteenth-century British urban society in social, economic, political and religious terms. Many studies have tried to demonstrate that they were a segregated group, explicitly or implicitly using a 'ghetto' model. More recently it has been stressed that this is only a partial picture and the diversity of experience of the Irish in Britain has been emphasized. The Irish took up a wide range of occupations in British towns: all larger urban centres had plenty of low-skilled employment while some, in addition, had specific labour-market features such as heavy industry, textiles or construction, which attracted the Irish. Some towns, notably Bristol, Dundee, Edinburgh, Hull and Newcastle, were more liberal in their response to the Irish than the main reception centres like Glasgow, Liverpool and Cardiff. In London, with no dominant manufacturing industry, a high proportion of the Irish worked in the service sector.

There has been considerable debate over the nature of Irish communities in British cities. The economics of the housing market forced them into low-rent slums where they displaced other slum-dwellers. However, social class and employment opportunities were more significant than ethnicity in determining patterns of Irish settlement. Irish families might dominate individual alleys, courts and streets but not whole neighbourhoods yet, while the Irish lived in mixed neighbourhoods, they did interact heavily among themselves, using networks of friends and kin.[20] There was a high turnover of Irish families in such residential areas but their mobility was mostly over very short distances within, rather than between, districts.

While the Irish were resented for accepting low wages and, in the view of many, driving down working-class wages more generally, and while their religion and politics may at times have been suspect, there is little indication of hostility to them on racial or ethnic grounds. The popular image of the good-natured Paddy – brave, impetuous, spontaneous but on the down side prone to drunkenness and violence – was a stereotype accepted by both Irish and English. The Irish were over-represented in the crime statistics, not entirely due to police prejudice, but much of the violence generated by them was directed within their own community, in pursuit of regional rivalries early in the nineteenth century and sectarian divisions later on. The Irish, by the third quarter of the nineteenth century, had become invisible immigrants, their appearance and dress being indistinguishable from the working classes in general.

Other immigrant groups were more readily identifiable and aroused more hostility. Nineteenth-century Britain was, nevertheless, a relatively liberal society, attracting political refugees as well as (predominantly) economic migrants. As well as the Irish significant numbers of East European Jews, Germans, Italians and smaller numbers of Chinese, black Africans, Indians and other groups also moved into Britain, often into traditional immigrant areas in major port towns, such as the East End of London.

German immigrants accounted for over a third of the nearly 90,000 people in England and Wales in 1871 originating from continental Europe. Many Germans were clerks, working in London to broaden their experience but German scientists, professional men and merchants were also prominent. Although there was resentment from some British clerks over the Germans undercutting wages, the Germans attracted less attention and hostility than other immigrant groups.

Jewish immigrants were probably better treated in Britain than in most other countries but many people were nevertheless unfriendly towards them. Sephardic Jews speaking Portuguese or Spanish had been present in Britain for centuries but the early nineteenth century brought a new influx of Ashkenazic Jews from Germany who spoke Yiddish. In London they were gradually absorbed into society, being admitted to the freedom of the city from 1830, with the first Jewish lord mayor appointed in 1855. Jewish immigration began to increase again in the 1870s and swelled rapidly after the pogroms in southern Russia in 1881–2 and in other parts of eastern Europe a few years later. In 1883 it was estimated that there were 44,000 Jews in London. By 1911 there were around 240,000 in Britain as a whole, the bulk of them in London's East End where their synagogues and specialist shops added a distinctive element to the character of the area. Their sober and industrious habits were admired but, as with the Irish earlier in the century, they were condemned for cutting wages. On the other hand there was suspicion of wealthy Jews who were considered to have undue influence in the financial sector and the press. Their dress, appearance and religion made them seem a separate group, within the nation but not belonging to it, pursuing their own agenda.

The pace of immigration increased greatly in the last twenty years of the nineteenth century. By 1901 there were some 82,844 people from Russian Poland, mainly Jewish, in England and Wales: they formed the largest European-born minority in Scotland, a country which was also popular with incomers from Lithuania, many of whom became coal-miners. The Italian community, polarized into those from the industrial north and from the poor, rural south, also grew markedly in the 1890s.

Immigrants from continental Europe, the empire and beyond inevitably moved mostly into low-wage occupations and low-rent housing vacated by earlier generations of immigrants such as the Irish. Some found suitable niche occupations such as German bands, or Italian ice-cream sellers, musicians and entertainers. In 1891 the Irish accounted for 14 per cent of the personnel of the British army and by 1911 there were over 1,000 Italian-run ice-cream shops in Scotland. Some Indians, Chinese and Africans arrived as sailors and stayed. Much of the movement was concentrated into the last thirty years of the nineteenth century before the Alien Restriction Acts of 1905 and 1919 curtailed the flow. In 1871 Britain had 157,000 residents born outside the empire. By 1911 this had risen to 428,000 – only 1 per cent of the population but more prominent for being heavily concentrated in areas like the East End.

Conclusion

Past studies of migration in nineteenth-century Britain have tended to focus on the exotic and atypical rather than the commonplace. In reality, short-distance movements within the everyday spheres of action of most people were far more common than long-distance moves though it is dangerous to impose twenty-first-century perceptions of distance on nineteenth-century society. Moves of over 50 km accounted for only about one-fifth of all migration throughout the nineteenth century. The circular and cyclical movement of many people demonstrates the importance of attachment to particular places and a desire to return to familiar localities. Most places, and most regions, gained and lost people with only modest net outflows or inflows. To this extent this might seem to reduce the importance of migration in nineteenth-century society but the sheer amount of movement that occurred demonstrates its central significance in people's lives.

NOTES

1. D. Grigg, 'E. G. Ravenstein and the "laws of migration"', *Journal of Historical Geography*, 9 (1977).
2. C. G. Pooley and S. D'Cruze, 'Migration and urbanization in North-West England c.1760–1830', *Social History*, 19 (1994).
3. W. Zelinsky, 'The hypothesis of the mobility transition', *Geographical Review*, 61 (1971).
4. C. G. Pooley and J. Turnbull, *Migration and Mobility in Britain Since the Eighteenth Century* (London, 1998).
5. Pooley and D'Cruze, 'Migration and urbanization'.
6. Pooley and Turnbull, *Migration and Mobility*.
7. P. J. Perry, 'Working class isolation and mobility in rural Dorset, 1837–1936: a study of marriage distances', *Transactions of the Institute of British Geographers*, 46 (1969).
8. R. A. Houston, 'Geographical mobility in Scotland 1652–1811: the evidence of testimonials', *Journal of Historical Geography*, 11 (1985).
9. S. Banks, 'Nineteenth-century scandal or twentieth-century model? A new look at "open" and "close" parishes', *Economic History Review*, 41 (1991).
10. J. M. Neeson, *Commoners: Common Right, Enclosure and Social Change in England 1700–1820* (Cambridge, 1993).
11. E. Richards, *A History of the Highland Clearances* (London, 1982 & 1985).
12. A. G. Crosby, ed., *The Family Records of Benjamin Shaw, Mechanic of Dent, Dolphinholme and Preston, 1772–1841* (Lancashire and Cheshire, 1991).
13. C. W. Withers, 'Highland migration to Dundee, Perth and Stirling 1783–1891', *Journal of Historical Geography*, 11 (1985).
14. K. D. M. Snell, 'Settlement, Poor Law and the rural historian: new approaches and opportunities', *Rural History*, 3 (1992).
15. N. Landau, 'Who was subject to the Laws of Settlement? Procedure under the Settlement Laws in eighteenth-century England', *Agricultural History Review*, 49 (1995).
16. D. Baines, *Emigration from Europe, 1815–1930* (London, 1991).
17. C. Erickson, *Leaving England: Essays on British Emigration in the Nineteenth Century* (London, 1994).
18. E. Richards, 'Voices of British and Irish migrants in nineteenth-century Australia', in C. G. Pooley and I. D. Whyte, eds, *Migrants, Emigrants and Immigrants: A Social History of Migration* (London, 1991).
19. C. Holmes, *John Bull's Island: Immigration and British Society, 1871–1971* (Basingstoke, 1988).
20. L. H. Lees, *Exiles of Erin: Irish Migrants in Victorian London* (Manchester, 1979).

FURTHER READING

C. G. Pooley and J. Turnbull, *Migration and Mobility in Britain since the Eighteenth Century* (1998) provides a detailed, up-to-date survey of the key themes and questions relating to internal migration in nineteenth-century Britain. I. D. Whyte, *Migration and Society in Britain 1550–1830* (2000) covers the earlier part of the century. C. G. Pooley and I. D. Whyte, eds, *Migrants, Emigrants and Immigrants: A Social History of Migration* (1991) also focuses on the nineteenth century. For emigration see C. Erickson, *Leaving England: Essays on British Emigration in the Nineteenth Century* (1994). There is a substantial literature on the Irish in Britain, reviewed in G. Davis, *The Irish in Britain 1815–1914* (1991). For immigration C. Holmes, *John Bull's Island: Immigration and British Society, 1871–1971* (1988) is excellent for the later part of the century.

CHAPTER SEVENTEEN

Standard of Living, Quality of Life

JANE HUMPHRIES

Introduction

By the dawn of the nineteenth century, conventional chronology has the first Industrial Revolution as already twenty years old. Component changes were well under way including: the application of science to production; specialization of economic activity; production for national and international markets rather than for family or parochial use; movement of population from rural to urban communities; enlargement and depersonalization of the production unit; movement of labour from primary production to the production of manufactures and services; use of capital goods in production; and the emergence of new social and occupational classes. When these changes happen together and are sustained, they are almost always associated with an increase in the volume of goods and services produced. How did the changes that distinguish an industrial revolution interact with the increase in production to impact on the standard of living? More specifically, by what time and to what extent did working people benefit from the British Industrial Revolution? This question was debated almost contemporaneously with industrialization and continues to be contested to the present day. Why, given all this attention, has the debate remained unresolved? There are three interrelated reasons.

First, the historical evidence is not of sufficient quantity or quality to facilitate definitive answers. Industrialization in Britain took place before the establishment of national offices dedicated to the gathering and processing of social and economic data. Even an issue as basic as how many people lived through the Industrial Revolution is problematic. The first census took place in 1801 but not until forty years later was occupational enumeration attempted. Vital registration of births and deaths was not undertaken until 1837. For the end of the eighteenth century and earlier, historians have to rely on educated guesswork. How much and what people produced and how this changed over time is also difficult to gauge in the absence of censuses of production and national economic accounts. In the context of dramatic social and economic change, the anxious denizens of the Victorian state often organized one-off investigations. Royal commissions, government inquiries and private investigations provide important insights into economic change and its effects on working people. But the historical evidence is like a difficult coalface. There are rich, if faulted, seams of relevant material that yield information that is frequently discontinuous and inconsistent. The standard of living as traditionally understood in terms of the value of production or consumption per capita, or real wages, involves measurement and valuation. Thus historians need time-series data on output, population, consumption, wages, the structure of employment and prices. The demands on the evidence are relentless.

A second reason why the welfare effects of industrialization remain contested concerns the standard by which we are to judge trends. Are gains in living standards from 1780 to 1860 to be compared with what went before or what came after? Are they to be compared with the gains that other countries achieved at the same time or during their industrial revolutions, or even with a counter-factual scenario representing the gains that could have been achieved in different circumstances, specifically in the context of a more involved state? Authors are often unclear about their criteria and slide in a confusing way from one standard to another.

Compounding the problems of patchy evidence and shifting standards are deep conceptual difficulties. What exactly does the standard of living mean? Economists had tried to evaluate the standard of living in terms of *utility*, which was variously interpreted as pleasure, as desire fulfilment or as choice. None were successful in facilitating comparisons across time and between people. *Subjectivism* played a key role in this failure and prompted economists to adopt more objective considerations such as commodity possession or *opulence*. It was more plausible to identify someone as having a low standard of living because she was deprived of decent housing, or adequate food, or basic medical care, than because she was simply unhappy. Thus one approach was to pursue an *exclusionist* strategy, to focus attention on the material standards and exclude less tangible factors. A focus on opulence also permitted a quantitative assessment of the standard of living; we can measure changes.

Fixing on material standards does not circumvent the problems with subjectivism that waylaid the utilitarians. Evaluative judgements are inescapable if individual living standards are to be compared. Nor can it sidestep the reality that many qualitative things in addition to the goods and services available influence well-being: how hard people have to work, the strains and stresses placed on their social lives, and the nature of their living conditions, for example. The desirability of bringing these into consideration has prompted a second, *reductionist* strategy, which attempts to impute a monetary value to the important qualitative factors. Once reduced to a common standard of account, intangibles become palpable and can be included in a standard analysis. Recently opulence-based approaches to the standard of living have come under renewed criticism and a broader conception, indicated in the phrase *quality of life*, recommended.[1] Sen has reconsidered the quality of life, in terms of *human capabilities and functionings*, that is people's opportunities to lead the kind of life that they have reason to value, and evaluated changes with reference to this criterion.[2] These ideas underpin a third, *radical* strategy, which involves starting not from utility or opulence but from the conception of a necessarily multi-dimensional quality of life.

This chapter categorizes the recent literature in terms of these strategies interwoven with two further themes. The first concerns the shifts in well-being characteristic of the era and the dangers of fixating on average experience. The second concerns the constitutive plurality of the quality of life and the likelihood that components of well-being can change in opposite directions. The study identifies divergent trends among component indicators and uses them to gain further insight.

Opulence: The Exclusionist Strategy

Traditionally economic historians concentrated on a narrow conception of the standard of living, the material aspect or opulence.

National income per capita (PCI)

The obvious empirical counterpart to opulence is the value of the goods and services available at any time divided by the population to arrive at the intuitively appealing measure of income per head (PCI). Simple though it sounds the compilation of PCI involves tricky technical problems, a large number of component calculations and a significant input of quantitative information. Production estimates of national income involve valuing heterogeneous goods; and income estimates involve aggregating labour and property incomes. Arriving at a figure for PCI or even producing a set of current price estimates for benchmark years is only the beginning of the calculation. If such indicators are to be compared with counterparts for other times and places or even with each other they must be adjusted for changes in the value of money. Economic theory has provided some guidance to technical issues, though conceptual problems often remain beneath the surface. For example, how can new goods be included or improvements in commodities be registered and set against price changes? But for the economic historians the main problem is in wresting the required information from an intransigent historical record. For example, prior to the census of 1841 there is no occupational evidence on which to base estimates of labour income by broad sector so labour incomes in the first three decades of the nineteenth century require extrapolation from later data. Similarly estimates of property income have to be constructed on the basis of assessment information for income tax levied only from 1799 to 1815 and after 1842. Historians who have made signal contributions within this paradigm are keen to underline the limitations that such data deficiencies impose. The calculations are 'controlled conjectures' not 'definitive evidence'.[3]

Most estimates by modern historians draw on initial calculations by Deane and Cole which in turn were heavily reliant on the best guesses of informed contemporaries.[4] This original quantitative overview of British growth suggested a definite outline for the Industrial Revolution (see table 17.1). Per capita growth accelerated in the last few decades of the eighteenth century. Growth was rapid and accompanied by structural change in the first decades of the nineteenth century but slowed down by 1840. Recent work has benefited from some new sources of data. These include Wrigley and Schofield's improved estimates of population based on parish register data; Lindert's findings on the structure of occupations, which drew on burial records; Feinstein's work on capital formation; and Harley's on industrial growth.[5] But improvements in recent estimates of PCI and its growth derive more from greater realism in the assumptions that structure the calculation than from the availability of

Table 17.1   Estimates of growth of National Product

	Deane and Cole's estimates (%)		Crafts' estimates (%)	
	National Product	National Product per capita	National Product	National Product per capita
1700–60	0.66	0.45	0.69	0.31
1760–80	0.65	−0.04	0.70	0.01
1780–1801	2.06	1.08	1.32	0.35
1801–31	3.06	1.61	1.97	0.52

Source: N. F. R. Crafts, *British Economic Growth During the Industrial Revolution* (Oxford, 1985).

superior empirical evidence. Recent work has revised the outline of growth, suggesting that the acceleration was more gradual and growth considerably lower over the period as a whole.[6] This view of the speed and pattern of change has become the new conventional wisdom with implications for the story of well-being. Slower growth, particularly before 1820, meant that there was less scope for consumption to rise.

Even within the traditional real-income or opulence approach to well-being it is obvious that PCI may not be the most appropriate indicator. The flow of goods and services includes many commodities that do not enhance living standards and indeed may be harmful – the armoury produced for the French wars, for example. Moreover, an overriding interest in welfare might suggest focusing attention on poor and wage-dependent people to the exclusion of the affluent. Such considerations along with the promise of greater transparency and perhaps reduced demands on the historical record attracted economic historians to real wages as a measure of improvements in welfare.

Real wages and real earnings

Real wages were one of the earliest kinds of quantitative evidence offered in the standard-of-living debate. They represented new 'scientific' evidence that took the wind out of the sails of the pessimist case and left proponents of pessimism rather lamely relying on 'intangible' factors to offset the apparent growth in material standards.

Did real-wage indices require less in the form of measurable historical inputs? Wage series for workers in different sorts of employment were available. It is true that such data were in current prices and so, like estimates of income, needed adjusting for changes in prices if trends were to be detected. Moreover case studies of specific occupations in particular locations could be challenged by other case studies that demonstrated opposing trends. What was needed was a series that represented all workers. The data demands escalated.

Such a series requires the collection of nominal-wage series for workers in enough different occupations to represent the whole labour force. These must then be weighted according to the importance of each trade in the total labour force. The wage trends of agricultural labourers who made up a large share of the labour force had to play a bigger role in the overall trends than those of proportionally less numerous civil servants.

Lindert and Williamson put together nominal-wage series for workers in many different occupations.[7] Much of the raw material was readily available and had already been used by economic historians. In fact there was little disputation of the main trends in *nominal* wages. The action was in the movements in the price indices that turned the nominal series into *real* wages by making clear what the money could buy. Lindert and Williamson accompanied their amalgamation of the evidence on nominal wages with a new cost-of-living index, which made three advances. First, the coverage of goods was superior because goods such as raw materials which did not enter final consumption were excluded and other important items such as rent that had hitherto been omitted were included. Second, the price data were better because they avoided institutional prices for textiles which were readily available but did not capture the prices paid by consumers and more importantly may not have moved in line with market prices. But in the absence of information on retail prices, Lindert and Williamson remained reliant on wholesale prices, which it was reasonable to assume moved in tandem with prices paid by consumers. Third, the weights assigned to the price changes of individual goods were revised to reflect their relative importance in working-class budgets, for example rent was assigned a large weight to capture its importance in expenditure. The net effect of these changes was that their price index fell somewhere between earlier optimistic and earlier pessimistic indices for the period 1788–92 to 1820–6, but thereafter suggested super-optimistically that the cost of living fell more than 50 per cent from the end of the Napoleonic Wars until mid-century.

The new super-optimistic estimation of price trends had powerful implications for assessments of real wages. Overall Lindert and Williamson's series suggested that nothing much happened until around 1810. There was some improvement between 1810 and 1814 followed by deterioration for most groups between 1815 and 1819. But thereafter there was continuous improvement up to 1851 for all occupational groups with the biggest improvement for white-collar workers. The gains estimated were bigger than optimists had previously claimed: over 60 per cent for farm labourers, over 80 per cent for 'blue-collar workers' and over 140 per cent for all workers.

But these optimistic conclusions were very dependent on Lindert and Williamson's evaluation of price trends and their cost-of-living index soon came under fire. Crafts argued that Lindert and Williamson's reliance on cotton prices to reflect trends in textile prices overstated the decline in the cost of living and gave the resulting estimates of what wages could buy an optimistic bias. Lindert and Williamson responded to Crafts's criticisms, and their revised cost-of-living index did mute the gains after 1820, reducing growth for 'blue-collar' workers from 84 per cent to 62 per cent. But their main conclusions remained intact. The story was one of stagnation before 1820 and growth thereafter.

Although the debate between Lindert and Williamson and Crafts focused on trends in *prices* and what they meant for living standards, the coverage of the labour force in their nominal-wage series was incomplete and excluded sectors and occupations of particular importance in the transition to a modern economy, for instance the woollen and worsted industries and handloom weavers.[8] It also covered only adult males and made no allowance for changes in the composition of the labour force within particular industries.[9] But perhaps more important in keeping the debate alive were the inconsistencies between Lindert and Williamson's confident optimism and the pessimism of other opulence-based indicators, such as consumption, as well as gloomy trends in more novel indicators such as height measurements.

Thus Feinstein in the most ambitious study of real-wage trends yet sought to extend the coverage of the nominal-wage series and deal with some of the outstanding problems with the cost-of-living index.[10] His aim was to construct an index of annual earnings intended to cover all manual workers, male and female, from 1770 to 1880. Annual estimates of the movements in earnings were compiled for more than twenty separate occupations, accounting for some 80 per cent of wage-earners in Great Britain in 1851. Apart from data on the earnings in coal-mining collected by Mitchell, Feinstein had little new information to draw upon and remained heavily dependent on the well-known estimates compiled by Bowley and Wood, also used by Lindert and Williamson.[11] A number of the existing indices, notably those for cotton-spinning and weaving, building and engineering, and shipbuilding, were extended to 1770 from their later starting-point in Bowley or Wood. But additional series were compiled for female agricultural labourers, workers in the wool and worsted industries, tailors, boot- and shoemakers, merchant seamen, railwaymen, other transport workers, male and female domestic servants, general labourers and the army and navy.

Feinstein's series measured average earnings assuming full employment in each sector. They should therefore capture changes over time in the composition of the labour force by age, gender, skill or region, and include overtime and incentive pay. They also included an estimate of the value of perquisites in occupations where these were important. Nonetheless the weight of the shared component series taken from Bowley and Wood (over 50 per cent in 1770 and more than 40 per cent in 1850) ensured that Feinstein's and Lindert and Williamson's indices moved together. Again the action was in the estimates of price trends not in trends in nominal wages.

In his cost-of-living index, Feinstein drew on better information on rents and a wider range of clothing prices, so escaping the over-reliance on the average value of exported cloth. He also included more and different food items. Horrell's systematic survey of household budgets underpinned changes to the expenditure shares.[12] In line with best practice a fixed-weight index was calculated. Separate indices for short sub-periods were chained together so that for each sub-period the quantity weights were close to expenditure patterns. The cumulative impact of these changes was substantive, diminishing the extent of the price decline after the end of the Napoleonic Wars until 1851 from the 51 per cent estimated by Lindert and Williamson to about 37 per cent. Since it was the fall in prices that had delivered the gains in living standards, this revision has important implications.

Feinstein's results vanquished the earlier optimism (see table 17.2). Average full-employment real earnings crawled up from the 1770s to the 1830s, made some better progress in the mid-thirties, but then fell back in the depression of 1838–42. It was not until the mid-1840s that real earnings grew steadily. By mid-century real earnings were roughly 28 per cent higher than they had been on the eve of the Industrial Revolution and where they had lingered for so long. More substantial gains had

Table 17.2   Real earnings 1770–1882 (five-year averages; 1778–82 = 100)

	Real earnings assuming full employment	Real earnings adjusted for unemployment
1770–2	95	96
1773–7	94	95
1778–82	100	100
1783–7	103	103
1788–92	106	106
1793–7	106	106
1798–1802	100	101
1803–7	112	112
1808–12	101	100
1813–17	102	99
1818–22	109	106
1823–7	112	110
1828–32	112	109
1833–7	123	121
1838–42	117	113
1843–7	126	124
1848–52	136	132
1853–7	128	128
1858–62	137	137
1863–7	143	143
1868–72	149	149
1873–7	167	168
1878–82	176	175

Source: C.H. Feinstein, 'Pessimism perpetuated: real wages and the standard of living in Britain during and after the industrial revolution', *Journal of Economic History*, 58 (1998).

to wait until the 1860s and, more importantly, after the decline in prices in 1873. The generation that lived through the industrial dawn saw little or no improvement in their real earnings, and though their children may have lived long enough to see some gains it was not until the third generation that an improvement was palpable.

Feinstein noted that the picture looked even bleaker if account was taken of other adverse features of the period including the increasing adulteration of food, the rising dependency ratio associated with rapid population growth and the deleterious effects of urbanization. Other changes too may have impacted on well-being, for example changes in the intensity and hours of work and the scaling-back of poor relief with its implications for the well-being of the most vulnerable. These points relate back to the inherent limitations of the real-income approach. To the extent that relevant quantitative information on these aspects of well-being is available it may be possible to bring them into the analysis, the agenda of the reductionists. But first we must conclude our survey of traditional approaches.

Consumption

The scaling back of the growth rate in PCI by the macro-economic historians had reduced the scope for increases in consumption. Crafts's index of real consumption per head derived from the application of macro-economic identities to his index of real GDP, suggested an increase of about 50 per cent from the end of the Napoleonic Wars to mid-century. This was alarmingly out of line with the initial deductions of the real-wage optimists, which had suggested gains of over 140 per cent for all workers. Why would growth in consumption per head so lag behind growth in real wages? Other evidence on consumption was also perplexing. Mokyr used trade statistics to show slow rates of growth of per capita consumption of imported sugar, tea and tobacco.[13] Such working-class luxuries were expected to grow rapidly if real wages were increasing. Thus the recent more pessimistic estimates of real-wage increases removed a puzzling inconsistency between various different indicators of opulence. But, alas, a new set of inconsistencies emerged. As the received opinion on real wages became pessimistic with the publication of Feinstein's magisterial work, economic historians working on consumption joined forces with intellectual and social historians to argue for a *consumer revolution* in the second half of the eighteenth century. While intellectual and social historians used literary and cultural evidence to trace out a shift in attitudes to goods, economic historians focused on probate inventories. Itemized accounts of commodities prepared for probate documented the widespread dissemination of durable consumer goods, such as china, cooking utensils and clocks, in the seventeenth and first half of the eighteenth centuries, a development that was completely out of sync with the new pessimism on the standard of living. Consumption historians now threw down a challenge to the pessimist view of the standard of living.

One clue as to how these divergent trends might be reconciled came from DeVries.[14] Although each generation from the mid-seventeenth to the late eighteenth centuries left behind more and better possessions, the value of these goods did not increase as a proportion of overall estates. Perhaps what was happening was a reallocation of expenditures in favour of durables, maybe in response to their relative cheapening. Another loophole involved timing. Probate inventories were not routinely recorded after 1730. To track the dissemination of consumer goods during the Industrial Revolution and to confirm ongoing gains, economic historians were reliant on King's comparison of pauper inventories of the late eighteenth century with earlier probate inventories.[15]

On the other hand, Horrell's scrutiny of working people's household budgets concluded that any gains in income were spent on more and better food. There was little room for increased expenditure on the new goods of the Industrial Revolution. If domestic demand for manufactures played a causal role in the Industrial Revolution that demand had to come from the upper and middling classes. Here Horrell indicated another possible way to reconcile the pessimist view of well-being with an apparent consumer revolution. Perhaps the Industrial Revolution saw an increase in inequality with wage gains going disproportionately to the skilled within the working class and to the expanding ranks of the middling sort. This would be consistent with the occupational wage trends, which had shown considerable variation with some groups losing ground and others pulling ahead.

Family incomes

Real-wage indices usually focused on adult male remuneration. Feinstein included women and juveniles, who made up a significant component of the labour force. He calculated not the average real earnings of adult males but the average real earnings of all workers. His series therefore takes account of shifts in the age and gender composition of the labour force but it does not capture an important determinant of the standard of living: the number of people dependent on average earnings. For example if working-class children started work at a younger age then this would dilute the labour force and given their relatively low pay put downward pressure on Feinstein's index. However if more children working had no effect on adult earnings, children's employment could boost family income and enhance living standards. Alternatively if women and children became less able or inclined to work for wages over the course of the Industrial Revolution, Feinstein's index would rise given the greater importance of relatively high-earning men, but more people would be dependent on those men and their earnings.

The inability of standard approaches to capture the effect of shifts in dependency rates prompted Horrell and Humphries to focus on family incomes.[16] Using evidence from a large number of documentary sources they compiled estimates of total family incomes for families of different sizes, living in different regions and headed by men in different jobs. These seemed broadly in line with the scaled-back version of the optimists' real-wage data, though, for the period as a whole, family incomes grew less than did male earnings. The implication is that dependency increased and welfare gains imputed from male earnings overstated actual improvements. Moreover since Horrell and Humphries relied on the Lindert and Williamson cost-of-living index as the best then available their conclusions were not entirely independent. If their estimates of nominal family incomes and male earnings are deflated by Feinstein's improved cost-of-living index, the results are more pessimistic.[17] Horrell and Humphries also explicitly considered the distribution of family incomes, finding that industrialization brought with it greater inequality among families.

Summary

Thus economic historians employing traditional measures of living standards approached a relatively pessimistic consensus about the extent and speed with which the working class benefited from the Industrial Revolution. Consensus was driven by the need to reconcile the evidence on a number of different indicators of opulence and to fit the different pieces of the industrialization jigsaw together. But dissatisfaction remained with the inherent narrowness of opulence-based measures and their inability to capture changes long held to have affected working people's well-being many of which were closely associated with the process of industrialization. Attention turned to how to broaden the approach to include these worrying intangibles.

Opulence Plus Intangibles: The Reductionist Strategy

The reductionist strategy, by imputing values, positive and negative, to all factors held to impact well-being and figuring the resulting addition or offset in their calculation of trends, sought to broaden the traditional approach to include the hitherto intangible. Three applications are described.

Unemployment

The lack of reliable information on the extent of involuntary unemployment in this period had long been a problem for economic historians working with traditional indicators of well-being, particularly real wages. Their input data were often wage *rates*, usually per week. To move to earnings involved making assumptions about the number of weeks worked. For adult males this was interpreted as making assumptions about the incidence of unemployment. Although there were no reliable figures, agricultural historians had demonstrated the existence of widespread under- and unemployment in the rural South-East and industrial historians had documented the severity of trade recessions in the industrial districts. Moreover the incidence of unemployment was not constant but probably increased as the economy became increasingly industrialized and market-oriented.

Initial attempts to gauge unemployment involved regressing estimates from unemployment insurance data for the late nineteenth century on a number of conditioning variables and then using the estimated relationship and the values taken by the regressors earlier on to predict unemployment outside the documented period.[18] In contrast to such top-down estimation strategies, other authors constructed individuals' actual lifetime earnings experience, though of course whether these were representative remained open to doubt.[19]

Again Feinstein provided the best attempt to figure unemployment and short-time working into his calculations. Cyclical unemployment was assumed to influence only building, mining, manufacturing and transport. A series by Gayer, Rostow and Schwartz, which classified recessions according to their severity, was extended using additional secondary materials on the trade cycle, so that each year could be graded according to the state of the labour market. Matching these grades with an absolute unemployment percentage was much harder. It involved a careful use of evidence on unemployment in the second half of the nineteenth century and ad hoc adjustments based on the views of business-cycle historians, estimates of industrial production and on 1815–17 demobilization figures.[20] The procedure was arbitrary but what mattered for trends in earnings was not the precise level assigned to unemployment each year but its broad trend.

Again in the absence of direct information, Feinstein estimated the impact of winter unemployment in agriculture according to estimates compiled by Boyer from the *Rural Queries*, a survey conducted in 1832 by the Royal Commission on the Poor Law.[21] Feinstein assumed that it only affected wage labourers (and not yearly farm servants or family labour) in areas of predominantly arable farming.

Feinstein's real-earnings series adjusted for unemployment can be compared with its unadjusted equivalent in table 17.2. Unemployment pulled the real-earnings index below its unadjusted counterpart in recessions (for example 1813–22), and dampened growth over the whole period as the adjustment for cyclical unemployment is applied to a progressively larger proportion of the labour force with the expansion of the industrial sector. Thus figuring unemployment into the index adds grist to the pessimist mill.

The urban penalty

Industrialization involved the movement of activities and population from the countryside into towns and cities that grew ahead of the provision of housing and sanitation, with horrible effects on living conditions. While any number of gut-wrenching descriptions testify to these disamenities, how they might be evaluated was less obvious. So the urban penalty usually headed a list of intangibles that undermined the precision of real-wage or PCI estimates.

Williamson made the first attempt to measure the urban penalty and set it off against real-wage gains.[22] The problem was to impute a value to the poor living conditions. If information on living conditions, living costs and wages in both rural and urban locations were freely available, and migration costs negligible then workers would move from country to town to take advantage of any wage premium over and above the higher living costs. As they did so wages would rise in the countryside as workers became less available, and decline in the urban area as the supply of labour increased. The rural – urban movement would only stop when the pay differential *exactly* compensated migrants for the urban penalty and differences in living costs. Additional migrants would lower the differential still further and so not be sufficiently compensated for the deterioration in living conditions that they would experience. Realizing this they would not move. Cross-section comparisons of English towns with different levels of urban disamenity, as proxied by infant mortality rates and population densities, allowed the isolation of the wage premium that was simply compensation. By imputing a value to the urban penalty from labour-market data, economic historians avoided the dangers of ahistorically referencing their own standards instead of trying to uncover how the workers of the Industrial Revolution themselves felt. Williamson found that, relative to rural wages, premiums of 10 to 30 per cent were necessary to induce workers to face the urban penalty in the industrial North. Further work in this tradition was even more pessimistic. Brown constructed estimates of real earnings for factory workers and handloom weavers in the North-West and adjusted these for the higher costs of urban living.[23] His findings showed virtually no improvements in the living standards of these workers until the 1840s and perhaps not until mid-century.

The element in wages needed to compensate the growing number of workers who lived in towns and cities for urban disamenities must be set against any secular wage growth before inferring a gain in the standard of living. If somewhere between 10 and 25 per cent of the urban wage provided compensation for disamenities, and this is subtracted for the one-third of the population living in towns of more than 20,000 in 1851, average real earnings at that date would be reduced by between three and eight percentage points.[24]

Of course these calculations leave open the question of whether wage premiums did or could compensate workers for urban blight. Migrants were unlikely to have the information and knowledge needed to evaluate the effect on them and their families of various alternative urban destinations, especially as this might take many years to become manifest. Nor did they have the financial reserves needed to resist a move to the city if unemployed elsewhere. Recent work on both heights and infant mortality suggests that whatever wage increments bought and however these goods were distributed within migrants' families, it was insufficient to offset the checks that the urban disease environment afforded to physical growth and infant survival.[25] In this fundamental sense the costs were uncompensated.

Working time

Another longstanding problem encountered in attempts to track the standard of living was the claim that industrialization caused working people to work longer and harder. Hence not all wage gains were net gains as workers had sacrificed leisure, which surely improved the quality of life, to obtain them. But the costs of longer and harder work proved very hard to quantify. Estimates of both the lost leisure time and its value are needed if net benefits are to be isolated. For the pre-industrial period and the Industrial Revolution, records of either the number of hours worked per day or days per year are scarce and scattered. Historians resorted to literary materials, regulations, occasional government reports and employment records. Such evidence illustrated the argument that in pre-industrial times work was irregular and uneven. 'St Monday' symbolized a leisurely start to a working week that often ended in a storm of effort as workers struggled to complete tasks.[26] With an increasing division of labour and larger-scale capital, workers had to become more regular and disciplined. The drive for surplus value motivated employers to extend the hours as well as intensify work. Thompson's evidence was not convincing to modern economic historians who preferred more systematic testing. Nor did surveys of rules and regulations and case studies of employment build consensus.

Economic historians turned to the indirect evidence offered by nutritional standards, or contradictory trends in real wages and probate inventories, or comparisons of annual full employment income with daily wage rates, all of which were made to yield inferences about time-use. Inferences can even be teased from the seasonality of conception, the timing of 'crowd events' and the scheduling of weddings. While suggestive such evidence did not clinch the issue. What was needed was direct evidence on patterns of labour and leisure among the population at large. This was provided by Voth's ingenious use of court records.[27] From the witness statements of more than 2,800 men and women, Voth extracted all mentions of time use for three periods (1749–63, 1799–1803 and 1829–30) and two locations, London and the North. At every opportunity he recorded what a particular individual was doing at a particular time.

The court records reveal the timing (by hour, day and month) of crime, but also the structure of daily life as lived by the working men and women who happened to witness crime. Voth can estimate when they got up and went to bed, when they started work and stopped. Schedules can be compared over time and between London and the North. In London, an approximately twelve-hour working day appeared to lengthen and then contract, while the initially longer hours in the North were further extended by 1830. The court records also facilitated estimation of the working week and year.

Non-random variation in the numbers working by weekday, while suggestive, is not sufficient to demonstrate the existence of St Monday. To this end Voth constructed a dichotomous variable, 1 if the witness was working, 0 otherwise, and then regressed it on a set of other characteristics including the days of the week, so uncovering the probability of daily working. For London, the odds of observing somebody in work and its statistical significance suggests that St Monday ceased to be celebrated between 1760 and 1830. The latter days of the week, when workloads purportedly increased, show higher than average work probabilities. In the North there is no evidence of St Monday, either before or after 1800, nor of increasing work frequency by Friday or Saturday. In the 1750s, holy days saw a strong reduction in the probability of observing somebody at work both in London and in the North. By 1800 this effect had vanished completely in London but lingered in the North. Alternative methods of aggregating hours per year and combining the results for London and the North provided seven different indexes of annual hours but all indicated upward pressure: annual hours increased somewhere between 14 and 32 per cent.

Why did people work longer hours? Voth's preferred explanation is the increasing attractions of consumption. A wrinkle in his consumer revolution neatly resolved the contradiction between the current pessimist consensus on wages and the apparent dissemination of consumption goods. It was precisely the gap between the *ability* to spend as determined by wage trends and the *desire* to spend that drove labour input. The mirror image of the increased hours of work is the leisure foregone. Valued according to market wages as implied in the economic theory of labour markets, accounting for the lost leisure erodes even further the estimated real-earnings improvements over the first seventy years of industrialization.

Summary

In their original references to intangibles the classical writers on the Industrial Revolution tried to reassert a broader concept of the standard of living in place of opulence and in this way to keep the pessimist case alive. However, merely listing intangibles whose actual value was unknown appeared a feeble response to the apparently scientific, objective and concrete measures of material gain.

A new generation of quantitative historians has not only scaled down the material gain but also, through ingenuity and perseverance, put some price tags on the intangibles. Rescued from the margins of history, the intangibles now appear in the central accounts. Ironically modern cliometrics has breathed new life into the pessimist case.

From the Standard of Living to the Quality of Life: The Radical Strategy

Recent theoretical work has heralded a renewed emphasis on a broader conception of the standard of living.[28] But for economic historians this broadening had to fit into the recently established hegemony of quantitative methods. There was no going back to lists of qualitative determinants of 'the quality of life'.

Heights have been taken as a summation of all influences on economic welfare. Trends in physical stature thus afford insight into the quality of life. Economic historians have also learned from development economists' attempts to identify universally valued human functionings, the measurement of which can be combined in an overall index of *human development* (HDI). What should be included in the index remains an open question both in the development and historical contexts.[29]

Table 17.3 Indicators of living standards in Industrial Revolution Britain and composite indices

	GDP per capita	Life expectancy at birth	Adult literacy	Schooling (average years' duration)	HDI	H(FWG)	H(K)
1760	1803	34.2	48.5	1.4	0.272	167.4	n.a.
1780	1787	34.7	49.5	1.5	0.277	168.0	166.1
1800	1936	35.9	52.5	1.8	0.302	168.9	165.6
1820	2099	39.2	54.2	2.0	0.337	170.7	165.9
1830	2209	40.8	57.5	2.3	0.361	170.7	166.1
1850	2846	39.5	61.5	2.7	0.407	165.3	165.2

HDI Human Development Index (see text).
H(FWG) Height of recruits born at this date when 20–23 (from R. Floud, K. Wachter and A. Gregory, *Height, Health and History: Nutritional Status in the United Kingdom, 1750–1980*, Cambridge, 1990).
H(K) Height of recruits born at this date when 20–23 (from J. Komlos, 'The secular trend in the biological standard of living in the UK, 1730–1860', *Economic History Review*, 46, 1993).
Source: N. F. R. Crafts, 'Some dimensions of the "quality of life" during the British industrial revolution', *Economic History Review*, 50 (1997).

Heights

Heights indicate net nutritional standards, that is calories and protein consumed, adjusted for environmental demands in terms of disease, climate and work effort. As a measure of 'outcomes' it appeared to answer critics who rejected incomes and real wages as inputs into rather than constituents of well-being. Furthermore the availability of heights data for times and places when information about incomes and prices was thin, promised to facilitate comparative analysis on an unprecedented scale. Considerable resources were devoted to the project. However the analysis of large amounts of data, laboriously extracted from the historical record, has prompted few general conclusions. Why?

First, the empirical evidence is unclear. Information on heights survived for two main populations: soldiers and convicts. The most commonly used data is the compilation of heights of recruits into the British Army and Royal Marines, and boys entering the Marine Society and Sandhurst. On the basis of this same data, Floud et al. argued that heights increased over most of the period, while Komlos found that they fell (see table 17.3).[30] The disagreement relates to a basic property of the data. The armed forces imposed minimum-height regulations. Men who were too short were rejected. Consequently the distribution of recruits' heights suffers from 'left-hand truncation'. The bit of the distribution covering those men who fell below the minimum standard is missing. Means calculated from truncated distributions provide biased estimates. While standard statistical procedures provide some guidance about how to deal with truncation so as to salvage reliable estimates of average heights, the problems are deepened because standards changed over time and were enforced with a strictness that varied with the need to recruit. The convict data, which are not censored in this way might be judged more reliable. They show a decline in average height.[31] In addition to these problems with identifying an overall trend, the changes appear small, often too small to justify any strong claims, and long-term trends are often overshadowed by short-term variation of equivalent or even greater magnitude, which are hard to interpret.

In addition to these empirical problems, economic historians began to worry whether heights really did respond to and therefore proxy for material conditions. When both measures were available, heights and incomes were not highly correlated, at least in the eighteenth and nineteenth centuries. In cross-sections individuals from (poorer) rural areas proved taller than their (richer) urban counterparts. Clearly food availability and disease environment played a role over and above opulence. This finding favoured the interpretation of those historians who argued that stature measured a broader *biological standard of living*. But increased height, unlike other possible biological indicators such as reduced mortality and morbidity, imparted little direct benefit. Worse still, when historians explored the various indicators of biological well-being, although life expectancy and infant mortality appear correlated with height over the long run and in modern times, this was not the case for the period of industrialization.

Historians continue to measure heights and to use stature as a meaningful output variable, though with decreasing confidence that they can map from this to either opulence or a broader conception of the standard of living. Perhaps stature's most useful role is in identifying relatively deprived groups within populations.[32]

Composite Indices of Human Development

Crafts constructed a conventional composite HDI index, which combined measures of income, life expectancy and educational attainment (a weighted average of literacy and schooling). The components are combined in a single index according to rationale laid out in the *Human Development Report 1994*. HDI and its component indicators are shown in table 17.3 where they can be compared with the evidence on heights. HDI suggests modest growth over the period of industrialization, consistent with a weak optimist position. Alternatives, which incorporated political and civil rights as components of the standard of living, suggested the same trend improvement, as do other more sophisticated indices, which take account of gender differences and income inequality.[33]

Thus moving from opulence-based indicators to the measurement of quality of life does not necessarily strengthen the pessimist case in the standard-of-living debate. But the seeming tension between this result and the pessimistic picture built up from the piecemeal extension of traditional measures to include various intangibles is partly a mirage. Crafts's HDI is based on component indicators accessible in 1997. Since then alternatives have become available. A case can be made for including Voth's findings on working hours, Feinstein's new pessimistic real-wage indices, and perhaps even some data on heights. A composite index based on some or all of these indicators would exhibit different trends both within sub-periods and across the Industrial Revolution as a whole.[34]

Summary

Strategies to break away from traditional opulence-based measures of the standard of living have unsettled the developing pessimist consensus. The evidence on heights has produced an independent unresolved debate about trends, with perhaps some reason to prefer the less optimistic reading. But the compilation of HDI and extended composite indices has suggested a modestly optimistic trend, which seems at odds with other evidence. The development of historical composite indices is however in its infancy and their sensitivity to component indicators, which often move in disparate ways, suggests that a variety of outcomes are possible according to what is included and how it is measured. The availability of new indicators, several of which have contributed to resurgent pessimism, suggests that it would be possible to develop alternative composite indices with a closer affinity to a more pessimistic perspective.

Conclusion

In the last twenty years or so the standard-of-living debate has come a long way. Economic historians have shown perspicacity and creativity. They have succeeded in broadening their approach without sacrificing quantification. In doing so two new research agendas have been opened up.

The first concerns the distribution of well-being over the course of the Industrial Revolution. Both standard measures of opulence (real wages, incomes) and alternative indicators of the quality of life (height) have suggested a range of experience around the average trends. It is becoming easier to identify the losers in this new industrial world, indeed even measure the extent to which they lost, as Brown does for example with those fabled underdogs, the handloom weavers.[35] Indeed some of the new measures of the quality of life may be better suited to answering outstanding questions about inequality and deprivation than they are to charting average trends. The second concerns the conception of development as the freedom to live a valued life, which directs historians' attention to political, legal and social capabilities.

While the overall tenor of recent research has converged on a new pessimism, composite indices cast a chink of optimist light on the gathering gloom. However, the sensitivity of composite indices to what is included, and how the components are measured and aggregated, epitomizes the inherent complexity of the standard-of-living question. And this, rather than their combative spirits, is why economic historians continue to debate it.

NOTES

1. A. Sen, *The Standard of Living* (Cambridge, 1987).
2. A. Sen, *Development as Freedom* (New York, 2000).
3. N. F. R. Crafts, *British Economic Growth During the Industrial Revolution* (Oxford, 1985), p. 9.
4. P. Deane and W. A. Cole, *British Economic Growth, 1688–1959* (Cambridge, 1962).
5. E. A. Wrigley and R. S. Schofield, *The Population History of England, 1541–1871: A Reconstruction* (London, 1981); P. H. Lindert, 'English occupations, 1670–1811',

Journal of Economic History, 40 (1980); C. H. Feinstein, 'Capital formation in Great Britain', in P. Mathias and M. M. Postan, eds, *The Cambridge Economic History of Europe*, vol. 7, *The Industrial Economies: Capital, Labour, and Enterprise* (Cambridge, 1978); C. K. Harley, 'British industrialization before 1841: evidence of slower growth during the industrial revolution', *Journal of Economic History*, 42 (1982).

6. Crafts, *British Economic Growth*; C. K. Harley, 'Harley on British economic growth, 1688–1959', EH.Net Review, September 2001.

7. P. H. Lindert and J. G. Williamson, 'English workers' living standards during the industrial revolution: a new look', *Economic History Review*, 36 (1983).

8. R. S. Neale, *Writing Marxist History: British Society, Economy and Culture since 1700* (Oxford, 1985).

9. S. Horrell and J. Humphries, 'Old questions, new data and alternative perspectives: families' living standards in the industrial revolution', *Journal of Economic History*, 52 (1992).

10. C. H. Feinstein, 'Pessimism perpetuated: real wages and the standard of living in Britain during and after the industrial revolution', *Journal of Economic History*, 58 (1998).

11. B. R. Mitchell, *Economic Development of the British Coal Industry* (Cambridge, 1984).

12. S. Horrell, 'Home demand and British industrialization', *Journal of Economic History*, 56 (1996).

13. J. Mokyr, 'Is there still life in the pessimist case? Consumption during the industrial revolution, 1790–1850', *Journal of Economic History*, 48 (1988).

14. J. DeVries, 'Between purchasing power and the world of goods: understanding the household economy in early modern Europe', in R. Porter and J. Brewer, eds, *Consumption and the World of Goods* (London, 1993).

15. P. King, 'Pauper inventories and the material lives of the poor in the eighteenth and early nineteenth centuries', in T. Hitchcock, P. King and P. Sharpe, eds, *Chronicling Poverty: The Voices and Strategies of the English Poor* (Basingstoke, 1997).

16. Horrell and Humphries, 'Old questions'.

17. S. Horrell and J. Humphries, *Household Budgets and the Standard of Living in the Industrial Revolution* (Cambridge, forthcoming).

18. J. G. Williamson, *Did British Capitalism Breed Inequality?* (London, 1985).

19. Neale, *Writing Marxist History*; Horrell and Humphries, 'Old questions'.

20. Feinstein, 'Pessimism perpetuated'.

21. G. Boyer, *An Economic History of the English Poor Law, 1750–1850* (Cambridge, 1990).

22. J. G. Williamson, 'Urban disamenities, dark satanic mills, and the British standard of living debate', *Journal of Economic History*, 41 (1981).

23. J. C. Brown, 'The condition of England and the standard of living: cotton textiles in the northwest, 1806–1850', *Journal of Economic History*, 50 (1990).

24. Feinstein, 'Pessimism perpetuated'.

25. P. Johnson and S. Nicholas, 'Male and female living standards in England and Wales, 1812–1857: evidence from criminal height records', *Economic History Review*, 48 (1995); P. Huck, 'Infant mortality and living standards of English workers during the industrial revolution', *Journal of Economic History*, 55 (1995).

26. E. P. Thompson, 'Time, work-discipline, and industrial capitalism', *Past and Present*, 38 (1967).

27. H.-J. Voth, *Time and Work in England, 1750–1830* (Oxford, 2000).

28. Sen, *Standard of Living*; M. C. Nussbaum and J. Glover, eds, *Women, Culture and Development: A Study of Human Capabilities* (Oxford, 1995).

29. P. Dasgupta and M. Weale, 'On measuring the quality of life', *World Development*, 20 (1992); N. F. R. Crafts, 'Some dimensions of the "quality of life" during the British industrial revolution', *Economic History Review*, 50 (1997).

30. R. Floud, K. Wachter and A. Gregory, *Height, Health and History: Nutritional Status in the United Kingdom, 1750–1980* (Cambridge, 1990); J. Komlos, 'The secular trend in the biological standard of living in the UK, 1730–1860', *Economic History Review*, 46 (1993).

31. S. Nicholas and R. H. Steckel, 'Heights and living standards of English workers during the early years of industrialization', *Journal of Economic History*, 51 (1991); Johnson and Nicholas, 'Male and female'.

32. S. Horrell, J. Humphries and H.-J. Voth, 'Stature and relative deprivation: fatherless children in early industrial Britain', *Continuity and Change*, 13 (1998).

33. Crafts, 'Some dimensions'.

34. H.-J. Voth, 'Living standards and the urban environment', in R. Floud and P. Johnson, eds, *The Cambridge Economic History of Modern Britain*, vol. 1, *Industrialisation, 1700–1860* (Cambridge, 2003).

35. Brown, 'Condition of England'.

FURTHER READING

Not surprisingly, given the importance of the issues and the duration of the debate, there are several existing excellent surveys of the standard-of-living question. A. J. Taylor, ed., *The Standard of Living in Britain in the Industrial Revolution* (1975) surveys the debate up to the point of its publication and reprints several classic contributions. S. Engerman updates this survey and reflects on the implications of the debate in 'Reflections on "the standard of living debate": new arguments and new evidence', in J. A. James and M. Thomas, eds, *Capitalism in Context: Essays in Economic Development and Cultural Change in Honour of R. M. Hartwell* (1995). H.-J. Voth, 'Living standards and the urban environment', in R. Floud and P. Johnson, eds, *The Cambridge Economic History of Modern Britain*, vol. 1, *Industrialisation, 1700–1860* (2003) covers much of the same ground as this chapter but is geared to an audience of economists rather than historians and provides much more technical detail. Finally C. H. Feinstein, 'Pessimism perpetuated: real wages and the standard of living in Britain during and after the industrial revolution', *Journal of Economic History*, 58 (1998) provides a succinct summary of the debate in the introduction to his magisterial work on real wages.

G. N. Von Tunzelmann, 'The standard of living debate and optimal economic growth', in J. Mokyr, ed., *The Economics of the Industrial Revolution* (1985) gives substance to the question whether or not well-being could have risen faster in different circumstances. He explores the counter-factual scenarios implicit in classic studies such as that by the Hammonds, before working through his own hypothesis that welfare would have improved more rapidly if growth had been less capital-intensive.

That different economic historians can look at industrialization and its consequences through different frames is brought out in several exchanges between economic historians representing different schools of thought. Readers should contrast the perspective and assumptions of J. G. Williamson, 'Urban disamenities, dark satanic mills, and the British standard of living debate', *Journal of Economic History*, 41 (1981) with those of S. Pollard, 'Sheffield and sweet auburn – amenities and living standards in the British industrial revolution: a comment', *Journal of Economic History*, 41 (1981) for example, or more generally the viewpoint of R. M. Hartwell, reprinted in A. J. Taylor, ed., *The Standard of Living in Britain* (1975) with that of E. P. Thompson, 'Time, work-discipline, and industrial capitalism', *Past and Present*, 38 (1967).

CHAPTER EIGHTEEN

Class and the Classes

MARTIN HEWITT

Importance of Class

Questions of class are fundamental to nineteenth-century British history. Class was a pervasive part of contemporaries' world-view, and class distinctions were deeply embedded in the social fabric. For much of the century class was not only the single most important form of social categorization, but also the bedrock of understandings of political and social change, and of the narratives which were constructed around them. For contemporaries, the history of the nineteenth century was written above all in the shifting fortunes of the classes, the eclipse of the aristocracy, the triumph of the middle class and the challenge of the working class.

Inevitably, historians in the twentieth century have come to see these grand movements as powerful organizing myths rather than as accurate descriptions of what 'really happened'. Nevertheless, class has remained a crucial analytical tool, and even though in the last decade or so there has been a significant reaction against many of the usages of class, the energy expended by opponents of the concept only serves to reinforce the fact that, at present, a serious desire to understand the nineteenth century implies a sustained effort to consider the role(s) of class.

Until recently, the concept of class had been most systematically deployed in the exploration of the history of the working class. However, this chapter takes a broad approach, considering all classes, and their inter-relations, and asks a series of questions. How far is it possible to see distinct social classes and in what ways have the composition and significance of these classes changed over time? How far did such classes generate discrete cultures, identities, value systems and ideologies, which shaped the nature of social and political conflict? How and why, in an era marked by often violent and dramatic social upheavals, did nineteenth-century Britain achieve what has been described as a 'viable class society'? In responding to these questions, this chapter seeks, notwithstanding powerful arguments to the contrary, to contend for the continued relevance of class as a mode of analysis.

What Is Class?

Of course 'class' is a slippery term which carries a great deal of contradictory theoretical baggage, and which is used by historians in very different ways. Some of these complexities are explored by the entry for class in Raymond Williams's *Keywords*.[1] Class can be used for largely descriptive purposes, as the basis for the definition of series of social or economic classifications or strata. It can be used in a more analytical way to indicate social collectivities with the potential to be historical agents. It has also been incorporated into philosophies of history as a foundational category, and as a fundamental motor of change. Effective evaluations of the significance of class require careful consideration of the precise ways in which it is, and might be, deployed.

As a descriptive category, the notion of class had wide usage before 1800 in classificatory systems across the sciences. As a term of social description it rapidly gained purchase in the early nineteenth century, although not with any consistency. Divisions of society into a number of broad but unitary classes co-existed with pluralist notions of loosely aggregated classes (such as the 'labouring classes'), and with specific applications to more narrowly defined groups (the 'class' of tenant farmers, for example). Nevertheless, the distinction made by Ricardo early in the century between those groups who obtained their income from rent, from profit and from wages encouraged the emergence of the tripartite division of the landed or upper class, the industrial or middle class and the working class as the most common formulation. This has persisted despite a number of attempts to develop more complex models, identifying various social groups, such as artisans, the 'lumpenproletariat', the gentry or the 'petit bourgeoisie', as distinct classes.

Part of the appeal of Ricardo's classes was that they were not merely descriptive categories but also represented distinct relationships to the economy, and hence different interests. It was on this foundation that Marx and Engels constructed the theory of class which proved most influential both (in a loose sense) for contemporaries and (often in a more precise sense) for twentieth-century historians. Marx and Engels argued that out of the material existence of such classes (class *in* itself), there would emerge a collective consciousness of class identity and interest (class *for* itself). They also suggested that history was itself the unfolding product of successive stages of class conflict which by the nineteenth century had in Britain reached the stage of struggle between the middle and working classes. They envisioned the ultimate overthrow of middle-class dominance and the establishment of a just classless society. In the aftermath of the late-twentieth-century collapse of communism as a force in the world order such ideas hold small purchase, but they help to explain the agendas and arguments of much nineteenth-century social and labour history, as well as the sense of needing to move to new approaches and questions which are characteristic of the early twenty-first century.

In ways both frustrating and fruitful Marxist theory was ambiguous about the precise nature of the relationship between economic structures and political ideologies, between 'base' and 'superstructure', between 'class *in* itself' and the self-conscious and agential 'class *for* itself'. Early Marxist historiography tended to assume relatively direct relationships, but from the 1960s, under the influence especially of Williams and E. P. Thompson, historians of class have tended to be less interested in dissecting its economic foundations than in exploring the uncertain and contingent ways in which class manifested itself in society, politics and culture.

Other theorists have attempted to dilute the unassailable primacy given to economic circumstance in the Marxist system, suggesting that a more effective mode of social analysis requires the addition of other aspects. So, for example, Max Weber suggested that class was one of three fundamental determinants of social identity and political action, along with status and party. He also suggested that class itself needed to be broken down into economic class, which defined groups by their relationship to the market (and which could be divided into more than three), and social class, which drew together related economic classes to provide the alignments of class conflict. Historians and especially historical sociologists have occasionally made use of the notion of elites or oligarchies, as developed in the writings of Vilfredo Pareto and Gaetano Mosca, to explore the extent to which social divisions are best understood as derived not from wealth or relationship to the mode of production, but from access to power, and to focus attention on the importance of competition within social groups or classes as well as between them.

There have always been historians who have rejected the efficacy of any form of class analysis, largely on the basis that class simply did not gell with the historical record: that economic processes did not create clear differences of interest between a small number of broad groups; that even if discrete social and economic divisions could be crudely drawn, these were never sufficiently clear in practice to support coherent shared perceptions of class identity.[2] Nevertheless, class has continued to dominate historical analysis not least because of the apparently limited ability of alternative theoretical frameworks to comprehend nineteenth-century social structure and conflict.

Class as Social Description

At the very least, few historians have been able or willing to abandon entirely the language of class as a tool of social description. Whereas eighteenth-century society can be effectively delineated in terms of various ranks or vertically integrated interest groups, portrayals of nineteenth-century society overwhelmingly use class divisions, and most often frame their questions in terms of the changing composition and relative fates of these classes. Inevitably, the precise definition of class boundaries is fraught with difficulty, and at times the problems are notoriously sidestepped, as by the nineteenth-century census which contented itself with broad sectoral classifications. Nevertheless, it is possible to outline a schema of class, both as conceived by contemporaries and as deployed by historians. It should be noted that although the criteria are primarily economic, they include other characteristics, including status and lifestyle.

The nineteenth-century upper class has been the least studied of all the classes, although over the last couple of decades this has begun to change. The problems are partly definitional. Historians write of the 'ruling class', the 'aristocracy', the 'upper class' or the 'landed class'. The aristocracy, the roughly 500 British peers or even the approximately 2,000 titled families, was more of a caste than a class. Conventionally, therefore, definitions of the upper class include the broader 'squirearchy' whose income derived from substantial landed estates, and the wider group of younger sons and their offspring, inserted, because of the restrictions of inheritance of estates and titles to the eldest male, into positions of profit and authority in the state system, the army, the church and the financial institutions. It was this far more complex network of kinship, privilege and connection, in which family, status and breeding were more important than wealth or even occupation, often attacked in the early nineteenth century as 'Old Corruption', and developing into the close alignment of land, commerce and finance which characterized the later nineteenth century, which constituted the upper class.

Similar problems confront any attempt to define the middle class. For a long time, it was symbolized by the industrial manufacturer of the Midlands and the North, associated in particular with 'Manchester School' doctrines of free trade and laissez-faire. Yet it has always been recognized that realities of a class which included between 15 and 20 per cent of the population were more complicated than this. Although an income of between £300 and £1,000 secured comfortable middle-class circumstances, in terms of wealth the class ranged from the great moneyed through the middle section of lesser manufacturers, commercial and professional men to the lower middle classes who struggled to keep up their position on incomes of only around £100 per annum. In terms of status there were significant divisions between the commercial and entrepreneurial middle class reliant on profits, the professional middle class whose income derived from fees, and the 'white collar' occupations which drew salaries. Nevertheless, collectively these groups were marked by characteristics which distinguished them from the classes above and below: property, but property vulnerable to market conditions; the importance of appearances, which required the keeping of servants and the public commitment to certain codes of respectability; work, but 'brain work' rather than manual work; and – at least between the two Reform Acts – possession of the vote.

Looked at from below, there was real and (absolute) division 'between those who, in earning daily bread, dirtied their hands and face and those who did not'.[3] As a result, historians have spent less time discussing the boundaries of the working class and more time considering its internal divisions, between artisan and factory hand, skilled and unskilled, rural and urban, respectable and rough. In recent years the force of all of these divisions has been questioned. It is clear that the nineteenth-century working class comprised a favoured group who were able to command premium wages, a much wider cohort who enjoyed relatively stable employment, albeit at lower wages, and a shifting mass forced to rely on casual labour, charity and the limited social provision provided by the Poor Law. Nineteenth-century rhetoric often presented these as largely distinct and self-contained groups. However, it is increasingly clear that individuals and families often moved in and out of these strata depending on economic or life cycles, or on the constant processes of attrition and erosion which brought many once favoured occupations low in the course of the century, or occupied positions which straddled these apparent boundaries.

Trajectories of Class

These classes were of course far from stable. Conventional interpretations for a long time emphasized the steady eclipse of the upper classes in the face of the emerging middle classes, presenting them as buffeted politically by the 1832 Reform Act, and economically by the 1846 repeal of the Corn Laws and the subsequent deterioration in the position of British agriculture. It is now recognized, however, that the coherent *British* upper class of the early nineteenth century was a relatively recent creation, benefiting from dramatic increases in income from land (which doubled from 1790 to 1820), and confident into the 1830s in its wealth, status and power.[4] The great landowners continued to grow richer for most of the nineteenth century, especially through the systematic exploitation of their non-agricultural assets, mineral rights and urban development. In an important series of studies of the configuration of wealth in nineteenth-century Britain, Rubinstein has demonstrated that until the 1880s more than half the really wealthy men in Britain were landowners, and that the bulk of non-landed wealth came not from the new industrial middle class but from commerce, and from the financial activities of the City, sectors with strong ties to the upper classes.[5] Rubinstein's figures have generated heated technical controversies; but their broad picture has not been seriously challenged.

The pre-eminence which the upper classes enjoyed at the start of the century was progressively if slowly eroded. The dismantling of the system of 'Old Corruption' threw the aristocracy back onto reliance on the land, while new forms of wealth emerged to rival them. Although the repeal of the Corn Laws in the 1840s did not bring the immediate collapse in incomes from land many had predicted, from the 1880s economic conditions finally began to deteriorate quickly and markedly. Agricultural prices collapsed, land rental values followed suit. Death duties placed new burdens on inherited real wealth.[6] After 1880 the rate of awards of titles and honours to new wealth increased rapidly, part of a process that contemporaries saw as the reconstitution of the upper classes into a more cosmopolitan and international plutocracy.

This combination of durability and adaptability meant that the middle class did not achieve the collective pre-eminence imagined by contemporaries preoccupied more by huge factories than huge fortunes. Not until 1880 do wealthy businessmen seem finally to have outnumbered wealthy landowners, and many of these fortunes were rooted in the City and commerce, and were still dwarfed by the largest landed ones. Especially after 1850 there was a considerable increase in the range, collective organization and general income levels of the professions. Even so, they never comprised more than about 2 per cent of the whole population, and many eked out a precarious living at the margins of gentility amidst the rapidly expanding lower middle class. By 1850 the expansion of retailing had fuelled the growth of the 'shopocracy', which was often able to achieve considerable local political influence. Thereafter expansion in white-collar employment meant that by 1911 14 per cent of the occupied population were in lower-middle-class occupations. Although these groups saw some modest improvements in the final decades of the century, many continued to struggle to sustain a 'respectable' lifestyle on incomes which were less than those in the upper reaches of the working class.

The changing nature of the experience of the working class continues to be much debated. There is little doubt that over the century it became predominantly urban and wage-earning. By 1871 there were more domestic servants than farm-workers. In 1901 85 per cent of the labour force was in dependent employment, and 75 per cent of the total were manual labourers. Even so, for much of the century vastly greater numbers were employed in small-scale manufacturing and workshop settings than in large-scale units of production. Indeed, the core industrial occupations never provided more than 40 per cent of the British workforce. The overall economic fate

of the working class has been the subject of sustained historical debate.[7] It is generally accepted that the century brought improvements in working-class standards of
living, but that they were slow, uneven and limited. At the end of the century social
surveys suggested that between a third and quarter of the working class were living
in some form of poverty. Such improvements in incomes as there were came at a
cost: an erosion of customary practices and protections, a loss of control over work
processes and an intensification of work pressure. One consequence of these pressures would seem to have been a narrowing of occupational distinctions and wage
differentials in the final quarter of the century. Another was a more sustained challenge to the authority of the other two classes than at any time during the century,
not excluding the previous peak of agitation during the Chartist period of the 1830s
and 1840s.

Social Mobility

How fluid was this society? The Victorian myth of self-improvement suggested almost
unlimited prospects of advancement for the thrifty and industrious. Widespread
middle-class anxieties seem to confirm the dangers of movement in the opposite
direction. The reality was more static. Part of the usefulness of class is the extent to
which class position does seem to have defined disparities of opportunity.

Although the British aristocracy was theoretically an open elite, constantly replen-
ished from the ranks of talented commoners, in practice mobility into and out of
the aristocracy was extremely limited. The vast bulk of peerage creations during the
century were for existing landed and gentry families. Nevertheless, there was sufficient movement of new men of wealth into ownership of substantial landed estates
to sustain the notion of an increasingly open landed elite.[8] Much the same can be
said for the industrial middle class.[9] First-generation manufacturers typically emerged
from existing mercantile and gentry groups, and as the century progressed rising
capital requirements further narrowed chances of movement from working to the
substantial middle class. There was sufficient truth in the myth of the self-made indus-
trialist to sustain it, but mobility down across this divide was much easier than mobility upwards across it.

At the same time, the boundary between the upper ranks of the working class and
the lower middle class did become more porous. Education provided a mechanism
of advance here, and the changing occupational structure, the rise of semi-skilled
jobs, the shift from informal to formal modes of training, as well as the increasingly
urbanized workforce, all encouraged greater exchange of personnel between the
classes. Nevertheless, 'mobility was heavily structured'.[10] Opportunities were profoundly unequal, most mobility was over short social distances, and the key barrier
was between those dependent on manual labour, and a heterogeneous middle and
upper class of salaried employees, businessmen, professionals and landowners.

Class as Consciousness

Such essentially descriptive characterizations aid us in portraying the changing shape
of nineteenth-century society, but they do not necessarily tally with contemporary
experiences. To understand this we must consider the extent to which these social

groups came to conceive of themselves as living in a society divided between distinct classes, and to identify themselves as members of one of these classes, bound by common experiences and sharing common ideologies.

It was established as long ago as the 1950s that the first three decades of the nineteenth century saw a dramatic expansion of the use of languages of class. In *The Making of the English Working Class* (1963), the single most influential study of class in nineteenth-century Britain, Thompson argued that this period saw the creation of socially distinct and politically aware classes. Subsequent studies traced the parallel emergence in these decades of a new middle-class identity. By the 1830s, it was argued, British society had largely learned to think of itself as divided first and foremost along class lines.

Although this position never commanded universal assent, it set the parameters of debate until the 1990s. Only then was it subjected to sustained attack. Taking their cue from new interpretations of the Industrial Revolution as much steadier and more gradual than had once been thought, a number of historians have suggested that the new languages of class were little more than the rhetorical by-products of particular political conflicts. Wahrman argued that the 'middle' or 'middling' classes were conjured not to represent a new social type, but to enable claims to be made about legitimacy – that the 'middle' was the ground of moderate reasonable men, whose opinions ought to be politically dominant.[11] Likewise, Joyce presented the language of class not as the dominant mode of social or political description, but merely as one among several.[12] As a result, we must now recognize both that the emergence of languages of class did not of itself necessarily indicate the emergence of the classes themselves, and that throughout the century conceptualizations based on class co-existed, perhaps uncomfortably, with a number of other identities or distinguishing forces.

Nevertheless, the traditional accounts have not been demolished entirely. Even if class languages remained one source of identity among several, even if class was not conceived of in rigorously consistent ways, this does not undermine the extent to which in the years around 1830 class overwhelmingly displaced hierarchy as the single most important mode of analysis. The inhabitants of the country, not just politicians and agitators, but social investigators, clergymen and novelists, displayed a social vision dominated by class, and indeed came to act along lines of class distinction in ways which effectively bridged – even if they did not efface – previously entrenched divisions of politics, religion and ethnicity. Society, especially in the new towns and cities, politics, especially as it related to debates over the right ordering of the franchise, and economics, in terms of the organization of employment relations, all came to be conceived of in terms of class.

How far this sort of 'class consciousness' was associated with distinct class ideologies is another matter. The Marxist tradition identified precise ideological positions appropriate to specific classes: in simple terms, an individualist middle class would face a collectivist working class. Unfortunately, evidence suggests that in the nineteenth century such oppositions were partial and intermittent at best, and much of the literature on class has arisen from the attempt to explain such 'failures'. The irony is that in measuring attitudes against complicated ideal types this literature has obscured the extent to which as broad social groups the classes were defined by distinct sets of values and beliefs.

Class as Conflict

If nothing else, class identities had become powerful motivating myths by the end of the first third of the century. As a result they became, notwithstanding limitations and fluctuations, a key node of activism. As conflict tends to privilege binary oppositions, such activism did often create alternative divisions, the people versus the elite, the productive versus the unproductive; but these identities were expedient renditions of class identities or instrumental claims to cross-class alliances, rather than fundamentally incompatible positions. They reflected the way in which the political process was concerned both with drawing on existing constituencies and also with defining new ones. They do not detract from the critical place of class.

In the agitation for parliamentary reform before the 1832 Act, divisions between middle- and working-class identities had, at least partially, been subsumed in a shared sense of political exclusion; but the deliberately calculated readjustments of the 1832 Act laid the ground for sharper distinctions. During the later 1830s and 1840s extraparliamentary politics was dominated by two movements, Chartism and the campaign against the Corn Laws, both of which sought to trade primarily on specific class interests, while also paying lip-service to wider cross-class constituencies. Even so, this moment of apparent national class conflict was short-lived. Neither the Anti-Corn Law League nor the National Charter Association were able to sustain the politics of class conflict beyond the 1840s. Their successors, such as the Financial and Parliamentary Reform Association or the National Reform League, were unable to mobilize the class constituencies to which they appealed.[13] Reform associations, such as the various socialist groups of the 1880s and 1890s, and umbrella organizations of trade unions, organized after 1868 under the remit of the Trades Union Congress, all drew strength from and attempted to mobilize languages of class, but all were recognized as sectional rather than class-based movements. At a national level, politics remained characterized by conflict between cross-class political parties rather than by class-based parties.

Before the mid-1880s class conflict was most visible not in national but in more intimate local contexts. In many of the new towns and cities conflict in the first third of the century was bound up in the efforts of a new middle class to wrest control of the institutions of local government from entrenched gentry elites, followed by their effective defence of this newly acquired authority against the claims of the working class.[14] The coherent identity of these groups was cemented through the complex network of institutions and associations which developed from the 1820s onwards, an enlarged local press, literary and scientific societies, philanthropic and charitable institutions, occupational and work-based unions. Society was saturated with forms of action predicated on class diagnoses of social and cultural problems (notwithstanding the fact that they were not always articulated in class vocabularies), and attempts to bridge or defend the apparent chasm between the classes.

In the final years of the century, class divisions and class conflict re-emerged at the national level. The 'discovery' of the slums of East London acted on the national consciousness in ways similar to the exposés of 'the condition of England' in the 1830s. The activity of socialist organizations such as the Social Democratic Federation and the Socialist League, coupled with the re-energizing of radical politics more generally through the formation in 1893 of the Independent Labour Party, and the rapid spread of organizations such as the Clarion movement, helped create a context in which the previously craft-dominated trade-union movement was able, even if only temporarily at first, to extend its coverage to previously neglected and unorganized groups. At the same time, the split of the Liberal party over Ireland in the 1880s accelerated the longstanding process of realignment which created the Conservative party as the party of property, albeit with important working-class constituencies, and the Liberal and then Labour parties as the parties of progress and labour.

The Limits of Class Assertion

Such a picture of muted class conflict, especially at the national level, raises questions as to how far the configuration of power and authority which prevailed in 1800 was challenged or modified during the course of the century, questions as to the ultimate significance of class conflict as a generator of change. Close attention suggests much greater stability in class positions than contemporaries often assumed.

Above all, the century was marked by aristocratic endurance, not just in terms of wealth and economic clout, but socially and politically. Until 1900 the British political system remained, notwithstanding its periodic reforms, a largely aristocratic system. The upper class dominated the House of Commons until the 1870s and every cabinet before 1905, and was still providing a third of all MPs into the twentieth century. Figures like W. H. Smith, the newsagent who achieved cabinet rank in 1877, remained very much the exception, and a place in government continued to be beyond the reach of the small number of working-class MPs until after 1900. Although after 1870 both Liberals and Conservatives made considerable efforts to incorporate working-class voters, not least through political clubs, their intention was to mobilize them, not to accord them influence. Admittedly, mid-century reforms of the civil service ostensibly made it more open to the sons of the middle class, and by mid-century the magistrates' bench in urban and industrial areas had been success-fully penetrated, but the composition of national and local 'establishments' changed only slowly, and in many areas the upper class and its clerical allies continued to dominate. Only in the later 1880s, as a result of reforms such as the County Coun-cils Act (1888), was the power of the upper class in rural localities seriously eroded.

Few would now accept the argument that the relative stability of mid-nineteenth-century Britain rested on the triumph of middle-class values.[15] Despite the repeal of the Corn Laws in 1846, there was little by way of legislative action to sustain the fiction that the middle class determined the shape of policy, even if they remained content to leave government in the hands of the traditional elites. Aristocratic policy continued to prevail. The strategy of pressure from without, which had appeared to serve the middle class so well in its opposition to slavery and the Corn Laws, perhaps because of the fragmentation of the middle-class voice from the 1840s, proved rather unsuccessful thereafter. Although after 1867 working-class pressure did achieve some significant liberalization of the laws relating to trade unions, the legal backlash of the 1890s culminating in the infamous Taff Vale judgment of 1901, which made unions liable to pay damages to an employer for losses arising out of an industrial dispute, demonstrated the fragility of these gains.

Class Accommodations

In the 1850s, Palmerston celebrated Britain as 'a nation in which every class of society accepts with cheerfulness the lot which Providence has assigned to it'. The paradox of a society in which class was pervasive, and yet direct class conflict appeared to be successfully diffused, and in which the dominant group of 1800 proved able to retain much of its power and authority, has preoccupied historians for much of the last half-century, and prompted the formulation of an impressive array of explanatory theories.

Greatest attention has been directed at answering, in the broad sense, the question posed by McKibbin: 'Why was there no Marxism in Great Britain?'[16] The greater prosperity and stability of the British economy after mid-century undoubtedly played a part, but prosperity was neither sufficiently reliable nor general to offer a sufficient explanation. Much attention has been given to the entrenched sectionalism of the working class, the wide differences of income levels and modes of living between the richest and the poorest. Within Marxist historiography such ideas were given a specific twist in the 'labour aristocracy theory', the suggestion that the stability of industrial society was reinforced by the buying off of that strata of skilled workers which would otherwise have formed the natural recruiting ground for working-class leaders. Material causes apart, much attention has also been given to ideas of 'social control', that working-class militancy was undercut by various mechanisms of social discipline, school, religion, police, even structures of paternalistic control established by factory-owners.

None of these ideas are convincing. It has proved impossible to identify with any clarity who the 'labour aristocracy' actually were or that the upper strata of the working class operated as a brake on working-class assertion. Models of social control have been widely questioned through detailed studies which have demonstrated the apparent ineffectiveness of all the institutions usually credited with effecting social discipline. As a result, in recent years most emphasis has tended to be given to more ideological approaches, which argue that, for much of the century, it is impossible to differentiate significantly between the political, social or even economic analyses of the working class on the one hand and those of the middle class on the other. Strategies of collaboration around a viable if often strained consensus generally proved more attractive than strategies of conflict.[17]

Less attention has been devoted to explaining the limits of middle-class assertion. It has long been recognized that the far greater demands placed on entrepreneurs in the supervision of their enterprises, and the deliberate and quite rational decision of many to concentrate their efforts within local contexts, considerably limited the number of industrialists achieving positions of national influence. However since the 1980s attention has tended to focus on arguments about the cultural weakness of the English middle class, advanced in the early 1960s, but spectacularly reformulated in 1981 by M. J. Wiener's *English Culture and the Decline of the Industrial Spirit 1850–1980*. Wiener argued that nineteenth-century Britain was marked by a feeble industrial or entrepreneurial culture, and a powerful anti-industrial aristocratic culture which continued to lure the industrial middle classes away from business to enjoy the delights of landed life, educate their children in the classics and a contempt for science, and turn their back on industry. Although studies of social mobility have questioned Wiener's suggestions of wholesale 'gentrification', and his arguments about the cultural weakness of the richest elements of the middle class have been much disputed, the largely contemporaneous work of Rubinstein bolstered Wiener's picture of an industrial middle class not only less wealthy but also less culturally secure than had previously been believed.

Perhaps the most suggestive theory to emerge out of these broad debates is the notion of 'gentlemanly capitalism', mostly fully developed by Cain and Hopkins in the context of explanations of nineteenth-century imperialism.[18] They argue that the weakness of the middle class was economic not cultural: rooted in the hegemonic position of the financial and services sector, dominated by the City of London, and deeply interlocked with the upper-class society of London and the Home Counties. Not only did this sector provide opportunities for the accumulation of wealth on an even greater scale than industry, but it enabled it to be done in a context which still offered scope for time to be devoted to public service, which perpetuated 'gentlemanly' ideals of trust and distance from the production process itself, and which cemented ties between landed wealth and the commercial elites. The nexus of 'gentlemanly capitalism' thus facilitated a slow and seamless transition from the land-based upper class of the first half of the century to the financial and commercial upper class which had substantially replaced it by the early twentieth century.

Class as Culture

Recognition of the uneven trajectories of class assertion during much of the century, and the powerful forces of class accommodation, along with the growing preoccupation of social history with questions of 'culture' as the vital mediating sphere between social position on the one hand and political action on the other, have encouraged a much greater attention to ideas of class cultures. In turn this has prompted a greater interest in the final third of the nineteenth century as the period in which coherent and consolidated classes in a national sense were finally created.

The basic argument is not novel. For the working class it was comprehensively developed in the 1960s by Hobsbawm, who argued that only after 1870 is it possible to see the emergence of common national cultural forms which give the working class a distinct identity: football as a spectator sport, the commercial music hall, fish and chips, the seaside holiday, the flat cap. Subsequent studies explored the ways in which these were aspects of an all-encompassing 'life apart' which set the late-Victorian working class apart from the classes above it, and helped to provide it with a shared sense of experience, albeit one which was often more fatalistic and consolatory than radicalizing. These studies have been supplemented by others which have demonstrated that it was in these years that industrial advances were finally creating a workforce gathered into large units of production, and governed by national processes of collective bargaining. From this, it is suggested, flowed a new and more all-encompassing sense of class identity, and ultimately, according to Joseph Chamberlain in 1906, the 'conviction, born for the first time in the working classes, that their social salvation is in their own hands'.[19]

More recently similar arguments have begun to be advanced for the nineteenth-century middle class. Gunn has suggested that it is possible to see in final third of the century the consolidation of common patterns of bourgeois public culture in urban Britain, while both Malchow and Trainor have argued that the period from the 1880s onwards brought a transformation from largely localized or provincial middle-class identities to the more homogeneous and national culture which characterized the period after 1914 (especially in the upper strata of the middle class), based on more integrated patterns of education in the new public schools, on the ethos and ideology promulgated by them, and on patterns of consumption and leisure.[20]

To some extent these processes also mark the breaking down of the boundaries between the nineteenth-century upper and middle classes. But at the same time, it is possible to see parallel processes enhancing the integration of the upper class at the same time as they blurred its boundaries. The economic crisis of rural society, the increasing social pull of London, improvements in transport and communication which made travel to and from country estates progressively easier, encouraging both greater residence in London and the country-house weekend, all served to diminish upper-class rootedness in local societies and enhance its sense of being a national elite.

The 'cultural turn' has contributed not merely to new chronologies of class formation, but also to a richer understanding of the ways in which class operated through the century. Studies by Epstein and Morris have drawn attention to the degree to which the development of a language of class was only one element in the 'making' of a class society in the first half of the century. By focusing on the construction of common practices, such as the 'subscriber democracy' which formed the backbone of middle-class voluntarism, and the way in which collective identities were cemented by increasingly ritualized and symbolic elements of public culture, dinners, meetings and civic celebrations, these authors have significantly expanded our understanding of the building blocks of class.[21]

Above all, the cultural turn has renewed attention to the extent to which ultimately, as E. P. Thompson always argued, class is about shapes in society. Nineteenth-century Britain was a class-based society because it was possible for acute social observers to recognize that the classes lived entirely different kinds of lives, married different kinds of spouses and had different aspirations, different possibilities and different limitations. These differences manifested themselves in various ways. They were spatial: while there continued to be considerable residential mixing between classes, the century progressively brought greater segregation. They were also demographic: although the evidence is limited and far from absolute, it seems reasonably clear that despite the steady decline of the kinds of occupational intermarriage which had been a characteristic of the early part, throughout the nineteenth century there were high levels of intermarriage within classes and relatively low levels of marriage crossing class boundaries. Differences were also linguistic: pronunciation and vocabulary marked class origins. Finally, they were physical: the classes dressed differently, they had different stature, different standards of personal hygiene, even different qualities of teeth.

Class as Myth

Not all the work inspired by the new cultural history has served to bolster understandings of the century in class terms. Quite the reverse, for some of the most influential work produced within this framework has sought rather to challenge the utility of 'class' as a primary conceptualization of nineteenth-century history. In doing so it has transformed a longstanding tradition of scepticism about the utility of class from pedantic conservative empiricism into a radical critique of the dominant modes of social and labour history.

This critique has come, in Britain, to be labelled the 'linguistic turn', in part because its foundational text was Stedman Jones's *Languages of Class* (1983): the first important attempt to apply postmodern epistemologies to nineteenth-century Britain. In fact, with a few notable exceptions the scholarship of the 'linguistic turn' has been less interested in a close study of language than in challenging traditional trajectories of analysis which have seen politics and culture as the reflection or refraction of underlying social and economic 'realities'. Experience, it is argued, does not exist prior to its recognition and interpretation, but is constituted in the very act of making sense, so that language, social forms and cultural practices as much form experience as are formed by it. And given this, there can be no justification for privileging the social and economic category of 'class', which, far from being the 'master category', is only one among a range of competing identities, race, gender, nationality or 'the people'.

Partly under the influence of this scholarship, and partly as a result of other trajectories, the scholarship of the 1990s has raised broad questions about the narratives which had been constructed around class. Of course traditional Whiggish accounts of heroic struggles for power and recognition, privileging leaders and institutions, had already been questioned. However, more fundamental questions have come to be asked about the significance of key events – such as the Reform Acts of 1832 and 1867 – which have continued to structure stories of class. Developments such as the Co-operative Movement, which had previously been marginalized because they did not fit easily into orthodox explanations of class and class conflict, have begun to be re-evaluated. Conventional pantheons of heroes and villains have been recast. Above all, there is a greater awareness that the history of class is itself a history of stories, the stories which individuals, institutions and social collectivities tell about themselves.

Feminist scholars in particular have taken up the spirit of such attacks on class to challenge the traditional interpretations. They have elucidated the extent to which the traditional account of the making of the working class ignored the extent to which class identities were framed in overwhelmingly masculinist ways, and were used to bolster assumptions and practices, such as the notion of the 'family wage', which involved the systematic subjection of women, both within the workplace and the home.[22] Such arguments built on insights into the way in which the formation of middle-class culture in the early nineteenth century was predicated in large part on substantial reworking of distinctions of the public and the private, and the construction of an ideal of domesticity which defined the role of women primarily in terms of the home.[23]

These contributions sparked a great deal of debate within British history in the 1990s, itself part of, although not always very effectively integrated into, a broader scholarly debate about the utility of class in historical analysis. However, although these exchanges generated considerable heat, they have in fact as yet had relatively little impact on historical scholarship in practice. Historians of the middle class and – to a lesser extent – labour historians have provided a robust defence of the importance of class and a willingness to attend to the broader range of identities and the complex nature of their constructions and interactions championed within the linguistic turn.

Class and the Future

So what of the future? Given current understandings, how useful is the concept of class, and in what ways can we expect to see it employed in the coming years? It seems unlikely that class will be abandoned for descriptive purposes. Not only does it remain the single most important contemporary (that is, nineteenth-century) mode of social categorization, but it has no serious rival as a way of aggregating social and economic categories into meaningful collectivities. This said, it may be that there is a greater tendency in future not only to make greater use of subdivisions of the traditional three-class model, but also to abandon the attempt to sustain unitary languages of class, having recourse instead to more flexible pluralist notions of classes.

Such a shift will, of course, call into question the continuation of attempts to comprehend the history of the nineteenth century around the classes as historical agents, and the privileged position which has frequently been accorded to class conflict as a historical dynamic. This will necessitate further moves away from understandings of class as a relatively unproblematic derivation of social or economic realities, and the old and increasingly unhelpful agendas derived from a desire to explain the failure of the history of class relations in nineteenth-century Britain to accord with a priori (usually Marxist) interpretations of historical development.

Instead the study of class formation and class action will need to be underpinned by a much broader range of attention to cultural and textual practices, self-constructions, social and political narratives, associational forms and public rituals. It may finally be that the impetus provided by the 'linguistic turn' will encourage close attention not just to abstract social vocabularies, but the articulation and reception of languages in specific social and cultural contexts, and to the complex symbolic economies of place, performance and power which complemented them.

Conclusion

The argument of this chapter has been that despite (indeed perhaps because of) current controversies, a grasp of the complex functions of class remains crucial to a proper understanding of nineteenth-century Britain. By class we need to understand not a specific relationship to the economy, nor merely a self-designated collective identity, but a way in which the world was ordered, imaginatively, linguistically, economically, socially, culturally and politically. Such ordering at no time produced hard and fast, absolute divisions: throughout the century class remained fluid, subjective and uncertain, constantly cut across by other identities and structures. Class was never all-embracing: many institutions, practices and aspects of life largely operated outside its definitions. Class conflict was partial, uneven and intermittent, augmented in times of crisis, subdued in times of prosperity and, without question, at times the assumption of class conflict has been allowed an unjustifiably dominant role in the setting of the agendas of historical scholarship and the formulation of its analyses. Even so, as much as anything, it is class which gives nineteenth-century Britain its identity:

the emergence of comprehensive class identities, the ascendancy of class-based visions of contemporary society, the persistent anxieties about class relations and the prevalence of class as a motive for social and political action.

NOTES

1. R[aymond] Williams, *Keywords* (London, 1983), pp. 60–9.
2. D. Cannadine, *The Rise and Fall of Class in Britain* (New York, 1999).
3. R. Roberts, *The Classic Slum: Salford Life in the First Quarter of the Century* (Manchester, 1971), p. 6.
4. L. Colley, *Britons: Forging the Nation 1707–1837* (London, 1992), pp. 155–64.
5. W. D. Rubinstein, *Men of Property: The Very Wealthy in Britain since the Industrial Revolution* (London, 1981).
6. D. Cannadine, *The Decline and Fall of the British Aristocracy* (New Haven, CT, 1990).
7. See J. Humphries, 'Standard of living, quality of life', chapter 17 in this volume.
8. D. Brown, 'Equipoise and the myth of an open elite: new men of wealth and the purchase of land in the equipoise decades, 1850–69', in M. Hewitt, ed., *An Age of Equipoise? Reassessing Mid-Victorian Britain* (Aldershot, 2000).
9. F. Crouzet, *The First Industrialists: The Problem of Origins* (Cambridge, 1985).
10. A. Miles, *Social Mobility in Nineteenth- and Early Twentieth-Century England* (Basingstoke, 1999), p. 177.
11. D. Wahrman, *Imagining the Middle Class: The Political Representation of Class in Britain, c.1780–1840* (Cambridge, 1995).
12. P. Joyce, *Visions of the People: Industrial England and the Question of Class, 1848–1914* (Cambridge, 1991).
13. G. R. Searle, *Entrepreneurial Politics in Mid-Victorian Britain* (Oxford, 1993).
14. J. Garrard, *Leadership and Power in Victorian Industrial Towns 1830–1880* (Manchester, 1983).
15. As advanced by H. Perkin, *Origins of Modern English Society* (London, 1968).
16. R. McKibbin, *The Ideologies of Class: Social Relations in Britain, 1880–1950* (Oxford, 1990).
17. E. F. Biagini, *Liberty, Retrenchment and Reform: Popular Liberalism in the Age of Gladstone 1860–1880* (Cambridge, 1992).
18. P. J. Cain and A. G. Hopkins, *British Imperialism: Innovation and Expansion, 1688–1914* (Harlow, 1993).
19. E. J. Hobsbawm, *Worlds of Labour: Further Studies in the History of Labour* (London, 1984), p. 258.
20. S. Gunn, *The Public Culture of the Victorian Middle Class: Ritual and Authority in the English Industrial City 1840–1914* (Manchester, 2000); H. L. Malchow, *Gentlemen Capitalists: The Social and Political World of the Victorian Businessman* (London, 1991); R. H. Trainor, *Black Country Elites: The Exercise of Authority in an Industrial Area, 1830–1900* (Oxford, 1993).
21. J. Epstein, *Radical Expression: Political Language, Ritual, and Symbol in England 1790–1850* (Oxford, 1994); R. J. Morris, *Class, Sect and Party: The Making of the British Middle Class, Leeds 1820–1850* (Manchester, 1990).
22. A. Clark, *The Struggle for the Breeches: Gender and the Making of the British Working Class* (London, 1995).
23. L. Davidoff and C. Hall, *Family Fortunes: Men and Women of the English Middle Class 1780–1850* (London, 2002).

FURTHER READING

For an introduction to the larger debates surrounding class in Britain see P. Joyce, ed., *Class* (1995) and N. Kirk, ed., *Social Class and Marxism: Defences and Challenges* (1996). The complex etymology of the term is discussed in Raymond Williams, *Keywords* (1983). The best recent general survey is D. Cannadine, *The Rise and Fall of Class in Britain* (1999), though it can usefully be supplemented by R. J. Morris, *Class and Class Consciousness in the Industrial Revolution 1780–1850* (1976) and A. J. Reid, *Social Classes and Social Relations in Britain, 1850–1914* (1992). Any student of the working class must eventually consider E. P. Thompson, *The Making of the English Working Class* (1963). Of the numerous textbook accounts, perhaps the most stimulating is R. Price, *Labour in British Society: An Interpretative History* (1986). A useful modern survey is D. M. MacRaild and D. E. Martin, *Labour in British Society, 1830–1914* (2000). The nineteenth-century middle class is still without a substantial single-volume survey. S. Gunn and R. Bell, *Middle Classes: Their Rise and Sprawl* (2002) gives a general overview, while L. Young, *Middle-Class Culture in the Nineteenth Century: America, Australia and Britain* (2002) provides a comparative cultural survey. Otherwise readers can get a sense of the conflicting views on the nature and role of the middle class from D. Wahrman, *Imagining the Middle Class: The Political Representation of Class in Britain, c.1780–1840* (1995), H. L. Malchow, *Gentleman Capitalists: The Social and Political World of the Victorian Businessman* (1991) and R. H. Trainor, *Black Country Elites: The Exercise of Authority in an Industrialized Area, 1830–1900* (1993). For the rich see W. D. Rubinstein, *Men of Property: The Very Wealthy in Britain since the Industrial Revolution* (1981), while the aristocracy proper is surveyed by D. Cannadine, *The Decline and Fall of the British Aristocracy* (1990) and, in comparative perspective, by D. Lieven, *The Aristocracy in Europe, 1815–1914* (1992).

CHAPTER NINETEEN

Economic Thought

NOEL THOMPSON

Research on the history of economic thought in general, and that of the nineteenth century in particular, has burgeoned in the post-war period and with this has come a formidable volume of literature, which has assumed two forms. The first, usually by and for economists, is particularly concerned with discussing writers and schools of thought in terms of their contribution to the development of the discipline of economics. Here the focus is on what has been added in terms of the precision of economic analysis, the coherence of theoretical systems and the sophistication of analytical tools constructed and deployed. This is the benchmark by which past writers are judged and such literature is indeed often judgemental. It has also been characterized by a mathematical modelling of the thought of political economists; though whether this has added to our historical understanding of their work or whether it tells us more about the ingenuity and predilections of the model builders is a moot point. Then there is that literature which is the product of those who might be labelled intellectual historians, where the onus has been on understanding the work of writers through its precise historical contextualization; something which has usually involved a recreation of the mental universe inhabited by a political economist or school of political economy.[1]

These different emphases and approaches to reconstructing and reading the past have their respective merits and have, in different ways, added to our understanding of the theoretical framework within which nineteenth-century economists worked, the analytical tools they deployed, the influences that shaped their thinking, the assumptions upon which their writing was based, the ideological biases that infused it and its prescriptive implications. The purpose of this chapter is to show how they have done this and to what effect in terms of our understanding of the political economies of both the major nineteenth-century writers and particular schools of economic thinking.

We begin with one of the dominant figures of early-nineteenth-century political economy, David Ricardo. Ricardo was seen by his contemporaries, and has often been portrayed by subsequent commentators, as the progenitor of a dismal science. This derived from his view that, as recourse was had to land of decreasing fertility to feed a growing population, so the productivity of agricultural labour would diminish, the cost of labour's subsistence (or natural rate of wages) would rise, the rate of profit would fall, growth would decelerate and, ultimately, the economy would arrive at a stationary state. At this juncture capitalist entrepreneurs would earn profits just sufficient to keep them in business at existing levels of activity, labour would receive a bare subsistence wage and the whole of the rest of the national product would accrue to the landowning class. It was this bleak vision of the imminent future that, for Ricardo, pointed to the imperative need to abandon agricultural protection, allowing the least fertile domestic land to be taken out of cultivation and the rate of profit to rise.

A number of writers have, however, challenged both the view that Ricardo saw the stationary state as, in any practical sense, imminent and that he believed that the wage rate invariably tended towards subsistence. For Hicks and Hollander the Ricardian wage rate was variable, determined by the forces of supply and demand in the labour market.[2] Where, therefore, the rate of capital accumulation was greater that the rate of population growth, demand would outstrip supply and wages would rise above a subsistence level. Only with the advent of the stationary state, they argued, did Ricardo believe that a natural subsistence wage rate would prevail. Yet such views have been criticized in turn because of the damage which their acceptance would inflict on the Ricardian model, the overriding concern of which, it was argued, was to establish the connection between worsening conditions of production on the land and falling profitability. This would be called into question were the notion of variability to be accepted and that of the subsistence wage as a potent centre of gravity relinquished.[3] Also called into question as a consequence of this would be the compelling Ricardian case for the repeal of the Corn Laws.

As to the stationary state, it has been argued that, even without the repeal of the Corn Laws, Ricardo did not see it as imminent. Thus, the point has been made that Ricardo was well aware, for example, of the productivity gains that could follow from an improvement of agricultural techniques. And, with free trade in grain, it is clear that he considered that Britain could enjoy a period of sustained economic growth with real wages rising well above their natural subsistence rate. Growth might ultimately slow once the fertile, cultivable land available had been exhausted but this lay some considerable time in the future. Yet against this, the fact remains that there is textual evidence to support the view that Ricardo believed that there existed strong population pressures tending to raise the cost of labour/real wages, with all the deleterious consequences that would have for profitability and the growth rate.

Much post-war Ricardian scholarship was stimulated by the publication of his *Works and Correspondence*.[4] This was particularly so with respect to Ricardian value theory. Schumpeter saw in Ricardo a writer who, in purveying a labour-embodied theory of value, had neglected the determinate role of supply and demand and, in particular, the subjective factor in the determination of price.[5] Sraffa, however, editor of the definitive edition of Ricardo's works, highlighted the theoretical sophistication of Ricardian value theory and portrayed it as anticipating in significant ways his own fundamental critique of the neo-classical theory of value. Subsequently Hollander, in opposition to both, challenged the notion that Ricardian theory was incompatible with neo-classical supply/demand analysis.[6] Specifically, he made much of what he saw as Ricardo's preparedness to admit a variable wage rate determined by the forces of supply and demand and placed him in a value-theory tradition that ran from Smith through Mill to Marshall, rather than from Ricardo through Marx to Sraffa. However, the problem with such an interpretation, as noted above, is that a Ricardo who did attach importance to a variable wage rate would be a Ricardo who inflicted substantial damage on the kind of economic model he sought to build; one that linked the inexorable rise in the labour cost of subsistence to falling profitability, the stationary state and the repeal of the Corn Laws.

Contemporary Ricardian scholarship has therefore engendered many more debates and differences of interpretation than it has resolved. Disputes still rage over the theory of value that Ricardo articulated, the potency of the natural subsistence wage as a centre of economic gravity, whether he believed that the rate of profits in the agricultural sector must inexorably decline and whether, in any case, he saw that rate as the essential determinant of the profit rate for the economy as a whole. Controversy has also centred on whether Ricardo had a pessimistic or an optimistic view of Britain's economic trajectory and the continuities and discontinuities of Ricardian political economy with neo-classical economics.

Along with Ricardo and John Stuart Mill, Malthus is seen as one of the canonical triumvirate of classical political economy. It is now some time since he was portrayed as a plagiarist, a sycophant, a bought advocate of the landowning interest and a purveyor of the demographic core of a dismal science which anticipated the mass of the population spending their lives in a condition of misery and vice. But charges of this kind, levelled against him by writers such as Southey, Hazlitt, Sadler, Carlyle, Cobbett, Ruskin, Marx and Engels certainly damaged and diminished his reputation in the century following his death. Important here too was the fact that his view of population as tending to outstrip the means available for its subsistence was seen as contrary to the experience of Western industrial nations in that period. Even by the 1830s and 1840s it seemed apparent to contemporaries such as Senior and Torrens that the British economy was generating a growing material abundance that rendered Malthusian pessimism historically redundant. Further, in the nineteenth century, his views on the inherent tendency for capitalist economies to experience periodic general depressions were seen by many as contributing to a stream of economic crankery fed by those who had failed to grasp the verities of Say's Law and the essentially self-equilibrating nature of the macro-economy.

As regards Malthus's macro-economics, Keynes contributed to a process of rehabilitation that has continued to the present.[7] For Keynes, Malthus had confronted the reality, after the Napoleonic Wars, of an economy in depression and had constructed a theoretical explanation that anticipated some at least of what the former offered in his *General Theory*. Unsurprisingly, many subsequent writers tended to discuss the extent to which Malthus should be seen as a proto-Keynesian. Some have been certain as to the quasi-Keynesian nature of Malthus's explanation of the post-war depression, and his discussion of sustainable economic growth that more nearly resembles the dynamic equilibrium theories of the post-1945 period. Others have, however, criticized the obsession with discussing Malthus in relation to Keynes, seeing it as obstructing the consideration of Malthus on his own terms. Rashid, for example, has emphasized the importance of the notion of satiation in Malthus's explanation of deficient demand, suggesting that those who construct a proto-Keynesian Malthus have neglected the centrality of this to his macro-economics.[8]

As to his writings on population, many of Malthus's contemporaries disputed the empirical basis of his views and in the last three decades this has been subjected to some rigorous empirical testing. Wrigley and Schofield have seen merit in a Malthusian explanation of population trends in Britain over a period from the mid-sixteenth to the late nineteenth century.[9] But others have cast doubts on the explanatory power of the Malthusian model. Thus Mokyr has questioned its applicability to what some have seen as the classic Malthusian scenario of pre-famine Ireland.[10]

By some the charge of pessimism has been seen as warranted. But others have made much of Malthus's stress, in the second (1802) and subsequent editions of his *Essay on Population*, on moral restraint as a means of limiting population growth by means other than those preventive and positive checks involving vice and misery. In this regard Malthus has sometimes been seen as conceding to Godwin his essential point that the application of human foresight and reason could make for a more perfect society. Also, Hollander has presented Malthus's notion of learned prudence, and his increasing acceptance of the benefits of technological change, as suggesting a belief in the possibility of material progress for the population as a whole.[11]

Charges of pessimism also touch on another aspect of Malthus's political economy that provoked contemporary ire and has, more recently, elicited the interest of scholars, namely his theology. For some contemporaries the 1798 edition of the *Essay* with its suggestion of vice and misery as the sole checks of population growth, seemed to cast doubt on the idea of a beneficent Deity. More recent scholarship has, though, categorized Malthus's position as that of a Christian moral scientist who, post-1798, articulated a theodicy in which population pressure promoted the virtues of striving and restraint. In this regard some have seen Malthus's work as part of the emergence of a distinctively Christian political economy that combined classical political economy with Anglican theology.[12]

From the outset Malthus's work has incited controversy and will undoubtedly continue to do so. However, what the last three decades of scholarship have done is to ensure that such debate can proceed both on a more informed basis and in a manner that rebuts many of the myths and much of the demonology of the past.

If Malthus and Ricardo were the titans of early-nineteenth-century political economy, it was Mill's *Principles of Political Economy* that, by the mid-century, exerted a hegemonic influence. The mid-Victorian standing of the work was not, however, to save Mill from subsequent rough treatment at the hands of some late-nineteenth- and twentieth-century commentators. Thus Schumpeter, like Jevons before him, saw Mill as having embraced and compounded the errors of the Ricardian labour theory of value and distribution. At the same time Mill was regarded by Schumpeter as struggling to reconcile Ricardian economics with the supply-and-demand analytical framework of Say, with its anticipation of some of the theoretical insights of late-nineteenth-century neo-classical economics; building on the foundation of Ricardian economics while, at the same time, seeking to accommodate ideas and constructs that were incompatible with the Ricardian model. In Schumpeter's reading we have, therefore, an economic philosopher seeking to break free of the limitations of an inherited theoretical system, with inconsistency and incoherence an inevitable consequence. Mill was also seen by him as having contracted the Ricardian vice of highly abstract a priori reasoning, that resulted in models built on unrealistic assumptions, deploying highly artificial concepts and claiming an authoritative, scientific status for the policy prescriptions they generated.[13]

However, in the last three decades scholarship has suggested a greater unity and coherence in Mill's economic and social thinking than earlier commentators have allowed. As regards his relationship to Ricardo, it has been argued that in terms of the theoretical framework of the *Principles* Mill was a consistent Ricardian, with his qualifications to the model having been anticipated by Ricardo himself. Here one should also note Hollander's view that the political economy of Smith, Ricardo and Mill had, at its core, a common conception of an economic world, driven and organized by the interaction of supply and demand in a recognizably neo-classical way; a world where prices, the allocation of resources and the distribution of rewards were simultaneously determined by the interaction of market forces.[14] Such a view has been much disputed but those who do adhere it necessarily accept the consistency of Millean and Ricardian political economy.

As regards accusations of methodological inconsistency and/or adherence to a rigid a priorism, these too have come under critical fire. Once again the Hollander continuity thesis has led its adherents to a view of Ricardo, Mill and Smith as embracing a common economic methodology that gave due importance to the empirical. Here it has also been noted that, on methodological matters, one of the most profound influences on Mill was that of Dugald Stewart, a prominent disciple and popularizer of Smith; someone who could certainly not be accused of rigid a priorism. More generally de Marchi has argued that while there is an inescapable a priori element in the political economy of Mill, he was neither opposed to empirically based economic laws nor to seeking empirical verification of his theories.[15] In this regard the empirical was seen as an essential complement to the deductive. Such scholarship, informed in particular by the Toronto edition of Mill's *Works*, has portrayed Mill as a thinker whose political economy has a coherence and unity born of a clearly articulated methodology and understanding of the economic world and the way it worked.[16]

As to those who have sometimes been seen as the lesser figures of the classical school, while Marx dismissed many as hired prizefighters and some subsequent commentators have viewed them as Ricardian or Smithian clones, the process of rehabilitation may be said to have begun with the work of Seligman.[17] However, it is largely in the post-1945 period that the positive reassessment of their contribution to the history of economic thought can be said to have gathered momentum. In this literature writers such as Longfield, Torrens, McCulloch and Senior have been shown to be thinkers who struck out their own solutions to theoretical and practical problems rather than simply explicating the ideas of a Ricardian, or any other, orthodoxy.[18]

The scholarship of the post-war period has not only furnished a more profound understanding of the political economy of individual writers but also a finer insight into the manner in which classical ideas informed policy debates and decision-making in early-nineteenth-century Britain. Such work has destroyed forever the notion of classical political economy as an ideology of laissez-faire and highlighted too the diversity and sophistication of the classical response to policy issues and the complexity of the manner in which that response was mediated by politicians and the political process.[19] Such scholarship has also created a fuller and more sophisticated appreciation of the manner in which the political economy of classical writers on theoretical and practical questions was mediated by popularizers. Work on economic articles in the *Quarterly*, *Edinburgh* and *Westminster* reviews and *Blackwood's* and *Fraser's* magazines has identified their authorship and elucidated their substance.[20]

Further the work of Gordon and others has given us a clearer picture of the impact and influence of political economy within parliament.[21]

As to the early-nineteenth-century anti-capitalist and socialist critics of classical economics, much of the scholarship has focused on establishing their intellectual pedigrees and the traditions of thinking within which they can be most appositely located. Specifically, much discussion has revolved around whether they can or cannot be seen as precursors of Marx. Labelling them 'Ricardian socialists' has implied that, like Marx, they used the theoretical foundations of Ricardo's *Principles* to construct their theories of labour exploitation and thence their general indictments of capitalism; those who have denominated them Owenite or Smithian have, however, suggested their political economy was profoundly different from that of Marx and pointed them prescriptively in a very different direction.[22]

Recent scholarship has also focused greater attention on their eighteenth-century roots with some attempting to locate their work in a tradition of political radicalism originating in the late eighteenth century and remaining relatively unchanged into the Chartist period.[23] Yet while such work often provides a necessary corrective to the fixation with these writers' relation to Marx, it is difficult to square with the distinctively economic understanding of exploitation and class that they frequently deployed.[24]

It is generally agreed that, around the 1870s, what may be termed mainstream economic thinking in Britain underwent a change in scope, emphasis, theoretical constructs used and analytical tools deployed. The extent and profundity of that change, whether it represented a fundamental break with classical economics, why it occurred and the reasons for its occurring when it did are, however, questions which have elicited no comparable unanimity.

The characteristics of the change have been clearly detailed. At its theoretical core was an increasing emphasis on subjective factors, maximizing behaviour and the use of the concept of the margin – marginal utility/marginal productivity – in the theorization of cost/price determination and the distribution of factor rewards. Along with this went a rejection of the cost-of-production value theories of a labour theory of value kind, a change in focus from macro- to micro-economic questions (though whether this was intrinsic to marginalist economics has been disputed) and a shift from the classical concern with social collectivities, such as classes, to an analytical prioritization of the economic behaviour of individuals and/or the individual firm. Some have also viewed this change in mainstream economics as characterized by a switch from practical to more purely theoretical concerns: the thrill of the intellectual chase becoming more compelling than its practical outcome.

For some commentators all this merited the sobriquet 'the marginal revolution'.[25] But others challenged this stressing of the continuities between classical and neoclassical economics.[26] Such conflicting views had already been put forward by late-nineteenth-century economists, Jevons claiming to have revolutionized the discipline of economics, while Marshall stressed the continuities between his position on key theoretical questions and those of his classical predecessors. And subsequent commentators, like Marshall, have also pointed to the fact that many of the insights of marginal economics had been articulated prior to the 1870s. But in this regard others have made a distinction between the theoretical insight that remains just that and the theoretical breakthrough which is then systematically elaborated. Here the fact that political economists such as Longfield, Senior and others anticipated some of the elements of post-1870 marginal economics does not make its emergence any less of a watershed.

The point has been made too that if Jevons's *Theory of Political Economy* (1871) was the first shot in a revolution, it was a revolution that was slow in gathering momentum. For it was not until Marshall's *Principles of Economics* (1890) that there emerged 'a widely comprehensible solution to the problem of cost – price relationships that the marginalists had been seeking for twenty years'.[27] However it should be said that while Kuhn might use a gestalt metaphor to convey the speed of paradigm shifts and intellectual revolutions, few historians of economic thought would consider the time which elapsed between the publication of the *Theory* and the *Principles* as crucial to determining whether 'revolution' is an appropriate description of the emergence of marginalist economics.

Nevertheless, in recent years scholars of the history of neo-classical economics have been loath to use this epithet. At the same time most accept that the work of Jevons in Britain, Menger in Austria and Walras in France did constitute some kind of pivotal point in the development of economic theory: a point when mainstream economics began to assume a recognizably modern form; when it self-consciously acquired the methodological characteristics of a social science; when it began to use a mathematical articulation of theory which rendered it less accessible to a lay audience; and when, correspondingly, it began to acquire the sociological and institutional characteristics of a distinct profession.

Why this occurred and why it occurred when it did has been much debated. Some have stressed factors exogenous to the discipline, with some Marxist writers seeing the marginalist onslaught on the labour theory of value as precipitated by the late-nineteenth-century emergence of a Marxian economics which had that at its theoretical core.[28] In addition, some socialist writers have suggested that in its stress on the individual and, in particular, the individual consumer, marginal economics represented a conscious rebuttal of the notion of class conflict at a time when it was an endemic and intensifying feature of contemporary capitalism. Others, though, have argued that there is no intrinsic ideological bias in marginalist economics. And, indeed, its reception by the European Left varied considerably from outright hostility to acceptance and use for the theoretical elaboration of socialist positions.[29]

More generally, in terms of exogenous explanations of its incidence, there have been suggestions that the emergence of neo-classical economics can be linked to a certain stage of economic development and, particularly in Britain, to the end of the rapid period of mid-Victorian growth and the emergence of the more problematic economic conditions of the last quarter of the nineteenth century. In such circumstances, it has been argued, questions of how growth might be accelerated (those addressed by classical political economists) were likely to be displaced by questions of how to maximize utility or output with scarce resources (those with which neo-classical writers were concerned).

Such exogenous explanations have, however, found less favour than those which have sought to explain the emergence of marginalist economics in terms endogenous to the discipline. Here emphasis has sometimes been placed on the theoretical crisis undergone by classical economics in the 1860s, as regards both its theories of value and distribution, with much being made of Thornton's refutation, and Mill's subsequent abandonment, of the wages-fund doctrine that was central to the classi-cal explanation of what determined the natural wage rate.[30] Others have suggested that there is evidence prior to this that classical economics was in crisis and that by the 1860s marginalist economics was a paradigm shift waiting to happen. Here much has been made of the fact that the change occurred almost simultaneously in the very different socio-economic and institutional circumstances prevailing in Britain, France and Austria.

Jevons's own view that his subjective, 'final' (marginal) utility explanation of the determination of the rate of exchange of commodities and its articulation in terms of differential calculus represented a decisive break with his classical predecessors has therefore been regarded critically by many. The fact that he was not the first to apply the concepts of the margin and utility to the problem of price determination has already been noted. In addition it has been made clear that he was not the first eco-nomist in Britain to apply mathematics systematically to economic questions.[31] Recent scholars have also demurred at a previous tendency to interpret Jevons's *Theory* as an embryonic formulation of what was ultimately to emerge as a mature neo-classical theory of price. Rather, it has been argued, the *Theory* should be seen as 'a transi-tional work', 'as far removed from Marshall as it is from Ricardo'; with Jevons's real break with classical economics being that of applying the calculus of pain and plea-sure to *all* aspects of economic life.[32] Such views do not, though, play down the sig-nificance and originality of Jevons's contribution to the value theory of the emerging social science of economics. For it is accepted by most commentators that, with and after Jevons, the part played by use value and demand and supply in the determina-tion of exchange value was given a more systematic and coherent treatment than it had been prior to the 1870s.

Further, the work of post-war scholars on Jevons has also shown that he made sig-nificant contributions to the development of late-nineteenth-century theoretical and applied economics in other spheres than that of value theory. These included the con-struction of index numbers, business-cycle analysis, work on the relation between natural resources and economic growth, and his discussion of the appropriate role for the state in the economic life of the nation. Such studies have made plain that viewing Jevons's work solely from the perspective of a 'marginal revolution' risks obscuring our appreciation of his overall achievement as an economist.

As to the influences on Jevons, these have been shown to reflect both the range of his intellectual interests and the fact that he came to a study of economics from outside the discipline. Recent writers have stressed the centrality of Bentham's hedon-istic calculus to his writing on value and other aspects of his political economy; in particular his labour-supply theory.[33] Others have pointed to his initial training in natural science as something that influenced both his methodology and the analyt-ical tools he used – most obviously his mathematical exposition of economic theory. Research has also shown Jevons's knowledge of, and sensitivity to, developments in the natural sciences, as well as the logic and philosophy of science; the ideas of Boole and de Morgan proving influential as regards the latter.

The leader of the new school of scientific, mathematically articulated, micro-based economics, who emerged after the death of Jevons, was Alfred Marshall. His status as leader was recognized by contemporaries and acknowledged by subsequent com-mentators; a leadership confirmed, institutionally, by his occupation of the Chair of

Economics at the University of Cambridge from 1885 to 1908. Marshall's *Principles of Economics* went through eight editions in his lifetime and exerted the same kind of doctrinal authority as had Mill's *Principles of Political Economy*. The breadth of its theoretical vision and its creation of what, post-Kuhn, might be termed a research agenda, gave Marshall his unchallenged reputation as Britain's leading economist and inspired that younger generation of scholars who were to be denominated the Cambridge School. On price theory, time-period analysis, the theory of the firm, capital theory, international-trade theory and monetary theory, subsequent commentators have emphasized the significance and originality of his contribution to the development of neo-classical economics and also to the professionalization of the discipline of economics in Britain.[34]

As to intellectual debts and his relationship with contemporary economists, these have been considered in detail by many scholars; something all the more needful as Marshall himself was not always forthcoming in his acknowledgement of those from whom he drew inspiration.[35] Here it has become clear that Marshall owed more to continental influences and the work of writers such as Cournot and von Thunen than to home-grown political economy such as that of Jevons's *Theory*. In addition, it has become apparent that Marshall's thinking, while indebted to British utilitarianism, was also influenced by contemporary evolutionism and German idealism; though in what proportions scholarship has not always made apparent.

In terms of his methodology, while Marshall stressed the importance of examining those economic regularities generated by the self-interested pursuit of gain, scholars have also shown that Marshall was well aware of the richness and variety of human motivation and the qualifications that must be made to whatever conclusions were drawn from his theoretical work. His mode of reasoning was in the a priori, deductive tradition of Ricardo but characterized by a methodological ecumenism; or, as J. N. Keynes put it, a 'deductive political economy guided by observation'.[36] His analysis was also marked by a partial equilibrium/comparative static approach, yet he had 'no interest in pushing the statistical approach to its logical conclusion in general equilibrium analysis'.[37] The picture that emerges, therefore, is one of a cautious, undogmatic thinker, quick to qualify, rethink and revise in the light of new empirical evidence; the advocate of a broad economic science, sensitive to the methodological limitations of the economics that he himself was in the forefront of constructing. And it is surely this sensitivity, and his consequent inclination to revise theoretical positions in the light of what he saw as rapidly changing economic circumstances that, in some measure, must account for the literary procrastination which made for what some have seen as a singularly limited flow of publications after the magisterial *Principles*.

If post-war research has added considerably to our understanding of the fundamental contribution of Marshall to the conceptual and theoretical framework of neo-classical economics, it has also added to our appreciation of other late-nineteenth-century economists; in particular our understanding of the work of Edgeworth and Wicksteed.[38] Further, it has also thrown considerable light on the political economies of those who challenged the neo-classical bid for disciplinary hegemony. Here work on writers such as Ashley, Cliffe Leslie, Hewins, Ingram and Cunningham has documented the *methodenstreit* precipitated by an English historical school that called into question the essentially deductive methodology of neo-classicism; a methodological struggle which, if it lacked the vigour and duration of its continental counterpart, did result in historical economists establishing their claim to the field of economic history, though it left neo-classical economists a near-monopoly over the sphere of mainstream economics.[39] As to the reasons for the emergence of the English historical school, few have added significantly to Coats's explanation of it as a product of middle-class social guilt, an antipathy to an aggressive industrialism and a moral revulsion against the poverty in the midst of plenty that a relatively untrammelled industrial capitalism had created.[40]

The challenge of late-nineteenth-century British Marxism to mainstream economics has been seen as largely a product of Hyndman in works such as *The Historical Basis of Socialism in England* (1883) and *The Economics of Socialism* (1896). In general it is also agreed that the distinguishing characteristics of Hyndman's Marxism, in particular its crude determinism, its dismissive attitude to the efforts of trade unions, its anti-religious sentiments, its intimations of violent revolution and its jingoistic imperialism, made it less palatable to the British Left than the Marxism purveyed to its counterparts in continental Europe. Different views have been expressed as to the originality, or otherwise, of Hyndman's theoretical contribution to the development of Marxian political economy and on the extent to which that contribution was consistent with what Marx himself had written. As to the former some have argued, however, that Hyndman's explanation of economic crises was a relatively sophisticated piece of theorizing that deserves more attention than it has hitherto received.[41]

Yet Hyndman's merits and demerits aside few would disagree that amongst *fin de siècle* socialist political economies, it was Fabianism that proved most influential. Of course it has been argued that, as regards the social and economic policies of the early Labour party what has sometimes been labelled Fabian had a different ideological provenance and certainly influences other than Fabianism helped shape that group's policy prescriptions. But, that said, it is generally recognized that Fabian political economy did have a material influence on Labour's economic literature in the inter-war period and on the conduct of economic policy by the second minority Labour government (1929–31).

In terms of Fabianism's theoretical core, it has long been accepted that it derived from an extension of Ricardian rent theory from land to other factors of production.[42] But it has also been suggested, not least by some of the early Fabians, that neo-classicism was profoundly influential, and George Bernard Shaw certainly claimed to have been weaned off the Marxian labour theory of value by Wicksteed's critique in the pages of *To-day* (1884). Yet while Shaw might trumpet the modern, scientific neo-classical character of the socialist political economy he purveyed, the fact is that the Fabian theory of profit, interest and rent deployed the concept of the margin in a manner more Ricardian than neo-classical.

Amidst late-nineteenth-century socialist political economies there was also the anarcho-communism of William Morris. Here the extent and nature of Morris's Marxism has been disputed. In the case of Meier, Morris was located in a Marxist-Leninist tradition of socialist thinking; with E. P. Thompson, his view as to the Marxist credentials of Morris altered between the first and second editions of his study of the latter's life and thought.[43] However, it is clear that, even if a Marxist appellation is apposite, it must be accepted that what we have is a very Morrisian or, perhaps, Ruskinian Marxist. Certainly much scholarship on Morris has made apparent the importance of Ruskin's influence in terms of Morris's conversion to socialism, the nature of his critique of capitalism and, in particular, the vision of the socialist future articulated in *News from Nowhere* (1890).[44]

Finally, there was the challenge to mainstream economics that came from the emergence in late-nineteenth-century Britain of a New Liberal political economy sensitive to the macro-economic failings of late-Victorian capitalism and the need for a more active interventionist role for the state if these were to be circumvented. As regards this redefinition of liberalism it is recognized that the work of writers such as Hobson and Hobhouse was fundamental.[45] In relation to the former, the work of Allett has made evident that he was not just a heretic in his challenge to Say's Law and his critique of imperialism but that he questioned the whole methodological and philosophical basis of contemporary mainstream economics, looking to the construction of a political economy that was ethically informed and which took on board the insights of other disciplines such as sociology, psychology and moral philosophy.

This chapter has sought to convey the richness, diversity and innovative character of the scholarship that has informed work on the history of nineteenth-century economic thought. It is a field of research that has attracted the attention of economists, historians, sociologists, philosophers, social anthropologists and others. This is what has given the scholarship its multifaceted character and helped to spawn the diversity of interpretations and methodological approaches by which it is characterized. And if the latter have sometimes served to make this area of research a battleground, they have also generated the intellectual excitement and outstanding historical research by which it is distinguished.

NOTES

1. D. Winch, *Riches and Poverty: An Intellectual History of Political Economy, 1750–1834* (Cambridge, 1996).
2. J. Hicks and S. Hollander, 'Mr Ricardo and the moderns', *Quarterly Journal of Economics*, 91 (1977).
3. T. Peach, 'David Ricardo: a review of some interpretative issues', in W. Thweatt, ed., *Classical Political Economy: A Survey of Recent Literature* (Boston, 1988).
4. P. Sraffa, ed., *The Works and Correspondence of David Ricardo*, 9 vols (Cambridge, 1951–2).
5. J. A. Schumpeter, *A History of Economic Analysis* (Oxford, 1954).
6. S. Hollander, *The Economics of David Ricardo* (London, 1979).
7. J. M. Keynes, *Essays in Biography*, in D. Moggridge, ed., *The Collected Writings of John Maynard Keynes* (London, 1972).
8. S. Rashid, 'Recent literature on Malthus', in W. Thweatt, ed., *Classical Political Economy: A Survey of Recent Literature* (Boston, 1988).
9. E. A. Wrigley and R. S. Schofield, *The Population History of England, 1541–1871: A Reconstruction* (London, 1981).
10. J. Mokyr, 'Malthusian models and Irish history', *Journal of Economic History*, 40 (1980).
11. S. Hollander, 'The wage path in classical growth models: Ricardo, Malthus and Mill', *Oxford Economic Papers*, 36 (1984).
12. A. Waterman, *Revolution, Economics and Religion: Christian Political Economy, 1798–1833* (Cambridge, 1992).

13. Schumpeter, *History of Economic Analysis*.
14. S. Hollander, *The Economics of John Stuart Mill*, 2 vols (Toronto, 1997).
15. N. de Marchi, 'John Stuart Mill, interpretations since Schumpeter', in W. Thweatt, ed., *Classical Political Economy: A Survey of Recent Literature* (Boston, 1988).
16. W. Robson, ed., *The Collected Works of John Stuart Mill*, 21 vols (Toronto, 1963).
17. E. Seligman, 'On some neglected economists', *Economic Journal*, 13 (1903).
18. L. Moss, *Mountifort Longfield: Ireland's First Professor of Political Economy* (Ottawa, 1976); D. P. O'Brien, *J. R. McCulloch: A Study in Classical Economics* (London, 1970).
19. B. Hilton, *Cash, Corn and Commerce: The Economic Policies of the Tory Governments, 1815–30* (Oxford, 1977).
20. F. W. Fetter, 'Economic articles in the *Quarterly Review*', *Journal of Political Economy*, 66 (1958).
21. B. Gordon, *Political Economy in Parliament, 1819–1823* (London, 1976); F. W. Fetter, *The Economist in Parliament: 1780–1860* (Durham, NC, 1980).
22. G. Claeys, *Machinery, Money and the Millennium: From Moral Economy to Socialism, 1815–60* (Cambridge, 1987).
23. G. Stedman Jones, *Languages of Class: Studies in English Working Class History, 1832–1982* (Cambridge, 1983).
24. N. Thompson, *The Real Rights of Man: Political Economies for the Working Class, 1750–1850* (London, 1998).
25. T. W. Hutchison, 'The "marginal revolution" and the decline of English classical political economy', in R. D. C. Black, A. W. Coats and C. D. W. Goodwin, eds, *The Marginal Revolution in Economics: Interpretation and Evaluation* (Durham, NC, 1973).
26. M. Blaug, 'Was there a marginal revolution?', in R. D. C. Black, A. W. Coats and C. D. W. Goodwin, eds, *The Marginal Revolution in Economics: Interpretation and Evaluation* (Durham, NC, 1973).
27. A. Campus, 'Marginal economics', in J. Eatwell et al., eds, *The New Palgrave: A Dictionary of Economic Thought*, vol. 3 (London, 1987).
28. J. Henry, *The Making of Neoclassical Economics* (London, 1990).
29. I. Steedman, *Socialism and Marginalism in Economics, 1870–1930* (London, 1990).
30. Hutchison, 'Marginal revolution'.
31. J. Henderson, *Early Mathematical Economics: William Whewell and the British Case* (London, 1996).
32. R. D. C. Black, 'William Stanley Jevons', in J. Eatwell et al., eds, *The New Palgrave: A Dictionary of Economic Thought*, vol. 2 (London, 1987).
33. S. Peart, *The Economics of W. S. Jevons* (London, 1996).
34. J. Maloney, *Marshall, Orthodoxy and the Professionalization of Economics* (Cambridge, 1985).
35. D. Reisman, *Alfred Marshall's Mission* (Basingstoke, 1990).
36. J. N. Keynes, *The Scope and Method of Political Economy* (London, 1890), p. 72.
37. J. Whitaker, 'Alfred Marshall', in J. Eatwell et al., eds, *The New Palgrave: A Dictionary of Economic Thought*, vol. 3 (London, 1987), p. 353.
38. J. Creedy, *Edgeworth and the Development of Neo–Classical Economics* (Oxford, 1986); I. Steedman, 'Introduction', to P. Wicksteed, *An Essay on the Co–ordination of the Laws of Distribution* (London, 1987).
39. A. Kadish, *The Oxford Economists in the Late Nineteenth Century* (Oxford, 1982); G. Koot, *English Historical Economics, 1870–1926: The Rise of Economic History and Neo-Mercantilism* (Cambridge, 1987).
40. A. W. Coats, 'The historist reaction to English political economy, 1870–90', *Economica*, 21 (1954).
41. M. Howard and J. King, *A History of Marxian Economics, 1883–1929* (London, 1989).

42. A. M. MacBriar, *Fabian Socialism and English Politics, 1884–1918* (Cambridge, 1962).

43. P. Meier, *William Morris: The Marxist Dreamer* (Hassocks, Sussex, 1978); E. P. Thompson, *William Morris: Romantic to Revolutionary* (London, 1977).

44. P. D. Anthony, *Ruskin's Labour: A Study of Ruskin's Social Theory* (Cambridge, 1983).

45. S. Collini, *Liberalism and Sociology: L. T. Hobhouse and the Political Argument in England, 1880–1914* (Cambridge, 1979); J. Allett, *New Liberalism: The Political Economy of J. A. Hobson* (Toronto, 1981).

FURTHER READING

As to general texts, J. Eatwell et al., eds, *The New Palgrave: A Dictionary of Economic Thought* (1987) provides an outstanding resource for an understanding of individual thinkers and major schools of nineteenth-century economic thinking and can be read in conjunction with J. A. Schumpeter, *A History of Economic Analysis* (1954), to allow British economic thought to be set in a broader European context.

The literature on classical political economy is enormous but W. Thweatt, ed., *Classical Political Economy: A Survey of Recent Literature* (1988) will give the reader a sense of the currents of research activity, and the controversies that have informed it, at least up until the 1980s. D. Winch, *Riches and Poverty: An Intellectual History of Political Economy, 1750–1834* (1996) provides an excellent discussion of the historical context and the theoretical and prescriptive concerns of major classical writers, while for individual thinkers it is difficult to ignore the work of S. Hollander, *The Economics of David Ricardo* (1979) and *The Economics of John Stuart Mill* (1997); though readers should be aware of the nature of the revisionist narrative that he is seeking to construct.

The origins, nature, significance, consequences and progenitors of the 'marginal revolution' are all considered in R. D. C. Black et al., eds, *The Marginal Revolution in Economics: Interpretation and Evaluation* (1973), while D. Reisman, *Alfred Marshall's Mission* (1990) furnishes a lucid discussion of the pivotal figure in the neo-classical economics that emerged. As to competing currents of economic thinking in late-nineteenth-century Britain, A. Kadish, *The Oxford Economists in the Late Nineteenth Century* (1982) provides a scholarly discussion of the English historical school while J. Allett, *New Liberalism: The Political Economy of J. A. Hobson* (1981) throws light on the late-nineteenth-century reconfiguration of the political economy of classical liberalism.

As to socialism, N. Thompson, *The Real Rights of Man: Political Economies for the Working Class, 1775–1850* (1998) provides a short introduction to the major figures of the early-nineteenth-century period, while A. MacBriar, *Fabian Socialism and English Politics, 1884–1918* (1962), M. Howard and J. King, *A History of Marxian Economics, 1883–1929* (1989) and E. P. Thompson, *William Morris: Romantic to Revolutionary* (1977) deal respectively with the political economies of Fabianism, Marxism and anarcho-communism.

Part IV

Society and Culture

CHAPTER TWENTY

Religion

MARK A. SMITH

The nineteenth century was clearly a period in which religion claimed a significant role in the lives of English men, women and children of all ages and at all levels in the social structure. There remains considerable debate, however, about the fortunes of the churches that organized most of the religious activity in nineteenth-century England, the nature of the changes that took place within them, the character of the beliefs that they fostered in the population at large and the extent to which England might still be characterized as a religious society at the end of the century. The last twenty years have been particularly fertile in the development of new perspectives on these issues and recent historiography has thrown doubt on the received views and traditions which, nevertheless, continue to dominate textbooks and popular accounts of the subject.

The Problems and Reform of the Established church

The Church of England, which remained much the largest church throughout the period, is traditionally regarded as having entered the nineteenth century in some disarray because of its failure, in the preceding century, to respond to the demographic and economic changes that were transforming English society. The influential work of historians like Gilbert and Ward, published in the 1970s, stressed the incapacity of the church arising from structural weaknesses in its diocesan and parochial systems.[1] Partly as a consequence of legal obstructions and partly because of difficulties in the distribution of the church's financial resources, the parish system in particular had not been adequately extended to the expanding industrial towns in which the population was increasingly being concentrated. The church was further weakened by evidence of neglect and even corruption among its clergy. The bishops, often selected for political reliability rather than pastoral or administrative excellence, were distracted by their political duties at Westminster and hampered by the primitive state of diocesan administrations and so could not exercise adequate supervision of their clergy. In any case, the property rights of the patrons and holders of benefices made it virtually impossible for the majority of bishops to influence the character of ministers appointed to serve in their dioceses or to exercise effective discipline over them when they were in place. At a parish level the church was weakened by the prevalence of pluralism and non-residence among the clergy and low standards of liturgical and pastoral provision. Perhaps even worse than the manifest structural weaknesses of the church was the complacent attitude of churchmen in the later Hanoverian period, which resulted in little or nothing being done about its problems until the shock of the collapse of the 'Anglican' constitutional settlement between 1828 and 1832 created both the conditions and the will for reform.

Into the vacuum produced by the incapacities of the Establishment rushed the Nonconformist denominations: especially the Baptists, Independents or Congregationalists and a variety of Methodist groups. Energized by the evangelical revivals of the second half of the eighteenth century, these churches benefited from an extroverted spirituality and a relative freedom from attachment to fixed ecclesiastical structures. They found a territory ripe for expansion, particularly among the artisans of the new towns. The Church of England, in consequence, lost its virtual monopoly over public religious practice in England and the stage was set for the creation of a pluralistic religious culture in which the boundaries and even the existence of an established church would be a major object of contestation.

The historiographical consensus about the incapacity of the established church also underpinned the work of K. A. Thompson, Brose and Best, who sought to analyse the reforms of the church instigated by parliament in the 1830s and 1840s through the medium of the Ecclesiastical Commission.[2] Here the Establishment was presented as having been saved, almost despite itself, by commissioners who were determined to envision it not as a ramshackle collection of essentially local institutions but as a whole. Moreover, this whole was one within which resources could be transferred to the points of greatest need by a vast effort of modernizing bureaucratic rationalization supported by maps, statistics and commissions of inquiry. The commissioners instigated legislation to remove the worst irrationalities of the diocesan structure, making the church much easier to manage, and initiated a process of reform that continued into the next century. In the teeth of essentially self-interested opposition based on obsolescent appeals to the antiquity of the church's institutions and to the rights of property, they trimmed back expensive cathedral establishments and thereby released resources that were used to expand the parochial ministry of the church. Legal obstacles to the creation of new parishes were cut down and controls on pluralism and non-residence tightened up. The commission itself, which was made a permanent body in 1836, represented an organ for central management in the church unprecedented since the seventeenth century. As a result of this whirlwind of modernization the church entered the second half of the century leaner, fitter and far more able efficiently to fulfil its core pastoral responsibilities.

In the 1980s and 1990s, however, this historiographical consensus began to be challenged – initially as a result of a re-evaluation of the church of the eighteenth century. The intellectual power, or even hegemony, of the supporters of the Establishment was asserted by Clark to the extent that he wished to describe later-Hanoverian Britain as a confessional state or even an *ancien régime*.[3] At a pastoral level, attention was drawn to the work of reformist bishops like Horsley and a new appreciation was developed of the virtues as well as the vices of the Hanoverian parish system.[4] Most notably, an influential volume of essays edited by Walsh, Haydon and

Taylor suggested that abuse and neglect were neither as widespread nor as serious as had often been assumed and that, despite its structural weaknesses, the Establishment could be a vital institution at parish level.[5] They also demonstrated that the established church retained the capacity to make a creative and substantially successful response even to the challenges of industrialization and urbanization by mobilizing local energy and resources to extend its pastoral ministry. A series of works published in the 1990s explored the capacity of the church to reform itself. Burns described an attempt to revive the institutions and ethos of the dioceses and to make them more pastorally effective.[6] Key diocesan institutions were undergoing a process of reform long before parliament began to take an interest in the diocesan system: the bishop's visitation, for example, was becoming more frequent, more comprehensive in the information it sought and above all more 'diocesan', as bishops began to use the information at their disposal to deliver charges which both presented an image of the current state of the diocesan community and launched policy initiatives. Offices like that of rural dean and archdeacon were revived or re-activated in many dioceses, as were ruridecanal chapters which provided an opportunity for clergy to meet together. The net effect of this process was to create a sense of common interest across the diocese that Burns labelled diocesan consciousness. Perhaps most significantly, Burns demonstrated that the sort of appeals to antiquity and tradition, which earlier writers on the Ecclesiastical Commission had tended to view as simple obstructions to the creation of a more efficient establishment, played a crucial part in legitimating the parallel process of reform which he describes as a diocesan revival. Other research demonstrated both that the later-Hanoverian Establishment continued to adapt to changing pastoral circumstances and that the new structures introduced by the Ecclesiastical Commission were difficult to implement and may have had ambiguous effects on the church – especially in stifling initiative at the local level.[7] The result of this reappraisal has been a much more complex representation of the Church of England in the first half of the nineteenth century. The straightforward narrative, in which neglect and failure were followed by a period of modernization and reform of a moderately utilitarian kind which produced a more efficient establishment better able to compete in the pluralistic denominational market-place of Victorian England, still commands a good deal of attention. However, it has been modified, and is perhaps gradually being replaced, by a recognition of the pastoral effectiveness of the later-Hanoverian church and the flexibility of its local structures. There is also a growing appreciation that the parliamentary reforms of the 1830s and 1840s need to be understood as only one part of a complex of reform projects in this period, many of them generated by the church itself and often legitimated on other than utilitarian or pragmatic grounds.

The Oxford Movement and Ritualism

It has long been recognized that the assertion of the integrity and spiritual independence of the church by the Oxford Movement or Tractarians represented a further key element in the response of churchmen to the reform crisis. Traditionally regarded as beginning in 1833 with Keble's protest against the government's remodelling of the Church of Ireland, the movement is often presented as a romantic re-appropriation of the past in reaction to modern liberalism and utilitarianism. In this view it represented an attempt to reassert the High Church tradition in the Establishment with a stress on the catholicity of the church's doctrine and constitution, the apostolicity of its bishops and its unique role as a *via media* between the errors of Protestantism and of Rome. This tradition had been overlaid by the Erastian spirit of the eighteenth century and the older generation of High Churchmen were too cautious in temperament to reassert it. It was therefore left open to the young enthusiasts of Oxford – particularly Newman and Froude – to seize the initiative and to begin to encourage the church to recover its Catholic heritage and sacramental spirituality. The movement is seen to have had a ready affinity with the Victorian vogue for medievalism and thus to have linked naturally to the ecclesiological enthusiasm for Gothic architecture and, later, to the attempts of the ritualists to recover as much as possible of the splendours of the church's medieval ceremonial. Already one of the most intensively worked-over areas in the study of nineteenth-century British religion, the historiography of the Oxford Movement has continued to grow over the last fifteen years or so, with Newman alone attracting two new substantial biographies.[8] The most significant reappraisal of the Tractarians as a whole has been by Nockles, who paid close attention not just to the theology and activity of the Tractarians themselves but also that of the older High Church or 'Orthodox' tradition from which they are assumed to have emerged.[9] In so doing, he revealed the Oxford Movement to be not so much an extension or intensification of the Orthodox tradition as a radical departure from it. The discontinuities became particularly apparent in a comparison of the Orthodox and Tractarian attitudes to antiquity and to the nature of the church. For the Orthodox, the fathers of the first four centuries of the Christian church were held in particular honour as a guide to the interpretation of scripture – a position consciously set on the one hand against the unqualified right of private judgement which they associated with extreme Protestantism and on the other against the claims of the modern Church of Rome to mediate an authoritative interpretation. Within Orthodox apologetic, the Fathers were deployed in a static defensive role to shore up the Anglican divines of the seventeenth century. For the Tractarians, however, the theology and practice of the early church, as they understood it, became an absolute standard against which the contemporary Church of England was to be measured – and frequently found wanting. Similarly, for the Orthodox, while the possession of a line of bishops in unbroken succession from the apostles was important for the well-being of the church, it was not a key test without which a church could not be regarded as a genuine part of the 'Church catholic' (a federation of territorial churches of which the Church of England was part). Within this frame of reference, both English Roman Catholics and Protestant Dissenters were regarded as schismatic. Continental reformed and Roman Catholic churches, on the other hand, were seen as true but defective churches – the reformed churches lacking an apostolic episcopate and the Romans a reformed doctrine. The Church of England was regarded as having been providentially favoured with both a sound doctrine and a Catholic constitution and to represent a *via media* between extreme Protestantism and Roman Catholicism. It was nevertheless, clearly a church of the Reformation and the Orthodox were notable for their resistance to attempts to admit Roman Catholics within the pale of the British constitution. For the Tractarians, however, the possession of apostolic succession was an essential mark of a true church. The continental reformed bodies were, therefore, not to be regarded as part of the Catholic church and the Anglican *via media* was not between Rome and extreme Protestantism but between Rome and Protestantism as a whole. These differences of view led to a cooling of relationships between the Tractarians and older High Churchmen and to suspicions that the Oxford Movement represented a Roman fifth column within the established church. This view seemed to be confirmed by the theological trends discernible within some of the later tracts and by the secession to Rome of a number of leading figures in the movement.

The spread of Tractarian ideas into the parishes from the middle of the nineteenth century is often associated with the attempts to change the ceremonial practice of the Church of England known as ritualism. Although the early Tractarians themselves appear to have been relatively indifferent to the use of elaborated ritual, the impetus for it did stem from a characteristic Tractarian doctrine. This was a theology of the eucharist in which Christ was understood to be present – not, as in the traditional Anglican understanding, spiritually in the hearts of the believers gathered around the table, but objectively in the elements of bread and wine themselves. The consequent growth in the spirituality of eucharistic devotion converged with Victorian antiquarianism and a more positive evaluation of Rome to encourage the development of ritual both for its own sake and because of its alleged efficacy in attracting the poor and the illiterate into church. The continuing resonance of the ensuing conflict between ritualists and the more Protestant sections of the church has made it difficult to disentangle the history of ritualism in the nineteenth century from more current concerns. Consequently the story has tended to be told from a historiographical perspective closely linked to the development of the Anglo-Catholic tradition. The resulting narrative has stressed conflict between devoted ritualist pastors – many of them working in slum parishes – and vitriolic Protestants unashamed to use prosecution and persecution in an unavailing attempt to hold back the Anglo-Catholic tide. Recently, however, Yates has attempted a reappraisal of ritualism which, while recognizing the devotion and commitment of many of its proponents, has also drawn attention to its tendency to permanent revolution, as each new generation of ritualists pushed the experiment further.[10] This made it difficult, even for sympathetic bishops, to accommodate ritualism within the church. The ultimate effect of ritualism, by undermining the role of the Book of Common Prayer as a focus for unity, was to turn the Church of England into a far more pluralist body than could have been imagined at the start of the century.

The Evangelicals

In contrast to the continuing historiographical enthusiasm for the Tractarians and their heirs, evangelicalism – much the largest component tradition in English Christianity throughout the nineteenth century – has received relatively little attention. Evangelicalism had significant representation among the most active clergy and laity in the established church including such figures as Sumner, Wilberforce and Shaftesbury. Evangelical theology and spirituality also predominated among the largest of the Nonconformist churches – especially the Baptists, the Independents and the many strands of Methodism. It is likely that at least two-thirds of churchgoers in mid-nineteenth-century England attended evangelical churches. Necessarily, therefore, evangelicalism was a diverse movement marked by considerable variations

in both theology and practice. Although references to evangelicalism can be found
in studies of individuals or in denominational historiographies, attempts to consider
it as a whole have been rare and there has been a particular paucity of published work
on the later nineteenth century. The outstanding exception remains Bebbington's
attempt both to identify the common characteristics of evangelicalism from the mid-
eighteenth to the twentieth centuries and to describe major stages in its development
with reference to broader cultural trends.[11] In Bebbington's analysis, which has been
widely adopted by other scholars, evangelicalism is characterized by a combination
of four characteristics. First, conversionism: for evangelicals a direct experience of
being justified by grace through faith in Jesus Christ marked the boundary between
being a Christian and a non-Christian. Much evangelical preaching and activity
was directed towards fostering conversion and evangelical parents often watched
anxiously for signs that such a work of grace was under way in the lives of their
children. However, in most evangelical circles, it was not required that conversion
should be a sudden datable experience rather than a gradual awakening to faith.
Alongside the evangelical emphasis on conversion ran another key doctrine: that of
assurance. For evangelicals, individuals could expect not only to receive salvation
through the grace of God but also to be assured that they had received it. The confidence which flowed from this spirituality added to the conviction with which evangelicals confronted their task in the world. The second characteristic identified by
Bebbington was Biblicism – a commitment to the idea that the Bible was the authoritative source of spiritual truth in matters of faith and practice. The Bible was the key
to evangelical spirituality: most evangelical preaching took the form of the exposition of a biblical text and the Bible also lay at the centre of evangelical devotion in
the home. While they agreed on its reliability as a means of conveying spiritual truth,
however, evangelicals held a wide range of views on the nature of the inspiration of
scripture. The third characteristic was crucicentrism: an emphasis on the cross of
Christ and the doctrine of the atonement usually understood in substitutionary terms
– the idea that Christ died on the cross in the place of sinners and thus satisfied the
justice of God on their behalf. For evangelicals the atonement stood at the heart of
the gospel and gratitude for the atoning death of Christ was the strongest possible
motive not only for pursuing personal holiness but also for undertaking good works
in the world. This led directly to the fourth characteristic – that of activism. Nineteenth-century evangelicalism was strongly activist in its orientation, not just in its
adoption of an ever widening range of strategies for propagating the gospel, but also
in pursuing a huge variety of philanthropic and political causes, from the abolition
of slavery to the proper observance of the Sabbath. It was this characteristic that
made evangelicalism so prominent in nineteenth-century society and that led to its
being satirized by authors like Dickens.

For Bebbington, while these four characteristics formed the common core of evangelicalism, their form and application varied as churches responded to broad changes
in their cultural environment. He suggests that, partly influenced by romanticism,
evangelicalism was by the 1830s developing a heightened supernaturalism. This manifested itself, in more robust views of the inspiration of scripture, in a sharper confrontation with forces regarded as inimical to the gospel – especially Catholicism both
within and without the established church. It also fostered revivalism and the pursuit
of holiness by faith, which was the hallmark of the Keswick conventions and a wider

holiness movement in later-nineteenth-century evangelicalism. The same romantic temper issued in a greater stress on the second advent of Christ, often as part of a pre-millennialist eschatological scheme which replaced the more optimistic post-millennialism of the Wilberforce generation and which suited a period, in the last third of the nineteenth century, when evangelicalism seemed to be losing ground. Similar changes are detected by Hilton, who has suggested that British society passed, in the mid-nineteenth century, from an era dominated by the doctrine of the atonement to one moulded by the doctrine of the incarnation – a development which had important consequences for the shape of social and economic thought.[12]

Protestant Nonconformity and Roman Catholicism

The Protestant Nonconformists and Roman Catholics who represented roughly half the churchgoers in England by the mid-nineteenth century have, like the evangelicals, failed to attract a proportionate share of historiographical interest. This problem is less apparent in the case of the Methodists. Partly in response to the controversial theses of Halévy and E. P. Thompson as to its counter-revolutionary effects, Methodism has been the subject of high-quality work from historians including Hempton.[13] The history of Roman Catholicism and of old dissenting churches, especially the Congregationalists and the Baptists, has often been dominated by traditional denominational concerns about the development of institutions and the role of particular individuals. However, in parallel with this traditional historiography, students of Protestant Nonconformity, in particular, have shown an interest in its culture and politics.[14]

This interest has been intensified in the last twenty years, stimulated by the thesis proposed by Helmstadter that, between the early 1830s and the mid-1880s, Nonconformity espoused a set of religious, political and social attitudes dominated by individualism.[15] The assertive individualism of the Nonconformists in this period was reflected in their predominantly Arminian or moderately Calvinist theologies, in social views which stressed the importance of individual effort and self-improvement and in political campaigns, like that for the disestablishment of the Church of England, which sought to remove restrictions on individual freedom. According to Helmstadter, this unified world-view came under severe challenge in the last twenty years of the century as biblical criticism and the decline of atonement-centred theology undermined the evangelical basis of Nonconformity, and collective or state-centred solutions to social problems began to marginalize the emphasis on self-help and the individual conscience. Helmstadter's view of mid-nineteenth-century Nonconformity has been refined in a recent analysis of dissenting politics by Larsen.[16] Like Helmstadter, Larsen stressed the close link between dissenting politics and theology. However, he identified not just a general evangelicalism but rather an independent ecclesiology as the root of the political attitudes of the Congregationalists and Baptists which were characterized by a commitment to religious freedom and equality and a suspicion of state interference in almost all areas of action. In this respect they differed from groups like Wesleyans and evangelical churchmen, who shared their evangelical soteriology but not their distinctive view of church polity.

Helmstadter's approach has been challenged elsewhere. Bebbington and Parsons have questioned the primacy of individualism within mid-nineteenth-century

Nonconformity, pointing out the importance of the communal features of Nonconformist culture.[17] These included the vital role of the family in transmitting Nonconformist tradition, a point particularly emphasized by Binfield, which, together
with the communal life of the chapels themselves, created an emphasis on mutuality
within the Nonconformist value system.[18] Bebbington and Parsons both question the
extent to which Nonconformist political ideas and policies were dominated by an
emphasis on freedom of choice, pointing, for example, to a trend towards involving
the state via legislation to control the drink trade or to enforce Sabbath observance.
Nonconformists were also willing to pursue corporate solutions to social problems –
either privately in the form of organizations for mutual support, such as provident
societies, or in public life via local or national attempts at social reform – of which
the 'civic gospel' promoted by Nonconformists in Birmingham is only the most
famous example.

The debates surrounding Roman Catholicism have also in part been concerned
with establishing the identity of the Catholic community and the nature of its cultural stance. To what extent was the Roman Catholic church in England, 'a medieval
survival or a modern revival'?[19] The Roman Catholic church of the early eighteenth
century was dominated by the surviving Catholic gentry and aristocracy who
imparted to it a generally reserved tone and a cautious attitude towards Rome. Significant changes were, however, under way by the 1790s. A wave of émigré priests
fleeing the French Revolution reinforced the Catholic missions in England, which
following the Relief Acts of 1778 and 1791 enjoyed official toleration. More important, however, was the rapid acceleration of immigration from Ireland, especially following the potato famine of the 1840s since a large majority of the immigrants were
at least nominally attached to the Roman Catholic church. The incorporation of these
settlers into the English Catholic community was the most urgent task facing the
Catholic church after 1830 and was to prove far from straightforward. Not only were
there enormous logistical problems in providing churches and priests for the new
Irish congregations but there were also significant differences in the religious culture
of the two groups. The immigrants, from a predominantly rural Irish background,
espoused a Catholicism centred on domestic worship and pilgrimages to local shrines,
often associated with a lively supernaturalism which was far removed from the
relatively austere English version centred on regular attendance at Mass and the
confessional.

It is generally agreed that the success of the Catholic church in marrying together
these disparate religious cultures laid the foundation for a remarkable boom in its
fortunes in the second half of the century. Rather more controversial, however, is the
nature of the new Catholic culture that emerged after the restoration of the Catholic
hierarchy. Some historians have stressed the triumph of Ultramontanism.[20] Partly
inspired by the zeal of Oxford converts like Manning and partly by the influence of
continental religious orders like the Redemptorists and Passionists a revolution was
worked in Catholic devotional practice. Alongside a new exaltation of the papacy,
new devotions to the Virgin and the saints were fostered and new practices like the
'forty hours' adoration of the sacrament were introduced from Italy. However, the
notion of an Ultramontane devotional revolution has been challenged by Heimann
who argues that it is better to see the devotional changes of the second half of the
century as a revival of the native English tradition. Thus while some new devotional

practices were introduced, the most popular ones, including the Benediction service and the use of the rosary, were in fact old favourites from the English devotional tradition. For Heimann, the most significant development in the second half of the nineteenth century was the adoption of a style of Catholic revivalism which bore more than a passing resemblance to its Protestant equivalent: 'It was the adoption of an excitable approach to sin and grace, not the introduction of Italian or continental forms of devotion *per se*, which marked a departure in Victorian Catholic piety from the more gentlemanly tone of the eighteenth century.'[21]

English Religion in the Later Nineteenth Century

The perception of a Roman Catholic boom in the second half of the nineteenth century is an exception to a long tradition in the historiography of English religion which tends to see this as a period of change, often of decline, and even of crisis. For Bebbington, the 1860s onwards was a period in which the predominant evangelical religion of the earlier part of the century was beginning to lose ground. For Hilton, this was the point at which an atonement-centred religious culture began to give way to one centred on the incarnation. For Helmstadter, the last quarter of the century marked the dissolution of the old Nonconformist cultural synthesis. For some writers, the most important factors at work in this period related to long-term changes in society – a process of secularization which is discussed below. Other historians have concentrated on more specific intellectual and cultural changes – often symbolized by the so-called 'Victorian Crisis of Faith'; there is a particularly large literature on the latter phenomenon.[22] Two broad themes may be discerned in this mass of literature – one relating to the problem of doubt in the last third of the century and the other to a broad trend to liberalization within most sectors of English religion.

The growth of religious doubt has generally been seen to arise from a combination of three factors which together undermined a pre-existing religious orthodoxy – science, biblical criticism and a moral critique of Christian doctrine. The debates concerning the relationship between theology and science in this period have frequently been presented in the form of a simple model of conflict – a conflict decisively won by the champions of the new science. This model remains foundational to popular representations of the topic, but a richer and more complex account has, since the late 1970s, begun to supplant the straightforward conflict model in the scholarly literature. Moore has stressed the variety of theological responses to Darwin and demonstrated that versions of Darwinian evolution were rapidly co-opted not only by liberal but also by some conservative theologians who regarded the Darwinian theory as strengthening rather than weakening an orthodox teleological and providential view of the universe.[23] Turner, while accepting the existence of conflict at some levels within Victorian debate on the relationship between science and theology, has helpfully located it as part of the story of the professionalization of the Victorian scientific community which required that the cultural prestige of theological metaphysics be replaced by scientific naturalism.[24] The adherents of the latter consequently tended to exaggerate the degree of conflict in order to promote their cause. Similarly, in the case of biblical criticism, historians have begun to move away from a simple linear view in which older assumptions about biblical inerrancy and verbal inspiration were gradually supplanted by modern biblical criticism – albeit primarily in the moderate form espoused by Lightfoot, Westcott and Hort. Within the evangelical tradition at least, there was no consensus on the nature of biblical inspiration and the popularization of hard-edged theories of plenary inspiration and verbal inerrancy was largely a response to the presentation of critical views of the Bible in journals like *Essays and Reviews* (1860). In seeking to explain a sense of religious crisis in the last third of the century, therefore, attention has tended to shift away from the 'conflict between religion and science' or 'the bible and criticism' and towards what Altholtz has described as 'the warfare of Conscience with Theology'.[25] According to this view, the most fundamental challenge to Christianity in the late-Victorian period was a principled ethical objection to its doctrine and its view of human nature. In particular, the apparently vengeful picture of God that emerged from a reading of the Old Testament, the doctrines of everlasting punishment in hell and the substitutionary atonement of Christ came under fire from people who regarded them as objectionable and unjust. Here, orthodox presentations of the faith were being judged and found wanting against moral standards largely formed by Christianity itself.

If the issue of religious doubt became acute for late Victorians, perhaps especially those in the upper middle classes, the phenomenon of liberalization was even more widespread and pervasive. To some extent this was a matter of theology as both Nonconformists and Anglican broad-churchmen began seriously to engage with the cultural changes they saw around them and to seek to reconstruct the faith on new foundations and with new emphases – most notably the doctrine of the incarnation. Johnson has linked this process to the development of professional theological education among the Nonconformists.[26] Such developments were often linked to a more optimistic view of the moral perfectibility of human nature and of the progress of human society and to an emphasis on the social implications of Christianity which issued in movements like Christian Socialism. However, even more widespread than theological liberalization was a liberalization of life in the churches. This was often associated with a culture of leisure as, seeking new points of contact with their communities, churches began to offer a range of sporting and other leisure facilities. Green has gone so far as to argue that a combination of the liberalization of spirituality, over-investment in church buildings and the elaboration of their associational culture ultimately undermined the long-term viability of the churches.[27]

The Impact of the Churches

The extent of the impact of the churches on nineteenth-century society in general and on the working classes of the growing towns and cities of Victorian England in particular remains perhaps the most hotly debated topic in the field. In the traditional view, most of the nineteenth-century churches were essentially middle class in orientation and made relatively little impact on the bulk of the population.[28] This view was modified by Gilbert. He suggested that, in the early period of industrialization, new urban workers, dislocated from their traditional rural way of life and experiencing anomie, which he defined as 'a generalised feeling of insecurity, rootlessness, and social fragmentation reflecting a dearth of familiar institutions, associations and unifying social activities', found the churches attractive as substitute communities.[29] However, the main beneficiary of this process was not the established church, which was slow to respond to the opportunity, but rather Protestant Nonconformity and especially its newer evangelical strands. The opportunity was limited, however – churchgoing tended to be restricted to artisans and the more respectable industrial workers – and the role of the churches as substitute communities diminished as the new towns stabilized and began to develop their own sense of community and neighbourhood.

From the 1970s the debate was informed by local studies of particular towns and cities.[30] These studies, while presenting a rather diverse picture of the state of religion, have tended increasingly to stress the particularly active form of Christianity which was to be found in the nineteenth-century town and city. There was a wide range of churches. Some were large and well staffed and they developed a range of organizations and agencies to tackle a variety of urban problems, both social and spiritual. Others were less socially prominent but appealed to a section of the population of a particular neighbourhood often from the poorer sections of the working classes. Urban areas were also notable for the plethora of non-church-based religious organizations that could be found operating there. These included undenominational Sunday schools and ragged schools, branches of national societies for distributing religious literature and, in the largest towns and cities, autonomous home mission societies, like the London City Mission whose agents carried out extensive programmes of domestic visitation concentrated in the poorer areas of the city. This sort of activist energy was a characteristic of the 'aggressive approach' popularized by the influential Scots evangelical Chalmers, who taught that it was futile simply to wait for the people to come to church and that the church had to go out to draw the people in. The local studies have also tended to undermine traditional perceptions of the churches as predominantly middle-class affairs supported by some of the more respectable among the working classes. Instead a study of church membership lists and, for the Nonconformist denominations, baptism registers has convinced most scholars working in this field that church congregations tended broadly to reflect the social structure of the neighbourhoods in which they were situated. Thus while it remains common ground that the middle classes as a whole were generally over-represented and adult male unskilled workers were often under-represented, it is now recognized that most congregations in nineteenth-century England would have been numerically dominated by the working classes.

This new consensus about both the high levels of religious activity and the broad social composition of the churches has been reinforced by a strong challenge to the persistent view that the towns and cities of industrial England represented a pastoral problem to which the churches of the nineteenth century proved unequal – a view often based on analyses of the 1851 religious census. Brown distinguished between two main lines of interpretation of urban religion: an older 'pessimistic thesis' and an alternative 'optimistic thesis'.[31] A review of the evidence for vitality in urban religious culture, including the relationship between the churches and civic government, led Brown to side with the optimists but his most important contribution was his challenge to the commonly accepted statistical evidence for a correlation between higher levels of urbanization and lower levels of churchgoing. This has been confirmed by the most recent statistical analysis of the 1851 religious census which concluded that, except perhaps in the most extreme cases like London, nineteenth-century urbanization had no detrimental effect on levels of churchgoing.[32]

Christianity, Women and Domestic Religion

In addition to re-evaluations of the impact of the churches on the towns and on the working classes, the 1980s also saw new attention being paid to the role of women in nineteenth-century religion. The most influential early work linked evangelical religion to the development of separate spheres for men and women of the middle classes.[33] The new interest in women and religion was often the result of the use of new sources of evidence. Work on the membership lists of Nonconformist churches and of Anglican organizations such as communicant guilds indicated that women often outnumbered men in a ratio of 3:2 in such organizations and sometimes 2:1 or even 3:1. While it is likely that the ratios were higher even in congregations than in membership or among communicants, it is significant that it was mostly women who took the greater step of commitment. Perhaps more importantly, the exploitation of oral source material for the later nineteenth and early twentieth centuries has allowed historians to discuss women's perspectives on religion which are often poorly represented in more conventional ecclesiastical sources. Roberts drew attention to the pervasive influence of religion on the lives of many of the Lancastrian women she studied, and Williams demonstrated both the importance to women in Southwark of a distinctive amalgam of orthodox Christianity and folk-religion and the vital role played by those women in transmitting the religious culture to their families.[34]

Other writing in this field has concentrated on investigating some of the links between religion and the cultural construction of gender, on female forms of religious activity like the work of Anglo-Catholic sisterhoods, or the vast range of female philanthropy.[35] Important work has also been undertaken on religion in the home – an arena in which women could develop, especially in the sectarian Methodist groups of the early nineteenth century, powerful ministries of prayer, exhortation and preaching.[36]

Christianity and Empire

The 1990s saw a revival of interest in the relationship between religion and national and imperial identities within Britain in the nineteenth century. This revival was in part stimulated by the publication of Colley's *Britons* which suggested that a sense of common Protestantism often expressed in opposition to a continental (usually French) Catholic 'other' was one of the major foundations for the development of a British national identity in the eighteenth and early nineteenth centuries.[37] The theme of anti-Catholicism in the nineteenth century has continued to attract interest.[38] Wolffe has argued that anti-Catholicism remained a significant force both at the popular cultural level and at the level of politics into the second half of the nineteenth century. He also suggests that it played an important role in the development of the Conservative party. Work on the relationship between religion and national identity, while giving full weight to the role of the institutional churches as a focus of activity, has tended to emphasize the sphere of 'popular religion', pointing, for example, to the role of the commemoration of the deaths of major figures, especially in the later nineteenth and early twentieth centuries, in promoting a convergence between popular religious and patriotic sentiments.[39]

Some interest has also been shown in the development of links between the churches and the military institutions of the imperial state. Anderson argued that the conflicts of the mid-nineteenth century, especially the Crimean War and the Indian Mutiny, marked a sea change in attitudes to the army among the religious public.[40] Increasing attention was paid to missionary and welfare work among the troops and a series of biographies promoted the idea of the Christian military hero – a tradition continued via such figures as Henry Havelock and General Gordon. More recent writing has also suggested that the churches themselves might be regarded as having gone through a process of semi-militarization in the later nineteenth century. Some popular hymns were suffused with military imagery and did not always make it clear that their reference was to a spiritual battle, while youth organizations like the Boys' Brigade and the Church Lads' Brigade featured drills, bands and annual camps alongside a more traditional emphasis on Bible study and church attendance. In 1911 the Church Lads' Brigade established a formal link with the Territorial Army. It is easy to overestimate the degree of militarization of the churches but organizations like the Church Lads' Brigade did prove fertile recruiting grounds in the early months of the First World War and the mix of popular patriotism with a diffused sentimental Christianity may have contributed to a willingness to participate.

Secularization

The theory of secularization has been the most powerful influence on the historiography of English religion in the last half century. It has shaped most of the writing on the impact of the churches on nineteenth-century society and its influence has been particularly marked on discussions of the churches and urbanization, the nature of popular religion and the changing nature of church-centred religion in the late nineteenth century. Secularization theory asserts that there is a connection (often regarded as a necessary and even irreversible connection) between the modernization of society and a decline in the social significance of religious institutions, ideas and practices. This view underlay Wickham's classic study of Sheffield and was made explicit by Gilbert, who located the beginning of significant secularization in the early Victorian period.[41] However, as more optimistic accounts of the state of religion in urban contexts began to come to the fore in the 1980s, secularization theory in the British context came under increasing challenge. Some authors responded to this debate by pushing the arrival of serious secularizing forces to the end of the nineteenth century. Others began to question the notion of secularization altogether since, however elegant and persuasive it appeared at a theoretical level, it did not seem to fit the empirical evidence.[42] Brown's *Death of Christian Britain* sidestepped the traditional terms of debate in favour of a concentration on changes in the role of the discourses of Christianity in forming the identity of individuals in the nineteenth and twentieth centuries.[43] According to this analysis, the nineteenth century saw the triumph of an evangelical 'salvation economy' and also a new view of women as the prime foci and transmitters of religious values within society. This created a set of discourses within which most women continued to construct their own identities until well after the Second World War. Secularization, understood as the destruction of Britain's religious culture, is thus located in the late 1950s and 1960s as the power of the evangelical discourse was eroded by pop culture, second-wave feminism and the replacement of traditional ethical concerns with new issues centring on peace, gender and the environment. These changes had a profound effect on the construction of female identity – removing a key foundation for the maintenance of a Christian culture and its transmission to a future generation. Brown's contribution remains controversial, however, and it is probable that the applicability of traditional secularization theory or other theories of religious change will continue to form an important part of the debate about nineteenth-century religion for some time to come.

NOTES

1. A. D. Gilbert, *Religion and Society in Industrial England: Church, Chapel, and Social Change 1740–1914* (London, 1976); W. R. Ward, *Religion and Society in England 1790–1850* (London, 1972).
2. K. A. Thompson, *Bureaucracy and Church Reform: The Organizational Response of the Church of England to Social Change, 1800–1965* (Oxford, 1970); O. J. Brose, *Church and Parliament: The Re-shaping of the Church of England, 1828–1860* (Stanford, 1959); G. Best, *Temporal Pillars: Queen Anne's Bounty, the Ecclesiastical Commissioners and the Church of England* (Cambridge, 1964).
3. J. C. D. Clark, *English Society 1660–1832: Ideology, Social Structure and Political Practice during the Ancien Regime* (Cambridge, 2000).
4. F. C. Mather, *High Church Prophet: Bishop Samuel Horsley and the Caroline Tradition in the Later Georgian Church* (Oxford, 1992).
5. J. D. Walsh, C. Haydon and S. Taylor, eds, *The Church of England c.1689–c.1833* (Cambridge, 1993).
6. R. A. Burns, *The Diocesan Revival in the Church of England c.1800–1870* (Oxford, 1999).
7. F. Knight, *The Nineteenth-Century Church and English Society* (Cambridge, 1995); M. A. Smith, *Religion in Industrial Society: Oldham and Saddleworth, 1740–1865* (Oxford, 1994).
8. I. Ker, *John Henry Newman: A Biography* (Oxford, 1990); S. Gilley, *Newman and his Age* (London, 1990).
9. P. B. Nockles, *The Oxford Movement in Context* (Cambridge, 1994).
10. N. Yates, *Anglican Ritualism in Victorian Britain 1830–1910* (Oxford, 1999).
11. D. Bebbington, *Evangelicalism in Modern Britain* (London, 1989).
12. B. Hilton, *The Age of Atonement: The Influence of Evangelicalism on Social and Economic Thought, 1795–1865* (Oxford, 1988).
13. E. Halévy, *A History of the English People in 1815* (London, 1938); E. P. Thompson, *The Making of the English Working Class* (London, 1963); D. Hempton, *Methodism and Politics in British Society 1750–1850* (London, 1984) and *The Religion of the People: Methodism and Popular Religion c.1750–1900* (London, 1996).
14. C. Binfield, *So Down to Prayers: Studies in English Nonconformity 1780–1920* (London, 1977).
15. R. Helmstadter, 'The Nonconformist conscience', in P. Marsh, ed., *The Conscience of the Victorian State* (New York, 1979).
16. T. Larsen, *Friends of Religious Equality: Nonconformist Politics in Mid-Victorian England* (Woodbridge, 1999).

17. Bebbington, *Evangelicalism in Modern Britain*; G. Parsons, 'From dissenters to free churchmen', in G. Parsons, ed., *Religion in Victorian Britain*, vol. 1, *Traditions* (Manchester, 1988).

18. Binfield, *So Down to Prayers*.

19. S. Gilley and W. J. Sheils, *A History of Religion in Britain* (Oxford, 1994), p. 347.

20. E. Norman, *The English Catholic Church in the Nineteenth Century* (Oxford, 1984).

21. M. Heimann, *Catholic Devotion in Victorian England* (Oxford, 1995), p. 146.

22. Much of this material is helpfully summarized in G. Parsons, ed., *Religion in Victorian Britain*, vol. 2, *Controversies*; vol. 4, *Interpretations* (both Manchester, 1988).

23. J. R. Moore, *The Post Darwinian Controversies: A Study of the Protestant Struggle to Come to Terms with Darwin in Great Britain and America 1870–1900* (Cambridge, 1979).

24. F. Turner, 'The Victorian conflict between science and religion: a professional dimension', in Parsons, ed., *Religion in Victorian Britain*, vol. 4.

25. J. L. Altholz, 'The warfare of conscience with theology', in Parsons, ed., *Religion in Victorian Britain*, vol. 4.

26. D. A. Johnson, *The Changing Shape of English Nonconformity 1825–1925* (New York, 1999).

27. S. J. D. Green, *Religion in the Age of Decline: Organisation and Experience in Industrial Yorkshire, 1870–1920* (Cambridge, 1996).

28. E. R. Wickham, *Church and People in an Industrial City* (London, 1957); K. S. Inglis, *Churches and the Working Classes in Victorian England* (London, 1963).

29. A. D. Gilbert, *The Making of Post-Christian Britain* (London, 1980).

30. H. M. McLeod, *Class and Religion in the Late Victorian City* (London, 1974); J. Cox, *The English Churches in a Secular Society: Lambeth 1870–1930* (Oxford, 1982); J. N. Morris, *Religion and Urban Change: Croydon, 1840–1914* (Woodbridge, Suffolk, 1992); Smith, *Religion in Industrial Society*.

31. C. G. Brown, 'Did urbanization secularize Britain?', *Urban History Yearbook 1988*.

32. K. D. M. Snell and P. S. Ell, *Rival Jerusalems: The Geography of Victorian Religion* (Cambridge, 2000).

33. L. Davidoff and C. Hall, *Family Fortunes: Men and Women of the English Middle Class 1780–1850* (London, 2002).

34. E. Roberts, *Working Class Barrow and Lancaster 1890–1930* (Lancaster, 1976); S. C. Williams, *Religious Belief and Popular Culture in Southwark c.1880–1939* (Oxford, 1999).

35. S. Gill, *Women and the Church of England from the Eighteenth Century to the Present* (London, 1994); R. B. Shoemaker, *Gender in English Society 1650–1850* (London, 1998); S. Mumm, *Stolen Daughters, Virgin Mothers: Anglican Sisterhoods in Victorian Britain* (London, 1999); F. K. Prochaska, *Women and Philanthropy in Nineteenth-Century England* (Oxford, 1980).

36. D. M. Valenze, *Prophetic Sons and Daughters: Female Preaching and Popular Religion in Industrial England* (Princeton, 1985).

37. L. Colley, *Britons: Forging the Nation 1707–1837* (London, 1992).

38. D. G. Paz, *Popular Anti-Catholicism in Mid-Victorian England* (Stanford, 1992); J. Wolffe, *The Protestant Crusade in Great Britain 1829–1860* (Oxford, 1991).

39. J. Wolffe, *Great Deaths: Grieving, Religion, and Nationhood in Victorian and Edwardian Britain* (Oxford, 2000).

40. O. Anderson, 'The growth of Christian militarism in mid-Victorian Britain', *English Historical Review*, 86 (1971).

41. Gilbert, *Making of Post-Christian Britain*.

42. S. Bruce, ed., *Religion and Modernization: Sociologists and Historians Debate the Secularization Thesis* (Oxford, 1992).

43. C. G. Brown, *The Death of Christian Britain: Understanding Secularisation, 1800–2000* (London, 2001).

FURTHER READING

The historical literature relating to nineteenth-century religion in England is vast. A good place to begin, therefore, is with one of the introductory surveys, such as W. O. Chadwick, *The Victorian Church* (1971), now a little dated in a number of respects but beautifully written and still well worth reading. Also helpful are the relevant volumes of K. Hylson-Smith, *The Churches in England from Elizabeth I to Elizabeth II* (1996–8), covering the periods 1689–1833 and 1833–1998, which reliably survey much of the historiography, and the essays in part III of S. Gilley and W. J. Sheils, *A History of Religion in Britain* (1994). A further useful resource is provided by the Open University series on *Religion in Victorian Britain*: vols 1, 2 and 4, edited by G. Parsons, and vol. 5, edited by J. Wolffe, comprise a number of essays, some of an introductory and some of a specialist nature, which together provide a good introduction to the field, though perhaps somewhat over-weighted towards certain topics, especially the 'Victorian crisis of faith'.

In addition to the monograph literature already surveyed in this chapter, much important material is to be found in periodicals especially specialist journals like the *Journal of Ecclesiastical History* and the *Journal of Religious History* and also the collections of papers to be found in *Studies in Church History*, published annually by the Ecclesiastical History Society. Also well worth consulting are the journals of denominational history societies such as the *Proceedings of the Wesley Historical Society* which contains material on the various branches of Methodism. The series produced by county record societies, for example the *Hampshire Record Series*, also include much material of value to the study of nineteenth-century religion as do a number of the volumes produced by the Church of England Record Society.

CHAPTER TWENTY-ONE

Literacy, Learning and Education

PHILIP GARDNER

In 1882, Francis Adams wrote a notable account relating the story, as he saw it, of the 'struggle for National Education' which culminated in the landmark Education Act of 1870. The title of Adams's book is every bit as illuminating as is its substance – the *History of the Elementary School Contest in England*.[1] Few images better evoke the character of nineteenth-century education than that of contest or struggle. The allusion applies, moreover, not only to the constellation of events which made up the educational past. It also marks many of the subsequent histories, from that of Adams onwards, within which such events have been configured, interpreted and related. The representation of the educational past, no less than that past itself, has often been a sharply contested business.

It is not hard to allow ourselves immediately to be drawn to the contentious features of educational history from, on the one hand, an institutional aspect or, on the other, from an ideological one. Both are manifestly important. The notion of contest has, however, another and less grandiose dimension which has often been little considered in standard educational histories and with which, in consequence, we should start. Though its best-known forms are to be traced at the level of policy development, implementation and commentary, the ramifications of the struggle for education in the nineteenth century found their ultimate expression in the educational experiences of its recipients themselves. For the greater part of the century, schooling was a relatively costly commodity that had to be purchased in a diverse and often weakly regulated market-place. This was not a problem for established wealth, with its traditional links with the ancient public schools and universities for the classical education of its sons, and its access to a plentiful supply of home tutors for its daughters. Neither did it present a difficulty for newer industrial wealth, able to choose from an expanding range and variety of private and proprietary schools and academies, many of which offered a more modern curriculum with a technical or scientific inflection. But for the majority of the population, that sixth-sevenths of society for whose educational provision the state had come to accept responsibility by 1870, the acquisition of learning was always a hard struggle.[2]

Such struggles were not fought for hegemony either over the form of education or over the nature of its representation, but for access to the elements of learning as a fundamental source of personal benefit, enrichment and pleasure in the lives of individual citizens. They were struggles to bring together within individual lives, in John Harrison's magnificent phrase, 'learning and living'. This recognition has come to exert a significant influence on historical scholarship in recent years, opening new lines of research which have widened a traditional focus upon educational policy and institutional formation to engage questions of the cultural meaning and usage of learning by its beneficiaries. Conceptually, such approaches have turned to the inclusion of issues of educational demand as well as supply, to the recognition of schooling as merely the formal element in a much broader array of informal and unsystematic opportunities for learning, to a concern for the uses of literacy and not only for its extent – in short, to an understanding of education as it was inscribed within individual lives rather than projected upon them.

Any focus upon the course of most nineteenth-century educational lives – those outside the economic and cultural elites – shows the characteristically episodic, fractured and contingent character of the great majority of individual experiences in the pre-1870 period. The nature and the significance of their educational experiences for those who attended the elite or middling reaches of private schooling in the nineteenth century are richly and extensively documented. The other end of the educational continuum is much more obscure. There are, however, tantalizing and evocative clues to be found in contemporary blue books, particularly in the volumes of the Children's Employment Commission. The great value of sources such as these – and one not yet sufficiently drawn upon by scholars – lies in their representative quality. Their succession of glimpses into the abbreviated and promiscuous educational lives of hundreds of otherwise unrecorded young people gives us a vivid composite picture of the educational opportunities and expectations which prevailed for the greater part of the century.

Sarah Pearce, for example, a 13 year-old munitions worker from London related that she

> [w]ent regularly to a week school, since she was four or five years old, till she came to work here . . . Can read 'very well', quite long words in the Bible. Can write on the slate very well. Mother is just teaching her to write a letter on paper in the evenings after work. Can 'add and take from and do sums with them two lines'.[3]

However they were initially gleaned, the subsequent exploitation of the prized elements of learning varied widely from case to case as the memorials of these teenage coal-miners from the 1840s show. John Watson had started at the pit at the age of 6; he '[o]nly knows his a, b, c; cannot write at all. Goes to no school now . . . Was at school before he went down the pit for a year and could read the Bible then; now he has forgotten everything.'[4] James Brady did 'not know exactly what age I am. It is 16, 17 or 18 . . . I cannot read much, some little. I have read the Testament. I have read the Spelling-Book and Ready-ma-daisy (Reading Made Easy).'[5] Isaac Tipton first went underground when he was 7: 'I am 16 years of age . . . I read middling . . . I read the Bible sometimes . . . I have read Reading Made Easy. I have read about Turpin and Jack Sheppard; I have read about Robin Hood. I read song-books . . .

I have read a bit of Robinson Crusoe. I have read about the pigs and cows dying of distemper.'[6]

Such fragments convey something of the mark, from the modest to the more notable, which education and learning might make upon the lives of working people in the first half of the nineteenth century. Such variety, however, should not obscure a more general appreciation of the surprising extent of the popular demand for education in these years. This was a demand which rested upon a number of factors: a deep residual appreciation among many for the importance of personal acquaintance with the scriptures; the burgeoning of increasingly cheap popular literature, whether sensational, improving or political in character; and a valuation of individual literacy as mediated by varying traditions of family, community and regional expectation. It was a demand which was seldom driven by any instrumental anticipation of occupational mobility as a consequence of the mastery of literacy and learning. Such were direct occupational requirements for relatively few working-class employments in the early stages of industrialization and urbanization. Indeed, there is powerful accumulated evidence to show that literacy rates, especially among women and girls, declined significantly at those moments and in those areas where industrial development was at its most rapid and extensive. The greater the pace of economic change, the more traditional valuations placed upon learning struggled to commend themselves in new occupational and domestic circumstances. And yet, though almost entirely divorced from any hope of occupational advance – the idea of education as representing an opportunity for 'getting on' belongs to the end of the century and not its beginning – the popular desire for education remained profoundly in evidence.

This is an important recognition which has a major historiographical implication. Educational histories, whether they have conceived the growth of mass schooling in terms of social progress or of class domination, have overwhelmingly been written in terms of the development of formalized educational supply and its gradual systematization. Given the balance of the evidence available to research, it is unsurprising that this traditional approach remains very influential and continues to produce forceful and sophisticated historical syntheses.[7] Nonetheless, the need for work which starts from the other end of the equation, from the nature, extent and consequences of popular demand for education, remains a pressing one.

Some of the most impressive advances in recent educational history have concentrated upon the struggles of remarkable individuals to win an education for themselves in the most unpropitious of circumstances. For such men and women, driven by what Sanderson once called 'the self-igniting desire for scholarship', the struggle for knowledge amounted to a life-long passion and a periodic release from toil, if no escape from it.[8] Intense personal narratives of the quest for education are the stuff of nineteenth-century working-class autobiography. Until the pioneering work of Vincent, Burnett and, more recently, Rose, historians seldom drew much upon this remarkable, extensive and still emerging genre.[9] Nevertheless, though working-class autobiographies offer an unparalleled insight into local educational landscapes, these sources have to be handled with some care. The furious, heroic struggles of those – most famously, perhaps, such as Thomas Cooper or William Lovett – to win an education in the face of adversity and disadvantage are admirable and inspiring but they do not represent the commonality of working-class experience. To the extent that we celebrate the astonishing achievements of such figures, we run some risk of underestimating the considerable importance which a more modest level of educational demand continued to hold for very large numbers of working families just above the level of most desperate poverty. Such families were widely castigated for their cultural and moral priorities by educational reformers such as James Kay-Shuttleworth, appointed in 1839 as the first secretary to the Committee of the Privy Council on Education, the modest first step on the road to a central administrative agency for education. Such criticism turned, however, less often on the charge of fundamental illiteracy and more usually castigated the shallow, salacious or unimproving ends to which learning skills were seen to be directed.

In a period of expansion in the availability and range of reading materials in popular circulation, educational reformers were agreed that it was the uses of literacy that were paramount, and particularly the potential for sober learning as a bulwark against immorality, recklessness and crime. This is why, as the century progressed, schooling rather than learning became the central concern of policy reform. Schooling was increasingly conceptualized not merely as a site for organized learning, but for learning of a sort which might reform the sensibilities of children raised within a parental culture widely perceived as morally deficient. If, in the twentieth century, the process of formal schooling would come to be discussed in terms of partnership between school and parent, such a relation made little sense throughout the nineteenth century – including most of the school-board period – with parents widely perceived as the most persistent obstacle to educational advance. Though there were very important differences in the ultimate outcomes they looked to from educational advance, the working-class autodidact and the middle-class educational reformer shared in common the perception of education as a fundamentally transformative force rather than an ameliorative one. Lovett's frustration with working-class attitudes to learning and its uses, expressed most eloquently in his manifesto for educational reform, *Chartism: A New Organisation of the People* (1840), had something in common with that expressed by Kay-Shuttleworth.

The truth is that the most passionate representatives of the autodidactic tradition were outstandingly gifted and intense intellects trapped in a time which cheated and squandered their exceptional talents. But it is misleading to see them as, in some sense, presenting the antithesis of a generally brutalized or unlettered popular culture, as islands of learning in a sea of ignorance. Rather, they occupy the pinnacle of an educational continuum at the centre of which probably clustered the majority of working people for whom learning was a modest source of local status, shared pleasure and individual solace, rather than being an all-consuming passion. That such individuals did not achieve, or aspire to achieve, the great feats of celebrated self-taught scholars was a function of the lack of those effective structures of support, encouragement and direction which the majority needed if their own talents were to blossom. Such structural advance came only in the closing quarter of the century as increased public spending, the enhanced quantity and quality of trained teachers and, above all, the introduction of compulsory school attendance, all made their mark.

With such advantages, the impulse to learning which, fifty years before, had been able to energize only an outstanding few was now felt much more widely by a new generation of intensely able but humbly born boys and girls who, in the words of one of their number, Ellen Wilkinson – born in 1892 and subsequently to become the first minister of education in a majority Labour administration – were 'keen, intelligent, could mop up facts like blotting paper, wanted to stretch our minds in every direction'.[10] Yet the notion that an organized and comprehensive national system of education was the key to unlock human capital and unleash general social mobility came to be understood only once such a system was already in place; it was not the motor which led to its creation. Once the lesson was grasped, however, those like Wilkinson found formal education increasingly represented a realistic escape route from a narrow and disadvantaged start in life. By the end of the century, the numbers who were travelling along this route were still very small. From the perspective of the more meritocratic age which was to follow, progress by the close of the century could be seen as slight, with the horizontal barriers of established educational provision scarcely dented. But from the perspective of those involved in the contemporary administration of education, the change appeared immense and profound. In the optimistic words of E. K. Chambers of the Board of Education, 'educational barriers between class and class no longer existed at the beginning of the twentieth century'.[11]

The most informative of working-class autobiographies – at least for the educational historian – are those which relate stories of exceptional personal achievement or social mobility as a consequence of educational experiences which were, in the context of their time, relatively conventional ones. This is because such accounts necessarily allude to the details of generally prevailing educational structures and influences as much as they relate to the intellectual brilliance of their protagonists. A fine example of such a life is that of Sir Henry Jones, born in 1852, the son of an impoverished village shoemaker from North Wales, who rose to become Professor of Moral Philosophy in the University of Glasgow. The exact combination of events which led to Jones's elevation were singular. But many features of his educational experience would have been familiar to countless working-class peers who were not destined for his rare success. What then does Jones's story have to say to us about the constellation of opportunities for learning which a humbly born mid-nineteenth-century child might encounter?

The first point to note, and one that has been particularly well made in the meticulous research of educational historians such as Marsden and Stephens, is the profound significance of regional, local and occupational distinctions in determining exposure to educational influences.[12] In Jones's case, though the family's circumstances were always very hard, he tells us that within it 'learning' was held in 'high esteem'. His parents had had very little schooling themselves but the whole family were regular attenders at the Sunday school, 'in Wales . . . an institution for adults as well as for children'. The most significant component of his education came at the village school which he attended assiduously from the age of $4\frac{1}{2}$ until the age of 12, with nothing permitted 'to break the regularity of our attendance'. But if this sustained opportunity for learning was welcome, the experience of formal schooling amounted to no intellectual turning-point, the schoolmaster being 'very cruel and very ignorant'. This modest entry to the world of learning, moreover, exacted a cultural as well as a pecuniary charge, the school subscribing to the common practice, followed in Scotland as well as throughout Wales, of excising the use of language other than English. In this way, the accelerating advance of literacy in the nineteenth century can be seen to represent a movement towards cultural homogeneity and a unifying national identity, and not merely the generalization of neutral learning skills.

> The speaking of [Welsh] was strictly forbidden . . . The master every morning handed over to a child . . . a small block of wood, through which a string passed. That child was to watch and listen till he heard someone speak Welsh . . . Then the "Welsh stick" was passed on, and every child who held it had either a stroke of the cane, or two verses of the Bible to learn.[13]

Midway through his thirteenth year, Jones left school, followed his father's footsteps 'and put on my little shoe-maker's leather apron'. And here, his formative educational life might have ended, to be extended thereafter only through episodic private reading. He now had no model to follow, no idea of what further avenues to other realms of learning might exist. Such was the completeness of the hierarchical separation of different regimes of education. But in concert with a small group of likeminded boys, Jones formed a self-help group to advance their combined learning in some useful way; 'we met together once a week in the squire's gas-works to learn short-hand'. Though directionless and unguided, the little group nonetheless 'had our aspirations'. Even in this most traditional of rural settings, there was a perception of a world of unknown opportunity and challenge beyond, and an awareness that learning was the key to finding it; 'somehow or other there was always something "intellectual" going on amongst us'.

Jones and his two siblings were frequent performers at the regular 'penny readings', held in the village school, through which the villagers entertained and elevated themselves during the long winter evenings. At the age of about 14, now a skilled and practised shoemaker, one of Jones's performances at the 'penny readings' caught the eye of the wife of a wealthy local farmer, Mrs Roxburgh. Thereafter, he was a frequent visitor to the Roxburgh home – 'There I saw, for the first time, a floor covered by a carpet' – to learn from his benefactor's conversations and to borrow from her library. This new phase in his education lasted for three or four years. Despite the burgeoning new learning to which it led, Jones remained content with his lot as a shoemaker though his patron continually pressed upon him that he 'should be "something better than a shoe-maker" . . . shoemakers as a rule were an intemperate and low set. I ought not to be one of them: I ought to become a minister'. Jones could resist this prospect chiefly because his new learning had not yet punctured the cultural expectations which his secure familial and occupational background had bequeathed to him. 'Looking to the future I saw nothing out of place. I was not only to be the best shoe-maker in all the country round, but an elder in the chapel, and one of the neighbourhood's real but uncrowned leaders'. He had not yet become dissatisfied with his lot. Ultimately, however, the gulf between the world of home and work and the new world opened up by his continuing flirtation with learning came to be an unbridgeable one. The realization came to him in a moment of revelation of the sort which is not at all unusual in working-class autobiography. On a rare outing to the local market town to view a travelling menagerie, Jones noticed some of his workmates from his father's shoemaker's shop lounging at the door of a public house. This otherwise banal sight shocked the intellectual sensibility that had until then had not seemed to disturb the settled routine of his artisan existence.

> [I]t was by far the most startling event in my whole life. I was stunned and helpless. The things that Mrs Roxburgh had told me were true! My shop-mates *were* disreputable! Their companionship in the workshop would verily be both unbearable and ruinous . . . The views which Mrs Roxburgh had been pouring into my soul week by week and year by year had now accumulated like dammed waters. And now the dam had broken and I was swept away as by a flood . . . My whole life seemed to me to have been a mistake. It lay in ruins around my feet . . . Only one thing remained. I would become 'something better than a shoe-maker' or I would die in the attempt.[14]

In these words, Jones announced the start of an odyssey from one educational world to another. He had no clear idea of what his ultimate destination would be, but only that it would be defined by the quest for learning itself. Many, of whom only a few remain known to history, made the same journey, each necessarily in their own way. But the example of Jones's experience is important in highlighting some of the key elements which were necessary to render the struggle a successful one. Personal ability and determination were essential starting-points but, on their own, they could not be enough. The fundamental tools for a life of independent learning – the ability to write, to reckon and, in popular perception overwhelmingly the most important, to read – were best obtained through a substantial and uninterrupted period of formal schooling. School, as was the case for Jones, might not offer an environment of great intellectual challenge or invigoration, but it presented, nonetheless, a generally enjoyable experience. Nineteenth-century elementary schooling was not usually the wholly tyrannical affair of popular imagination and the evidence suggests that for most children it presented a more palatable prospect than premature labour or life on the street. The most critical factor in the sustained development of learning came through the subsequent stimulation of the basic skills learned in the schoolroom. As the evidence of the Children's Employment Commission shows, many young people found that their command of basic skills evaporated on leaving school. In this respect, Jones was fortunate, his growth as a self-improver being supported in the home, in the Sunday school, in his religious affiliation to the local chapel and in the company of like-minded peers. But all of these advantages would have amounted to little without a powerful catalyst to accelerate and organize learning and to orient it towards a tangible goal. For many, particularly in the early decades of the century, such a stimulus came from political radicalism, from the struggle for 'really useful knowledge', from the Co-operative Movement or from Chartism. For others as was the case, if in a modest way, for Jones, the critical agent came in the form of a sympathetic, knowledgeable and influential local patron, charmed by the prospect of liberating and advancing a captive intellect. Such an agent was essential both for opening new cultural dimensions of learning but also for establishing the crucial personal connections required for moving into unfamiliar social milieux.

The first step on the social ascent which would lead to Jones's ultimate academic celebrity is where we should leave his story, for the subsequent trajectory of his career thereafter becomes exceptional. This initial step, however, was one which was shared with many thousands of others for whom it represented the height of respectable

ambition for a girl or boy from a poor family. Jones became a pupil teacher, a classroom apprentice on the road to qualification as a trained and certificated teacher and,
as such, a traveller on one of the earliest and most important routes for occupational
mobility in the second half of the nineteenth century. In fact, we might configure
the symbolic and practical importance of the pupil teacher still more widely to stand
as one of the most significant and dynamic manifestations of nineteenth-century
popular schooling. Developed in the late 1830s by Kay-Shuttleworth and formalized
by government action in 1846, pupil teaching has been persuasively construed as 'the
earliest attempt of the State . . . to undertake the direction and control of elementary
education'.[15] Indeed, we might see the emerging figure of the pupil teacher as one
of the most significant devices woven into the larger fabric of educational change
across the century. In systemic terms, pupil teaching formed the bow wave of popular
educational advance, with the academic expectations of pupil teachers constantly
nudging upward to encroach upon curricular provinces traditionally available only to
those from more elevated backgrounds.

   At the start of the nineteenth century, Britain was far from being an unschooled
or illiterate society. In fact, there were schools everywhere – including ancient
endowed schools in varying stages of decline, newer charity schools, parish schools,
infant schools, the ubiquitous Sunday schools and private schools of every description from the meanest dame school to the most select academy. Such a variety was
reflected in an endemic looseness and ambiguity in contemporary definitions of
'school' and 'scholar'. This is one of the reasons why modern histories which aspire
to the establishment of numerical certainties in nineteenth-century education have
such a difficult task. In this respect, quantitative approaches cannot be separated from
qualitative; the calculation of statistics of nineteenth-century schooling cannot escape
the original definitional assumptions which rendered quantification an interpretive
process and not a neutral one. Many educational institutions were of very poor
quality, both materially and academically; some were ephemeral; most were very
small; relatively few did not charge fees. On each of these criteria, amongst others,
the nation's schools could be seen to form one vast continuum of provision into
which users dipped as and when they could and at the level they could best afford.
The notion of learning, moreover, had not yet been collapsed into that of schooling
and the idea of the school had to compete alongside other, informal traditions of
learning in the home or the local community. Between them, the available opportunities for learning supported a level of basic literacy – defined by the ability to sign
the marriage register – approaching 50 per cent for women and between 60 and 65
per cent for men. These were proportions which remained relatively stable from the
late eighteenth century until the 1840s, which saw the beginning of a general and
consistent upward trend culminating in the achievement of an effectively universal
literacy by the end of the century.[16]

   From the earliest years of the century, the most immediate and urgent problem
of schooling provision resulted from a chronic shortage of suitable teachers to staff
formal elementary schools. The majority of these were supplied, as an integral aspect
of their pastoral mission, by organized religion and predominantly, of course, by the
Church of England. In accordance with the prevailing hermetic imperative governing educational provision, the teachers for each grade of schools characteristically
came from that class of society to which such schools were directed. This cultural

consonance meant that working-class private schools, for example, were often chosen by working-class parents above alternative options, apparently superior in quality and certainly cheaper in cost. But whilst the maintenance of a hierarchical organization of schools according to social distinction did not seem at all objectionable to those concerned with educational policy, it was accompanied by a recognition, new to the early nineteenth century and most succinctly evidenced in the reports of local statistical societies, of the transformative potential of mass schooling. In this sense, Johnson's assertion that 'the education of the poor was . . . one of the strongest of early Victorian obsessions' is well judged.[17] To the degree that schools were increasingly perceived – whether by the churches or, in a quite different way, by utilitarian reformers – as key sites for the moral reformation of a parental culture interpreted as deficient, dangerous and 'vicious', then questions of teacher quality and supply became critical. Teachers had to be morally reliable agents as well as effective ones. This implied the need for a cadre of teachers drawn ideally from the middling or the professional classes. But the remuneration, social status, conditions of service and the prospects of the work meant that teaching held no attractions for members of these groups. Recruitment therefore had to continue to come primarily from the working class itself. However, if such recruits were to secure the tasks with which they were charged, then they too would require to pass through a transformative process. They would, in other words, have to be trained. This was an expectation, it should be added, that was not seriously entertained in respect of the secondary sector until nearly a hundred years later. The nineteenth century therefore became the century of the trained elementary teacher, a characteristically isolated figure, earnest and misunderstood, lampooned and ridiculed from above, regarded from below with a combination of admiration and distrust.

Trained teachers would not appear overnight. How could an effective supply of schooling be put in place in the meantime? This was not yet a question directly for the state but for the traditional voluntary suppliers of schools, the churches and their associated educational societies who took the lead in seeking to provide new schools, particularly in those urban areas of most rapid growth. The brilliant solution of these bodies to the problem of teacher supply was the introduction of schools run on the monitorial system. Here, hundreds of children could say their lessons under the gaze of a single trained teacher, surveying the assembled ranks from an elevated vantage point at the head of the great barn-like edifice which such an organization required. The body of scholars was notionally, less often physically, subdivided into numerous graduated groupings, each under the immediate tutelage of a senior pupil, a monitor, a 'conduit-pipe of knowledge', who schooled his or her charges according to principles and practices inculcated at a daily preliminary meeting of teacher and monitors.[18] The clear and widely rehearsed analogy between schools organized on such lines and, on the one hand the factory, on the other the panopticon, has provided an obvious but frequently fruitful point of departure for modern historical analyses adhering, respectively, to Marxian social theory in the 1960s, 1970s and 1980s or, more recently, to the non-narrative approaches associated with Foucault. The epistemological status accorded to substantive histories guided by either of these theoretical orientations can be contested. What cannot be doubted, however, is that each has had a significant and welcome methodological impact in reminding us, through their respective insistence upon ideology or discourse, of the dangers of literal or uncritical readings of nineteenth-century educational sources which traditional correspondence histories have assumed and asserted.

Pupil teaching was essentially a rationalization and development of the monitorial strategy into a national programme which, at the age of 13, offered to the brightest and the best of elementary scholars a five-year apprenticeship under the guidance of their erstwhile headteachers. The scheme was an expression of the same thinking which also produced the half-time system for scholars by which child workers divided their waking hours between the classroom and the mill. It reminds us that the idealized relation between protective teacher and dependent pupil which would come to govern the educational life of the twentieth century was a construction that was established only in the closing decades of the nineteenth. But the pupil-teacher system was important in another respect. Its financial and administrative configuration confirmed the complex relation which, from the 1830s, the state had chosen to follow in educational policy. From the early years of the nineteenth century, the question of the schooling of the people, and particularly of the urban working class, was a substantial policy concern. In particular, the need for both the enhancement and the systematization of educational provision were recognized on all sides. What divided opinion was the practical question of how these goals were to be achieved. A radical minority urged the adoption of a system of state-run compulsory schooling on the continental model. Such a strategy, however, could be followed only if the traditional providers of popular schooling – the churches and their associated educational societies – were pushed aside by the agency of the state. Such a costly and politically dangerous course was rendered unnecessary precisely because its very prospect, together with the reality of vigorous local denominational competition to supply new school places, stimulated a process of unprecedented school building – the elementary school 'contest' – particularly in areas of rapid industrial and urban growth.

From the 1830s, therefore, the fundamental assumption which guided education policy for the rest of the century had been adumbrated. The job of the state was to supply from the centre only those systemic elements which were not, or could not be, supplied by the voluntary effort of the churches. Its task was to support and to subsidize, but also to investigate, to guide, to set national standards, to inspect and, famously in the Act of 1870 and its Scottish equivalent of 1872, ultimately to 'fill the gaps' where voluntary agency appeared unable to keep up. If novel in scope and sheer scale, the principle of addressing such gaps, it should be noted, was not entirely new in 1870, having earlier stimulated legislative action in the 1830s to secure, however inadequately, indirect forms of compulsory schooling for pauper children and child labourers through poor law and factory legislation. The state, in other words, perceived a new obligation to intervene on behalf of those who stood outside the generality of those marginally better-off populations to whom voluntary effort – with the notable exception of the philanthropic ragged-school movement – chiefly addressed itself.

Despite the 1846 pupil-teacher reforms, the single most significant characteristic of mid-nineteenth-century educational provision – though certainly considerably less true of the more uniform Scottish experience – was its fundamentally unsystematic structure and form. In the second half of the century however, systematization began to develop at an increasing pace, driven by accelerating social and political pressures which proved historically difficult to reconcile. The former operated through the institutionalization of highly visible and explicit hierarchical gradations, based on class and increasingly upon gender distinctions. This meant that schools came, more than they had ever done before, to function as badges of distinctive social status and indices of normative educational expectation. The latter reflected a growing recognition by the state that the supply of schooling, at least in so far as it applied to the working class, required effective regulation and standardization in the interests of maintaining an expanding and progressive policy agenda. This included the accommodation of new idealized constructions of childhood which, contingent upon the falling demand for child labour, redefined both its duration and the degree of its dependency upon the world of adults; the nurturing of a citizenry sufficiently educated to discharge its new political duties in a period of progressive electoral reform; and the defence of enhanced levels of economic efficiency and technical sophistication in the face of mounting international competition in trade and industry. The degree of the relative success or failure of contemporary policy in each of these areas has provoked considerable historical debate, with the last, the question of the linkage between the culpabilities of late-nineteenth-century public policy in education and the origins of a supposed subsequent national economic decline, proving particularly lively.

In terms of its historical significance for the development of national education, the 1870 Education Act occupies a paramount position in all accounts. But any assessment of the provenance or the impact of the 1870 Act cannot be confined merely to technical systematization, to the tidying up of local deficiencies in school supply, or to the acceleration of the pre-existing upward trend in literacy rates. Though it was by no means solely responsible for them, the Act was also implicated in profound changes in social and political perceptions of the place of popular schooling in national life. H. G. Wells's famous assertion that the Act was designed 'to educate the lower classes for employment on lower-class lines . . . with specially trained, inferior teachers' established an enduringly influential strain of radical functionalism in the literature of educational history which placed at its centre the mechanical device of 'social control'. The link between social inequality and differentiated educational opportunity was, and remains, a powerful one. But 'social control' has proved itself to be far too crude an instrument with which to address a process which was increasingly a channel for growth, agency and production as well as for limitation, structure and reproduction. Expectations of education in the second half of the nineteenth century were always more complex than this. On the supply side, the late-Victorian anxiety over notions of liberal or organic citizenship indicated a leading role for education in maintaining a balance between what Reeder has seen as 'the prudential concern for a stable moral order and the progressive concern to promote modernising social and cultural forces'.[19] The development and influence of elite political discourses of national educational reform are complex but eminently discernible; Reeder, for example, pursues the debate through the contemporary writings of, amongst others, Lowe, Playfair, Green and Sadler.

Movements in the nature of the popular demand for schooling are far more poorly understood and are considerably less easy to chart. For citizens of the 'schooled society' of the twentieth and twenty-first centuries, the nature and the extent of the change in popular opinion during the last quarter of the nineteenth century are difficult to appreciate fully. The normative association of a progressively extended period of childhood defined by the assured experience of compulsory formal schooling has constituted the expectation of every British child for more than a century. It has seemed to be, and has become, natural. But the forging of this link was a very hard-won political achievement, reflecting that elemental movement in which Lowndes saw the origins of an educational transformation which he eloquently dubbed 'the silent social revolution'.[20] In its impact upon the behaviour and attitudes of the masses of children and parents whom it influenced so spectacularly, historians have given the origins of this revolution surprisingly little detailed attention. This story, of the winning of popular acquiescence for schooling that was rendered generally compulsory (in 1880) before it was made generally free (in 1895), is likely to be an immensely complex one. It will demand a greater emphasis not only upon the ways in which national schooling was newly represented in popular imagination but also upon the sites – particularly the classroom itself – where such representations were constructed and commemorated.

Looking back from the 1880s, with the most successful of the large urban school boards beginning the work of building popular support within working-class constituencies, Francis Adams contrasted the dominating national mood in education at the close of the century with that at its beginning. Then, he wrote, education 'had been played and coquetted with by sects, and interests and cliques, but it had never got down to the people'.[21] One of the most remarkable features of the school-board period was its success in 'getting down to the people' through the process of building real, if seldom very demonstrative, bonds of popular loyalty between locally elected school boards, publicly provided schools and their working-class users. That powerful combination of negative and positive impulses – class suspicion and parental autonomy – which, a few years before, had kept some publicly subsidized church schools half empty and had sustained a long tradition of independent working-class private schooling, began to fade. The inculcation of what Thomas Gautrey of the School Board for London thoughtfully noted as the 'school habit' changed the face of child-thronged Victorian cities – and, to a significantly lesser degree, the face of the countryside – along with the sensibilities and expectations of working-class parents. These were changes which were achieved incrementally, inch by inch, the cumulative result of thousands of unmarked daily confrontations between parents, teachers, children, policemen and school-attendance officers at street corners, front doors and school gates. After 1870, the idea of education and of learning was regularized, subsumed by the experience of schooling as a formal progress through a series of specified 'standards'.

If many liberal educational historians have understood the school-board period as simply a speeding up in an essentially benign process of national educational development, an important tendency associated with the work of Simon has conceived these years in far more radical terms, as part of a broader conflict analysis of nineteenth-century education. Simon sees the school-board years as a period in which popular educational demand and local policy came closer than they had ever been, producing the potential for the building of an alternative structure of national education that eschewed the traditional principles of exclusion and separation, and prefiguring an egalitarian, comprehensive system of education. A motif for this interpretation comes in the words of Thomas Smyth, giving evidence before the Cross Commission of 1888: 'We feel that [board schools] are our own, more or less; that they are really practically in the highest sense of the thing the beginning of a national system of schools'.[22] Between them, the argument goes, the agency of the school boards, the increase in public spending and the depth of local popular support stimulated improvements in the quality of educational provision. These were particularly exemplified by further reforms in pupil teaching and by the appearance of higher-grade schools with curricula that were not only more advanced but also more technically oriented. Each of these developments threatened the inherited hierarchical structure of national schooling and Simon's analysis sees the legislative demise of the school boards as the culmination of a central policy designed by, and in the interests of, political and economic elites to restore traditional horizontal divisions in education.

The role of the central agency of the state in the development of nineteenth-century education has constituted one of the most venerable debates in the field of educational history. The most interesting of these debates have generally been those which have addressed the British case in terms of its own historical development rather than as a deviation from an idealized developmental model in which the British experience is seen to exhibit 'late' or 'delayed' state involvement. From a liberal viewpoint, the cause of the 'delay' has been seen to revolve principally around the 'religious difficulty', in which the vested educational interests of the churches for many years dissuaded more aggressive public intervention.[23] From a more radical perspective, the problem has rested more with a variety of the 'peculiarities of the English' argument with its identification of an associated non-revolutionary path towards the formation of a modern state apparatus.[24] In the neo-liberal view, the entire effort of the educational state from 1870 onwards is conceived as a catastrophic and unnecessary mistake, as 'better never than late'.[25] This view rests upon a provocative if misconceived problematization of contemporary distinctions between private and public agency in the nineteenth century, and upon a flawed educational arithmetic which insists that any deficiencies in the pre-1870 provision of schooling were capable of resolution through the renewed efforts of private agency without the intervention of the state. More interesting treatments are those which operate under a more explicitly historicist impulse – that is to say, which seek to interpret historical events through the eyes of the past rather than through the ideological predilections of the present. Thus, Silver seeks to alert us to the critical importance of the 1860s as the decade to which we should particularly attend for clues to explain the general and deep-seated shifts in popular thinking on education in subsequent years.[26]

Nineteenth-century educational reform was directed primarily and most urgently towards the reconfiguration of popular schooling. By the close of the century, a vocal lower-middle-class constituency could indeed protest that their educational interests had been squeezed between the operation of an exclusive private market in secondary and higher education for the rich and an increasingly costly public subvention for the elementary education of the poor. Reform in secondary and higher education, if less dramatic than for popular schooling, was driven by the same cumulative trend towards systematization, modernization and the alleviation or circumvention of religious obstacles to expansion. Moreover, across all branches of education – with the exception of the great public schools, where reform was largely generated internally, partly in response to new parental demands – change conformed to a common strategic pattern. Legislative or administrative reform in each case followed in the wake of detailed and extensive enquiries by influential Royal Commissions: the Clarendon Commission of 1852–3 investigating the state of the ancient universities; the Newcastle Commission of 1861 on the state of popular education, and its successor, the Cross Commission of 1888; the Schools Inquiry Commission of 1868 on the endowed secondary schools; the Samuelson Report of 1882–4 on technical education; and the Bryce Report of 1895 on secondary schooling. Several careful and constructive traditional historical treatments of the reform of the university and secondary sectors of education, their attendant examination structures and their progressively closer relation to a system increasingly perceived in national terms, have been produced in recent years. But, still more significantly, this field has increasingly been dominated by the exercise of powerful and immensely instructive revisionist accounts drawing upon feminist theory – unquestionably the most important advance in the writing of educational history in recent years. Initially such work drew principally upon patriarchal or essentialist paradigms, emphasizing the recovery of the distinctive, exclusionary educational experiences of girls and women, but latterly there has also been a turn towards the insights of post-structuralism, towards the re-problematization of foundational gender categories and a new emphasis upon the significance of language in the construction of educational history.

Feminist histories of nineteenth-century education have drawn particular attention to formal learning as a key site for the transformation of the mid-century ideology of 'separate spheres', most spectacularly evidenced in the influential writings of Ruskin. The struggle for the establishment of girls' high schools, for the systematic training of women teachers and for access to higher education, as well as the progressive feminization of the elementary teaching profession following the Revised Code provisions of 1862, all announced education in the second half of the nineteenth century as a unique site where women's personal, social and professional ambitions and aspirations could draw upon the experience of an established and functioning sphere of genuine professional status and authority. This was an experience, however, which led not to the heroic masculine model of the inspired individual pedagogue or omnipotent educational administrator, but to the development of interpersonal networks for educational advance and the achievement of spaces for the exercise of a different kind of educational agency. It was an experience, in other words, within which the complex intersection of the public and the private could be both personally and collectively renegotiated. And if it took the struggles of women on their own behalf in the late nineteenth century to notify men that the liberating promise of education and learning could not in the end be stopped up or differentially parcelled out – as the autodidacts of the early years of the century had also known – it has taken the pioneering work of women educational historians of the late twentieth century to remind us of the rich complexities and continuing consequences of this fact.

NOTES

1. F. Adams, *History of the Elementary School Contest in England* (Brighton, 1972).
2. J. Hurt, *Elementary Schooling and the Working Classes 1860–1918* (London, 1979), p. 5.
3. P.P. 1863 xviii, *Children's Employment Commission (1862). First Report of the Commissioners. With Appendix*, p. 115.

4. P.P. 1842, xvi, *Reports from Commissioners (2). Children's Employment (Mines)*, p. 617.

5. P.P. 1842, xvi, p. 86.

6. P.P. 1842, xvi, p. 84.

7. R. D. Anderson, *Education and the Scottish People, 1750–1918* (Oxford, 1995).

8. M. Sanderson, *The Universities and British Industry, 1850–1970* (London, 1972), p. 396.

9. D. Vincent, *Literacy and Popular Culture: England 1750–1914* (Cambridge, 1989);
    J. Burnett, ed., *Destiny Obscure: Autobiographies of Childhood, Education and Family
    from the 1820s to the 1920s* (London, 1982); J. Rose, *The Intellectual Life of the British
    Working Classes* (New Haven, CT, 2001).

10. E. Wilkinson, 'Ellen Wilkinson, MA, MP', in M. Oxford, ed., *Myself When Young, By
    Famous Women of To-day* (London, 1938), p. 404.

11. P.P. 1907, lxiv, *General Report on the Instruction and Training of Pupil-Teachers,
    1903–1907, With Historical Introduction*, p. 14.

12. W. E. Marsden, *Unequal Educational Provision in England and Wales: The Nineteenth-
    Century Roots* (London, 1987); W. B. Stephens, *Education, Literacy and Society: The
    Geography of Diversity in Provincial England* (Manchester, 1987).

13. H. Jones, *Old Memories* (London, 1923), pp. 29, 13, 30, 32.

14. Jones, *Old Memories*, pp. 35, 54–5, 66, 69, 72–3.

15. P.P. 1907, lxiv, p. 3.

16. D. Mitch, 'The role of human capital in the first industrial revolution', in J. Mokyr, ed.,
    The British Industrial Revolution (Boulder, CO, 1993), p. 275.

17. R. Johnson, 'Education policy and social control in early Victorian England', *Past and
    Present*, 49 (1979), p. 96.

18. P.P. 1898, xxvi, *General Report on the Instruction and Training of Pupil-Teachers,
    1903–1907, With Historical Introduction*, p. 1.

19. D. Reeder, ed., *Educating Our Masters* (Leicester, 1980), p. 29.

20. G. A. N. Lowndes, *The Silent Social Revolution* (Oxford, 1937).

21. Adams, *History*.

22. B. Simon, *Education and the Labour Movement, 1870–1920* (London, 1965), p. 123.

23. M. Sturt, *The Education of the People: A History of Primary Education in England and
    Wales in the Nineteenth Century* (London, 1967).

24. A. Green, *Education and State Formation: The Rise of Education Systems in England,
    France and the USA* (London, 1990).

25. E. G. West, *Education and the Industrial Revolution* (London, 1975).

26. H. Silver, *Education as History: Interpreting Nineteenth- and Twentieth-Century Educa-
    tion* (London, 1983), pp. 81–99.

FURTHER READING

Concise and incisive introductory surveys include M. Sanderson, *Education, Economic Change and Society in England 1780–1870* (1995), W. B. Stephens, *Education in Britain 1750–1914* (1998) and G. Sutherland, 'Education', in F. M. L. Thompson, ed., *The Cambridge Social History of Britain, 1750–1950*, vol. 3, *Social Agencies and Institutions* (1990). A comprehensive critical survey of past and present trends in educational historiography can be found in W. Richardson, 'Historians and educationists: the history of education as a field of study in post-war England', *History of Education*, 28 (1999). G. McCulloch and W. Richardson, *Historical Research in Educational Settings* (2000) has made a useful start to the addressing of methodological problems and approaches in the history of education. R. Lowe, ed., *History of Education: Major Themes* (2000) is an invaluable multi-volume collection of seminal articles exploring central themes in the modern history of education.

M. Sturt, *The Education of the People: A History of Primary Education in England and Wales in the Nineteenth Century* (1967) offers a solid and resilient account of the liberal interpretation of nineteenth-century educational growth. A radical alternative reading can be found in B. Simon, *Education and the Labour Movement* (1965) and *The State and Educational Change: Essays in the History of Education and Pedagogy* (1994). Simon's approach has stimulated a good deal of work in similar vein, with M. Vlaeminke, *The English Higher Grade Schools: A Lost Opportunity* (2000) an impressive recent example. I. Copeland, *The Making of the Backward Pupil in Education in England 1870–1914* (1999) is an attempt to apply a Foucauldian approach to a substantive historical problem and may be compared with J. Hurt, *Outside the Mainstream: A History of Special Education* (1988) which takes a more traditional reconstructionist perspective.

Analyses of the institutional growth of an administrative machinery for national education are provided by A. S. Bishop, *The Rise of a Central Authority for English Education* (1971) and G. Sutherland, *Policy Making in Elementary Education 1870–1895* (1973). For trends in the development of literacy, as well as for discussion of technical and interpretive problems in such work, see W. B. Stephens, *Education, Literacy and Society: The Geography of Diversity in Provincial England* (1987) and D. Mitch, *The Rise of Popular Literacy in Victorian England* (1992). For outstanding accounts illuminating the popular uses of literacy rather than the progress of institutional provision, see D. Vincent, *Literacy and Popular Culture: England 1750–1914* (1989) and J. Rose, *The Intellectual Life of the British Working Classes* (2001), together with R. D. Altick, *The English Common Reader: A Social History of the Mass Reading Public 1800–1900* (1998). W. E. Marsden, *Unequal Educational Provision in England and Wales: The Nineteenth-Century Roots* (1987) is an original and revealing investigation accentuating the profound importance of regional and local factors in patterns of urban educational activity, whilst P. Horn, *Education in Rural England 1800–1914* (1978) has produced the most detailed account of local schooling.

For the development of secondary education, see D. Allsobrook, *Schools for the Shires: The Reform of Middle-Class Education in Mid-Victorian England* (1986); for higher education, R. D. Anderson, *Universities and Elites in Britain since 1800* (1992) is a good starting-point while S. Rothblatt, *The Modern University and its Discontents* (1997) is stimulating and perceptive. For the teaching profession, A. Tropp, *The Schoolteachers* (1957) is essential. For changing perceptions of childhood, see H. Hendrick, *Child Welfare: England 1872–1989* (1994). From an extensive literature on the education of girls and women, see C. Dyhouse, *Girls Growing Up in Late Victorian and Edwardian England* (1981), J. Purvis, *A History of Women's Education in England* (1991) and J. Goodman and S. Harrop, eds, *Women, Educational Policy-Making and Administration in England* (2000).

CHAPTER TWENTY-TWO

The Press and the Printed Word

ALED JONES

The many forms of printed communication produced during the nineteenth century, which included formats as diverse as ballads, broadsides, chapbooks, newspapers, magazines and books, have long provided historians with valuable entry points into a wide range of subject areas in modern British history. These include histories as seemingly disparate as those of gender, class, technology, commerce, transport, religious belief, literacy and education, fiscal policy, government and political organization, social control, biography, family life, leisure and popular taste. Historians, however, have long argued that, as well as being a valuable source for the study of these subjects, the products of the printing press need also to be regarded as participants in, rather than simply observers of, the transformation of Victorian society. The notion that the press was an agent of change, and was constitutive of meaning in the sense that it both embodied and helped to shape popular perceptions of the world, to a large extent explains the growing volume of studies published during the second half of the twentieth century. These began with a trickle of seminal works by Webb, Altick, Raymond Williams and others in the 1950s and 1960s, and which have now led to the broad and multi-directional streams of published research, within and outside specialist journals, and across several disciplines, that are available to us today.[1] This chapter aims to capture some of the flavour of that work, and to show how the history of print may offer fresh ways of approaching some of the questions historians ask about British history in the nineteenth century.

The expansion of print in nineteenth-century Britain was made possible in part by the availability of new composing and steam-printing technologies, and by the development of improved methods of distribution, especially by means of better roads and, later, the railways. Population growth, urbanization and the growing prosperity of the industrial and commercial sectors of the economy, enriched by the expansion of national and colonial markets for British manufactured goods, further fuelled demand for print, and the information and opportunities for educational and cultural advancement it contained. Newspapers in particular were poised to take advantage of these circumstances, and quickly developed elaborate forms of news-gathering and new outlets for commercial advertising which positioned them favourably in the growing market-place for printed goods. Until the middle of the century, however, these pressures for growth were constrained by a number of powerful fiscal and ideological forces. Most significantly, legislation intended to raise revenue for the Treasury and, simultaneously, to control the growth of a cheap, popularly accessible and often politically radical newspaper press had made print, especially news print, extremely expensive. To a lesser extent, the lack of free and universal educational provision may also have restricted demand among the poor, although evidence suggests that, during the first half of the century, the level of publication of printed material lagged behind surprisingly high levels of popular literacy, especially if literacy is defined principally as the ability to read.

Stamp Acts introduced in 1712 imposed a tax on each copy of a periodical publication carrying news, an obstacle to growth that was accompanied by a flat-rate duty on advertisements and on paper. These duties were steadily increased until, by 1815, they stood at 4d stamp tax on every copy of a newspaper, 3s 6d for every advertisement they carried, and a further 3d per pound weight of newsprint. Under this fiscal regime, a new copy of *The Times*, for example, would cost 7d to buy. These taxes were rendered even more stringent by the emergency anti-seditious legislation of 1819 (the 'Six Acts'), while other forms of regulation, including a financial security deposit imposed on printers by successive libel laws, acted as further restraints on the operation of a 'free-market' press. Reaction against these restrictions proliferated during the 1820s and the early 1830s, when radical journalists in particular led the campaign against the stamp duty by producing and distributing hundreds of illegal, unstamped newspapers – Wiener records 562 such titles produced in the period 1830–6, their prices ranging from 1d to 3d per issue.[2] Many were outspokenly oppositional, demanding the reform not only of the press laws, but also of an unrepresentative political system, and attacked the inequalities of power and wealth that manifestly existed in British society. Some drew inspiration from Cobbett's *Political Register*, first launched in 1802, which became a stridently radical news-sheet in 1809, selling some 40,000 copies for 2d each by the end of the Napoleonic Wars. Cobbett continued to edit the paper until he died in 1835, shortly before the Stamp Act was reformed. He and Hone, imprisoned for printing 'scandalous libels' in 1818, were two of many precursors of the illegal press campaign of the 1830s who not only challenged political orthodoxies but also extended the demand for serials that began to resemble the combination of news, comment and entertainment which were to be found in newspapers, the first of which had appeared in England in 1701. Carrying such evocative titles as the *Poor Man's Guardian*, established by Hetherington in July 1831, the *Radical* (1831–2), the *Republican; or, Voice of the People* (1831–2) and the *Destructive* (1833–4), these and other titles produced by such leading figures of the reform movement, notably Carpenter, Watson and Cleave, were important, some have argued essential, elements of the popular politics that led to both the Chartist and the free-trade movements in early- and mid-nineteenth-century Britain.

It would be misleading, however, to characterize the entire phenomenon of the unstamped press as being driven by demands for radical reform, or indeed to regard those that were as being solely geared to the achievement of political and social change. Many drew lavishly on the existing traditions of the penny chapbooks and the police gazettes, such as Smith's *Bawbee Bagpipe* of 1833, which mixed political

radicalism with fiction and, by later standards, crudely reproduced graphics. Furthermore, in the early months of 1832, at least eighteen penny satirical papers could
be found being produced in London – sporting titles like *Figaro in London* (1831–9)
or the *Devil's Memorandum Book* (1832). Thus the ballads, song-books (which later
in the nineteenth century grew in popularity alongside that of the music hall) and
chapbooks that had been the dominant popular print forms of the eighteenth century
bequeathed significant elements of their styles and formats to the newspaper and
magazine serials that gained large-scale readerships from the 1830s onwards.

Sparks has argued that the press, being 'a portmanteau term' with few unifying
characteristics other than a mechanical means of production, 'is produced for different social classes', and that newspaper titles are used and consumed differently
depending on the class and cultural contexts in which they are read.[3] This analysis is
persuasive with regard to the radical unstamped papers, and the particular styles and
discursive strategies employed by their editors. Yet it remains difficult to demarcate
social boundaries in the reading habits of serials in general at this time. Evidence suggests that less well-off readers could and did gain access to the contents of the higher-
priced newspapers by employing a variety of methods which included the reading
aloud of newspapers in public houses, the formation of newspaper clubs where the
high costs of titles might be shared by a circle of readers, the purchase of newspapers for lower prices in the days after they were printed, and the growing availability of reading rooms and libraries which included a range of newspaper and magazine
titles. Many of those concerned and threatened by the social and political messages
being put out by the cheap radical and satirical weeklies came to the view that social
stability might best be assured by adopting a strategy of making 'respectable' newspapers even more widely available, primarily by reducing their price. Partly in response
to these pressures, in 1836 the duty on newspapers was reduced from 4d to 1d. This
was, in many respects, a hollow victory for the advocates of a 'free press', since governments continued to restrict diversity, partly by means of a more aggressive enforcement of the law. Following the passing of the 1836 Act, the volume of newspaper
titles gradually increased, as did their circulations, while the number of radical, anti-
establishment titles fell drastically. Perhaps the most important and popular radical
journal of the first half of the nineteenth century, the Chartist *Northern Star*, it should
be noted, was launched in 1837 as a legal, stamped newspaper.

As the vibrancy of the unstamped became transformed into the commercial speculation of the post-1836 newspaper market, the 'key to popular literature' was not
radical or revolutionary politics, but melodrama.[4] Again, the older forms of the news
broadside, the printed ballad and the 'dying confessions' of condemned prisoners, so
widespread in late-eighteenth- and early-nineteenth-century popular culture, became
absorbed into the journalism of a more commercialized newspaper sector from the
1830s. This can be seen in the extensive column-space in newspapers that was
devoted to verse, serialized fiction, book and theatre reviews, and imaginatively
recounted crime reports, as well as in their political and cultural comment, home and
foreign news items and advertising. This was especially true of the popular Sunday
newspapers, which grew in importance from the 1840s.[5] There can be little doubt
that the three major Sundays, *Lloyd's Newspaper* (1842), *News of the World* (1843)
and *Reynolds's Newspaper* (1850), which had led the way in new forms of reporting

for a popular readership, including those in the armed forces, provided the cheapest and the most convenient, readable and appealing forms of journalism for working-class readers during the middle decades of the century.

The most powerful title of the entire first half of the nineteenth century, however, was *The Times*, established in 1785. Under the editorship of two hugely influential and successive editors, Thomas Barnes (1817–41) and John Thadeus Delane (1841–77), it had assumed a dominant position in terms of the size, remuneration and distribution of its reporting staff, its access to information and its political clout. Only the Peelite *Morning Chronicle* (1769), the *Morning Post* (1772), the *Standard* (1827) and the Liberal *Daily News* (1846) posed any significant challenge to its supremacy, and each lagged far behind *The Times* in terms of its circulation. More substantial periodicals, which appeared less frequently than the newspapers, were also much in evidence. At the beginning of the century, this sector was dominated by such quarterly journals as the *Edinburgh Review* (1802) and the *Quarterly Review* (1809), both of which enjoyed circulations of thirteen to fourteen thousand copies in the 1810s, and which provided platforms for Whigs and Tories respectively to reach Britain's educated reading public. Monthly literary and political magazines became popular from the middle of the century, while fortnightlies followed in its final decades and political weeklies in the 1900s. What is truly striking about these periodicals is their diversity, and the human industry they embodied, in areas as wide-ranging as religion, music, medicine, every conceivable form of political movement and pressure group, not to mention imaginative writing and reviewing. Some titles reflected the growing professionalization of highly specific occupational groups, such as medicine in the *Lancet* (1823), while others staked out particular political positions, including the free trade organ the *Economist* (1843). *Household Words* (1850) became a forcing-house for new fiction, *Punch* (1841) pioneered satirical writing and illustration, a charivari in print, while the *Illustrated London News* (1842) hugely expanded the possibilities of pictorial journalism. A number of these ventures were closely associated with book publishing. Macmillan's, for example, had been set up in 1843 to publish books, but launched the highly successful *Macmillan's Magazine* in 1859.

The expansion of print during the first half of the century, however constrained that growth may have been by legislation, was nonetheless the subject of a lively debate. By effectively introducing a new order of information, popular print in particular altered the boundaries of social knowledge in what were understood at the time to be some potentially destabilizing ways. In other words, more readers were gaining access to a broader range of information and argument than had ever been the case before. Whether or not such a process was regarded as socially progressive depended on the perceived nature of the publications under scrutiny and the capacity of those who read them to adopt the good and resist the bad. Social reformers and conservatives alike were divided in their opinion, but one of the most striking manifestations of this anxiety about the possibly ruinous consequences of licentious print on the moral and social order appeared in 1826 under the banner of the 'march of intellect' and the Society for the Diffusion of Useful Knowledge (SDUK), founded by Henry Brougham. The circulation of its most popular publication, the *Penny Magazine*, exceeded 200,000 in 1832, though the enterprise collapsed into debt in 1846 when the hugely ambitious venture was drawn to a close. However, during those twenty years, a popular market for print, in all its forms, had effectively been created, and there can be no doubt that the activists of the SDUK had played their role in doing so. This is particularly true of the book trade. The SDUK launched its Library of Useful Knowledge in 1827, under the energetic leadership of Charles Knight. His attempt to saturate the market for print with 'wholesome', educational material succeeded, not so much in reducing labour militancy after the socially turbulent 1830s, but rather in publicizing the notion that enlightening literature for the 'masses' could be produced relatively cheaply.[6] Although the evidence points to a largely aspirational, middle-class readership, the argument had at least been made that a popular market existed for books, as well as for newspapers and magazines. In this manner, social activism around issues of moral improvement was itself one of the prime initiators of the new print world that came into being during the first half of the century. While it remains far from clear whether the SDUK won its war against the 'licentious' and 'seditious' press of cheap fiction, crime reporting from court cases, pornography, republicanism and political radicalism, there can be little doubt that print as a form of communication affected in some important ways the older oral traditions of popular culture and politics. For example, as the debating societies and literary salons of the bourgeoisie proliferated among workers in both London and the provinces, it is evident that the subjects of their discussions were often drawn from the pages of periodicals and newspapers. In these and other ways, print contributed to the process of opening up new areas about which people talked – about sport and morals as well as politics and market prices. By the same token, however, the proliferation of print in its mid-nineteenth-century forms may have also helped to ensure that there was less room in the culture for the public airing of other 'dangerous' discourses, such as sexuality or revolutionary politics. In these ways, the coming of popular print may be said to have contributed substantially to the transformed public sphere that had emerged in Britain by the middle of the century.

Other forces, too, were at work in broadening the market for print, and in particular for books. Elaborately illustrated prophetic and historical almanacs drew significant readerships, while the development of steam printing to replace hand production during the 1840s extended print's capacity to reach further into the reading population. The part-publication of fiction, popularized from 1836 by Dickens's *Pickwick Papers*, and the reduction by half of the average price of books between the 1820s and 1850s (albeit from an artificially high level), further increased the willingness of readers to devote some at least of their disposable incomes to the purchase of books. Much of this reading matter, however, had less to do with the dour improving texts of the SDUK than with the growing popularity from the late 1840s of melodramatic and Gothic romances, and woodcut-strewn crime and penny weekly serial novels. Some were openly plagiarized versions of the more successful authors, such as 'Bos's *The Penny Pickwick*.

The second half of the century saw the continued growth of new titles in all formats, and an accelerated trend in the reading and buying of newspapers, magazines and books. Circulating libraries, of which 1,000 were in operation by the middle of the century, by securing discounts from publishers paradoxically had the effect of keeping the price of books high. In 1852, however, a form of booksellers' protectionism known as 'underselling' was abolished, and discounts began to be offered in an open competition for buyers of books. The appearance of cheap reprints further expanded the market for inexpensive fiction, one that was soon to be dominated by George Routledge's Railway Library and the W. H. Smith railway bookstalls. These included pirated editions of American novels, then still unprotected by British copyright laws, and which led in 1852 to the phenomenal success in Britain of Harriet Beecher Stowe's *Uncle Tom's Cabin*. In addition, a more didactic body of material was produced from the late 1840s by Cassell, perhaps the most successful inheritor of the approach initially adopted by Brougham and Knight in the SDUK. Thomas Hardy, for example, taught himself German from Cassell's *Popular Educator*. The continued availability of printed reading matter in coffee houses, Mechanics' Institutes and village reading rooms further extended book readership, but, increasingly, reading became a more private and domestic affair as prices were reduced. Vincent has estimated that while in the 1840s a penny would buy a 250-word broadside, by the 1860s it would buy a 7,000-word serial, a 20,000-word novel by the 1880s and, from 1896, entire editions of classic works.[7]

The tax on news, though, remained a problem with significant political dimensions. The campaign to abolish the remaining 1d stamp duty on newspapers, and the remaining advertisement and paper taxes – collectively stigmatized in bourgeois laissez-faire as well as in plebeian radical politics as the 'taxes on knowledge' – became a *cause célèbre* within reforming circles, where opinion was increasingly in favour of freeing commercial activity from fiscal controls. Encouraged by the repeal of the Corn Laws in 1846, free traders in parliament, allied to some, though by no means all, newspaper proprietors and editors, continued to apply pressure on governments and the Treasury until the advertisement duty was abolished in 1853, the Stamp Act in June 1855 and the paper duty in 1861. Though resisted by *The Times* and the Provincial Newspaper Society, who sought to protect their established titles from cheaper competition, the coming of free trade in periodical print nevertheless opened up huge possibilities for both old and new titles. Coming as it did during a period of acute news-hunger brought about by the Crimean War, the impact of repeal was immediate. A wave of speculative activity led to a sudden and dramatic growth in the number of titles on the market, while the extension of railway lines and services, then under way in even the most remote areas, accelerated their distribution throughout the islands of Britain. Prices fell, advertising revenues rose and, most importantly, freedom from taxation made it possible for the first time to employ such new technologies of production as rotary, web-fed printing machines, which were wholly impractical in an age when every sheet of newsprint needed to be separately taxed. The fiscal deregulation of newspapers in the years between 1853 and 1861 led to the launching of such new titles as the *Daily Telegraph*, which first appeared on 29 June 1855 and promptly halved its price to 1d, the *Saturday Review* and a further sixteen major provincials, including the *Sheffield Daily Telegraph*. But the reforms also enabled many of the older titles to engage more actively in the market. The *Manchester Guardian*, founded as a weekly in 1821, became a daily in response to the changed competitive environment of 1855, as did the *Liverpool Post* and the *Scotsman*.

The mid-century reforms led to major changes in the structure and content of the newspaper press, and as well as in its scale and geographical reach. Fast and accurate news-gathering became a more urgent, and more profitable, necessity. The Reuters news agency, which took early advantage of the completion in 1850 of the new telegraph cable connecting the stock-exchanges of Paris and London, opened an office in London in 1851 and had by 1857 extended its reach as far as Russia. In 1859, *The Times* published its first major Reuters scoop, which signalled the beginning of a sophisticated, international news communication system. This was further accelerated when a cable link connecting Europe with the USA was laid in 1866, although Reuters had already been supplying American news to the European market for several years before that, including regular accounts of the Civil War and the Lincoln assassination. In Britain, Liberal journalists established the Central Press Agency in 1863, and, when it was bought by Conservative interests in 1870, set up an alternative National Press Agency in 1873. News agencies and the availability of cheap telegraph communication, nationalized as part of the Post Office in 1870, also contributed to the appearance in the 1870s of new halfpenny evening papers in the larger urban centres. Agencies also for a time stimulated the provincial weeklies, providing them with news, parliamentary sketches and speeches, features, fiction, even advertising. The practice of 'split printing' enabled editors of local newspapers to buy a proportion, normally a full half, or four pages, of their weekly text from specialist agencies already set up on stereotype plates. Others could buy popular fiction relatively inexpensively from such syndicated fiction agencies as Tillotson's of Bolton. Readers of provincial weeklies, particularly in the period between the 1850s and 1890, could thus gain regular access to a wide range of national and international news, as well as to some of the most popular authors of their day, in addition to local stories and comment.

Journalism also became more professionalized. The Provincial Newspaper Society, formed in 1836 (and renamed the Newspaper Society in 1889 when London newspaper proprietors joined the association), agitated successfully for the right of newspaper editors to stand for local elections and to become magistrates, and made significant amendments in their favour to the libel laws in 1881 and 1888, while the Press Association was founded in 1868, initially to fight the monopoly activity of the pre-nationalized telegraph companies. Both organizations sought to improve the social status of their industry, as did the Institute of Journalists, founded in 1884 as the National Association of Journalists, and the Society of Women Journalists, formed in 1895. New divisions of labour in the publishing industry, such as the emergence of sub-editors, and the training of reporters, created new hierarchies of skill, income and status which signified, by the final decade of the century, that the speculative boom of the immediate post-1855 period, led by what Lee termed 'a host of nobodies,' had been transformed into a far more concentrated phenomenon with 'modern' industrial practices.[8]

Curran has argued that this reform process had an 'ugly face' since the subsequent concentration of ownership and control reduced the diversity of the press and increased the power of the richest and most politically influential sections of late-Victorian society.[9] The paradox of fiscal deregulation was that it had both extended the potential for a diverse and democratic press, and accelerated the mechanization of production which, given the nature of the market economy, tended towards monopoly. Whereas type, for instance, had earlier been set by hand on wooden blocks, the introduction of composing machines in the 1860s vastly increased the speed at which type could be set. The revolutionary linotype machine, first used on the *New York Tribune* in 1886, and which was introduced into Britain in the 1890s, was by 1900 used to typeset twenty of the London dailies, and a further 200 provincial newspapers. As composing was speeded up, so was the capacity of rotary printing machines, a process which began to be electrified in Britain from 1884. As a consequence of these and other technological changes, Lee calculated that whereas it would take £25,000 to establish a London daily in 1850, that sum had quadrupled to £100,000 within twenty years.[10] Individual proprietors gave way to joint-stock companies, 4,000 of which were formed in England and Wales during the second half of the century. Correspondingly, the money-making potential of newspaper-publishing, particularly by means of selling advertising space, grew exponentially during the 1880s and 1890s. While the *Manchester Guardian* made profits of more than £20,000 per year from the 1860s, a London daily like the *Daily Telegraph* could turn an annual profit of some £120,000 in the 1880s. Capital accumulated by the more commercially successful titles, together with more efficient production and distribution methods, also began to change the pattern of consumer demand. Most strikingly, the balance between the London and the provincial newspapers, and between the evening and morning dailies, was transformed. Although the number of provincial dailies increased from 43 to 171 between 1868 and 1900, Brown has demonstrated how the London newspapers, increasingly concentrated in Fleet Street, became a national press both in terms of the distribution of their readership, and the geographical coverage of their news.[11]

Partly as a consequence of these broader changes, historians have argued that a new kind of journalism appeared during the last twenty years of the century. Prefigured by such popular titles as the *People* (1881), the *Daily Graphic* (1890) and George Newnes's *Westminster Gazette* (1893, printed on green paper), the 'Northcliffe revolution' may be said to have started on 4 May 1896 with the appearance of Alfred Harmsworth's halfpenny morning, the *Daily Mail*. It cost £500,000 to set up, but sales on the first day reached 400,000, and Harmsworth, later Viscount Northcliffe, announced that he had found a 'gold mine'. Newspapers were now big business, and the *Daily Mail* and other titles of its kind accelerated a process of concentrating media ownership that would, in the early twentieth century, be regarded by many as a major political problem, even a challenge to its nascent democracy.

Those anxieties had preoccupied many cultural and political critics for much of the nineteenth century, but the forms adopted by popular print in the 1880s and the 1890s came under particular scrutiny. The strikingly bold typography and the focus on human interest stories and interviews, which drew heavily on North American journalism, stimulated a range of critical responses. Arguably the most cogent and influential assault on the 'New Journalism' was published by Matthew Arnold in the May 1887 issue of the *Nineteenth Century*. In it, he berated the style and content of such newspapers as Stead's *Pall Mall Gazette* and O'Connor's *Star*, as well as, by implication, the journalism of such earlier pioneers of the genre as Yates and Greenwood. Its 'feather-brained' and wistful superficialities, which pandered to the undereducated, threatened to undermine cultural standards and the ethical basis of British society. However, a robust defence of the new style of 'independent' journalism had been made by Stead while serving his sentence in Holloway prison for abduction following his exposure in the *Pall Mall Gazette* of child prostitution in London. Published as 'Government by Journalism' in the *Contemporary Review* in 1886, his audacious polemic argued that the printing press had converted Britain into an 'assembly of the whole community'. Newspapers had become 'the organs by which the people give utterance to their will', and went on to propose that newspaper editors, by being 'nearer the people' were their true democratic representatives. 'An editor', Stead announced, was 'the uncrowned king of an educated democracy'.

Such hyperbole touched a raw nerve in late-Victorian Britain. The problems of democracy, political representation and the tensions between 'culture' and 'anarchy' were central to the ways in which the press, and the uses which readers made of it, were understood. The extensions to the franchise in 1867 and 1884 had increased the pressure on Conservative political leaders to challenge the Liberal dominance of the provincial press, especially in such cities as Newcastle, Birmingham and Manchester where Liberal editors and newspaper-owners were tightly enmeshed within the political worlds of their respective municipal corporations, and used them to project themselves into national, and even international, arenas. Joseph Cowen, editor and owner of the *Newcastle Daily Chronicle*, was not only a core member of the Newcastle political elite, but supported nationalist uprisings in Italy and in 1873 became the city's Liberal MP. In Birmingham, links between Joseph Chamberlain, as mayor and MP, and John Thackeray Bunce, editor of the *Birmingham Daily Post* from 1870 until 1899, provide further evidence of the symbiosis of politics and journalism at both regional and national levels. The *Manchester Guardian*, with roots deep in Manchester Liberalism, was transformed by C. P. Scott, its editor from 1872 until 1929, from a provincial into a national title. Elsewhere, provincial newspapers were owned and controlled by local industrialists: Colman owned the *Ipswich Express*, Tillotson the *Bolton Evening News* and, in Cardiff, coal-owner the Marquess of Bute had been responsible for launching the *Western Mail*.

These links between the press and political and economic power, at both local and national levels, stimulated arguments about the kind of knowledge that the press produced and disseminated, and the effects it might have not only on the individuals who read it but also on the broader nature of the society itself, arguments which continued to resonate throughout the twentieth century and into the twenty-first. Theorists associated with 'mass society' sociology and Frankfurt School philosophy, the latter being a despairing Marxist response to both the rise of Nazism in the interwar period and the triumph of Western consumerism that followed its defeat, saw in the commercialized media a flattening of human diversity and possibility into a compliant 'one-dimensional' culture which further entrenched the hegemony of the most powerful social groups and institutions. Williams, on the other hand, while acknowledging that the 'long revolution' of print had destroyed much of the richness of late-eighteenth- and early-nineteenth-century popular culture, continued to see in forms of cultural production and popular political action a capacity for resistance, both in the marginalized opposition press and in the unpredictable and autonomously critical ways in which readers responded to mainstream journalism.[12] Habermas, too, in his classic studies of the public sphere, allowed for the possibility that an active, participatory civil society might still emerge in media-saturated late-industrial societies, an emancipatory 'cultural modernity' based on widely distributed knowledge and rational thought which might challenge the 'functional' modernity of the technologies of the state and the market.[13] Both Williams and Habermas, in different ways, opened up a space in which it was possible to theorize the power of the printed word in ways that might enable the human subject, the reader, to use the press for

purposes potentially at variance with the intentions of its writers, editors and con-
trollers, the presumed 'gatekeepers' to our knowledge of the world.

In an altogether different context, Anderson, in his study of the rise of modern
nationalism, postulated the theory that the press, or 'print language', acted as a
vehicle for the emergence of some modern forms of national identity.[14] Reading newspapers that referred broadly to the same body of knowledge, the same news and
sporting stories, was a 'ritual' which many millions could participate in daily, and
which helped map their cultural worlds. The very different histories of the periodical press in the English provinces, and in Scotland, Wales and Ireland, and the historical tensions that emerged between the efforts made to maintain distinctive press
identities in these areas and the almost uniquely centralized 'national' British press
symbolized by Fleet Street suggests that much might be gained by applying
Anderson's insight to the cultural history of the British Isles. By the same token, the
roles performed by the press in developing and maintaining, as well as in resisting,
the British Empire and its dominions continue to attract the attention of historians.
The growth of an international English-language network for news-gathering and
exchange, together with new trans-national forms of media ownership, based on a
highly diverse range of British territorial possessions overseas, further sought to
underpin the cultural cohesion and the political unity of Britain's vast late-nineteenth-
century empire, from Australia to Canada, and from India to the Caribbean. At the
same time, imperial governors and governments understood the double-edged potential of the 'vernacular', non-English-language journalism of their domains, which
might act as either 'a safety valve' for cultural sensitivities and controlled criticism,
or as effective and popular tools of anti-imperial sedition. When threatened by the
latter in its Indian territories in 1878, Britain imposed the first of a series of Vernacular Press Acts which severely restricted the publication of news and comment in
Indian languages. A decade later, a correspondent to *The Times* pointedly remarked
on the benefits for social order that might result from the employment of the same
repressive legislation to curtail the radical Nonconformist Welsh-language press in
North Wales. The analytical possibilities and complexities of language have also preoccupied the work of cultural historians of the 'postmodern turn'. The ensuing elision
of historical and literary critical methods of enquiry has led to a renewed interest
in melodrama and satire in nineteenth-century journalism, and to the effects of
periodical print on public debate and the exercise of power.[15] Others have traced the
continuities between serial publications and books, in authorship and content, which
promises a more holistic approach to the history of print culture and the transmission of ideas in nineteenth-century Britain.[16]

Finally, research into the history of the press and the printed word in Britain in
the early twenty-first century will change in one fundamental respect. The completion of the Newsplan 2000 project to microfilm all British newspapers and to make
local copies available in local libraries, will have a major long-term impact on the uses
made of the nineteenth-century press, especially, perhaps, by local and family historians.[17] But the digitization programme planned for these serials will not only render
them even more widely available, but, crucially, will also provide them to readers in
a form that is electronically searchable. This will further transform the ways in which
historians and others will read the nineteenth-century newspaper press, and the 'web

of print' of which it formed such a richly significant part. Above all, the application of such technologies to what were initially regarded as ephemeral, disposable products, meant to be read then thrown away, indicates the value that has subsequently been placed on them as important, astonishingly wide-ranging and complicated records of the past. These require both careful preservation and the elaboration of ever more fruitful ways in which their content, language, style and purposes may be explored and their meanings debated. If the general directions taken by twentieth-century studies of the nineteenth century's rich legacy of popular print indicate anything, it is that the diversification of subject areas and approaches in modern history have also provided some exciting new entry points into the study of the press itself.

NOTES

1. R. K. Webb, *The British Working Class Reader* (London, 1955); R. D. Altick, *The English Common Reader: A Social History of the Mass Reading Public 1800–1900* (Columbus, OH, 1998); Raymond Williams, *The Long Revolution* (London, 1961).

2. J. H. Wiener, *A Descriptive Finding List of Unstamped British Periodicals, 1830–1836* (London, 1970). See also J. H. Wiener, *The War of the Unstamped: A History of the Movement to Repeal the British Newspaper Tax, 1830–1836* (Ithaca, NY, 1969) and P. Hollis, *The Pauper Press: A Study in Working-Class Radicalism of the 1830s* (Oxford, 1970).

3. C. Sparks, 'Goodbye, Hildy Johnson: the vanishing "serious press"', in P. Dahlgren and C. Sparks, eds, *Communication and Citizenship: Journalism and the Public Sphere* (London, 1991), p. 63.

4. L. James, ed., *Print and the People 1819–1851* (London, 1976), esp. pp. 83–6.

5. V. Berridge, 'Popular Sunday papers and mid-Victorian society', in G. Boyce et al., eds, *Newspaper History: From the Seventeenth Century to the Present Day* (London, 1978), pp. 247–64.

6. Altick, *English Common Reader*.

7. D. Vincent, *Literacy and Popular Culture: England 1750–1914* (Cambridge, 1989), p. 211.

8. A. J. Lee, *The Origins of the Popular Press in England, 1855–1914* (London, 1976).

9. J. Curran and J. Seaton, *Power Without Responsibility: The Press and Broadcasting in Britain* (London, 1981), pp. 36–42.

10. A. J. Lee, 'The structure, ownership and control of the press, 1855–1914', in G. Boyce et al., eds, *Newspaper History: From the Seventeenth Century to the Present Day* (London, 1978), p. 119.

11. L. Brown, *Victorian News and Newspapers* (Oxford, 1985).

12. Williams, *Long Revolution*.

13. J. Habermas, *The Structural Transformation of the Public Sphere* (Cambridge, 1989).

14. B. Anderson, *Imagined Communities: Reflections on the Origin and Spread of Nationalism* (London, 1983).

15. P. Joyce, *Visions of the People: Industrial England and the Question of Class, 1848–1914* (Cambridge, 1991).

16. For a notable recent example, see L. Brake, *Subjugated Knowledges: Journalism, Gender and Literature in the Nineteenth Century* (London, 1994).

17. J. Lauder, 'Partnerships in preservation: the experience of the NEWSPLAN 2000 project', International Federation of Library Associations and Institutions (IFLA) 2002 Conference proceedings, online at www.ifla.org.

FURTHER READING

In addition to the texts referred to in the notes above, the following studies provide some indication of the diversity of approaches adopted by recent historians towards the expansion of print in the nineteenth century. D. Griffiths, ed., *The Encyclopedia of the British Press 1422–1992* (1992) was the first of its kind and contains a vast range of useful information, and D. Linton and R. Roston, eds, *The Newspaper Press in Britain: An Annotated Bibliography* (1987) remains a vital bibliographic resource. S. E. Koss, *The Rise and Fall of the Political Press in Britain*, vol. 1, *The Nineteenth Century* (1981) is still the most exhaustive study of the changing relationship between newspaper journalism and Britain's major political parties. A broader study of periodical print culture may be found in J. Shattock and M. Wolff, *The Victorian Periodical Press: Samplings and Soundings* (1982) and L. Brake et al., *Investigating Victorian Journalism* (1990). The 'new journalism' is approached from a number of disciplinary directions in J. H. Wiener, ed., *Papers for the Millions: The New Journalism in Britain, 1850s to 1914* (1988), while theories of the nineteenth-century press have received critical attention by M. Hampton in, for example, ' "Understanding media": theories of the press in Britain, 1850–1914', *Media, Culture and Society*, 23 (2001). Readers may also wish to consult a number of scholarly journals dedicated to the history of print, including *Publishing History*, *Victorian Periodicals Review* and *Media History*.

CHAPTER TWENTY-THREE

Crime, Policing and Punishment

HEATHER SHORE

Introduction

The nineteenth century is host to a set of enduring myths about the establishment and development of the criminal justice system in Britain. On the face of it, it is certainly true that, during this century, urban, borough and county police forces were established, the state penal system was massively expanded, the roots of juvenile justice were put into place and the legal system overhauled. Yet, these shifts, as a number of historians have pointed out, were neither so inevitable nor necessarily so innovative as they have sometimes been portrayed. By the end of the century, justice had travelled, and become a very different creature to what it had been at the end of the eighteenth century. How far that journey was a progression or rather a more prosaic evolution will be explored in this chapter.

Traditional histories of crime[1] have been overtaken by the substantial body of work that has been developed since the 1970s. Most recently, research on cultural responses to crime, violent crime, gender and crime, juvenile crime, and provincial policing continue to develop the historiography. Overwhelmingly, this has been a social history of crime, with the political content largely subdued. Thus whilst some researchers have concentrated on the interplay between the mechanics of criminal justice and social change, many have sought to provide a history from below, tracing the experience of the accused at the hands of the criminal justice system.[2] However, the overarching presence in much recent history of crime is the state, which took an increasingly active role in the development and augmentation of criminal justice policy during the nineteenth century. As a result, the boundaries between the centre and the localities were redefined, and in many cases, undermined. Many practices, particularly in the case of policing, carried out at local levels and by local initiatives were, during the course of the century, formalized into something approaching a national system. Moreover, a recognizable body of penal professionals, many from the influential voluntary sector, were incorporated into the criminal justice system, supporting the new bureaucracy that was put in place by the state, particularly by the Home Office and the prison service.

In the late twentieth century the influence of the social sciences, the development of quantitative methodologies, the use of textual analysis and the micro-approach, and the impact of cultural studies and postmodernity have resulted in a rich historiography of crime, punishment and policing. In contrast to the approach of traditional historians who tended to concentrate their research on elite sources, the new research has been strongly located in the archives. Historians of the justice process have explored the substantial archival survivals of quarter-session and petty-sessions records in order to reconstruct the experience of the offender in the criminal justice system. Related textual sources have been fruitfully utilized in a number of studies, for instance on child abuse and capital punishment.[3] Where elite sources have been used the development of new theoretical methodologies has encouraged historians to apply a more critical lens to documents created by government. The problematization of sources such as the parliamentary blue books and the statistical series created from 1857 has had a significant impact on the way historians have approached the study of crime.[4] A number of sources, only partially utilized hitherto, are now informing research. The records of the county sessions, of the summary courts, the coroner's court, and newspapers are being used to study inter-personal violence, and there is new work on a number of its forms, such as assault, rape, domestic violence and gang violence.[5] Finally, the records of the county and borough police forces have been used to re-direct the focus of historians away from the Metropolitan Police.[6] The possibilities for historians of crime, whilst not limitless, are still far from being exhausted. Equally it can be argued that the substantial research which has been undertaken has contributed to the making of a field that is now well established. The following sections will delineate this very wide field in a few basic brush strokes, with the intention of providing an insight into the shifting landscape of criminal justice in the nineteenth century.

Definitions of Criminality

During the course of the nineteenth century criminals were to be increasingly subject to classification and labelling. Contemporaries noted the apparent proliferation of 'criminal types' and the 'criminal classes' with the result that more sharply defined and linguistically determined ways of describing the criminal were developed. In the vast majority of cases, this was done through the passing of legislation: for example, the Juvenile Offenders Act (1847) and the Habitual Criminals Act (1869). Whilst neither juvenile offenders nor habitual criminals were an invention of the nineteenth century, it could be argued that contemporaries responded to crime in divergent ways from their early modern predecessors.[7] The notion of a separate criminal class, with its own language, culture and spatial identity, increasingly took hold from the early to mid-nineteenth century. This view of a distinct criminal culture was to be further influenced by imperial and racial discourses, by the impact of the natural sciences which increasingly viewed the criminal and delinquent in pathological terms, and by the rise of mass immigration, particularly of Jewish settlers from the 1880s. Moreover, this shifting public attitude was reinforced by legislation that stressed the distinctiveness of criminality. Public attitudes were partially influenced by the periodic panics about crime and disorder.

At the beginning of the century, contemporaries were aware of the rise of population, and the increasingly urban nature of society. In the metropolis, middle-class fears about the poor informed at least in part the passage of the Vagrancy Act (1824) and the New Poor Law (1834). The need to control the poor had been made all too clear with the problems of public order entailed by the outbreaks of Luddism in the Midlands and North in the 1810s, the 'Peterloo massacre' of 1819 and the Swing disturbances in the agricultural districts of southern England during the early 1830s. Whilst for most of the century urban riots were never to be as threatening as they had been during the eighteenth century, political radicalism in response to the push for reform, and particularly the rise of Chartism in the 1830s and 1840s, helped to develop the threatening spectre of a insurrectionary poor. Later in the century the problem of the unemployed, and the influence of socialism, were underlined by riots in the West End and central London; and the 'Bloody Sunday' meeting in 1887 of the Social Democratic Federation in Trafalgar Square was broken up by police and troops. Problems of public order, whether in the form of urban riots or rural agitation, were increasingly politicized in the nineteenth century. Moreover, they posed a challenge for the new police, who frequently policed both riot and public order.[8] In the context of the Northern industrial factory towns, and the East End of London, the police were arguably seen as enforcers of order.[9]

Gatrell and Petrow have argued that the increased ability and willingness of the state to police crime during the course of the nineteenth century brought about in some cases the creation, and in other cases the stronger identification, of specific categories of criminal.[10] This was exemplarized by the Habitual Criminals Act (1869), which was accompanied, in the later nineteenth century, by a growing apparatus with which to record, identify, measure and classify the criminal. However, prior to this, the emphasis was less on the criminal individual, and more on the type of crime in which he or she was engaged. Juvenile crime, violent crime and professional crime all concerned contemporaries to a greater or lesser degree.

Juvenile Crime

Juvenile delinquency was perennial, of course; however, from the early nineteenth century it was increasingly being singled out as a social problem. In 1815 the Committee for Investigating the Causes of the Alarming Increase of Juvenile Delinquency in the Metropolis was formed, and the report that it published the following year opened the floodgates to a rush of select committees, investigations and pamphlets concerned with juvenile crime. Recent work has suggested that the main motivations behind this groundswell was a mixture of generational fears, coincident with the end of the Napoleonic Wars, a refocusing of attention on the outdated prison system, and the growing influence of reform.[11] Increasingly, the need to separate children from adults throughout the whole of the criminal justice system became paramount. In the 1820s a number of acts were passed which were partially designed with the juvenile in mind. The Malicious Trespass Act (1820), the Vagrancy Act (1824) and the Larceny Act (1827) allowed for varying forms of summary processing to be resorted to in the case of petty crimes and minor theft. Overwhelmingly these acts singled out the trivial and mundane crimes which juvenile offenders were most likely to commit. Moreover, the passage of the 1829 Metropolitan Police Act reinforced this process by focusing the early energies of the new police on petty offences and more vulnerable offenders.[12] The development of summary jurisdiction and juvenile justice in Britain went hand in hand, a relationship that was formalized with the passage of the Juvenile Offenders Act (1847), which allowed children under the age of 14 to be tried in petty sessions summarily, and a further Act of 1850 which permitted the age limit to be raised to 16. From this point on criminal children were increasingly diverted to summary jurisdiction, although the Juvenile Court was not established until the early twentieth century, under the 1908 Children's Act. The legislative journey of the later nineteenth century was to focus almost wholly on the institutional care of the juvenile.

From the late eighteenth century, philanthropists had urged the need for separate accommodation for juvenile offenders. The image of the child in the unreformed prisons, and increasingly, in the company of adult offenders more generally, was a source of anxiety for commentators by the early nineteenth century. Strategies to deal with juveniles in institutions developed in two ways. On the one hand, the state felt that the new prisons and penitentiary, the apparatus of reform, were adequate to house and to reform juvenile offenders. Peel's Gaol Act (1824) allowed for greater classification and separation of juveniles. Institutions would be rebuilt or refurbished with separate juvenile-specific accommodation. However, this legislation was often approached permissively. Many county institutions simply did not have either the manpower or the space to put Peel's measures into place. On the other hand, the philanthropic sector established a number of refuges and schools where juvenile offenders could be given useful training. Ultimately the passage of the Industrial and Reformatory Schools Acts (1854–7) incorporated elements of both the state and voluntary systems. The principle of separate confinement of juvenile offenders was to be finalized in 1876 under the Education Act, which established day industrial schools and truant schools. As a result of the reformatory movement of the later century, there was a significant decline of children in prison, and most children placed in prison were there on remand, or in lieu of paying a fine. This was addressed by the Industrial Schools Act (1866), which detained such children in the workhouse, and more successfully in the Youthful Offenders Act (1901), which empowered the courts to remand a child 'into the custody of any "fit person" . . . who is willing to receive him'.[13]

Violent Crime

Concern for the future generation was to conjure up the spectre of the juvenile offender growing into the adult burglar or violent robber. Indeed, violence was a frequent preoccupation of Victorian society. Discussion of violent crime in the past has frequently focused on homicide. The murder rate has traditionally been regarded as a reliable guide to homicide, since it is the most frequently reported offence, and often cleared up. Yet analysis of nineteenth-century crime statistics is subject to a number of difficulties.[14] Moreover, concentrating only on homicide masks the extent of the most prevalent forms of violence in nineteenth-century society; assault, often in or around the public house, domestic violence and malicious wounding were frequent forms of inter-personal violence.[15] Most violence took place between people who were related or known to each other; common forms of homicide and attempted homicide were those between husbands and wives, or parents and children.[16] There were periodic panics about violent crime during the nineteenth century, and various historians have argued that this was a result of the growing intolerance towards violence and disorder.[17] The Ratcliff Highway murders of 1811, where two families were bludgeoned to death in east London, sent shock-waves through the country, inspiring much middle-class and literary commentary as to the broader social and cultural meanings of the crime. In the mid-nineteenth century, growing concern about the ticket-of-leave probation system, and a rash of violent assaults, prompted a panic about garrotting, manipulated in part by the contemporary press. The 'moral panic' which resulted had a significant effect on criminal justice. The panic of 1862 was intensified by the 'garrotting' of the MP Hugh Pilkington in Pall Mall in July of that year, resulting in an increase in the number of prosecutions for street robbery. A Security from Violence Act, known more prosaically as the Garrotter's Act, was passed in 1863, imposing flogging as the penalty for robbery and attempted robbery with violence, in addition to a sentence of imprisonment or penal servitude.[18] It also prompted moves towards the greater classification and identification of known offenders, culminating in the passage of the Habitual Criminals Act (1869). The final dramatic violent crimes of the nineteenth century were the unsolved Whitechapel murders of 1888. Although these have become the preserve of gaslight aficionados and cultural theorists, they refocused the attention of contemporaries, already eastbound, onto the problems of poverty and prostitution.

Historians of the *longue durée* have posited a decline in violence over time; yet more recently they have turned their attention to changing attitudes to violence in the nineteenth century. They have suggested that the change was not so much in the amount of violence, but rather in the language used to describe that violence.[19] The influence of the natural sciences, and of biologically determined explanations for crime like phrenology, anthropometry and later eugenics, was significant. Thus, the increasing tendency to categorize and discuss the criminal in a pathological sense allowed for the development of a discourse in which criminality was described as an inherent characteristic of the poor. This can be seen most graphically in later-nineteenth-century responses to immigration. By this time the supposed linkages between aliens and crime had become much more pronounced. This was reflected in contemporary attitudes which characterized certain forms of violence as being of foreign origin, or 'un-British'. The garrotting panic of 1862 was seen in these terms, the garrotte itself being a Spanish execution device. Whilst moral panics may have been concerned with more exotic forms of violence, intolerance of more prosaic everyday violence was increasing in the later nineteenth century. In particular, violence towards women was much less tolerated. More men were being tried for such violence, and receiving more substantial sentences.[20] Similarly, Jackson's work on the 'discovery' of child sexual abuse in the Victorian and Edwardian periods also indicates a shift in attitudes, although, particularly in terms of the courtroom, understandings and responses to abuse were complex, and often contradictory.[21]

Professional Crime

Whilst interpersonal violence has recently attracted the attentions of historians, contemporaries often had a more amorphous sense of brutality and danger. The garrotter was only one of a range of characterizations which can be found in Victorian popular literature. The violent robber, the burglar, the ticket-of-leave man and the gang were all popular stereotypes in the typologies of crime and criminality which were being constructed during the course of the nineteenth century. The brutal villains of fiction to be found in the Newgate novels of the early nineteenth century, and the rising genre of detection towards the end of the period, made for a tangible subterranean brutality which could have frightening echoes in real life. Increasingly the violence in society came to be seen as immensely threatening. Thus, allusions to the criminal class who inhabited the dens, rookeries, stews and alsatias of the poorest parts of the country became common from the mid-century. And, whilst fears about criminal sub-cultures have most frequently, and understandably, been based on the metropolis, Glasgow, Cardiff, Liverpool, Birmingham, and most of the ports and other growing urban and industrial conurbations, had areas identified as belonging to the criminal class.[22] In reality, the identification of certain areas as 'criminal districts' owed much to concerns about public health and sanitation issues, and to increased police surveillance. Whilst such areas had always been present, the portrayal of criminality became more intense in the later nineteenth century. The combination of more effective policing, the rise of social evangelicalism, the impact of imperial racist discourses, and the emergence of a threatening casual labour class, all helped bring attention to the 'criminal classes'.

Even in the early nineteenth century Metropolitan Police select committees were littered with concerns about 'hardened' criminals, and what we would now call 'professional' criminals. At this time considerable anxiety was expressed about the corruption of young boys and girls by older criminals, a theme returned to by Dickens in *Oliver Twist*. The image of organized gangs of juvenile pickpockets was to remain stalwart in the Victorian depiction of urban crime. In rural areas as well the gang was an active criminal stereotype: 'rural' crimes such as poaching and horse-stealing, and in coastal areas smuggling, were typically said to be carried out by organized gangs. How far such gangs were simply a product of the over-active Victorian imagination is difficult to assess. In the cities and large towns, it seems clear that the juxtaposition of the poor to their more comfortably-off neighbours was keenly felt. Certainly, the great mass of theft was petty and opportunistic, but this was not simply a hand-to-mouth economy. It is likely that in both rural and urban areas the black economy had some impact. The 'fence', or the receiver of stolen goods, pulling the strings of a web of criminal associates was, once again, a familiar stereotype in Victorian sensational literature. More prosaically, the 'fence' was a figure in the local community, male or female, often working in the old clothes trade, pawn shops, or as publicans or lodging-houses keepers, and not averse to dipping into the black economy.[23]

Prostitution

Clearly criminal networks, in both the city and the countryside, did have some sort of reality. How much of a threat they really posed to Victorian society, and how much they had in common with the criminal underworlds of the popular imagination cannot be known. Often Victorian commentators were imbued with a sense of thwarted morality, and the criminal, the juvenile delinquent and the prostitute contributed to a general social unease about the underside of society, the 'Nether World', as George Gissing pronounced it (*The Nether World: A Novel*) in 1889. Whilst the prostitute and the criminal were not mutually exclusive categories, concerns about the sexual networks of the metropolis were to dominate much contemporary discussion of poverty from the mid-nineteenth century.

Sexual immorality had long been a pressing issue for urban elites and city fathers. In the eighteenth century, the Society for the Reformation of Manners had been extremely active and often successful in their campaign to rid the streets of London, Bristol and other urban centres of the idle and disorderly. Overwhelmingly, these were disorderly women, and such campaigns to control women's deviant sexuality were to be frequently repeated during the course of the next century. The Society for the Reformation of Manners had exhausted itself by the late eighteenth century, but was superseded by the Society for the Suppression of Vice in the early nineteenth, which could name Patrick Colquhoun, the police reformer, amongst its vice-presidents. Historians of prostitution have concentrated their energies on the second half of the nineteenth century;[24] understandably so, since the work of William Acton, the campaigns of Josephine Butler and the Ladies National Association, and the impact of the Contagious Diseases Acts (1864, 1866, 1869) all belong to this period. During the later nineteenth century the common prostitute, always a figure of public censure, underwent a double-edged onslaught. On the one hand, she was subjected to the proddings of medical science, under the directions of the Contagious Diseases Acts; on the other hand she was to be rescued and reformed through philanthropic endeavour. Moreover, the levity of the police as regards prostitution was an object of some irritation to the reformers. Prostitution in itself was not a crime, and soliciting could be difficult to prove. As a result the police were not always compliant in the crusade against prostitution. Even later in the century, when the horror of the Whitechapel murders had turned the nation's attention to the problems of prostitution, the police continued to be accused of tolerating it. The Metropolitan Police favoured a policy of containment in an area which they could keep well policed.[25] This was in direct contrast to the police in Scotland, who were notably more assiduous.[26]

Policing

The role of the police evolved rapidly over the course of the nineteenth century. However, by the latter part of the century, they were still subject to a considerable amount of public criticism. Much has been written, in recent years, to undermine the traditional Whig narrative of police reform in the nineteenth century. The watersheds of police reform were, in essence, the 1790s and 1820s–1830s. In 1795 Colquhoun published *A Treatise on the Police of the Metropolis*, and in 1792 the Middlesex Justices Act had been passed, establishing seven police offices for London, manned by stipendiary magistrates. In 1798 (generally attributed to the influence of Colquhoun), a private police was set up to guard the commerce of the river Thames; in 1800 this organization was taken over by the government and remodelled as the Thames River Police. The later period was marked by the passage of the Metropolitan Police Act (1829), the Rural Constabulary Act (1839) and the County and Borough Police Act (1856). Recent research has concentrated on two areas. Firstly, it has focused on the continuities between the old police and the new: Paley in particular, has undermined the myth of an unpoliced society prior to the 1829 Act, and describes a system that was, within its limits, surprisingly effective at the parish level.[27] Secondly, it has considered the evolution of law enforcement outside London. Because it was the seat of government, because of its size and concerns about metropolitan crime, London tended to host most new initiatives in policing. However, the concentration on London belies the extent of policing experiments in other parts of the country. The Cheshire Police Act had also been passed in 1829, and many provincial towns had efficient police forces by the 1830s. In Scotland, for example, private Police Acts had proliferated in the burghs in the early nineteenth century.[28] More generally, the combination of the Lighting and Watching Act (1833) and the Municipal Corporations Act (1835) gave local authorities in Britain a considerable amount of power and leeway to reorganize their systems of police.

The historiographical shift to considering provincial police reform has necessarily broadened research on issues connected with rural policing. Philips and Storch have shown how crucial the permissive 1839 Constabulary Act was in rural areas. The county gentry put their resolve firmly behind Peel's message of crime prevention, and whilst the installation of a police force was made piecemeal and more gradually in the countryside, by the mid-nineteenth century it was clear that both urban and rural England and Wales had seen the transition to a 'policed' society.[29] The Welsh were particularly quick to embrace the legislation. The impact of the Rebecca riots of 1839 and 1843–4, together with fears about Irish immigrants and vagrants, meant that in most Welsh counties the basis for a professional police force had been laid well before the compulsory Act of 1856.[30] In Scotland the police developed roughly in step with that of England and Wales, though early developments were made in rural areas largely as a response to concerns about vagrancy. An Act was passed in 1833 enabling the establishment of a 'General System of Police' in the burghs. A compulsory Act was passed in 1857, and like the Welsh, few Scottish counties had to be compelled to set up police forces.[31]

After the mid-century, developments in all three countries followed a similar path to a more centralized and rationalized police force. However, the police were not greeted universally with open arms, and resistance has been well documented. Storch's work on police resistance in class-conscious working-class communities, particularly those of the northern textile towns, shows how they opposed the presence of the police through extra-parliamentary means, such as anti-police riots.[32] However, working-class victims of crime could also see the advantages of the 'new police'. One of the major effects of the establishment of the police was the transference of the prosecution process from the victim to the police. As a result working-class people were more willing to report petty crime, and even to involve the police in domestic altercations.[33] By the end of the nineteenth century, the police were a central institution in British society. Moreover, it was not only in preventive policing that developments had occurred. The emergence of more specialized branches of police work was to be a major feature of the later nineteenth century.

Detection

If the history of the police has been a central concern to historians of crime, the history of detection has received much less attention. The detective department of the Metropolitan Police was established in 1842, upon the recommendation of the police commissioner, Sir Richard Mayne. Two inspectors and six sergeants were appointed for detective work, and, after some expansion and a good deal of corruption, was reorganized as the Criminal Investigation Department (CID) in 1878. Calls for a separate detective force had been a long time coming. In the previous century, John Fielding had been vociferous in his campaigning for some sort of criminal intelligence network, recognizing that there needed to be both some sort of central clearing-house for information, and much closer links between parochial and county law-enforcers. He also recognized the importance of using newspapers in tracking down and capturing criminals. However, Fielding's ideas, although he had some limited success, were reminiscent of the secret police or armies of absolutist continental Europe, and provoked considerable hostility. In the early nineteenth century, detection continued to be a part of policing, but took a second place to prevention. The use of detectives and *agents provocateurs* in the early nineteenth century is an area which calls for further exploration. Until this is done, our main knowledge of police detection rests on the developments of the later nineteenth century.

The expansion of the detective force was greatly boosted by the scare about ticket-of-leave men in the 1860s, in response to which a departmental committee was appointed to investigate policing in 1868. This coincided with the Habitual Criminals Act (1869), which reflected the increasing categorization and identification of criminals. Detectives were strongly implicated in this work. A further factor was the activities of the Fenians, who had been responsible for a series of 'outrages' in the late 1860s. As a result, in 1869, full-time divisional detectives were established. Within a decade the department was reorganized under the aegis of the CID after the scandal following the 'Trial of the Detectives'. In April 1877, five men were convicted of fraud and forgery in the Turf Fraud case. Four senior central detectives, Chief Inspectors Clarke, Palmer and Druscovitch, and Inspector Meiklejohn, were implicated, and as a result a commission was appointed to inquire into the state of the detective branch.[34] The branch was reorganized under the leadership of a Director of Criminal Investigation, Howard Vincent, in 1878; within six years the Metropolitan Police district CID had expanded from 280 to 800 officers. County studies of provincial detectives still await their historians, despite the fact that in the late nineteenth century provincial towns were comparatively well served with detectives. Whilst in the Metropolitan Police the percentage of police employed in detective work was 2.4 per cent, in Birmingham it was 4.5 per cent, in Liverpool and Glasgow 3.5 per cent and in Manchester 2.7 per cent.[35] The unwillingness to invest more resources in detective work was partly a product of the structure of the CID, which was divided between central and divisional detectives. The relationship between the centre, at Scotland Yard, and the periphery, in the outlying divisions, was not always smooth, and the CID was to continue in this relatively decentralized manner until the twentieth century. By the late nineteenth century the scope of the CID was expanding, with the adoption of new forensic technologies such as fingerprinting, and the establishment of the Anthropometry Department from 1895. The political role of the CID was realized in the founding of the Special Branch in 1883. Originally organized as a response to Fenianism, by the late 1880s the Branch had became involved in broader matters of national security. Whilst in many ways it can be seen as separate from the CID, except for a short period during and immediately after the First World War, the Special Branch remained a part of the CID.

Prosecution

One of the major transitions in the history of policing during the nineteenth century, as we have already seen, was their increasingly important role in the prosecution process. However, the precise process of how this change occurred has been largely ignored by historians. Possibly the key role of the 'new police' in controlling petty street crime suggested a broader interpretation of their guardian role. As Emsley states, 'overwhelmingly the police dominated the prosecution of offenders against public order, public decency and public safety'.[36] Moreover, the police were much more likely to contribute to or lead the prosecution process where the victim was weak, poor or vulnerable in some way. The eighteenth-century criminal justice system had not always worked for the poor and vulnerable. The costs of prosecution were prohibitive for many who could not afford legal advice, nor to lose valuable wages. As a result the entrepreneurial system of law enforcement flourished, with rewards and gratuities for informers often providing the incentive to deal with crimes through extra-legal means. This system was countered by legislation passed during the later eighteenth and early nineteenth centuries that allowed expenses towards the cost of prosecution. By the time of Peel's Criminal Justice Act of 1826, expenses were paid to all prosecutors where there was a conviction, to witnesses, and in the case of some misdemeanours as well as felonies. However, financial considerations were not the only factor to encourage prosecution. The increasing abolition of the capital sentence during the early nineteenth century, for example for picking pockets in 1808, and in 1820 for shoplifting, meant that people were more willing to consider prosecution. It has become a truism that the capital sanction in the eighteenth century was more an exercise in hegemony than real threat; however, victims and prosecutors were not always happy with pursuing a capital prosecution.[37] The availability of secondary punishments such as transportation and the increasing tendency to use longer-term prison sentences, combined with a growing revulsion particularly towards public executions, meant that by the time of the abolition of public execution in 1868, capital punishment was reserved only for the most heinous of crimes.

Punishment

Overwhelmingly, the greatest transition between the eighteenth and nineteenth centuries was in the arena of punishment. Accordingly, the varieties of punishment and the processes which drove the motor for change have been the focus of much historical work. The impact of Foucault's *Discipline and Punish* can be seen in recent work which has investigated the cultural history of the death penalty in the nineteenth century.[38] More conservatively, McConville has written the definitive administrative history of penal development, and the reorganization of local prisons in Britain.[39] The scope of punishment in the nineteenth century can be roughly divided into three phases. Firstly, there was the search for secondary punishments from the later eighteenth century. Before this time, sanctions other than execution had taken the form of fines, corporal punishment, short terms of imprisonment in the unreformed prisons and houses of correction, transportation to the American colonies, and punitive public sanctions such as the stocks and the pillory. This system was not without its problems, but sufficed until the emergence of debates about capital punishment and the state of the prisons in the later part of the century. Despite traditional historians' dramatic reconstructions of the bloodiness of eighteenth-century criminal justice, it has now become a truism that the rise of capital statutes, from the period of the 1688 revolution in government and monarchy, was not a meaningful one. Many of the statutes created in the eighteenth century referred to very specific acts such as destroying Westminster Bridge, or were simply re-formulations of older Tudor and Stuart legislation.

The second phase put theory into practice, with the legislative attack on capital punishment on the one hand, and the substantial programme of penitentiary building and refurbishment of existing institutions on the other. This middle phase was also marked by an increasing tension between ideas about reformation in relationship to punishment. Whilst reformation was hardly a new concept, nineteenth-century institutional regimes focused on more or less practical strategies to reform the prisoner. The third phase saw the end of Australian transportation and the adoption of penal servitude, the growth of the industrial and reformatory school movement, the further decline of capital punishment and abolition of public execution, and the early formulation of some sort of probation system.

Transportation to Australia between 1788 and 1867 represented the most vivid phase of the long history of penal transportation from Britain. When the outbreak of hostilities caused relationships with the American colonists to break down in 1776, the rotting hulks were used as a temporary expedient. By the 1780s it was clear that the hulks were insanitary and unsatisfactory, resulting in the search for an alternative. On the one hand, this provoked the move towards the reformed penal system at home; on the other hand, transportation was again suggested as a viable solution. Subsequently, the penal colonies at New South Wales, Van Diemen's Land, and from the 1850s Western Australia, became the main destinations for those convicted of more serious felonies during the early to mid-nineteenth century. The ideological rationales for transportation were well matched by economic pragmatism. For the British government, penal reformers and the elite, transportation was a fine solution. Not only did it banish such unsavoury elements of society from view, but it provided a flexible workforce with which to establish the new colony. Moreover, for any consciences that might need salving, it provided a reformatory experience – criminals, convicts, even the formerly condemned, could be reformed, and emerge as new colonial citizens. With this in view, we should not be surprised that the convicts were overwhelmingly male and overwhelmingly young. Male prisoners in their late teens and early twenties formed a substantial workforce – those with agricultural backgrounds, or skilled workers, such as bricklayers, masons and blacksmiths, did best in this environment. The unskilled fodder, more likely to be urban and/or youths, fared worst.

The backlash against transportation occurred on both sides of the world. In Australia the fledgling colony had developed an identity, and both free settlers and reformed convicts wanted to be distanced from the colony's penal beginnings. In Britain, transportation had been the subject of criticism almost from its inception. However, from the 1830s pressure was stepped up, resulting in the Molesworth Committee of 1837/8 which produced a devastating critique of the system. Moreover, objections to transportation were paralleled by new developments in the British penal system. During the early nineteenth century Britain embraced what has been designated the 'great confinement'. The old system, which combined a mixture of physical sanctions, with financial penalties and short spells in institutions, was replaced with a system that was to become dominated by penal servitude. For much of the nineteenth century, penality was under review, with contemporaries seeking for balance between punishment and reformation.

Perhaps the most startling element of the new penality was the emergence of the penitentiaries, realized in the building of Millbank Penitentiary in 1816. The idea of the penitentiary was to combine the disciplinary regimes of silence and separation with educational and religious instruction. A Penitentiary Act had originally been passed in 1778, with the object of erecting two national penitentiaries (one for males, one for females) which were to be centrally administered. For a variety of reasons, but not least the disruption of the Napoleonic Wars, the scheme took several decades to materialize fully. The war itself was to contribute to the shifting opinions of the government regarding penality. The administration of substantial numbers of prisoners of war for a relatively long period undoubtedly influenced plans for the national penitentiaries. Moreover, the ideals of Jeremy Bentham's Panopticon were also incorporated in the recommendations of the Holford Committee, which met to reconsider the penitentiaries in 1810. Bentham's philosophical views were profoundly important to penal development in Britain. His architectural realization of the prison was closely bound with adherence to three principles: the rule of lenity, which signalled the move from bodily suffering associated with the old penal system; the rule of severity, which posited the principle of less eligibility; and the rule of economy, that the system should essentially be cost-effective. The Holford Committee generally shared these views, and to a greater or lesser degree they underpinned the regimes established in Britain's institutions over the next few decades.

The system that was to evolve by the end of the nineteenth century had learnt from the lessons of the past. Whilst elements of the silent and separate system could still be found, the worst excesses of the penal experiments of the early nineteenth century were removed. That system had not lived up to its reformatory promise, solitary confinement had had a counter-productive effect on the morale of prisoners, and a number of highly publicized cases of suicide and insanity brought it into discredit. The separation of prisoners, to be engendered by the classification of different categories of prisoner, particularly through the Gaol Acts of the 1820s, had more success though, as we have already seen, theory was not always put into practice. Despite this, the principles of Benthamite penality were to be echoed in the Penal Servitude Acts of 1853, 1857 and 1864. Penal servitude differed from a sentence of imprisonment in a number of ways, and was envisaged as a direct replacement for transportation, with seven years' transportation equalling seven years' penal servitude. Essentially penal servitude consisted of a mixture of separate confinement and hard labour, followed by probation in the form of a ticket-of-leave. It was kept for those convicted of more serious crimes (those who would previously have been transported) and thus went hand in hand with the Habitual Criminals Act (1869), and the Prevention of Crimes Act, which was passed in 1871 and tightened supervision of convicted criminals.[40] The perception of a threatening 'criminal class' which can be identified particularly with the later nineteenth century enabled a system which increasingly labelled and categorized convicts. However, the system was not rigorously enforced. Once again problems of expense, particularly in the provinces, meant that local elites were often reluctant to enforce legislation which created problems of supervision and accommodation. Worries about the ticket-of-leave, or convict licence system, were greatly exaggerated during the peaks of the garotting panic in 1862. Public anxiety was matched by the frustration of the police in keeping track of ticket-of-leave men. In Birmingham, for example, the police were only able to find fourteen out of an estimated eighty to a hundred ticket-of-leave men.[41] Whilst police supervision was to improve towards the end of the century, the Penal Servitude Act of 1864 attempted to redress the situation by specifying a minimum sentence of five years for first, and seven years for subsequent, offences.

Debate about penal servitude was overwhelmingly concerned with the male convict. This is not to say that other categories of convict were to be ignored in the penal equation. Juveniles, as we have already seen, were to be catered for with the developing reformatory school system. The thrust of juvenile justice in the early nineteenth century had been somewhat contradictory. Whilst urging the removal of children and youths from the existing prisons, reformers were also advocating the use of institutional solutions for both convicted children and those deemed 'at risk'. The result of this was that juvenile offenders were, by the 1830s and 1840s, less likely to be acquitted, and much more likely to be institutionalized in one form or another.[42] Women were also increasingly subjected to the vagaries of a broad policy of institutionalization. One of the key elements of separation had been the division of male and female convicts. Consequently disciplinary arrangements for female convicts were distinct from those of their male counterparts.[43] Moreover, female offenders were increasingly pathologized during the course of the nineteenth century. Thus a broad shift can be identified from around the middle of the century where female criminality was interpreted as biological or psychological disorder.[44] This view was profoundly to influence the experience of women convicts, and penal regimes for women tended to be more centrally shaped by 'moral' issues such as sexuality, alcoholism and feeble-mindedness.

Ultimately the criminal justice system in the nineteenth century underwent a series of shifts. Whilst historians no longer see all these necessarily as either sudden breaks with the past, or as progressive developments, it is recognized that certain paradigms are crucial to the way students and researchers alike understand crime in the past. Hence, the increasing visibility and intervention of the state, the shifting form and function of policing as representatives of that state, the nature of institutionalization in society, and the significance of the impact of cultural understandings and responses to crime, all contribute to a more nuanced history of crime and policing in the nineteenth century.

NOTES

1. For example J. J. Tobias, *Crime and Industrial Society in the Nineteenth Century* (London, 1967).
2. M. Ignatieff, *A Just Measure of Pain: The Penitentiary in the Industrial Revolution, 1750–1850* (London, 1978); V. A. C. Gatrell, *The Hanging Tree: Execution and the English People 1770–1868* (Oxford, 1994); D. Philips, *Crime and Authority in Victorian England: The Black Country, 1835–60* (London, 1977); H. Shore, *Artful Dodgers: Youth and Crime in Early Nineteenth Century London* (Woodbridge, 1999).

3. L. A. Jackson, *Child Sexual Abuse in Victorian England* (London, 2000); Gatrell, *Hanging Tree*.

4. H. Taylor, 'Rationing crime: the political economy of criminal statistics since the 1850s', *Economic History Review*, 51 (1998).

5. S. D'Cruze, ed., *Everyday Violence in Britain, 1850–1950: Gender and Class* (Harlow, 2000).

6. D. Philips and R. Storch, *Policing Provincial England, 1829–1856: The Politics of Reform* (London, 1999).

7. J. A. Sharpe, *Crime in Early Modern England, 1550–1750* (Harlow, 1999), pp. 5–10.

8. C. Emsley, *The English Police: A Political and Social History* (Harlow, 1996).

9. R. D. Storch, 'The plague of blue locusts: police reform and popular resistance in northern England, 1840–1857', *International Review of Social History*, 20 (1975).

10. V. A. C. Gatrell, 'Crime, authority and the policeman-state', in F. M. L. Thompson, ed., *The Cambridge Social History of Britain, 1750–1950*, vol. 3, *Social Agencies and Institutions* (Cambridge, 1990); S. Petrow, *Policing Morals: The Metropolitan Police and the Home Office, 1870–1914* (Oxford, 1994), pp. 83–113.

11. P. King, 'The rise of juvenile delinquency in England, 1780–1840: changing patterns of perception and prosecution', *Past and Present*, 160 (1998); Shore, *Artful Dodgers*.

12. S. Magarey, 'The invention of juvenile delinquency in early nineteenth century England', *Labour History*, 34 (1978).

13. L. Radzinowicz and R. Hood, *A History of English Criminal Law and its Administration from 1750*, vol. 5, *The Emergence of Penal Policy in Victorian and Edwardian England* (London, 1986), pp. 627–8.

14. Taylor, 'Rationing crime'.

15. D'Cruze, ed., *Everyday Violence*, pp. 1–19.

16. C. Emsley, *Crime and Society in England, 1750–1900* (Harlow, 1996), pp. 41–5.

17. J. Davis, 'The London garrotting panic of 1862: a moral panic and the creation of a criminal class in mid-Victorian England', in V. A. C. Gatrell, B. Lenham and G. Parker, eds, *Crime and the Law: A Social History of Crime in Western Europe since 1500* (London, 1980); P. King, 'Punishing assault: the transformation of attitudes in the English courts', *Journal of Interdisciplinary History*, 27 (1996).

18. Radzinowicz and Hood, *History of English Criminal Law*, p. 692.

19. D'Cruze, *Everyday Violence*, p. 19.

20. M. J. Wiener, 'The Victorian criminalisation of men', in P. Spierenburg, ed., *Men and Violence: Gender, Honour, and Rituals in Modern Europe and America* (Ohio, 1998).

21. Jackson, *Child Sexual Abuse*.

22. D. J. V. Jones, *Crime, Protest, Community and Police in Nineteenth-Century Britain* (London, 1982), pp. 105–8.

23. Shore, *Artful Dodgers*.

24. P. Bartley, *Prostitution: Prevention and Reform in England, 1860–1914* (London, 2000); J. R. Walkowitz, *Prostitution and Victorian Society: Women, Class and the State* (Cambridge, 1980).

25. Bartley, *Prostitution*, pp. 161–8.

26. L. Mahood, *The Magdalenes: Prostitution in the Nineteenth Century* (London, 1990).

27. R. Paley, ' "An imperfect, inadequate and wretched system?": policing London before Peel', *Criminal Justice History*, 10 (1989).

28. K. Carson and H. Idzikowska, 'The social production of Scottish policing, 1795–1900', in D. Hay and F. Snyder, eds, *Policing and Prosecution in Britain, 1750–1850* (Cambridge, 1989), pp. 270–1.

29. Philips and Storch, *Policing Provincial England*, pp. 36–57.

30. D. J. V. Jones, *Crime in Nineteenth Century Wales* (Cardiff, 1992), pp. 201–38.

31. Carson and Idzikowska, 'Social production', p. 274.

32. Storch, 'Plague of blue locusts'.

33. Jones, *Crime in Nineteenth Century Wales*, p. 214.

34. Petrow, *Policing Morals*, pp. 57–8.

35. Petrow, *Policing Morals*, p. 62.

36. Emsley, *Crime and Society*, p. 191.

37. D. Hay et al., *Albion's Fatal Tree: Crime and Society in Eighteenth Century England* (London, 1975).

38. M. Foucault, *Discipline and Punish: The Birth of the Prison* (London, 1977); Gatrell, *Hanging Tree*; R. McGowen, 'Civilising punishment: the end of the public execution in England', *Journal of British Studies*, 33 (1994).

39. S. McConville, *A History of English Prison Administration*, vol. 1, *1750–1877* (London, 1981).

40. Petrow, *Policing Morals*, pp. 75–82.

41. Radzinowicz and Hood, *History of English Criminal Law*, p. 250.

42. Shore, *Artful Dodgers*, pp. 115–17.

43. McConville, *History of English Prison Administration*, pp. 425–8.

44. L. Zedner, *Women, Crime, and Custody in Victorian England* (Oxford, 1991).

FURTHER READING

There is now a substantial historiography on the development of crime and criminal justice in Britain during the nineteenth century. The best starting-point is C. Emsley, *Crime and Society in England, 1750–1900* (1996). There have also been a number of excellent monographs. Amongst the best are: C. Conley, *The Unwritten Law: Criminal Justice in Victorian Kent* (1991); D. Philips, *Crime and Authority in Victorian England: The Black Country, 1835–60* (1977); V. A. C. Gatrell, *The Hanging Tree: Execution and the English People 1770–1868* (1994); and M. J. Wiener, *Reconstructing the Criminal: Culture, Law and Policy in England, 1830–1914* (1990). On the development of the police see: C. Emsley, *The English Police: A Political and Social History* (1996); S. H. Palmer, *Police and Protest in England and Ireland, 1780–1850* (1988); and C. Steedman, *Policing the Victorian Community: The Formation of English Provincial Police Forces, 1856–80* (1984). The introductory chapter to R. Reiner, *The Politics of the Police* (1992) is also useful. On the development of the penal system S. McConville's complementary volumes, *A History of English Prison Administrations* (1981) and *English Local Prisons 1860–1900: Next Only to Death* (1995), cover much ground, though these are fundamentally orthodox accounts. M. Foucault, *Discipline and Punish: The Birth of the Prison* (1977) and M. Ignatieff, *A Just Measure of Pain: The Penitentiary in the Industrial Revolution, 1750–1850* (1978) offer more challenging interpretations. On the nature of criminality and specific groups of offenders, G. Pearson's classic work on delinquency, *Hooligan: A History of Respectable Fears* (1983), can be read alongside L. Mahood's work on Scotland, *Policing Gender, Class and Family: Britain, 1850–1940* (1995). On women and gender see L. Zedner, *Women, Crime and Custody in Victorian England* (1991) and the appropriate chapters in M. L. Arnot and C. Usborne, eds, *Gender and Crime in Modern Europe* (1999).

CHAPTER TWENTY-FOUR

Popular Leisure and Sport

ANDY CROLL

Few subject areas have grown with as much vigour as the history of British leisure and sport. In the 1960s and early 1970s, it was an historiography still in its infancy, and suffering from something akin to an inferiority complex. Those historians practising in the field were often acutely aware of the prejudices of their peers and invariably felt moved to justify their work in lengthy prefaces and introductions. They emphasized how their findings were of scholarly significance and pointed out how a study of recreations and amusements could shed light on a variety of weighty matters. Today, few students of leisure history feel the need to defend their work in such a fashion. Whereas once they could see themselves as shaking up a conservative historical establishment, now leisure historians are an accepted – and respected – group within the profession. The Young Turks have transformed themselves into a burgeoning professoriate. In the process, they have produced some of the most exciting and innovative historical work to appear in recent years. Much of it has been concerned with the nineteenth century, a period that was quickly identified as being of critical importance in the development of modern leisure. What follows is a consideration of some of the debates that have done most to shape the historiography since its inception back in the late 1960s and early 1970s. The significance of 'class' as a means of understanding key developments in the history of leisure will be discussed, as will the generation of alternative analytical frameworks. The chapter concludes with a consideration of the ways in which the second generation of scholars can build upon the achievements of the first. For the moment, however, attention is turned to one of the major questions that has exercised leisure historians since the earliest days: the problem of explaining 'change over time'.

Massive Disruptions and Impressive Continuities

From the outset, leisure historians were concerned to develop chronologies that could make sense of the far-reaching transformations that had been wrought during the course of the nineteenth century. There were profound shifts in the ways in which leisure was conceptualized, in the place it occupied in everyday life, and in the types

of recreations and sports that were popular. Whereas late-Victorian sports and entertainments such as football, rugby and the music hall appeared to historians to be
reassuringly familiar, the blood sports and rustic amusements of the early nineteenth
century seemed exotically different. One challenge was to construct a chronological
framework that could account for such major cultural changes over what was a
relatively short period of time. In so doing, the 'modernization' of leisure became
an attractive organizing concept.

As scholars set about tracing the decline of the 'traditional' and the birth of the
'modern', so the century appeared to be marked by major turning-points and moments
of massive disruption. Forces of modernization were identified as having 'undermined'
and even 'attacked' a once buoyant set of popular recreations. As portrayed by a
number of historians, this pre-industrial popular cultural formation was essentially rural
in character, uncommercialized in nature and shaped by the exigencies of an agricultural society. Moreover, it had ostensibly changed little over the course of hundreds of
years as the leisure calendar moved in close sympathy with the seasons of the year. For
generations, feast days and holy days had been marked by pastimes such as ploughing
contests, wakes, cockfights and football. This was a highly localized world, with the
village and the parish serving as the prime sites within which leisure was played out.
The face-to-face nature of this society ensured that there was a large degree of understanding between different ranks and orders. At worst, the gentry tolerated the boisterous pastimes and diversions that so entertained their poorer neighbours. At best,
such figures were active patrons of customary popular recreations.

A 'pessimistic' school of historians singled out the Industrial Revolution and the
growth of towns as the prime culprits responsible for the disruption of this traditional leisure culture. The most developed statement of this case was penned by
Robert Malcolmson. He painted a vivid and detailed picture of how the modernizing forces of industrialization and urbanization worked to undermine popular recreations. New working practices ushered in by the rise of the factory system severely
reduced the number of hours that most workers had for leisure. The birth of a class
society, and the associated souring of social relations, meant that the patronage of
the social elite was withdrawn from many customary pastimes. Meanwhile, urbanization was seen to have played a doubly corrosive role. In the first place, the expansion of the built environment brought about the loss of common land that had long
been used for leisure purposes. Secondly, urban growth was accompanied by increased
residential segregation along class lines. Whereas leisure pursuits had often brought
rich and poor together in the pre-industrial villages, now the great industrial towns
with their slums and suburbs encouraged the evolution of class-specific leisure cultures. Against such a context, there arose new understandings of what constituted
civilized behaviour that provided the middle class with the ideological justification it
needed to 'attack' the more distasteful aspects of customary leisure. The establishment of the Society for the Prevention of Cruelty to Animals in 1824, and its successful efforts to end the annual bull-run through the streets of Stamford in the
1840s, was one example of this assault; the activities of the Society for the Suppression of Vice (formed in 1802) was another. The result was a such a severe withering
of the 'traditional' culture as to lead to a 'vacuum of leisure' in the second quarter
of the century.[1] By the century's mid-point, a once richly variegated popular culture
had been reduced to institutions such as the beershop and the gin palace.

This pessimistic reading of the developments of the first half of the nineteenth century dovetailed neatly with arguments that were being elaborated by historians interested in the mid- and later Victorian periods. But now the emphasis was on growth and innovation. This storyline appeared all the more dramatic given the apparent nadir in popular leisure reached during the 1830s and 1840s. If the trauma of 'modernization' had brought about the severe demise of many 'traditional' recreations and entertainments, new ones were to be created that were better suited to the demands of an industrialized, urbanized, class society. 'Modern' leisure rose like a phoenix from the ashes, possessed of prodigious powers of expansion and invention. The renaissance was especially marked in the years after 1870. So striking were the developments that some argued it was a 'revolutionary' era as leisure and sport became more diverse and occupied an enhanced place in the life of the nation. Briggs contended that, by the end of the century, it was possible to think in terms of there being a 'mass entertainment industry' in place.[2]

In contrast to the earlier period, rather than being threatened by the forces of modernization, leisure now drew sustenance from them. Urbanization, industrialization and commercialization appeared as heroes of the piece. The gathering together of large centres of population had the effect of creating mass audiences apparently hungry for entertainment. This demand for leisure was crucial in stimulating entrepreneurs to invest heavily in new forms of recreation and amusement. Hedonistic urban dwellers were enabled to move around and between the large towns and cities in their pursuit of pleasure courtesy of advances in transport such as the railway and the tram. Industrialization was beneficial in other ways too as new technologies were applied to leisure. Thus, the steam press, in conjunction with the railway, broke down the localism that characterized 'traditional' recreations. Now entertainments and sports could become ever more national in scope. Meanwhile, rising real incomes meant more people now had greater funds to spend on their pastimes and amusements. Finally, leisure had gone from being seen as something that was threatening and shot through with dangerously radical overtones, to being conceived of as a necessary feature of the good, civilized life.[3] A consequence of this was a willingness on the part of the authorities and employers to countenance increasing the leisure time available to the working class. Working hours began to drop across a number of trades and occupations, and the number of holidays increased. Bank holidays were introduced in the 1870s, for instance. And 'modern' conceptions of what constituted a working week gradually became the norm as leisure became a more integrated part of everyday life.

Examples abounded of new forms of 'modern' leisure activities developing during the second half of the century. The music hall is often cited as the classic instance of the transforming power of unfettered commercialization. In the 1820s and 1830s, singing and entertainment took place on an informal basis in lowly beerhouses and drinking-places. As first enterprising landlords, and then breweries, began to realize the increased profits that could accrue from investing in purpose-built facilities, the specialist music hall was born. However, it was just one amongst many forms of leisure that had life breathed into them during these years. Seaside resorts grew so fast that they became one of the most important nodes of urban growth during the later decades of the century. Cramped and dark beerhouses made way for well-lit, spacious public houses. Theatres went from being small, portable wooden structures to sumptuous spaces of dramatic pleasure. Consumption itself became a leisure activity. Fish-and-chip shops appeared for the first time, teashops boomed, sales of newspapers, cigarettes and even pianos rocketed, while the department store proclaimed the arrival of a new sort of shopping experience. Meanwhile, there was a 'revolution' in sport. The numbers of sports increased significantly, they were ever more organized and commercialized, and attracted larger numbers of participants and spectators. From football to fox-hunting, curling to croquet and badminton to bowls, the story is the same: expansion, greater organization and an increased profile.

Taken together, these two accounts of change over time portrayed the nineteenth century as being marked by turning-points and deep fault-lines. Decades of terminal decline were apparently followed by an interregnum in which there was 'vacuum' of leisure. This, in turn, was followed by an era of vigorous growth and innovation. Notwithstanding the convincing manner in which the two arguments complemented each other, another reading of events was quickly elaborated. This alternative chronology placed greater stress on the gradual nature of the changes that beset leisure during the period. The 'pessimistic' interpretation of the early industrial years came under the heaviest and most sustained attack, although more recently historians of late-Victorian leisure have seriously quizzed the extent to which the notions of a 'revolution' and untrammelled growth accurately describe developments in the post-1870 decades.

Very early on, a number of the assumptions underpinning Malcolmson's analysis were called into question. As much as it was a critique of the specifics of his argument, this re-evaluation also stood as a criticism of the 'modernization thesis' that informed so much of his and other historians' work. For example, the pessimists' use of the terms 'traditional' and 'modern' was highly problematic. In the first place, it represented an arbitrary labelling of popular cultural practices, and indeed whole societies, that could prove highly misleading. Malcolmson's evocation of the society that had preceded industrialization was certainly flawed. In his account, pre-industrial England emerged as an essentially static society that had changed little over many generations. Yet, as Golby and Purdue pointed out, early modern Britain was far more dynamic than Malcolmson had suggested. Market relations had long since made their presence felt in the countryside, and to that extent, it was the *survival* of older popular pastimes into the late eighteenth century that was worthy of comment, not their imminent decline; they had already outlived the circumstances in which they had originated.[4] Secondly, the modernization thesis set up the idea that the 'traditional' and the 'modern' were mutually exclusive with the former necessarily and inevitably giving way to the latter. This overlooked the fact that so-called 'traditional' pastimes could still be found in 'modern' settings. Even the blood sports, the recreations that came under the heaviest pressure from reformers during the early Victorian years, could be found alive and well – albeit less popular – in the ostensibly 'modern' late nineteenth century. Indeed, the more historians looked, the more they found such examples of adaptation, synthesis and continuity. 'Modern' football had much in common, if one chose to see it, with the varieties of folk football that had been played in the first half of the century; similarly, 'traditional' prizefighting and 'modern' boxing were closely related; and for all the differences that separated the purpose-built public houses from the beershops of the early industrial period, they shared much in terms of the basic functions they discharged. Meanwhile, the urban poor often had little choice but to amuse themselves in ways that would have seemed familiar to their 'traditional' predecessors, given that their poverty effectively excluded them from the realm of commercialized entertainment.

As the criticisms mounted, so the idea of the 'vacuum in leisure' separating a period of atrophy from one of growth looked increasingly untenable. Just as the later Victorian years contained more 'survivals' than one might reasonably expect if the modernization thesis was correct, so there were clear instances of evolution and even innovation during the first half of the nineteenth century. A number of pre-industrial fairs enjoyed new leases of life with the arrival of the steamboats and rail-ways. Sports such as cricket and pedestrianism grew in strength. Entertainments such as the pantomime were re-made during the early industrial age, while the circus was invented during the period. And publicans replaced the gentry as key patrons of popular culture. So striking were these and other developments that Cunningham contended it was more accurate to think of the period from the 1780s through to the 1840s as one in which leisure grew rather than declined.[5]

This underscoring of the impressive continuities that bound the first half of the century with the second represents an important advance on the 'discontinuity thesis'. Although less dramatic than narratives built around the ideas of fracture, disruption and transformation, it is a more sophisticated analysis of the complex processes which underlie cultural change. That said, we need to be careful not to throw the baby out with the bathwater. The nineteenth century did see tremendous changes in the realm of leisure. Too much emphasis on the continuities can obscure that which genuinely was novel and play down the significance of remarkable phenomena such as the sports booms of the later Victorian years. Furthermore, while the notion of a leisure vacuum writ large is fundamentally flawed, it is worth noting that in certain places, such as the frontier industrial towns and iron districts of South Wales, leisure amenities and opportunities were noticeable by their absence during the 1830s and 1840s, partic-ularly when compared with the more bountiful situation that obtained at the end of the century. Any understanding of change over time needs to pay due attention to both the continuities *and* the changes which necessarily can be found in all periods of history.

Class Analysis: The Dominant Paradigm

One of the great strengths of the historiography of leisure has been its openness to outside influences. Historians have frequently borrowed concepts and explanatory models from other disciplines. In seeking to explain the ritualistic nature of many sports, for instance, anthropological ideas of 'thick description' – first developed by Clifford Geertz in his study of the Balinese cockfight[6] – have been pressed into service. Norbert Elias's arguments about a 'civilizing process' have been employed by historians of sport to make sense of changes in levels of violence over time, while, as we shall see later, the sociological concept of 'social control' has featured heavily in much of the literature. Meanwhile, historians have been influenced greatly by scholars working in the field of cultural studies. Thus, a concern to uncover mean-ings and values and to 'decode' popular cultural practices has become a major theme. However, notwithstanding the diverse range of theoretical and conceptual tools drawn from a variety of disciplines, the extent to which class analysis has dominated is striking. This reflects the subject's origins in the 'new' social and labour history projects that developed so vigorously in the 1960s and 1970s, and is testament to the degree to which various brands of Marxist thought have served as intellectual touchstones for so many leisure historians.

From class cultures of leisure to class consciousness

That 'class' appears regularly as a term of social description is, of course, unremarkable in many ways. After all, as social historians have long made plain, the nineteenth century saw the 'birth' or the 'making' of a class society. Even non-Marxists have been quite content to place class at the centre of their histories of Victorian society. And given the extent to which class clearly shaped nineteenth-century leisure, an approach that left it out would be deficient indeed. Vast tracts of the landscape of leisure bore its imprint. For example, where one chose to consume alcohol was a statement of class difference. The bourgeoisie had their private clubs and suburban homes, while the public house was left to become the working-class leisure institution par excellence. The taking of holidays by the seaside was a practice moulded by concerns about 'social tone' and status. Certain resorts catered specifically for the workers whilst others were geared to the demands of a more genteel clientele. Some of the bigger seaside towns – such as Blackpool – managed to accommodate various classes through careful social zoning. Audiences in music halls and theatres were distributed throughout the auditoria by a finely gradated pricing system that worked to separate the classes. Meanwhile, sports were fully implicated in the class system. Football was, in Hobsbawm's words, 'a mass proletarian sport' by the mid-1880s.[7] Boxing enjoyed a similarly close relationship with the working class. And rugby league had its very origins in a clash of class cultures in the 1880s and 1890s when a middle-class elite showed itself to be implacably opposed to the incursion of professional values that was the corollary of rugby union's proletarianization. Other games, such as golf and lawn tennis, became the preserve of the bourgeoisie. Occasionally, governing bodies acted formally to maintain the status of their membership. Thus, during the second half of the century, both the Amateur Rowing Association and the Amateur Athletics Association passed edicts excluding 'artisans and mechanics' from their ranks. More common, and just as effective, was the less formal method of 'black-balling' applicants deemed 'unsuitable'. Even children's leisure was differentiated by class. Bourgeois offspring were likely to spend their leisure time playing with toys and pursuing rational pursuits in the home under adult supervision. Working-class children spent their free time in the streets in the company of their peers. If toys featured at all in this boisterous leisure culture, they were those that could be played with outside, such as hoops, skipping ropes and spinning tops.

Given that so many leisure pursuits were located on one side or other of the line separating the classes, we should not be surprised that historians were content enough to use class as term of description. However, they rarely stopped at that point. For built into the descriptive label were important analytical charges, not least of which was the notion that pastimes were imbued with 'class' values. Thus, when Hobsbawm described football as a 'proletarian sport' he was doing something subtly, yet significantly, different from merely stating it was a sport played and watched by large numbers of working people. He was making the point that the very act of supporting a team in a stadium packed with thousands of other working-class fans, had the potential to raise levels of class consciousness. Likewise, in Smith's exploration of the cultural and social meanings that attached themselves to Welsh boxers, he began by noting that boxing was '*the* working-class recreational activity in industrial Wales'. As such, it could be studied to throw light upon the Welsh working class itself, its value systems and its relationships with other social groups.[8] A host of other sports, amusements and leisure institutions – once defined in class terms – could be similarly analysed. Drinking in pubs, playing in brass bands, singing in choral societies, betting 'on the dogs', pigeon fancying, all were instances of popular cultural practices that could be understood as being inscribed with class meanings.

Recognition that leisure could play a formative role in the production of class consciousness came most fully in debates about the nature of the so-called 'traditional working-class culture' that coalesced in the late-Victorian era. Proceeding from the proposition that political consciousness extended far beyond the sphere of party politics, historians such as Hobsbawm and Stedman Jones cast their nets wide in an effort to gauge the values and meanings that infused the thought-world of the British working class. Popular cultural practices were accorded a prime place in their analyses. Arguments were formulated that not only noted the class-based character of leisure during these years, but which also underlined the tendency for working-class recreations to be ever more 'homogenized'. Unlike earlier eras, in which regional and local differences were often profound, now a range of sports, entertainments and amusements were carried out on a national basis. Workers up and down the country partook of a popular culture that still attested to the importance of the local, yet which was ever more integrated and standardized. It also served as constant reminder of their distinctiveness vis-à-vis the bourgeoisie.

The precise nature of the meanings encoded in this enclosed world of late-Victorian working-class leisure has been disputed. According to Hobsbawm, class consciousness could be found 'everywhere', from the football stadium to the fish-and-chip shop. Moreover, in the twentieth century, it had the potential to be converted into support for the organized labour movement. Stedman Jones was rather more gloomy, underlining the 'inward-looking', 'defensive' and 'conservative' aspects to the values generated in this realm of mass entertainment. The trivialities of an increasingly commercialized culture ensured it was a watered-down version of the more politically charged artisanal culture that had preceded it.[9] Historians of particular leisure practices sometimes agreed. Thus Russell suggested that while popular music-making could have a radicalizing effect, 'the major thrust . . . was probably in a conservative direction'; it competed with the labour movement for individuals' time and money and even managed to build 'delicate' links between the classes.[10] Likewise, McKibbin saw much in working-class leisure that drew resources away from the labour movement, but took issue with Stedman Jones's idea that it was part of a 'culture of consolation'. Sports and hobbies had their own rich meanings that brought satisfaction and afforded an opportunity for mental stimulation. In short, they represented something much more fulfilling than mindless escapism from the drudgery of work.[11]

Such divergent views highlight the difficulties involved in 'reading-off' political meanings from leisure. However, what is of interest here is that no matter how much the proponents disagreed about the details, all were agreed about the central issue, namely that a raft of 'class' meanings resided in the realm of popular leisure.

Class Conflict, 'Social Control' and Working-Class Agency

Another important set of debates also placed class at centre stage. Complementing those concerned with issues of class difference and consciousness, these arguments were focused on the role of class in determining the social relations of leisure. Once again, the gravitational pull exercised by Marxist ideas was decisive. As scholars set about pondering how different social groups related to each other in the realm of leisure, they constructed narratives that turned around notions of class struggle. In addition to possessing their own leisure cultures, classes were also brought into conflict with each other as the bourgeoisie set about re-making popular recreation. Thus, class struggle was not merely the concern of historians of work, politics and industrial relations. On the contrary, it formed the very weft and warp of the social history of leisure too.

The middle class emerged as important players in the drama, for it was they who became experts at 'problematizing' all manner of leisure pursuits. Indeed, in the first instance, the so-called 'problem of leisure' was decidedly bourgeois in character. By the 1820s, the middle class began to enjoy increases in disposable incomes and leisure time. However, such an apparently happy situation was not without its drawbacks. For non-work time could encourage idleness, an unacceptable state of affairs for a group that prided itself on its adherence to the work ethic. In such circumstances, recreation could only be justified if it was 're-creation' – a process that improved and ennobled the citizen and reinvigorated the tired worker's body and mind. The idea that leisure time had to be spent in a 'rational' fashion quickly became installed at the heart of middle-class thinking. It required bourgeois pleasure-seekers to categorize amusements according to their supposed moral worth. Certain practices were unquestionably civilizing – such as the singing of choral music, for instance. Others were irredeemably 'demoralizing' – such as the drinking of alcohol to excess.

Not content with policing its own use of leisure, the middle class was also keen to ensure that the proletariat was spending its free time in an uplifting fashion. In fact, in the case of the working class, the problem was all the more acute, for so many of the pastimes and amusements of the workers seemed to be dissolute and degrading. An exercise in social engineering began, with bourgeois worthies convinced of the ability of 'rational recreation' to save the working class from their immoral ways. As H. A. Bruce, then a stipendiary magistrate in Merthyr Tydfil, put it in 1850:

> To me the simplest, most natural, most efficacious instrument of redemption seems to be, to provide, or to assist the working classes to provide, those means of innocent pleasure, of social enjoyment, at which moral and mental improvement rather insinuate themselves than are enforced – where recreation may lead on insensibly to refinement, and pursuits commenced for the mere purpose of amusement and relaxation, may gradually improve the manners, elevate the tone, and expand the intellect of those, who little suspect the transformation they are undergoing.[12]

Little wonder, when confronted with such statements, that historians of leisure felt able to talk about a 'social control' project being carried out. They chronicled the various bourgeois-sponsored initiatives that had the aim of attracting the workers away from their taverns and beershops. Mechanics' Institutes, free libraries, temperance societies, Sunday schools, coffee taverns and museums were opened, public parks

were laid out, choral societies and brass bands were formed. And if techniques of
'moral suasion' failed to work, there were those who were willing to use the law to
bring about the civilization of the workers. Acts of Parliament were introduced which
targeted popular recreations while leaving those of the well-heeled untouched. The
1835 Cruelty to Animals Act could be used to bring to an end the Stamford bull-
run, but was apparently powerless when it came to the upper-class pursuit of fox-
hunting. Likewise, the Welsh Sunday Closing Act of 1881 managed to shut
working-class pubs whilst leaving bourgeois clubs open for business. Meanwhile, as
by-laws were introduced that sought to regulate the streets, the 'new' police were
introduced as agents of class rule to ensure that the writ of the middle class ran in
even the most working-class of neighbourhoods.[13]

This drive to 'rationalize' working-class leisure was seen as a clear instance of power
operating along class lines. However, an important feature of the historiography was
the extent to which working-class resistance was asserted. The middle class may have
been cast as the group with their hands on many of the most impressive levers of
power, but true to their credentials as authors of 'history from below', leisure historians were keen to emphasize the ability of the workers to make their own history.
Here a strong 'culturalist' influence could be discerned, with E. P. Thompson's ideas
resonating most strongly throughout the field. His insistence that the working class
was present at its own making, and was responsible for the creation of a working-
class culture that was rich, distinctive and enduring found widespread acceptance
amongst leisure historians generally.[14] They pointed out how often middle-class
schemes to elevate and educate the workers came to naught. Far from being a blank
slate upon which the bourgeoisie could write their own meanings, the working class
possessed its own set of values – so much so, that scholars have recently begun to
note how the assumptions governing 'rational recreation' were modified as middle-
class reformers slowly began to appreciate that the working class wanted more from
their leisure than lectures and 'worthy' pastimes. By the 1890s, some were even
beginning to re-think the strategy of encouraging alternatives to the public house,
deciding instead to use the pub itself as a means of improving the workers.[15]

It should be noted that fault has been found with the 'social control' thesis on
both empirical and theoretical grounds. Firstly, it tends to gloss over the fact there
was a sizeable group within the working class possessed of a strong desire to 'self-
improve' and spend its leisure time in a rational fashion. The bourgeoisie never had
a monopoly on respectable behaviour. Secondly, it can overstate the extent to which
the ruling class was in agreement about the 'problem' of popular leisure. By the later
Victorian years there is evidence to suggest that, while elements of the middle class
were as sanctimonious and pious as ever, significant numbers of the rest of the bourgeoisie were becoming less earnest and more attuned to the fun that could be had
from recreation. Thirdly, critics point out that the mechanisms of social control were
highly imperfect. The police, for instance, might be seen as agents of middle-class
rule, but they were largely drawn from the working class itself, and could exercise
their own discretion when it came to enforcing the law. Finally, there are theoretical
problems with the idea of social control, not least of which is that it can be seen to
be everywhere simply because there was no serious uprising in the second half of the
century. Even when there were outbreaks of disorder or moments of resistance against
the latest attempt to reform popular leisure, these can be interpreted as evidence of

a state that was willing to let the working class get its own way occasionally if only to make it feel as if it was being listened to. Thus, a breakdown in social order could actually be evidence of a successful piece of social control. Under such circumstances, the concept is emptied of any real explanatory powers.[16]

In the face of these criticisms, historians of leisure turned increasingly to Gramscian notions of 'hegemony', 'consent' and 'negotiation', as a rather more sophisticated means of analysing such phenomenon as the drive towards rational recreation. Whatever the merits of the various concepts employed to make sense of the lived history, the real strength of the debates lay in their recognition that leisure was a field implicated in wider power relations between the classes. This proved to be an immensely fruitful way of approaching (especially) the mid- and late-Victorian periods, the era in which Britain's reputation as a 'class' society was being cemented. Nevertheless, whilst class analysis has become the predominant paradigm shaping the literature, recent years have witnessed an increased awareness of its limitations as a master explanatory category.

Beyond Class? Alternatives and Complements to Class Analysis

One could be forgiven for thinking that class analysis was everywhere in the historiography. Whether used as a term of description or as a means of understanding the social relations of leisure, class has shaped the historical literature in a way that no other concept has managed to do; and with good reason. Class, after all, clearly mattered. However, historians have begun to appreciate the need to allow other explanatory categories into their histories. In part, this has been a widespread phenomenon affecting most historians of nineteenth-century Britain to varying degrees over the last decade. The rise of postmodernism is especially noteworthy in this respect. By attacking some of the primary building blocks of historical practice (including the concept of class), postmodern scholars have been especially adept at plunging whole disciplines into crisis. In comparison with some subject areas, particularly social and labour history, leisure history has emerged from the debates about the 'linguistic turn' relatively unscathed. Whether or not this is a good thing is a matter that will be returned to later. For the moment, it is enough to note that historians of leisure have managed to look beyond class – albeit often in tentative ways – even without the help of the postmodernists.

Notwithstanding its many virtues as a tool of analysis, the shortcomings of class are becoming more apparent. Even as a means of describing the leisure world of nineteenth-century Britain it has its weaknesses, not least of which is its tendency to reduce a complex history to overly simple terms. While labels such as 'working-class' pastimes and 'middle-class' sports undoubtedly reveal truths about the past, they cannot pretend to capture the nuances of the lived history. In fact, the very best of leisure historians have always known that while class may have strongly influenced cultural values, it never determined them completely. Thus, to write about 'middle-class' attitudes to sport can obscure as much as it illuminates. Certainly, amateurism may usefully be seen as a middle-class ideology, but only if it is recognized that it was possible to be middle class and think that professionalism in sport was perfectly acceptable. Indeed, in particular regions of the country – such as the North of England and industrial South Wales – just such bourgeois attitudes can be discerned.

A whole host of factors should be brought into play – including age, religious affiliation, ethnicity, educational credentials, language and status – when researching the
history of ostensibly 'working-class' or 'middle-class' leisure cultures. Class certainly
set limits on what it may have been possible to think, but even the most obviously
class-determined culture always allowed contradictory thoughts to flourish.

In the light of the failings of the 'social control' thesis, historians of leisure were
receptive to lines of argument that moved away from an over-reliance upon class.
Long before the arrival of the 'linguistic turners', scholars were paying close attention to the language employed by contemporaries when discussing leisure. They
observed how the discourse of 'improving' organizations such as temperance societies and chapels was invariably drained of class meaning. Instead, a socially inclusive
and consensual discourse – often invoking notions of 'respectability' – was deployed
that could unite the 'labour aristocrats' with their middle-class betters. The more
they looked, the more respectability appeared to be a worthy rival to class itself.
Indeed, according to Best, one of the concept's most enthusiastic champions, the
gulf separating those who were and were not respectable represented 'the sharpest
of all lines of social division . . . a sharper line by far than that between rich and poor,
employer and employee, or capitalist and proletarian'.[17]

Leisure historians were necessarily implicated in arguments over respectability, for
use of leisure time was seen a major factor in the moulding of 'character'. 'Roughs'
were likely to get drunk in public, swear, gamble and generally fritter away their
leisure hours; their respectable counterparts, on the other hand, were more inclined
to use their free time in a rational, improving manner. The most suggestive intervention in the debate came from Peter Bailey, a leisure historian. He contended that
respectability should be viewed as a social role rather than a cultural absolute.[18] Bailey
was unconvinced by the image of a substratum of the working class that was
respectable for ever and a day. Instead, it was more accurate, he suggested, to see
respectability as a role that could be performed when it suited the working class to
do so. Such an argument generated new insights into working-class reactions to the
rational recreation movement. Workers could 'play' at being respectable in a strategic and instrumental fashion. For example, when 'muscular Christians' began
setting up church football clubs in an effort to save working-class souls, their efforts
were met with great enthusiasm on the part of many youths. However, all the evidence suggests that while the hopes of reformers were initially high, in fact the experiment simply produced more working-class footballers; congregation sizes remained
constant. Keen sports fans were more than able to speak the language of respectability and rational recreation in order to get the help necessary to set up their own teams
and leagues.

Bailey underlined the importance of respectability while holding onto class as an
analytical tool. Working-class understandings of respectability could, it seemed, vary
significantly from bourgeois ideas. Class has proved similarly resilient in the face of
the rise of women's and gender history. Indeed, so entrenched was class analysis that
it took a remarkably long time for the historiography to bear any signs at all of the
heightened sensitivities to gender that had become evident throughout other subject
areas. Too often, when discussing leisure, historians merely generalized from the
experiences of men. However, recently scholars have begun to take gender seriously,
a move that has highlighted how misleading a male-centred version of leisure history

can be. Take, for example, debates about the growth of leisure in the mid- and late-Victorian periods. If women are excluded from the narrative, the storyline is one of increased recreational opportunities for all – a veritable democratization of leisure. But if one looks at the history of working-class women, an altogether different tale emerges. Parratt has highlighted how working-class leisure in late-Victorian and Edwardian England was deeply fractured along gender lines. While many working-class men may well have been able to participate in the world of commercialized leisure, working-class women were severely hamstrung by their precarious position in the labour market. Those that did get jobs outside the home often found themselves in poorly paid, insecure, unskilled occupations. Consequently, they were unable to build up the resources, in terms of time and money, to partake of the expanding world of commercialized entertainments. Those who remained at home were in an even more unfavourable position. Their labours were rarely thought of as constituting 'proper' work and thus their claims to the pleasurable compensations of leisure were easily dismissed.[19] In the light of studies which focus attention upon the experiences of women, the notion of an ever expanding leisure world is shown to be highly misleading. At best, it captures the experience of those working-class men who were fortunate enough not to belong to the sizeable ranks of the urban poor.

Middle-class women were also treated as second-class citizens. Yet, notwithstanding the real inequalities suffered by bourgeois women, it seems clear that the higher up the social scale a woman was, the greater her ability to enjoy at least some of the benefits of the much-vaunted democratization of leisure. Take sport, for example. As the 'cult of athleticism' developed in the mid-Victorian public schools for boys, notions of 'manliness' and male character were increasingly fused with sporting activities. Women were cast in passive roles, supposedly offering their menfolk support from the sidelines. Nevertheless, it was working-class women who suffered most in the face of such ideas. Their lowly position in the dual hierarchies of class and gender marginalized them for most of the period. In contrast, middle-class women appear to have been better placed to break into various sports. Reformers of female education looked to transpose many aspects of the curricula in boys' schools into the girls' equivalents. At first, exercise was of a gentle nature but exertion levels rose as the century wore on. By the 1880s, gymnastics was a common feature of most school curricula, while by the end of the century, girls were introduced to an ever widening range of team sports including rounders, hockey, fencing, lacrosse, lawn tennis and cricket. Although none of this amounted to anything like equal treatment for bourgeois women, class was still of critical importance in the gender-divided world of sport.

Yet despite the obvious power of class analysis, the deficiencies of an approach that fails to recognize the gendered nature of leisure are slowly being realized. It is no longer enough simply to note that nineteenth-century leisure was 'male-dominated'. Even the most masculine of leisure institutions – the pub – has been reappraised. Bailey has reminded us that while women customers may have been few and far between, at the heart of this 'male-dominated' environment stood the barmaid. Her femininity brought a sexual charge to the act of drinking. Thus gender, as well as class, shaped the culture of the public house in ways that have rarely been acknowledged.[20] Meanwhile, other historians have applied gender insights that can make us rethink male-oriented definitions of leisure itself. Melanie Tebbutt's history of 'gossip' is significant in this respect. She concentrated attention upon an activity that most leisure historians had completely ignored. In the process, she confirmed how working-class women had little opportunity to enjoy the commercialized mass entertainments of the later Victorian years. These, of course, were the entertainments that had so bewitched scholars and had come to define the very essence of late-nineteenth-century leisure in the historiography. Yet Tebbutt showed how working-class women were able to use what scarce resources they had for leisure in a creative and rewarding fashion. A few precious minutes snatched during a day of otherwise unremitting hard toil were turned into meaningful social exchanges.[21] This is not to say that gossip should be seen as adequate compensation for the inequalities endured by such women. But it is to suggest that our understandings of what constituted leisure need to be expanded if historians are to capture more adequately the complexities of the past. Gender analysis has the potential to do just that.

More of the Same?

The last forty years have witnessed the vigorous growth of leisure history. From its uncertain beginnings, it has flourished into a respected area of historical research. In the process, the nineteenth century has commanded the lion's share of leisure historians' attention. As a consequence, our understanding of how recreations and sports developed during what was clearly a crucial period has deepened immeasurably. The processes by which older amusements and diversions either fell into abeyance or adapted to new surroundings are more easily grasped once the distorting lens of the 'modernization thesis' has been placed to one side. We are better able to appreciate the ways in which the social relations of leisure were conducted. The 'social control' paradigm did much to focus attention upon leisure's implication in a power network shaped by the demands of a class society. And historians are now beginning to explore other means by which social conflict and difference were structured in the realm of leisure. However one gauges it, the achievements of recent decades are legion. And there are plenty of nodes of historiographical growth to keep the next generation of historians fully occupied. While we know much about urban popular culture, its rural equivalent has long been neglected. The same goes for social groups other than the working class. Some, at last, are being let into the fold. Women are amongst the most significant of these, although the middle class too is now receiving the serious attention that it deserves. Meanwhile, the range of leisure activities and sports that are been researched are increasing exponentially.

Nevertheless, for all this industry and fine work, warning bells are ringing. As the historiography has developed, it has begun to suffer from a 'hardening of the categories'.[22] More of the same – albeit about different sports, entertainments or social groups – may not be enough to retain the vitality of the field. Bailey has suggested some ways forward that break out of the existing problematics. In particular he has urged historians to pay more attention to the 'experience' of leisure. What of the dreams and fantasies that contemporaries invested in their pastimes and amusements? How might notions such as 'pleasure' and 'fun' have changed over time? These are important issues that serious-minded academics have generally shied away from. Yet by considering more carefully the meanings bound up in the language of pleasure, by attending to the various vocabularies of fun deployed throughout the century, whole new vistas in the history of leisure may be opened up.

Historians may be helped in such a venture by the recent 'linguistic turn'. For all its failings, some of which are profound, postmodernism has at least asked historians to think carefully before essentializing all manner of apparently straightforward 'experiences'. Certainly the social history paradigm has been invigorated by its (sometimes bruising) encounters with postmodernists. Yet there has been remarkably little in the way of engagement between leisure and sports history and the linguistic turners. This is to be regretted. As Jeffrey Hill's work on aspects of twentieth-century leisure has demonstrated, if the worst excesses of postmodern theory are avoided, new insights into the meanings of popular cultural practices can be gleaned.[23] While there is no obvious Victorian equivalent of Nick Hornby's *Fever Pitch* to consult, if scholars approach their sources imaginatively it may yet be possible to uncover the 'emotional economy' that underpinned, for instance, sports such as football and rugby.

Of course, the apparent lack of interest displayed by leisure historians in postmodernism might be a blessing in disguise. It could be that scholars have simply decided that a body of thought with such ahistorical (and even anti-historical) tendencies is not for them. However, an alternative explanation is that the historiography is becoming too self-referential and disconnected from the mainstream. This was a danger that James Walvin identified back in 1984 in relation to sports history. In the very first edition of the *British Journal of Sports History*, he reflected on the value of having a journal dedicated solely to the history of sport. Walvin was unconvinced about the need for the new organ. Sports history's claims to autonomy were 'strictly limited', he argued. Its true home was the social history project, for there it could be located within a wider interpretative framework. This was necessary if the studies of sports historians 'are to be any more than yet another quasi-antiquarianism masquerading as serious social history'.[24] The same can be said about leisure history generally. That social history has been fully exposed to the icy blasts of postmodernism, while leisure history has been seemingly insulated from them, is perhaps a worrying sign that the two historiographies are going their separate ways. There can be little doubt that the very best historians of nineteenth-century leisure and sport have always looked to place their findings in the widest possible context and been open to new ideas. Such openness is needed again if the next generation of leisure historians is to be as successful and exciting as the first.

NOTES

1. R. W. Malcolmson, *Popular Recreations in English Society, 1700–1850* (Cambridge, 1973), p. 170.
2. A. Briggs, *Mass Entertainment: The Origins of a Modern Industry* (Adelaide, 1960).
3. H. Cunningham, *Leisure in the Industrial Revolution, c.1780–c.1880* (London, 1980), pp. 177–8.
4. J. M. Golby and A. W. Purdue, *The Civilisation of the Crowd: Popular Culture in England 1750–1900* (Stroud, 1999), ch. 1.
5. Cunningham, *Leisure*, ch. 1.

6. Clifford Geertz, 'Deep play: notes on the Balinese cockfight', in *The Interpretation of Cultures: Selected Essays* (London, 1993).

7. E. J. Hobsbawm, *Worlds of Labour: Further Studies in the History of Labour* (London, 1984), p. 185.

8. D. Smith, *Aneurin Bevan and the World of South Wales* (Cardiff, 1993), p. 320.

9. Hobsbawm, *Worlds of Labour*; G. Stedman Jones, *Languages of Class: Studies in English Working Class History, 1832–1982* (Cambridge, 1983), ch. 4.

10. D. Russell, *Popular Music in England, 1815–1914: A Social History* (Manchester, 1987), p. 241.

11. R. McKibbin, *The Ideologies of Class: Social Relations in Britain, 1880–1950* (Oxford, 1990).

12. H. A. Bruce, *On Amusements as the Means of Continuing and Extending the Education of the Working Classes* (Cardiff, 1850).

13. R. D. Storch, 'The policeman as domestic missionary: urban discipline and popular culture in northern England, 1850–80', *Journal of Social History*, 9 (1976).

14. E. P. Thompson, *The Making of the English Working Class* (London, 1963).

15. D. W. Gutzke, 'Gentrifying the British public house, 1896–1914', *International Labor and Working-Class History*, 45 (1994).

16. Stedman Jones, *Languages of Class*, ch. 2.

17. G. Best, *Mid-Victorian Britain 1851–75* (London, 1979), p. 282.

18. P. Bailey, 'Will the real Bill Banks please stand up? Towards a role analysis of mid-Victorian working-class respectability', *Journal of Social History*, 12 (1979).

19. C. M. Parratt, *'More Than Mere Amusement': Working-Class Women's Leisure in England, 1750–1914* (Boston, MA, 2001).

20. P. Bailey, 'Parasexuality and glamour: the Victorian barmaid as cultural prototype', *Gender and History*, 2 (1990).

21. M. Tebbutt, *Women's Talk? A Social History of 'Gossip' in Working-Class Neighbourhoods, 1880–1960* (Aldershot, 1995).

22. P. Bailey, 'The politics and poetics of modern British leisure: a late twentieth-century review', *Rethinking History*, 3 (1999), p. 155.

23. J. Hill, 'The legend of Denis Compton', *The Sports Historian*, 18 (1998).

24. J. Walvin, 'Sport, social history and the historian', *British Journal of Sports History*, 1 (1984).

FURTHER READING

The best introduction to the historiography, and essential reading for all serious students of leisure history, is P. Bailey, 'The politics and poetics of modern British leisure: a late twentieth-century review', *Rethinking History*, 3 (1999). For a compelling survey of developments in the nineteenth-century, see H. Cunningham, 'Leisure and culture', in F. M. L. Thompson, ed., *The Cambridge Social History of Britain, 1750–1950*, vol. 2, *People and Their Environment* (1990). Cunningham's *Leisure in the Industrial Revolution, c.1780–c.1880* (1980) is still an important work. J. M. Golby and A. W. Purdue, *The Civilisation of the Crowd: Popular Culture in England 1750–1900* (1999) is another admirable survey. Fans of sports history are well served by R. Holt, *Sport and the British: A Modern History* (1989) and N. Tranter, *Sport, Economy and Society in Britain, 1750–1914* (1998). For classic examples of the social history of leisure, see P. Bailey, *Leisure and Class in Victorian England: Rational Recreation and the Contest for Control, 1830–1885* (1987), B. Harrison, *Drink and the Victorians: The Temperance Question in England* (1971) and J. K. Walton, *The English Seaside Resort: A Social History, 1750–1914* (1983). All highlight how the history of leisure, at its best, has always been about more than just leisure. J. Lowerson, *Sport and the English Middle Classes, 1870–1914* (1993), M. Huggins, 'Second-class citizens? English middle-class culture and sport, 1850–1910: a reconsideration', *International Journal of the History of Sport*, 17 (2000) and C. M. Parratt, *'More Than Mere Amusement': Working-Class Women's Leisure in England, 1750–1914* (2001) are fine examples of how leisure historians are now studying groups that have hitherto been marginalized. Meanwhile, J. Hill, 'British sports history: a postmodern future?', *Journal of Sport History*, 23 (1996) makes the case for an application of some of the insights generated by the 'linguistic turn'.

CHAPTER TWENTY-FIVE

Health and Medicine

KEIR WADDINGTON

The history of medicine has been seen, all too often, as a ghetto; separate from political, social or economic history. Early accounts were inward-looking and doctor-oriented. They embodied a positivist view, concentrating on great men and scientific advances. Since the 1960s, scholarship has endeavoured to break away from this Whiggish mould by exploring the social relations of medicine. The emergence of a radical sociological critique of medicine in the 1970s through the work of Foucault, Szasz and Illich further challenged perceptions.[1] These scholars argued that medicine was a form of repression, a way of defining deviance, which exercised a socio-political strategy of power and authority in the name of apparently value-free science. Buttressed by this revisionist critique, the social history of medicine moved to adopt a more problem-oriented approach, drawing on concepts from demography, gender studies and ethnography. Gradually, new accounts started to dismantle both heroic and anti-heroic narratives. Medical histories moved to address broader questions of culture, society and politics and their relationship with health, adding to debates on the social construction of everyday life. Calls were made for medical history from below and the number of regional studies grew. Although the breadth of research increased to embrace providers, patients, institutions and rationales, certain trends remained. Issues surrounding professionalization and the construction of power and knowledge continue to represent important themes, as does the role of the state. These preoccupations have provided continuity but have not prevented medical history from becoming, over the last thirty years, a vibrant field that has come to address political, social and economic issues.

This chapter adopts a critical view of the historiography in order to explore a series of interlocking themes. It re-examines what was represented by health and medicine, in order to investigate practices, institutions and the role of the state. The intention is not to provide a narrative, but to question existing chronologies, the status of medicine and the nature of care.

Health and Illness

Experiences of illness are essentially personal and are hard to quantify. Historians have therefore tended to concentrate on mortality with its paper trail of records. Whilst a fall in mortality after 1870 has been detected, death rates tell us little about non-fatal illnesses and only hint at incidences of ill-health. James Riley has attempted to measure this hidden history of sickness. By looking at the records of friendly societies, he has suggested that incidences of sickness fell during the nineteenth century.[2] However, with membership of these societies restricted to those who could afford to subscribe, his assessment paints only a partial picture, one contradicted by Poor Law and other contemporary evidence (diaries and letters) which imply that sickness continued to be a feature of everyday life for many even at the end of the century. Experiences of ill-health involved not just grave ailments but also minor complaints, and depended on a range of factors that included season, location, class, age, gender and ethnicity. For example, levels of sickness were greater in the North and in cities. Across the country, industrialization and urbanization took their toll on health. Many towns were constructed on a whim by developers, with builders sacrificing quality for speed. When the Health of Towns Commission investigated in the 1840s, it found the urban environment characterized by accumulations of filth. Overcrowding, sewage and pollution were part of urban topography. Rural conditions were little better. Large variations existed between affluent and poor districts, something contemporaries did not fail to notice. Slums and 'epidemic streets' were feared as sources of contagion, concerns that were directed at houses, ethnic groups (particularly the Irish) and individuals. Only gradually were urban conditions improved.

In these conditions, new diseases like cholera took hold and reached epidemic proportions, while existing infectious diseases became endemic. Overcrowding multiplied opportunities for infection; migration assisted the spread of disease, as did social customs that encouraged regular visiting; and new workplaces and working practices brought with them new diseases, many of which were disfiguring. However, the public's imagination was captured not by the mundane experiences of sickness but by the epidemics that swept Britain. Although epidemics have been associated with high mortality, more fell ill than died. They left a physical and psychological wake, with the onslaughts of cholera the most striking. Like plague before it, cholera was an occasional invader with four outbreaks between 1831 and 1866. The progress of the disease was frightening; it was hardly surprising therefore that it became invested with a terror which one contemporary described as 'cholerapobia'. Less sensational were the outbreaks of 'fever' in the 1830s and 1840s or the epidemics of typhoid in the 1840s and 1860s. With a decline in epidemics after 1860 other, less sensational diseases – cancer, heart disease and diabetes – emerged to take their place as the major causes of death. This reflected a transition towards chronic and degenerative diseases, although uncertainty over the extent to which these had been previously underdiagnosed complicates the picture. Why this transition occurred is open to considerable speculation, with explanations covering improved nutrition, limitation of family size, and social intervention.

For most, the experiences of sickness were dominated not by epidemics but by colds, headaches, flu and diarrhoea, the latter a common affliction during the summer. Minor and chronic illnesses were widespread and helped mask the early stages of serious conditions. Poor domestic and personal hygiene, compounded by impure and inadequate water supplies, increased the risk. Food-poisoning was a constant danger, though in most cases the result was indigestion. For many, poverty and deprivation were intertwined with sickness, factors that accounted for high levels of ill-health among the poor.

Women generally fared better than men. However, many doctors subscribed to the view that 'the man who does not know sick women does not know women'. They felt that women were driven by their reproductive cycle, linking their biology to weakness and sickness. Certain diseases were labelled female maladies, whilst women were seen as especially prone to others. This construction of pathological weakness served a purpose, assisting in the definition of gender roles. It did not reflect social realities. Whilst women suffered longer periods of illness than men they fell sick less often. Yet this assessment ignores the rigours of childbirth. Women in the 1890s remembered weakness and suffering associated with pregnancy and childbirth, with the latter the most important cause of female ill-health. Poor women fared worse than their richer sisters.

If location, class and gender shaped ill-health, contemporaries also pointed to a connection between behaviour and illness. Disease continued to be seen as symbolic of misdeeds or as the natural outcome of vice, attitudes that did not translate into an exclusively class-centred concern with the poor. Tuberculosis, for example, at one time romanticized, became associated with depravity and indulgence, and VD with sexual vice. Labels were sought to explain disease and were applied to behaviour (such as masturbation) that was perceived as deviant. Disease was readily associated with particular character types, not only in the popular imagination, but also in medicine as moral and social explanations were put forward.

Surrounded by illness, many became fatalistic or indifferent. For the poor, the dread of being deprived of work encouraged them to ignore diseases or to embrace promises of cure. Others, particularly the middle classes, became obsessed with health. Lectures and pamphlets related health to cleanliness and civilization. Intellectuals both sentimentalized illness and lamented their poor health. In response, they suggested models for the healthy citizen that combined the physical and the spiritual. For others, disease or invalidism was to be embraced. The sick-role gave privacy and a degree of authority, particularly for women. Sickness could therefore serve a number of functions for the individual and for society. Only by the end of the century did health begin to be perceived as a normal state, as a romantic glorification of suffering was rejected in favour of healthy pursuits.

The Fringe and the Orthodox

This concern with disease underpinned the ecology of care. Health, or the promise of health, had become a commodity, providing the foundation for an expanding medical market. Ideas of hygiene and good health became important features of advertising, particularly for products like Pears soap. Societies were established to provide care and promote health. An array of healers flourished alongside this philanthropic effort, with ability to pay shaping the dimensions of care. Although the fortunes of such groups fluctuated, for orthodox practitioners the nineteenth century has been seen as an era of professionalization.

Although definitions of professionalization have been broadly divided between a functional and structural approach, in both medicine has been seen as representing the paradigm of the process of professionalization. However, neither model is entirely satisfactory in explaining the way in which doctors came to see themselves as belonging to an increasingly respectable profession. Studies of alternative medicine have highlighted problems with occupational closure, those of medical education the absence of a single portal or body of knowledge. Research has pointed to the insecurities of Victorian practitioners, how they were not always able to exert control over their work, and to their diverse attitudes. For members of an increasingly self-conscious occupation, the trappings of professionalization proved harder to obtain than a belief that medicine represented a profession.

While doctors by 1900 could lay claim to the credentials of the professional gentleman, the process was not a linear one. Studies in the 1980s questioned the view that orthodox practitioners before the 1858 Medical Act conformed to a tripartite hierarchical model divided between physicians, surgeons and apothecaries. Boundaries were already blurred, encouraged by the growing demand for medical care and the self-interest of practitioners. Works by Waddington and Loudon have moved away from an iconoclastic approach that saw the period between the 1815 Apothecary Act and the 1858 Act as one of uninterrupted progress in which a defined profession emerged.[3] Instead, they have stressed continuity, arguing that a rank-and-file composed of surgeons and apothecaries (or increasingly both) had already cut across existing structures before 1800. This group came to represent a growing class of general practitioners (GPs) catering to the middling orders, eager to reform the elitist licensing bodies and to press for protection. The result was intra-professional strife, not least among the rank-and-file which, if united by its exclusion, was divided by politics and religion. By the 1860s, doctors had become loosely divided between GPs and an elite group of hospital consultants. In the process, the elite had consolidated their position. However, this polarity can be overdrawn. Whereas those holding hospital posts endeavoured to attend the wealthy, their work was entrenched in general practice. Many doctors combined a range of duties that included general practice and an institutional appointment. While this heterogeneity points to an increasing medicalization of society as the number of opportunities for doctors expanded, it also represented a rational strategy in the face of competition.

Doctors certainly felt beleaguered. Complaints were repeatedly voiced about what was perceived as competition and low incomes. The rise of the dispensing druggist, offering cheap care, triggered calls for reform, but druggists were not the only competitors. Quacks, those pretenders to medical skill, were cast as a national evil made worse by their success. They offered convenient remedies, but whilst quacks continued to peddle their nostrums, new groups of alternative practitioners emerged. Linked to radical dissent, they drew on heterodox theories of pathology and therapeutics to claim a holistic approach. Each argued in its own language that regular medicine was wrong, with adherents claiming that they offered a better, more natural system. This was an alternative science; one bound up with social, cultural and political movements. Popular, in part because of their cheapness, alternative practitioners threatened the legitimacy of orthodox medicine and challenged its attempts at monopoly. Of these alternative medicines, homoeopathy appeared the most dangerous to doctors and the most alluring to the public. Based on the ideas of Samuel

Hahnemann, who advocated that 'like cures like', homoeopathy embraced a holistic view and small dosages in contrast to the heroic practices of allopathic medicine. Homoeopathy was not the only movement to attract attention. For example, herbalism served a largely working-class clientele; hydrotherapy became a middle-class vogue. The boundaries between these, and other alternative medicines such as mesmerism, and those espoused by regular practitioners were fluid and often socially constructed. To see them as conceptual or epistemological opposites is to overstate divisions. Alternative practitioners, like their orthodox cousins, assimilated a scientific rhetoric to enhance their status, whilst they reinvigorated ideas from allopathic medicine. Both stressed the healing power of nature and the importance of a rational understanding of disease. Nor were regular practitioners averse to using alternative therapies, for example employing patent medicines or hydrotherapy. Only as access to professional medicine improved and confidence in orthodox practitioners rose, were attempts to marginalize alternative practitioners successful.

Doctors' anxieties followed the fortunes of the medical market and reflected attempts to gain a professional monopoly. Competition was intense, both from alternative practitioners and from the surge in the number of orthodox practitioners. In this environment, doctors attacked the real and imagined threat posed by irregulars to their livelihoods and authority. Rather than being motivated by social change and scientific advance, many saw in their abolition a solution to the financial and status problems facing medicine. Attacks on quacks merged with intra-professional quarrels as GPs attempted to improve their status. After over half a century of campaigning, the 1858 Medical (Registration) Act was a disappointment. For historians, however, it has been seen as a defining moment in the professionalization of medicine. In establishing a medical register and the General Medical Council (GMC), it demarcated the legal boundary between orthodoxy and fringe. However, it failed to outlaw alternative practice. Although state posts were restricted to registered doctors, competition persisted. The Act did not create a single portal of entry or settle the problem of an acceptable body of knowledge. In insisting on the need for practitioners to hold a qualification from one of the licensing bodies in order to register, it merely recognized existing practices and maintained established hierarchies.

If quackery became a convenient label with which to attack competitors, quacks were not the only threat. Women also posed a problem. Opposition to female practitioners arose from an interaction of material concerns and social and medical constructions of femininity. Efforts to exclude women from the profession formed an important part of the masculinization of medicine and doctors' strategy of occupational closure. The story of women's struggle to enter medicine is often one of a few dedicated individuals facing opposition from a profession that willingly constructed pseudo-scientific theories which played on social prejudices. A more nuanced account suggests that eighteenth-century female practitioners were marginalized and that women's attempts to gain entry to medicine after 1840 focused initially on confrontational, inclusionary strategies. These were replaced by legalistic tactics and a move to found an all-female medical school in London. Although opposition was never total, only a few hospital schools became co-educational. Once women were admitted, opposition shifted slightly to restrict career opportunities (mainly to paediatrics or gynaecology), leaving the few who did qualify isolated and under hostile scrutiny.

The impression of unity produced by the 1858 Medical Act concealed a lack of integration between Welsh, Scottish and English practitioners. Hierarchical differences existed between urban, suburban and rural practices, and between GPs and consultants. The debate over outpatient abuse, where it was felt that voluntary hospitals wrongfully admitted patients who could pay, saw GPs accuse consultants of stealing patients. In turn, consultants accused GPs of being greedy. These divisions point to insecurities in the medical profession that reflected its low status. Before 1850, doctors were regularly satirized as mercenary, brutal and ignorant. In espousing heroic or contested treatments, they allied themselves to unpopular remedies. Dissection, made necessary by the growing emphasis on morbid anatomy, further damaged medicine. Dissection offended taboos surrounding death and generated deep cultural and spiritual anxiety, while the process of obtaining bodies through grave-robbing associated medicine with criminal and immoral practices. When body-snatching became murder – as in the notorious case of Burke and Hare – the public was outraged. The 1832 Anatomy Act, in creating a legal supply of cadavers, did little to relieve tensions, and by targeting the bodies of unclaimed paupers, made dissection appear a punishment for pauperism. It was not only dissection that aroused anger and fear. Campaigns against the Contagious Diseases Acts (introduced to control the spread of venereal disease) portrayed doctors as vehicles of instrumental rape, and the furore surrounding vivisection suggested that they were cruel.

By the 1880s, doctors were in a stronger social position. In part, this arose from structural changes in medicine. The formation of medical societies, associations and journals helped developed a sense of professional belonging and common identity. The GMC sought to police medicine, adopting standards of ethical and professional behaviour that reflected notions of propriety which appealed to the middle classes. It also worked to systematize medical education and replace apprenticeship with hospital training. Although what doctors should learn remained the subject of intense debate, changes in the medical curriculum and the move into medical schools encouraged the development of shared professional values. However, educational change was only part of the answer. With character, breeding and a cultured education believed to be essential to success, doctors adopted prevailing concerns with character and moral vigour. Science also played a prominent role. Before the 1850s, science had been used in the struggle against alternative practitioners as a means of asserting legitimate knowledge. Subsequently, science was increasingly used in a different way to enhance the status of medicine. For contemporaries, science was a source of cultural authority, provided it was not the same science deplored by anti-vivisectionists. If few patients judged practitioners on their knowledge, doctors readily co-opted a language of science for their professional ends. In the process, medicine's status rose allied to changes in medical ideas and surgical practices that underlay a growing confidence in doctors' judgements.

The growing status of medicine and its ability to diagnose disease gave doctors a role in interpreting a range of social issues including sexuality, race and poverty. By 1900, doctors began to talk openly of belonging to a profession. However, it would be unwise to see a complete transformation in their status. Patients continued to dictate terms and sections of the working classes remained sceptical, preferring non-professional and alternative practitioners. With the profession overpopulated, doctors were seldom in a strong position. Although they felt that science gave them a legitimate voice in constructing social concerns, this did not mean that their claims went unchallenged as demonstrated by the anti-vivisection movement. In *The Doctor's Dilemma* (1906) George Bernard Shaw could still view doctors as little better than licensed butchers who wrote absurd prescriptions, exploited hypochondriacs and manufactured lucrative illnesses. Neither had doctors gained control over those institutions (such as the hospital) naturally associated with medicine, raising questions about their authority. Medicine had come a long way by 1900 in acquiring the trappings of professionalization. However, if orthodox medicine was in the ascendant, concerns about competition, status and authority persisted.

The Sciences of Medicine

The growing prominence of medicine in nineteenth-century society reflected in only a small way its therapeutic ability. Doctors were more concerned with the alleviation of sickness, as cure often proved elusive. Although customary skills of bedside medicine remained important, new ways of understanding disease did take hold as medical knowledge was refashioned. Rather than representing a period in which scientific medicine flourished, notions of what represented good science fluctuated in the nineteenth century. Confidence in medicine grew slowly. Most sought self- or family diagnosis and household remedies first before visiting a doctor, with perceptions of treatment influenced by familial or community networks, religious beliefs or moral stances. Patients picked their practitioners according to their income and availability; using social over medical criteria. Orthodox, alternative and self-medication were used side – by side. Orthodox practitioners did not, therefore, have it all their own way.

Self-medication, through either folk or patent medicines, was an important source of treatment, especially in rural districts where access to doctors was limited. Publications like Cox's *Companion to the Family Medicine Chest and Compendium of Domestic Medicine* went into numerous editions. Opium mixtures sold widely and quacks plied their nostrums. Patients suffering from VD, unwanted pregnancy or impotency – conditions about which they might be too embarrassed to consult their family doctor – became targets, with the promise of quick cures free from embarrassment. Whilst attempts were made to portray these as dangerous, the endorsements and boasts attached to patent medicines had a powerful appeal, especially when doctors could claim no greater success. New mass-production techniques ensured that money was to be made, placing patent medicines in the vanguard of a commodity culture. Sales increased tenfold and outlets expanded, providing the background for companies like Boots the Chemist. Wholesale and manufacturing chemists expanded beyond personal enterprises into pharmaceutical companies. Demand remained high and controls minimal, much to the chagrin of doctors who, fearing competition, disapproved of self-medication.

In the face of self-medication and heterodox ideas, doctors tried to claim a better understanding of disease. Faith in humoral medicine and symptom-based nosologies was being eroded by 1800 as doctors adopted a system of bedside medicine that correlated pathological signs with clinical symptoms, asserting their authority over the definition of disease. Historians have seen this change as rooted in Paris and argued that this new, more self-confident 'scientific' approach formed the foundation of hospital medicine and medical education. Only gradually has a revisionist view emerged that has contested the centrality of Paris. Like France, British doctors were also interested in pathological anatomy. In addition, French doctors were influenced by British ideas. Questions might also be asked about the extent to which this shift enabled doctors to assert their authority. For Jewson, the patient's narrative, which had dominated clinical encounters, was relegated as doctors sought information about illness from clinical signs.[4] In the process, he felt that the clinical authority of the doctor was elevated and that physical examination, previously rare, started to form the basis of a new approach. Here the stethoscope became a symbol of this type of medicine and doctors' ability to 'see' what previously had been hidden. However, doctors carried on reproducing lay beliefs in their accounts and history-taking remained a central element in the medical encounter, suggesting that the transformation was not as sudden as has been proposed.

It was not just the understanding of disease that altered. Specialization, if controversial, reoriented practice, marking a conceptual growth rather than a revolution. A shift in the medical gaze to individual organs as the locus of disease encouraged specialization, whilst the rise of the hospital and the creation of new diagnostic tools like the opthalmoscope gave more room for specialists, even though a generalist culture continued to dominate. In surgery, new methods linked to physiological principles emerged to broaden the prospect of intervention as a surgical concept of disease asserted itself. The surgeon was increasingly cast as hero, with anaesthesia hailed as a triumph. However, it was not immediately or universally employed and continued to prove contentious, especially when used in childbirth. Surgeons from the 1830s had already become more ambitious and were to go on to invade areas of the body previously seen as inoperable. For all surgeons' claims, outside the hospital surgery remained characterized by minor operations, the province of the GP rather than of the heroic surgeon.

The understanding of the process of infection shifted after 1840. The microscope offered new means of observation, while Rudolf Virchow's theory of cellular pathology marked a final abandonment of humoralism, although ideas about evolution, natural selection and inheritance continued to fuel disagreements about the role of environment and heredity in disease. Experimental physiology had a harder reception in face of anti-vivisection sentiments and an established faith in anatomy. Whereas experimental physiology raised questions about the nature and ethics of medical science, the work of Louis Pasteur in France and Robert Koch in Germany in the 1860s gave a new dimension to disease. The resulting reinvigoration of pathology and the development of bacteriology altered the value of science for doctors. Cells and germs provided much greater analytical purchase than earlier explanations based on hereditary factors or miasma. If British doctors appeared to take second place to their counterparts across the Channel in the construction of these ideas, debate about germ theories and their implications for medicine was still intense in Britain. However, this did not mean that germ theories or bacteriology had triumphed by 1900. Although a broad consensus emerged on the need for science in medicine, the type of laboratory knowledge represented by bacteriology was epistemologically different from the ideas many doctors had been exposed to in the 1850s and 1860s. Many resisted the laboratory in favour of a style of medicine that valued observation.

Antiseptics provide an example of the conflict engendered by germ theories and the way in which germ practices provided a mechanism whereby 'germs' were given a greater role. The surgeon Joseph Lister offered one solution to the problem of wound management at a time when several were being suggested. Opposition to his complicated methods stimulated interest in germs as surgeons moved to achieve antisepsis. Lister's ideas were modified as surgeons found it easier to incorporate an approach that emphasized the need to keep wounds clean. This did not mean that Listerians felt obliged to take any less of the credit, arguing that antisepsis had revolutionized surgery.

While debates over antisepsis and germ theories enthused learned societies and journals popularizing scientific medicine, the laboratory had less impact on medical practice. Doctors may have used science to bolster status, but this did not mean that science was integrated with the bedside. Faith was retained in individual experience and observation. Only a minority asserted the necessity of the laboratory. By the 1880s, this group had become more confident as consensus grew about the role of bacteria. Often it was the diagnostic benefits of the laboratory, rather than the new ideas shaping pathology and bacteriology, that eased their introduction. By the 1890s, the bench and the bedside were beginning to be perceived as analogous spheres as bacteriology started to displace other disease models. However, there was no sudden switch from physiological or empirical notions. Despite growing interest, Britain could boast few bacteriologists or laboratories beyond those used in teaching or public-health analysis. Equally, the benefits of these new sciences proved disappointing; it was only with the development of the diphtheria antitoxin in 1894–5 that confidence grew, promoting the search for other antitoxins.

In the acceptance of these ideas, generational gaps existed. Diagnostic aids, for example, were more likely to be used by younger practitioners so that new instruments were only slowly incorporated. Traditional ideas remained strong, with clinical history-taking outweighing physical examinations or later laboratory tests. Although disease concepts were modified, medicine continued to be centred on symptomatic diagnosis, much of which was imprecise or overlapped with lay ideas. Treatments were all too often rooted in practical utility, economic resources and the structure of a practitioner's clientele. For example, working-class patients encountered lower levels of examination and received a more limited range of medicines than middle-class patients. Notions of propriety and decency ensured that women were seldom properly examined, allowing many complaints to go untreated. However, practices did alter. Homoeopathy and the idea that doctors should assist nature challenged heroic dosages. Faith in bloodletting also declined in favour of supportive treatments. In most cases, doctors mixed the old with the new. Some were just as likely to use leeches as morphine. It did not help that effective drugs only emerged in the 1870s and 1880s as a by-product of the German chemical industry. At the same time, interest in antisepsis spread beyond the hospital with chemists and companies from the 1880s starting to distribute a range of antiseptics which were taken up by GPs. These new approaches often meant that older treatments were given a new rationale.

Although by 1900 doctors and patients had become more positive about medicine's ability to diagnose and manage disease, what type of medicine was desirable remained disputed. Advances in medicine concealed substantial gaps in the understanding of the way in which the body worked or how disease should be cured. Despite discoveries, improvements in care remained largely the result of better patient management through improved hygiene, isolation and greater emphasis on diet and convalescence. On these grounds, the nineteenth century should not be seen as a period of unrivalled progress in scientific medicine. If medicine might appear more 'modern' by 1900, much remained to be discovered.

Charity and Self-Help

In this shifting structure of practice, the hospital was the institution that came to be intimately associated with medicine. Histories have moved beyond simplistic narrative accounts to look at the hospital as a complex social and economic institution. Instead of seeing medical change at the centre of the phenomenal expansion in the number of hospitals after 1800, accounts now point to the role played by concerns about urban conditions, social mobility, and a shift in the nature of benevolence. A combination of these forces ensured that, by 1850, most cities had a general hospital. However, distribution remained uneven and hospitals were essentially urban institutions. Diversity intensified as new institutions emerged: the teaching hospital, the specialist hospital and later the cottage hospital, which extended institutional provision in towns and rural areas. Of these, specialist hospitals proved the most controversial. They evolved in response to specialization and demands for care of groups (children, pregnant women) traditionally excluded from hospitals. However, at their centres were enterprising doctors. Excluded from general hospitals by a nepotistic system of appointments, they took the initiative. Institutions were established for all manner of ailments, organs and patients. Philanthropists and large sections of the medical profession viewed them as damaging but, despite criticism, the number of specialist hospitals grew, with institutions for children and women especially popular. By the 1890s, most large cities could boast several specialist hospitals. Doctors gradually started to modify their opposition and general hospitals opened specialist departments, though many were constructed more as sources for instruction than care.

Hospitals should not be seen as part of Foucault's carceral archipelago. They evolved from an interaction of philanthropic enthusiasm, demand for care and professional interests, into places where reputations were made and medical knowledge constructed and disseminated. Hospitals not only provided a forum in which professional identities were developed, but also an arena for a type of medicine typified by observation, physical examination and morbid anatomy. However, despite a gradual process of medicalization, they continued to serve an important function for their founders and supporters. A focus for civic pride, local benevolence and the formation of class identities, hospitals were hailed as the most successful manifestations of institutional philanthropy. Despite signs of crisis after 1860 as the cost of care outpaced philanthropic resources, the voluntary ideology that underpinned hospitals remained entrenched. Only those on the periphery seriously suggested state intervention. Medicalization might have ensured that lay governors had to defer increasingly to medical opinion, but they remained firmly in control.

Hospitals became sites for training, innovation and experimentation (particularly in surgery and pathology), and were central to debates over the value of science. In nursing, they acted as a stimulus and focus for reform, aiding the reconceptualization of the hospital as a medical space. Reforms, initiated by nursing sisterhoods and part of a conception of the hospital as a moral space, saw nursing transformed from a mainly small-scale, untrained and private enterprise into a respectable occupation. Florence Nightingale has taken much of the credit. However, the process was not as straightforward as that. Revisionists have undermined the 'Nightingale Myth' so as to move away from triumphalist accounts. They have raised questions of gender and class, revealing the problematic nature of nurses' claims to professionalization. The timing of change and the type of nurse believed to have emerged differed from the view propounded by conventional accounts, and from what contemporary reformers wanted. While the Nightingale School at St Thomas's provided a model, lady probationers proved problematic and were quickly replaced by hospital-trained nurses. Reforms to increase the authority of the matron, appropriate a technical discourse and assert a holistic tradition to counter the subordination favoured by doctors were only partially successful. By the end of the nineteenth century, nursing was still sex-stereotyped, divided and poorly paid, while the last decades of the century witnessed a clash over the means to secure professional status. Nursing reforms also resulted in inter-professional conflict over spheres of authority. These disputes point to the manifold tensions between different groups in the hospital.

Despite their role in medicine, hospitals only admitted a limited number of patients. Emphasis was placed on the acute rather than the chronic sick, with hospitals favouring the ill-defined 'deserving' poor. In reality, restrictions were overlooked by doctors. Demand for care frequently outstripped resources, with many institutions providing local and, in some cases, national facilities. Access was extended by membership of friendly societies, by medical charities and by churches, all of which sought admission rights. In addition, hospitals were magnets for casualties. Rising admissions encouraged the expansion of outpatient facilities, whilst middle-class demand for care was, in part, met by controversial schemes for paying patients. Several processes were at work. Changes in the image of the hospital made them more attractive as places of treatment, prompted by improvements in surgery and nursing, new diagnostic and surgical facilities, and growing confidence in medicine. However, an increase in admissions was not without concern. Contemporaries became convinced that rising patient numbers represented an abuse by those who could afford to pay. Rumour was enough to confirm these fears at a time when an abuse of charity was feared to be widespread. Several solutions were put forward, including the appointment of enquiry officers, the forerunners of hospital social workers.

It would be unwise to focus on hospitals as the only source of medical philanthropy. GPs regularly subsidized poor patients. Convalescent homes were established, whilst charitable dispensaries flourished in manufacturing towns, outnumbering hospitals in the North. Easy to found, dispensaries proved popular and responded quickly to urban needs. Despite their relatively limited catchment areas, they were important local resources, offering diagnoses and medicines as well as surgical and obstetric care. However, with hospitals able to secure a monopoly of teaching and research by the late nineteenth century, dispensaries went into decline with much of their work subsumed by outpatient departments.

Amidst these institutional solutions was a host of medical charities offering assistance and advice. This philanthropic effort was supplemented by a growing number of institutions based on self-help and the insurance principle. Collective responses formed an important part of health care, although the low-paid were less well placed to make them. Taking advantage of an oversupply of doctors, various forms of workers' associations and clubs emerged to cover injury and sickness, linked to the principle of weekly contributions. Their size, form and function varied considerably: some were established by doctors, others around workshops or factories. Although many such organizations were local in character, several large affiliated Northern orders emerged of which the Oddfellows, Buffaloes and Foresters were the biggest. Men dominated, with few societies accepting women in large numbers. Members were expected to take responsibility for their own health and care was provided through contracts with local doctors giving practitioners a guaranteed income. Given the nature of the medical market, competition for posts was stiff but, with increasingly professional confidence, doctors demanded higher fees, resulting in the 1890s in 'The Battle of the Clubs'. Conflict was hardly surprising. Working men and their dependants made increasing use of these organizations and contemporaries felt they played an important role in preventing poverty from ill-health. From the point of view of doctors, the clubs undercut private practice.

Medical charity and self-help organizations represented a central component of the nineteenth-century ecology of care. They were visible manifestations of interest and concerns about health, while they offered important services. However, in terms of patient numbers they were never in a position to rival private practice or the state.

A Therapeutic State?

The concept of a mixed economy of welfare has led historians to talk of a moving frontier between the state and voluntary sector in Victorian Britain. Notions of contribution rather than entitlement remained vital, with a voluntary ethos central to civil society. State intervention proved problematic, but the nineteenth century saw the state take an increasing responsibility for the nation's health. Tensions emerged between central and local government; between intervention and the laissez-faire tenets of British politics; and between civil servants and other bodies. A permissive rather than an obligatory approach dominated, with later mechanisms for compulsion seldom applied. Consequently, changes in social policy were not thoroughly implemented. Much was left to local initiatives; in the process local government was transformed as health was incorporated into the municipal gospel. However, what was achieved was not a precursor to the welfare state. Intervention was a response to the visible problems of urbanization, infectious disease and poverty. Only from the 1880s onwards did intellectual and collectivist approaches begin to point to a need for a broader system of state welfare.

The growing role of the state in public health reflects this tension between the need to intervene and countervailing political and economic philosophies. Public health took on the qualities of a moral and scientific crusade. It became one solution to the problems created by urbanization and industrialization; one bound up with moral conceptions of redemption. Efforts were made to merge civic pride and local philanthropy with concerns about the urban environment reached evangelical proportions. A new moral economy of surveys and statistics along with fear and guilt influenced these attempts to clean up cities. Panics generated by epidemics played a smaller role, highlighting the need for action rather than motivating reform.

Although part of a European trend, Britain's public-health experiences are often seen as paradigmatic. While heroic accounts have become marginalized, the history of public health continues to embody a sense of improvement interwoven with debates about mortality change following McKeown's provocative thesis that the latter was linked to changes in the standard of living and nutrition.[5] The story is therefore a familiar one.

The work of Sir Edwin Chadwick, the doyen of sanitarians in the 1830s and 1840s, is often seen as the starting-point for the public-health movement. Architect of the New Poor Law, Chadwick linked poverty and disease and set about conducting an investigation as part of attempts to reduce the financial burden of destitution. The resulting *General Report of the Sanitary Conditions of the Labouring Classes of Great Britain* (1842) was not a sudden departure. It reflected a growing consensus and broader philanthropic goals that underlay early-nineteenth-century investigations into the state of society. This is not to undervalue Chadwick's efforts, which sustained a reforming sanitarian ideology. The *Report* established a statistical connection between environment and diseases, asserting a miasmatic interpretation whereby filth, 'bad air' and disease were interconnected. Prevention was cast as a matter of sanitation, subordinating concerns about the individual and poverty. Chadwick's view was embodied in the permissive 1848 Public Health Act, which created the General Board of Health under him. From Chadwick's brand of sanitary reform, with its unpopular stamp of centralization, the adoption of an epidemiological approach has been detected as doctors gained control following Chadwick's replacement by John Simon. This chronology suggests that under Simon a broader conception of state medicine was asserted until the merger of the public health and Poor Law administration under the Local Government Board (LGB) saw Simon resign in 1876. State medicine was subsequently overshadowed in favour of a preventive approach. A further shift has been seen in the 1890s, with bacteriology promoting a move to categorize individuals into risk populations. Certain diseases became notifiable in 1889 with notification made compulsory in 1899. Debate about infectious-disease control intensified with notification, stimulating local public health services.

However, it was often the rhetoric and not the substance that changed. For example, sanitarian ideas remained prominent throughout the nineteenth century, especially at a local level where sanitary engineering projects and concerns about filth dominated. Neither were ideas uniform or the transition between them smooth. A competing and complex range of assumptions characterized approaches to public health and explanations of disease transmission.[6] With no clear divide between miasmatic interpretations and contagionism, the public-health movement drew on both. Early failures in bacteriology initially reinforced existing ways of looking at disease; only in the 1890s did bacteriology gain a hold, displacing epidemiology as the science of public health.

Despite the growing influence of the central authority, public health remained a local problem and utilized the traditional institutions of local government. Under the 1848 Public Health Act, a system of local inspection was created through the appointment of medical officers of health (MOHs). Compulsory appointments followed first in London and later in provincial districts, creating a body of public-health practitioners. Local action depended on the efforts of the MOH, whose duties included investigation, identification of nuisances and overcrowding, notification and isolation.

Strong regional and urban differences prevailed, reflecting local physical, social, cultural or economic factors. While some authorities embraced sanitary reform others, such as Birmingham, waited until obliged to act. Rather than reflecting opposition, this represented disorganization, disagreements over the best course, 'bewilderment and frustration with technical and legal complexities and fear of taking a wrong step'.[7] What was achieved was often immense. By the 1880s, MOHs were asserting their identity as preventive practitioners and shaping provision. Their work was assisted by civic pride, which saw an expansion of activities aided by cheap loans from the LGB. Definitions of public health expanded to include, for example, parks, streets and public baths. It became linked to municipal socialism, serving to transform local government so that by 1900 national legislation was beginning to follow local initiatives. The impact of these measures, as Hardy and Szreter have argued, played a central role in mortality decline.[8]

Public health was not limited to drains and clean water, particularly as MOHs expanded their areas of concern. Compulsory measures were introduced through incremental means to enforce smallpox vaccination and through the Contagious Diseases Acts designed to screen, isolate and treat prostitutes suffering from venereal disease. At a structural level, attention was directed at housing and living conditions. Building regulations became part of efforts to combat poor housing and promote sanitation. Provisions under the 1872 Food, Drink and Drugs Act and the 1875 Public Health Act saw MOHs become involved in questions of food safety. Many also distributed tracts and gave public lectures on health-related issues. Given the scale of this work, MOHs were assisted by a range of local functionaries and philanthropists who provided information and support which proved 'essential to the effective functioning of the local preventive authorities'.[9]

Although public health remained essentially local, perceptions of centralization and interference generated hostility. Compulsory regulations stimulated popular resistance, especially in the case of compulsory vaccination and the Contagious Diseases Acts. At a more prosaic level, domestic privacy was prized and 'the intrusion of the preventive administration was widely resented or resisted through all levels of society'.[10] Disease notification was opposed and cases of notifiable disease were concealed. At another level, demand rose. Public baths and disinfection stations were popular. Pressure was brought to bear on local authorities by working-class organizations keen to extend public works and public-health schemes. Public health therefore evoked mixed feelings but, often locally, it was seen as a source of pride.

The other side of the state's efforts to intervene was less popular and more subdued. The Old and the New Poor Law offered care for those who could not afford to pay, or were excluded by charities as 'undeserving'. Until its repeal in 1834, the Elizabethan Poor Law of 1601 provided the foundations for a diverse system of parish-based medicine. Provision for the outdoor poor covered all aspects of primary care with parish doctors offering domiciliary medical attention, prescriptions, midwifery and minor surgery. These services were often little different from those available to the local community given that local practitioners accepted contracts.[11] In addition, parishes provided artificial limbs and spectacles, along with food and alcohol. Subscriptions to medical charities gave access to institutional facilities and, in a few cases, parishes established infirmaries, though systematic medical relief was limited to the English Midlands, South and East.

Concerns about the Poor Law reached fever pitch in the first decades of the nineteenth century. Much has been written on the debates and investigations that followed and the inception of the New Poor Law in 1834. While it has been seen as punitive and initially dominated by the problem of rural unemployment, assessments also point to a system of medical care that evolved into something approaching a state hospital system. From the start, sickness eroded the principles reformers had sought to enshrine in the 1834 Act to discourage pauperism, as it was anticipated that the sick poor should be subjected to a less severe regime. Medical services were developed in a piecemeal and pragmatic fashion. Although under no obligation to offer medical care, with sickness a major cause of poverty, most unions appointed medical officers. They became key figures in shaping care, acting as liberal gatekeepers. Workhouses were built and by the 1860s contemporaries felt that they had come to represent state hospitals. However, given the level of opposition to the 1834 Act, the idea that relief should be restricted to the workhouse was never feasible. Unions (particularly in Wales) resisted building workhouses: many persisted in granting out-relief and subscribed to local medical charities. Consequently, institutional services (especially in rural districts) compared unfavourably with the medical relief available to the outdoor poor.

Development was often hampered by a system forced to treat the chronic patients that other institutions refused to admit and by the deterrent social philosophy and desire for economy that underlay the 1834 Act. Gaps existed between the needs of the sick poor and the willingness of the ratepayers to fund medical care. Facilities varied greatly between unions, giving the New Poor Law its characteristic diversity. In Manchester, for example, the infirmary admitted three times as many patients as the voluntary hospital and could boast good standards of care. In other unions, a propensity for parsimony saw relief restricted, while old or inadequate buildings continued to be used. A system of tender ensured that it was frequently cost rather than skill that dominated appointments. Low levels of pay and requirements in many unions that medical officers should supply medicines discouraged the better-qualified from applying. Medical officers were overstretched and subservient to Guardians and Relieving Officers who would often ignore or countermand their recommendations. In addition, the heavy workloads experienced by medical officers led to incidences of neglect.

Efforts were made to raise standards, fuelled by charitable reformers and medical officers keen to improve their position. The 1860s was a pivotal decade as criticism of medical services mounted. The deaths of two paupers in a London workhouse and two damning inquiries into conditions saw the government pass the 1867 Metropolitan Poor Law Act. This acknowledged the state provision of medical care, while a renewed crusade against out-relief saw the emphasis shift back towards institutional solutions. Pressure was applied to close unsuitable buildings and erect new ones with loans made available to facilitate this. Additional sick wards or a fever ward were often added, whilst larger unions built separate infirmaries. Measures directed at London were slowly emulated elsewhere. Expansion was not limited to workhouses. Unions in the 1870s experimented with the creation of dispensaries, although the number formed was restricted by financial and moral concerns, while the 1866 Sanitary Act and the 1867 Metropolitan Poor Act encouraged the creation of isolation hospitals.

Despite efforts at reform, problems remained. The administration of relief was cumbersome and continued to be restricted by notions of deterrence, parsimony and ignorance. Rural infirmaries were poorly equipped. Other unions, swayed by the crusade against out-relief, limited medical care to a loan basis. Medical officers were overworked and underpaid and there was little systematic effort to ensure that minimum standards were maintained. Tensions with Guardians further frustrated efforts, especially as the dimensions of care often depended on the ambition and enthusiasm of the medical officer.

While Poor Law medical services were hampered by the stigma of pauperism, evidence suggests that they were not a last resort. Popular attitudes made a distinction between indoor and outdoor relief and the conditions under which they were granted. From the start, medical services were used by the working classes, a position recognized in 1885 when legislation allowed medical relief to be granted without the recipient losing the right to vote. One report in 1896 noted that there appeared to be no limit to the number of sick who were willing to use the medical skill and nursing provided by workhouse infirmaries.

A growing willingness to use Poor Law medical services and the expansion of public-health services pointed to the increasing involvement of the state in health care. However, although large sums were invested, and a comprehensive programme of intervention was initiated, the state remained a reluctant participant.

Conclusion

Looking back over Victoria's reign, doctors felt confident that medicine had made great strides. They pointed to anaesthetics, antiseptics and the overall fall in mortality as triumphs and claimed that medicine had become more scientific. Improvement for them was cumulative and continuous and it was argued that the new understandings of aetiologies and mechanisms of disease had enabled doctors to be more effective in prevention, diagnosis and intervention. Certainly the status of medicine had risen. By 1900, health and medicine had moved from the periphery to the centre of social and political life. Metaphors of health and disease provided a way of conceptualizing society. Orthodox medicine had been legitimized by the state with doctors playing an increasing role in shaping public policy and morals. However, formal health care remained patchy, whilst medicine's overall effect in combating ill-health, as opposed to reducing levels of infectious disease through public health, was probably small. Old and new continued to exist side by side and, for all the growing confidence expressed by practitioners in their art, doctors remained anxious about competition. If modern medicine had not yet emerged in the nineteenth century, the foundations had been laid.

NOTES

1. M. Foucault, *Madness and Civilization: A History of Insanity in the Age of Reason* (London, 1967) and *Birth of the Clinic: An Archaeology of Medical Perception* (London, 1973); T. Szasz, *The Manufacture of Madness: A Comparative Study of the Inquisition*

and the Mental Health Movement (New York, 1970); I. Illich, *Medical Nemesis: The Expropriation of Health* (London, 1975).

2. J. C. Riley, *Sick not Dead: The Health of British Workingmen during the Mortality Decline* (Baltimore, 1997).

3. I. Waddington, *Medical Profession in the Industrial Revolution* (Dublin, 1984); I. Loudon, *Medical Care and the General Practitioner 1750–1850* (Oxford, 1986).

4. N. Jewson, 'Medical knowledge and the patronage system in eighteenth century England', *Sociology*, 8 (1974).

5. T. McKeown, *The Modern Rise of Population* (London, 1976).

6. M. Pelling, *Cholera, Fever and English Medicine, 1825–1865* (Oxford, 1978).

7. C. Hamlin, 'Muddling in bumbledom: on the economy of large sanitary improvements in four British towns, 1855–1885', *Victorian Studies*, 32 (1988), p. 60.

8. A. Hardy, *Epidemic Streets: Infectious Disease and the Rise of Preventive Medicine, 1856–1900* (Oxford, 1993), pp. 289–94; S. Szreter, 'The importance of social intervention in Britain's mortality decline c.1850–1914: a reinterpretation of the role of public health', *Social History of Medicine*, 1 (1988).

9. Hardy, *Epidemic Streets*, p. 6.

10. Hardy, *Epidemic Streets*, p. 269.

11. J. Lane, *The Social History of Medicine: Health, Healing and Disease in England, 1750–1950* (London, 2001), p. 45.

FURTHER READING

There are a number of recent works which provide a critical overview of nineteenth-century medicine. W. F. Bynum, *Science and the Practice of Medicine in the Nineteenth Century* (1994) offers a comparative study of the foundations of 'modern medicine', while C. Lawrence, *Medicine in the Making of Modern Britain, 1700–1920* (1994) is an interpretative account of how doctors created a role for themselves. There are a number of studies of professionalization of which I. Loudon, *Medical Care and the General Practitioner 1750–1850* (1986) and A. Digby, *The Evolution of British General Practice 1850–1948* (1999) are the most insightful. The role of women is further explored by A. Witz, *Professions and Patriarchy* (1992). For nursing A. M. Rafferty, *The Politics of Nursing Knowledge* (1996) is a good analysis of reform, while a revisionist account of the impact of Florence Nightingale is put forward by M. Baly, *Florence Nightingale and the Nursing Legacy* (1997). Less has been written on alternative medicine, but R. Porter, *Quacks: Fakers and Charlatans in English Medicine* (2000) does explore the transition from quackery to alternative medicine. The literature on the laboratory and medical science is best approached through J. H. Warner, 'The history of science and the sciences of medicine', *Osiris*, 10 (1995), while C. Lawrence, 'Incommunicable knowledge: science, technology and clinical art in Britain 1850–1914', *Journal of Contemporary History*, 20 (1985) explores how doctors used science. For germ theory, the revisionist account by M. Worboys, *Spreading Germs: Disease Theories and Medical Practice in Britain, 1865–1900* (2000) is perhaps the best new scholarly account. Although many of these works do look at hospitals, B. Abel-Smith, *The Hospitals 1800–1948: A Study in Social Administration in England and Wales* (1964) is still a classic account. However, a more critical view is offered by L. Granshaw, ' "Fame and fortune by means of bricks and mortar": the medical profession and specialist hospitals in Britain 1800–1948', in L. Granshaw and R. Porter, eds, *The Hospital in History* (1989) and by K. Waddington, *Charity and the London Hospitals 1850–1898* (2000). M. A. Crowther, *The Workhouse System, 1834–1929* (1981) offers a sophisticated analysis of Poor Law medical services. Much has been written on public health, though A. Wohl, *Endangered Lives: Public*

Health in Victorian Britain (1983) remains a lively general survey. C. Hamlin, *Public Health and Social Justice in the Age of Chadwick: Britain, 1800–1854* (1998) is a revisionist account, while A. Hardy, *Epidemic Streets: Infectious Disease and the Rise of Preventive Medicine, 1856–1900* (1993) and S. Szreter, 'The importance of social intervention in Britain's mortality decline c.1850–1914: a reinterpretation of the role of public health', *Social History of Medicine*, 1 (1988) represent the new orthodoxy.

CHAPTER TWENTY-SIX

Sexuality

LESLEY A. HALL

Continuities, Shifts and Questions of Periodization

The historiography of sexuality in the nineteenth century is dominated by the Victorians. The preceding more than a third of a century is sometimes simply subsumed into 'Victorianism', as if Victoria's shadow embraced the entire century; and the earlier decades of the nineteenth century, although a period during which major transitions took place, are much less investigated than the latter part. These decades have been predominantly characterized in two conflicting ways, either as the last gasping stretch of the 'long eighteenth century', or as a mere prelude and overture to the Victorian Age. They were both.

A sexual 'long eighteenth century' can be extended well into the young queen's reign: for many of the aristocracy, though some were profoundly influenced by morally reforming movements, the Victorian era as experienced by the middle classes hardly existed, though arguably aristocratic libertinism did become more privatized and discreet. In the early decades of the century a republican and anti-religious 'radical underworld', as McCalman described it, employed libertine discourses and scurrilous obscene satire for politically revolutionary purposes.[1] This alliance between political radicalism and unconventional sexual morality is usually assumed to have been disintegrating by the 1820s, as political radicals became more interested in respectability, libertine satire mutated into cynically commercial pornography, and the libertine sub-culture became depoliticized.

However, the 1820s saw the first suggestions of neo-Malthusianism, which placed a revisionist slant on the gloomy prognostications of Thomas Malthus by suggesting that human ingenuity might intervene in the apparently inevitable connection between sexual intercourse and conception. While this may be read as intrinsically part of the 'radical underworld', in generating a fertile relationship between theories of political economy and the 'secret knowledge' of contraceptive methods associated with prostitutes and libertines, it might also be interpreted as 'Victorian' in its use of applied science. Richard Carlile in his *What is Love* (1826) posited a radically revised pattern of relationships between the sexes, which the 'preventive measures' advocated by his neo-Malthusian colleague Francis Place would facilitate.[2] These ideas permeated the Owenite wing of social reform and continued to be, if in a sometimes rather subterranean way, influential in a developing socialist movement. This ideal-istic and democratized, even somewhat millenarian, vision of transformed sexual relationships was a very different proposition from libertinism, in particular in its positioning of women not merely as objects of male lascivious desire but as potentially sexual subjects themselves. Libertine discourse itself sometimes struck notes of critique.

Intimations of 'Victorianism' as popularly understood can be traced well back into the eighteenth century. Fears of the dire effects of 'onanism' (masturbation) emerged in the early 1700s. Institutions for the victims of sexual vice – repentant prostitutes, abandoned babies and sufferers from venereal diseases – were being founded by the mid-century. Ideologies of passive womanhood and aggressively phallic manhood had emerged before 1800. The evangelical movement within the established church led to the activities of 'vice societies' aiming at cleaning up the streets from flagrant pros-titution, sodomites and obscene representations, and the work of the original, epony-mous, clean-up-Shakespeare bowdlerizer, Thomas Bowdler himself. Gloom was cast over the dawning new century by the conclusions of Malthus (1798) on the outcome of unrestrained procreation.

The effect on society, and on perceptions of the age in general, of the change of monarch in 1837 was considerable. The young queen and her consort established a royal domestic circle very different from the courts of her predecessors. The new image of the monarchy was one with which middle-class respectability could iden-tify. Victoria herself, however, was far from a stereotypical Victorian: all the evidence suggests that she was quite the reverse of the model Victorian wife who was supposedly only interested in sex to gratify her husband and in order to achieve motherhood.

Recent studies have indicated a significant shift in attitudes, and indeed behaviour, later in the century, from around 1870. It was from this date that the population began to decline: how and why are still the subjects of considerable debate.[3] Op-position to the attitudes embodied in the Contagious Diseases Acts of the 1860s cohered into a multi-strand movement for their repeal, which evolved into an influ-ential social purity movement aimed at bringing society to the single moral standard already expected of respectable women. There was a gradual development of an endeavour to understand the complex phenomena of sexuality in the light of devel-opments in science, most notably perhaps Darwin's *Origin of Species*. Alternatives to the assumed heterosexual norm and marriage as an expected part of the life cycle became apparent. Several scandals made homosexuality visible to a wider public. If lesbianism remained more occluded, 'New Women' of the final decades of the century were critiquing and even rejecting marriage, and spurning male dominance.

Vile Victorians?

Many sound and well-researched studies have shed a good deal of light on the com-plexities and intricacies of sexual attitudes and behaviour in Victorian Britain. Nonetheless, every few years, it seems, someone produces yet another volume which promises to overturn 'accepted stereotypes' of Victorian repression which one would have thought long modified. *The Vile Victorians* forms part of a series of lighthearted introductions to history for young people: this has certainly been one of the most influential ways of thinking about the Victorians and sex, embodied in such titles of early studies in the history of Victorian sexuality as Ronald Pearsall's *The Worm in the Bud* (1969). Hypocrisy has been assumed to be the key-note: the central image might be a Victorian patriarch who holds lengthy family prayers before breakfast, and married, relatively late in life, a virginal bride with whom he has an infrequent and inhibited sex life and who now spends much of her time lying on a sofa exhausted by childbearing and the strain of marriage to such a man; he flogs his sons to maintain discipline, keeps his daughters as useless and ignorant as possible, turns pregnant housemaids out of doors with no pay and no character, keeps a mistress in a discreet establishment, and probably also has sex with under-age prostitutes. This image conflates many different kinds of Victorian: at the very least, not all Victorian middle-class (or even upper-class) males habitually resorted to prostitutes or kept mistresses, for economic reasons as well as concerns of morality or health.

Detailed biographical studies of individual Victorians or specific groups are a major way in which these simplistic, caricatured, assumptions may be undermined. A brief look at the lives of some of the best-known Victorians may confirm some of the clichés while shattering others. Charles Dickens, while hymning the virtues of domesticity and family life, was repelled by his wife's fecundity and increasing girth. He compelled her to accept a separation, and took up with a young actress named Ellen Ternan many years his junior, who was forced into a life of meticulous concealment after becoming his mistress. Dickens, one of the vociferous moralists of his time, led this life of concealed sin, while with considerable irony, Mary Ann Evans, who wrote under the name George Eliot, and was regarded as one of the most distinguished moral voices in Victorian literature, openly lived a life many people defined as immoral. She chose to unite her life with George Henry Lewes, a man already married but legally unable to divorce his wife. The lives of individual Victorians were far more complex than the received picture. If few lived up to the high ideals of manly or womanly conduct advanced in prescriptive literature, in few cases do we see the kind of knowing hypocrisy which the popular image suggests.

An increasing number of studies of actual Victorian lives of a range of individuals and networks demonstrate how difficult it is to talk in terms of the 'typically Victorian' when it comes to sexual behaviour and conduct. Startling arrangements often emerged in the context of divorce cases and murder trials, when the light of publicity was suddenly shone upon the hidden recesses of private lives.

Whores and Madonnas?

Victorian prostitution still exerts the fascination that it exerted over its contemporaries, as does Victorian womanhood more generally. It is often assumed that the Victorians recognized two distinct kinds of women: the pure and chaste, and the unchaste fallen. Although there remains considerable scope for research in this area, it is possible to argue that the situation was rather more complex than the frequently repeated stereotype allows.

Victorian social observers tended to exaggerate the amount of prostitution occurring in the rapidly expanding cities of the nineteenth century. Middle-class men might presume working-class women to be prostitutes through misreading behavioural codes of different classes, assuming, for example, that women frequenting places of public amusement were there on business as prostitutes rather than for harmless recreation. A Home Office file contains protests by the local vigilance association in 1886 that Clapham Common was infested with prostitutes and nightly 'disgusting exhibitions of vice'. The local police asserted to the contrary that the Common was frequented by respectable females and courting couples, and the few prostitutes conducted themselves discreetly. Protestors seem to have assumed that women out in public after dark were up to no good and canoodling couples on park benches were vicious fornicators rather than respectable young people with nowhere else to do their courting.[4]

Quite apart from such misapprehensions, estimates of the total numbers of prostitutes by various observers often included women who were very dubiously definable as such, for example those having casual sexual relationships for their own pleasure as well as, or rather than, for profit, or living in monogamous relationships without legal marriage. The definition of the prostitute was not, in fact, clear-cut. One of the most famous of nineteenth-century observers, William Acton, mentioned the frequent route taken out of prostitution into respectable marriage. Walking the streets might be a brief phase through which girls passed, if they were lucky accumulating a little capital in order to set themselves up in business, or an occasional recourse by women following trades which underwent seasonal fluctuation. However, it would appear that by the end of the century definitions had hardened and this fluidity was less viable.

A perhaps unexpectedly subtle apprehension of the meaning of prostitution and the nuances of 'good' and 'bad' women in Victorian England was the belief in what might be defined as the partial or retrievable fall. There was a quite widespread view that a single slip by a woman should not damn her to a career of vice and degradation. Numerous institutions attempted to differentiate between women who had fallen once, as the result of seduction or even rape, from women who made an habitual career of selling themselves. Barret-Ducrocq tells the stories of the women who argued that they had made a single slip, either seduced under promise of marriage, or been the victims of rape, in order to place their illegitimate offspring in the Foundling Hospital.[5] Frost reveals that women seduced in what they supposed to be anticipation of marriage received a good deal of sympathy from judges and juries before whom breach-of-promise cases were tried.[6] Acton himself clearly distinguished the 'young housemaid or pretty parlour-maid' who 'with shame or horror bears a child to the butler, or the policeman, or her master's son' from 'streetwalkers and professional prostitutes', and wrote to the *Lancet* advocating the employment of these unfortunates as 'Unmarried Wet-Nurses' to enable them to earn an honest living.[7]

Even the professional prostitute was not necessarily spurned as wholly irredeemable. Well before the Contagious Diseases Acts put prostitution on the political agenda, an active movement aimed at rescuing prostitutes from their life of sin. However, although the rhetoric of rescue was often one of kindliness and compassion to fallen sisters, stringently disciplined conditions of considerable severity, meant to inculcate remorse and repentance, were characteristic of the institutions established for their reception.

The boundary between protection and punishment was thus rather hazy, and rescuing and policing prostitutes were not dichotomous activities but among a range of strategies pursued by individuals and organizations concerned about the 'social evil'.

The major gap in attitudes towards prostitution was between those who did, in fact, see it as a difficult moral and social problem, though they might dispute remedies, and those who took what Mason has termed the line of 'classic moralism' based on an acceptance of the double moral standard as 'natural', and prostitution an ineradicable and necessary institution of society.[8]

There were a number of curious inconsistencies in the ways in which the legal system treated women in connection with sexual crimes. Studies of rape and sexual violence (and textbooks of forensic medicine), however, indicate that although these were a pervasive menace, and rape considered a heinous crime, convictions were remarkably few and there was pervasive male paranoia about false accusations. Class as much as gender, and the vague, but to contemporaries clearly understood, category of 'respectability', were significant elements in the outcome of trials. 'Respectable' men who sexually harassed, molested or raped domestic servants or female employees (or even small children) seem to have been regarded as incapable of a crime defined as the act of a bestial, sub-human, underclass.

Yet women seduced under promise of marriage were accorded considerable sympathy when suing for breach of promise: Frost suggests that their values were shared by the householders on the jury, who had no hesitation in awarding damages against vile seducing cads who had exploited a decent woman's affections. Also, though defined as cads, and made to pay, the men were not criminalized or identified as sub-human beasts.[9] The other area in which a perhaps unexpected sympathy was extended to female transgressors was in the case of infanticide: proof was hard, but judges and lawyers also tacitly accepted that the parlous economic and social circumstances of such women mitigated their crime, although there were attempts by the medical profession to take a more serious line.

Beneath the Crinoline

Some writers seem fascinated, rather like the Victorian scientific male, by the Victorian woman. There is what sometimes seems an almost prurient interest in what was going on under those cumbersome crinolines. The fact that some women are on record as having managed to discover and enjoy sexual pleasure is taken, by a rather dubious process of generalization, to mean that the Victorian woman in general was a right little raver.[10] While stereotypes of the 'lie back and think of England' and 'ladies don't move' kind have the status of urban legend, the evidence should be approached cautiously and critically. Women were operating within a system in which the beliefs and expectations of males about their own sexuality, as well as that of women, had a significant impact.

The evidence for the views of the Victorian male about the sexuality of the Victorian female (there is rather little evidence about the opinions of the female herself until very late in the century) is conflicting and ambiguous in the extreme, and strongly inflected for class and ethnicity. But, even when middle-class men were thinking about middle-class women, opinions could be very varied. Women might be perceived as possessing desires which could constitute a demanding and dangerous temptation, or as appropriately cold in the manner described by perhaps that most quoted authority, Acton, submitting to their husbands for reasons of domestic harmony and desire for motherhood. There was also an ideal of mutual sexual delight and pleasure, though this cannot be read as uncomplicatedly 'pro-sensual', since it was hedged around with the necessity of formal marriage ties and even within them regulated and rationed. There could also be an unthinking male assumption, of which the pseudonymous 'Walter', author of the pornographic classic *My Secret Life*, is probably the best example, that of course women had orgasms automatically through the kind of penetrative sex that was pleasurable for the male. The antithesis to this complacent belief is perhaps the confession received in 1920 by Marie Stopes from an elderly man, that forty years previously, as a young husband, he 'was frightened and thought it was some sort of fit' when his wife had an orgasm.

A complex of entangled mid-Victorian meanings about female sexuality was revealed during the 1860s in the furore caused by Dr Isaac Baker Brown, who advocated (and performed at his London Surgical Home) clitoridectomy to eradicate female self-abuse, which he believed the cause of many maladies. There is no satisfactory evidence that clitoridectomy was ever routinely prescribed by Victorian medical men for 'female disorders' such as hysteria and, indeed, one wonders if many doctors could reliably have located the clitoris. The attitudes to women and female sexuality expressed during the meeting of the London Obstetrical Society which led to Baker Brown's expulsion, do not reveal any simple and monolithic set of beliefs among a group of men often assumed to have been rigorously defining and policing the female body as an object of medical authority and intervention. It was regarded as a foul insult to British womanhood to argue, as Baker Brown did, that they practised self-abuse at all, at least in the numbers he claimed. Horror was also registered, however, at his performing of a 'mutilating operation' with serious consequences for future married life.

Male Fears

Victorian female sexuality needs to be located in the wider context of ideas about the place of sexuality in marriage and the life of the individual, and in particular in the context of male attitudes towards their own sexuality. This was by no means straightforward. While libertine sub-cultures undoubtedly existed, it should not be assumed that the average nineteenth-century male had no compunction about, for example, habitual resort to prostitutes. The customers of prostitutes are shadowy figures about whom little is known – for example, how many of them there were, how often they purchased sexual favours, why they did so and what services they required.

One reason why men might have been chary of indulging in bought sex even if they had no personal moral revulsion was fear of venereal diseases. These diseases were stigmatized – sufferers were excluded from most hospitals – but for large parts of the century were not necessarily considered to be enormously serious. The most common conditions, gonorrhoea and syphilis, normally remit spontaneously, and thus appeared to respond to medical intervention. While syphilis did, in fact, produce long-term consequences in its victims and their children, the full extent of the effects of tertiary syphilis was not recognized until the advent of the Wasserman test in 1905, although, from clinical observations alone, by the 1890s many doctors were ascribing numerous problems to its ravages.

Concern over the high level of sexually transmitted diseases in the army and navy, in which physical fitness and readiness for defence of the nation was at a premium, led to the introduction of the Contagious Diseases Acts during the 1860s, under which prostitutes in designated port and garrison towns could be compulsorily medically examined and if found to be infected, incarcerated until cured (both diagnosis and 'cure' were highly unreliable given the state of clinical knowledge and the conditions of examination). While some sectors of public opinion welcomed these Acts, and even argued for their extension for the benefit of the civilian population, there was also a strong outcry against them from a consortium of interests: an emerging feminist movement considered that they typified male blame and degradation of womankind; the working-class movement saw them as biased against the young women of that class; religious interests saw them as making the world safe for immorality; and civil libertarians objected to the compulsory (and humiliating) examinations and incarceration without trial of women who had committed no crime (it was not a crime to be a prostitute: 'causing a nuisance' and 'being disorderly' were the formulae deployed to police their activities). Even some doctors felt that tackling an infectious disease by controlling only one-half of the population involved was not good sanitarian science.

Many men, nervous of taking diseases associated with immorality to a regular doctor, resorted to the plethora of quacks who promised quick discreet treatment without the use of mercury (which caused unpleasant symptoms itself). The quacks did not confine themselves to providing spurious remedies for sexually transmitted diseases. They also offered to repair the ravages caused by habitual self-abuse (masturbation), and in particular to cure the disease of 'spermatorrhoea', the morbid emission of semen, allegedly caused by sexual excess: the oozing away of this vital fluid was believed to lead to serious debilitation. The medical profession took it very seriously – the *Lancet* published articles on the subject, and gave positive reviews to books on it. Anxious men resorted to painful physical remedies such as cauterization and the wearing of spiked rings to prevent unwanted erection and emission. Masturbation not only led, it was believed, to this physical wasting, but by the 1860s was also believed to result in insanity, although almost immediately there was a retreat from this position and assignment of blame for causing mental distress to the point of lunacy to the panic-mongering publications of quacks. Advertising was rife and took many forms: it would have been hard for a young man to escape it.

'Excess' even in conjugal relations was deemed perilous to health. By the later decades of the century concern over the economic burdens of offspring as well as potential health risks caused many men to restrict sexual indulgence within marriage.[11]

Men feared sexual temptation. During the parliamentary debates of the early 1880s on the raising of the age of consent to 16 (from 13, the recent advance over 12 which had been standard since Elizabethan times), concern was expressed over the danger from 'designing harpies' of 14, already 'corrupted', to naive males of a superior social class several years their senior. Men also feared false accusations and blackmail. There was a pervasive male belief that the making of false accusations of rape was rife and that these far outnumbered the justified cases. They were also at risk of being accused of making homosexual advances or even committing sodomy, and blackmailed on this account: the crime being regarded as so horrendous and disproving it so difficult made it a boon to the extortionist even before the passage of the Labouchère mendment to the 1885 Criminal Law Amendment Act, which criminalized all male–male sexual contacts in public or in private, with a penalty of two years in prison with hard labour. The Victorian male was therefore not a being confident in effortless superiority but more a creature in conflict and sexually imperilled.

The Convergence of the Twain

The sexual nervousness of the Victorian male had implications for conjugal relations. In many cases he must have been a twitchy and inhibited partner, both anxious about the possible deleterious outcome of sexual activity, and operating under various preconceptions, unlikely to be beneficial, of the appropriate way to approach a 'good' woman of his own class.

It is sometimes assumed that Victorians were having sex about as much as people today. This view can be naive, or it can suggest differing perceptions of the private and the mentionable and the role of codes of discretion. Others have argued that in fact the Victorians were having sex less – again, this can be a naive assumption, that what people say and what they do are entirely consistent, or rather more nuanced in its consideration of the influence of sexual discourse and indeed of practical constraints (such as the lack of effective contraception) on actual behaviour.

The assumption that if the Victorians were not having sex as often as we, in the early twenty-first century, think healthy and desirable, often goes along with the belief that if so, they must have been sad, sick, repressed and unhappy people. Szreter paints a rather gloomy picture of the sex life of the late-nineteenth-century middle-class household which resulted in the noticeable decline of the population from 1870 onwards. He places considerable emphasis on the role of abstention from marital coitus in reducing family size, but rather conflates deliberately contraceptive abstinence with the pervasive ideology of marital continence, which would reduce the probability of conception (without that being the deliberate aim).[12]

An assumption often made by modern writers is that the pleasure of sex is quantitative: that more must be better, and that the important element is the gratification of desire. It is helpful to think of the Victorians as differently sensual: Margaret Gullette's study of changing perceptions of male mid-life sexuality usefully delineates some of the ways in which such a system might have worked.[13] John Maynard presents fascinating case-studies including the Catholic convert poet Coventry Patmore and the very anti-Catholic muscular Christian, social reformer and novelist Charles Kingsley.[14] Patmore is best known for his poem of courtship and early married life, *The Angel in the House*, but sexuality provided a central metaphor for religious experiences in his mystical later works. Sex, contained and expressed within Christian marriage, seemed to Kingsley also a God-given pleasure, and his well-documented courtship was full of mutual anticipations of the fulfilled pleasures of the marriage bed.

Neither writer, however, was praising simple indulgence, but a sexual praxis in which periods of abstinence were central, and in which anticipation seems to have been at least as highly eroticized as eventual gratification. Patmore placed enormous value on the state of desire, regarding it as the intensest experience of the sexual. There is some rather curious evidence that he practised a form of masturbation providing the pleasures of arousal without those of satisfaction.

By the end of the century there was a feminist assertion of the rights of the wife within marriage. Immense importance was placed on women's physical inviolability, and their absolute right to refuse unwanted advances, as well as to be the arbiter of when to bear children. Some writers argued that contraception was merely an excuse for the unbridled expression of male lust. However, Bland has pointed out that the ideal of 'psychic' (rather than physical) love did carry an implication of pleasure and draws attention to the similarity between the language deployed in this connection and that used by the Malthusian League in pro-contraception rhetoric, suggesting the possibility that the 'rational' use of prevention could be assimilated to the expression of 'pure and psychic love' on the physical plane.[15]

Alternative Positions

Nineteenth-century sexuality, however, was not exclusively about heterosexuality and positioned along the twin axes of marriage/prostitution. Even within heterosexuality there was resistance to the institution of marriage, ranging from protests against the legal position of women within it, to outright rejection. From Richard Carlile in the 1820s to the Legitimation League in the 1890s, there was a persistent, if sometimes rather muted, free-love tradition. In some cases this did mean being open to multiple relationships: it was a utopian desire to eschew jealousy which led George Lewes to condone his wife's relationship with Thornton Hunt, removing any later possibility of divorce. However, it seems mostly to have meant monogamous unions intended to be enduring without the intervention of the church or the imprimatur of the state. There was nonetheless a good deal of stigma attached to free unions. Mary Ann Evans chose seclusion rather than deal with social snubs when she went to live with Lewes. Edith Lanchester was actually incarcerated in a lunatic asylum by her family for proposing to enter an unsanctified relationship with a socialist comrade. Radical Malthusian doctor Charles Robert Drysdale and his partner, pioneer medical woman and feminist Alice Vickery, seem to have chosen not to marry on principle, but kept this a dark secret out of concern for their medical careers. The penalties for sexual nonconformity could be considerable in social and professional terms. But they were not actual criminal penalties.

At the beginning of the nineteenth century sodomy between males was a capital offence, although the actual prosecution of cases and execution of sodomites was very sporadic. In 1861 the Offences Against the Person Act section on 'Unnatural Offences' removed the capital penalty and substituted life imprisonment. However, the lesser offence of 'attempted sodomy' was employed to cover a wide range of male–male sexual acts. Cocks illuminates the extent to which even before the alleged 'blackmailers' charter' of the Labouchère Amendment of 1885, men who had sexual relations with other men were harried by the police and victimized by blackmailers.[16]

Cities such as London had a burgeoning homosexual sub-culture. There was also a pervasive cult of 'Greek love' among educated males, intended to be an idealized affection rather than anything more carnal. The plethora of all-male environments fostered attachments ranging from the intensely emotional to the fleetingly physical, and indeed the abusive.

The Labouchère Amendment to the Criminal Law Amendment Act of 1885 remains the subject of historical controversy. Was it a deliberate move against all homosexual activity? Was it a badly drafted (because the subject was one no-one wanted to discuss in detail) attempt to extend the protection the Act gave to young girls to their masculine contemporaries? Or did 'Labby' actually intend this amendment as a wrecking measure? The record is unclear. What did happen was that the police gained clearer grounds for prosecuting cases without the requirement to demonstrate clear evidence of sodomy or an attempt at it. The penalties for sodomy as such remained on the books, but the vast majority of prosecutions for homosexual 'crimes' subsequently took place under the 1885 Amendment.

While most homosexual activity was discreetly contained through policing measures and summary jurisdiction rather than jury trials, there were a number of famous cases which brought it, however concealed in euphemism, to public attention. In 1870 'Fanny' Boulton and 'Stella' Park were arrested for being in drag and tried for conspiracy to commit sodomy. During the trial new ideas of identity entered the debate. Both were acquitted and the police criticized. In 1889–90 there was the Cleveland Street Scandal, in which boys employed by the Post Office were found to be moonlighting by 'going to bed with gentlemen' at an establishment in Cleveland Street. A number of aristocrats were named. It has been suggested that the reluctance of the government to pursue this case was motivated by a desire to conceal a member of the royal family patronizing the establishment, but it seems more likely that it was felt that publicity in this unseemly matter was to be avoided if possible. The most famous case, of course, was that of Oscar Wilde, in 1895, whose speech on 'the love that dares not speak its name' had the courtroom cheering. Sordid revelations about working-class 'renters', however, rather undercut this ideal vision of male–male love. In 1897 male soliciting was further penalized under the Vagrancy Act. If homosexuality was gradually becoming more visible, this was perhaps at the cost of being further stamped on.

Meanwhile a few individuals were endeavouring to make a case for the toleration of the 'invert/uranian/intermediate'. The literary man John Addington Symonds wrote two brief essays, *A Problem in Greek Ethics* (1883) and *A Problem in Modern Ethics* (1890), which he had printed privately and sent to those he thought interested or sympathetic. The socialist, pacifist, vegetarian Edward Carpenter produced a pamphlet on *Homogenic Love and its Place in a Free Society* (1894). However, when he proposed publishing this as one chapter of his *Love's Coming of Age* in 1896, the publisher took fright and refused it. The doctor and literary figure Havelock Ellis, unlike the previous two not himself homosexual, but married to a woman predominantly lesbian, responded favourably to the suggestion that he and Symonds should write a work on *Sexual Inversion*, which fitted in with the ambitious project which became Ellis's *Studies in the Psychology of Sex* (1897–1927). After various misadventures, this work appeared under Ellis's name alone, was caught up in a police raid for anarchist literature, and the bookseller was prosecuted for obscenity in 1898. The latter pleaded guilty, preventing a defence of the work on the grounds of its intentions (which were praised in contemporary medical journals).

Women, however, enjoyed legal impunity in homosexual relations. As a result the history of women who were sexually active with other women is even more obscure than that of the mass of homosexual males, and much of the evidence only permits speculation. The idea of life-long female devotion in a quasi-marital relationship was overtly honoured in the early nineteenth century in the respect given to the relationship between the 'Ladies of Llangollen', Sarah Ponsonby and Lady Eleanor Butler, who had eloped together rather than submit to marriage, and whose modest home in rural Wales was visited by many well-known figures of the day. The diaries of Anne Lister, a Yorkshire landowner and gentlewoman, have been decrypted to reveal a woman completely conscious of the physical nature of her desire for other women and detailing her actively sexual affairs with them. Occasional cases came to light of women who had successfully masqueraded as men, sometimes to the extent of actually marrying another woman. Women were permitted a good deal of emotional expressiveness in their relationships with other women, and even a degree of physical intimacy (kissing, hugging, sharing beds), but the extent to which this ever blossomed into consummated sexual relations is a matter of debate. Also a matter for conjecture is the nature of the households set up by 'New Women' rejecting marriage and choosing to share their lives with a companion of their own sex with similar ideals.

There is a persistent mistaken belief that in its original form the Labouchère Amendment included the criminalization of lesbianism, struck out through the personal intervention of Victoria, who could not believe that any woman would be so lost to a sense of decency. The Criminal Law Amendment Act of 1885 was not creating new crimes but extending the parameters of existing offences such as the seduction of young girls and sex between men. The queen in this anecdote seems to be exemplifying the age's incapability of conceiving that women could be sexual without men. This generalization is not wholly true, of course: Victorian erotica includes a plethora of woman/woman sex and/or flagellation, but, as Marcus commented, this typified 'pornutopian' inversion of the assumptions of Victorian respectability.[17] It has also been argued that a tacit understanding that such things happened can be discerned in the responses to various scandals of the day, but 'knowing silence' is hard to grasp as historical evidence.

Taking Sex towards a New Era

The Contagious Diseases Acts of the 1860s precipitated enormous debate. By the 1880s the campaign to repeal the Acts had grown into a mass movement aiming at a much broader moral regeneration of society. Nonetheless, opposition was still considerable. While the Acts were suspended in 1883, attempts to pass a law raising the age of consent for girls encountered a good deal of resistance. However, a series of sensationalist articles in the *Pall Mall Gazette* by its editor, W. T. Stead, culminating in his practical demonstration of how easy it was to purchase a child and export her to a foreign brothel, led to enormous public outcry and the passage of the Criminal Law Amendment Act, 1885, raising the age of consent to 16, tightening up existing laws on brothel-keeping, and including the Labouchère Amendment discussed above. The following year the Contagious Diseases Acts were quietly repealed, having created an unintended discursive explosion around the subject of sex in society.

The social-purity movement which emerged from the repeal campaign (embodied in a variety of organizations, not always working harmoniously together) undertook a wide-ranging programme of improving society, from initiating censorship cases, through proactive work on the sexual abuse of women and children, to the demand for the sexual enlightenment of the young. Though sometimes positioned as antithetical to the new science of sexology concurrently emerging, a strong case can be made that these two movements were less distinct than supposed and that they had more in common with one another than with the smug assumptions of 'classic morality' about the trans-historical inevitability of the double moral standard. Women's protests against the laws on marriage and the Contagious Diseases Acts contributed to a destabilization of existing categories of 'normal' and 'natural' which favoured the explorations of writers such as Carpenter and Ellis beyond the confines of accepted heterosexual normality. Moral activists like Ellice Hopkins were also theorizing sexual relations. While women (and also male social purity activists) were often writing in modes (for example the religious) or genres (such as handbooks on sex education for children) which are overlooked when constructing the scientific genealogy of sexology, in the British context it may well be argued that if Darwin was the father of sexual science, through positioning reproduction as essential to evolution, its mother was Josephine Butler, the charismatic leader of the Ladies' National Association for the Repeal of the Acts.

In conclusion, the main point to be borne in mind when contemplating sexuality in nineteenth-century Britain is the extraordinary complexity of the subject and the very contradictory attitudes and behaviour manifested throughout the century.

NOTES

1. I. D. McCalman, *Radical Underworld: Prophets, Revolutionaries and Pornographers in London, 1795–1840* (Cambridge, 1988).
2. M. L. Bush, *What is Love?: Richard Carlile's Philosophy of Sex* (London, 1998).
3. S. Szreter, *Fertility, Class and Gender in Britain, 1860–1940* (Cambridge, 1996).
4. 'Annoyances on Clapham Common', Home Office file, HO45/9666/A45364, Public Record Office.
5. F. Barret-Ducrocq, *Love in the Time of Victoria: Sexuality, Class and Gender in Nineteenth Century London* (London, 1991).
6. G. Frost, *Promises Broken: Courtship, Class and Gender in Victorian England* (Charlottesville, 1995).
7. W. Acton, 'Unmarried wet-nurses', *Lancet*, 1 (1859).
8. M. Mason, *The Making of Victorian Sexual Attitudes* (Oxford, 1994).
9. Frost, *Promises Broken*.
10. P. Gay, *The Bourgeois Experience – Victoria to Freud*, vol. 1, *Education of the Senses* (London, 1983).
11. Szreter, *Fertility, Class and Gender*.
12. Ibid.
13. M. M. Gullette, 'Male midlife sexuality in a gerontocratic economy: the privileged state of the long midlife in nineteenth-century age-ideology', *Journal of the History of Sexuality*, 5 (1994).
14. J. Maynard, *Victorian Discourses on Sexuality and Religion* (Cambridge, 1993).
15. L. Bland, *Banishing the Beast: English Feminism and Sexual Morality, 1885–1914* (London, 1995).
16. H. Cocks, *Nameless Offences* (London, 2003).
17. S. Marcus, *The Other Victorians: A Study of Sexuality and Pornography in Mid-Nineteenth Century England* (New York, 1966).

FURTHER READING

The fullest and so far the most satisfactory discussion of Victorian sexuality and sexual attitudes is M. Mason, *The Making of Victorian Sexual Attitudes* and *The Making of Victorian Sexuality* (both 1994). These give significant attention to the pre-Victorian roots of 'Victorianism', but unfortunately conclude at 1870. On prostitution, venereal diseases and the Contagious Diseases Act, J. R. Walkowitz, *Prostitution and Victorian Society: Women, Class and the State* (1980) remains an essential resource. L. Bland, *Banishing the Beast: English Feminism and Sexual Morality, 1885–1914* (1995) is the best and most solidly researched account of feminist interventions into debates on sexuality.

On sexual violence and the abuse of women, there are two excellent recent studies: S. D'Cruze, *Crimes of Outrage: Sex, Violence and Victorian Working Women* (1998) looks at the place of violence and sexual assault in (primarily) the lives of working-class women, while L. A. Jackson, *Child Sexual Abuse in Victorian England* admirably tackles this sensitive topic (2000). A. J. Hammerton, *Cruelty and Companionship: Conflict in Nineteenth Century Married Life* (1992) deploys legal materials on divorce and separation to illuminate the murky private arena of marital relations.

On extra-marital and non-marital relationships, historiography has concentrated on the female victims. F. Barret-Ducrocq, *Love in the Time of Victoria: Sexuality, Class and Gender in Nineteenth Century London* (1991), using previously unexamined materials from the Foundling Hospital, is empirically rich but maddeningly under-theorized. L. Mahood, *The Magdalenes: Prostitution in the Nineteenth Century* (1990) and P. Bartley, *Prostitution: Prevention and Reform in Britain, 1860–1914* (2000) look at institutions for the rescue/reform of prostitutes in Scotland and England. The life of prostitutes outside this institutional framework is harder to recapture, but F. Finnegan's study of York prostitutes, *Poverty and Prostitution: A Study of Victorian Prostitutes in York* (1979), remains valuable.

H. Cocks, *Nameless Offences* (2003) uses queer theory in close analysis of archival sources to examine the intersection between developing homosexual sub-cultures and institutions of social control. It gets beyond the focus on causes célèbres to look at routine police harassment and containment of non-elite homosexuals.

CHAPTER TWENTY-SEVEN

The Arts

PATRICIA PULHAM

Alfred, Lord Tennyson's 'The Palace of Art', published in *Poems* (1832), speaks of a mythical architectural wonder in which the poet's soul resides in splendid isolation. Here, in this cultural retreat, art replaces reality: geography, history and culture are all represented in paintings that hang on its sumptuously decorated walls. But Tennyson's poet soon finds that such imitations of life are not enough; that his soul (personified as female) must descend from her gilded seclusion to live in 'a cottage in the vale' where she might repent her pride and arrogance. Yet she begs that her palace towers be allowed to remain, and suggests that in time, when she has 'purged her guilt', she may 'return with others' to enjoy its beauties.[1] Tennyson's poem, playing with the notion of a romantic poet who finds that his solitary existence, in which the glories of art are elevated above the earthly cares of a prosaic world, is no longer fitting, highlights a democratic movement in art which was to function as one of the defining features of the nineteenth century. During this period, many of those 'palaces of art' (both literal and figurative) hitherto inaccessible to the general public would open their doors, and those lofty souls belonging to the poets, painters, novelists, dramatists, musicians, sculptors and architects of the age would indeed return to them 'with others' whose tastes would shape and re-shape their contents by their consumption and patronage of the arts.

It has been well documented that the development of industrial towns and cities had a significant impact on both geographical and social mobility in the nineteenth century. Tempted by the promise of work, many agricultural labourers and their families were to move from the country to the city, and for those with vision and foresight there was money to be made which might elevate them above their working-class roots. In the arts, these changes created new audiences with differing economic means and varying requirements and, in the rising middle classes, new patrons and a new audience with leisure time at its disposal. This chapter examines the effects of these new consumers on the production of art in the nineteenth century, and on those intermediaries: publishing houses, circulating libraries, galleries, theatres and government bodies, who strove to please, or in some cases to control, a rapidly changing and ever increasing public.

Poetry

In 1798, William Wordsworth and Samuel Taylor Coleridge published *Lyrical Ballads*, a collection of poems which, while conforming in subject matter with many contemporary poems to be found in the *Gentleman's Magazine*, the *Monthly Magazine* or the *Scot's Magazine* and dealing with such subjects as rural poverty and social outcasts, was widely criticized for employing the language of the common man. Wordsworth defended his poetry in a preface that accompanied the 1800 edition and outlined his objectives, which were to make ordinary life interesting, to depict natural characters and, finally, to heighten the reader's social conscience and personal awareness of human relationships. Poetry, traditionally associated with elevated language and classical allusion is here seemingly 'democratized' in Wordsworth's hands. Yet it is vital to remember that Wordsworth's words were being addressed to what was still a relatively 'exclusive' readership, and his own reluctance to participate in the widening of that readership is evident in his response when asked to contribute to *The Keepsake* annual in 1829. The annuals were to become one of the nineteenth-century's success stories and one of the primary outlets for budding as well as established poets. Sporting titles such as *Friendship's Offering*, *The Literary Souvenir*, the *English Bijou Almanack*, bound luxuriously in silks and sometimes embossed with jewels, these collections created an illusion of exclusivity belied by their ubiquity and were aimed primarily at a female market. Featuring short stories, essays and poems, but valued more perhaps for the steel engravings of sentimental or pastoral subjects they were often commissioned to accompany, the annuals were, ostensibly, morally acceptable reading for young ladies that had the added attraction of a certain social cachet. As a result they found an avid clientele in young women readers of the middle classes, epitomized by Rosamond Vincy in George Eliot's *Middlemarch* (1872). Therefore, Wordsworth, who in 1802 had defined the poet as 'a man speaking to men', found himself, in *The Keepsake* for 1829, addressing a predominantly female audience.[2] The reasons for this compromise are made clear in a letter from Wordsworth's daughter, Dora, to Maria Jane Jewsbury. Referring to the considerable sum of 100 guineas for twelve pages of verse which was to be Wordsworth's remuneration Dora wrote that, as a result of their pecuniary constraints, her father did not feel justified in refusing this generous offer, despite suffering a sense of degradation at having to accept it. Evidently the financial compensations were too tempting to refuse. However, it is worth looking at the wider context in which this decision was made. As the nineteenth century progressed, poetry began to lose its hold on the popular imagination, and was rapidly replaced by a rising interest in the novel. Faced with the public's growing indifference and haunted by insecurities fostered by the financial crisis of 1826, publishers were reluctant to publish first editions of poetry. By the 1830s and 1840s Edward Moxon was one of the few publishers in England of new collections of poetry by individual poets and his firm survived mainly due to his precaution that poets should agree to underwrite part of the publishing costs incurred. For those unable to do so, the annuals provided an alternative, and, during the early years of his career in the 1830s, Tennyson too, in spite of his professional dissatisfaction with the annuals, was among those who used the medium for his own ends: three short poems of his appeared in *The Gem*; there were sonnets in *Friendship's Offering* and *The Yorkshire Literary Annual*; and a poem in *The Tribute* was the germ for *Maud*. Others whose work appeared in these annuals include Scott, Shelley, Coleridge and Southey, and it is worth noting that these annuals were instrumental in bringing these names to new audiences. During the Romantic period, when these poets began their careers, people were more likely to have read Scott than any other poet, and Shelley and Coleridge did not achieve popularity until later in the Victorian period.

For female poets of the first half of the nineteenth century, these annuals proved a godsend. Felicia Hemans and Letitia Landon contributed regularly to a number of titles, and poems by Elizabeth Barrett Browning are to be found among the pages of *Finden's Tableaux* for 1838, 1839 and 1840, and of *The Keepsake* for 1855 and 1857. The annuals were instrumental in creating a literary community for these women and their professional relationships are clearly visible in the poems themselves, for Letitia Landon's eulogy, 'Stanzas on the Death of Mrs Hemans' (1835), finds its echo in Barrett Browning's 'Felicia Hemans' (1838), dedicated to Letitia Landon, and in 'L.E.L.'s Last Question' (1844). Yet, the annuals' marketing strategy, aimed primarily at the female consumer, served to undermine the literary value of women's poetry, and male writers in particular voiced their disdain for the annuals even as they reaped the financial benefits of their contributions. This adverse response to the annuals is perhaps best explored in relation to the question of separate spheres. In the nineteenth century, critics such as John Ruskin and Alfred Austin were concerned to voice their definitions of sexual roles. For Ruskin, man was formed for activity, woman for passivity, and Austin was to lament the fact that women had seemingly escaped the privacy of the home and were dangerously ubiquitous in the public sphere. Vehicles like the annuals, while retaining the accoutrements of the private feminine sphere – the silks and jewels of its covers and the fostered intimacy of reading – nevertheless provided a platform for the female poet. As the century progressed, writing poetry began to seem 'like woman's work, even though men were supposed to do it'.[3] From this, it is easy to draw the conclusion that the male poets' contempt for the annual form is due, in part, to fears of feminization, and it is interesting to note that, while many Victorian poets including Tennyson, Robert Browning and Algernon Charles Swinburne often retreated to a classical, medieval or renaissance past in their poetry, many women poets began to speak of contemporary concerns. At the head of this contingent is Barrett Browning who, in her novel-length poem *Aurora Leigh* (1856) writes that a poet's 'sole work' should be to 'represent the age/Their age' and not some distant past.[4] This realist perspective is often followed by poets like Augusta Webster and Amy Levy, who discuss such subjects as syphilis, illegitimacy and the fallen woman in their works. In their poetry, unfortunate women can tell their stories unglossed by the transforming eye of the male poet.

In *Aurora Leigh*, Barrett Browning was also to question the rigidity of traditional forms of poetry and, faced with the popularity of the annual form, other poets did likewise, experimenting with an increasing variety of poetic genres in the hope of reclaiming the reader's attention. In this literary climate, the divisions between poetic forms became increasingly blurred. Whereas in the past epic and tragedy had led the field, closely followed by elegy and lyric, now the lines were less clearly demarcated. In 1868–9 Robert Browning produced *The Ring and the Book*, a collection of poems which tells the same story from a variety of perspectives, recalling the narrative technique of early detective fiction, while containing both epic and lyric qualities. In his

Idylls of the King, Tennyson, too, was to play with poetic genres. Choosing an epic subject, that of the Arthurian court, he avoids the restrictions of the epic form by supplying the reader with a number of poems which give fragmented, yet interrelated, glimpses of the court, thus focusing our attention on his chosen protagonists. Similarly Tennyson's *The Princess*, a poem in mock-heroic style, plays with the epic subject of the quest: the story of the princess, set in a chivalric past, is framed by a contemporary narrative and is punctuated by lyric interjections. But the most significant genre which evolved in the nineteenth century is the dramatic monologue: a genre of which Robert Browning became the indubitable master in such poems as 'My Last Duchess' (1842), 'Fra Lippo Lippi' (1855) and 'Andrea del Sarto' (1855); a genre influenced by the rise of the novel, and the popularity of drama in the preceding century. Nineteenth-century poetry is characterized by variety: it offers a multiplicity of styles and genres, ranging in subject matter from the nonsense poems of Edward Lear and Lewis Carroll to the Christian poetry of Christina Rossetti and Gerard Manley Hopkins, and spans a time line which stretches from the classical and medieval past recalled in the poetry of Tennyson and Swinburne, to the contemporary Darwinian doubts expressed by Matthew Arnold: an eclecticism of genre, theme and tone, reflecting the educational and social range of its audience.

The Novel

The rise of the novel represents one of the most significant literary changes in the nineteenth century. The term 'novel' did not become widely used until the end of the eighteenth century, which had seen the progression of the form through autobiographical narratives and the epistolary novel. According to Watt, historians of the novel have defined 'realism' as the genre's distinguishing feature, and we can trace its development via works such as Defoe's *Robinson Crusoe* (1719) and Samuel Richardson's *Clarissa* (1747–8) in the eighteenth century, and in the more conventional novels of Jane Austen's oeuvre (1811–18).[5] In the nineteenth century, this realist perspective materialized in various forms: the historical novel, the social-problem novel and the community novel. At the heart of all three forms is the question of self and society: whether distanced romantically in the past as in Scott's *Waverley* (1814); confronted by the contemporary concerns of the industrial towns and cities as in Elizabeth Gaskell's *Mary Barton* (1848); or faced with the social mores of a provincial community like Eliot's *Middlemarch*. In the mid-Victorian era the topical issue of social obligation dominated the novel. While the Victorian underclass had often claimed general interest in such novels as Charles Dickens's *Oliver Twist* (1838), it was the representation of the working classes which was to monopolize the public's attention during this period. The working classes, mobilized by the trade unions, began to rally against political impositions such as the Poor Law of 1834, and in 1837, the People's Charter demanded the vote for every man at 21, the ballot and other political reforms. The instability of the working classes, expressed through the Chartist movement, gave rise to middle-class fears and the question of social responsibility was hotly debated. Contributing to this debate were what have come to be known as the 'Condition of England' novels. Among these are Gaskell's *Mary Barton* and *North and South* (1854–5), Dickens's *Hard Times* (1854), Disraeli's *Sybil* (1845) and Charles Kingsley's *Yeast* (1851), novels which, while depicting the degradation of poverty, tread carefully on the sensibilities of their middle-class audiences. Like these authors, Eliot too merged the private lives of her characters with those of the community amid real events such as the Reform Bill of 1832. Yet, unhampered by the need to expose, or comment on, a particular 'question', Eliot, in such novels as *Middlemarch*, is able to explore her characters in greater depth, affording them a psychological complexity that significantly contributes to the domestic realism in her text. And Eliot was not alone: in the latter part of the century Thomas Hardy would create a rural realism in his Wessex novels; Dinah Craik had earlier found a ready readership for her works *John Halifax, Gentleman* (1857) and *A Life for a Life* (1859); and with such novels as *The Heir of Redclyffe* (1853) and *The Clever Woman of the Family* (1865), Charlotte Yonge was to achieve considerable popularity for her representations of family life; she was later admired by Henry James whose displays of psychological acuity in his own realist fictions are testament to his admiration.

The role of self and society was also to become the focus of the 'sensation' novel, a term borrowed from the theatre's 'sensation drama' which staged melodramatic events within the family circle. These novels centred on questions of morality with bigamy, adultery, illegitimacy, duplicity and murder forming the defining elements of the genre. Arguably, these themes relate to the tensions caused by the urban unknowability of the growing towns and cities: a tension which manifests itself in the preoccupation with identification and classification that increases significantly in the nineteenth century. In these novels, the fears that walk the city reverberate within the family home and manifest themselves in concerns with sexuality, madness and the alien intruder, resonating interestingly with the violence and terror that earlier characterizes the Brontë novels: *Jane Eyre* (1847), *Wuthering Heights* (1847) and *The Tenant of Wildfell Hall* (1848). Wilkie Collins's *The Woman in White* (1860), Mary Elizabeth Braddon's *Lady Audley's Secret* (1861–2) and Ellen Wood's *East Lynne* (1861) fulfil all expectations of the genre which became a close cousin of not only early detective fictions such as Collins's *The Moonstone* (1868), but also of the fantastic novels published in the late nineteenth century such as Robert Louis Stevenson's *The Strange Case of Dr Jekyll and Mr Hyde* (1886), Oscar Wilde's *The Picture of Dorian Gray* (1891) and Bram Stoker's *Dracula* (1897). At the nineteenth century *fin de siècle* these novels return once again to those concerns with demonology, science and psychology which are to be found in novels of the late eighteenth and early nineteenth centuries such as Matthew Lewis's *The Monk* (1795), Mary Shelley's *Frankenstein* (1818) and James Hogg's *Confessions of a Justified Sinner* (1824). The end of the century also saw the development of a form of 'Boys' Own' adventure novel, exemplified by H. Rider Haggard's *King Solomon's Mines* (1885) and Rudyard Kipling's *Kim* (1901), that concerned itself with the far-flung reaches of the British Empire, reclaiming the novel from the domestic milieu that had defined much of the period's literature.

From its inception, the novel had generated a general unease centred on the suitability of reading matter for certain audiences. Many nineteenth-century novels were originally published as 'three-deckers', in other words in a three-volume set costing 31s 6d, which was considered the appropriate form in which to publish first editions. However, the purchase of a three-decker novel proved beyond the means of most readers and it was common to rent volumes from the circulating libraries which sprang up to meet public demand. The most famous of these was Mudie's, which dominated the field from the mid- to the late-Victorian period. The influence of the circulating library system was considerable and shaped both the way in which people read, and the way in which novelists wrote. Readers were restricted to the reading of a novel in three 'instalments', and novelists had to fit their novels into the three-volume system or settle for much lower prices from the publishing companies who colluded with the circulating libraries. Such libraries, and in particular Mudie's, were to have another significant effect. Advertising itself as 'Mudie's Select Library' ensured that Mudie's attracted its clientele from the middle classes, but such an advertisement also carried a certain moral tone which ultimately controlled the content of the novels accepted for distribution. Yet it would be reductive to view the accessibility of the novel purely from the perspective of the circulating libraries, for not all fiction was published in the three-decker form, particularly that which was aimed at the working-class market. In the early part of the century, the most popular of these were chapbooks and broadsheets which contained poems and prose offerings and could be purchased for a penny or less. Later, a new form emerged which serialized fiction in weekly parts costing one or two pennies per issue. Dickens took this idea and developed it by publishing novels in monthly parts costing a shilling, but still continued to publish some of his own novels in weekly magazines such as *Household Words* and *All the Year Round*. By mid-century, quick, cheap, small reprints of novels, made possible by innovations in printing technology, began to appear, often sold at railway stations for between a shilling and 2s 6d, which became known as 'railway novels' or 'yellowbacks', and, in the 1860s, paperback editions were issued costing as little as sixpence. By the end of the century the novel had crossed the boundaries of class, and settled in the democratic niche of popular fiction.

Painting

Whilst Turner's Romantic landscapes retained their hold on the nineteenth-century artistic imagination for much of the period, the realist movement, prevalent in fiction, also had its effects on art, resulting in a 'realistic' mode termed 'genre' painting, popular in the 1830s, which centred on scenes of everyday life, primarily interiors. Paintings such as Thomas Webster's *The Boy with Many Friends* (1841) is typical of this style, and Victoria herself is depicted in a scene of domestic bliss by Sir Edwin Landseer in *Windsor Castle in Modern Times* (1841–5). Literature had another, and more direct, effect on art which resulted in the literary genre painting for which an episode from a well-known play or novel would be the inspiration. Among these is William Mulready's *Choosing the Wedding Gown* (1846), which is taken from Oliver Goldsmith's *The Vicar of Wakefield* (1766). Seventeenth- and eighteenth-century literature such as that of Pepys and Defoe proved to be prime sources for such paintings, and the continuing popularity of Scott's novels contributed to an artistic interest in the literary and historical past, particularly that of Scotland. Even the *Keepsake* annuals were to be influential in inspiring a type of portrait painted in what came to be known as the *Keepsake* style, showing beautiful, alluring women, often dressed in historical costume, emulating the popular engravings of the annual form.

This interest in the past was also expressed in the historical paintings which became one of the most popular and enduring genres of the period. In these paintings the

Victorian public looked for the greatness of their national past and a reaffirmation of their contemporary morality. They also enjoyed the glamour which could be supplied by historical figures such as the Duke of Buckingham whose life and death are portrayed in two paintings by Augustus Leopold Egg (1853–5). Despite the ostensibly realist premise of these paintings, certain subjects were avoided and poverty was rarely depicted. George Frederick Watts was among the few artists to contravene this unwritten law and, in the late 1840s and early 1850s, he painted a number of paintings including *The Irish Famine* (*c*.1850), which shows a poverty-stricken family sitting by the roadside, surrounded by a cheerless landscape. In contrast, the contemporary urban middle class was everywhere to be seen, painted by a number of artists including William Powell Frith and George Elgar Hicks in such paintings as *Dividend Day at the Bank of England* (Hicks, 1859) and *The Derby Day* (Frith, 1856–8), showing them at work and at play. Some artists extended the genre by providing a 'narrative' – painting a series of scenes depicting a story, such as Egg's trilogy *Past and Present* (1858) and Hicks's triptych, *Woman's Mission* (1863), both of which centre on the moral virtue of the Victorian woman. However, when we think of nineteenth-century art one group of painters comes immediately to mind: the Pre-Raphaelites.

Formed in 1848, the Brotherhood comprised John Everett Millais, William Holman Hunt, Thomas Woolner, Frederic George Stephens, James Collinson, Dante Gabriel Rossetti and his brother Michael. Disliking the popular taste exhibited at the Royal Academy, the Pre-Raphaelites, as their name implies, were influenced by the art of the early Italian painters, and, prompted by their interest in John Ruskin's ideas, as propagated in the early volumes of *Modern Painters* (1843–60), brought naturalistic detail and bright colour to such subjects as *The Girlhood of the Virgin Mary* (Dante Gabriel Rossetti, 1848–9) and *Christ in the House of his Parents* (Millais, 1849–50). Later, they would bring their distinctive style to bear on modern subjects as in Hunt's *The Awakening Conscience* (1853–4). The critical response to their work was initially unfavourable, but Ruskin espoused their cause, and his support encouraged a public reassessment. While the Brotherhood was short-lived, ending in 1853, Hunt, Dante Gabriel Rossetti and Millais continued to work independently, and the influence of their various styles can be traced in the work of artists of the Aesthetic Movement which enlivened the art scene in the latter part of the nineteenth century. Embracing Victor Cousin's philosophy of 'art for art's sake', the aesthetes rejected genre painting, and the narrative art which had dominated the Victorian period. Instead, form, line and colour became of paramount importance, and the fluid lines of the human form – male, female or androgynous – lent itself to the sensuality of artistic expression in Dante Gabriel Rossetti's own later works, and in the canvases of Albert Moore, Frederic Leighton, Edward Coley Burne-Jones, James Abbot McNeill Whistler, Simeon Solomon and George Frederic Watts.

The viewing of art had become a widespread leisure pursuit. From the 1830s onwards many new exhibition societies were formed, both in the provinces and in London. In the capital, public exhibitions had been dominated by the Royal Academy, founded in 1768 by Sir Joshua Reynolds, whose annual summer exhibition displayed works which were for sale, and gave artists scope to paint subjects outside those commonly requested by private commissions. However, by the 1870s the Academy had become a source of frustration to innovative artists, as exhibition depended on the selection of a jury which had become increasingly conservative and which often served its own interests. During the 1860s and 1870s the wealthy aristocratic artists, Sir Coutts Lindsay and Blanche, Lady Lindsay, both had work rejected by the Royal Academy and felt that other important artists such as Burne-Jones, Whistler and Hunt were inadequately represented there. Lindsay felt that 'high art', that art which concerned itself with the work of Renaissance masters, or used classical allusion in its composition, was being rejected in favour of paintings pleasing to the popular taste. Evidently, there was a class issue at work here, for, at this time, classical literature and a knowledge of Renaissance art would still have been primarily the privilege of the upper classes. In response, the Lindsays opened the Grosvenor Gallery in New Bond Street on 1 May 1877 and, within two months of opening, the gallery was being referred to as a 'palace of art'. Eschewing the crowded hanging practices of the Royal Academy, the Grosvenor Gallery hung its paintings with careful attention to aesthetic effect, and provided space so that each painting could be seen to its best advantage. The artists who showed at the Grosvenor were in general second-generation Pre-Raphaelites, although some of the first generation, including Dante Gabriel Rossetti and Hunt, also showed. Millais and his fellow academician Leighton used the Grosvenor as an alternative to the Royal Academy, and the gallery also provided a much-needed forum for women artists including Louisa Stuart, Lady Waterford, Princess Louise (Victoria's daughter) and Evelyn Pickering De Morgan. While the Royal Academy's audience encompassed the middle classes, the audience at the Grosvenor remained composed predominantly of aristocrats and the London avant garde. However, the Grosvenor did take part in Sunday openings designed to encourage a wider audience who might be otherwise engaged (working) at other times. Nevertheless, these democratic openings, which gave free admission to the poor, particularly those of the artisan class, took place later in the London season so that their presence might not coincide with that of the art-world glitterati.

So who were the purchasers of nineteenth-century art? Owing to economic changes a considerable shift had taken place. In the eighteenth century, most art had been commissioned by private purchasers who came, in the main, from the aristocracy. In the nineteenth century this social monopoly of art began to alter considerably. The rising middle classes, often enriched by the spoils of industry, became a significant force in the world of art-collecting and influenced art production. Genre painting, for example, owed its popularity to the tastes of the merchants and manufacturers whose patronage contributed to the process of supply and demand. While the nobility continued to buy art, their purchases would be determined by the connoisseurship their education encouraged. New art was, more often than not, purchased by a middle-class patron, usually male, from a second- or third-generation middle-class family enriched by commerce or trade, whose base might be in London or in the provinces. Unequipped by his education to determine the finer points of traditional art, this type of patron would buy what he liked, often influenced by the nationalistic, moral or religious content of the paintings, and commissioned works accordingly. Conscious of the fact that, for an illiterate community, the visual image held an educative power, many such patrons were also instrumental in supporting art exhibitions aimed at the lower classes. It seems that, despite the concerns of the artists and distributors of 'high' art, Victorian art was firmly placed in the hands of a new public unhindered by its social or educational shortcomings.

Theatrical and Musical Entertainment

This popular movement extended to the theatre and influenced the kinds of performances that found favour with the public. The patent theatres, in existence since the Restoration, proved inadequate when faced with a growing clientele whose tastes extended beyond the classical repertory commonly played at such houses. What this new audience wanted was spectacle, excitement, music and dancing, and unlicensed theatres began to challenge the patent theatres by meeting their needs. In the early nineteenth century, a number of these began presenting musical concerts, ballets, gothic dramas, melodramas and pantomimes. Their success led to the rise of an increasing number of minor theatres such as the Lyceum (1809), the Surrey (1810), the Sans Pareil (1806), later renamed the Adelphi, and the Coburg (1816), later called the Royal Victoria. The success of these minor theatres led the patent theatres to reconsider their programmes, and gradually they began to cater for public taste by mounting expensive spectaculars incorporating complex mechanical 'special effects' to draw the crowds. Eventually, in 1843, a Bill was passed in parliament effectively freeing the independent theatres. Variety was the name of the game, and for the next twenty years these theatres would offer a miscellany of entertainment ranging from domestic plays and melodramas to burlesques, providing up to six hours of diversion for only a few shillings. The tastes which prevailed in literature were echoed in the playhouses. Domestic 'realism' had its own hold on the theatre and thrived on plays which portrayed the joys and sorrows of everyday existence, while reflecting contemporary morality, such as the extremely successful nautical play, Douglas Jerrold's *Black Ey'd Susan* (1829). Thanks to innovators such as Thomas Robertson, this realism extended to staging techniques resulting in the 'cup-and-saucer' dramas which eschewed conventional painted backdrops in favour of real furniture, and doors and windows that could be opened by the actors. Similarly, sensation fiction became locked in a reciprocal process with the theatre and, in the course of the nineteenth century, novels such as *East Lynne* and *Lady Audley's Secret* were dramatized. Sensation drama also became inextricably linked with melodrama which used music to intensify the emotions depicted on stage, and employed spectacular devices to enthral its audiences.

Music was employed in quite a different manner in the productions of Gilbert and Sullivan which presented the public with a palatable mixture of comedy and tragedy together with a combination of light and serious music which ensured their success. The origins of *HMS Pinafore* (1878), *Patience* (1880) and *The Mikado* (1885) can be traced back to burlesque, and Gilbert and Sullivan's later works have obvious associations with musical comedies which, like their own operettas, proved particularly popular among the middle classes. Characterized by a contemporary realism, and sprinkled with popular song, musical comedies, like the music hall, supplied middle-class young ladies with tuneful fodder with which to entertain their captive listeners in the comfort of homes where they might display their musical accomplishments on the family pianoforte.

Unlike musical comedy, however, the music hall was a working-class phenomenon and, although in the latter part of the century it was to attract a cross-section of society through its doors, social divisions were subtly enforced by the cost of seats in different locations. Music halls became popular during the mid-nineteenth century and grew up in the industrial towns, and in London itself. They began as 'singing saloons' in pubs, and the popularity of such entertainment ensured an expansion which was to lead to the opening of the first music halls, among which were the Star in Bolton (1832), the Polytechnic in Salford (*c.*1840) and the Canterbury (*c.*1848) in London. By the 1890s, the music halls had become variety theatres which catered for diverse audiences, but initially they were the leisure-pursuit of choice for working-class audiences of both sexes. The evening's entertainment divided into three main categories: music and theatre, circus tricks, and information sections which included the display of inventions. Programmes included songs which spoke not only of generalities – love, marriage, family, patriotism, work and play – but also covered subjects of specific interest to the working classes such as urban life and housing conditions. Yet there were also music halls which included 'higher' forms of music such as classical music and opera in their schedules. While classical music and opera may seem out of place among circus tricks and inventions, it is important to remember that the hurdy gurdy, the barrel piano and the barrel organ which provided street music would have included popular pieces in their repertoire, and that the lower social classes were themselves often active in choirs, bands and orchestras. Moreover, the inclusion of such music would reflect the proprietor's 'refinement', and would attract middle-class customers to the halls. In the early years, the composition of the music-hall audience was influenced by the predominating trade in the region in which a hall was situated, but remained mainly working class, or lower middle class at most. In London, divisions also occurred according to area. In the West End, halls would be frequented by aristocrats, students and bohemians; suburban halls drew a more varied audience from the immediate vicinity such as shopkeepers, mechanics, labourers, soldiers and sailors; and minor music halls in the poorer areas would cater for the lower classes, the range of entry fees available reflecting the pockets of their clientele.

For most of the century, other 'higher' forms of musical entertainment, such as Grand Opera, remained the preserve of the upper classes. However, until the arrival of Wagner in the latter part of the century, interest in the medium was determined less by the opera itself than by the fame of individual opera singers such as Giulia Grisi, the soprano, who made her English debut in 1834, and Jenny Lind, known as the 'Swedish nightingale', who achieved lasting fame in England following her English debut in 1847. Opera continued to be sung in Italian, German or French, as English opera was marked by a tinge of provinciality which had no home in the London opera houses. Yet, despite the elitism implicit in such linguistic exclusion, Wagner, sung in German, was to attain a popularity among the lower echelons of society. While opera aficionados rejected Wagner's energetic style, the 'common people' of the pit and the gallery clamoured for more, and opera houses complied, some occasionally surrendering their programmes to his work. It seems that success in opera, like that in literature and painting, was no longer determined by the discerning few, and depended instead on the tastes of a new and developing public.

Sculpture and Architecture

In contrast to the popular arts discussed so far, sculpture remained, for much of the nineteenth century, trapped in an artistic limbo which resulted in unexceptional public and funerary monuments. Sculptors such as John Gibson and Francis Chantrey were neo-classicists concerned with those properties outlined by Winckelmann in *History of the Art of Antiquity* (1764), who advocated a stillness and serenity which prohibited that artistic self-expression which fosters sculptural diversity. However, this view of sculptural 'perfection' was to change, thanks in part to Alfred Stevens, whose travels in Italy had brought him into contact with Italian High Renaissance sculpture in which form and line contributes to expression and movement. Stevens was instrumental in breaking down the barriers between 'high' and 'decorative' art. His main concern was the expressiveness of sculpture itself, regardless of whether its purpose was monumental, industrial or architectural. The energy and flow of his figures can be seen in such works as *Valour and Cowardice* and *Truth and Falsehood* (1857–75), which form part of the Wellington Monument in St Paul's Cathedral. While Frederic Leighton's *Athlete Wrestling with a Python* (1877) is the statue which is often seen as marking a departure in Victorian sculpture, it is clear that Stevens's earlier work already displayed the physical power and movement that characterizes Leighton's figure.

Stevens's sculpture, and that of others who followed this 'new style', transformed not only 'high' art, which by the 1880s included such works as Alfred Gilbert's *The Kiss of Victory* (1878–81) and William Hamo Thornycroft's *The Mower* (1884), but also the 'lesser' arts such as architectural carving which brought sculpture within the vision of the people. In the latter part of the nineteenth century such decorative arts attained a higher status due mainly to the establishment of official design schools, which contributed to a reassessment of the term 'art', and raised public consciousness. In 1837 the Government School of Design was installed at Somerset House at which Stevens taught architecture, perspective and modelling in 1845. It was the first of many similar schools established in Britain whose purpose was to train students from the age of 12 in order to supply the needs of the decorative industries. These students were not destined to be artists in the conventional sense, but to become designers and craftsmen. Their success not only raised the profile of such work, but also encouraged the popularity of these arts among the lower social classes, and were instrumental in 'improving' their tastes and their knowledge. These training schools, while attempting to foster an excellence that would rival French production, eschewed traditional French training which incorporated the use of live models in drawing classes, and it was not until 1871 when the Slade School was opened, that this form of training was introduced. During this time, the Royal Academy remained staunchly traditional, still placing sculpture in a subordinate position to painting. However, with the accession of Leighton to the presidency in 1878, things began to change, and it too set up a separate school of modelling for architects. This was an appropriate move, for the concerns regarding sculptural production were often voiced in an architectural context. In his essay 'British Sculpture: Its Condition and Prospects' (1861), William Rossetti lamented the way in which sculpture and modelling had been isolated. He argued for a reassessment of sculpture, and suggested that its future would be best served by incorporating it into city buildings where the public might see it.

This debate is itself embedded in a larger one concerning the nature of the buildings themselves. During the nineteenth century, professional architects were involved in a longstanding dispute regarding the appropriate style for public architecture. In the early years there was a general consensus of opinion which acknowledged that certain styles befitted certain types of buildings: public buildings should be Grecian; domestic buildings Jacobean; churches Gothic. Until 1837, the architectural field was led by Sir John Soane whose aesthetic designs had been extremely influential. When Soane died, there was no leading light to replace him and it was not until 1849, when Ruskin published his *Seven Lamps of Architecture*, that this place was filled. While the classical tradition continued in the work of William Wilkins and George Basevi, and was advocated by George Vivian and Joseph Gwilt, Ruskin's views were to have a substantial impact. Guiding the architect with his seven lamps which were defined as Sacrifice, Truth, Power, Beauty, Life, Memory and Obedience, Ruskin encouraged the use of ornament for its own merits, original materials, considerations of light and shade for emphasis, the imitation of natural forms, enduring architecture and the preservation of the past. For Ruskin, architectural style should be heterogeneous, accepted by architects and public alike, and the work of a 'School' thus not subject to idiosyncrasy. For Ruskin, the ideal style could be located among those already in existence, and particularly in the Christian-Gothic style which had hitherto been reserved for religious architecture. Ruskin's influence can be traced in the Gothic revival which took place as the century progressed, notably in the Houses of Parliament (Augustus Welby Pugin and Charles Barry, 1836–65) and in the St Pancras Station Hotel (Gilbert Scott, 1868–74). However, Ruskin's vision would never be fully achieved, and those styles deemed appropriate for individual buildings in the early part of the century would remain in favour, with the greatest variation taking place in private residences whose style depended on the whim of the owner.

Implicit in these debates was the necessity for interior and exterior decoration which could only be supplied by the carvers and sculptors whose arts were viewed with a certain disdain by the purveyors of 'high' art, and are generally overlooked in critical analyses. The problems experienced by such artisans is exemplified by the difficulties experienced by sculptors involved in the decoration of the Houses of Parliament and the Albert Memorial who found that the architects considered their work extraneous and not intrinsic to their projects. In spite of this, one has only to walk through the streets of London and the other major cities in Britain to find that nineteenth-century sculpture, decorative or commemorative, is everywhere to be found: in the niches of our richest buildings; forming landmarks; reminding us of the famous and the dead at the end of glorious vistas, or in the quiet side-streets of our city centres. Like those other 'palaces' of art we have visited in this essay, the sculpture palace is no longer isolated in a lofty location: its doors have opened to a viewing public which walks through its rooms with a sense of those social and democratic freedoms formulated in the nineteenth century.

NOTES

1. A. Tennyson, 'The Palace of Art', *The Poems of Tennyson*, ed. C. Ricks (Harlow, 1969), vol. 1.
2. P. J. Manning, 'Wordsworth in the *Keepsake* 1829', in J. O. Jordan and R. L. Patten, eds, *Literature in the Marketplace: Nineteenth-Century British Publishing and Reading Practices* (Cambridge, 1995).

3. D. Mermin, 'The damsel, the knight, and the Victorian woman poet', *Critical Inquiry*, 13 (1986), p. 67.
4. E. Barrett Browning, *Aurora Leigh*, ed. K. McSweeney (Oxford, 1993), Book V, II, pp. 202–3.
5. I. Watt, *The Rise of the Novel* (London, 1987).

FURTHER READING

I. Armstrong, *Victorian Poetry: Poetry, Poetics and Politics* (New York, 1993).
Ashley, L. R. N., ed., *Nineteenth-Century British Drama: An Anthology of Representative Plays* (Lanham, 1988).
P. Bailey, *Popular Culture and Performance in the Victorian City* (Cambridge, 1998).
S. Beattie, *The New Sculpture* (New Haven, CT, 1983).
M. Bright, *Cities Built to Music: Aesthetic Theories of the Victorian Gothic Revival* (Columbus, 1984).
J. Bristow, ed., *The Cambridge Companion to Victorian Poetry* (Cambridge, 2001).
M. W. Brooks, *John Ruskin and Victorian Architecture* (London, 1987).
A. Byerly, *Realism, Representation, and the Arts in Nineteenth-Century Literature* (Cambridge, 1997).
D. Cherry, *Painting Women: Victorian Women Artists* (London, 1993).
T. J. Collins and V. J. Rundle, eds, *The Broadview Anthology of Victorian Poetry and Poetic Theory* (Ontario, 1999).
V. Cunningham, ed., *The Victorians: An Anthology of Poetry and Poetics* (Oxford, 2000).
C. Dakers, *The Holland Park Circle: Artists and Victorian Society* (New Haven, CT, 1999).
D. David, ed., *The Cambridge Companion to the Victorian Novel* (Cambridge, 2001).
B. Denvir, *The Late Victorians: Art, Design and Society 1852–1910* (London, 1986).
M. Ffinch, *Gilbert and Sullivan* (London, 1993).
D. E. Gerard, *David Elwyn, John Ruskin and William Morris: The Energies of Order and Love* (London, 1988).
S. M. Gilbert and S. Gubar, *The Madwoman in the Attic: The Woman Writer and the Nineteenth-Century Literary Imagination* (New Haven, 1979).
S. Gurney, *British Poetry of the Nineteenth Century* (New York, 1993).
S. Hudston, *Victorian Theatricals: From Menageries to Melodrama* (London, 2000).
A. Jenkins, *The Making of Victorian Drama* (Cambridge, 1991).
A. Kettle, *The Nineteenth-Century Novel* (London, 1981).
D. Kift, *The Victorian Music Hall: Culture, Class and Conflict* (Cambridge, 1996).
A. Leighton, ed., *Victorian Women Poets: A Critical Reader* (Oxford, 1996).
D. S. Macleod, *Art and the Victorian Middle Class: Money and the Making of a Cultural Identity* (Cambridge, 1996).
M. Meisel, *Realizations: Narrative, Pictorial, and Theatrical Arts in Nineteenth-Century England* (Princeton, 1983).
G. Needham, *Nineteenth-Century Realist Art* (New York, 1988).
P. G. Nunn, *Problem Pictures: Women and Men in Victorian Painting* (Aldershot, 1995).
R. Pearsall, *Victorian Popular Music* (Newton Abbot, 1973).
E. Prettejohn, ed., *After the Pre-Raphaelites: Art and Aestheticism in Victorian England* (Manchester, 1999).
B. Read, *Victorian Sculpture* (New Haven, CT, 1982).
R. Robbins and J. Wolfreys, eds, *Victorian Identities: Social and Cultural Formations in Nineteenth-Century Literature* (London, 1996).

D. Skilton, ed., *The Early and Mid-Victorian Novel* (London, 1993).

L. Smith, *Victorian Photography, Painting and Poetry: The Enigma of Visibility in Ruskin, Morris and the Pre-Raphaelites* (Cambridge, 1995).

G. Stamp, *Victorian Buildings of London 1837–1887: An Illustrated Guide* (London, 1980).

J. Steegman, *Victorian Taste: A Study of the Arts and Architecture from 1830–1870* (Cambridge, MA, 1970).

J. Treuherz, *Victorian Painting* (London, 1993).

D. Vlock, *Dickens, Novel Reading and the Victorian Family Magazine* (Basingstoke, 2001).

I. Watt, *The Rise of the Novel* (London, 1987).

B. Zon, ed., *Nineteenth-Century British Music Studies* (Aldershot, 1999 & 2001).

Chapter Twenty-Eight

The Sciences

Iwan Rhys Morus

When the physicist William Thomson – ennobled as Baron Kelvin of Largs for his services to British science and industry – died in 1907, he was buried with due pomp and circumstance in Westminster Abbey. Recalling the event in his *Life* of the great man a few years later his biographer – physicist and popular scientific writer Silvanus P. Thompson – took the opportunity to reflect on the occasion's significance for British science. The nineteenth century, he declared, had 'intellectually, been the golden age, not of art or of poetry, not of drama or of adventure, but of science'. This was an assessment that many of his scientific contemporaries would have shared. It seemed that by the end of Victoria's reign science had come to play a central role in British culture. Kelvin's funeral was a moment of poignant significance for them since his career seemed to epitomize so much of what they thought their science had accomplished. He had played a key role in establishing the key sciences of electro-magnetism and thermodynamics. His activities had straddled science and industry. He had been at the centre of many of the past century's most significant scientific and cultural debates. His career demonstrated that, however contested that role might have been, science had played a crucial part in the making of nineteenth-century culture.

Historians of science would largely agree with this assessment of the central role played by the sciences in moulding Victorian material and intellectual culture. It is plain that science mattered to the Victorians. New historiography has demonstrated that, far from being relegated to a cultural cul de sac, nineteenth-century science had significant connections with and consequences for a whole range of concerns embracing art, industry, literature, politics and religion. Historians may still debate the extent to which nineteenth-century science had a discernible impact on the British economy, but the relationship was certainly a matter of ongoing concern and dispute for Victorian men of science and other cultural commentators. Novelists and other literary figures littered their writings with scientific references as a matter of course. What scientists said about the operation of natural law was routinely regarded as having important consequences for social organization. The debate surrounding Darwinism was only one of many in which natural philosophical claims and discoveries were endowed with immense theological consequences. Both in metropolis and provinces, engagement with science through membership of scientific societies, attendance at popular lectures, exhibitions or museums, reading popular accounts or just keeping up with the latest scientific gossip in the press was common. The term 'British' needs to be taken with a pinch of salt in this context, however. Whilst we now know a great deal about such activities in England and, to a lesser degree, Scotland, we know much less about Ireland and hardly anything about Wales.

Historians of science have gained new insights into the central place the sciences had in nineteenth-century British culture by rethinking the way they understand science.[1] Rather than viewing science as an abstract body of knowledge operating according to its own internal and self-contained logic, historians now look at science as an open-ended set of practices. This change of perspective has focused attention both on the material and social resources that sustain scientific activity and on the reciprocal relationship between the sciences and broader culture. We are now far more aware, for example, of the intimate connections between nineteenth-century science and issues of gender, race and class. Nineteenth-century science – in terms of its practitioners at least – was a largely male, middle-class activity. For most of the century women and working-class participants struggled to gain entry, though there are notable exceptions like Michael Faraday and Mary Somerville. Participation in scientific activity was often an exercise in self-fashioning. Aspirants in science had to play their cards carefully in order to establish their position securely. Audiences mattered, not just as passive consumers of scientific facts but as active participants who played a vital role in constructing the sciences' place within nineteenth-century British culture.

Historians have also become increasingly aware of the pivotal place the nineteenth century holds in the history of British science itself. Traditional histories of science have focused much of their attention on the Scientific Revolution of the sixteenth and seventeenth centuries, hailing that as the birth of modern science. As this perspective has come under increasing scrutiny, historians of science have started to recognize the nineteenth century's significance in this respect. It seems clear that it was during this period that the trend towards scientific specialization started to take place. Professionalization is an awkward term for historians of nineteenth-century British science since, for much of the period, the majority of practitioners were certainly not professionals in any obvious contemporary sense and even many self-declared reformers were opposed to any such idea. It is nevertheless clear that increasing numbers of scientists throughout the century were actively engaged in trying to carve out a distinct cultural space for the practice of science – this is where the origin of the English word 'scientist' itself is to be found. New links were forged between science and industry during our period. Most significantly of all, the Victorians were largely responsible for forging the optimistic link between science and progress which, though somewhat tarnished, remains with us today.

Institutions and Audiences

The sciences' institutions underwent massive transformation during the course of the nineteenth century, both in terms of the emergence of new ones and the overhaul of more ancient establishments. The Royal Society of London had been founded as early as 1662 but many natural philosophers regarded it as overdue for reform by the first half of the nineteenth century. A trend for local literary and philosophical societies in provincial cities had started with the foundation of the Manchester Literary and Philosophical Society in 1781 and this continued into the following century.[2] Metropolitan societies – the most successful being the Royal Institution – started appearing at about the same time. Specialist scientific societies splintered away from the Royal Society. Battles for reform and the overhaul of natural philosophical teaching raged at the ancient universities as the new London University and its provincial and Scottish counterparts increasingly offered scientific training to the sons of the industrial middle classes. Looking at these institutions and at the audiences for the science they had on offer can tell us a great deal about the sciences' place in nineteenth-century culture; the ways in which scientists visualized the role their disciplines might play in Victorian society and the ways in which they might carve out careers for themselves; and what nineteenth-century British society at large saw science as being able to deliver.

A key juncture in the re-framing of the sciences' cultural place came with the establishment of the British Association for the Advancement of Science (BAAS) in York in 1831. That meeting was the outcome of months of negotiation between the local instigator, the Rev. William Vernon Harcourt, and others both in London and elsewhere, concerning the organization and purpose of what everyone agreed should be a major new movement for the defence and dissemination of British science. The 'British Ass' was soon firmly under the control of self-proclaimed gentlemen of science who were keen to ensure the dominance of their version of science as a benign and progressive edifice unthreatening to both church and state.[3] Following a visit by Samuel Taylor Coleridge to the BAAS gathering at Cambridge in 1833, William Whewell coined the word 'scientist' to describe this new class of devotees in the search for natural knowledge. The movement's leaders were keen to encourage a broad-based membership, even welcoming women so long as they stayed in the audience and away from the stage. They were just as keen to avoid controversy. Charles Babbage's plans for a statistical section were squashed for just that reason.

It was central to the BAAS ethos that it met annually in different cities scattered across the kingdom, though never in London despite (or perhaps because) of the increasing role played in its organization by the metropolitan scientific elite. They kept a firm grip on the reins through their domination of the association's council and the sectional committees in charge of the various specialist disciplines. Large audiences assembled for these annual gatherings, where earls and bishops rubbed shoulders with engineers, industrialists, doctors, clerics and, of course, the plain curious. Local and national papers devoted acres of newsprint each summer to recording the proceedings. Charles Dickens famously satirized the event's eclecticism with his Mudfog Association for the Advancement of Everything. The BAAS soon acquired significant lobbying power, playing a key role in the deliberations of successive Royal Commissions on scientific and technical education. It also played an increasingly important role in its own right as a dispenser of scientific funds as the century moved on. Despite its leaders' managerial efforts the BAAS's annual meetings could sometimes become the focus of major controversy. A famous example was John Tyndall's presidential address to the 1874 meeting in Belfast where his materialist message caused much gnashing of Presbyterian teeth.

The 'British Ass' was by design an umbrella organization cobbled together to keep under one roof as much of British science as its organizers deemed desirable or possible. During the first half of the century transformations were taking place in the institutional structures of British science that made that task more difficult. Starting with the foundation of the Geological Society of London in 1807 and accelerating with the foundation of the Astronomical Society in 1820, disciplinary specialization seemed increasingly to be the order of the day. Throughout the 1820s and on into the 1830s and 1840s debate raged about the relationship between these new disciplinary bodies and the parent Royal Society of London, especially with regard to access to government patronage. Inextricable from these debates was the question of the man of science's cultural identity. A new generation of vocationally minded gentlemen like Babbage, John Herschel and Leonard Horner were increasingly anxious to dissociate themselves from what they regarded as the corruption and nepotism surrounding the Royal Society. This was what underlay Babbage's vitriolic attack on British scientific institutions in his *Reflexions on the Decline of Science in England* (1830). Babbage looked to French scientific institutions established under the Revolutionary and Napoleonic regimes as exemplars of enlightened scientific organization.

Whilst few of his contemporaries shared Babbage's enthusiasm for French institutions, his disenchantment with the state of British science was more widespread. From the perspective of metropolitan savants at least, the move to establish the BAAS was, in part, a response to the perceived inadequacies of the Royal Society. The new generation of vocational specialists advocated new standards of expert discipline in the practice of their sciences. They wanted the Royal Society's ruling clique of (as they saw them) amateurish dilettantes replaced by meritocrats like themselves. By the end of the 1840s the new generation had taken over, reforming the Royal Society and dominating its council. As well as being battles about the control of the Royal Society debates like these between the 1820s and 1850s were about the cultural place of science. What kind of practice should science be and who should be its practitioners? Scientific gentlemen in London, Cambridge and Oxford had different perceptions on such issues from those in the provinces, particularly those in the rapidly industrializing cities of the North and Midlands. Views in such places about relationships between science and industry for example, might be very different from those held by a Cambridge don like Whewell.

Battles for reform were under way at Cambridge and Oxford as well. At Cambridge undergraduates founded the Analytical Society to introduce new continental mathematical techniques to the Mathematics tripos. It was a political as much as a scientific campaign. They wanted to turn the ancient university into a place that provided training for the sons of business-minded industrialists as well as the sons of the gentry. By the 1840s and 1850s increasingly strident calls were heard at both Cambridge and Oxford for more formal teaching and examination in the natural sciences. The Cambridge Natural Sciences tripos was established in the 1850s. Following the Devonshire Commission's report on scientific and technical education in the late 1860s Cambridge took the lead, establishing the Cavendish laboratory in 1874. Teaching in the natural sciences had been central to the curriculum at London University – that 'godless institution on Gower Street' – since its foundation in the 1820s. The same was true of its Anglican competitor King's College on the Strand.

The sciences were at the centre of teaching at the secular Queen's Colleges established in Ireland in the 1840s. As colleges and universities got going in industrial cities like Manchester, the prospect of science education was a key part of their appeal to their prospective constituencies.[4]

London's Royal Institution (RI), founded in 1799 to promote natural knowledge as the key to improvement, played a key role in establishing an audience for science amongst the metropolis's middle and upper classes. The RI's Friday evening discourses, established by Faraday in the 1820s, rated high amongst the social events of the London Season. The RI's successes led to the establishment of rivals like the London Institution, eager to cash in on cultivated London's increasing desire for similarly cultivated science. Lower down the social scale popular lectures in natural philosophy competed with theatrical productions and exhibitions to cater for the public craze for edification and entertainment. Outside London, local 'Lit & Phils' flourished for much of the century. South Wales got its own Royal Institution in the 1840s. The model established at London's Royal Institution of popular lectures, scientific soirées and *conversaziones* was widely emulated. The Great Exhibition of 1851 played an important part in creating an audience enthusiastic for technological and scientific display. Its success was emulated by a succession of such exhibitions in London and elsewhere across Britain throughout the rest of the century.

Exhibitions like the Crystal Palace and the small metropolitan Galleries of Practical Science that preceded it did not always provide an image of science that matched the vision of elite gentlemen of science. The picture of science – as a useful and practical activity – offered in such places was more populist (and sometimes more egalitarian) than the view offered by disciplined specialists. From the 1820s onwards at least some promoters of the Mechanics' Institutes movement tried to insist that workers should educate themselves in science rather than be satisfied by the carefully sanitized knowledge handed down by their middle-class patrons. The same impulse underlay the Owenite Halls of Science. However much scientific leaders tried to keep a lid on politically radical readings of science, the genie kept on escaping from the bottle. Radical socialists and Chartists during the 1830s and 1840s used science's materialist message to damn the elites. Later in the century T. H. Huxley, representative of a new breed of 'professional' scientist, used lectures at working men's institutes to woo thousands with his brand of materialist anti-clericalism. For this new generation, the image of science as a gentlemanly vocation fostered by reformers earlier in the century was itself in need of a radical overhaul.

New developments in printing throughout the century generated a new mass taste for scientific literature. Scientific journals at the beginning of the century were few and far between and largely aimed at a select audience. By the end of the century the market had expanded beyond recognition. From the 1820s onwards crusading organizations like the Society for the Diffusion of Useful Knowledge and their rivals at the Society for the Promotion of Christian Knowledge competed to bring cheap tracts and magazines filled with carefully packaged natural knowledge to a mass audience. Evangelical campaigners such as the Religious Tract Society later in the century were equally anxious to promote their own alternative visions. There were plenty of other alternatives to mainstream science. The science of phrenology flourished throughout the century, providing a materialist account of mind for radical reformers. From mid-century spiritualism was in the ascendancy, giving comfort to those uncomfortable with scientific materialism.[5] Phrenologists and Spiritualists alike took advantage of new printing technologies to spread their message and to offer their own accounts of what science was, how it should be organized and how its practitioners should act. Scientists, both old-style reformers and the new professionals, often reacted furiously to these upstarts, but could do little to stop the dissemination of their subversive messages to receptive audiences.

Physics for the Empire

The mourners at Lord Kelvin's funeral would certainly have regarded British physics as one of the nineteenth century's greatest success stories. At the beginning of the century there was no such science as physics. By its end physics was the queen of the sciences. Physicists were confident that they held the keys to the secrets of the universe. The science they produced in many ways epitomized Victorian values. It was, as French philosopher and physicist Pierre Duhem scoffed, the physics of the factory floor, practical and wedded to mechanical principles even in its flights of theoretical fancy. Physicists regarded themselves as playing a key role in Britain's imperialist endeavours. Thermodynamics was quite literally the science of the steam engines that powered the nation's industrial supremacy. Maxwellian electromagnetism was the science of the telegraph networks that guaranteed that Britain's economic dominance was matched by political control. The physics that guaranteed the efficiency of British steam engines explained the sources of energy powering the sun and stars as well. For some of them, like James Clerk Maxwell, the fact that molecules looked like precision-engineered manufactured articles was proof not only of the existence of a Cosmic Engineer, but that he operated according to the same principles as they did in their laboratories.

At the beginning of the century, natural philosophers like the flamboyant Humphry Davy at the Royal Institution made names for themselves with spectacular demonstrations of nature's powers. Davy showed his genteel RI audience how the newly invented voltaic battery could be used to rip matter apart and investigate its innards. His erstwhile apprentice Faraday followed in his footsteps. Faraday's electromagnetic investigations during the 1830s and 1840s established him as one of Europe's premier natural philosophers as well as establishing the RI's reputation as a centre for physical research for most of the rest of the century. Faraday argued that his experiments showed how electromagnetic lines of force filled all space. Outside the august precincts of the RI, popular electricians like William Sturgeon argued that the universe was made of electrical machines like the ones they demonstrated to their audiences. They put their productions on show at venues like London's Adelaide Gallery of Practical Science. This was a way of demonstrating the electrical nature of the universe and their own mastery of it. It was also a way of demonstrating their science's utility. Electrical machines could make Nature useful to humanity, as well as lucrative for their inventors.[6]

By the 1840s electricity was regarded by many as the key not only to unlocking Nature's secrets but to making Nature pay as well. Natural philosophers built and investigated the workings of instruments like the voltaic pile, or Faraday's electromagnetic apparatus, that seemed to be examples of the conversion of one kind of natural power into another. When the Mancunian brewer's son James Prescott Joule first started experimenting in the late 1830s his interest lay in finding out just how efficient electromagnetic engines could be. This engineering approach to natural philosophy led to his experiments on the mechanical equivalent of heat. It also led to his work being sidelined by metropolitan scientists until it attracted the attention of Thomson. Born in Presbyterian Belfast and bred in industrial Glasgow, Thomson like Joule was interested in work and waste as processes in nature as well as industry. There were a number of attempts during the 1840s to make sense of the relationships between the forces, like the Welshman William Robert Grove's theory of the correlation of physical forces. By the beginning of the 1850s Thomson, with his Cambridge mathematical training, and an interest in engines shared with his engineering brother James, was in the process of bringing it all together in a new science of energy.[7]

Thomson and Joule were part of a new generation of natural philosophers mainly from Northern Ireland, Scotland and the industrial north of England who were interested in forging links between natural philosophy and engineering. The new theory of the conservation of energy that would dominate British physics for the rest of the century came out of this industrial sensibility applied to science. Thomson, Professor of Natural Philosophy at Glasgow and P. G. Tait, another Cambridge product and Professor of Mathematics at Queen's College Belfast before moving on to Edinburgh, wrote the monumental *Treatise on Natural Philosophy* as a bible for this new physics. Not only did the science of energy show how to make physics useful, it turned it into a weapon to defend Protestant Victorian values against the infidel. Thomson used his dynamical theory of heat to show that the geologist Charles Lyell and the evolutionist Charles Darwin were wrong. The laws of physics demonstrated that the Earth could not have existed long enough for their views on gradual geological development or natural selection to hold true. Thanks to popularizers like Balfour Stewart and others the conservation of energy was used to explain everything from the origins of the universe to the inadvisability of women's emancipation. Later commentators were fascinated by the picture energetics painted of the eventual heat death of the universe.

The new physics' main protagonists were, with few exceptions, products of the new regime of mathematical training that developed in Cambridge during the second quarter of the century. The Analytical Society's efforts to introduce the latest continental mathematical techniques into the University's curriculum had been successful. At the same time the increasing rigour of the tripos examinations fostered the development of a flourishing local industry of mathematical coaches to prepare ambitious students for academic success. The aim of a Cambridge mathematical education was to produce rigorously trained minds fit to go out and govern the empire. As a side-effect it produced a succession of mathematical physicists as well. As new university physics departments were established across the British Isles and the dominions in the second half of the nineteenth century, they were largely staffed by Cambridge graduates, imbued with Cantabrigian notions of the proper practice of physics and what kind of person was needed to do it. This was an unambiguously male culture. Only male minds and bodies, it was widely imagined, could stand up to the kind of testing mental and physical regime that produced mathematical physicists. Women's participation in the Mathematics tripos was strongly opposed, even (or maybe particularly) after a Newnham College student, Phillippa Fawcett, beat that year's senior wrangler in 1890.[8]

British physics laboratories were also bastions of male culture for much of the century. Until the middle of the century institutional research and teaching laboratories were comparatively rare. Faraday at the Royal Institution had a purpose-built laboratory but the same could not be said of his contemporaries in London's academic institutions. Thomson at Glasgow towards the end of the 1840s was one of the first to make laboratory training in research part of the teaching curriculum. By the 1870s laboratory space and laboratory training was an increasingly common feature of university physics. At the same time an increasing emphasis on the importance of precision measurement was developing as a central feature of Victorian laboratory culture. At Cambridge's Cavendish laboratory, under the directorship of Maxwell's successor Lord Rayleigh, rigorous training in the disciplines of electrical measurement was the order of the day. Rayleigh was in the process of transforming the Cavendish into a standards laboratory, devoted to producing accurate measurements of standard electrical units for the British telegraph industry. It was regarded as a major triumph for British physics and electrical engineering when the Cavendish ohm (the unit of electrical resistance) was accepted as the international standard in 1882. Critics and supporters alike regarded laboratories like the Cavendish as having more than a little in common with factories.

Physics laboratories were not the only places of scientific production that some thought bore an uncanny resemblance to Victorian factories. When George Bidell Airy (another Cambridge wrangler) was appointed as Astronomer Royal in 1835 he was determined to impose an industrial regime on the Royal Greenwich Observatory. Airy was an admirer of the factory system and thought the division of labour would work as a means of improving the efficiency of carrying out astronomical calculations as it would for pin-making. Airy also investigated the possibility of making use of new technologies like photography as a way of doing away with the vagaries of individual human observers. He played a key role in bringing telegraphy to Greenwich too, as a means of co-ordinating astronomical observations between observatories – and introducing the Greenwich time signal as well. By the second half of the century photography was playing an increasingly important role in British astronomy as expeditions set out across the globe to try and capture elusive celestial phenomena such as the solar eclipse. Astronomers like William Huggins and Norman Lockyer introduced apparatus like the spectroscope to analyse light from the sun and distant stars and determine their chemical composition. Using apparatus like this straight from the physics laboratory and lecture theatre, astronomers could bring celestial phenomena to new audiences and explain them using the new vocabulary of Maxwellian electromagnetism and the universal ether.

Maxwell's mathematical treatment of electromagnetism was widely regarded, along with Thomson's development of thermodynamics, as one of the cornerstones of Victorian physics. Maxwell, a Scottish laird and another product of Cambridge's Mathematics tripos, had made his name by taking Faraday's speculations about lines of electrical force in space and turning them into a coherent mathematical theory. Like Thomson and Tait's *Treatise*, his *Treatise on Electricity and Magnetism* (1873) tried to provide the framework for a whole new science. Maxwell and his followers regarded themselves as providing the theoretical tools that explained everything from the operations of the British telegraph network to the propagation of light through apparently empty space. Maxwellian theoreticians, in a debate that reached its culmination at the BAAS annual gathering in 1888, argued that they, rather than practically minded electrical engineers, were the ones who truly understood how telegraphs worked.[9] This was also the year in which Liverpool's Professor of Physics Oliver Lodge was pipped to the post by the German Heinrich Hertz with his demonstration of the existence of electromagnetic waves travelling through space. It was a discovery widely regarded as providing the ultimate vindication of Maxwell's theories and the mathematical speculations of his followers such as Joseph Larmor and the autodidact Oliver Heaviside.

Hertz's discovery was also widely reckoned to have conclusively proved the existence of the electromagnetic ether – the space-filling immaterial medium that stored and propagated electromagnetic energy. Finding the properties of the ether and reducing them to simple mechanical principles became the Holy Grail of late-nineteenth-century British physics. It was one of the targets that Duhem had in mind with his quip about British physics and factory culture. For physicists like Larmor, Lodge or George FitzGerald the existence of the ether was more than an article of faith. It vindicated what they saw as the British approach to physics. It stood for the way late-Victorian physicists thought their science embodied Victorian values of hard work, self-discipline and progress. Not only did their physics provide the material and intellectual tools for governing the empire with steam engines and telegraphs, it also used those tools in the same way that God used them to administer the universe. More prosaically, many late-nineteenth-century physicists also thought their discipline was the model science. Its combination of rigorous mathematical analysis and self-disciplined precision measurement was the blueprint for progress elsewhere.

Life, Nature and Society

For most, if not all, of the nineteenth century it was taken for granted that the state of nature delivered important messages for the state of society. There was a natural order of things and uncovering that order in the natural world could lead to an enlightened understanding of how society ought to be ordered. This was why sciences like geology and, later, Darwin's theory of evolution by natural selection were so controversial. Controversy aside, however, geology and natural history were amongst the most popular of nineteenth-century scientific pursuits. Collecting and arranging geological and natural historical specimens was widespread amongst all classes. Natural history societies were amongst the most common local scientific organizations. However, by the end of the century the life sciences were also becoming laboratory disciplines. Experimental physiologists looked to physics (and to the Continent) for inspiration in making their science conform to new standards of what it meant to be scientific. It was a heavily contested transformation. Doctors were dubious as to what they might learn from these new, laboratory-based practices. Antivivisectionists saw animal experimentation as outrageous evidence of the soulless materialism of scientific culture.

Widely regarded as a foundational text for modern geological practice, Charles Lyell's *Principles of Geology* (1830–3) laid out a radical new theory for understanding the Earth's development. According to Lyell's uniformitarian doctrines geological change could only be regarded as the outcome of slow, gradual processes extended over indefinite periods of time. His opponents' efforts to describe such changes in terms of past cataclysms and catastrophes he dismissed as so much superstitious special pleading. Others, like William Buckland in his *Reliquae Diluvianae* (1823), insisted that there was good geological evidence for such past upheavals, including the biblical flood. The debate was still simmering in the 1860s and 1870s with Thomson's efforts to put Lyell and his disciples in their place over the age of the Earth. Issues like this mattered especially since they seemed to bear on questions of biblical interpretation. William Paley's *Natural Theology* (1802) was massively influential in convincing many nineteenth-century practitioners that it was impossible to engage in natural historical activity without also engaging with issues of Divine design. The eight *Bridgewater Treatises*, commissioned by the Royal Society in the 1830s to lay out the evidence for God's benevolent design throughout creation were similarly influential, provoking a *Ninth Bridgewater Treatise* in vehement opposition from Babbage.

Much as they might disagree over interpretation, the gentlemanly fellows of the Geological Society largely agreed on geological practice. Geology was about stratigraphy – identifying and mapping the different layers of rock that made up the surface of the Earth. Gentlemanly geologists like Lyell, Buckland, Adam Sedgwick and Roderick Impey Murchison devoted considerable resources in both time and money to geological excursions to study rock across Britain, Ireland and the Continent. Sedgwick and Murchison showed that this seemingly prosaic activity could be just as controversial as scriptural interpretation as they battled vigorously over the proper identification of the boundary between Cambrian and Silurian strata of rocks.[10] Geologists cultivated extensive networks of local informants who could lead them to the most interesting locations. They, as gentlemanly specialists, remained strictly in charge of interpretative matters however. Under the direction of Henry de la Beche the state-funded Geological Survey established in the 1830s, thanks to de la Beche's friendship with Sir Robert Peel, set about the ambitious task of providing a geological map of the entire country.[11] The Survey provided the model for similar efforts in different parts of the empire. From the 1850s the Royal School of Mines provided a steady supply of trained geological surveyors, mapping the past and assessing its economic potential.

In the life sciences during the 1820s and 1830s medical students returning from studies abroad introduced radical new ideas. Lamarckian ideas about transmutation and Geoffroy St Hilaire's ideas about morphological unity seemed to have revolutionary implications for English and Scottish students brought up on Paley's natural theology. These new French ideas appeared to do away completely with any idea of a divine and benevolent plan for the organization of nature and the relationship between species. They fitted in neatly with an increasing number of doctors' discontent with the state of their profession. Along with other agencies of 'Old Corruption' the elite medical corporations looked ripe for reform in the 1820s and 1830s and new continental notions about progressive development were grist for this radical mill. This philosophical anatomy was championed by, amongst others, Robert Knox of Burke and Hare notoriety, banished to London from Edinburgh after the graverobbing scandal. The anatomist Richard Owen, Hunterian Professor at the Royal

College of Surgeons, led the attack against anatomical radicalism, putting forward his ideas about shared morphological features between species as evidence of a common archetype rather than a common origin. It was a way of trying to make the new anatomy fit in with the English tradition of natural theology and the argument from design.[12]

The 1840s saw the most serious attack yet on British certainties about the relationship between Nature and its Creator. In 1844 the anonymously published *Vestiges of the Natural History of Creation* proved an instant bestseller. Its author marshalled an impressive array of the latest findings from anatomy, astronomy, geology and natural philosophy to support their view of a universe in a state of constant progression. According to this model everything in the cosmos was in the process of continual development. New solar systems were developing out of stellar dust, new geological formations were continually taking place on Earth and new higher life forms were continually developing out of lesser species. An unspoken corollary was that new and more enlightened social and political systems would inevitably emerge. The *Vestiges* (written by Edinburgh publisher Robert Chambers) was slammed by the gentlemen of science as evidence of what might happen if anyone other than the expert elite were permitted to interpret the findings of natural philosophy. It was so badly argued, according to Sedgwick, that it might have been written by a woman (he had Ada Lovelace, Byron's daughter, in mind). The imbroglio shows two things: just how sensitive early Victorian gentlemen of science could be to potential materialist and radical readings of their work and how anxious they were to maintain that only they had the proper credentials to interpret their findings correctly.[13]

One gentleman of science perturbed by his fellow specialists' response was Darwin. By the mid-1840s Darwin was privately convinced that evolution was a fact of nature. His voyage around the globe on the *Beagle* had provided him with first-hand evidence and his reading of Malthus's *Essay on the Principle of Population* (1797) had provided the mechanism. According to Malthus, unchecked human populations would expand exponentially, rapidly outgrowing available resources. The result would be inevitable disease, famine and war. Unusually for a Victorian scientist, Darwin turned the social principle back on to nature arguing that this was the mechanism that produced evolution as well. Life was a constant battle for resources and only the best-adapted individuals and species would survive. When the *Origin of Species* was eventually published in 1859 it caused a furore. Not even Lyell could accept the new theory's ramifications. Darwin skirted around the issue of human origins but few of his readers and fewer of his critics missed the implications. Cartoonists promptly dressed him in a monkey-suit to illustrate his theory's absurdities.

Tradition has it that 'Darwin's Bulldog' – T. H. Huxley – saw off the religious opposition to Darwinism when he demolished Soapy Sam Wilberforce at the BAAS 1860 meeting. In reality, contemporary observers of the debate were far less sure who had emerged victorious. Darwin's defenders, such as Huxley or the naturalist J. D. Hooker, were usually of the younger generation of Victorian scientists, less concerned than their elders about the spectre of materialism. Huxley invented the word 'agnostic' to describe his position with regard to spiritual matters. Others, like the zoologist and Catholic convert St George Mivart, were attracted by natural selection's simplicity but repelled by its implications. They struggled to find an accommodation that embraced both God and Darwin. Similarly the socialist Alfred Russel Wallace, Darwin's co-discoverer of natural selection, soon parted company with him over Darwin's emphasis on competition rather than co-operation. By the end of the century Darwinism was in decline.[14] His evolutionary mechanism of natural selection attracted dwindling support. Instead, a new and more respectable version of Jean Lamarck's theory of transmutation was coming into vogue. Neo-Lamarckianism with its inbuilt sense of developmental direction seemed more attractive to progress-minded Victorians than the blind chance of Darwin's theories.

Some of Darwin's staunchest supporters were to be found in newly established university departments of experimental physiology. This was largely a new discipline in late-nineteenth-century Britain. For much of the century, British investigators tended to favour anatomical rather than physiological research. However, by the 1860s and 1870s the new generation was looking to the Continent for inspiration, just as radical doctors had done half a century previously. Huxley was instrumental in these debates as well. British biologists had to adopt the experimental method if they wanted to dignify their pursuits with the title of science. Huxley played a key role in establishing his protégé Michael Foster as Professor of Physiology at Cambridge in 1883. Foster was a product of University College London, itself a bastion of radicalism earlier in the century. At Cambridge he was instrumental in putting together a research school in physiology.[15] Huxley, and fellow-members of the informal 'X Club' such as the physicist Tyndall, fought ruthlessly – and largely successfully – to impose their vision of radical materialism on British science. To establish their own expert authority they had to make sure that others – be they Anglican clerics or conservative doctors – got out of the way.

The new experimental physiology's uncompromising materialism seemed a step too far to many of the late-Victorian public. By the closing decades of the nineteenth century the anti-vivisection movement was in full swing. The practice of animal experimentation was increasingly represented as a typical example of the excesses of scientific materialism. Scientists were so obsessed by their research that they were blind to the suffering they caused. Prominent campaigners like the feminist Frances Power Cobbe wielded considerable influence, arguing that physiologists were no better than bear-baiters or cat-skinners. Vivisection was an expression of scientific nihilism. Cobbe and her fellow-campaigners carried enough clout in the corridors of power to demand a royal commission to call the vivisectionists to account. The result was the 1876 Cruelty to Animals Act which restricted animal experimentation to those licensed to perform them. Huxley and his crew regarded the Act as an insult – a suggestion that scientists were not fit to keep their own house in order. The anti-vivisection movement, like the contemporary vogue for spiritualism, was in many ways an expression of deep concern about the direction of late-nineteenth-century science. It is not surprising that many of the activists in both movements were women, largely excluded from and uncomfortable with the predominantly male world of *fin de siècle* professional scientists.

Conclusions

This has been a necessarily brief and partial overview. Hardly anything has been said about chemistry. One reason for this is that nineteenth-century chemistry has not attracted as much attention as the physical and life sciences. For similar reasons very little has been said about what we would now call the social sciences. A great deal of work remains to be done in these areas to make sense of such sciences' cultural connections. However, enough has been said here to give some sense of the main thrust of Victorian science, the kinds of issues that concerned its practitioners and their audiences and the ways in which they regarded scientific issues as having a direct and immediate impact on broader cultural concerns. The traffic was not all one way. If novelists and other literary types picked up on the latest scientific issues, scientists were in tune with literature as well.[16]

This is not to suggest that nineteenth-century science was part of a common culture. It seems rather unlikely that any such thing existed for science to be a part of it. What does seem clear however is that science – and claims to be scientific – carried considerable cultural capital for a wide variety of different groups. Being able to present one's activities as science carried considerable weight. This chapter has inevitably devoted most of its attention to those aspects of nineteenth-century scientific thought and practice that prospered and became the orthodox position. It should be clear however that this orthodox position was continually contested throughout the century. Alternative sciences such as mesmerism, phrenology and spiritualism thrived throughout the period. Different social groups and classes offered radically different accounts of what science was about, how it should be practised and who its practitioners should be. The nature of the relationship between science and society was continuously being questioned and redefined. Moreover, the scope of scientific activity broadened dramatically during the course of the century. By the end of the century the rise of provincial universities, the development of new technologies like the telegraph, and the forging of new links between science and industry meant that far more people than at its beginning might describe themselves as men (and they were still mostly men) of science.

NOTES

1. B. Lightman, ed., *Victorian Science in Context* (Chicago, 1997).
2. I. Inkster and J. Morrell, eds, *Metropolis and Province: Science and British Culture, 1780–1850* (1983).
3. S. F. Cannon, *Science in Culture: The Early Victorian Period* (New York, 1978); J. Morrell and A. Thackray, *Gentlemen of Science: The Early Years of the British Association for the Advancement of Science* (Oxford, 1981).
4. R. Kargon, *Science in Victorian Manchester: Enterprise and Expertise* (Baltimore, 1977).
5. R. Cooter, *The Cultural Meaning of Popular Science: Phrenology and the Organization of Consent in Nineteenth Century Britain* (Cambridge, 1984); L. Barrow, *Independent Spirits: Spiritualism and English Plebeians, 1850–1910* (London, 1986).
6. I. R. Morus, *Frankenstein's Children: Electricity, Exhibition and Experiment in Early-Nineteenth-Century London* (Princeton, 1998).
7. C. Smith and M. N. Wise, *Energy and Empire: A Biographical Study of Lord Kelvin* (Cambridge, 1989); C. Smith, *The Science of Energy: A Cultural History of Energy Physics in Victorian Britain* (London, 1998).
8. A. C. Warwick, *Masters of Theory: Cambridge and the Rise of Mathematical Physics* (Chicago, 2003).

9. B. Hunt, *The Maxwellians* (Ithaca, NY, 1991).

10. J. A. Secord, *Controversy in Victorian Geology: The Cambrian–Silurian Debate* (Princeton, 1986).

11. M. Rudwick, *The Great Devonian Controversy: The Shaping of Scientific Knowledge amongst Gentlemanly Specialists* (Chicago, 1985).

12. A. Desmond, *The Politics of Evolution: Morphology, Medicine, and Reform in Radical London* (Chicago, 1989).

13. J. A. Secord, *Victorian Sensation: The Extraordinary Publication, Reception and Secret Authorship of* Vestiges of the Natural History of Creation (Chicago, 2000).

14. P. J. Bowler, *The Eclipse of Darwinism: Anti-Darwinian Evolution Theories in the Decades around 1900* (Baltimore, 1983).

15. G. Geison, *Michael Foster and the Cambridge School of Physiology* (Princeton, 1978).

16. G. Beer, *Open Fields: Science in Cultural Encounter* (Oxford, 1996).

FURTHER READING

Readers interested in the development of scientific culture generally should start with S. F. Cannon, *Science in Culture: The Early Victorian Period* (1978) and follow with J. Morrell and A. Thackray, *Gentlemen of Science: The Early Years of the British Association for the Advancement of Science* (1981). B. Lightman, ed., *Victorian Science in Context* (1997) provides a good survey of contemporary approaches. A. Winter, *Mesmerized: Powers of Mind in Victorian Britain* (1998) provides insights into popular and 'alternative' Victorian science. Many of the key issues in the cultural history of British physics are dealt with in C. Smith, *The Science of Energy: A Cultural History of Energy Physics in Victorian Britain* (1998) and A. C. Warwick, *Masters of Theory: Cambridge and the Rise of Mathematical Physics* (2003). B. Hunt, *The Maxwellians* (1991) deals with the rise and development of electromagnetism. C. Smith and M. N. Wise, *Energy and Empire* (1989) provides a biographical study of Lord Kelvin that also provides a wealth of information concerning the culture of British physics more generally. An important discussion of the rise of physics laboratories and their place in industrial and imperial culture is found in S. Schaffer, 'Late Victorian metrology and its instrumentation: a manufactory of ohms', in R. Bud and S. Cozzens, eds, *Invisible Connections: Instruments, Institutions and Science* (1992). Readers interested in finding out more about nineteenth-century geological controversies should look at M. Rudwick, *The Great Devonian Controversy: The Shaping of Scientific Knowledge amongst Gentlemanly Specialists* (1985) and J. A. Secord, *Controversy in Victorian Geology: The Cambrian–Silurian Debate* (1986). Early British debates about evolution are examined in A. Desmond, *The Politics of Evolution: Morphology, Medicine and Reform in Radical London* (1989). The literature on Darwin is huge. A. Desmond and J. R. Moore, *Darwin* (1991) is an excellent place to start. Responses to Darwin are the focus of P. Bowler, *The Eclipse of Darwinism: Anti-Darwinian Evolution Theories in the Decades around 1900* (1983). G. Beer, *Open Fields: Science in Cultural Encounter* (1996) suggests some interesting ways of linking Victorian science and literary culture. C. E. Russett, *Sexual Science: The Victorian Construction of Womanhood* (1989) and E. Showalter, *The Female Malady: Women, Madness and English Culture, 1830–1980* (1987) point to ways in which both physics and the life sciences were used to construct notions of gender throughout the Victorian period.

PART V

The United Kingdom

CHAPTER TWENTY-NINE

Politics in Ireland

CHRISTINE KINEALY

Ireland's political history has a contemporary significance that is unusual within British history. The impact of Ireland's past on current political developments was illustrated in 1993, at the signing of the Downing Street Joint Declaration, when it was announced that the people of the North and the South needed to 'overcome the legacy of history'. During the signing of the Good Friday Agreement in 1998, British prime minister Tony Blair cautioned that 'the hand of history is upon us'. Such statements suggest that Irish history informs political actions, but that it was defined by continuous conflict between Protestants and Catholics. This interpretation, however, only emerged in the late nineteenth century. The course of Irish historiography changed again when Ireland was partitioned in 1921: an outcome that was neither inevitable nor demanded by nationalists or unionists in the nineteenth century.

The creation of two new political states after 1921, and the consequent break-up of the United Kingdom, signalled the commencement of a reinterpretation of Protestant history wherein past triumphs against Catholics (usually commencing in 1641) had ended in ultimate victory, that is, the gaining of a Protestant state. For nationalists, the outcome was more opaque; whilst twenty-six counties had won a measure of independence, the cost had been partition. In the newly created Free State, partition was followed by civil war (1922–3). Hence historians in the post-partition period were grappling not only with the birth of a new state, but also with uncertainty as to whether it marked the end of the nationalist struggle or merely the commencement of a new one. Many Irish historians – both north and south of the border – looked to British academia for guidance, embracing developments taking place in London which sought to make historical research objective and value-free. Such an approach was a welcome antidote to nationalist sentiment or rancour. At the same time, a number of Irish academic historians believed that they should challenge or 'revise' the nationalist myths which had emerged since 1850. In doing so, they laid the foundation for an orthodoxy which dominated historical writing in Ireland until the 1990s. Whilst by the 1960s British history had evolved to take account of new methodological and theoretical approaches, in Ireland revisionism remained entrenched. Moreover, research on aspects of Ireland's violent past was largely ignored by historians in the Republic, whilst the main concern in Northern Ireland was with unionist history.

This chapter outlines the main changes in the Irish political historiography of the nineteenth century, in particular historical revisionism and the attempts to challenge it. The significance of partition is also examined, since it created a challenge for unionist historians because the fears of their predecessors that home rule would be granted had been shown to be false. The historiography of nineteenth-century politics is explored through a number of key events, themes and personalities which have dominated the writing of Irish history in this period, such as the 1798 uprising, the role of the Orange Order and the growth of nationalism and unionism. At the same time, areas which have received relatively little attention have been addressed. The division of historical writing into nationalist and unionist historiography reflects the increasing polarization of both Irish politics and historical memory after 1850. Since the 1990s the domination of the revisionist orthodoxy has been undermined. Significantly many of the challenges to revisionism came from historians outside Ireland, or from academics engaged in different methodological approaches which had been less constrained by the revisionist debate.

Historiography

The scholarly writing of nineteenth-century Irish political history originated in the nineteenth century itself with the pioneering work of the Irish historian W. E. H. Lecky (1838–1903). Lecky's sympathetic portrayal of Grattan's parliament, his criticisms of aspects of British rule in Ireland and his refutation of the English historian J. A. Froude's unfavourable views of the Irish people won him the support of many contemporary nationalists during the period of home-rule agitation. Lecky, however, was opposed to the home-rule movement, and was elected a Unionist MP in 1895. Lecky's life, together with the complexity of his views and the debates which they engendered, were a foretaste of the controversies that both dominated and distorted much historical writing in the twentieth century.

Between the 1930s, revisionism was the prevailing orthodoxy within Irish historical writing. It emerged from the attempts by British historians to make history scientific, source-based, objective and value-free, and is associated with the University of London's Institute of Historical Research. Herbert Butterfield, the doyen of this approach, placed sceptical empiricism at the centre of scholarly research. Ironically (as it proved in Ireland) he also cautioned that 'the study of the past with one eye, so to speak, upon the present is the source of all sins and sophistries in history'.[1] A number of Irish historians had been trained either in the London Institute or in other British universities and they brought this Whig interpretation back to Ireland. In Ireland, the new revisionist approach had to adapt to a post-colonial and post-partition society which was anxious to exorcize some of the ghosts of a violent past. At the same time, historians had to accommodate and make historical sense of a political settlement that had not been part of the demands of either nationalists or unionists in the nineteenth century. Two influential pioneers of revisionism were T. W. Moody, Professor of History at Trinity College, Dublin after 1939, and Robert Dudley Edwards, who became Professor of Modern Irish History in University

College, Dublin five years later. They were the first editors of *Irish Historical Studies*, a journal founded in 1938 to raise the profile and professionalism of history-writing. It also established strict guidelines for the writing of Irish history, and included a series of articles entitled 'historical revisions', a purpose of which was to challenge received nationalist wisdoms, which they believed implied that Irish history since the twelfth century had been a continuous trajectory of oppression by Britain. Together, Moody and Edwards dominated Irish history in the south of Ireland for forty years and set an agenda for the study of Irish history in both Dublin and Belfast.

The foundation of *Irish Historical Studies* established a landmark in making Irish history more professional. Because one of the primary concerns of the early revisionists was to discredit romanticized nationalist interpretations of Ireland's past, some of the new writing provided an antidote to an over-simplistic view of the new state as being Catholic and Gaelic, such as was evident in the nationalist writings of Alexander Martin Sullivan (1829–84), Alice Stopford Green (1847–1929) and Daniel Corkery (1878–1964). The writings of John Mitchel, a republican nationalist in the 1840s, were also a favourite target for revisionists. Despite his being exiled to Bermuda at the beginning of 1848, his writings ensured that the tradition of armed insurrection continued, both in the *Jail Journal* (1854) but more comprehensively in *The Last Conquest (Perhaps)* (*c.*1862). For revisionists, Mitchel's polemical approach and his denunciation of the British government for the Great Famine represented a particularly dangerous brand of nationalist writing. However, Mitchel could not be accused of adopting either a Catholic or a Gaelic approach; he was an Ulster Presbyterian, who followed in the non-sectarian republican tradition of 1798.

Nonetheless, revisionism appeared to offer a useful tool for understanding Anglo-Irish relations in a period when the political connection with Britain was ambiguous (until the unilateral declaration of a republic in 1948, the Free State remained part of the British Commonwealth). However, rather than being value-free or objective, much of the writing associated with the revisionist interpretation was either anti-nationalist or avoided issues which referred to negative aspects of Ireland's colonial past. There was also a reluctance to discuss violent aspects of the national conflict (or the resistance to it) with emphasis placed on the constitutional rather than the physical-force movement. Consequently the uprisings in 1798, 1803, 1848, 1867 and 1916 were regarded as largely irrelevant to the achievement of political independence. In its crudest form, therefore, revisionism served a propagandist function that was just as politically motivated as some earlier English accounts of colonialism or nationalist accounts of conquest had been.

One of the consequences of revisionism was to stifle, rather than enrich, intellectual debate. Despite an expansion of historical research in Ireland from the 1970s into areas such as labour history, social history, popular culture and women's history, the imprint of revisionism remained. Moreover, after the commencement of the 'Troubles' in 1969, revisionism provided historians, politicians and the media alike with a moral prism through which to understand Ireland's nationalist past and ignore its uncomfortable present. The renewed paramilitary campaign in the North gave the revisionist approach a new significance in Irish politics. Critics of revisionism accused it of adopting such an approach in the interests of conciliating Ulster unionists or of maintaining Anglo-Irish relations, although this was denied by its proponents. Furthermore, its anti-nationalist stance reflected the prevailing political climate within the country, whilst it continued to distance Irish history from other theoretical approaches, including feminism, Marxism, post-colonialism and postmodernism. Consequently, instead of providing an interpretative framework for understanding Ireland's colonial past, and explaining the complexity and diversity of nationalism or unionism, much of the writing sought to distance itself from such issues. The small size and intimacy of the Irish academic community also impeded dissension. Thus, by the 1980s, an historiographical consensus appeared to have been achieved, yet revisionism had widened the gap between academic and popular history.

Two historians associated with the new wave of revisionist writing were Ronan Fanning and Roy Foster. Fanning explained how Irish history differed from that elsewhere because the myths surrounding it were 'designed to legitimize violence as a political weapon in a bid to overthrow the state'.[2] Ireland's violent past had become a violent present and, unlike more evasive proponents of revisionism, he admitted that the state in the Republic of Ireland (and in Northern Ireland) would support the revisionist project in order 'to buttress and legitimize their own authority'. A more comprehensive and influential repositioning of Irish historiography was provided by Foster's revisionist template of Irish history.[3] Foster described nationalist history as a morality tale based on popular myths which, in turn, had their roots in the writings of antiquarians and folklorists. He also inverted traditional nationalist interpretations: the Famine was of less significance in Irish economic and social development than the agricultural disruption that followed the end of the Napoleonic Wars in 1815; landlords were rehabilitated and recast as victims themselves; the Land War of 1879 to 1882 was described as a revolution in rising expectations and grounded in economic greed; and the Fenians were 'typical' Victorians, with the movement providing a vehicle for leisure pursuits rather than the spread of revolutionary activities. Political ideology, conflict, trauma and idealism had been surgically removed, whilst the emphasis on religious and cultural differences suggested that, in the nineteenth century, the real divide was not between Ireland and Britain, or rich and poor, but between eastern Ulster and the rest of the country. Significantly, unionist or Protestant mythology was not held up to the same robust scrutiny by revisionists as nationalist history. By the 1980s, therefore, revisionism had challenged and undermined most of the nationalist and popular assumptions about Ireland's past – from the Norman conquest to the Plantation of Ulster, from Grattan's parliament to the Land War, from the Easter Rising to the commencement of the Troubles – and it concluded that things were not as bad as had been depicted by nationalists. At the same time, the contribution of physical force as a way of achieving independence had been removed. Yet, after thirty years of domination, this approach had not convinced the wider public, and some students trained in revisionist methodology also rejected it.

An authoritative challenge to the domination of revisionism was made by Brendan Bradshaw, an Irish-born historian whose main research interest was the sixteenth century and the emergence of a Catholic identity among both English settlers and native Irish. He placed ideology, particularly national consciousness, at the centre of understanding this period. By doing so, Bradshaw realized that he was 'swimming against the current of historiographical consensus' in the 1970s.[4] His research findings coincided with a new wave of IRA violence in Northern Ireland but despite academic opprobrium, Bradshaw continued to assert that 'the revisionist enterprise reintroduced a biased perspective, quite as distorting as that of the romantic nationalists but more insidious, because it masqueraded under the name of scholarly detachment'. Bradshaw's contribution to historical debate could not be ignored following the appearance of an article in *Irish Historical Studies* in 1989. His inclusion in a journal that had been associated with revisionism since its inception suggested a move away from the influences of the founding generation of the orthodoxy. In it, Bradshaw accused revisionist discourse of having written the trauma and catastrophe out of Irish history, by its refusal to engage with topics such as the rebellion in 1641 and the Great Famine in the 1840s. Bradshaw's accusations provoked both heated debate and denial amongst Irish historians.[5] But his conclusions found resonance with a new generation of young researchers who believed that his criticisms also had a wider applicability to Irish historiography in general.

The diffusion of post-revisionist interpretation was helped by the emergence of the popular magazine *History Ireland* in 1993, which bridged the gap between traditional and more progressive scholarly interpretations of Irish history. Also, at the beginning of the 1990s a new generation of writers emerged, some of whom lived outside Ireland and who were less constrained by the prevailing ideological boundaries. Other methodological approaches, notably literary and cultural criticism, pointed to new directions for historical analysis. Moreover, the emergence of 'New British History' meant that the traditional anglocentric view of earlier historians was no longer acceptable. It also marked a move towards an inclusive history rather than separate national histories, although a search for language that was regarded as politically neutral was reflected in the shift from the descriptor 'British Isles' to 'North Atlantic Archipelago' to 'the three kingdoms' or, occasionally, 'Greater Britain'. The paramilitary ceasefire in Northern Ireland in 1994 and the commencement of the peace process also contributed to an opening up of historical debate throughout Ireland and Britain. However, these developments highlighted the level of self-censorship in Irish history before the 1990s. The new writing coincided with the anniversary of the Great Famine in 1995, and it was in this area that the challenge to revisionism was to prove the most difficult to refute.

The domination of revisionism had also stifled the development of academic debate in areas that were engaging academics elsewhere. The development of Irish women's history, for example, only emerged in the late 1970s. Recent research has demonstrated the significant involvement of women in a variety of political activities, ranging from Mary Ann McCraken in 1798, to Anna Parnell in the 1880s, to the members of the Ulster Women's Unionist Council at the beginning of the twentieth century. The emergence of alternative approaches to traditional history was slow to take root in Ireland, however, leading Margaret Ward in 1991 to appeal to Irish historians to build on the use of gender as a tool for historical analysis and as a way of rethinking mainstream history.[6] Nonetheless, women's history continued to remain separate from, rather than part of, the main body of historical writing, although Liz Curtis's study of Irish political development after 1798 provided a rare example of a historian synthesizing politics with gender issues.[7]

Revisionism also affected Marxist debate in Ireland. Some Marxists viewed revisionism as a neo-imperialist orthodoxy whilst others did not regard British imperialism as central to Irish political development. A further difficulty arose in applying historical materialism to Ireland and demonstrating the relationship between nationalist and socialist revolution. The attempts by James Connolly, the labour leader executed in 1916, to show that the national struggle was driven by class struggle was adopted by later Marxist academics. It is in the writing of unionist rather than nationalist history, however, that Marxists have made most impact. Since the 1970s, a new generation of Marxists have criticized earlier ones for being sympathetic to nationalist interpretations. They also criticized them for disregarding the uneven development of capitalism in Ireland, particularly the uniqueness of north-east Ulster, and its significance in political development. But these writers have, in turn, been criticized for applying Marxist methodology to justify the ideology of unionism. They have also been accused by their left-wing critics of supporting democratic rather than republican aims in the North. Furthermore, through their interest in the cultural identity of unionists and loyalists, and justification of partition, they have been criticized for applying – overtly and covertly – a two-nation approach to Irish political history. Collectively, however, their work increased understanding of loyalist cultural development and of Ulster economics and politics, areas which had largely been marginalized by Dublin-based historians.

Whilst Irish historiography at the beginning of the twenty-first century has broken free from the stranglehold of revisionism, a number of historians who associated themselves with this approach regard post-revisionist interpretations as being nationalism in another guise. Yet apprehension that the post-revisionist challenge would give rise to a proscriptive dichotomy or might become the new orthodoxy appeared groundless, as the removal of the revisionist domination allowed debates over interpretation to flourish, and opened rather than closed discussion on many of the previously contested or marginalized areas of Irish history. Consequently, much of the recent research has been less constrained by ideological imperatives than that of the preceding generations.

Partition and History in Northern Ireland

The partition of Ireland shaped Irish historiography. Between 1920 and 1970 Northern Ireland history was dominated by unionist historians, who articulated a largely Protestant version of history, grounded in assumptions of northern distinctiveness and superiority, and the need to defend themselves against the common enemy. When viewing history through this prism, separation – in the form of partition – appeared to have been inevitable. Like the revisionist interpretation, it was shaped by contemporary political concerns, which were superimposed on a partisan reading of past events. As Walker has demonstrated, the unionist view of history promoted the seventeenth century as the key period in the development of a Protestant and unionist consciousness, through focusing on the events of 1641, 1689 and 1690 – which were recalled in popular memory as triumphs of Protestantism over Catholicism. The Protestant interpretation of history was widely accepted by academics and non-academics, as well as by unionists and nationalists alike in the late twentieth century.[8] Yet interest in the seventeenth century only emerged in the late nineteenth century in response to the threat of home rule. It sought to provide a Protestant view of history that was rooted in conflict and division with Catholics and thus reflected a contemporary concern with intensifying political polarization between nationalists and unionists, a demarcation that was increasingly based on religious division. The foundation of Northern Ireland in 1920 ('A Protestant state for a Protestant people') reinvigorated this Protestant view of history.

However, there were a number of problems and omissions associated with this interpretation. Even the nomenclature caused problems, with Ulster (the historic nine counties) and Northern Ireland (the six-county state formed in 1920) often used interchangeably, even by respected historians. In a similar way, the term British Isles – which has no political validity – was used by some historians who were reluctant to engage with the complexities of the colonial relationship. In addition, the Protestant interpretations were usually only concerned with confrontations, and thus did not explain the differences within Protestantism (which were a dominant feature until the 1830s); Protestant support for the repeal of the union or for republican nationalism; and instances of co-operation between clergy of all denominations. Taking this broader view of Irish history, partition does not appear to have been inevitable, whilst comparisons with other European countries have demonstrated how the views of religious and political minorities can be accommodated within one state.

More balanced histories of Northern Ireland were provided by a generation of writers in the 1970s and 1980s, but their endeavours to appear impartial were judged by some nationalists to be attempts at covert unionism. From the 1970s also, unionist history was well served (both in quantity and quality) by historians but the debates about unionist identity and origins remained largely confined to academics and rarely impacted on the political discourse of unionists. At the end of the 1980s, there were attempts to foster a more nuanced approach to the history of Northern Ireland by recognizing the different cultural (as opposed to political) traditions within the community. This approach was pioneered by Leland Lyons in 1979 who argued that attempts at political solutions to the Irish situation had ignored the collision of cultures on the island.[9] Ten years later, the adoption of this perspective in Northern Ireland received the official backing of the British government through the creation of a Cultural Traditions Group, its purpose being to 'explore ways of promoting a better understanding of, and a more constructive debate about, our different cultural traditions in Northern Ireland'.[10] The impact of this approach was most evident in histories of Northern Ireland, particularly in attempts to locate unionism in a cultural context and to demonstrate the differences within unionist identity. Ironically, whilst post-revisionism meant that politics were being written back into nationalist history, the importance of cultural rather than political differences was being highlighted in unionist history.

Following the creation of the Northern Ireland state, nationalist history in the North was less well served by academic historians. This situation changed slowly after 1970, partly in response to the renewed conflict but also because a new generation of Catholic/nationalist historians emerged who had benefited from the opening up of third-level education. Overall, the role of Ulster Catholics and Protestants in the national struggle continued to receive relatively little scholarly attention. In the 1990s Eamon Phoenix, using previously unexplored sources, provided a thorough and incisive study of Catholics in the north of Ireland.[11] His work covered a period when hopes were fleetingly raised, with home rule being agreed to in 1912, and promptly dashed, when only six years later a partition was imposed. Unusually also, Phoenix's narrative neither began nor ended in 1920, thus allowing a portrayal of both the causes and consequences of partition. He also examined how Catholics in the north-east coped with being a minority in a unionist-dominated state, concluding that their treatment in the decades after partition sowed the seeds for conflict in the 1960s.

The paramilitary ceasefire in 1994 and the peace process changed the emphasis of some history-writing concerning the north of Ireland and resulted in a fresh interest in cultural pluralism. Although a more nuanced view of Northern Ireland emerged in the late twentieth century, the distinctiveness of the area remained a dominant theme for some historians. The view of two distinct tribes is central to the work of Dudley Edwards on the Orange Order which relies on polemic and assertion.[12] Increasingly, however, a simplistic unionist view of history may be hard to sustain as more scholarly study is undertaken on aspects of Ireland's past that united rather than divided the denominations.

The 1798 Uprising

The political history of the nineteenth century begins in the 1790s. This was a pivotal decade in Irish politics with the formation of the United Irishmen in Belfast in 1791 marking the emergence of republican nationalism and an attempt to make Irish politics non-sectarian. The decade also witnessed an increase in sectarianism in Irish politics, especially amongst the lower orders, which resulted in a number of factional clashes. One such conflict in County Armagh in 1795 resulted in the formation of the Orange Order, an avowedly anti-Catholic, sectarian organization. The uprising in 1798 was a failure for the United Irishmen and their non-sectarian ideals; for the Orange Order it marked an early victory and an opportunity to present themselves as not only loyal, but a valuable counter-revolutionary force. The bicentenary of the 1798 uprising in 1998 marked a reappraisal of its significance, benefiting from both the general broadening of historical debate in Ireland and the peace process.

The early historiography of the United Irishmen tended to be driven by the ultimate failure of the uprising rather than by the ideological context within which it had existed and which, in turn, it had helped to shape. One of the most perturbing questions regarding this uprising was the extent to which it manifested sectarian tendencies. Nineteenth-century accounts viewed the rebellion in 1798 as being driven by Catholic peasants, with little recognition given to Protestant involvement (apart from in sectarian conflicts). In the 1990s, work placed the uprising within the secular context of a period of popular politicization and international radicalism.[13] It also located the 1790s in Ireland in the light of earlier revolutions in America and France, although the seventeenth-century historian Nicholas Canny argued that 1798 was part of a longer historical continuum that had roots in 1641.

Modern work concentrates on the popular politicization of the 1790s and the climate of revolution in Ireland during a period of European upheaval. Moreover, the ideologies associated with that decade are viewed positively, being seen as the beginning of the struggle for democracy in Ireland. Yet there remains a lack of historiographical consensus on the uprising. Some of the new writing rehabilitates the United Irishmen as marking the birth of Irish nationalism (although the republican and violent aspects of the uprising are sometimes played down). However, these positive interpretations have been challenged by the more traditional approach which continues to question the secular aspects of the uprising but identify anti-Protestant elements within it. As with the Great Famine, the precise death toll during the rising is not known, although much of the writing in the early 1990s concurred that it was in the region of 30,000. Overall, in addition to stressing the international context of the uprising, the new research demonstrates that rebellion meant different things to diverse social groups in each part of the country.

Some of the most exciting writing on the 1798 uprising concerns groups who have been invisible in the historiography, notably the role of women in radical politics.[14] The way in which memory and commemoration have been incorporated into historical remembrance has also been explored using the experience of 1798.[15] In contrast to the recent interest in the 1798 uprising, the 1848 rebellion continues to be neglected by Irish historians. At the same time, the influence of Irish radicals on British political developments – in the 1790s and 1840s, during the Fenian uprisings in 1867, in various general elections, during the home rule agitation and following the 1916 uprising – remains relatively unexplored.

The Act of Union

The nineteenth century commenced with the passing of the Act of Union, legislation that changed the constitutional face of England, Ireland, Scotland and Wales. It also created the United Kingdom and marked the abolition of the Irish parliament in Dublin. Opposition or loyalty to the Union shaped the political profile of Ireland in the following century, although allegiances were not static; the Orange Order, for example, had opposed the Union, whereas the hierarchy of the Irish Catholic church had supported it. Within a few decades, their respective positions had reversed. The Protestant ascendancy in Ireland was strengthened initially by the Union, through their involvement in local government and national politics, and because of their possession of land. By the end of the century the system of landholding had undergone a radical change, with Catholic peasant proprietors replacing the Anglo-Irish landlord class. Furthermore, in the decades following the Union, sectarian divisions hardened, whilst political and religious affiliations became increasingly inseparable. Union also changed the direction of British political discourse, with some British politicians becoming unwitting casualties of it, from Pitt, responsible for the legislation, to Gladstone, who attempted to reverse it. Yet, the significance of this legislation has largely been marginalized by Irish historians and ignored by many British ones, regardless of the emergence of the 'New British History'. The question of the extent to which the Union changed or extended the concept of Britishness therefore remains unanswered.

Union with Ireland proved difficult to achieve as members of the Irish parliament were reluctant to vote themselves out of existence. The way in which Irish politicians were persuaded to accept the disappearance of their parliament has divided historians. Although bribery and coercion were an integral part of British political life, and therefore a conventional tool to be employed in winning Irish support, the degree to which they were utilized to achieve the Union (especially in financial terms) was unusual. Geoghegan, however, regards the large expenditure as pragmatic and typifying a wartime mentality.[16]

At the time, the population of Ireland accounted for approximately one-third of the total United Kingdom population; by the end of the century, it accounted for only one-tenth. Yet, especially in the political arena, Ireland continued to be a stimulus for change. Support for Irish home rule, for example, not only influenced similar movements in Scotland and Wales, but also in other parts of the empire. The Government of Ireland Act of 1920 – a compromise imposed from London – created two parliaments where prior to 1800 only one had existed. Ironically also Irish unionists, who had argued most vigorously for the continuation of the Union, achieved self-government before any other part of the United Kingdom. The Act also marked a first stage in the break-up of the United Kingdom and, eventually, of the British Empire. Compared with the unions with Wales and Scotland, the Irish union was short-lived, yet pivotal to understanding political development within the United Kingdom in the nineteenth and twentieth centuries.

Catholics and Nationalists: Heroes or Nationalist Hagiography?

If unionists have looked to the seventeenth century for their political justifications and ideological roots, some nationalist writing has traced a longer continuum of oppression and conflict going back to the twelfth century. Both interpretations are selective: neither nationalism nor unionism has had a continuous history of popular support; the religious and economic divisions within Ireland have not always been clear-cut; and the political settlements achieved after 1920 were neither inevitable nor anticipated. Much of this view of Ireland's past has its origins in the late nineteenth century, which marked the beginning of an attempt to link the contemporaneous conflict with a continuous struggle dating back to an earlier century.

By playing down the national struggle in Ireland, revisionism severed Ireland from being part of what was a European-wide movement. Nationalism (and revolutionary struggle) was a powerful force in nineteenth-century Europe, resulting in the emergence of a system of nation-states. To a large extent also, the national struggle characterized the political history of Ireland in the nineteenth century. Yet few publications on nationalism in nineteenth-century Europe include Ireland within the parameters of their study. In Ireland also, the national struggle has tended to be characterized as being a *Catholic* struggle – by both revisionists and an earlier generation of nationalist writers. However, the most important and radical leaders, including Wolfe Tone, Isaac Butt, John Mitchel, William Smith O'Brien and Charles Parnell, were Protestant. They did not view Irish nationalism in isolation, but linked it with republican or nationalist movements elsewhere. Even Daniel O'Connell, who bound the repeal movement most closely with Catholicism, was also involved in various British radical movements including the abolition of slavery, the reform of parliament and Jewish emancipation. Significantly, O'Connell was greatly admired by liberals and radicals throughout Europe and America. Why, therefore, were Catholicism and Irish nationalism often viewed as synonymous?

Since the Reformation Irish Catholics had been regarded as a threat to both the interests of the Protestant minority in Ireland and to the security of the monarchy and the British state. But if the seventeenth century was defined by attempts to make Ireland Protestant, the nineteenth century witnessed a diametrically opposed attempt to undo that process both by British politicians (who regarded it as an essential component of justice for Ireland) and by nationalists (who increasingly viewed Catholicism as an integral part of Irish identity). O'Connell dominated Irish politics in the first half of the nineteenth century. The most comprehensive studies of him were published in the 1970s and 1980s when constitutional rather than republican politics were regarded as acceptable. As Oliver MacDonagh demonstrated, one of O'Connell's greatest achievements was to give both an ideological coherence and an organizational structure to the demands for Catholic emancipation and repeal of the Union.[17] The high point of his political career was winning Catholic emancipation in 1829 and his biographers have generally drawn a distinction between his pre- and post-1829 achievements. However, O'Connell's political astuteness was also apparent in 1835 when he allied, through the Lichfield House Compact, with the Whigs and reformers within the British government to further his aims. O'Connell's achievement was also to provide a structure, organization and political coherence rare within other European nationalist movements at the time. In European terms, his achievements were unique in creating a mass movement from a largely illiterate, Irish-speaking peasant society – which won a substantial victory against the sophisticated machinery of the British state. At the time of his death in 1847, however, the repeal movement was in disarray and the country was in the midst of the Great Famine. The vacuum created by his death was filled by a republican uprising in 1848 led by a radical group known as Young Ireland. The Young Ireland uprising, like that of 1798, was part of a wider period of revolutionary upheaval throughout Europe. Many of the leaders of Young Ireland were Protestant and they argued that the Protestant ascendancy should not simply be replaced by a Catholic ascendancy. Although the 1848 uprising created a bridge between the physical-force movements of 1798 and those of 1867 and 1916 it has largely been ignored by historians.

One of the weaknesses of O'Connell's tactics was that he moved Irish nationalism closer to a form of denominational exclusiveness owing to his close association with the Catholic church. Moreover, the victories of Catholics in the early nineteenth century, together with the depiction of the 1798 uprising as being a sectarian conflict, alarmed Protestants and reawakened memories of seventeenth-century strife. O'Connell's failure to win the support of Protestants was mirrored by later nationalists such as Parnell and Patrick Pearse, who either underestimated or ignored the demands and fears of the Protestant/unionist population. Assessments of Parnell's contribution tended to focus on the tragic ending of his career, following the O'Shea divorce in 1889. The achievements and failures of Parnell cannot be understood without reference to the wider British political context. The role of Gladstone, who supported land reform and home rule, was particularly significant. Despite his considerable contribution to Irish affairs, recent studies have focused on his perceived shortcomings, notably his failure to appreciate or appease the concerns of Ulster unionists. Gladstone's concern for Ireland is thus reduced to a misplaced obsession. In areas such as this, the role of the 'New British History' could prove valuable in moving interpretations away from a predominantly anglocentric view of events.

The 1916 rising in Ireland has traditionally been the most contested rebellion of the long nineteenth century. For nationalists, 1916 is a sacred memory, whereas some revisionist historians have viewed it as being based on the ideas of sacrifice and redemption and indelibly linked with a Catholic vision of nationhood, rather than being part of a republican tradition that commenced in 1798. Revisionists have claimed a 'post-nationalist' position, suggesting that Irish historiography had reached a stage whereby it was unnecessary to justify either the nationalist project or the achievement of independence. This has been hotly contested, with critics arguing

that received wisdom (and accepted fallacies) are not restricted to nationalist inter-
preters and that the Rising probably had more popular support than has generally
been depicted by revisionists.

Orangeism and the Growth of Unionism

Irish Protestants have often been cast in a conservative mould: as evangelicals worried
by the growth of the Catholic church; as defenders of the Union, willing to fight
to defend it; or as members of the Orange Order, combining anti-Catholicism with
an aggressive defence of the Union. The term Protestants is often used in such a way
also as to imply an homogeneous group, which was not the case. The two main
Protestant denominations were Anglican and Presbyterian and, until disestablishment
in 1869, the Anglican church was the state church. In the early decades of the nineteenth century the political distinctions between the two groups were clear on some
issues; for example, Presbyterians had been the main supporters of the United Irishmen, whilst the Orange Order was almost exclusively Anglican. The perceived threat
posed by Catholic emancipation, however, had led Presbyterians and Anglicans to
form a Protestant alliance in the 1830s. It was not until the 1880s, however, that
Irish politics, most clearly in the province of Ulster, had polarized along Protestant
and Catholic or unionist and nationalist lines. Walker has argued that by the time of
the general election in 1886 'for the first time in Ulster politics the population split
on a firmly denominational basis'.[18] Not only had the religious divide intensified, but
a geographic divide had emerged between *Ulster* and *Irish* politics, reflected in the
language of parliamentary debate which no longer referred to the 'Irish Question'
but increasingly to the 'Ulster Question'.

There were also considerable differences between the smaller Protestant denominations, Methodists, Moravians, Baptists and Quakers. The Quakers were universally
admired for their role in giving relief during the Great Famine, in contrast to the
role of evangelical Anglicans and Presbyterians who used the tragedy as an opportunity to proselytize. Whilst there is a new interest in dissenting voices amongst Ulster
Protestants it still remains a relatively under-explored area. The recent research on
the 1798 uprisings has highlighted the role of Presbyterians in the formative years
of republican nationalism. However, Campbell's most comprehensive survey has
identified a radical Protestant tradition from the Plantation of Ulster to partition.[19]
Jackson has offered an inclusive view of Irish political developments since 1798, synthesizing unionist and nationalist narratives and viewing them from both Belfast and
Dublin perspectives.[20] Jackson's strength lies in his expertise in unionist history, an
approach with which few historians in the Irish Republic appear to feel comfortable.
Moreover, Jackson's methodological approach and ideological and philosophical
influences are broad, borrowing from Marxist, nationalist, revisionist and postmodernist approaches.

As with Union, so the Protestant minority viewed the introduction of Catholic
emancipation as a threat. Moreover, it had been forced through parliament by two
Protestant sympathizers – Wellington and Peel. Who, therefore, could be trusted to
defend Protestantism? Emancipation was a massive psychological victory for Catholics
in general, and O'Connell in particular. But emancipation also changed the balance
of political power, especially as various governments after 1830 advocated 'justice for

Ireland'. These changes reminded Protestants of their minority status in Ireland. The safe Protestant majority which had resulted from the Act of Union was more than offset, therefore, by the government which wanted to conciliate Catholic opinion. The view of Ulster as being different – and superior – also began to be articulated in the 1840s especially in the wake of the catastrophe of the Famine. By the 1880s, with the emergence of home rule, these separatist beliefs were directly impacting on the formulation of unionist policy.

The extent to which Ulster had a separate identity divides historians. Was it a nation, with its own unique history, traditions and culture? Or was this separate identity a nineteenth-century intervention? Jackson has argued that a separate Ulster nation which was 'cohesive, Protestant and particularistic', and with its own history, did exist in the late nineteenth century in the north-east of the province.[21] Loughlin, however, has rejected the idea of Ulster as a separate nation, arguing that this consciousness did not exist amongst Ulster Protestants.[22] Instead, he argues that Ulster unionists were an ethnic group but not an ethnic nationality. He also points out that the idea of being British was complicated by the fact that, whilst the Union made Protestants part of a religious majority in the United Kingdom, they realized that a sizeable portion of the British people at the end of the nineteenth century sympathized with the aspirations of the Irish Nationalist Party. Moreover, the actions of Gladstone demonstrated the perfidy of the British government. The crown was the only thing to which they could give unequivocal allegiance, especially after the disappearance of empire in the twentieth century.

The Orange Order

The actions of the Orange Order at the end of the twentieth century, especially in Drumcree, have overshadowed its early history, yet its history has been dominated by conflicts over the right to march along so-called traditional routes. The history of the Orange Order, which started as an agrarian defence organization but became the backbone of the unionist movement, provides an insight into Irish politics in the nineteenth century. Nonetheless, the Order has been poorly served by modern historians, with Hereward Senior's 1966 publication remaining a classic, although he ends his study in 1836, when the Grand Lodge voluntarily dissolved following the publication of an unfavourable parliamentary report. His account was also written before the commencement of the Troubles and the Orange Order's increasingly defensive stance, culminating after 1994 in the stand-off in Drumcree. One of the strengths of Senior's study is that he places the Orange Order in its international context and suggests that the only thing lodges in Ireland, Britain, America, Canada and India had in common was their anti-Catholicism. One of his conclusions is that whilst both the various Whig and Tory governments disliked popular movements, Orangeism was tolerated, especially by the Tories, because it 'offered the government a last resort should its other resources become exhausted . . . They were thus a barrier to revolution and an obstacle to compromise'.[23]

The Orange Order was founded in 1795 in County Armagh, although the roots of loyalist sectarianism lie earlier. Its establishment coincided with the emergence of non-sectarian republicanism in Ireland and, like the United Irishmen, Orangeism emerged from contemporary debates on democracy and political power. Since its

formation, the Orange Order has contributed to the creation of a Protestant identity, especially through its involvement in unionist politics. The new Northern Ireland
state also identified itself as both Protestant and Orange. Yet, few studies have been
made of the Order and the limited literature has tended to be largely uncritical or,
in the case of Dudley Edwards's account, polemical.[24] Whilst her publication does
provide a contemporary insight into the working of the Orange Order and other loyalist institutions, the historical background is weak. She fails to account for the
strength of the Order outside Ulster in the early nineteenth century; in 1798, for
example, there were thirty-six Orange lodges in Dublin.

The most incisive recent work is Bryan's anthropological study that also provides
a historical overview of early political parades.[25] He argues that Orange parades were
central to the development of a Protestant ethnic identity and to the demarcation
between Protestant and Catholic communities. Bryan's textured study also shows
that whilst Orangeism ostensibly brought together people from different economic
and social backgrounds, the upper classes (landlords, merchants, ministers) used the
Order as a way of maintaining their authority and hegemony. The attitude of the
British authorities also changed throughout the nineteenth century, alternately
regarding the Order as a useful counter-insurgency tool or as a threat to law and
order/stability. The concepts of respectable Orangeism and traditional rights have
also been employed to depoliticize the parades and marginalize the role of sectarianism. Respectability, however, was more difficult to sustain when Orangeism was
not endorsed by state bodies.

Ireland and Empire

Understanding the involvement of Ireland (or any colonial nation) in empire is
inevitably a fraught issue. In this area the historiography is small, with few studies of
the British Empire including Ireland. Nonetheless, a question central to the historiography of the nineteenth century is: was Ireland a colony or, if not, what was its
place within the British Empire? For nationalists, the answer is generally clear-cut:
Ireland was England's first colony, whilst after 1920 the Free State was characterized
as being post-colonial. More recently, colonial discourse theory has suggested that it
is possible to be both colonizer and colonized, whilst some feminist theory has
blamed the strong patriarchal elements in modern Irish society on the colonial legacy.
An unequivocally anti-nationalist interpretation of Ireland's role has been provided
by Stephen Howe.[26] The targets of Howe's wrath are many, including historians who
view the Irish experience as exceptional, rather than applying a comparative analysis.
Howe also argues that it is incorrect – especially since the Union – to regard Ireland
as a British colony. In turn, his critics have accused him of promoting a neo-conser-
vative and imperialist interpretation of Ireland's past. A more balanced view of Ireland
and empire is provided by Keith Jeffrey, who argues that understanding empire is
crucial to understanding Ireland in the nineteenth century and even later on the
grounds that 'Ireland, as part of the metropolitan core of the Empire, supplied many
of its soldiers, settlers, administrators'.[27] He suggests that one of Ireland's paradoxes
resided in her status: being simultaneously imperial and colonial. The role of Irish
soldiers in the British army demonstrates one aspect of this paradox. In the early nineteenth century Irishmen accounted for approximately 40 per cent of all conscripts.

Victoria's visit to Ireland in 1900, to raise troops for the Boer War, demonstrated the importance of Irish soldiers in the imperial project, notwithstanding the backdrop of nationalist agitation.

Conclusion

Since the mid-1990s much progress has been made in the scholarly revision of Irish history, although more remains to be done to reveal the variety, complexity and ambiguities of nineteenth-century Ireland. In addition to the emergence of post-revisionism, there has been a concurrent growth in new research, which has helped to move the historical debate beyond the parameters of a revisionist and post-revisionist binary opposition. The opening up of historical debate has been helped by the expansion in university provision in Ireland, the birth of the Celtic Tiger, and the commencement of the peace process. Revisionism, in turn, is developing new approaches to deal with the challenges, occasionally by denying the existence of revisionism or, as Foster has done, accusing its challengers of promoting a view of Ireland's past which is just as sentimental as that of early nationalist accounts.[28] Significantly, Foster dates the emergence of revisionism to the 1960s and regards its main purpose as 'dismounting the lachrymose myths' of Irish nationalist history. In contrast, he regards his Protestant heritage as giving him 'immunity' from romantic nationalism. The main object of Foster's scorn is popular-memory or personal-accounts history which he regards as sympathetic to nationalist aspirations. He attacks with equal ferocity Gerry Adams, Frank McCourt and Famine commemorations, yet fails to explain how the public engages with both popular and academic history. Despite Foster's earlier appeals for Irish history to be inclusive, his own view remains academic and anti-nationalist. Moreover, his failure to engage equally with either Protestant nationalism or with the myths of a unionist past demonstrates that some aspects of Irish historiography remain locked in their own version of telling tales about Ireland's political past.

NOTES

1. H. Butterfield, *The Whig Interpretation of History* (London, 1973), p. 30.
2. C. Brady, ed., *Interpreting Irish History: The Debate on Historical Revisionism 1938–1994* (Dublin, 1994).
3. R. Foster, *Modern Ireland, 1600–1972* (London, 1988).
4. B. Bradshaw, 'The emperor's new clothes', in *Free Thought in Ireland* (Belfast, 1991), p. 18.
5. Brady, *Interpreting Irish History*.
6. M. Ward, *The Missing Sex: Putting Women into Irish History* (Dublin, 1991).
7. L. Curtis, *The Cause of Ireland: From the United Irishmen to Partition* (Belfast, 1994).
8. B. Walker, *Dancing to History's Tune: History, Myth and Politics in Ireland* (Belfast, 1996), pp. 1–14.
9. F. S. L. Lyons, *Culture and Anarchy in Ireland 1890–1939* (Oxford, 1979), p. 1.
10. M. Crozier, ed., *Cultural Traditions in Northern Ireland: Varieties of Irishness* (Belfast, 1989), p. vii.

11. E. Phoenix, *Northern Nationalism: Nationalist Politics, Partition and the Catholic Minority in Northern Ireland 1890–1940* (Belfast, 1994).

12. R. Dudley Edwards, *The Faithful Tribe: An Intimate Portrait of the Loyal Institutions* (London, 1999).

13. D. Keogh and N. Furlong, eds, *The Mighty Wave: The 1798 Rebellion in Wexford* (Dublin, 1996).

14. D. Keogh and N. Furlong, *The Women of 1798* (Dublin, 1998).

15. L. M. Geary, ed., *Rebellion and Remembrance in Modern Ireland* (Dublin, 2001).

16. P. M. Geoghegan, *The Irish Act of Union: A Study of High Politics 1798–1801* (Dublin, 1999).

17. O. MacDonagh, *The Emancipist: Daniel O'Connell 1830–1847* (London, 1989).

18. B. Walker, *Ulster Politics: The Formative Years 1868–1886* (Belfast, 1989), p. 255.

19. F. Campbell, *The Dissenting Voice: Protestant Democracy in Ulster from Plantation to Partition* (Belfast, 1991).

20. A. Jackson, *Ireland, 1798–1998: Politics and War* (Oxford, 1999).

21. A. Jackson, *The Ulster Party: Irish Unionists in the House of Commons 1885–1911* (Oxford, 1989), p. 10.

22. J. Loughlin, *Ulster Unionism and British National Identity since 1885* (Leicester, 1995), pp. 33–4.

23. H. Senior, *Orangeism in Ireland and Britain 1795–1836* (London, 1966), p. 284.

24. Dudley Edwards, *Faithful Tribe*.

25. D. Bryan, *Orange Parades: The Politics of Ritual, Tradition and Control* (London, 2000).

26. S. Howe, *Ireland and Empire: Colonial Legacies in Irish History and Culture* (Oxford, 2000).

27. K. Jeffrey, ed., *'An Irish Empire'? Aspects of Ireland and the British Empire* (Manchester, 1996), p. 1.

28. R. Foster, *The Irish Story: Telling Tales and Making it up in Ireland* (London, 2001).

FURTHER READING

There is an extensive literature on the 1790s, which includes N. Curtin, *The United Irishmen: Popular Politics in Ulster and Dublin, 1791–1798* (1994) and D. Gahan, *The People's Rising: Wexford, 1798* (1995). Little research has been undertaken on the 1848 uprising, but more work has been done on its leader, including R. Davis, *Revolutionary Imperialist: William Smith O'Brien 1803–1864* (1998) and R. Sloan, *William Smith O'Brien and the Young Ireland Rebellion of 1848* (2000). The most comprehensive research on O'Connell remains that done by O. MacDonagh, which includes *The Emancipist: Daniel O'Connell 1830–1847* (1989). A lively overview of Irish radicals in provided in T. Eagleton, *Scholars and Rebels in Nineteenth-Century Ireland* (1999). A sophisticated understanding of the context within which Orangeism emerged has been propounded in C. D. A. Leighton, *Catholicism in a Protestant Kingdom: A Study of the Irish Ancien Regime* (1994). Research on Catholic/Protestant co-operation is more unusual but a comprehensive view of the radical Protestant tradition is provided in F. Campbell, *The Dissenting Voice: Protestant Democracy in Ulster from Plantation to Partition* (Belfast, 1991). Gendered approaches to Irish history tend to be rare despite a lively literature, including M. Ward, *The Missing Sex: Putting Women into Irish History* (1991) and M. Luddy and C. Murphy, *Women Surviving: Studies in Irish Women's History in the Nineteenth and Twentieth Centuries* (1990).

CHAPTER THIRTY

Economy and Society in Ireland

CHRISTINE KINEALY

Revisionism

Since the 1930s, revisionists have been rewriting the nationalist interpretations of history, which they viewed as simplistic and politically influenced. One indication of this trend was the absence of Famine research in the pages of the authoritative *Irish Historical Studies*, founded in 1938. Its first editors, T. W. Moody and Robert Dudley Edwards, set the tone for subsequent decades in challenging what they regarded as received nationalist myths about Irish history and about Britain's relationship with Ireland, and the Famine was seen as a prime example. James S. Donnelly has suggested that their anti-nationalism also may have been shaped by the fact that many of this generation of scholars were educated in British universities.[1] These scholars, and those sympathetic to this view, also influenced the teaching of history in Irish universities, notably in Trinity College and University College, Dublin, where Moody and Dudley Edwards continued to teach up to the 1970s. As a result, subsequent generations of Irish scholars who received their graduate training in Irish universities had been nurtured within the revisionist environment. Moreover, whereas historical debate in universities in Britain and elsewhere after the 1960s had been enriched by new methodologies and areas of research, within Ireland revisionism not only remained in the ascendant but had been invigorated by political developments in the north of Ireland. It had also found new champions in a younger generation of historians, notably Roy Foster and Ronan Fanning.

By the 1980s revisionism was the dominant orthodoxy in the teaching, researching and writing of Irish history. Its supremacy was evident in Foster's description of Cecil Woodham-Smith, author of *The Great Hunger*, as a 'zealous convert' to a nationalist perspective.[2] But rather than just demythologizing Irish history, revisionism increasingly attacked nationalist versions of history, especially the way in which history had been taught in schools after 1921. Fanning argued that the expansion in economic and social history after the 1950s was because Irish historians were uncomfortable with examining their recent political history.[3] Furthermore, the upsurge of IRA violence after the 1960s made nationalist myth more dangerous and current.

The advent of the 'Troubles' in Northern Ireland meant that those who challenged the revisionist orthodoxies were likely to be branded as nationalist or republican sympathizers, which after 1969 was politically unacceptable in both Ireland and Britain. Consequently, revisionism also imposed a form of unspoken censorship on its critics. However, its opponents criticized it for sanitizing and removing the cataclysmic aspects of Irish history. One of the weakest aspects of the revisionist approach to nineteenth-century Ireland was its failure to engage with the Famine, an event which had been a watershed in both the economic and social development of Ireland, whilst having a significant impact on the development of Britain, North America and Australia. This omission was to a large extent to prove the Achilles' heel of the revisionist orthodoxy.

The Great Famine

The Great Famine (referred to by nationalists as the Great Hunger) was one of the most lethal famines in recent history yet revisionist accounts were cautious, partial and averse to engaging with the fact that over one million people had died of hunger or hunger-related diseases within the richest empire in the world. It was also a watershed in the development of modern Ireland yet, until the mid-1990s, it was the subject of little scholarly research whilst general histories played down its significance. Consequently, until the 1990s the history and memory of the Great Hunger was poorly served by Irish historians who had either ignored or marginalized it. Before 1994, only two substantial publications were available: the sanitized and uneven *The Irish Famine* and the vibrant, thoroughly researched, but academically panned, *The Great Hunger*.[4]

The idea for a substantial study of the Great Hunger to mark its centenary in 1945 did not originate with Irish academics but was the brainchild of the then Taoiseach, Eamon de Valera. He also provided a subvention to two Dublin historians to produce a comprehensive narrative of the Famine, but the end result was a collection of essays which took so long to produce (almost twelve years) that the centenary anniversary had passed. The overall approach of the collection edited by Dudley Edwards and T. D. Williams was so delicate that little sense of loss, devastation or trauma was conveyed. The introduction set the tone for the overall placatory nature of much of the volume, especially in relation to the role of the British government. It reproached folk memory for interpreting 'the failure of the British government in a sinister light', explaining that '[t]he scale of the actual outlay to meet the Famine and the expansion in the public-relief system are in themselves impressive evidence that the state was by no means always indifferent to Irish needs'.[5] More damagingly perhaps, from the outset it was decided that the thorny issue of mortality should be side stepped, although they admitted that 'many, many had died'. By avoiding the issues of mortality and culpability, controversy was averted. However, intellectual honesty had been compromised. De Valera was also disappointed, preferring the more robust approach of Woodham-Smith, whilst one of the book's editors described it privately as 'dehydrated history', perhaps suggesting that even those who propounded a revisionist interpretation were not convinced by it.[6]

The Great Hunger engaged directly with the thorny issues of the devastation caused by the Famine and the culpability of various groups, including Irish landlords and British ministers. Nonetheless, *The Great Hunger* did not receive academic acceptance within Ireland, being accused of providing inadequate context and of being over-simplistic. However, some of the criticisms made against Woodham-Smith's interpretations could also have been directed at the Edwards and Williams volume. Despite being denounced or ignored by Irish historians, *The Great Hunger* sold massively and was reprinted frequently, making it one of the best-selling history books of all time. In addition to the dislike of Woodham-Smith's interpretations, less cerebral considerations may have been at work in the academic reaction to the book, with academic historians possibly envious of its commercial success. Moreover, this publication informed a generation of people about the tragedy, and contributed to a redesignation from Great Famine to Great Hunger by those who rejected the revisionist interpretation.

Yet the publication of *The Great Hunger* marked an end, rather than a beginning, of famine research. The book had exposed the gulf between popular memory and an academic orthodoxy based on revisionism which no Irish historian seemed willing to either explain or bridge. Following the outbreak of the conflict in Northern Ireland after 1969, politics and history became even more ideologically charged as the battle for hearts and minds took on a new significance. The most gifted champion of 'new' revisionism was Foster, who defended the response of the British government to the food shortages. He also averred that the Famine was not a significant turning-point in Irish history, arguing:

> Traditionally historians used to interpret the effects of the Famine as equally cataclysmic: it was seen as a watershed in Irish history creating new conditions of demographic decline, large scale emigration, altered farming structures and new economic policies, not to mention an institutionalized Anglophobia amongst the Irish at home and abroad.
>
> As a literal analysis, this does not stand up, at least insofar as economic consequences are concerned. . . . If there is a watershed year in Irish social and economic history it is not 1846, but 1815, with the agricultural disruption following the end of the French wars.[7]

The Famine's place in Ireland's social and economic development was of less significance, therefore, than the ending of the Napoleonic Wars. Significantly also, his portrayal was subsumed in a general chapter on Ireland before and after the Famine. Moreover, by describing the Famine as a 'Malthusian apocalypse' Foster suggested that over-population was the real cause of the Famine. Malthus himself, however, had not viewed Ireland as being on the brink of demographic disaster. Furthermore, Foster ignored the fact that the most densely populated county in Ireland was County Armagh, in the north-east of the country, an area which, in a subsequent publication, he claimed 'escaped lightly'.[8]

Yet, despite having little basis in research, by the early 1980s a number of orthodoxies had emerged regarding the Great Hunger. The revisionist interpretation, in varying degrees, suggested that the Famine was inevitable, that it was not a watershed in the development of modern Ireland and that the British government had done all it could to provide relief, in the context of the time. This interpretation further strengthened the dominant revisionist approach in Irish history. By the late 1980s its domination appeared unassailable. The stranglehold of revisionism acted as

a form of invisible censor, as historians who questioned or disagreed with revisionism could be denounced as nationalists or republican sympathizers. Not surprisingly,
therefore, some of the most sustained and dynamic challenges to revisionism came
either from outside Ireland or from academics or writers outside the discipline of
history.

Brendan Bradshaw accused revisionists of not writing on the cataclysmic episodes
in Ireland's history, using the Famine as an illustration because it demonstrated
'more tellingly than any other episode of Irish history the inability of practitioners
of value-free history to cope with the catastrophic dimensions of the Irish past'.[9] He
castigated Daly's overview of the Famine for failing to engage with the unpalatable
reality of the catastrophe 'by assuming an austerely clinical tone, and by resorting to
sociological euphemism and cliometric excursi, thus cerebralising and thereby de-
sensitizing the trauma'.[10] Bradshaw's attacks on revisionism, in turn, resulted in his
being castigated (both personally and professionally) by some fellow-academics.

The 150th anniversary of the onset of potato blight demonstrated a latent interest in the Famine both in Ireland and amongst the Irish diaspora that was both unexpected and unprecedented. The coincidence of the anniversary with a paramilitary
ceasefire was also significant in promoting a new openness when discussing the
Famine. Consequently, a number of historians associated with revisionism also repo-
sitioned themselves: Mary Daly explained that '[n]ow that we are in a cease-fire
situation, we can talk about aspects of history which we may previously have felt
uncomfortable with'.[11] Official recognition was also given by the government of the
Irish Republic through the establishment of a Famine Committee to promote commemorative events and selected publications.

The sesquicentenary also resulted in a wave of publications, many of which
engaged with the awfulness of the tragedy. One of the first of this new wave of writing
concluded that

> the response of the British government to the Famine was inadequate in terms of human-
> itarian criteria and, increasingly after 1847, systematically and deliberately so . . . There
> was no shortage of resources to avoid the tragedy of a famine. Within Ireland itself,
> there were substantial resources of food which, had the political will existed, could have
> been diverted, even as a short-term measure to feed a starving people.[12]

The findings of much of the new research were closer to the interpretative analysis
of Woodham-Smith than to the positions of her critics. Local studies also demonstrated the impact of the Great Hunger on communities, families and individuals –
adding a human dimension which had sometimes been lost when mortality had been
reduced to a statistic. The peak of Famine publishing occurred between 1994 and
1997, when more books were produced than in the previous 150 years. Significantly,
many of the publications favoured an interpretation that was closer to the traditional
nationalist version than to the revisionist one. After 1997, however, 'famine-fatigue'
had allegedly set in and publishers believed that the market-place was saturated with
publications on the topic. Despite this commercial curfew some substantial Famine
books did appear, which contained fresh perspectives on the Great Hunger and
demonstrated that much remained unknown and a great deal remained to be explored
or said about the Famine.[13]

Despite the vast amount of new research after 1994, a historiographical imbalance remained. Much of the reassessment of the Famine continued to focus on the south and west of the country, whilst the tragedy's impact on the north-east was ignored. The impact on Protestants was similarly disregarded, thus the long-established view of the Famine as being an exclusively Catholic tragedy was also reaffirmed. However, MacAtasney's pioneering study of the Famine in Lurgan and Portadown, two predominantly Protestant (and also major linen-producing) towns, has demonstrated that excess mortality cut across denominations, whilst mortality in the Lurgan workhouse at the beginning of 1847 equalled that of some of the most distressed parts of the country.[14] His research further illustrates that even parts of eastern Ulster which were regarded as being industrialized and advanced experienced poverty and distress similar to that in other parts of the country.

The Irish Economy

The Irish economy in the nineteenth century was generally perceived to be impoverished and under-productive. For English politicians and economists, therefore, civilizing Ireland increasingly meant not only anglicizing and Protestantizing the population, but making it a nation of capitalists and wage-labourers. The eastern counties of Ulster, however, were regarded as an exception to this pattern. The twin evils in agricultural production were believed to be the failure of landlords, especially absentees, to invest in their estates, coupled with high dependence on the potato. Yet, by the 1840s, potatoes accounted for only 20 per cent of all agricultural output, whilst other parts of the sector were buoyant, with large amounts of corn, livestock and dairy goods being produced, mainly for export to Britain.

The decline of the Irish economy and its failure to industrialize in the early nineteenth century was blamed by nationalists on the Act of Union. The Union had brought about free trade within the United Kingdom and a gradual integration of economic institutions, with protective duties on Irish manufactured goods being removed in the 1820s. But did economic union damage or stimulate the Irish economy? For traditional nationalist writers such as George O'Brien, the decline of the Irish economy dated from the Union and the loss of an independent government.[15] The fact that O'Brien was writing in the turbulent years between the 1916 rebellion and the partition of Ireland gave him an unique perspective in Irish historiography. He presented the Irish economy in the late eighteenth century as successful, and like many nineteenth-century nationalists attributed its growth to Ireland having its own parliament (Grattan's semi-independent parliament of 1782–1800). He believed that this interpretation provided overwhelming evidence in favour of parliamentary independence at the beginning of the twentieth century. One of the main themes of O'Brien's writings was that Union deprived Ireland of her ability to develop an industrial base as she was unable to compete with the industrial might of Britain.

In 1966 Raymond Crotty laid the foundations for the revisionist view that the impact of the Act of Union and the Famine in the development of the modern Irish economy were of less importance than the agricultural crisis following 1815.[16] Rather, the years that followed the ending of the Napoleonic Wars were regarded as the watershed period in Irish economic development. Moreover, according to Crotty, the backwardness of the Irish economy prior to 1845 suggested that a Malthusian sub-sistence crisis was unavoidable, and if the potato blight had not occurred, the pop-ulation would have declined anyway. Crotty influenced the writing of a generation of Irish economic historians who gave little importance to the Famine in Ireland's development. Foster's avowedly revisionist rewriting of Irish history from the early seventeenth century similarly played down the significance of the late 1840s in Irish economic development, echoing the conclusions of Crotty twenty years earlier. Fur-thermore, the main significance of the Famine was that, as a result of the diminished population, the standard of living rose, with Irish per capita income rising more rapidly than English in the late nineteenth century. The social cost of this economic growth, however, was high: population declined rapidly after 1845 and by 1900 had fallen to approximately half of its pre-Famine level. Within both the United Kingdom and Europe, the Irish demographic decline was unique and suggests a different form of impoverishment.

The main challenge to these orthodoxies came from an American econometric his-torian.[17] By applying sophisticated econometric analysis, Joel Mokyr confirmed that between 1800 and 1845 sections of Irish society were poor (and some getting poorer) and some sectors of the Irish economy were underdeveloped, yet he concluded that a famine was not inevitable. His revised estimates of Irish national income also showed that Irish income was rising prior to 1845 and reinforced his argument that a sub-sistence crisis was not inevitable. Moreover, Mokyr denied that the Malthusian model of inevitability had any relevance to population decline in Ireland. Within Ireland, Cormac Ó Gráda, like Mokyr, applied econometric analysis to accepted orthodoxies about the Irish economy, and the Famine in particular, and thus undermined many earlier revisionist orthodoxies. In relation to the Crotty – Foster assertions that 1815 was of more significance than 1846, Ó Gráda, whilst not denying the crisis that fol-lowed the end of the wars was serious (and Europe-wide) warned that 'there is a danger of magnifying a combination of the kind of temporary dislocation that often accompanies war's end and a series of poor harvests into a secular condition'.[18] He went on to say '[t]he Famine is the main event in modern Irish history, as import-ant to Ireland as, say, the French Revolution in France or the first Industrial Revo-lution to England'.[19] A further point made by some of the new economic historians was that many criticisms of the Irish economy were culturally derived and made from the standpoint of outsiders; the ubiquitous dung-heap placed outside rural cabins, for example, shocked many visitors but provided rich manure that was part of an effi-cient agricultural cycle. Moreover, the benchmark used for judgements on the Irish economy was the British model, Britain being the self-professed workshop of the world by 1851.

The economic history of Ulster in the nineteenth century is often treated in his-toriography as being distinct from that of the rest of Ireland, especially in the post-Famine decades. The economic growth of parts of the province was remarkable: in the seventeenth century Ulster was widely regarded as the poorest province in Ireland, but by the early nineteenth century it was the most prosperous region in the country. However, the use of the geographic term Ulster is misleading as not all of the nine counties within the province developed equally and the border counties of Donegal, Cavan and Monaghan had more in common with counties such as Sligo, Queens or Roscommon than with the eastern counties of Down and Armagh.

The fact that the most industrialized part of Ireland also contained the highest proportion of non-Catholics (95 per cent of Protestants lived in Ulster) appears to support a link between Protestantism and economic performance (or as it was inverted in Ireland, the link between Catholicism and idleness). For example, Kennedy and Ollerenshaw claim that '[a]nother distinctive feature of Ulster was, and remains, the presence of a substantial Protestant population. Indeed it is difficult to exaggerate the significance of Protestant influence on the economic, social and political evolution of Ulster'.[20] The contention that industrial success was linked with Protestant superiority has been challenged by Ó Gráda, who linked economic performance with sectarianism or discrimination in the form of 'rent dissipation in the quest for privilege, reduced work effort from disadvantaged workers and entrepreneurs (to be balanced against more effort from the gainers), selective emigration, or higher transactions costs born of mutual mistrust'.[21] Little attention has been paid, either, to the fact that poverty existed within areas which were generally regarded as being doubly favoured by being both industrialized and Protestant; poverty was endemic amongst all denominations in Belfast in the nineteenth century.[22]

Land and Landlords

In the nineteenth century, the principal basis of power (and conflict) in Ireland continued to be land. The land question, therefore, is central to understanding both economic and political relations in the nineteenth century. It emerged as a political problem in the 1840s, as recognized by the groundbreaking government inquiry known as the Devon Commission (1843–5), but the Famine distorted any action that might have taken place. In the latter years of the Famine also, mass evictions and the Encumbered Estates courts purged vulnerable tenants and indebted landlords respectively. Understanding the land question helps to make the response to the Famine more comprehensible in relation to evictions of the poor and the replacement of impoverished landlords. Philip Bull's work places the cataclysmic events of the 1840s in a longer context.[23] He tries to understand the complex relationship between land and politics, especially nationalist politics in the nineteenth century. He suggests that by the end of the nineteenth century (where his research is strongest) a pattern of relationship had been forged which meant that attempts by various British governments (both Liberal and Conservative) to introduce radical reforms were wasted. Moreover, land agitation had combined with the national struggle creating mass mobilization in which landlords were an easily identifiable enemy and portrayed as a barrier against progress. Land reforms when they came, therefore, were too late. Consequently, Irish agriculture remained underdeveloped, and the anti-landlord tradition embedded. But Bull's thesis is occasionally weakened by his attempt to bolster his argument by polarizing the two sides rather than exploring the complexities of the situation. He is also weak on Ulster, where a form of tenant protection known as the Ulster Custom existed. Ulster was also the home of the early tenant-right movement, largely due to the efforts of W. S. Crawford and James McKnight. An insightful study of Ulster land tenure and social relations has been provided by Frank Wright's ultimately pessimistic view of Catholic and Protestant relations in Ulster in the eighteenth and nineteenth centuries, which still resonated in the twentieth century.[24]

The extent and significance of evictions continues to be a dividing line between revisionist and non-revisionist historians. Whilst nationalist historiography generally painted landlords as villains, revisionist accounts have remoulded them as victims. Revisionists believe that Irish landlords rarely undertook capricious evictions, but rather that they also were victims of the landholding system, especially after the Famine when rents were too low. The failure of Irish agriculture to modernize was mainly due to the resistance of tenants to change.[25] However, the low spending of landlords and the lack of investment in their estates is rarely explained or criticized in the revisionist accounts. More recent writing has taken a more nuanced approach to landlords and evictions, especially during the Famine years. The volume and callousness of the evictions perpetrated by many (but not all) landlords during the Famine has been well documented by Donnelly, who estimated that over the space of six years approximately 70,000 families were legally and permanently ejected from their homes.[26]

Much of the writing on landlords and land tenure has focused on the period between 1850 and 1914. Ideas about the relations between landlords and tenants have been dominated by the 'Solow – Vaughan thesis'. Barbara Solow and W. E. Vaughan have suggested, with varying degrees of emphasis, that the Land War, which took place intermittently after 1879, was unnecessary, achieved little for the tenants, and probably increased rather than averted evictions.[27] Vaughan's more recent research on landlords and tenants, although unsurpassed in its knowledge of sources, restates many of the arguments associated with the revisionist interpretation.[28] He asserts that after the Famine neither rents nor eviction levels can be considered to be exceptionally high in Ireland. He also suggests that, before 1870, tenant right worked well, as it was underpinned by a form of moral economy which acted as a check on the undue power of landlords. Agrarian violence, therefore, was not so much caused by landlord and tenant conflict, as by internal and intra-community feuding. He argues that rent, which everybody paid, rather than evictions, which affected far fewer people, were what defined landlord – tenant relations. Significantly, he plays down the impact on tenants of the agricultural depression of 1879–82 and the accompanying mass emigration, but for the tenants the widespread crop failure may have been a reminder of the Famine. The significance of the Land War after 1879 is similarly played down: instead Vaughan suggests that by the 1870s the discrepancy between rents and output was so great that a crisis was inevitable. Charles Parnell and Michael Davitt merely harnessed this discontent for their own political ends. In common with earlier revisionist writings, ideology is removed from Irish history and replaced with economic motives. Simply, Vaughan suggests that Irish landlords failed because they were not sufficiently capitalistic or ruthless. Landlords could have survived the Land War but they were vulnerable to economic fluctuations. Vaughan continues to contend that, given the prevailing conditions, the number of post-famine evictions was surprisingly low, averaging fewer than 500 ejectments annually. But, for areas where evictions were carried out, the local impact was devastating. The psychological impact of ejectment, especially when tied in with political grievances, was strong, and Parnell and Davitt deftly harnessed this feeling into support for the Land League. Evictions were recognized as a powerful propaganda tool by those opposed to them. A more interesting question perhaps is why Irish landlords were so generally despised even amongst those of their own class in the rest of the United Kingdom. The study of landlords, land tenure and evictions in Ireland would greatly benefit from more comparative analysis. Whilst one of the merits of revisionist writing has been to force a move away from a simplistic view of landlords as bad, and tenants as powerless victims, with little in between, writers such as Solow and Foster have reversed the polarity.

Religion

Religion in nineteenth-century Ireland was important, as a matter not just of faith but of loyalty and identity. Unlike other Western European countries where class or political affiliation increasingly cut across religious divides, in Ireland religion cut across class divides and consolidated political divisions. Much of the historiography has helped to reinforce rather than deconstruct the polarities associated with Catholicism and Protestantism. Despite the fact that approximately 80 per cent of the population was Catholic, between 1537 and 1869 the established state church was the Anglican church of Ireland. From the sixteenth century, religious conflict was a feature of Irish society. From that date also, Catholicism was equated with both Irishness and rebellion. The position of the Catholic church consolidated in the nineteenth century, accelerated by the rise of a Catholic middle class and attempts by various governments to conciliate Catholic opinion. Following the Famine, there was both a religious revival and a large church-building programme within all churches in Ireland. The massive fall in population and the rise in clergy and other religious orders reinvigorated the Catholic church in particular, whilst it moved closer to European modes of piety and structure. As Catholicism became organizationally stronger, it also became more socially conservative. The new class of peasant propri-etors which replaced the landlord class was also Catholic, thus reinforcing the hold of the church on the population and the political process. But whilst historians have engaged with the role of the churches before or after the Famine, less has been written about the churches during those years, in regard to either their response to the crisis, their engagement with other religious bodies, or their involvement with politics, notably the 1848 uprising.

Despite the pivotal role of religion and the various churches, much of the writing has been either unduly generalized or overly specialized. Much of the recent histor-iography on the Catholic church has been shaped by the pioneering works of S. J. Connolly and Emmet Larkin. The central conclusions of Connolly's work on the pre-Famine Catholic church, specifically on the unorthodox nature of religious practices in Ireland remains valid.[29] Larkin is associated with the 'devotional revolution thesis', using this phrase to explain the sudden and dramatic change in the way that popular religion was practised between 1850 and 1875. He also suggested that Paul Cullen, Archbishop of Armagh and Dublin between 1849–52 and 1852–78, was central to moving the Irish Catholic church close to both Rome and Ultramontanism, stating that:

> Cullen not only reformed the Irish Church, but, what was perhaps even more import-ant, in the process of reforming that church he spearheaded the consolidation of the devotional revolution. The great mass of the Irish people became practicing Catholics, which they have uniquely and essentially remained both at home and abroad to the present day.[30]

Other historians have moderated Larkin's claim, suggesting that the changes be viewed as part of a broader modernization of the Irish churches. Interest in the history of religion has grown since the early 1990s, yet Larkin's thesis – largely concerning the rise of organized religion and the closer links with Rome after the Famine – continues to exercise the minds of historians.[31]

Surprisingly, given the political and economic importance of both the Anglican and Presbyterian churches, relatively little has been written about them. The history of Protestant churches in Ireland has been overshadowed by the Catholic focus of many studies. Also, since the early nineteenth century, the designation 'Protestant' has been used generically to describe all non-Catholics, but generally meaning Anglicans and Presbyterians. Consequently, little consideration has been given to the distinctive development of the smaller religious bodies in Ireland, such as Methodists, Moravians, Baptists, Jews and others. Since the 1990s a number of individual studies have been produced, although the results of this research are rarely synthesized into more mainstream histories. Finlay Holmes has made the development of the Presbyterian church accessible to a non-Presbyterian readership.[32] However, his small history of the church, which covers 1642 to 1992, does not do justice to the complexity of its subject. Whilst it is insightful on the 1790s, it avoids more controversial aspects of Irish and Presbyterian history, such as the response to Catholic emancipation in 1829 and disestablishment in 1869, proselytism during the Famine, links with the Orange Order, and the attitudes of the church leaders to those who opposed unionism and partition. A similar approach is apparent in Alan Acheson's history of the Church of Ireland, which, as the state church until 1869, exerted influence disproportionate to the size of its congregation.[33] Essentially both are popular histories, and as general overviews they are useful but far from being comprehensive or definitive.

The view of Protestants as members of a faith rather than political entities has also been obfuscated by political developments: after 1850, for example, politicians tended to refer to 'Ulster Protestants', increasingly giving the impression that Protestantism in Ulster was different from that elsewhere in Ireland. In the wake of partition, this difference could be employed to justify the political division. As late as 1900, however, nobody in Irish or British politics could have foretold the partition and, when it did occur, it both surprised and disappointed pro-Union Protestants who lived outside the six severed counties. Whilst Protestants were most highly concentrated in Ulster, particularly the north-eastern counties, more recent histories tend to locate them within Ulster exclusively, rather than throughout the country where their importance in regard to economic and political matters was out of proportion to their numbers. Moreover, little has been written about the discrimination against Protestants evident in some areas such as Monaghan from the late nineteenth century and which reached a peak in the aftermath of the creation of the new Free State.

Evangelical Protestantism, rather than simply Protestantism, provided social cohesion amongst Protestants and a prism for viewing Catholicism as a false religion based on superstition and Catholics as the 'other'. The perceived superiority of their reformed church was also reinforced by political and economic factors. They could also see themselves as part of the imperial project – offering a civilizing influence in an alien and economically backward country. However, research on evangelical Protestantism, and its links with groups outside Ireland, remains limited. A general overview has been provided by David Hempton and Myrtle Hill, who have studied the complex interplay between evangelical religion and Protestant politics between 1740 and 1890.[34] Their work demonstrates that the rise in evangelicalism was often related to external factors: its growth in the 1790s was possibly in reaction to events in Ireland, but the French Revolution also offered a challenge to all organized religions within Europe. The evangelical crusade by Cooke in the 1820s also coincided with an internal challenge, as under the astute leadership of O'Connell, Irish Catholics demanded – and received – emancipation. Hempton and Hill suggest that the Great Revival after 1859 might have been a response to rapid industrialization, which accounts for its strength in the north of the country. They argue that, while evangelicalism did not create divisions within Ulster society, it was important in defining Protestant identity and cohesion amongst different classes of Protestants. Not all Protestants, however, enjoyed either the fruits of belonging to the British Empire or of religious affiliation, and the roles of disaffected, impoverished, radical or non-believing Protestants are often marginalized.

In contrast the role of Catholics in Ulster is harder to characterize. Two recent publications have addressed this question, both taking a long-term perspective on Catholic development. Oliver Rafferty regards Catholic history since 1603 as being one of continuous if intermittent oppression.[35] He concluded that Catholics in Ulster developed a sense of being under siege which gave them a strong, if erratic, sense of attachment to their church. This attachment, in turn, provided them with a distinctive identity. Rafferty's starting-point in the early seventeenth century – the period of the plantation – clearly marks an important disruption point for Catholics in the eastern counties of Ulster, but less so for Catholics who lived elsewhere in the province.

The starting-point of Marianne Elliott's social history of Ulster Catholics, which she commences in Gaelic Ireland, is that within the province of Ulster there was a distinctive Ulster Catholic tradition which separated it from the Catholic traditions developing elsewhere in Ireland.[36] From the seventeenth century she identifies a history defined by separation from and sectarianism towards their Protestant neighbours, although this is mitigated partially by numerous instances of co-operation. She suggests that since this period Ulster Catholics have been seeking an accommodation within what she frequently refers to as the British Isles. Although the approach to the subject was ambitious in its scope, she has been accused by critics of tailoring her conclusions to a post-partition mindset. In relation to the Famine, for example, she does not engage with some of the recent historiography (or primary sources) which demonstrated that the Famine had no respect for religious affiliation but killed poor Protestant and Catholic alike, whilst evangelical Protestants (who were generally middle class) used the hunger of the people in the west of Ireland as an opportunity to proselytize.[37]

Both Elliott and Rafferty agree that the development of Catholics in Ulster was distinctive from their progress elsewhere in Ireland, and therefore understate the discontinuities of the Catholic experience and the similarities with the experience of Catholics elsewhere: the Famine, for example, cut across geographical and denominational divisions; Catholics throughout Ireland supported both Catholic emancipation and home rule. Overall, the work of Elliott, Acheson and Holmes appears uncomfortable with some of the less pleasant aspects of all churches in the nineteenth century. Neither Rafferty's book nor Elliott's deals with the difference between Ulster and, after 1921, Northern Ireland, either using the terms loosely or in Rafferty's case summarily dropping the three counties of Monaghan, Donegal or Cavan following partition. Yet, if numerical superiority is what made the Catholic experience different, then only four counties fell into that category.

A small but important contribution to the historiography of religious practice in Ulster has been provided in a study of female piety in Ulster. Apart from its intrinsic interest, this work gives women a central position as practitioners, promoters and preservers of religious practices. Nor is Andrea Brozyna's study confined to any particular denomination, so similarities rather than differences can be explored. Interestingly, despite an obsession with a public display of differences between Catholic and Protestants, in reality the two had much in common. In particular, Brozyna identifies '[c]onservatism in matters concerning gender construction and understanding of gender roles'.[38] This publication is a reminder that, despite recent important work, too many publications on Irish economic and social history either continue to ignore women or treat them as appendages to the main narrative.

Some of the best writing on religion seeks to establish synergies between religion and politics, not just in Ireland but within a wider international context. Less ambitiously but just as revealing, some of the recent historiography also seeks to place Ireland in a broader British context.[39] John Wolffe is particularly interested is the interplay of religion and nationhood, although developments in Ireland are explored through an anglocentric lens. In contrast, the strength of Hempton's volume is that he frequently looks at the situation from the perspective of Ireland, although Scottish and Welsh readers might feel slightly neglected.

Emigration

Although large-scale emigration is often associated with the Famine and its aftermath, even before 1845 Ireland had one of the highest rates of emigration in Europe. Recent research demonstrates that, whilst the Famine was a watershed in emigration as in so many other things, pre-Famine (and pre-Union) emigration was important. There are some suggestions that outflow from Ireland in the seventeenth and eighteenth centuries was probably higher than after 1800, with Louis Cullen provoking a reassessment of traditional views by suggesting that migration in the 1760s and 1770s was the greatest watershed in the history of emigration.[40] At the same time, Cullen examines Europe as a destination for emigrants, rather than just the traditional transatlantic narrative. In addition, the majority of Irish emigrants were Protestant. Emigrants in the eighteenth century were more likely to be Ulster Presbyterians, who viewed themselves as Scots-Irish. Moreover, whilst North America was the favoured destination of many nineteenth century emigrants, the range of destinations was truly far-reaching. A number of recent studies have attempted to focus attention away from North America. The scale of emigration was growing after the 1830s but the Famine was clearly a trigger for the mass exodus.

Emigration, especially to North America, was a central feature of Irish life after the Famine. This was explored by Kerby Miller, whose research covered the period 1607 to 1921, with particular emphasis on the decades after 1845. During this period, an estimated seven million people emigrated to North America from Ireland. Miller concluded that Irish emigrants, in particular Catholics, regarded emigration as involuntary exile; this belief in turn shaped their experience in America where they adapted to their new life 'in ways which were often alienating and sometimes dysfunctional, albeit traditional, expedient and conducive to the survival of Irish identity and the success of Irish-American nationalism'.[41] Whilst the exile motif and the links with Irish-American nationalism might have been accepted or promoted by earlier generations of historians, Miller's contribution was that he based his conclusions on massive research, including 5,000 letters and memoirs, in addition to using poems, songs and folklore. The exploration of these non-traditional sources provided a model for using emigrants' letters as principal evidence.

The study of the Irish in South America and Africa is less advanced than that of emigrants in Britain or North America, although these and other areas are now being explored.[42] Much of the new research confirms the diversity of experience and the wide range of destinations reached by Irish emigrants, although the interest in transatlantic migration remains the most developed area of study. There is also a move away from seeing emigrants as merely victims, but also as survivors or 'winners'. However, the poverty and ill-treatment of many emigrants, who were subject to American nativism or general prejudice, meant that they probably did not regard themselves as winners. An area which remains relatively under-explored is how Irish emigrants, especially second-generation ones, reacted to other emigrants, such as Italians (many of whom were fellow-Catholics) and Jews, and to other disadvantaged groups, such as Native Americans and slaves.

The historiography of emigration from Ireland to Britain was for many years dominated by the pioneering work of Swift and Gilley.[43] Whilst their work was groundbreaking, it tended to focus on the experience of 'stereotypical' emigrants – poor, Catholic, unskilled and male. But their own recent writing and that of others is moving away from the traditional depiction. Debates regarding assimilation or 'ethnic fade', and the extent of ghettoization or integration continue, but Hickman has pleaded for a new research agenda which will break free from the segregation/assimilation model.[44] Despite the recent increase in research, emigration historiography has played down or ignored the role of women, despite the fact that (uniquely in Europe) women represented approximately half of the Irish emigrants in the nineteenth century.

Conclusion

Until the 1990s, revisionism dominated much of the writing of Ireland's nineteenth-century social and economic history. The final decade of the twentieth century witnessed an explosion in Irish historiography. The emergence of local history as a respectable field of academic study has encouraged the analysis of regional variations and this has been a feature of much Irish history in the 1990s. The control of revisionism over Irish studies has meant that many historical debates regarding Ireland in the nineteenth century are still relatively new, but the involvement of other disciplines and approaches has extended and enhanced the understanding of Ireland's social and economic development in the nineteenth century.

NOTES

1. J. S. Donnelly, *The Great Irish Potato Famine* (Stroud, 2001), p. 12.
2. R. Foster, 'We are all revisionists now', *Irish Review*, 1 (1986).
3. C. Brady, ed., *Interpreting Irish History: The Debate on Historical Revisionism 1938–1994* (Dublin, 1994).
4. R. D. Edwards and T. D. Williams, eds, *The Great Famine: Studies in Irish History, 1845–52* (Dublin, 1995); C. Woodham-Smith, *The Great Hunger: Ireland 1845–1849* (London, 1962).
5. Edwards and Williams, *Great Famine*, p. xi.
6. Brady, *Interpreting Irish History*.
7. R. Foster, *Modern Ireland, 1600–1972* (London, 1988), p. 318.
8. R. Foster, ed., *The Oxford Illustrated History of Ireland* (Oxford, 1989), p. 203.
9. Brady, *Interpreting Irish History*.
10. M. E. Daly, *The Famine in Ireland* (Dundalk, 1986).
11. Quoted in G. MacAtasney, *'This Dreadful Visitation': The Famine in Lurgan and Portadown* (Belfast, 1997), p. xv.
12. C. Kinealy, *This Great Calamity: The Irish Famine 1845–52* (Dublin, 1994), p. 359.
13. C. Ó Gráda, *Black '47 and Beyond: The Great Irish Famine in History, Economy, and Memory* (Princeton, 1999); Donnelly, *Great Irish Potato Famine*; C. Kinealy, *The Great Famine: Impact, Ideology and Rebellion* (Basingstoke, 2002).
14. MacAtasney, *'Dreadful Visitation'*, pp. 49–50.
15. G. O'Brien, *The Economic History of Ireland in the Eighteenth Century* (Dublin, 1918), pp. 398–406.
16. R. Crotty, *Irish Agricultural Production: Its Volume and Structure* (Cork, 1966).
17. J. Mokyr, *Why Ireland Starved: A Quantitative and Analytical Analysis of the Irish Economy, 1800–1859* (London, 1983).
18. C. Ó Gráda, *Ireland: A New Economic History 1780–1939* (Oxford, 1994), pp. 158–9.
19. Ó Gráda, *Ireland*, p. 173.
20. L. Kennedy and P. Ollerenshaw, *An Economic History of Ulster, 1820–1939* (Manchester, 1985).
21. Ó Gráda, *Ireland*, p. 330.
22. C. Kinealy and G. MacAtasney, *The Hidden Famine: Hunger, Poverty and Sectarianism in Belfast 1840–50* (London, 2000).
23. P. Bull, *Land, Politics and Nationalism: A Study of the Irish Land Question* (Dublin, 1996).
24. F. Wright, *Two Lands on One Soil: Ulster Politics before Home Rule* (Dublin, 1996).
25. Foster, *Modern Ireland*, pp. 408–10.
26. J. S. Donnelly, 'Mass eviction and the great famine', in C. Póirtéir, *The Great Irish Famine* (Cork, 1995).
27. B. L. Solow, *The Land Question and the Irish Economy, 1870–1903* (Cambridge, MA, 1971); W. E. Vaughan, *Landlords and Tenants in Ireland 1848–1904* (Dublin, 1984).
28. W. E. Vaughan, *Landlords and Tenants in Mid-Victorian Ireland* (Oxford, 1994).
29. S. J. Connolly, *Priests and People in Pre-Famine Ireland 1780–1845* (Dublin, 2001).
30. E. Larkin, *The Historical Dimensions of Irish Catholicism* (New York, 1981), p. 625.
31. S. J. Brown and D. W. Miller, eds, *Piety and Power in Ireland 1760–1960: Essays in Honour of Emmet Larkin* (Belfast, 1999).
32. F. Holmes, *The Presbyterian Church in Ireland: A Popular History* (Dublin, 2000).
33. A. Acheson, *A History of the Church of Ireland, 1691–1996* (Dublin, 1997).
34. D. Hempton and M. Hill, *Evangelical Protestantism in Ulster Society, 1740–1890* (London, 1992).

35. O. P. Rafferty, *Catholicism in Ulster 1603–1983: An Interpretative History* (Dublin, 1995).

36. M. Elliott, *The Catholics of Ulster: A History* (London, 2000).

37. Kinealy and MacAtasney, *Hidden Famine*, pp. 124–38.

38. A. E. Brozyna, *Labour, Love and Prayer: Female Piety in Ulster Religious Literature 1850–1914* (Belfast, 2000), p. 211.

39. J. Wolffe, *God and Greater Britain: Religion and National Life in Britain and Ireland 1843–1945* (London, 1994); D. Hempton, *Religion and Political Culture in Britain and Ireland: From the Glorious Revolution to the Decline of the Empire* (Cambridge, 1996).

40. L. Cullen, 'The Irish diaspora of the seventeenth and eighteenth centuries', in N. Canny, ed., *Europeans on the Move: Studies in European Migration 1500–1800* (Oxford, 1994).

41. K. Miller, *Emigrants and Exiles: Ireland and the Irish Exodus to North America* (Oxford, 1985), p. 4.

42. A. Bielenberg, ed., *The Irish Diaspora* (London, 2000).

43. R. Swift and S. Gilley, eds, *The Irish in Britain 1815–1939* (London, 1989) and *The Irish in the Victorian City* (London, 1985).

44. M. Hickman, 'Alternative historiographies of the Irish in Britain: a critique of the segregation/assimilation model', in R. Swift and S. Gilley, eds, *The Irish in Victorian Britain: The Local Dimension* (Dublin, 1999).

FURTHER READING

For further perspectives on the revisionist debate see C. Brady, ed., *Interpreting Irish History: The Debate on Historical Revisionism 1938–1994* (1994) and D. Ó Ceallaigh, ed., *Reconsiderations of Irish History and Culture* (1994). Famine publications which appeared after the conclusion of the publishing frenzy of 1995–7 include C. Ó Gráda, *Black '47 and Beyond: The Great Irish Famine in History, Economy, and Memory* (1999), J. S. Donnelly, *The Great Irish Potato Famine* (2001) and C. Kinealy, *The Great Famine: Impact, Ideology and Rebellion* (2002), each providing new perspectives on the Great Hunger. The prevalence of female representations in Famine literature is explored in M. Kelleher, *The Feminization of Famine: Expressions of the Inexpressible?* (1997). The activities of landlords continues to divide opinion. W. E. Vaughan, *Landlords and Tenants in Mid-Victorian Ireland* (1994) offers a generally sympathetic view of their role. Larkin's controversial devotional revolution thesis is explored in S. J. Brown and D. W. Miller, eds, *Piety and Power in Ireland 1760–1960: Essays in Honour of Emmet Larkin* (1999).

Recent studies of North American emigration have shown the diversity of experience of Irish-Americans, for example, in M. Glazier, ed., *Encyclopaedia of the Irish in America* (2000), and D. MacRaild, ed., *The Great Famine and Beyond: Irish Migrants in Britain in the Nineteenth and Twentieth Centuries* (2000), which moves away from the traditional view of emigrants in Britain as poor Catholics. M. Hickman, 'Alternative historiographies of the Irish in Britain: a critique of the segregation/assimilation model', in R. Swift and S. Gilley, eds, *The Irish in Victorian Britain: The Local Dimension* (1999) calls for a new approach to traditional emigration historiography.

CHAPTER THIRTY-ONE

Scotland

E. W. MCFARLAND

The minds of men were excited to new enterprises; a new genius, as it were, had descended upon the earth, and there was an erect and outward-looking spirit abroad that was not to be satisfied with the taciturn regularity of ancient affairs.

John Galt, Annals of the Parish, 1821

The cruelty and brutality of a city of endless streets. A city with a heart of stone and a frame of steel and iron; of ugliness and unfriendliness; of noise and clamour and dirt and garbage; an alien people streaming endlessly, unsympathetic, harsh-voiced. There was nothing soft in the city. Even in the parks the beauty of a leafy bough was imprisoned behind the iron bars of fence and paling.

James Barke, Land of the Leal, 1938

Somewhere between these two visions of hope and despair lies the making of modern Scotland. Historians have struggled to impose coherence on this sprawling century, rich in sources but giving rise to seminal questions of culture and self-image. Testament to their plight is the array of turning-points and watersheds with which they have punctuated their accounts. Was the 1832 Reform Act the beginning of the new society? – or the Disruption of 1843? Or did the Liberal crisis of 1886 mark a true defining moment? Sometimes it seems that novels, like Barke's *Land of the Leal*, rather than history texts are most at ease with the sweep of 'Scotland's century'. Yet dates are perhaps less important than the shared realization in the historiography of the speed and suddenness of change. There is also a measure of agreement on the dynamics that shaped the century: a fluctuating industrial economy, urbanization, evangelicalism, liberalism and imperialism.

Undoubtedly, historians of the nineteenth century have benefited from the growing maturity of Scottish historical writing generally from the 1970s onwards. Magisterial surveys, such as Devine's *Scottish Nation*, while reaching out to a broader public audience, have been able to draw on an impressive body of work in specialist monographs and essay collections.[1] The discipline has also been strengthened by an eagerness to look outwards, broadening the scope of comparison beyond Scotland's strong southern neighbour. This, in turn, has meant a less strident tone in asserting Scottish history as a distinctive field of study and a greater willingness to extend the scope of comparison to other social formations in Europe and beyond. The impact of linguistic and post-structuralist methodologies has been more restricted. Historiography has thus remained steadfastly within the narrative and empirical fold but, while the categories of 'class' and 'experience' tend to be invoked in an unproblematic fashion, issues of 'Scotland' and 'Scottishness' have moved into the foreground of historical debate. This is particularly true of the nineteenth century, a formative period in the emergence of a complex, yet clear, national identity.

Economy and Society

Out of choice and necessity, it was a very different nation that stood on the brink of the nineteenth century than had entered the 1707 Treaty of Union. The impact of the constitutional settlement on Scotland's future material advance has been one of the most hotly debated issues in Scottish history. The traditional view, espoused by historians of the Victorian period, was trenchantly upheld by Campbell who underlined the Union's centrality to modern Scottish economic history.[2] For Devine, however, the stress is on the 'texture' of Scottish society, including agricultural improvement and elite involvement in trade and industry. Meanwhile Whatley has refocused attention on the extent to which the Union 'shaped and overshadowed' economic, social and political life – the Union was beneficial in so far as some Scots seized on its terms and exploited them to their own advantage.[3]

Less controversial are the parameters of Scotland's industrial take-off. It was economic and social historians who led the renaissance of Scottish historical writing and the field still benefits from the solid empiricism of their pioneering studies.[4] The interpretation underpinning much of the historiography is one of 'convergence'. Industrialization and urbanization, it is argued, were British-wide forces, reducing the 'otherness' of Scottish society. Where Scotland did stand out, it is argued, was in the speed and concentration of her transformation. In contrast to England's evolutionary development, most historians agree that the trajectory of the Scottish economy in the early nineteenth century was truly dramatic. Indeed, it could be argued that Scotland underwent not one but *three* industrial revolutions. There is no shortage of statistical indicators in the secondary literature. In the first half of the century, the most dynamic sector was textiles, distinguished both by new technologies and by methods of organizing work. By 1820 there were some 120 cotton factories, concentrated in the west of Scotland, whose output value of £7 m already outstripped the country's total agricultural rental. In 1826 nine out of ten manufacturing workers were in textiles and the influence of the industry was beginning to spread beyond the central belt.

Rapidly, heavy industry was set to overtake textiles as the leading sector of the economy, thus ensuring that Scotland would soon outstrip the rest of Britain in terms of the scale of industrialization. The revolutionary triptych was formed by coal, iron and shipbuilding, with railways performing their accustomed multiplier effect. Coal production – from abundant reserves – grew from 3 m tons in 1830 to 7.4 m tons in 1851, with 76 per cent of this total produced in the west of Scotland. The next wave of economic modernization gathered momentum from strategic innovation in furnace design. The hot-blast process, by cutting production costs, gave Scottish iron the edge in British and overseas markets just as demand was set to soar. By 1840 Scotland was producing a quarter of British output, with foundries mainly located in the west-central districts of Ayrshire and Lanarkshire. Shipbuilding in turn benefited from cheap raw materials so that the Clyde could boast 66 per cent of the tonnage of British iron vessels by 1850.

The next stage in Scotland's 'economic miracle' was also courtesy of the heavy industrial sector. From mid-century the astonishing penetration of global markets began in earnest. Coal production surged from 7.4 m tons in 1854 to 14.9 m tons in 1870, mostly destined for the iron industry or for export. When pig iron production peaked in the early 1870s at a level of over 1.2 m tons, the nascent steel industry was able to compensate. Steel had close links with shipbuilding, and over the next three decades the proportion of world tonnage originating from the Clyde yards was to rise to almost one-fifth. Yet Scotland's highly integrated economy was to pay a hard price for its increasing reliance on exports in the shape of sensitivity to cyclical depressions. Shipbuilding, for example, suffered seven major cycles, averaging nine years between 1822 and 1879, with inevitable knock-on effects on related industries such as engineering.

By 1880, a more persistent decline in overseas demand coupled with a sharpening of competition, high interest rates and falling productivity encouraged far-reaching changes in the workplace. These included the increasing use of semi- and unskilled labour, standardized production systems and the introduction of semi-automatic machinery. Coal-mining, shipbuilding and engineering led the way, but smaller trades such as furniture-making and even fishing were drawn in. Recent research has revealed, however, that Clydeside employers were not necessarily more authoritarian than elsewhere in Britain, though late industrialization did mean that labour relations tended to be more 'primitive'.[5]

By the end of the century the world's second workshop was coming under pressure. Glasgow's economy was reckoned by contemporaries to be 'heavily smitten' and took a decade to recover, but the structural fault-lines in Scottish prosperity were more difficult to grasp. The extent of regional diversity is becoming increasingly apparent from the local-level studies that have flourished in recent years. Major urban centres such as Paisley, Dundee and Aberdeen continued to develop variegated industrial bases during the 1880s and 1890s, while Lowlands farming rose to the challenge of agricultural depression through flexible, high-quality production methods. Yet the Scottish economy as a whole remained seriously distorted with its overwhelming dependence on the great staple industries. For the present these remained profitable, but one small country's insistent presence in the world's markets could not continue indefinitely.

The modernization of the Scottish economy also moulded 'new Scots'. It has been estimated that a million new jobs were created by the expansion of the Victorian economy between 1841 and 1911. This in turn encouraged substantial growth in Scotland's population. It had already expanded to a figure of 2.447 million in 1831, but by 1911 it had doubled to 4.761 million. This was overwhelmingly a city population. With the exception of Poland, Scotland's urban growth rate was the highest in Europe. In 1900 the four major cities of Glasgow, Edinburgh, Aberdeen and Dundee alone accounted for one-third of the population, with the four industrial counties of the west containing an astonishing 44 per cent. This was one face of a demographic transformation, which in the nineteenth century had stripped rural parishes of their inhabitants, especially from Galloway and the south-west and from Moray to Berwick in the east.

Not all 'new Scots' were of course Scottish-born. Irish migrants had begun to claim a presence in Scottish society from the end of the previous century. They have also claimed the attention of a growing band of historians who have assisted our understanding of the contours and complexity of this population.[6] By 1841, 126,321 of Scotland's population were already of Irish birth, but famine in the middle of the decade greatly boosted migration. In 1851 more Irish migrants came to England and Wales than Scotland – 519,959 compared with 126,321 – but their impact was much greater in the Scottish case where they numbered 7.2 per cent of the population, compared with England and Wales's 2.9 per cent. The downturn in Irish agriculture in the 1870s encouraged a further wave of migration, so that by 1881 the Irish-born total in Scotland had reached 218,745 (5.9 per cent). As economic migrants they sought jobs and living space in the west of Scotland and Tayside where the first generation predominantly swelled the unskilled labour force.

Indeed, the cheapness and abundance of labour had been an essential component in Scotland's rapid industrialization. The presence of this large reserve army, however, proved a double-edged sword. Levitt and Smout's study of 1843 Poor Law data suggests that this was a low-income economy, with earnings subject to fluctuation during cyclical depressions.[7] This pattern persisted throughout the second half of the century. Rewards from the great economic boom were not evenly distributed and the gaps between employer and employee, skilled and unskilled, male and female remained sharply delineated. Data is imperfect, but although wage rates seem to have risen from the 1850s, cleavages continued to be evident according to skill levels, location and gender. It was also still the case by the mid-1880s that in key trades such as cotton, construction and shipbuilding, Scottish employees were substantially less well paid than their English counterparts – indeed it was not until 1900 that artisan wage levels began to move towards British levels. Even then, women's wages were still only 42 per cent of the male average – a baleful statistic in localities where female workers predominated. In the jute town of Dundee, for example, the resulting pressure on incomes reduced living standards by the end of the century to some of the lowest in Scotland.

When coupled with higher living costs the pattern of restricted wages generally ensured a low demand for services and consumer goods. In this sense, argues McCaffrey, heavy industry produced both a skewed economy and a skewed society.[8] Absolute poverty may have been diminishing from the 1870s, but awareness of economic disparities was sharpening. Scottish cities once impressive for their wealth and dynamism now drew comment on the scale of their social problems. Dramatically rising and fluctuating mortality in the 1830s and 1850s had given way to declining rates in the mid 1870s, but the process was slower than in England and Wales and the urban death rate remained stubbornly 45 per cent higher than the rural until the 1890s. The pattern of poor housing, poverty and squalor underpinning Scotland's economic miracle was dramatically captured in 1900 by the social campaigner John Ferguson who wrote in his polemical pamphlet, *Glasgow: The City of Progress*: 'The cities, Saturn-like, devour their offspring . . . The rural population is decreasing rapidly. Soon the supply of healthy parents from the country will be exhausted, and then the intellectual and physical decay of our noble nation must be very rapid . . .'. In the last instance, the dramatic expansion and concentration of Scotland's population must be set beside successive surges of emigration in the late nineteenth century. In recent years, the dominant thesis structuring our understanding of this movement of population has been Devine's identification of the 'paradoxes' at the heart of Scottish emigration.[9] Scotland saw a much higher proportion of her population emigrate than most European countries. Official statistics from the 1850s onwards suggest that she may have lost as much as 30.2 per cent of her natural population increase – especially to the United States – with outflows of twenty to thirty thousand per annum in the decades from 1875 to 1900. Yet, unlike other nations with high emigration rates, such as Norway and Ireland, Scotland was an established industrial, urbanized country. Moreover, the majority of emigrants were not coming from the poorer agricultural areas. Instead, by the end of the century, well over half of all emigrants on passenger lists originated from Scotland's industrial counties. The tradition of migration may have brought some positive benefits, for example, building trading links with established Scottish communities, but ultimately it must be viewed as a condemnation of the social and economic conditions left behind. The lack of protection from the succession of booms and slumps, and the limits of the Scottish Poor Law which made no provision for the able-bodied unemployed, were circumstances bound to fuel the search for 'betterment' in the new world.

Two Scotlands?

It was not only Lowlanders who left Scotland in the nineteenth century. Emigration from the northern counties, however, was driven by rather different dynamics. This example is indicative of broader methodological and conceptual issues. Historians have found it something of a challenge to treat Scotland as an integrated whole – scholarly collections still regularly contain their dedicated 'Highland chapter'. A notable exception is the integrated approach of Fraser and Morris, while Smout places the experience of Highlanders at the heart of his narrative.[10] The Highlands were exposed to similar forces to the rest of Scotland and bound into its emerging economy by internal migration, landownership and economic liberalism, yet their impact was mediated by a distinctive geography and cultural context. 'Convergence' here seems difficult to plot.

Recent commentators on the region typically begin by deconstructing their object of study.[11] Perceptions of the area, they stress, were under continuous revision from within Scotland. Prior to 1300, there was no contemporary awareness of a line dividing Scotland into Highland and Lowland regions. However, the long integration of the Highlands into the Kingdom of Scotland and later Great Britain developed alongside a sense of separateness and the growing delineation of a 'Highland problem' in terms of the poverty and 'lawlessness' of its inhabitants. Periodically in the nineteenth century, attempts were made by government to draw a 'Highland line' to regulate whisky production or limit crofting tenure. However, cultural perceptions do not easily translate into geographical boundaries. On the east coast, north of Inverness, and in southern Argyll, 'Lowlands' conditions were in evidence, with agricultural improvement and seasonal migration able to strike a balance with local resources. In the north and west a harsher terrain meant that landholding was more fragile and traditional society already open to dislocation by 1800.

The key dilemma was of how to control change, when the region's resource base was expanding more slowly than its population. Between 1801 and 1841 the population of the western seaboard of the Highlands grew by 53 per cent. In the southern and eastern areas where the increase was small, but significant, substantial single-tenant farms could be encouraged. In contrast, landed proprietors in the west, many of them clan chieftains who still shared their tenantry's Gaelic culture, had less room for manoeuvre. They responded in the form of crofting tenancies, based largely on potato culture. High prices for cattle and kelp further tempted these landlords to incur substantial debts in conspicuous consumption and speculative building schemes. By 1815 the vulnerability of the new crofting system was unmistakable. Cattle prices fell dramatically, the kelp industry collapsed and a demobilized male population returned to the Highlands. Impending bankruptcy drove some traditional proprietors, such as Mackenzie of Seaforth, from their estates, and encouraged others to consider alternatives such as clearance of the population and the rearing of sheep. By the 1830s the region was soon in crisis with the partial failure of the potato crop. Crofters increasingly met the challenge by seasonal migration, but this by no means addressed the root of the problem.

A much more serious threat was posed by the famine of 1846 whose effects persisted to the mid-1850s and beyond. By 1847 it was estimated that two-thirds of the food supply was lost. As in Ireland laissez-faire liberalism conditioned the official response, but the limited government initiatives, when combined with charitable interventions and the remittances from Highlanders overseas, were able to prevent a major mortality crisis. The longer-term impact was to replace individual relief with social engineering as clearance and emigration gained greater acceptance as solutions to the 'Highland problem'. The new emphasis was particularly attractive on estates like Ardnamurchan which were held by trustees for the creditors of the former landlords, who were obliged to treat land as an economic asset in the effort to offset debts. Richards has done much to revise the popular image of the Highlander's docility in the face of these evictions, but it is also important to remember that clearance was itself an uneven phenomenon.[12] The major clearances of the Famine years took place on the western mainland and the Hebrides, an area containing around 44 per cent of the population. Even here major evictions, involving the destruction of whole townships, was restricted to the Outer Hebrides and by 1860 had become rare.

For many Highlanders, emigration was the only course. In 1848 the *Scotsman* reported that, during the first six months of the year, 5,165 steerage passengers had left from the western Highlands for America. Yet not all were able to pay for their passage in this fashion. For this group, landlords and philanthropic bodies in the 1840s and 1850s organized programmes of assisted emigration. Between 1846 and 1856, at least 16,553 Highlanders emigrated through the Highland and Island Emigration Society, or the government's Colonial Land and Emigration Commission. These tended to be the poorer families from the areas where the Famine had left a legacy of destitution and poverty. In this way, emigration functioned as a safety valve once attempts to revive the Highland economy had failed.

In short, by the end of the nineteenth century depopulation became a major determinant of the nature of Highland society. For those who stayed behind, crofting remained a subsistence occupation, incapable of matching the aspirations of a younger generation coming into closer contact with Lowlands consumerism. Ironically, just as the old society was ebbing away, its symbols, costumes and emblems would be appropriated by Lowlanders as containing the essence of 'Scotland' in a world of change.

Religion

The embarrassment of churches found in any Scottish burgh is testament to the wealth of the Victorians who built them and to the disputative nature of their Presbyterianism. Scottish ecclesiastical history is a narrative of fragmentation, sectarian competition and disunity, but one in which there emerges a core of common beliefs that were shared by most practitioners. Indeed religious pluralism was the hallmark of a society with a strong Presbyterian identity.

The thrust of much revisionist work in the field has been to challenge the thesis that urbanization and industrialization necessarily hastened the decline of religiosity. Nineteenth-century Scotland, with its rapid and concentrated pattern of modernization, has provided a particularly useful test case for theories of secularization, as evidenced in studies by Brown and Hillis.[13] Paralleling the work of historians of British religion, these commentators have helped enlarge our understanding of the contours of religious adherence.

The established kirk was one of the main pillars of post-Union society, and had considerable practical authority in the fields of education and poor relief, but the eighteenth-century legacy was also one of repeated schisms – Burgers versus Antiburgers, Auld Licht versus New Licht. In the new century this religious kaleidoscope was suffused with a spirit of evangelism, a tendency reflected in most European churches. This was at the same time an intensely personal religion of the heart and a great crusading movement, which sought to build the Kingdom of God on earth. Both strands were present in the towering figure of Rev. Thomas Chalmers – evangelist and social reformer. The success of Chalmers' urban mission in Glasgow was revealing as to the extent of middle-class confidence in an age of transformation. The distribution of wealth might have a divine imprimatur, but it also imposed a duty of philanthropic endeavour upon the rich. The other major stronghold of evangelism in the first half of the century was the western Highlands and Islands, which were swept by successive evangelical revivals. To some extent, this was a by-product of Lowlands missionizing, but it also drew on deep indigenous roots, featuring the involvement of lay preachers – *Na Daoine* – 'the Men'. Here, by concentrating minds on individual salvation, evangelism conferred 'spiritual certainty' amidst the dislocation of clearance and resettlement.

This powerful intellectual and social force was also destined to split the established kirk asunder. During the 'Ten Years Conflict', evangelicals in the kirk had clashed with their more temporizing moderate opponents over lay rights to appoint parish ministers. A series of court cases from 1838 onwards widened the breach by raising fundamental issues concerning the supremacy of the church in spiritual matters. The General Assembly of 1843, held at St Andrew's Church in Edinburgh, provided the storm centre. After reading out his protest regarding the state's infringement of church rights, the retiring Moderator walked out followed by a mass of evangelical ministers and elders to form the 'Free Protesting Church' – later the Free Church of Scotland. Around 38 per cent of ministers and 40 per cent of members joined the new body, with congregations forming throughout Scotland. Within a year it could claim 470 new churches. With its social doctrines of self-help, integrity and individualism, it drew particular strength from crofters in the north-western Highlands, small farmers in the north-east, the lower middle classes in the major cities, and the descendants of dissenting Presbyterians in the Borders.

For Brown the 'Disruption' was 'the most spectacular event in modern Scotland'.[14] For others it holds even wider significance, heralding the beginning of the 'modern era' and sapping the strength of Presbyterianism in its later battles against secularization. Recent research, however, suggests a number of caveats. The Free church's success did weaken the claims of the established church to speak for Scotland. The church's traditional 'local government' role was also soon eroded, with the 1845 Poor Law Amendment Act transferring the parish churches' poor-relief powers to elected boards. By the early 1850s ecclesiastical influence in university affairs was also decisively curtailed, a pattern repeated in 1872 with the introduction of universal elementary education and the school-board system. However, it can also be argued that 'godly competition' for communicants actually helped the various denominations' ability to retain a foothold in the new society. The picture is an uneven one, given the nest of methodological difficulties involved, but Brown's data suggests little significant decline in church attendance in the Scottish cities between 1830 and the 1890s, although levels did fall after that date. Similarly, research by Hillis on nine Glasgow Presbyterian congregations in the mid-nineteenth century argues that while the unskilled working class was under-represented – the unfortunate 'unkirked' on whom much prayerful energy was spent – churchgoing among skilled workers remained buoyant. Indeed, in none of the Glasgow churches he studied did the working-class element fall below 55 per cent, and a considerably larger representation was evident in established-church congregations.[15] Membership of churches and their allied organizations can perhaps be interpreted more easily. Drawing on Sunday school data, for example, Brown indicates a steady rise in provision through most of the century. Church adherence in general, he argues, probably more than doubled between 1830 and 1914.[16] The churches also firmly retained control of the familiar rites of passage – baptism, marriage and burial – and were even able to reach out to potential new communicants through city missions, Bible and tract societies and revival meetings. The influence of American evangelists Moody and Sankey, who first toured Scotland in 1874, was vital in encouraging new forms of popular worship, as the metrical psalms and Scottish Paraphrases faced competition from rousing choruses on the harmonium.

Even the downturn of churchgoing towards the end of the century could not check the pervasiveness of religious values in Scottish society. The churches continued to influence public policy, either directly through their participation in inquiries such as the 1888–91 Housing Commission, or informally through the careers of men like Provost Samuel Chisholm of Glasgow. An unflinching United Presbyterian, Chisholm waged indiscriminate war during the 1890s on slum housing, barmaids and the drink trade. Furthermore, the web of Boys' Brigade companies, Youth Fellowship groups, Bands of Hope and Women's Guilds hosted by congregations of average energy had an inescapable influence on Scottish popular culture.

Participation in women's organizations, for example, encouraged a social role for Scottish women that was far from being exclusively private and passive. More generally, membership of these citadels of self-worth and mutual improvement fuelled the ethos of 'decency' – a powerful amalgam of social, economic and cultural signifiers that helped demarcate the 'rough' and 'respectable' working classes in the late nineteenth century.

Religion in Scotland also contained a more negative dynamic. Historians from the late 1980s have focused increasing attention on the incidence of sectarian conflict in the west of Scotland.[17] It was not only the Protestant churches in Scotland which retained an insistent presence in the nineteenth century – the Roman Catholic church also emerged stronger from contact with modernizing, secular forces. Before the dramatic rise in Irish migration, the Catholic population of Scotland had numbered less than 1 per cent of Scots concentrated in the southern Hebrides and the north-east Highlands. By 1833 however, it was estimated that the Western District alone, comprising Glasgow and its environs, had 44,000 Catholics. Handley's classic study suggested the church initially lacked the resources – and often the will – to deal with its new flock.[18] It was not until the late 1850s that Glasgow began to acquire the infrastructure necessary for a vigorous parish culture. The profile of Catholicism was also raised in controversial fashion by the promulgation of the doctrine of papal infallibility in 1870, followed by the restoration of the Scottish hierarchy eight years later. By the 1890s, there were 338,000 Catholics in Scotland with 244 chapels and over 180 schools.

There had existed a settled antipathy towards Catholicism in Scotland dating from the Reformation but, in the absence of a large Catholic population, this had assumed a 'theoretical' form directed at perceived threats of papal machination and unscriptural error. To this native tradition was grafted a more robust, imported strain. Although Catholicism became the dominant and distinguishing feature of the Irish community, a sizeable proportion, perhaps as many as one-third, were Protestants from the counties of Ulster. Settling in increasing numbers from mid-century, some of the community found a familiar point of contact in the Orange lodges which had created a foothold in the west of Scotland in the wake of the 1798 United Irishmen's rebellion. Despite the ambitions of its leaders, Orangeism found it difficult to shake off accusations of importing Irish party quarrels and consequently failed to penetrate the mainstream of Scottish society and politics. It did, however, provide an active goad in the 'frontier' areas of the west of Scotland, most notably the industrial settlements of Lanarkshire, where Protestant and Catholic jostled over territory and scant resources. 'Aggressive Christianity' in this form was certainly not the ideal envisaged by the douce churchmen on either side of the Disruption divide.

Politics and Identity

Issues of power, identity and mobilization have assumed considerable significance in contemporary Scotland. After a decade of historic constitutional debate, it was hardly surprising that for some commentators the political history of modern Scotland also stood in need of 'rehabilitation', if not re-writing. Scotland, it seems has not always been best served by her historians. Michael Fry has argued that her historiographical problems were rooted precisely in her status as a 'stateless nation'.[19] The paradigm of Whig history, which came to dominate during the nineteenth century, was one of democracy, peace and progress secured through British parliamentary institutions. Thus the need for a separate 'political' history for Scotland ended with the loss of her separate political status. The 'convergence' narrative with a British destiny at this point reaches its highest expression. Colin Kidd's contribution, however, is rather more subtle.[20] Individual Scots, he suggests, did not suffer marginalization in nineteenth-century historical culture, but the price paid for participation was their dismissal of most aspects of Scottish life before the Union – most notably the feudal and repressive nature of her political past. Yet the triumph of Anglo-Britishness was not complete, and left scope for 'subterranean' Scottish themes. Some historians, such as John Mackintosh, turned to cultural history, while the separateness of Scotland's religious experience meant that ecclesiastical history could even less be subsumed in the Anglo-British perspective.

Modern political historians have, therefore, had to cope with a fractured legacy. Working within a field of study that has traditionally been driven by an Anglo-British agenda, their challenge has been to understand Scotland's political history in its own terms. This is perhaps easier in the early part of the century before the 1832 Reform Act, a period of 'semi-independence' when the institutional settlement guaranteed under the Union Treaty was largely in place. W. Hamish Fraser effectively captures this volatile society.[21] Here the completeness of aristocratic hegemony meant that contradiction between economic and social dynamism and political stasis was sharply drawn. Fewer than 3,000 voters, for example, elected the 30 county members of parliament. With the burghs similarly a byword for corruption, politics were effectively 'managed' through the use of patronage. Yet the situation was ripe for dissent. The ideas of the Scottish enlightenment percolating through the universities and debating clubs encouraged rational thinking and distrust of the existing distribution of power. Meanwhile the first wave of ecclesiastical fragmentation over patronage issues encouraged suspicion of the elite and frustration with the old order – particularly among the new professional and commercial bourgeoisie in the towns. The protests, which accelerated from the 1790s, were also notable for their sophistication. Middle-class organizations, such as the Scottish Friends of the People, had epitomized 'orderly' protest with their local branch structure and network of conventions. Recurrent slumps in the Scottish economy between 1812 and 1830 drew in a broader social mix. Unprotected from economic crisis, key artisan groups initially sought a cushion in the form of trade societies, but when these failed they were willing to harness trade union organization behind more directly political objectives. The mass movement for reform which resulted was checked by the failure of the 'Radical War' of 1820 but during the rest of the decade debates continued over the nature of political economy as Britain turned increasingly to free trade.

For most mainstream surveys, however, the 'modern' political history of Scotland begins in 1832. Despite his concentration on developments among the main political parties in Scotland and on electoral politics, Hutchison's study has been particularly influential in shaping our understanding of later-nineteenth-century developments.[22] Scottish reform, he argues, adopted the principles of the English Act, but to sweeping effect, creating a new electorate of 64,000. Nevertheless, aristocratic power was far from broken, since the Scottish Act neither ended electoral malpractice, nor curtailed the influence of the propertied elite through unofficial as well as official channels. Urban elites also survived the 1830s, often by cultivating those who were likely to benefit from successive widening of the electoral process.[23] Yet the 1832 Act did mean a significant shift in power, in the sense that the governance of Scotland could no longer be the province of a single faction. By signalling that constitutional change was possible it renewed the debate on how political institutions should evolve in keeping with a dynamic society. The first fruit came in 1838 in the form of the Chartist movement in Scotland.

At first sight the historiography of Scottish Chartism is confusing. The current orthodoxy has highlighted that Scottish Chartism was identifiably 'different' from its English counterpart.[24] Commitment to the temperance crusade and the development of Chartist 'churches' marked it out, as did its willingness to build cross-class links and employ moral-force arguments. The latter stance may have reflected both the absence of a divisive measure similar to the 1834 English Poor Law and the relative lack of industrial unrest in the 1840s. While local studies suggesting significant regional differences in the degree of militancy may qualify this thesis, the strong impression remains that, despite the continuing restrictions on the working-class franchise, bitterness between the classes did not emerge after the First Reform Act. Instead both working class and middle class were united against the persistence of the aristocracy's exploitation of political privilege.

The theme of cross-class collaboration has been prominent in successive historical interpretations. When Scottish Chartism failed to revive in 1848, its legacy, it is argued, could safely be appropriated by reformers of all colours without isolating any section of society. Overwhelmingly, public debate in these decades was now to be propelled by the ecclesiastical and commercial concerns of the rising middle classes who had received the vote in 1832. The central role of religion in politics was not due to fascination with abstruse theology, but was instead the touchstone for a range of social, economic and political grievances, which could be equally cast as 'moral issues'. It was the Tories' great misfortune, however, to be in power as the Disruption unfolded, incurring the abiding wrath of the powerful new Free church lobby. Their position was further undermined by the campaign to repeal the Corn Laws, a cause which again proved highly popular in Scotland across the spectrum of political opinion.

In short, by the 1847 General Election the foundations had already been laid for the extraordinary dominance of the Scottish Liberal party who were to gain a majority of Scottish seats in every general election until 1900. Indeed, this was to be the defining feature of Scotland's political identity for the remainder of the century. Scotland's industrial economy had begun to mature and stabilize. During an era of buoyant, if volatile, economic fortunes, what motivated the worker politically was 'the desire to have equal rights with capital' – and for the moment the political system seemed receptive to this aim. In terms of leadership, it was Gladstone who ensured that the Liberal party would speak the language of 'the people' as opposed to the venial class-based interests of their aristocratic opponents.[25] As evident during his Midlothian campaign and on many other speaking tours in Scotland, the deep respect he aroused there was legendary. Liberalism's Grand Old Man was not above flattering the Scots, implying that they were capable of a higher level of political understanding and principle than the English, but above all he infused the cause with the language of mission, 'domesticating' the radicalism of former years, but successfully moulding and modernizing his own party's ideology in a period dominated by the steady democratization of the franchise through the acts of 1868 and 1884.

While tensions could arise over Whiggish Liberals' antipathy to trade-union demands, these were more than balanced by a series of unifying issues, apparently proclaiming the need for radical moral reform. Opposition to reckless and costly imperial expansion was perhaps the most dramatic of these, but working-class and middle-class Liberals also rallied, for example, around the temperance campaign to curb the liquor traffic. More variegated than a middle-class war on proletarian culture, this drew strength from the working-class values of prudence and self-respect. The campaign for state-funded education performed a similar function, leading to the foundation of a Scottish National Educational League in 1870. Education was indeed to offer a practical campaigning ground for other under-represented groups in Scottish society. The 1860s had seen demands develop from middle-class women for enhanced political participation, but while their suffrage pamphlets and petitions failed over the next thirty years, women's ambitions did find a measure of fulfilment in school-board participation and in the successful struggle to obtain access to higher education.

There seems little doubt, however, that the most energizing domestic issue in the 1870s and 1880s was land reform. This is an area that is encouraging significant new research, which has widened the focus to include the reciprocal, external linkages of Scottish radicalism. Land had the particular ability in Scotland of uniting the 'productive classes' against a parasitic aristocracy. It was clear from the fervid support given to the American land reformer Henry George on his first visit to Glasgow in 1882 that this was still a crusade close to the hearts of urban dwellers. George rapidly attained messianic status among his audiences. His book *Progress and Poverty*, selling over 100,000 copies in Britain during the 1880s, presented a picture of want in the midst of abundance that was familiar to its Scottish readers. Its 'Single Tax' platform, offered as an alternative to orthodox political economy, involved a refreshingly simple scheme for the punitive taxation of land values. This was more than mere fiscal re-adjustment, but contained a message of spiritual rebirth, heralding 'the Golden Age of which poets have sung and high-raised seers have told in metaphor!'

Influenced by George and his followers, the land campaign gathered greatest momentum in the Highlands. Here discontent had an additional practical focus in the game laws and in the precarious rights of tenant farmers. The cause could also draw strength from a rising generation of crofters whose folk memories invoked the evictions of the 1840s, while sparing them their directly demoralizing influence. It was also encouraged by the example of Irish land agitation and by the propaganda of home-grown activists such as John Murdoch, proprietor of the *Highlander* news-paper. Pushed to crisis point by the poor harvests of the early 1880s and the decline of alternatives such as herring-fishing, the response was rent strikes and public protests, including the so-called 'Battle of the Braes' in Skye in 1882. Clearly a sophis-ticated, political leadership cadre was developing in the Highlands. This was matched by the growth of a well-organized support network in the form of the Highland Land Law Reform Association whose branches linked the north with sympathizers in the Lowlands urban centres. Growing Liberal responsiveness prepared the way for the Crofter's Holding Act of 1886. Despite the initial misgivings of activists, this sig-nalled the beginning of a new era of stability in the Highlands.

Most commentators agree that 1879–80 marked the high watermark of popular Liberalism in Scotland. From this point onwards, traditional historiography has concentrated on the issue of 'decline' – questions of chronology featuring as much as competing explanations. Attention originally focused on the 1880s as the crucial decade of transition, with Liberalism debilitated by both organizational decay and internal dissent. More recently, the preference has been to highlight the early twentieth century as a point of no return. Perhaps a more appropriate question for the future historical agenda, however, is how this broad church managed to *retain* its relevance and power in an increasingly challenging climate.

The impact of the land issue pointed to some of the dangers ahead. Just as Georgite demands were impossible to resolve within the existing social and economic system, neither could they find full expression in Liberalism. For the candidate selection process in the constituencies remained dominated by more cautious counsels. It was significant that the frustration of land reformers rapidly found expression in breakaway candidatures, such as those of the Scottish Land Restoration League and 'Crofter's Party' candidates in the 1885 General Election. These independent forays set a precedent for labour interests within Scottish Liberalism who also felt marginalized in the party apparatus. The labour challenge though, was blunted by short-term factors such as the weakness of the Scottish trade-union movement and the restrictive impact of the pre-1918 franchise.[26]

More visceral was the Liberal party's remarkable ability to articulate progressive values which appeared uniquely Scottish. In this way internal feuding over the disestablishment of the Church of Scotland or Irish home rule, which accelerated during the 1880s, was not the severe handicap that might be assumed. In the case of disestablishment the struggle assumed the form of a competition between the supporters of the voluntaries and the Establishment over who was more committed to Presbyterian democracy and freedom of conscience. The political impact of home rule was undoubtedly more severe. For Whiggish elements, Gladstone's 1886 Bill was proof of the party's leftwards drift and represented a threat to the imperial markets that had underpinned Scottish prosperity. The most disillusioned elements left to form the Liberal Unionist party. The defection of large numbers of Protestant working-class voters to the new party again underlined the salience of religious issues in Scottish politics. The Liberal share of the popular vote dipped over the next few decades and the party struggled at the 1895 and 1900 elections. Yet the 'conjunctural crisis' of Irish home rule also had a positive impact. Local research is beginning to suggest how removal of the party's more cautious elements opened the way for a restatement of Liberalism's radical credo.[27] Typically, in 1891 the Scottish Liberal Association had proclaimed its support for universal male suffrage, substantial land reform, the eight-hour day and the abolition of the House of Lords. In short, Scotland may no longer have been a one-party state at the century's end, but Liberalism remained a coherent force that appeared well able to maintain its traditional heartland among crofters and skilled workers, while for the Scottish-Irish it remained the only party capable of delivering constitutional change.

Finally, one of the most contentious debates in political history has concerned Scotland's 'missing' nationalism. It was not only a self-confident nationalist historiography that was lacking during the nineteenth century. While other small, historic European nations were swept by the spirit of the *Risorgimento*, Scotland's response was the short-lived National Association for the Vindication of Scottish Rights. Established in 1853, this articulated financial grievances and campaigned against the eclipse of Scottish institutions and symbols, yet operated within a shared acceptance of Anglo-Britishness. Nor did it attract much popular support, fading quickly with the outbreak of the Crimean War.

Scotland's 'failure' here has been part of a much wider discourse unfolding from the 1970s around her 'unfinished' political identity. Most famously, Tom Nairn has characterized Scottish culture as a fragmented and deformed entity.[28] Scotland, he argues, suffers from a cultural neurosis, resulting from its cultural 'sub-nationalism'. There was nothing about the Scottish enlightenment that was explicitly 'Scottish', but instead it saddled Scotland with a British inheritance fixed by a commitment to the Union. What was left for Scots in the late Victorian period was the cultural backwater of 'kailyard' authors and tartan iconography, as they became obsessed with petty parochial concerns, yet seduced by the commercial opportunities of Union and empire.

In recent years the 'kailyard' thesis has experienced radical revision from a new generation of historians. Graeme Morton, for example, has suggested that while Scotland failed to meet the criteria for conventional bourgeois nationalism of the 'ethnic' or 'political' variety during the nineteenth century, it did exhibit an early form of modern 'civic' nationalism.[29] Post-Union Scots were forced repeatedly to reinvent their national identity in ways that did not require an independent parliament or conventional statehood – 'Highlandism' and 'tartany' was only one aspect of this. Drawing on the evidence of the voluntary structure of Scottish towns, Morton argues that during the 1860s a confident middle class also expressed their mobile identity through a web of civic institutions, some local, some referring to a Scottish context, some with a British character. From the 1880s onwards, the empire too became a focus for national self-esteem rather than self-immolation. Similarly, Richard Finlay offered an important early analysis of a distinctive *Scottish* imperial mission, finding expression in the exploits of Scottish regiments and missionaries and in the success of individual Scots as administrators, entrepreneurs and settlers, a theme also taken up by Fry.[30] The cult of 'Great Scots' functioned powerfully as a statement of continuity with a heroic past. The monuments raised in stone to Burns, Wallace and the Covenanters during the late nineteenth century were not the product of 'cultural sub-nationalism', but represented a complex sense of 'Scottishness'. This did not threaten the Union, but reminded Scots that Wallace's struggle ensured that Scotland could enter the 'imperial partnership' as an unconquered nation. Finally, this growing appreciation of the complexity of Scottish identity has also lead to a reassessment of Scottish literary and cultural history. The sentimental kailyard authors, such as J. M. Barrie, appealed to an international book-buying public rather than the home market. They were, besides, only a small part of a rich cultural scene stretching from Robert Louis Stevenson's novels to a reinvigorated Gaelic poetry tradition.

Conclusion

In the wake of devolution, Scots seem to have recovered an appetite for their past. For historians the challenge remains to offer a diet beyond the plaintive and picturesque. Once history's self-appointed 'gallant loser', the past three decades have seen Scotland's cherished mythology revisited and often actively revised. The Scotland which emerges from recent scholarship on the nineteenth century is indeed a nation scarred by social and economic upheavals, but one able nevertheless to channel and interpret change through the medium of her distinctive civil society, religious tradition and political culture.

As regards the future historical agenda, two areas stand out for development. The first is Scotland's 'exterior' history. After a long gestation period, Scotland's role in the imperial system is now beginning to engage scholars. Yet many questions here still require careful empirical work: how, for example, were Scottish empire-builders viewed by their imperial partners and by the peoples they helped rule? Complementing this, however, is a need for an 'interior' history of nineteenth-century Scots. We have advanced our understanding of their public world – their churches, parties and industries – but what of Scottish private lives? Sexuality, leisure and rites of passage are handled tentatively in existing scholarship, yet were immediate realities for Scottish men and women in the past. These too must find their historians.

NOTES

1. T. M. Devine, *The Scottish Nation 1707–2000* (Harmondsworth, 1999).
2. R. Campbell, *Scotland since 1707: The Rise of an Industrial Society* (Edinburgh, 1985).
3. Devine, *Scottish Nation*; C. A. Whatley, *Scottish Society, 1707–1830: Beyond Jacobitism towards Industrialisation* (Manchester, 2000).
4. A. Slaven, *The Development of the West of Scotland, 1750–1960* (London, 1975); S. Checkland and O. Checkland, *Industry and Ethos: Scotland, 1832–1914* (London, 1984).
5. R. Johnston, *Clydeside Capital, 1870–1920: A Social History of Employers* (E. Linton, Scotland, 2000), p. 205.
6. T. M. Devine, ed., *Irish Immigrants and Scottish Society in the Nineteenth and Twentieth Centuries* (Edinburgh, 1991).
7. I. Levitt and C. Smout, *The State of the Scottish Working Class in 1843* (Edinburgh, 1979).
8. J. F. McCaffrey, *Scotland in the Nineteenth Century* (Basingstoke, 1999), p. 85.
9. Devine, *Scottish Nation*, p. 469.
10. W. H. Fraser and R. J. Morris, eds, *People and Society in Scotland*, vol. 2, *1830–1914* (Edinburgh, 1990); T. C. Smout, *A Century of the Scottish People, 1830–1950* (London, 1987).
11. T. M. Devine, *The Great Highland Famine: Famine, Hunger and Emigration and the Scottish Highlands* (Edinburgh, 1988); E. A. Cameron, *Land for the People: British Government and the Highland Land Issue* (E. Linton, Scotland, 1996).
12. E. Richards, *The Highland Clearances* (Edinburgh, 2000).
13. C. G. Brown, *Religion and Society in Scotland since 1707* (Edinburgh, 1997); P. Hillis, 'Education and evangelisation, Presbyterian missions in mid-nineteenth century Glasgow', *Scottish Historical Review*, 66 (1988).
14. Brown, *Religion and Society*, p. 38.
15. Hillis, 'Education and evangelisation'.
16. Brown, *Religion and Society*.
17. T. Gallagher, *Glasgow: The Uneasy Peace* (Manchester, 1987).
18. J. E. Handley, *The Irish in Modern Scotland* (Cork, 1947).
19. M. Fry, 'The Whig interpretation of Scottish history', in I. Donnachie and C. Whatley, eds, *The Manufacture of Scottish History* (Edinburgh, 1992).

20. C. Kidd, *British Identities Before Nationalism: Ethnicity and Nationhood in the Atlantic World, 1600–1800* (Cambridge, 1999).

21. W. H. Fraser, *Scottish Popular Politics: From Chartism to Labour* (Edinburgh, 2000).

22. I. G. C. Hutchison, *A Political History of Scotland, 1832–1924: Parties, Elections and Issues* (Edinburgh, 1986).

23. I. Maver, *Glasgow* (Edinburgh, 2000).

24. Fraser, *Scottish Popular Politics*.

25. W. W. Knox, *Industrial Nation: Work, Culture and Society in Scotland, 1800–Present* (Edinburgh, 1999).

26. J. Smyth, *Labour in Glasgow 1896–1936* (E. Linton, Scotland, 2000).

27. C. M. M. Macdonald, *The Radical Thread: Political Change in Scotland, Paisley Politics 1885–1924* (E. Linton, Scotland, 2000).

28. T. Nairn, *The Break Up of Britain: Crisis and Neonationalism* (London, 1977).

29. G. Morton, *Unionist Nationalism: Governing Urban Scotland, 1830–60* (E. Linton, Scotland, 2000).

30. R. Finlay, 'The rise and fall of popular imperialism in Scotland, 1850–1950', *Scottish Geographical Magazine*, 113 (1997); M. Fry, *The Scottish Empire* (E. Linton, Scotland, 2001).

FURTHER READING

It is perhaps the compact nature of the object of study that has discouraged the fragmentation of modern Scottish history into competing sub-histories. This fundamental integrative approach, allied with the desire to reach a wider public beyond academia, has encouraged the production of a number of survey volumes in recent years. Of those addressing the nineteenth century directly, J. McCaffrey, *Scotland in the Nineteenth Century* (1999) tackles its subject with commendable economy. Some earlier contributions are also noteworthy. T. C. Smout, *A Century of the Scottish People, 1830–1950* (1987) remains a stylish and provocative introduction to the period. The essays in W. H. Fraser and R. J. Morris, eds, *People and Society in Scotland*, vol. 2, *1830–1914* (1990) have worn well, though many are now being overtaken by new scholarship.

The nineteenth-century experience is also covered in broader attempts at historical synthesis such as M. Lynch, *Scotland: A New History* (1991), W. W. Knox, *Industrial Nation: Work, Culture and Society in Scotland, 1800–Present* (1999) and T. M. Devine, *The Scottish Nation 1707–2000* (1999). Indeed, the latter's own 'back catalogue' deserves special mention, containing seminal material on Irish migration, the Highlands and the emigrant tradition (*The Great Highland Famine: Famine, Hunger and Emigration and the Scottish Highlands* (1988); *Irish Immigrants and Scottish Society in the Nineteenth and Twentieth Centuries* (1991)).

At the other end of the scale, the discipline has recently been enlivened by a series of local studies, which together offer an appreciation of the complexity behind some of the categories through which the century has been analysed. Representative of these are C. M. M. Macdonald, *The Radical Thread: Political Change in Scotland, Paisley Politics 1885–1924* (2000); I. Maver, *Glasgow* (2000); W. H. Fraser and C. H. Lee, eds, *Aberdeen 1800–2000: A New History* (2000); L. Miskell et al., eds, *Victorian Dundee: Images and Realities* (2000).

These are only a few of the monographs and specialist essay collections that have appeared over the past decade. The weight of contributions has tended to tilt away from economic and industrial studies, which predominated in the 1970s and 1980s, and towards attempts to understand Scotland's unique political and cultural legacy. Readers seeking an introduction to the 'pillars' of post-Union society would benefit from consulting: R. D. Anderson, *Education and the Scottish People, 1750–1918* (1995); C. G. Brown, *Religion and Society in Scotland since*

1707 (1997); E. Gordon and E. Breitenbach, eds, *The World is Ill Divided: Women's Work in Scotland in the Nineteenth and early Twentieth Centuries* (1990); C. Kidd, *British Identities Before Nationalism: Ethnicity and Nationhood in the Atlantic World, 1600–1800* (1999); G. Morton, *Unionist Nationalism: Governing Urban Scotland, 1830–60* (2000).

The *Scottish Historical Review* and the *Journal of the Social and Economic History Society of Scotland* remain the main journal sources for modern Scottish history. Finally, M. Lynch, ed., *The Oxford Companion to Scottish History* (2001) offers a valuable reference source, including biographies and key thematic essays.

CHAPTER THIRTY-TWO

Wales

MATTHEW CRAGOE

Of all the nations of the United Kingdom, Wales, in any meaningful sense, is the newest. Following the 1536 Act of Union, Wales effectively lost the trappings of nationhood, and it was only in the mid-nineteenth century that the urge for national distinctiveness was rediscovered. Even then, many contemporaries needed convincing that Wales really existed: as late as the 1880s, one Anglican bishop of St Davids could refer to Wales as 'little more than a geographical expression', whilst the *Encyclopaedia Britannica* was famously unaware of the claims of the principality to national status: 'For Wales,' it blandly advised its readers, 'see England'.

Since Wales's nationhood is of more recent origin than that of Scotland and Ireland, it is perhaps unsurprising that the study of the modern Welsh past is also a somewhat more modern preoccupation. Despite a few pioneering forays before 1939, it was only after the Second World War that historians began to reconnoitre the nineteenth century, and not until the 1960s that any systematic attention was devoted to the period. The intellectual climate of that era – with its heady call for 'history from below' – perhaps explains the populist outlook imposed on the discipline by its founding fathers. If, as Gwyn Williams complained in 1966, '[m]uch traditional Welsh history has been Welsh history with the Welsh left out', then it was clearly the business of scholars to write the 'Welsh' back into 'their' history.[1] Identifying who should be the subjects of this endeavour was not a difficult task: it was the 'ordinary' people. Williams himself, a product of industrial South Wales, viewed his professional function as being the 'people's remembrancer', and others identified just as closely with their subjects. As David Jones, son of an agricultural labourer from Montgomeryshire, made clear in his study of the Rebecca Riots: 'The riots are a part of the history of every Welsh man and woman. Until recent times we lived on the land, and the process of removal from it has been a painful one.'[2] The historian and his subjects were equal partners in this un-royal 'we': the history of Wales was to be the people's story.

Yet, though the ideological predisposition of its practitioners may offer one rationale for the outlook of modern Welsh historiography, it does not explain everything. This chapter will suggest that the 'Welsh people' on whom this history concentrates have another, more distinctive, 'nationalist' lineage, dating from the time when the Welsh 'nation' was rediscovered in the mid-1860s. As part of that process it was necessary to delineate precisely who was to be considered part of the Welsh 'nation', and who not. When twentieth-century historians set out to sketch the history of the Welsh people, they unwittingly allowed the older portrait to determine the contours of the new. As a consequence, modern interpretations of the Welsh past owe a great deal to the agendas of those involved in defining the original Welsh nation. The extent to which this focus on the history of the Welsh people – with their hybrid socialist and nationalist identity – has affected our understanding of the history of Wales, will be assessed through an examination of political and social history respectively.

The Nineteenth-Century Background

The origins of modern scholarship on Wales arguably extend back into the mid-nineteenth century when modern definitions of what 'Wales' was became current. By the late eighteenth century, 'Wales' had little meaning in a British context. The country had no distinctive political institutions (the Court of Great Sessions aside, and this was abolished in 1830), and was for all administrative purposes an extension of England. Geographically, Wales remained remote and poor, internal communications were difficult, and there was little sense of these thirteen counties sharing some indissoluble 'national' link. A distinct language, spoken chiefly by the poorer classes, was Wales's sole distinctive trait.

When contemporaries spoke of 'Wales', therefore, it was not a term with any political resonance. Instead, the word conjured up a series of romantic associations: the wild, untamed nature of the countryside; the innocent childlike nature of the people; the antiquity of the language. Wales was something that had happened long ago, in a distant romanticized past. 'Historical' accounts of Wales focused on bards, druids and Ancient Britons; the Anglican clergy, and educated aristocrats like Lady Llanover who patronized such antiquarian fantasizing, championed a view of a homogeneous, rural community which was increasingly out of step with the reality around them.[3]

During the early nineteenth century, Wales underwent a two-fold revolution. The first of these was that which marked the dividing line between modern and pre-modern Wales: industrialization. The iron industry transformed south-eastern Wales, revolutionizing trade, communications and settlement patterns: in just fifty years, the population of Merthyr underwent a six-fold increase, as the town mushroomed from about 8,000 souls in 1801 into a vast and incoherent mass of nearly 50,000 people fifty years later. The second revolution affected people across the principality. During the late eighteenth and early nineteenth centuries, many people in Wales found refuge from the neglect of the Anglican church in the ministrations of the burgeoning chapel movement. By the early nineteenth century, the Calvinistic Methodists had broken away from the Anglican church to form what would become a kind of 'triple alliance' with the Baptists and the Independents. Forged anew under the joint impress of industrialization and religious revival, the lives of ordinary people in Wales bore little resemblance to the idyllic musings of the antiquarians: the Welsh people were ripe for redefinition.

The catalyst precipitating that redefinition was, perhaps ironically, an external one. In 1846, the government appointed a royal commission to examine the state of education in the principality; mindful of the fact that the southern portion of the country had witnessed two high-profile disturbances in the previous ten years – the Chartist rising at Newport in 1839, and the Rebecca Riots which reduced west Wales to near-anarchy in 1842–3. The commissioners, also instructed to comment on the morals of the people, produced a highly critical report. The women they accused of unchastity, the men of lying and cheating, and the community as a whole of lamentable backwardness. As to causes, the Welsh language and the prevalence of dissent were singled out: these, it was claimed, deprived the people of wholesome intercourse with their (anglicized) social superiors and kept them ignorant of anything other than the religious controversies which dominated the Welsh-language press. In short, the report attacked the two essential elements in the cultural life of ordinary people in Wales: their religion and their language.

It would be too much to say that on the morning after the publication of the report, people in the principality awoke to find that they were, in some new and hitherto unsuspected way, 'Welsh'. Yet, in the twenty years after the appearance of the report, a protracted engagement by Welsh artists and thinkers with the problems raised by the commissioners helped forge a new identity for the Welsh people.[4] The scale of this redefinition, and the influence upon it of the commissioners' report, can most clearly be seen in the work of a man like Henry Richard. Richard was a notable figure in British radical circles, living in London and occupied as secretary of the Peace Society. He was also, however, a Welshman and, as a native speaker and an ordained Independent minister, was incensed at the commissioners' strictures on his countrymen. His fury found outlet in a series of letters to the *Morning Star*, an English newspaper, in which he sought to refute their worst charges.

Richard presented a view of the Welsh people diametrically opposed to that offered by the commissioners. Whereas the commissioners interpreted the prevalence of dissent and the Welsh language in a negative light, in Richard's eyes these were the very coping stones of Welsh morality and genius. The want of serious crime in the principality was attributable to the moral teachings of the chapel, whilst the flourishing Welsh-language press and eisteddfod movement were indicators of the people's strong interest in highly cultured pastimes. Far from being backward and immoral, as the commissioners suggested, the Welsh were loyal, decent, cultured and hard-working. Their shared moral sense bound them together, pastors and congregations alike, and gave them a collective identity: they were '*y werin*', something akin to the German Volk: innocent, cultured, one.

If there was villainy in Wales, it was not among the *werin* that it was to be found, insisted Richard, but among their so-called betters, the aristocracy and the clergy. The former, he argued, had become alienated from the people, abandoning the native tongue and turning their faces against the people's own religion, Nonconformity. The latter, the aristocracy's creatures, stung by the sight of empty churches and full chapels, had become the sworn enemies of the people. This alienation manifested itself in various ways. Swingeing rent rises and arbitrary eviction – particularly of any tenant who dared disobey his landlord's instructions at election time, as evidenced in Merioneth in 1859 – were represented as the daily experience of the *werin*. However, another manifestation of their alienation from the people had been the hostile testimony concerning Welsh morals and manners given to the commissioners in 1847. This proved definitively that the aristocracy and the clergy were no friends of the people: indeed, they stood against everything which defined the Welsh people. Whereas the Welsh people spoke Welsh and worshipped in the chapels, the aristocracy and clergy made a point of speaking English and worshipping in the church.

In effect, Richard's work schematized the cultural qualities of those who were to be considered members of the Welsh 'nation' (the Welsh-speaking, Nonconformists), and those who were not (the landed, Anglican aristocracy). This process of redefining what it meant to be 'Welsh' was – at an intellectual level – complete by 1867, when Richard's letters were published in a one-volume edition. And it is arguable that, in the annals of Welsh historical writing, this intellectual revolution has been a more significant turning-point than the Industrial Revolution. What has been of interest to historians ever since has, by and large, not been the history of events in the geographical region known as 'Wales', but of those events and themes which affected the 'Welsh' people. 'Welsh' history, in other words has followed the parameters laid down by Richard, and reflected a series of cultural decisions about who and what was worthy of inclusion in a history of 'Wales'.

Political History

Nowhere, perhaps, is the influence of the model of 'Wales' discussed in the previous section so clearly visible as in the field of political history. The fact that the subject receives sustained consideration only from the General Election of 1868, the first at which Richard's ideas played a part, and that attention thereafter focuses solely on the affairs of the Liberal party, which Richard had identified as the natural political home of the 'Welsh people', suggests a clear echo of the nineteenth-century arguments about who and what could properly be understood as 'Welsh'.

As in other areas of scholarship relating to the history of nineteenth-century Wales, interest in politics awoke in the 1950s and 1960s. There were some pioneering efforts in the 1930s: R. T. Jenkins produced a sketchy account of the rise of Welsh nationalism and Thomas Evans's *The Background to Modern Welsh Politics* offered interesting insights, though, as few of the great estate collections were yet open to the public, he was forced to rely largely on newspaper accounts for his primary material.[5] David Williams produced a study of the famous Chartist, John Frost, to mark the centenary of the Newport rising.[6] However, Williams stuck closely to his subject and offered only broadly contextualizing comments about the history of politics in early-nineteenth-century Wales.

It was from the late 1950s that nineteenth-century politics began to attract the attention of Welsh scholars. The fruits of this labour emerged in a succession of hugely influential articles and monographs during the 1960s which continue to provide the framework for accounts of Welsh political history today. The focus of these works, as might be expected, was 'the people', and the picture that emerged was distinctive. Popular engagement with politics had been intermittent before 1868, and had only become an all-consuming interest thereafter, fuelling the rise of the Liberal party to its late-century ascendancy in the principality.

In 1966, Gwyn Williams published the first in a succession of studies of politics in early-nineteenth-century Merthyr Tydfil. He drew a compelling portrait of a frontier urban community, 'radical from birth', staunchly republican during the

French Revolution and maintaining thereafter a radical tradition that would carry straight on into Chartism and beyond.[7] 'Politics' in Wales was, for Williams, an urban phenomenon, the property of the emergent urban working class. It involved an expression of hostility to privilege in all its forms, as the programme of the Merthyr Political Union in 1832, with its insistence that it would back only candidates willing to support the repeal of the Corn Laws, the abolition of both tithes and slavery, and the imposition of new taxes on property, indicated. By contrast, the countryside was a political wasteland during the first half of the century, characterized by the often 'grotesque concentration of landlordism'. No political action was possible here, he wrote: 'the sheer weight and penetration of deference politics pinned the people to the ground', meaning that politicization itself on the part of the people was 'something of a mass rebellion'.[8]

If Williams's account of the countryside owed something to Richard, the rest came straight from the mainstream of Marxist history. His work laid the foundation for understanding the essential background to what still registers as the culmination of one phase of political engagement by the Welsh people, the Chartist rising at Newport in 1839. After this point, however, as Williams somewhat regretfully explained, a new order imposed itself, centred around Nonconformity and respectability, a code of values at odds with the fiery independence of the industrial frontier.

The primary focus of Ieuan Gwynedd Jones's work has been the history of rural Wales. The bulk of his political essays have taken the form of constituency-based studies, notably of Merthyr, Cardiganshire and Merioneth during the 1850s and 1860s, but he also examined the considerable impact made on Welsh politics by the Liberation Society, which aimed at the disestablishment of the Anglican church. Jones argued that the years between 1850 and 1870 witnessed the birth of a new Welsh middle class in the countryside, bringing together the aristocracy of labour and the larger tenant farmers. This native elite, already powerful within the chapels as deacons and elders, now found a new sphere of activity: politics. The columns of the many newspapers that began to circulate following the repeal of the 'taxes on knowledge' in 1854 were open to them, and they were the group to whom the Liberation Society made a particular appeal. These men, 'the preacher, the college lecturer, the chapel deacons – very often men of outstanding gifts, educated and literate' – were 'in the highest sense the legislators of their times'. The famous election of 1868 saw their emergence from the shadow of landlord power: the Liberal victories at that election were 'evidence that . . . men had voted as individuals rather than, as in the past, as elements in communities taking their direction from their lord'.[9] A revolution had taken place in the Welsh countryside.

For all that Jones was interested in the formation of a middle class, there is no sense that this group acted apart from the interests of 'the people': they were *primus inter pares*, their fight was the people's fight. It is striking how, once again, the actions of the 'people' engaged on the Liberal side in politics are held to define the history of Wales; the historical experience of the elite and their supporters, for all that these people resided within in the geographical boundaries of the principality, is not accorded the same legitimacy. Indeed, the whole premise of Jones's influential work on Merioneth politics, which examined the alleged eviction of Liberal-voting tenants by Tory landlords after the 1859 election, perpetuates the Richardite notion that the elite only maintained control by oppressive means. The 'people' would naturally vote with the Liberals unless forced to do otherwise.

Jones's account of the new Liberal forces developing in Welsh society forms an essential prequel to the work of Kenneth O. Morgan, which deals with the period after 1868. It is given to few books to dominate the historiography of a period or subject as comprehensively as has *Wales in British Politics*.[10] For nearly forty years it has held sway as the standard work on politics in Victorian Wales and gone through three editions – a remarkable achievement for a monograph. Its primary focus is on the years after 1880, that period when the Liberal party turned Wales into a virtual one-party state. The early chapters trace the background, noting the growing Welsh support for Liberal radicalism, rooted in the prevailing Nonconformity of the people, and the impact of the notorious evictions in Merioneth (1859) and Carmarthenshire, Cardiganshire and Carnarvonshire (1868). These evictions fuelled the shift 'from radicalism to nationalism', which Morgan locates as occurring during the early 1880s and evolving rapidly thereafter into a demand for home rule. In the event, the nationalist moment came and went: by the late 1890s Welsh politics was concerned with a new force, socialism. Morgan's book ends with the Liberal party having achieved its long-sought goal of disestablishing the Church of England in Wales, but with its ability to maintain an ascendancy – particularly in the industrial areas – increasingly in doubt.

Morgan's account provided the kind of sustained analysis across time that the more episodic work of Gwyn Williams and Ieuan Gwynedd Jones, by its nature, could not. Its detailed interpretation of parliamentary politics, in particular, remains unchallengeable. Yet his study of post-1867 liberalism within Wales itself, like the analyses of radical Merthyr, or the unquiet countryside of Merioneth, shares a focus on the people's challenge to the authority of the Anglican and aristocratic establishment. It is clear that this is an account of how 'the people' came to control their own destiny. Discussing the great Liberal victories of 1868, for example, Morgan cautions against reading too much into the result. Most of those returned, he says, were Anglicans and landowners: 'the Welsh people remained unrepresented'.[11] It is a comment that is freighted with a series of unspoken assumptions, reminiscent of those underpinning Richard's comments considered earlier. In both cases, the 'Welsh people' are presented as the antithesis of the elite.

Perhaps the most significant counter to the model of political history set out in the 1960s has been David Howell's *Land and People in Nineteenth-Century Wales*, which offered a corrective to the prevailing view of the relationship between landlord and tenant.[12] Howell suggested that stories of ill-feeling between landlords and tenants had been greatly exaggerated by contemporary radicals, and maintained that, in general, tenants were quite happy to follow their landowner's lead at election time. And though there was evidence that this relationship broke down along a religious line in 1868, he argued that landlord pressure was not the only pressure brought to bear on tenants, there being well-documented allegations that Nonconformist ministers were 'riding' their supporters as hard as ever the landlords did. Howell's work thus posited a much more three-dimensional framework for the study of Welsh politics, offering a picture of the tenant farmer as an individual with political options – estate or chapel, with consequences attached to both. Although Howell's work has been described as being too 'pro-landlord' for the tastes of most Welsh historians, the thrust of his findings with regard to the political role of the landed estates has been supported in works on Cardiff and Carmarthenshire.[13]

Despite this, the pattern of history established by the historians of the 1960s survives in modern interpretations with very little qualification. In part, as noted earlier, the concentration on 'the people' reflects the determination of scholars in this generation to write the people back into their history, Welsh or otherwise. The current model, however, seems to go further, since it not only writes 'in' the 'people', but writes 'out' their opponents. Very little research has been done on the aristocracy and the Conservative party in Wales, despite the fact that, until the election of 1865, they routinely took a majority of seats in the principality. The omission may simply reflect the tendency of those who write history in Wales to be drawn towards the political left, but it may also be amenable to a more historiographical explanation. It is arguable that it reflects the model of the 'Welsh people' advocated by Richard in the 1860s. This model, it will be recalled not only defined what it meant to be one of the 'Welsh people' (Welsh-speaking, chapel-going, Liberal-voting), but also decreed that those that did not share those cultural qualities were not Welsh. The absence of the aristocracy and the Conservative party from the narrative of Welsh history may thus reflect not only the fact that scholars with an interest in 'the people' have another focus for their work, but that these groups are perceived, at some fundamental level, as not 'Welsh', and thus having no place in the history of 'Wales'. If this is the case, it will be the task of the next generation of Welsh historians to recognize the Richardite model for what it is – one more gambit in the ongoing politics of nineteenth-century Wales – and to revisit the political history of the principality with an aim of producing an account which balances the claims of all parties even-handedly.

Social History

If the pattern of political history suggests the possible influence of an older model of the 'Welsh people', can the same be said for social history? In fact, the range of scholarship in this area of Welsh studies is considerably more rich and varied than is true for political history. An examination of the literature available on the history of the countryside, for example, can be used to demonstrate the plurality of scholarly perspectives available. However, it will be also argued that even in the realm of social history there are areas in which the influence of the 'Welsh' model may be detected, notably in religious history. It is paradoxical that, despite the Welsh people being defined by their adherence to Nonconformity, little sustained scholarly attention has been paid to the social history of either the chapels or their leaders. This section begins, however, by examining the views of two historians who commenced their research on rural society in the 1960s: David Jones and David Howell.

David Jones became the foremost historian of crime in Wales, and, indeed, one of the leading authorities on the subject anywhere. For all that the rioters, thieves, poachers and other assorted miscreants thronging his pages hailed from the principality and were drawn from the non-aristocratic section of society, there is no sense in which his account of these people from Wales falls within the Richardite 'Welsh people' model. On the contrary. Jones's stated aim was to strip away the myths about this mythical 'nation' advocated by the likes of Richard, particularly that part of it which claimed the *werin* were crime free. Jones showed this was not true. Whilst serious offences such as murder might have been somewhat rarer in the principality than neighbouring England, there was plenty to indicate that, in other areas, they matched them blow for blow, crime for crime.

His work was primarily focused on the study of riot and disorder in the nineteenth century.[14] Perhaps the clearest statement of his interpretation of the countryside came in his examination of the Rebecca Riots.[15] His was not the first treatment of the riots but was distinctive in its tracing of the way in which the generation of Nonconformist propagandists working in the years after 1847, of which Richard was so important a part, had carefully airbrushed the picture of the recent Welsh past.[16] In contrast to their insistence that Rebecca was an isolated spasm of disorder in the history of a people otherwise peaceful and law-abiding, Jones located the riots against a background of more or less chronic crime, disorder, protest and moral policing carried out within the community itself: it was an escalation of existing patterns, but very much of its environment nonetheless. Thus, despite that veneer of respectability and orderliness which Richard attempted to draw over the countryside, Jones demonstrated how, as late as 1862, an adulterer might face the shaming ritual of a ride on the 'ceffyl pren' (the Welsh version of the skimmington ride), whilst crimes like arson and poaching remained familiar throughout the post-Rebecca generation. In Jones's hands, the familiar story of the Rebecca riots was used to illuminate the lower reaches of Welsh rural society in a new and challenging way.

Historical appreciations of the Welsh countryside were also being revolutionized by Howell's *Land and People*. Although its focus is primarily on the economic history of the countryside, its great strength is its even-handed treatment of all sections of the rural population, landlords, farmers and labourers alike. In addition, a healthy scepticism about the Richardite account of the oppression inflicted upon the *werin* by the aristocracy makes this a genuinely revisionist account of nineteenth-century Welsh society.

Howell saw rural Wales as witnessing a conflict between a landed aristocracy which – themselves anglicized – shared the English belief in agricultural improvement, and a native class of small tenant farmers with altogether different priorities. Drawing on sociological work, he argued that the economic and social outlook of the tenant classes betrayed a 'peasant mentality', and that the economic history of the Welsh countryside exemplified the problems of a peasant economy, focused on poverty, over-population and land-hunger.[17] The differences between the owners and occupiers of land did not end there, of course. The division was not simply one of economic perspective, but was coloured by linguistic and religious differences; yet Howell rejected any simple model of antagonism between the two groups and offered a clear-eyed account of how the chief parties to the agricultural compact negotiated these myriad differences.

For all that radical urban contemporaries such as Richard stressed the points of tension and breakdown in the relationship between landlord and tenant, Howell offered a more nuanced view. Particularly on the estates of the great landowners, he argued, conditions were very liberal, and there were only minor tensions over politics, personal religion or the landowners' confiscation of tenant-funded improvements to their properties. On small estates, however, the relative poverty of both landlord and tenant brought such tensions much more frequently 'to a near clash-ing point': in particular, the landowners' temptation to take advantage of the pre-vailing land-hunger and charge the highest possible rent for properties gave both parties much less leeway in difficult years.[18] On large and small estates alike, however, there was one issue on which the views of landlords and the rest of the rural com-munity really did differ, and where the power that resided in the hands of the former to enforce their own privileges caused great tension: the poaching of game. This said, Howell concluded that it was necessary to challenge much of the radicals' case against the landed classes, and to see that indictment for what it really was: a vehicle to promote the cause of the Liberal party.

Many of Howell's findings were echoed by John Davies's work on the Bute estate in and around Cardiff.[19] In particular, he showed clearly why life on the big estates might be far more comfortable for tenants, as he demonstrated the extent to which the Butes used income from non-agricultural sources to subsidize their more pater-nalistic handling of the agricultural sector – particularly the provision of new farm buildings and drainage. Evictions were rare, and tenants who paid their rents gener-ally continued to hold their properties for life. Farms, meanwhile, were never let by auction, and nor were prospective tenants vetted in terms of their politics or their religion. If farming standards remained low, Davies concluded, this was due more to the 'ancient prejudices' of the tenantry respecting the proper way to farm than to any deficiency in the management of the estate.

The social history of the countryside, therefore, provides an example of an area in which the specifically 'Welsh' model of nineteenth-century development has had little purchase: indeed, it has been ruthlessly extirpated. Other areas of social history, however, continue to suggest signs of its influence. The social history of religion is one such area. Surprisingly, given the prominence of religious adherence in Welsh social and cultural life during the nineteenth century – to men like Richard, Wales was defined by its faith: it was 'a nation of nonconformists' – this is an area of historical scholarship which is significantly underdeveloped. Whilst historians of England, Scotland and Ireland have produced sophisticated synthetic accounts of reli-gious life in their respective countries, Wales can offer little that is comparable.[20] And whereas, elsewhere, a rich monographic literature exists on many aspects of religious life, including the attitude of the working classes to matters of faith and the history of those called to minister in both churches and chapels, in Wales only fragments of the picture have yet been revealed.

These scattered works are not without importance. There is a definitive two-volume calendar of the returns from the Religious Census of 1851 and Ieuan Gwynedd Jones has produced a number of pieces examining the pattern of religious adherence in individual counties.[21] Cragoe has demonstrated that the revival of the Anglican church in Wales probably depended as much on its embrace of Welsh cultural mores as the active building programme undertaken during the Victorian period.[22] The language issue – which formed part of this cultural reorientation – has recently been the subject of a detailed exploration of the relationship of both Anglic-anism and dissent to the Welsh tongue.[23] The denominational press, meanwhile, the cornerstone of Welsh-language culture in this period, has been explored as part of a larger study of journalism in the principality.[24] There are studies both of the visual culture of Nonconformity and of the periodic religious revivals in Wales, those episodes of recurrent spiritual transfusion which maintained the life-blood of Welsh dissent.[25] Finally, key topics in which religious bodies of all persuasions had a stake have received extended treatment: the temperance movement and the history of education.[26]

Yet for all this, the subject lacks historiographical coherence, and certain areas have not been broached at all. Perhaps the most important of these is the history of the dissenting ministry in Wales. It is arguable that this neglect reflects two factors. The first may be the low ebb of scholarly interest in religious history during the 1960s and 1970s, the period when Welsh historical scholarship really took off. For left-wing historians, there were other battles to fight. More significantly, however, it might be suggested that the neglect of the Nonconformist ministers reflects another central assumption of the 'Welsh people' model preached by men like Richard. In Richard's account, the dissenting ministers were presented as typifying all the qualities possessed by the classless *werin*: they were Nonconformist, Welsh-speaking, literate and moral. They were of the people, the most representative of all their virtues. Might it be that, seen against the background of a 'Welsh people' who reflect their own qualities, the Nonconformist ministers have simply 'disappeared' from the sight of modern historians, and thus not appeared ripe for separate investigation?

The history of clergy in other parts of the United Kingdom suggests that there were in fact very real differences, educational, social and cultural, between pastors and their flocks. In England and Ireland, clergy, whether dissenting, Anglican or Catholic, seem to have come normally from the higher echelons of the communities they served – they were the sons of farmers or skilled workers rather than of labourers. The work of David Jenkins, which drew attention to real status divisions in Welsh society between those who held land and those who did not, suggests that this dynamic might have been at work in the chapels, too.[27] If dissenting clergy in Wales, like Irish priests, benefited from relationship to the 'landed' stratum of society, what of those who supported their authority in the chapels as deacons and elders: were they, too, farmers and craftsmen rather than the labourers? If so, what does this tell us about the social politics of religion in Victorian Wales, and of the agencies which enforced conformity to Nonconformity's rigorous moral tenets? And what role did the leading women in the congregation play? Questions of this sort have only recently been broached.[28]

Perhaps, as in political history, until the influence of the 'Welsh people' model is fully understood, and the inhabitants of nineteenth-century Wales are freed from the need to appear as a uniform mass, a religious history which offers a balanced view of all the forces competing in nineteenth-century society cannot be written. It is a striking irony that the best recent work on religious history in Wales deals not with the dissenting majority, but with the comparatively tiny Catholic community, a group who naturally fall outside the paradigm of the 'Welsh' model.[29] Paul O'Leary's focus on the Irish in Wales illustrates the way in which this community, though they faced periods of intense hostility, notably when large numbers arrived after the Famine, were able to develop their own range of social, cultural and religious societies and thus build a distinctive presence in the southern industrial towns. In his forensic examination of local sources, his broad-ranging engagement with the topic – so that the Catholic response to all sorts of things is considered – and, perhaps above all, his dialogue with the wider historiography of nineteenth-century social and religious history, O'Leary provides a model for other historians. At the very least, he high-lights how essential a thorough understanding of religious history is for any rounded appreciation of nineteenth-century Welsh social history.

Conclusion

In choosing to focus on the historiography of politics, the countryside and religion as vehicles through which to analyse some of the problems involved in writing the history of Wales, many important areas of recent research have been neglected. Yet these three topics are, arguably, fundamental to an understanding of the way in which the Welsh past is currently imagined. This is because they each bear a particular rel-evance to the model of 'Welsh' Wales created in the wake of the 1847 commission-ers' report and used by men like Richard. In the first place, Richard argued that the people, '*y werin*', possessed a natural cultural purity: an important device in convey-ing this was to represent them as essentially rural, an innocent Volk, unsullied by the corruption of the Industrial Revolution. Secondly, he described the way in which their virtue was informed and reinforced by their unswerving adherence to the tenets of Nonconformity, and stressed the extent to which the ministers were themselves equally members of the *werin*: leaders and led were at one. Finally, Richard had a political purpose: to de-legitimize the political opponents of the 'nation of noncon-formists', the aristocracy. What better way than by making the yardstick of political legitimacy, not the ownership of broad acres, but 'Welshness', and defining this in such a way that it would be impossible for the aristocracy to meet its requirements?

The model presented by Richard thus took a very particular stance on each of the three branches of history surveyed in this chapter: the countryside, religion and politics. And it is very striking that, of the three branches, the most comprehensive and even-handed is that field where the myths perpetuated by the nineteenth-century model have been most ruthlessly exposed, the history of the countryside. Very fine though the individual pieces of scholarship in other areas have been, it seems that until scholars working on politics and religion recognize the model for what it is, and dismantle it, there is little chance of emulating the achievement of the rural his-torians in producing an account offering breadth of coverage across the century and balance between the competing bodies under consideration. When this is done, it will be possible to argue that the 'history of Wales' does at last reflect faithfully the historical experience of the people of Wales.

NOTES

1. G. A. Williams, 'The Merthyr of Dic Penderyn', in G. Williams, ed., *Merthyr Politics: The Making of a Working-Class Tradition* (Cardiff, 1966), pp. 26–7.
2. D. J. V. Jones, *Rebecca's Children: A Study of Rural Society, Crime, and Protest* (Oxford, 1989), p. vi.
3. P. Morgan, 'The hunt for the Welsh past in the golden age', in E. Hobsbawm and T. Ranger, eds, *The Invention of Tradition* (Cambridge, 1983).

4. P. Morgan, 'Early Victorian Wales and its crisis of identity', in L. Brockliss and D. East-wood, eds, *A Union of Multiple Identities: The British Isles, c.1750–1850* (Manchester, 1997).

5. R. T. Jenkins, 'The development of nationalism in Wales', *Sociological Review*, 27 (1935); T. Evans, *The Background to Modern Welsh Politics, 1789–1846* (Cardiff, 1936).

6. D. Williams, *John Frost: A Study in Chartism* (Cardiff, 1939).

7. Williams, 'Merthyr of Dic Penderyn'.

8. G. A. Williams, *When Was Wales? A History of the Welsh* (London, 1985), pp. 198–9.

9. I. G. Jones, *Explorations and Explanations: Essays in the Social History of Victorian Wales* (Llandysul, 1981), pp. 293, 296.

10. K. O. Morgan, *Wales in British Politics, 1868–1922* (Cardiff, 1963).

11. K. O. Morgan, *Rebirth of a Nation: Wales, 1880–1980* (Oxford, 1981), p. 12.

12. D. W. Howell, *Land and People in Nineteenth-Century Wales* (London, 1977).

13. J. Davies, *Cardiff and the Marquesses of Bute* (Cardiff, 1981); M. Cragoe, *An Anglican Aristocracy: The Moral Economy of the Landed Estate in Carmarthenshire, 1832–95* (Oxford, 1996).

14. D. J. V. Jones, *Before Rebecca: Popular Protests in Wales 1793–1835* (London, 1973); *The Last Rising: The Newport Insurrection of 1839* (Oxford, 1985).

15. Jones, *Rebecca's Children*.

16. D. Williams, *The Rebecca Riots: A Study in Agrarian Discontent* (Cardiff, 1955).

17. D. Jenkins, *The Agricultural Community in South-West Wales at the Turn of the Twenti-eth Century* (Cardiff, 1971).

18. Howell, *Land and People*, p. 52.

19. Davies, *Cardiff and the Marquesses of Bute*.

20. E. T. Davies, *Religion and Society in Nineteenth Century Wales* (Llandybie, 1981).

21. I. G. Jones and D. Williams, eds, *The Religious Census of 1851: A Calendar of the Returns Relating to Wales* (Cardiff, 1976 and 1981); I. G. Jones, *Communities: Essays in the Social History of Victorian Wales* (Llandysul, 1987) and *Mid Victorian Wales: The Observers and the Observed* (Cardiff, 1992).

22. M. Cragoe, 'A question of culture: the Welsh church and the Bishopric of St Asaph, 1870', *Welsh History Review*, 18 (1996).

23. R. T. Jones, 'The church and the Welsh language in the nineteenth century', in G. H. Jenkins, ed., *The Welsh Language and its Social Domains, 1801–1911* (Cardiff, 2000).

24. A. G. Jones, *Press, Politics and Society: A History of Journalism in Wales* (Cardiff, 1993).

25. J. Harvey, *The Art of Piety: The Visual Culture of Welsh Nonconformity* (Cardiff, 1995); C. B. Turner, 'Revivalism and Welsh society in the nineteenth century', in J. Obelkevich, L. Roper and R. Samuel, eds, *Disciplines of Faith: Studies in Religion, Politics and Patriarchy* (London, 1987).

26. W. R. Lambert, *Drink and Sobriety in Victorian Wales c.1820–1895* (Cardiff, 1983); G. E. Jones, *Controls and Conflicts in Welsh Secondary Education, 1889–1944* (Cardiff, 1982); R. Smith, *Schools, Politics and Society: Elementary Education in Wales, 1870–1902* (Cardiff, 1999).

27. Jenkins, *Agricultural Community*.

28. R. Davies, *Secret Sins: Sex, Violence and Society in Carmarthenshire, 1870–1920* (Cardiff, 1996); M. Cragoe, 'Conscience or coercion? Clerical influence at the general election of 1868 in Wales', *Past and Present*, 149 (1995); I. Matthews, 'Debate: conscience or coercion? Clerical influence at the general election of 1868 in Wales', *Past and Present*, 169 (2000); M. Cragoe, 'Reply', *Past and Present*, 169 (2000).

29. P. O'Leary, *Immigration and Integration: The Irish in Wales, 1798–1922* (Cardiff, 2000).

FURTHER READING

Among the general introductions to Welsh history, G. A. Williams, *When Was Wales? A History of the Welsh* (1985) offers moments of searing insight, while J. Davies, *A History of Wales* (1993) is a stylish, reliable guide. No satisfactory history of nineteenth-century Wales yet exists, but for the later period there is no substitute for K. O. Morgan, *Rebirth of a Nation: Wales, 1880–1980* (1981).

Modern scholarship covers many subject areas beyond those included in the main essay. There is a well-established literature on urban history, with Merthyr Tydfil and Cardiff especially favoured. M. J. Daunton, *Coal Metropolis: Cardiff 1870–1914* (1977) is a text of the first importance, while A. Croll, *Civilizing the Urban: Popular Culture and Public Space in Merthyr, c.1870–1914* (2000) brings a challenging new perspective to bear. There are a number of very good monographs on the social history of Welsh industry including C. Evans, *'The Labyrinth of Flames': Work and Social Conflict in Early Industrial Merthyr Tydfil* (1993), R. M. Jones, *The North Wales Quarrymen, 1874–1922* (1981) and C. Williams, *Democratic Rhondda: Politics and Society, 1885–1951* (1996). Women's history has been opened up by A. V. John, ed., *Our Mothers' Land: Chapters in Welsh Women's History, 1830–1939* (1991) and the multi-volume social history of the Welsh language under the general editorship of G. H. Jenkins, especially *Language and Community in the Nineteenth Century* (1998) and *The Welsh Language and its Social Domains, 1801–1911* (2000), has brought sustained intellectual fire to bear on the history of nineteenth-century Wales.

CHAPTER THIRTY-THREE

British Identities

CHRIS WILLIAMS

The United Kingdom of Great Britain and Ireland came into being on 1 January 1801, following the passage of the Act of Union between Great Britain and Ireland during the preceding year. The state of Great Britain was itself of recent origin, having been created in 1707 by the Act of Union between England and Scotland. England had incorporated Wales as well following another, earlier, set of Acts of Union, in 1536 and 1543. Such 'unions' had been preceded by dynastic mergers: Henry Tudor's victory over Richard III at Bosworth Field in 1485 at least allowed the Welsh the comfort of believing that one of their own race sat upon the English throne and, following the death of Elizabeth I in 1603, the accession of James VI of Scotland as James I of England had replaced the 'Welsh' Tudor dynasty with that of the 'Scottish' Stuarts. The subsequent history of the 'British' monarchy was far from simple, as the events of the years 1649, 1688, 1715 and 1745 indicate, but it was stabilized under George III from 1760 and remains a key national institution to this day. However, the United Kingdom, as created in 1801, lasted just over one hundred and twenty years: in December 1922 Ireland was partitioned and the Irish Free State launched, leaving the United Kingdom as that of Great Britain and *Northern* Ireland. At the time of writing that eighty-year-old version of unitary state formation appears to be once more under pressure: referenda in 1997 have led to the establishment of a Scottish Parliament and a Welsh Assembly, whilst there is also an assembly in stuttering existence in Northern Ireland. Although none of these have developed into springboards for any further separatism, the possibility is no longer beyond contemplation. Devolution for at least some English regions, especially in the north, is on the political agenda, whilst the logic of membership of the European Community tends towards economic and political integration. Since the Second World War the last remnants of the once impressive British Empire have been dismantled and immigration by peoples of the former colonies has problematized previously complacent assumptions of ethnocentric (white) homogeneity. But, as the relevance of a 'British' identity to citizens of the contemporary United Kingdom has been subject to an apparently mounting set of challenges, so historians of the modern era have taken an increasing interest both in what defined and what was contained by 'Britishness'.

Approaching 'British' History

The first plea for 'British' history was made in the early 1970s by the New Zealand historian Pocock.[1] Himself somewhat melancholic at the manner in which the 'mother country', in pursuit of stronger European links, had turned its back on its former dominions, Pocock later argued that no 'true history of Britain' had ever been seriously attempted: '[i]nstead of histories of Britain, we have . . . histories of England, in which Welsh, Scots, Irish . . . appear as peripheral peoples when, and only when, their doings assume power to disturb the tenor of English politics'. Such an 'anglocentric' historiographical tradition had generated its opposite, 'anglophobic' tradition, in Wales, Scotland and Ireland. Neither tradition, Pocock suggested, was a satisfactory response to the 'plural history of a group of cultures situated along an Anglo-Celtic frontier and marked by an increasing English political and cultural domination'. British history had to be understood as interactive, interdependent, multicultural and, via the British Empire, constructed on a global stage. Although England's hegemony in this context could not be avoided, '[t]he fact of a hegemony does not alter the fact of a plurality'. In recognition of Celtic nationalist objections to the ostensibly unionist language of 'Britishness' Pocock optimistically coined the term 'the Atlantic archipelago' as a more neutral replacement. In a later essay he claimed that his approach revealed 'the ideological falseness of the claim of any state, nation, or other politically created entity to natural or historical unity', and positioned himself as both 'multinational' and 'antinational'.[2]

Although it was to be some years before Pocock's call to arms began to be heeded by historians of modern Britain, his essays continue to be the clearest and most profound statement in favour of 'British' history (the terminology of 'archipelagic' history not having caught on). Most subsequent scholars have found that, in using Pocock's ideas as a template for study, the latter have required only enhancement rather than wholesale revision. Thus Hugh Kearney, writing in the late 1980s, preferred to adopt what he termed a 'Britannic' approach, but meant by this 'the interaction of the various major cultures of the British Isles'.[3] His 'history of four nations' explicitly recognized that such national units (England, Ireland, Scotland and Wales) could themselves be dissolved into a number of distinctive cultures, and also that such cultures had the capacity to overlap national boundaries. Kearney believed that the concept of a 'national history' inevitably stressed difference: what marked one nation out from another (especially those on its borders). His 'Britannic' approach, by contrast, could more easily accommodate change over time and cultural interaction, and was capable of stressing how much the 'Britannic' cultures had in common.

Such an intellectually robust approach to British history did not sweep all before it. Kearney's single-volume survey from prehistory to the present could hardly be anything other than impressionistic, whilst less sophisticated works have somewhat crudely bolted together the separate histories of England, Ireland, Scotland and Wales and called the result British history.[4] There remained the suspicion, particularly on the so-called Celtic fringe, that this 'British' history was a Trojan horse of English history writ large, threatening the integrity of Irish, Scottish and Welsh histories that had been built up over decades through painstaking struggle against being patronized and marginalized. David Cannadine correctly drew attention to the Whiggish danger of the 'identificational teleology which merely and mindlessly claims that, at any given time, the British were actively engaged in the process of becoming more British than they ever had been before.'[5] In Norman Davies's *The Isles* one may identify a separate peril: that the historical dynamics of Irish, Scottish or Welsh identities are not subjected to the same level of deconstructive scepticism as that of 'British'.[6]

One issue on which most scholars do share a common approach is that of the nature of ideas of the nation, of nationality and of national and collective identity.[7] Many nineteenth-century scholars, writing at a time when nation-states were being formed across Europe, regarded the emergence of nations as the natural and logical outcome of centuries of human history. History was written in terms of the evolution and dispositions of 'national character' and nations were seen as fundamentally objective phenomena, based on specific essential criteria (if varying from case to case) such as language, religion, geography or 'race'. In recent decades modernist and postmodernist works have undermined many of these old certainties. Nations now tend to be seen as 'invented' or 'imagined', as manufacturing historical roots and traditions in the light of contemporary concerns or pressures.[8] What is held to constitute 'the nation' changes over time, as does any sense of a specific 'national identity'. Nations, far from being immanent in history, are historically and socially 'produced' and 'constructed', and are thus open to 'deconstruction' as well. Rather than an individual possessing a single sense of national identity, we now appreciate that each of us may have multiple, composite and overlapping identities (for example, Welsh and British, and perhaps European too). Different identities are deployed in different contexts and are thus 'situational'. For some scholars, identities are relational, generated through binary oppositions: we are defined by what we believe we are not. Others go so far as to challenge the notion of a unitary 'self' at all, suggesting that we have fragmented, multiple 'selves'. Certainly national identities have to interact along multiple axes with other identities, including those related to family, class, gender, religion, ethnic group and locality or region, all of which may have the potential to generate a sense of belonging to a wider collectivity. To a degree any given national identity is built from such identities, although they may well not be fully reconcilable. Political scientists distinguish between 'ethnic' and 'civic' forms of national belonging: the former generated by possession of certain traits (speaking a particular language, being an adherent of a particular religious faith) and the latter stemming from one's membership of a political community (being a voter, a 'citizen'), irrespective of one's broader qualities or characteristics. Gender theorists suggest that discourses of national identity often make ideological and symbolic use of women, and that women may experience national identity in fundamentally different ways from men.[9]

To be aware of the often recent, constructed origins of modern forms of national identity is not, however, to dismiss their power or relevance. One may agree with Eric Hobsbawm that 'no serious historian of nations and nationalism can be a committed political nationalist . . . [n]ationalism requires too much belief in what is patently not so', but this should not blind us to the fact that many people in the past were prepared to commit themselves thus, often to the point of sacrificing their lives.[10] Whatever the artificiality of national 'imaginings', they remain authentic facets of the human experience, and one has to be able to explain why people chose to belong to certain forms of the nation, while rejecting others. Moreover, although nationalism has often been regarded as a 'bourgeois' ideology, generated by the middle class in order to secure popular acceptance of capitalist state formations, it is necessary to appreciate that all such ideas are negotiated and contested by subordinate classes (workers, peasants) who are active in giving them new, and potentially subversive, meanings.[11] Finally, national identities are not completely 'invented' in the sense of being concocted out of thin air: they draw upon pre-existent traditions, myths, legends, beliefs and identities, even if they transform those into something fundamentally different. Any appreciation of nineteenth-century Britishness, therefore, must begin in the eighteenth century.

The Colley Thesis and its Critics

Linda Colley's *Britons: Forging the Nation 1707–1837* is a work rooted in the history of eighteenth-century Britain that nonetheless sets a powerful agenda for the study of British identities in the nineteenth century.[12] Lucidly written, stylishly illustrated, provocative and stimulating, it embodies a certain rhetorical and narrative force that invites agreement. Its impact has been profound and its stature, notwithstanding a barrage of criticisms, remains considerable.

Colley's argument is that it was in the period from the Act of Union of 1707 to the end of the Napoleonic Wars in 1815 that a powerful sense of British national identity was forged. This British identity should not be seen simply in terms of English domination imposed from the centre, nor should it be seen as replacing or suffocating other identities. Rather it was an artifice, an invention, superimposed onto those older alignments, which retained their own powers of attraction, albeit themselves shot through by regional and local attachments, and the relationship between old and new alignments was always fluid. Although Colley does not altogether discount the importance of certain *internal* homogenizing social, economic and cultural trends (the development of an advanced transport network, the success of free trade, the growth of the press and of postal communications, the rise in internal migratory movements), these were very much secondary to the generation of a sense of unity from *without*. For the twin pillars of British national identity in this period were war and Protestantism.

Britain was at war with France for much of the eighteenth and early nineteenth centuries. These wars were often global in their reach and serious in the threats they posed to the British state and empire. The French alliance with the American rebels deprived Britain of much of its first empire and although Britain was never subjected to a full-scale invasion, there were a number of invasion scares; contemporaries did not have the foreknowledge that British forces would be victorious at Trafalgar or at Waterloo. Wolfe, Nelson, Wellington all became national heroes, their images found on everything from woodcuts, fabrics and ceramics to inn signs. The Napoleonic Wars in particular allowed some British women, for the first time, a range of opportunities by which to manifest their patriotism: providing clothing, collecting money, making flags and banners, organizing committees and lobbying. Though they did so within the context of conventional separate-spheres ideology, their pro-war activism demonstrated that they also had a legitimate public role. As for British men, the same conflict witnessed an unprecedented mobilization of the lower orders in regular, militia and volunteer forces. At the height of recruitment there was close to half a million men in regular forces at home and abroad, and perhaps another half a million in territorial forces. Military training, Colley contends, was a more common working-class experience than factory work, political agitation or trade unionism. Men were drawn from all over the country, with especially high recruiting in urbanized and industrialized areas. Though possessed of no political rights, no formal stake in the status quo, Colley argues that the fact that the volunteers remained loyal to the unreformed British state indicates that it rested on a basis of consent rather than coercion: Britain remained free from civil war. Thus Colley rehabilitates a sense of British loyalism and patriotism as more than politically reactionary. E. P. Thompson's image of a potentially revolutionary nascent working class, biding its time during the Napoleonic years, is challenged: such people, Colley implies, were in the minority. Patriotism was multi-layered but also rational: it offered opportunities for profit and career advancement, for escape and excitement, for the claiming of social status, for the defence of one's homeland and family, and for advancing claims to civic and political participation.

France was not a threat just in terms of its imperial ambitions, but also in that it was the world's strongest Roman Catholic power. Since the Protestant Reformation of the sixteenth century, Colley argues, the English (and increasingly the Scots and Welsh too) defined themselves by their Protestantism. That Protestantism was at its most united when facing a Catholic challenge from without. Colley stresses the prevalence of a plebeian anti-Catholicism revealed through almanacs and popular literature such as Foxe's *Book of Martyrs* and Bunyan's *Pilgrim's Progress.* Such literature stressed the providential nature of British Protestantism and encouraged a belief that the British were God's chosen people.

Long-term war with a foreign, Catholic 'other' was accompanied by the building of a massive overseas empire, taking in more than a quarter of the world's population by the 1820s. This too contributed to a sense of British national identity. Not only did the empire provide profits and opportunities in which England's junior partners might share, but ruling over large numbers of non-white, non-Christian subject peoples generated a sense of innate British superiority, mission and values, reflected through a variety of popular cultural forms. An imperial governing class was formed that was authentically British in scope. The ranks of government and empire were opened to Scots, Welsh and Anglo-Irish, providing an arena in which national differences could be sunk in a broader imperial culture. Such elites intermarried and blended culturally, converging in wealth and lifestyles. Englishmen established landed estates in Wales and Scotland and the rise of the public schools, recruiting from across Britain, generated a common form of educational experience. Dual identities were more and more common and could be reconciled in an overarching loyalty to 'Britain'. 'British' manners and customs (such as fox-hunting) became adopted in contradistinction to continental (especially French) styles, the elite patronized domestic rather than foreign art, and (with the closure of the Continent through war after 1793) toured the mountainous districts of Britain rendered attractive by the romantic, the picturesque and the sublime. The monarchy was rehabilitated as a central part of British culture from the late eighteenth century onwards. George III was able to capitalize on the fact that he had been born and bred in Britain, and his illness in later life served to protect him from much criticism, whilst at the same time allowing for his multiple reinvention as 'Father of the People' and guarantor of British stability and prosperity. During the Napoleonic Wars royal visits and celebrations were used as a means of focusing patriotic identification in an essentially inclusive and non-partisan way.

Although Colley's chronological span continues until the accession of Queen Victoria in 1837, it is Wellington's victory over Napoleon at Waterloo in 1815 that marks the climax of her interlocking argument. Thereafter Britain was indisputably the greatest power in the world, with the largest empire. That level of security, and the fact that British Catholics had generally proved to be loyal subjects during the Napoleonic era, facilitated a subtle shift of attitude, especially within the governing class, towards the question of Catholic emancipation. Although when that came, in 1829, it was accompanied by much popular protest from ordinary Britons, toleration was growing and anti-Catholicism was less central to the definition of Britishness than it had been. During the same period there was significant popular involvement in pressing for parliamentary reform and for a moral stance on slavery: the passing of the Reform Act in 1832 and the emancipation of West Indian slaves in 1833 (following the abolition of the slave trade in 1807) facilitated a more enlightened self-image of Britain as the peaceful home of freedom and liberty, superior again in its orderly evolution to its former rival across the Channel. In Colley's formulation British national identity was in no way fixed by the long period of conflict with Catholic France: as she writes, 'most nations have always been culturally and ethnically diverse, problematic, protean and artificial constructs that take shape very quickly and come apart just as fast'.[13] What 'Britishness' means was therefore bound to change. But it is her contention that by 1815 Britain had been first defined as a nation by war, Protestantism and empire: the nation had been 'forged'.

Understandably, Colley's thesis has not gone unchallenged. Criticisms may be roughly grouped under four headings. First, she largely ignores Ireland, though there are occasional mentions of the Anglo-Irish governing class. She justifies this on the grounds that the Irish were seen by the mainland British as 'alien', largely on the basis of their Catholicism (though this does not take account of the Protestant population of Ulster) and that the Irish themselves were more resistant to being incorporated into an all-embracing British identity. The criticism remains that, given that after the Act of Union of 1800 Ireland was part of the United Kingdom, there is very little attention paid to what impact Ireland and Irishness might have had on prevailing notions of Britishness.

Secondly, it has been suggested that Colley elevates a monolithic 'Britishness' to the exclusion of any assessment of the continuing importance of other identities, particularly that of the English who enjoyed a distinctive nationalism of their own.[14] In focusing on wartime patriotism, Colley may be confusing rhetoric particular to that exceptional context with a more pervasive, deeper sense of Britishness. It is contended by some that a sense of a British identity was deployed in symbolic but very limited ways and that there was no official attempt to make Britishness the 'primary cultural identity' of British subjects: the British state was sufficiently flexible and plastic to allow a plurality of such primary identities to co-exist under its auspices.[15]

A third criticism has been that Colley exaggerates the degree of homogeneity both internally and externally. British Protestantism may have been by no means as united as the Colley thesis requires, with particular tensions within the Protestant churches of Wales and Scotland, and to argue that the French were invariably seen as 'other' underestimates the extent of Francophilia, especially amongst the British governing elite.[16]

Finally, in a detailed examination of wartime mobilization during the period 1793–1815, J. E. Cookson has taken issue with what he sees as Colley's simplistic conflation of loyalism and what he terms 'national defence patriotism'.[17] He stresses the varieties of patriotism, which could include radical and evangelical critiques of the existing order, and sees volunteering as more opportunistic and conditional and much less formative than Colley. He is also less sanguine as to the extent to which nationwide mobilization erased traditions of localism and social tensions.

For the purposes of understanding British identities in the nineteenth century Colley's work, therefore, offers a number of hypotheses rather than accepted conclusions. The argument for Britishness is an important one that should not be jettisoned easily, even, or especially, as it has become less fashionable in recent decades. In drawing attention to the importance of the forging of a (culturally) relatively homogeneous ruling elite, to the enhanced role of the monarchy, to the impressive (even if temporary) power of wartime patriotism, and to the externally generated solidarities of conflict with France, Protestantism and empire, Colley has placed a number of important themes at the heart of the debate about British identity. But at the same time there is insufficient flexibility within Colley's interpretative schema for different varieties of Britishness or pre-existent identities for us to accept her picture as wholly convincing. The idea that a highly variegated and culturally diverse, class- and status-ridden set of peoples on the cusp of industrialization would unite in attachment to a common and relatively coherent set of attitudes is not plausible. For, as much of the historical record demonstrates, the forces working for integration were frequently counterbalanced, or at least resisted, by those working for continued diversity.

Integration and Diversity

Apart from Colley, the only scholar to attempt an overarching book-length interpretation of British identity in the modern era has been Keith Robbins. His *Nineteenth-Century Britain* is a more thematic and discursive text than *Britons*, and certainly more circumspect in its conclusions.[18] Robbins starts with the premise that, while English history is central to the history of Britain, it is not synonymous with it, and he suggests that whereas the nineteenth century witnessed progressive integration between England, Scotland and Wales, this did not of itself eliminate continuing diversity. He uses the metaphor of a balanced 'blending' of English, Scots and Welsh to produce 'the British', but remains mindful of the fractured nature of those components, and of the plural character of identity. Like Colley, Robbins declines to encompass Ireland within his analysis, suggesting that the Irish could not be coerced or induced into Britishness. Unlike Colley, Robbins is more interested in those social, economic and political processes, often linked to industrialization and urbanization, that tended towards cultural homogenization. However his analysis does end with a conflict, the First World War, in which the unity of the British nation is once more being subjected to a fierce examination.

In what is an intellectual fertile text Robbins alights first upon the formation of the Victorian 'image' of Britain through, *inter alia*, landscape painting, cartography and travel writing and the steady erosion of regional differences and peculiarities in matters of diet, local fairs and holidays, and differing local time zones. Railway travel effectively 'shrank' Britain by reducing journey times between one end of the country and the other. Areas once considered inaccessible and mysterious became the familiar subjects of picture postcards as domestic tourism gathered pace. A survey of language, literature and music reveals continuing diversity within a broader uniformity. English steadily enhanced its position as the dominant British language throughout the century, but was shot through with differences of dialect and accent. It was challenged by the prevalence of Welsh across much of Wales and by Scots Gaelic in parts of the Scottish Highlands, although anglicization had significantly eroded both languages by the end of the nineteenth century, with less than half the Welsh speaking Welsh (and only 15 per cent being Welsh monoglots) by 1901, and only 5 per cent of Scots speaking Gaelic. Novelists such as Dickens reflected regional diversity and attained a British-wide popularity. Separate English, Scottish and Welsh musical traditions were linked in composition and performance.

Robbins also assesses religion, politics and sport (discussed separately below), business, education and the press. The nineteenth century witnessed the gradual development of a national retailing network, the rise of the City of London and the centralization of corporate decision-making in the capital, but at the same time neither banks nor railway companies were organized along national lines. The Scots retained their educational system and there were significant variations in the organization of Welsh schooling, but a common education system was in place across England by the end of the century. Increased working-class literacy gave the majority of the population more regular access to ideas and information. Although the provincial press flourished, the national (London) press grew in power, and was poised for a new era of dominance at the century's turn. Newspaper circulation and the postal system became capable of reaching all corners of the kingdom.

Robbins is careful not to impose a monolithic meaning on his material: different identities operated in different contexts. Contact between peoples had the potential both to heighten awareness of difference as well as to confirm integration: there was no uniform tendency operating across the board. Although the unifying bonds of Britishness were reinforced, the cultural pluralism that existed in their interstices continued to flourish. Possibly because it is more tentative, cautious, and open to different readings, Robbins's work has not attracted the same level of either approbation or criticism as Colley's. Other scholars have trod similar ground, extending and qualifying Robbins's work in the process. The next two sections investigate key dimensions of identity formation: those such as the monarchy, the political system and organized religion that involved conscious action designed to strengthen or challenge the bonds of British national identity; and those such as economic and social change and cultural practices that were, if less directed, no less significant in their longer-term impact. The remainder of the chapter addresses spheres of identity both more restricted and more expansive than that of Britishness – ideas of Englishness and of imperial identity – before examining some promising recent developments in national identity scholarship.

Loyalties in Common? Crown, Nation, Religion

The nature of popular attachment to the monarchy did not remain at the high level attained by George III in his latter years. His son George IV was much less popular, not least because of his very public and scandalous rift with his wife Caroline. William IV was hardly much more loved, and although Victoria's youth and femininity appealed, her marriage to Albert raised fears of Germanic influence at court. Albert himself did gradually overcome such prejudices, but the lengthy period of mourning entered into by Victoria after her husband's death in 1861 saw a mounting, if ultimately fragile, attachment to republican sentiments and anti-monarchical critiques. Victoria's rehabilitation in later life as Empress of India (1877) and imperial matriarch was largely successful, but it was not pre-ordained. However, during her reign, the monarchy did become more ostentatiously 'British' than ever before. While queen, Victoria is estimated to have spent seven years in Scotland (mainly at Balmoral), seven weeks in Ireland and seven nights in Wales, her children and other relatives supplementing these visits. Popular enthusiasm for the monarchy was not confined to England and, apart from the Fenians and Irish Republicans, there was little criticism of the Royal Family from a Celtic nationalist perspective. On the contrary, the Scots and Welsh in particular, but also British Catholics and Jews, placed great stress upon their loyalty to the crown. The late nineteenth century saw the elevation of the monarchy to a position above and beyond partisan conflict: the monarch became the quintessential symbol of Britishness and the conventional focus for patriotic celebration.[19]

As for patriotism, there has been considerable debate over the extent to which it was the property of the Right rather than the Left in nineteenth-century Britain. One explanation sees the radical patriotism of the eighteenth century continuing until the mid-nineteenth century when it lost momentum, the vocabulary of patriotic identification thereafter becoming much more the property of conservative politicians and ideologues.[20] This view has been challenged by other scholars who have used studies of the iconography of John Bull and of the political ideas of the radical and labour movements to qualify any such straightforward transfer of the meaning of patriotism.[21] It seems likely that, although it became harder for radicals to articulate their ideas in patriotic terms, especially from the late 1870s onwards, they did not cease to do so, and the discourse of patriotism resisted any simple appropriation by either Left or Right.

Below the level of the crown the political system remained an integrating force in British life. From the beginning of their unions Scots and Irish MPs and peers had been absorbed into Westminster and from 1801 there were 100 Irish MPs, forty-five Scots and twenty-four Welsh, alongside 489 English, a rough-and-ready approximation of the relative size of the differing electorates. The legitimacy and sovereignty of parliament was widely recognized and accepted, notwithstanding the separate legal system retained in Scotland. The political framework allowed for the representation of different interests and every voter was roughly equal, irrespective of what part of the kingdom they were from. Scottish electoral law was different, but Reform Acts were passed in both England and Wales and in Scotland in 1832. Scottish MPs and peers served in British cabinets, and politicians such as Gladstone – Scottish by descent, English by upbringing and education, married into a Welsh family and revered by Welsh liberals – appeared genuinely 'British'. Political parties organized across England, Scotland and Wales and most political issues crossed national borders, creating something of a common political culture. This is not to deny the salience of renewed senses of political Scottish and Welshness towards the end of the century, with the Scottish land agitation in the 1880s, the establishment of the Scottish Office in 1885 and the development of a close relationship between national identity and Liberalism in Wales after the 1868 General Election. Scottish and Welsh demands for 'home rule', however, were not only ultimately frustrated but also recognized, in their envisaged federalism, the continuing benefits of the British state and empire.

In the matter of religion one has to distinguish between the continuing uniting power of a militant anti-Catholic Protestantism on the one hand and the religious diversity that existed within the body of the Protestant faith on the other. Anti-Catholic sentiment was actually strengthened in the short term by the controversy over Catholic emancipation, and gained new impetus from the mid-1840s with the Maynooth agitation and with the increasing levels of Irish immigration into Britain as the potato famine bit harder.[22] The restoration of the Roman Catholic hierarchy across England and Wales sparked the 'papal aggression' crisis of 1850–1 and there were numerous anti-Irish and anti-Catholic riots in the course of the following decade. Anti-Catholic sentiment was strongest in urban Scotland, Lancashire and the West Midlands, where Irish settlement was most marked, but could be found almost anywhere, woven into popular celebrations such as Guy Fawkes' Day, arising out of clashes between evangelical 'missionaries' and the intended targets of their prose-lytism, sparked by labour-market rivalries, or mobilized as a vote-winner by the local Conservative party. Such sentiments were highly diverse and localized in their origins and motivations: this was not a 'movement', less still something officially sponsored, and increasingly it appealed to those at the bottom of the social hierarchy who thought they had most to lose from the arrival of equally poor Irish migrants. The sense in which Britain was a Protestant nation under serious threat from a foreign Catholic power steadily diminished, and explicit anti-Catholic prejudice became less and less acceptable in respectable circles. By the close of the nineteenth century it was a significant force only in Glasgow, south-west Scotland and Liverpool, its con-tribution to a sense of British national identity progressively more marginal.

The eventual decline in the salience of anti-Catholicism as a badge of British iden-tity ensured that the pluralistic, fissiparous and contentious nature of British Protest-antism gained prominence. Neither the Union of 1707 nor that of 1800 had sought to establish religious homogeneity, accepting a Presbyterian religious establishment in Scotland and the de facto popularity of Roman Catholicism in Ireland. In Wales the eighteenth-century Methodist revival and the power of the other Nonconformist churches ensured that the Anglican church's 'establishment' was both precarious and controversial. The 1851 religious census revealed the strength of Nonconformity across much of England as well as the uncomfortable fact that a substantial minor-ity of the population apparently did not attend church at all. Religious diversity was increasingly a 'British' experience, in that most denominations could be found in all parts of the island, but religion remained an important vehicle for the articulation of national identities, especially on the Celtic fringe. The Church of Ireland was dises-tablished in 1871 and considerable pressure built for the disestablishment of the Church of Wales (eventually taking force in 1920). The first specifically Welsh piece of legislation (the Welsh Sunday Closing Act of 1881) owed much to Wales's adopted self-image as a nation of Nonconformists. Religion and national character were frequently linked, but not only were they less frequently expressed in terms of 'Britishness' (there being few pressures towards British integration apart from anti-Catholicism), but even alignments with 'Welshness' or 'Scottishness' could be complicated by denominational ties that extended beyond national borders, and by schisms within denominations themselves (most notably, the disruption of the Scottish kirk in 1843). The British Isles remained 'a religious patchwork quilt of immense complexity', religion an ambivalent force in its impact on British identities.[23]

Social and Economic Change: A 'Balanced Blending'?

England was always the most populous component of the United Kingdom, but its share of the total increased from 54 per cent in 1801 to 74 per cent by 1901, substantially but not exclusively as a consequence of Ireland's demographic collapse. However, such absolute figures conceal the importance of mobility within Britain, which blurred the borders of national and ethnic identification. Substantial numbers of Irish people settled across Britain, and there was considerable migration from England into South Wales as well as much movement from country to town and from town to city within England, Scotland and Wales. It has been estimated that more than three-quarters of the population of Manchester, Bradford and Glasgow aged 20 and over in 1851 had been born elsewhere. Although the bulk of this internal migration was over relatively short distances, it nonetheless increased migrants' familiarity with parts of their homeland other than their place of birth, broadening horizons and gradually breaking down barriers. Intermarriage amongst English, Welsh and Scots, and between the English of different regions, was facilitated, especially amongst those of a Protestant faith. As for Irish Catholic immigrants, they tended to settle not in ethnically delimited 'ghettoes' but in streets and quarters that were also inhabited by the indigenous poor. Although anti-Irish prejudice and violence was common in the mid-nineteenth century, there was gradual acceptance and integration in most communities as living standards rose in the latter decades of the century. The Irish did not suffer so much from 'ethnic fade' as take their place in what was an increasingly diverse urban population. Non-Irish immigrants comprised at most about 1 per cent of the population, and being concentrated in certain ports and cities would only infrequently come to the attention of most Britons. As to their integration, much depended on their religion, race and the politics of the time: Germans and Italians tended to be relatively well received, Eastern European Jews, Chinese and black people less so. 'Integration' was not, of course, the same as assimilation: few such immigrants would have either seen themselves as British or been regarded as such by contemporaries. Explicit and widespread engagement with notions of multiculturalism would have to wait until the closing years of the twentieth century.

If demographic change and migration probably enhanced a sense of a common identity, it is less clear that industrialization did so. Most certainly, the Industrial Revolution was a British phenomenon. Polycentric, it took place in South Wales, central Scotland and Ulster as well as in the north of England and the Midlands. Britain steadily became a more integrated single market, with agricultural goods being transported over long distances to serve growing urban centres and combat local famines. But at the same time the image of industrialization progressively integrating regional economies into a single national economy is too simplistic. Historical geographers and economic historians have argued for an increasing differentiation between regions, at least up to the mid-nineteenth century.[24] Industrial regions generated their own regional labour and capital markets and transport networks, based upon the expansion of the canal system. Towns and cities such as Manchester, Birmingham, Newcastle and Sheffield became foci of economic growth and of regional identities. Many social protest movements from Luddism to Chartism had a marked regional character, as did most early trade unions and the Anti-Corn Law League. Only with the coming of the railways did long-term processes of integration become dominant. But regions themselves were fluid entities, not always contained by national borders or county boundaries. Thus industrialization in Glamorgan and Monmouthshire drew upon the rural hinterland not only of Wales but also of Gloucestershire, Somerset and Herefordshire, and upon the industrial and commercial capacities of Bristol. Industrialization in Flint and Denbighshire owed much more to the magnetic pull of Merseyside and Manchester than to any Welsh or North Welsh economy.

In the realm of social interaction, aside from war, sport offers one of the clearest indications of popular allegiances.[25] It is widely recognized as an important cultural domain for the articulation of feelings of belonging and difference and can play a crucial role in defining nationhood. Success in sport may be used for the assertion of claims of national or ethnic difference and of 'innate' characteristics. In nineteenth-century Britain sport became an important marker of national difference and a key vehicle for the parading of national pride, especially in terms of the 'four nations' of England, Ireland, Scotland and Wales. Towards the end of the century in Scotland association football, and in Wales rugby union, came to function as surrogate nationalisms, as means of expressing one's identity *vis-à-vis* the otherwise dominant English, the first England–Scotland soccer international taking place in 1872, and the first England–Wales rugby international in 1881. However, the fact that such sports were played with the English, and under a common code of 'decency', 'fair play' and 'sportsmanship', ensured that they were part of a common if competitive culture. Even cricket, which tends to be viewed as quintessentially English, was popular in both Wales and Scotland, although the relative strength of the game in England inhibited the development of any 'four nations' framework. By contrast, the 'root and branch' rejection of British sports by Irish cultural nationalists in the form of the Gaelic Athletic Association (from 1884) was a stark repudiation of any shared culture and an attempt to demarcate difference through sport. Nonetheless, many 'British' sports such as association and rugby football, athletics, tennis and hunting remained popular in Ireland.

Sport did not generate solely 'four nations' identifications. The pattern of popularity of association and rugby football tended to be highly region-specific, with strong elements of North–South rivalry in England paralleled by differing approaches to the question of professionalism. Even in the railway age, distance and the expense of travel inhibited all-England forums for sporting participation, and there was no such framework until after the end of the century in the two most widespread winter games of rugby and soccer. Domestic national rivalries could, additionally, co-exist with British sporting unities, as in rugby union with the British Lions touring team from 1888. A study of sport is extremely effective in revealing the layered, multiple nature of local, regional, national and supra-national identities circulating in nineteenth-century Britain.

Englishness

In discussing 'Britishness' one is inevitably faced with the problem of demarcating it from a sense of 'Englishness'. For Englishness was at the core of Britishness, even if it was not synonymous with it. It is very difficult to think of any 'British' trait that was not also considered to be an English one, very difficult to separate out Britishness from the political, economic and cultural hegemony of England. Much of what, for contemporaries, constituted the essence of Englishness – representative government, the sovereignty of parliament, political stability and the avoidance (in recent times at least) of violent revolution, freedoms of speech, religion and trade, a claim on an historic 'liberty', a confidence in 'progress' – was also at the heart of Britishness.

Work on the evolution of an English 'character' from the late seventeenth century through to the mid-nineteenth century has nevertheless identified certain cultural values that were not necessarily transferable to England's Celtic partners.[26] The English were held to be sincere, honest and decent, candid and frank if reserved, energetic and enterprising if eccentric, self-disciplined and dedicated to honest endeavour and honourable ambitions. The Englishman (and it was very much a masculine concept) was independent, individualistic, proud and self-reliant. Such characteristics were embodied in the manners and mores of the reformed public schools from the mid-century on, institutions which, along with the universities, inculcated a common code of 'gentlemanly' behaviour. It has been argued that, by the 1860s, as right-wing patriotic and imperial rhetoric gathered momentum, and as the status quo came under threat from both within (reform) and without (economic and imperial rivalry) this 'Englishness' was under stress: that two opposing models – one conservative, ethnocentric and chauvinistic, based on custom, tradition and prejudice, the other rational and liberal, based on notions of justice – were threatening to pull it apart.[27] Such a view has been countered by work which stresses the universalist and civilizational (rather than ethnocentric) nature of English self-imagery.[28]

The significance of cultural definitions of English identity is that they were purely cultural. 'English nationalism' is a misnomer for there was no nationalist movement, not even much of an interest in marking St George's Day or in flying his flag. Given the highly variable nature of the historical boundaries of the English state, and the hybridity of the occupants of the English throne, English qualities had always had to survive independent of the state structures of the day. By the late nineteenth century this culture was, however, becoming institutionalized.[29] The English language received an official imprimatur with the establishment of the *New English Dictionary* (later the *Oxford English Dictionary*); English history would be codified in the form of the *Dictionary of National Biography*; the idea of a canon of English literature, bearing English values, gathered support, scholars and students. All these developments were part of a process of national self-definition that enshrined the middle and upper classes as the bearers of national values, and invited England's Celtic partners to the party only in so far as they learnt the same rules and played the same game, either disposing of their cultural traditions or subsuming them within this refashioned Englishness. And whilst such an Englishness undoubtedly contained the potential to be bold, industrial, commercial and forward-looking, it appears that in the late nineteenth century it retreated behind a comforting myth of rural nostalgia.[30] England came to be defined not by the manufacturing powerhouses of the North, nor even by the commercial and financial vigour of the world's greatest city, but rather by the pastoral imagery of the rural South. English architecture, art, literature and music celebrated a society that was itself vanishing under the pressures of urbanization and agricultural modernization. Such an ideal did not need to confront the problems of American and German economic rivalry, but could take comfort in the organic continuities, harmonies and tranquillities of a timeless countryside.

An Imperial Identity

Although Colley's work on the eighteenth and early nineteenth centuries posits the significance of the empire to the forging of a sense of Britishness, both in terms of the widespread encounters with the non-white, non-Christian 'other' and in terms of the opportunities imperial expansion offered to England's junior partners in the United Kingdom, most work on imperial identities has concentrated on the last three decades of the nineteenth century, the age of the 'new imperialism' and the 'Scramble for Africa'. This is not to deny the relevance of empire for the earlier period, but it is to recognize that it was in the late-Victorian years that empire was inscribed most forcibly in British culture and politics. There is now a substantial array of texts that deal with imperialism and everything from education and music hall to sport and ideas of the natural world, from popular journalism and juvenile literature to military adventures and missionary activity (and missionary positions). Imperial signification was found in advertising imagery and marketing slogans, on cigarette cards and postcards, in youth organizations and in the vocabulary of popular speech, in museums and school textbooks. The most symbolic imperial occasions of this time were the Golden Jubilee of 1887, the Diamond Jubilee of 1897, Victoria's funeral in 1901 and the subsequent coronation of Edward VII. These spawned imperial paraphernalia including commemorative mugs and plates, toys and games, medals and banners, trinket boxes and scent bottles. One did not have to be a 'jingo' or a rabid imperialist to be affected and impressed by the constant reminders that one was at the centre of a global empire, and one did not have to be English either. Enthusiasm for and participation, real or vicarious, in the adventure of empire was as likely to appeal to the Scottish, Welsh or even Irish as it was to the English. The Scots and Irish were particularly prominent as emigrants, administrators and soldiers and overseas national differences were more likely to be blurred by a common identification as British. An imperial identity worked to strengthen ties between the constituent nations of the United Kingdom and to generate a sense of British national superiority and pride. No other people could forge its identity on such a worldwide scale, or could believe that its law, its wealth, its military might, its political stability, its particular brand of Christianity, were so worthy of export.[31]

An awareness of the power of popular imperialism in the late nineteenth century is not enough for some post-colonial historians. They have registered unease at the way in which explicitly 'British' history has remade Britain as a 'falsely homogeneous whole', the '*a priori* body upon which empire is inscribed' rather than as a part of the very discourse of empire-making itself. Britain, they allege, may only be understood as part of its own empire.[32] As yet, such assertion has not been sufficiently substantiated by scholarship for this to be taken much further, and one might legitimately prefer to see an imperial identity as available to but not always adopted by nineteenth-century Britons. It is not axiomatic that empire constructed national identity rather than projecting it onto a global stage, and one should certainly resist any attempt to reduce the diversity of imperial experiences to a single meaning. Furthermore, post-colonial perspectives tend to prioritize the dependent territories of the non-white empire in discussions of imperial ideology, whereas the primary conception of empire, at least from the metropolitan 'core', was probably one which saw it first and foremost as a family of English-speaking 'dominions', largely settled by the British themselves. Such territories not only shared a common language, but many core political and cultural values, extending to forms of religious observance and sporting competition.[33]

New Approaches

Some of the most fruitful work on British identities to have emerged in recent years has attempted to explore the meanings given to such identities by ordinary people. Stephanie Barczewski's study of the nineteenth-century elaborations of the legends of King Arthur and Robin Hood reveals the limitations to the cultural penetration of Britishness when confronted by a voracious, confident Englishness.[34] It draws on histories, novels, poetry, plays, ballads, operas, costumery, the iconography of paintings, stained-glass panels, decorative textiles and statuary, the naming of inns, ships, racehorses and friendly societies, and the development of tourism in Tintagel, Glastonbury and Nottinghamshire in a profoundly impressive engagement with the multi-layered nature of cultural meanings. The two legends were inserted, not without tension, into an explicitly English understanding of the national past which worked to exclude the other constituent parts of the United Kingdom. Whereas Robin Hood could easily enough be presented as a heroic Saxon freedom-fighter struggling against Norman oppression, Arthur (a Celt) had to undergo a more complex reconfiguration, with the contrast being drawn between the Arthur of history (British chieftain) and the Arthur of legend (King of England). This explicitly 'English' interpretation of the legends was itself riven by conflict, with the Arthurian legend's conservatism challenged by the implicit radicalism and egalitarianism of (a usually still loyal) Robin Hood, sometimes deployed in Luddite and anti-imperialist critiques. Barczewski's claim that her work reveals the dominance of 'Englishness' over 'Britishness' is insufficiently alive to the situationally varied nature of any such hierarchy, but nevertheless convincingly demonstrates that neither form of identity represented a single, coherent set of values and ideals.

If Barczewski tends to 'read off' popular beliefs from the forms taken by a range of texts, Morgan's investigation of the expression of national identities by nineteenth-century (mainly early- and mid-Victorian) travellers (in their writings) takes us much closer to individual perceptions of who they were and to which collective community they belonged.[35] It was when away from home, encountering new people and places, that individual and collective identities were most often thrown into sharp relief. Her evidence suggests that state ceremonial, pageantry and propaganda were only sporadically experienced and referred to, and that more 'banal' forms of national identification were touched upon in landscape, religion, manners, food and drink and recreational rituals. Rather than travellers operating with a single dominant national identity, they utilized a 'flexible repertoire', heavily dependent on context. Travellers in Britain itself tended to refer to themselves as English, Scottish or Welsh (Morgan excludes the Irish from her analysis) rather than as British. Overseas a British identity might come to the fore, but this was most likely to be expressed in relation to political, imperial, commercial and military capacities (and even then was often confused by the way in which 'English' often stood for 'British' in the eyes of foreigners). If defining themselves culturally, even overseas, such travellers tended to fall back on definitions as English, Scottish or Welsh. Morgan's material reveals that although British travellers emphasized a shared Protestantism when travelling in Europe, when in Britain they stressed the divisions within Protestantism. Travel around Britain also highlighted linguistic differences, both between English and the Celtic tongues, and of dialect and accent within English itself. Context, evidently, was everything: identities were consistently situational and relational: the 'alien' could be encountered in Britain as much as on the Continent or further afield.

One area that needs much more sustained investigation is the degree to which gender cut across national identities. Existing work on the late-nineteenth-century formulation of 'Englishness' suggests that it embodied essentially masculine qualities, such as leadership, courage, justice and honour, for which there was no satisfactory female equivalent. Rather, female qualities were perceived as being universal to womanhood, irrespective of nationality. Woman's contribution was to be in the preservation and perpetuation of the race through maternity and through the exercise of an appropriate domestic role, but women themselves had little opportunity to influence the way in which the nation itself was imagined. In fact, by the century's end, women were subject to a number of investigative discourses determined to discover the extent to which they were fulfilling their allotted roles. Colley's emphasis on women as active participants in the construction of their own understandings of national identity stands alone and unsupported in this context and future work on national identities needs a much more sustained engagement with how such concepts were gendered.[36]

Conclusion

In 1900, residents of England, Scotland and Wales probably had a stronger sense of a common British identity than had been available to their ancestors a century earlier. This British identity was not uniform, not without its contradictions, and was not necessarily hegemonic. It could accommodate a variety of different meanings and ideological positions, and it could co-exist with other, equally valid and often more potent identities, be those national, regional, local, religious or ethnic. The fact that elements of this 'Britishness' had been in the process of formation from at least early in the eighteenth century had meant that accommodating Irish Catholicism had never been critical to the development of the identity itself, whatever the strategic imperatives of the British state. So the fact that the views of many of the Irish population appeared irreconcilable with 'Britishness' did not pose a fundamental threat to its maintenance. Scottish and Welsh identities, on the other hand, appeared to be comfortably contained within a flexible structure that rewarded loyalty with opportunity, that allowed Scottishness and Welshness to 'nest' within a broader, imperial British-ness. The secession of the Irish Free State, when it came, did not do more than dent the self-image of a British imperial identity reforged, once more, in war against a con-tinental 'other'. The historical study of nineteenth-century 'British identities' has been almost as diverse and variegated as the historical nature of those identities them-selves. It remains a relatively new field, with paradigms still in the process of forma-tion and much groundwork remaining undone, particularly in the matter of popular understandings of national identity. With the apparently irresistible fragmentation of a contemporary sense of Britishness the subject faces the danger that its study will become unfashionable, as scholars retreat behind devolved boundaries, seeing 'British' history as somehow irredeemably unionist and imperialist. Given the volume of multiple cultural interactions and shared cross-border experiences in the nineteenth century itself, and given the stimulating if disparate nature of much of the writing on British history, that would be both a shame and a distortion of the historical record. Having expended so much energy in demonstrating the contingent, situ-ational and multiple nature of identity it would be a mistake for future scholars to succumb to the political imperatives of a single, hierarchical, construction of national identity.

NOTES

1. J. G. A. Pocock, 'British history: a plea for a new subject', *Journal of Modern History*, 47 (1975).
2. J. G. A. Pocock, 'The limits and divisions of British history: in search of the unknown subject', *American Historical Review*, 87 (1982).
3. H. Kearney, *The British Isles: A History of Four Nations* (Cambridge, 1989).
4. J. Black, *A History of the British Isles* (Basingstoke, 2003).
5. D. Cannadine, 'British history as a "new subject": politics, perspectives and prospects', in A. Grant and K. Stringer, eds, *Uniting the Kingdom? The Making of British History* (London, 1995), pp. 26–7.
6. N. Davies, *The Isles: A History* (London, 1999).
7. A. D. Smith, *Nationalism and Modernism: A Critical Survey of Recent Theories of Nations and Nationalism* (London, 1998).
8. E. Hobsbawm and T. Ranger, eds, *The Invention of Tradition* (Cambridge, 1983).
9. N. Yuval-Davis, *Gender and Nation* (London, 1997).
10. E. J. Hobsbawm, *Nations and Nationalism since 1780: Programme, Myth, Reality* (Cambridge, 1990), p. 12.
11. H. K. Bhabha, *Nation and Narration* (London, 1990).
12. L. Colley, *Britons: Forging the Nation 1707–1837* (London, 1992).
13. Ibid., p. 5.
14. A. Hastings, *The Construction of Nationhood: Ethnicity, Religion and Nationalism* (Cambridge, 1997), 61–4; G. Newman, *The Rise of English Nationalism: A Cultural History, 1740–1830* (London, 1987).
15. D. Eastwood, L. Brockliss and M. John, 'Conclusion: from dynastic union to unitary state: the European experience', in L. Brockliss and D. Eastwood, eds, *A Union of Multiple Identities: The British Isles, c.1750–c.1850* (Manchester, 1997).
16. T. Claydon and I. McBride, 'The trials of the chosen peoples: recent interpretations of Protestantism and national identity in Britain and Ireland', in T. Claydon and I. McBride, eds, *Protestantism and National Identity: Britain and Ireland, c.1650–c.1850*

(Cambridge, 1998); R. Eagles, *Francophilia in English Society 1748–1815* (Basingstoke, 2000), pp. 2–8.

17. J. E. Cookson, *The British Armed Nation 1793–1815* (Oxford, 1997).

18. K. Robbins, *Nineteenth-Century Britain: England, Scotland and Wales: The Making of a Nation* (Oxford, 1989).

19. R[ichard] Williams, *The Contentious Crown: Public Discussion of the British Monarchy in the Reign of Queen Victoria* (Aldershot, 1997).

20. H. Cunningham, 'The language of patriotism, 1750–1914', *History Workshop Journal*, 12 (1981).

21. M. Taylor, 'John Bull and the iconography of public opinion in England c.1712–1929', *Past and Present*, 134 (1992); M. C. Finn, *After Chartism: Class and Nation in English Radical Politics, 1848–1874* (Cambridge, 1993); P. Ward, *Red Flag and Union Jack: Englishness, Patriotism and the British Left* (Woodbridge, 1998).

22. J. Wolffe, *The Protestant Crusade in Great Britain, 1829–60* (Oxford, 1991); D. G. Paz, *Popular Anti-Catholicism in Mid-Victorian England* (Stanford, 1992).

23. D. Hempton, *Religion and Political Culture in Britain and Ireland: From the Glorious Revolution to the Decline of Empire* (Cambridge, 1996), 173; J. Wolffe, *God and Greater Britain: Religion and National Life in Britain and Ireland 1843–1945* (London, 1994).

24. J. Langton, 'The Industrial Revolution and the regional geography of England', *Transactions of the Institute of British Geographers*, New Series 9 (1984); P. Hudson, ed., *Regions and Industries: A Perspective on the Industrial Revolution in Britain* (Cambridge, 1989).

25. R. Holt, *Sport and the British: A Modern History* (Oxford, 1989).

26. P. Langford, *Englishness Identified: Manners and Character 1650–1850* (Oxford, 2000).

27. C. Hall, *White, Male and Middle Class: Explorations in Feminism and History* (London, 1992).

28. P. Mandler, ' "Race" and "nation" in mid-Victorian thought', in S. Collini, R. Whatmore and B. Young, eds, *History, Religion, and Culture: British Intellectual History 1750–1950* (Cambridge, 2000).

29. S. Collini, *Public Moralists: Political Thought and Intellectual Life in Britain 1850–1930* (Oxford, 1991); P. Dodd, 'Englishness and the national culture' in R. Colls and P. Dodd, eds, *Englishness: Politics and Culture 1880–1920* (Beckenham, Kent, 1986).

30. M. J. Wiener, *English Culture and the Decline of the Industrial Spirit* (Cambridge, 1981); A. Howkins, 'The discovery of rural England', in R. Colls and P. Dodd, *Englishness: Politics and Culture 1880–1920* (Beckenham, Kent, 1986).

31. J. M. MacKenzie, 'Empire and metropolitan cultures', in A. Porter, ed., *The Oxford History of the British Empire*, vol. 3, *The Nineteenth Century* (Oxford, 1999).

32. A. Burton, 'Who needs the nation? Interrogating "British" history', in C. Hall, ed., *Cultures of Empire: Colonisers in Britain and the Empire in the Nineteenth and Twentieth Centuries: A Reader* (Manchester, 2000), pp. 140–1; C. Hall, 'The rule of difference: gender, class and empire in the making of the 1832 Reform Act', in I. Blom, K. Hagemann and C. Hall, eds, *Gendered Nations: Nationalisms and Gender Order in the Long Nineteenth Century* (Oxford, 2000).

33. A. S. Thompson, *Imperial Britain: The Empire in British Politics c.1880–1932* (Harlow, 2000).

34. S. L. Barczewski, *Myth and National Identity in Nineteenth-Century Britain: The Legends of King Arthur and Robin Hood* (Oxford, 2000).

35. M. Morgan, *National Identities and Travel in Victorian Britain* (Basingstoke, 2001).

36. J. Mackay and P. Thane, 'The Englishwoman', in R. Colls and P. Dodd, eds, *Englishness: Politics and Culture 1880–1920* (Beckenham, Kent, 1986); A. Davin, 'Imperialism and motherhood', *History Workshop Journal*, 5 (1978).

FURTHER READING

L. Colley, *Britons: Forging the Nation 1707–1837* (1992) and K. Robbins, *Nineteenth-Century Britain: England, Scotland and Wales: The Making of a Nation* (1989) remain vital starting-points for the study of 'Britishness', complemented by both L. Brockliss and D. Eastwood, eds, *A Union of Multiple Identities: The British Isles, c.1750–c.1850* (1997) and A. Grant and K. Stringer, eds, *Uniting the Kingdom? The Making of British History* (1995). A reliable and stimulating single-volume history written from a 'Britannic' perspective is H. Kearney, *The British Isles: A History of Four Nations* (1989).

The interweaving of religion and national identities may be traced in two books by J. Wolffe: *The Protestant Crusade in Great Britain, 1829–60* (1991) and *God and Greater Britain: Religion and National Life in Britain and Ireland 1843–1945* (1994); and in D. Hempton, *Religion and Political Culture in Britain and Ireland: From the Glorious Revolution to the Decline of Empire* (1996). 'Englishness' is best studied in R. Colls and P. Dodd, eds, *Englishness: Politics and Culture 1880–1920* (1986), S. Collini, *Public Moralists: Political Thought and Intellectual Life in Britain 1850–1930* (1991) and P. Langford, *Englishness Identified: Manners and Character 1650–1850* (2000). Much on patriotism and popular imperialism may be quarried from R. Samuel, ed., *Patriotism: The Making and Unmaking of British National Identity* (1989) and J. M. MacKenzie, 'Empire and metropolitan cultures', in A. Porter, ed., *The Oxford History of the British Empire*, vol. 3, *The Nineteenth Century* (1999). Two impressive recent studies are S. L. Barczewski, *Myth and National Identity in Nineteenth-Century Britain: The Legends of King Arthur and Robin Hood* (2000) and M. Morgan, *National Identities and Travel in Victorian Britain* (2001).

Bibliography of Secondary Sources

Abbott, M., *Family Ties: English Families, 1540–1920* (London, 1993).

Abel-Smith, B., *The Hospitals 1800–1948: A Study in Social Administration in England and Wales* (London, 1964).

Acheson, A., *A History of the Church of Ireland, 1691–1996* (Dublin, 1997).

Acland, A., *Caroline Norton* (London, 1948).

Adams, F., *History of the Elementary School Contest in England* (Brighton, 1972).

Adas, M., *Machines as the Measure of Men: Science, Technology, and the Ideologies of Western Dominance* (Ithaca, NY, 1989).

Adelman, P., *Victorian Radicalism: The Middle-Class Experience 1830–1914* (London, 1984).

Alborn, T. L., *Conceiving Companies: Joint Stock Politics in Victorian England* (London, 1998).

Allen, R. C., *Enclosure and the Yeoman: The Agricultural Development of the South Midlands, 1450–1850* (Oxford, 1992).

Allett, J., *New Liberalism: The Political Economy of J. A. Hobson* (Toronto, 1981).

Allsobrook, D., *Schools for the Shires: The Reform of Middle-Class Education in Mid-Victorian England* (Manchester, 1986).

Altholz, J. L., 'The warfare of conscience with theology', in G. Parsons, ed., *Religion in Victorian Britain*, vol. 4, *Interpretations* (Manchester, 1988).

Altick, R. D., *The English Common Reader: A Social History of the Mass Reading Public 1800–1900* (Columbus, OH, 1998).

Anderson, B., *Imagined Communities: Reflections on the Origin and Spread of Nationalism* (London, 1983).

Anderson, M., *Family Structure in Nineteenth Century Lancashire* (Cambridge, 1971).

Anderson, O., 'The growth of Christian militarism in mid-Victorian Britain', *English Historical Review*, 86 (1971).

Anderson, R. D., *Universities and Elites in Britain since 1800* (Basingstoke, 1992).

Anderson, R. D., *Education and the Scottish People, 1750–1918* (Oxford, 1995).

Anstey, R., *The Atlantic Slave Trade and British Abolition, 1760–1810* (Cambridge, 1975).

Anthony, P. D., *Ruskin's Labour: A Study of Ruskin's Social Theory* (Cambridge, 1983).

Armstrong, I., *Victorian Poetry: Poetry, Poetics and Politics* (New York, 1993).

Arnold, D., ed., *Imperial Medicine and Indigenous Societies* (Manchester, 1988).

Arnot, M. L. and Usborne, C., eds, *Gender and Crime in Modern Europe* (London, 1999).

Ashley, L. R. N., ed., *Nineteenth-Century British Drama: An Anthology of Representative Plays* (Lanham, 1988).

August, A., 'How separate a sphere? Poor women and paid work in late-Victorian London', *Journal of Family History*, 19 (1994).

Bagehot, W., *The Collected Works of Walter Bagehot*, ed. N. St John-Stevas (15 vols, London, 1965–86).

Bagwell, P. S., *The Transport Revolution* (London, 1988).

Bailey, P., 'Will the real Bill Banks please stand up? Towards a role analysis of mid-Victorian working-class respectability', *Journal of Social History*, 12 (1979).

Bailey, P., *Leisure and Class in Victorian England: Rational Recreation and the Contest for Control, 1830–1885* (London, 1987).

Bailey, P., 'Parasexuality and glamour: the Victorian barmaid as cultural prototype', *Gender and History*, 2 (1990).

Bailey, P., *Popular Culture and Performance in the Victorian City* (Cambridge, 1998).

Bailey, P., 'The politics and poetics of modern British leisure: a late-twentieth-century review', *Rethinking History*, 3 (1999).

Baines, D., *Emigration from Europe, 1815–1930* (London, 1991).

Baly, M., *Florence Nightingale and the Nursing Legacy* (London, 1997).

Banks, O., *Faces of Feminism: A Study of Feminism as a Social Movement* (Oxford, 1981).

Banks, S., 'Nineteenth-century scandal or twentieth-century model? A new look at "open" and "close" parishes', *Economic History Review*, 41 (1991).

Bannister, R. C., *Social Darwinism, Science and Myth in Anglo-American Social Thought* (Philadelphia, 1979).

Barczewski, S. L., *Myth and National Identity in Nineteenth-Century Britain: The Legends of King Arthur and Robin Hood* (Oxford, 2000).

Barker, E., *Political Thought in England 1848 to 1914* (Oxford, 1918).

Barnett, A., ed., *Power and the Throne* (London, 1994).

Barret-Ducrocq, F., *Love in the Time of Victoria: Sexuality, Class and Gender in Nineteenth Century London* (London, 1991).

Barrett Browning, E., *Aurora Leigh*, ed. K. McSweeney (Oxford, 1993).

Barrow, L., *Independent Spirits: Spiritualism and English Plebeians, 1850–1910* (London, 1986).

Bartlett, C. J., *Great Britain and Sea Power 1815–1853* (Oxford, 1963).

Bartlett, C. J., 'Britain and the European balance 1815–48', in A. Sked, ed., *Europe's Balance of Power* (London, 1979).

Bartlett, C. J., *Defence and Diplomacy: Britain and the Great Powers, 1815–1914* (Manchester, 1993).

Bartley, P., *Prostitution: Prevention and Reform in Britain, 1860–1914* (London, 2000).

Baumgart, W., *Imperialism: The Idea and the Reality of British and French Colonial Expansion, 1880–1914* (Oxford, 1982).

Baumgart, W., *The Crimean War 1853–1856* (London, 1999).

Bayly, C. A., *Imperial Meridian: The British Empire and the World 1780–1830* (London, 1989).

Bayly, C. A., *Empire and Information: Intelligence Gathering and Social Communication in India, 1780–1870* (Cambridge, 1996).

Beales, D., 'The electorate before and after 1832: the right to vote, and the opportunity', *Parliamentary History*, 11 (1992).

Beames, M. R., *Peasants and Power: The Whiteboy Movements and their Control in Pre-Famine Ireland* (Brighton, 1982).

Beattie, S., *The New Sculpture* (New Haven, CT, 1983).

Bebbington, D., *Evangelicalism in Modern Britain* (London, 1989).

Beckett, J. V., 'The decline of the small landowner in eighteenth- and nineteenth-century England: Some regional considerations', *Agricultural History Review*, 30 (1981).

Beckett, J. V., *The Aristocracy in England, 1660–1914* (Oxford, 1986).

Beckett, J. V., *The Agricultural Revolution* (Oxford, 1990).

Beer, G., *Open Fields: Science in Cultural Encounter* (Oxford, 1996).

Bellamy, R., ed., *Victorian Liberalism* (London, 1990).

Bennett, T., *The Birth of the Museum: History, Theory, Politics* (London, 1995).

Bentley, M., *Politics Without Democracy 1815–1914: Perception and Preoccupation in British Government* (London, 1984).

Bentley, M., *The Climax of Liberal Politics: British Liberalism in Theory and Practice, 1868–1918* (London, 1987).

Bentley, M., 'Victorian politics and the linguistic turn', *Historical Journal*, 42 (1999).

Berg, M., *The Machinery Question and the Making of Political Economy 1815–1848* (Cambridge, 1980).

Berg, M., 'Women's work, mechanisation and the early phases of industrialisation in England', in P. Joyce, ed., *The Historical Meanings of Work* (Cambridge, 1987).

Berg, M., *The Age of Manufactures 1700–1820: Industry, Innovation and Work in Britain* (London, 1994).

Berg, M., 'Factories, workshops and industrial organisation', in R. C. Floud and D. McCloskey, eds, *The Economic History of Britain since 1700*, vol. 1, *1700–1860* (Cambridge, 1994).

Berg, M. and Hudson, P., 'Rehabilitating the industrial revolution', *Economic History Review*, 45 (1992).

Berridge, V., 'Popular Sunday papers and mid-Victorian society', in G. Boyce, J. Curran and P. Wingate, eds, *Newspaper History: From the Seventeenth Century to the Present Day* (London, 1978).

Best, G., *Temporal Pillars: Queen Anne's Bounty, the Ecclesiastical Commissioners and the Church of England* (Cambridge, 1964).

Best, G., *Mid-Victorian Britain 1851–75* (London, 1979).

Bhabha, H. K., *Nation and Narration* (London, 1990).

Biagini, E. F., *Liberty, Retrenchment, and Reform: Popular Liberalism in the Age of Gladstone 1860–1880* (Cambridge, 1992).

Biagini, E. F., *Gladstone* (Basingstoke, 2000).

Bielenberg, A., ed., *The Irish Diaspora* (London, 2000).

Billy, G., *Palmerston's Foreign Policy 1848* (New York, 1993).

Binfield, C., *So Down to Prayers: Studies in English Nonconformity 1780–1920* (London, 1977).

Bishop, A. S., *The Rise of a Central Authority for English Education* (Cambridge, 1971).

Black, J., *A History of the British Isles* (Basingstoke, 2003).

Black, R. D. C., 'William Stanley Jevons', in J. Eatwell, M. Milgate and P. Newman, eds, *The New Palgrave: A Dictionary of Economic Thought* (London, 1987), vol. 2.

Black, R. D. C., Coats, A. W. and Goodwin, C. D. W., eds, *The Marginal Revolution in Economics: Interpretation and Evaluation* (Durham, NC, 1973).

Blake, R., *The Conservative Party from Peel to Churchill* (London, 1970).

Blake, R., *Disraeli* (London, 1998).

Bland, L., *Banishing the Beast: English Feminism and Sexual Morality, 1885–1914* (London, 1995).

Blaug, M., 'Was there a marginal revolution?', in R. D. C. Black, A. W. Coats and C. D. W. Goodwin, eds, *The Marginal Revolution in Economics: Interpretation and Evaluation* (Durham, NC, 1973).

Blaut, J. M., *The Colonizer's Model of the World: Geographical Diffusionism and Eurocentric History* (Harlow, 1994).

Bock, G., 'Women's history and gender history: aspects of an international debate', *Gender and History*, 1 (1989).

Bogdanor, V., *The Monarchy and the Constitution* (Oxford, 1995).

Bolt, C., *Victorian Attitudes Towards Race* (London, 1971).

Bond, B., ed., *Victorian Military Campaigns* (London, 1967).

Bourne, K., *The Foreign Policy of Victorian England, 1830–1902* (Oxford, 1970).

Bowle, J., *Politics and Opinion in the Nineteenth Century: An Historical Introduction* (London, 1963).

Bowler, P. J., *The Eclipse of Darwinism: Anti-Darwinian Evolution Theories in the Decades around 1900* (Baltimore, 1983).

Boyer, G., *An Economic History of the English Poor Law, 1750–1850* (Cambridge, 1990).

Bradshaw, B., 'The emperor's new clothes', in *Free Thought in Ireland* (Belfast, 1991).

Brady, C., ed., *Interpreting Irish History: The Debate on Historical Revisionism 1938–1994* (Dublin, 1994).

Brain, R., *Going to the Fair: Readings in the Culture of Nineteenth-Century Exhibitions* (Cambridge, 1993).

Brake, L., *Subjugated Knowledges: Journalism, Gender and Literature in the Nineteenth Century* (London, 1994).

Brake, L., Jones, A. and Madden, L., *Investigating Victorian Journalism* (Basingstoke, 1990).

Brantlinger, P., *Rule of Darkness: British Literature and Imperialism, 1830–1914* (Ithaca, NY, 1990).

Brewer, J., *The Sinews of Power: War, Money and the English State, 1688–1783* (London, 1989).

Briggs, A., *The Age of Improvement 1783–1867* (London, 1959).

Briggs, A., *Mass Entertainment: The Origins of a Modern Industry* (Adelaide, 1960).

Bright, M., *Cities Built to Music: Aesthetic Theories of the Victorian Gothic Revival* (Columbus, 1984).

Brinton, C., *English Political Thought in the Nineteenth Century* (London, 1949).

Brinton, C., *The Political Ideas of the English Romanticists* (Ann Arbor, 1966).

Bristow, J., ed., *The Cambridge Companion to Victorian Poetry* (Cambridge, 2001).

Brock, M., *The Great Reform Act* (London, 1973).

Brockliss, L. and Eastwood, D., eds, *A Union of Multiple Identities: The British Isles, c.1750–c.1850* (Manchester, 1997).

Brooke, J., *King George III* (London, 1972).

Brooks, M. W., *John Ruskin and Victorian Architecture* (London, 1987).

Brooks, R., *The Long Arm of Empire: Naval Brigades from the Crimea to the Boxer Rebellion* (London, 1999).

Brose, O. J., *Church and Parliament: The Re-shaping of the Church of England, 1828–1860* (Stanford, 1959).

Brown, C. G., 'Did urbanization secularize Britain?', *Urban History Yearbook 1988*.

Brown, C. G., *Religion and Society in Scotland since 1707* (Edinburgh, 1997).

Brown, C. G., *The Death of Christian Britain: Understanding Secularisation, 1800–2000* (London, 2001).

Brown, D., 'Equipoise and the myth of an open elite: new men of wealth and the purchase of land in the equipoise decades, 1850–69', in M. Hewitt, ed., *An Age of Equipoise? Reassessing Mid-Victorian Britain* (Aldershot, 2000).

Brown, D. S., 'Palmerston and the politics of foreign policy 1846–1855', PhD diss., University of Exeter, 1988.

Brown, J. C., 'The condition of England and the standard of living: cotton textiles in the northwest, 1806–1850', *Journal of Economic History*, 50 (1990).

Brown, J. K., 'Design plans, working drawings, national styles: engineering practice in Great Britain and the United States, 1775–1945', *Technology and Culture*, 41 (2000).

Brown, L., *Victorian News and Newspapers* (Oxford, 1985).

Brown, S. J. and Miller, D. W., eds, *Piety and Power in Ireland 1760–1960: Essays in Honour of Emmet Larkin* (Belfast, 1999).

Brozyna, A. E., *Labour, Love and Prayer: Female Piety in Ulster Religious Literature 1850–1914* (Belfast, 2000).

Bruce, S., ed., *Religion and Modernization: Sociologists and Historians Debate the Secularization Thesis* (Oxford, 1992).

Bryan, D., *Orange Parades: The Politics of Ritual, Tradition and Control* (London, 2000).

Bull, P., *Land, Politics and Nationalism: A Study of the Irish Land Question* (Dublin, 1996).

Burnett, J., ed., *Destiny Obscure: Autobiographies of Childhood, Education and Family from the 1820s to the 1920s* (London, 1982).

Burns, R. A., *The Diocesan Revival in the Church of England c.1800–1870* (Oxford, 1999).

Burrow, J., *Evolution and Society: A Study in Victorian Social Theory* (Cambridge, 1966).

Burrow, J., *A Liberal Descent: Victorian Historians and the English Past* (Cambridge, 1981).

Burrow, J., 'Sense and circumstances: Bagehot and the nature of political understanding', in S. Collini, D. Winch and J. Burrow, eds, *That Noble Science of Politics: A Study in Nineteenth-Century Intellectual History* (Cambridge, 1983).

Burrow, J., *Whigs and Liberals: Continuity and Change in English Political Thought* (Oxford, 1988).

Burton, A., 'Rules of thumb: British history and "imperial culture" in nineteenth- and twentieth-century Britain', *Women's History Review*, 3 (1994).

Burton, A., *Burdens of History: British Feminists, Indian Women, and Imperial Culture, 1865–1915* (Chapel Hill, NC, 1994).

Burton, A., 'Who needs the nation? Interrogating "British" history', in C. Hall, ed., *Cultures of Empire: Colonisers in Britain and the Empire in the Nineteenth and Twentieth Centuries: A Reader* (Manchester, 2000).

Bush, M. L., *What is Love?: Richard Carlile's Philosophy of Sex* (London, 1998).

Butterfield, H., *The Whig Interpretation of History* (London, 1973).

Byerly, A., *Realism, Representation, and the Arts in Nineteenth-Century Literature* (Cambridge, 1997).

Bynum, W. F., *Science and the Practice of Medicine in the Nineteenth Century* (Cambridge, 1994).

Byrne, M., *Britain and the European Powers, 1815–65* (London, 1998).

Cain, P. J., *Hobson and Imperialism: Radicalism, New Liberalism and Finance, 1887–1938* (Oxford, 2002).

Cain, P. J. and Hopkins, A. G., *British Imperialism: Innovation and Expansion, 1688–1914* (Harlow, 1993).

Cain, P. J. and Hopkins, A. G., *British Imperialism, 1688–2000* (Harlow, 2001).

Caird, J., *English Agriculture in 1850–51* (London, 1968).

Cameron, E. A., *Land for the People: British Government and the Highland Land Issue* (E. Linton, Scotland, 1996).

Campbell, F., *The Dissenting Voice: Protestant Democracy in Ulster from Plantation to Partition* (Belfast, 1991).

Campbell, R., *Scotland since 1707: The Rise of an Industrial Society* (Edinburgh, 1985).

Campus, A., 'Marginal economics', in J. Eatwell, M. Milgate and P. Newman, eds, *The New Palgrave: A Dictionary of Economic Thought* (London, 1987), vol. 3.

Cannadine, D., *Lords and Landlords: The Aristocracy and the Towns 1774–1967* (Leicester, 1980).

Cannadine, D., 'The context, performance and meaning of ritual: The British monarchy and the "invention of tradition", c.1820–1977', in E. Hobsbawm and T. Ranger, eds, *The Invention of Tradition* (Cambridge, 1983).

Cannadine, D., 'The present and the past in the industrial revolution', *Past and Present*, 103 (1983).

Cannadine, D., *The Decline and Fall of the British Aristocracy* (New Haven, CT, 1990).

Cannadine, D., 'British history as a "new subject": politics, perspectives and prospects', in A. Grant and K. Stringer, eds, *Uniting the Kingdom? The Making of British History* (London, 1995).

Cannadine, D., *The Rise and Fall of Class in Britain* (New York, 1999).

Cannadine, D., 'Ornamentalism and the British Empire', *History Today*, 51(5) (May 2001).

Cannadine, D., *Ornamentalism: How the British Saw Their Empire* (London, 2001).

Cannon, J., *Parliamentary Reform 1640–1832* (Cambridge, 1972).

Cannon, S. F., *Science in Culture: The Early Victorian Period* (New York, 1978).

Carson, K. and Idzikowska, H., 'The social production of Scottish policing, 1795–1900', in D. Hay and F. Snyder, eds, *Policing and Prosecution in Britain, 1750–1850* (Cambridge, 1989).

Carter, I., *Farm Life in Northeast Scotland 1840–1914: The Poor Man's Country* (Edinburgh, 1997).

Caunce, S., *Among Farm Horses: The Horselads of East Yorkshire* (Stroud, 1991).

Chadwick, W. O., *The Victorian Church* (London, 1971).

Chalus, E., ' "That epidemical madness": women and electoral politics in the late eighteenth century', in H. Barker and E. Chalus, eds, *Gender in Eighteenth-Century England: Roles, Representations and Responsibilities* (London, 1997).

Chalus, E., 'Women, electoral privilege and practice in the eighteenth century', in K. Gleadle and S. Richardson, eds, *Women in British Politics, 1760–1860: The Power of the Petticoat* (Basingstoke, 2000).

Chamberlain, M., *'Pax Britannica'? British Foreign Policy, 1789–1914* (London, 1988).

Chandler, D. G. and Beckett, I. F. W., eds, *The Oxford Illustrated History of the British Army* (Oxford, 1994).

Chapman, S. D., *The Cotton Industry in the Industrial Revolution* (London, 1972).

Charlesworth, A., *Social Protest in a Rural Society: The Spatial Diffusion of the Captain Swing Disturbances of 1830–31* (Norwich, 1978).

Chartres, J., 'Rural industry and manufacturing', in E. J. T. Collins, ed., *The Agrarian History of England and Wales*, vol. 7, *1850–1914* (Cambridge, 2000).

Checkland, S. and Checkland, O., *Industry and Ethos: Scotland, 1832–1914* (London, 1984).

Cherry, D., *Painting Women: Victorian Women Artists* (London, 1993).

Chinn, C., *They Worked All Their Lives: Women of the Urban Poor in England, 1880–1939* (Manchester, 1998).

Chitnis, A. C., *The Scottish Enlightenment and Early Victorian Society* (London, 1986).

Claeys, G., *Machinery, Money and the Millennium: From Moral Economy to Socialism, 1815–60* (Cambridge, 1987).

Claeys, G., *Citizens and Saints: Politics and Anti-Politics in Early British Socialism* (Cambridge, 1989).

Clark, A., *The Struggle for the Breeches: Gender and the Making of the British Working Class* (London, 1995).

Clark, A., 'Gender, class and the constitution: franchise reform in England, 1832–1928', in J. Vernon, ed., *Re-Reading the Constitution: New Narratives in the Political History of England's Long Nineteenth Century* (Cambridge, 1996).

Clark, A., 'The New Poor Law and the breadwinner wage: contrasting assumptions', *Journal of Social History*, 34 (2000).

Clark, G. K., *The Making of Victorian England* (London, 1962).

Clark, J. C. D., *English Society 1688–1832: Ideology, Social Structure and Political Practice during the Ancien Regime* (Cambridge, 1985).

Clark, S., *The Social Origins of the Irish Land War* (Princeton, NJ, 1979).

Clarke, J., *British Diplomacy and Foreign Policy 1782–1865: The National Interest* (London, 1989).

Claydon, T. and McBride, I., 'The trials of the chosen peoples: recent interpretations of Protestantism and national identity in Britain and Ireland', in T. Claydon and I. McBride, eds, *Protestantism and National Identity: Britain and Ireland, c.1650–c.1850* (Cambridge, 1998).

Clowes, W. L., *The Royal Navy: A History from the Earliest Times to the Present* (London, 1897–1903).

Coats, A. W., 'The historist reaction to English political economy, 1870–90', *Economica*, 21 (1954).

Cocks, H., *Nameless Offences* (London, 2003).

Coleman, B., *Conservatism and the Conservative Party in the Nineteenth Century* (London, 1988).

Colley, L., *Britons: Forging the Nation 1707–1837* (London, 1992).

Collini, S., *Liberalism and Sociology: L. T. Hobhouse and Political Argument in England, 1880–1914* (Cambridge, 1979).

Collini, S., *Public Moralists: Political Thought and Intellectual Life in Britain, 1850–1930* (Oxford, 1991).

Collini, S., Winch, D. and Burrow, J., *That Noble Science of Politics: A Study in Nineteenth-Century Intellectual History* (Cambridge, 1983).

Collins, E. J. T., 'Migrant labour in British agriculture in the nineteenth century', *Economic History Review*, 29 (1976).

Collins, E. J. T., ed., *The Agrarian History of England and Wales*, vol. 7, *1850–1914* (Cambridge, 2000).

Collins, T. J. and Rundle, V. J., eds, *The Broadview Anthology of Victorian Poetry and Poetic Theory* (Peterborough, Ontario, 1999).

Colls, R. and Dodd, P., eds, *Englishness: Politics and Culture 1880–1920* (Beckenham, Kent, 1986).

Conacher, J. B., 'Party politics in the age of Palmerston', in P. Appleman, W. A. Madden and M. Wolff, eds, *1859: Entering an Age of Crisis* (Bloomington, 1959).

Conley, C., *The Unwritten Law: Criminal Justice in Victorian Kent* (Oxford, 1991).

Connolly, S. J., *Priests and People in Pre-Famine Ireland 1780–1845* (Dublin, 2001).

Cooke, A. B. and Vincent, J. R., *The Governing Passion: Cabinet Government and Party Politics in Britain, 1885–86* (Brighton, 1974).

Cookson, J. E., *The British Armed Nation 1793–1815* (Oxford, 1997).

Cooter, R., *The Cultural Meaning of Popular Science: Phrenology and the Organization of Consent in Nineteenth Century Britain* (Cambridge, 1984).

Copeland, I., *The Making of the Backward Pupil in Education in England 1870–1914* (London, 1999).

Cowling, M., *1867: Disraeli, Gladstone, and Revolution* (Cambridge, 1967).

Cox, J., *The English Churches in a Secular Society: Lambeth 1870–1930* (Oxford, 1982).

Crafts, N. F. R., *British Economic Growth During the Industrial Revolution* (Oxford, 1985).

Crafts, N. F. R., 'Some dimensions of the "quality of life" during the British industrial revolution', *Economic History Review*, 50 (1997).

Cragoe, M., 'Conscience or coercion? Clerical influence at the general election of 1868 in Wales', *Past and Present*, 149 (1995).

Cragoe, M., *An Anglican Aristocracy: The Moral Economy of the Landed Estate in Carmarthenshire, 1832–95* (Oxford, 1996).

Cragoe, M., 'A question of culture: the Welsh Church and the Bishopric of St Asaph, 1870', *Welsh History Review*, 18 (1996).

Cragoe, M., 'Reply', *Past and Present*, 169 (2000).

Cragoe, M., ' "Jenny rules the roost": women and electoral politics, 1832–68', in K. Gleadle and S. Richardson, eds, *Women in British Politics, 1760–1860: The Power of the Petticoat* (Basingstoke, 2000).

Creedy, J., *Edgeworth and the Development of Neo-Classical Economics* (Oxford, 1986).

Croll, A., 'Street disorder, surveillance and shame: regulating behaviour in the public spaces of the late Victorian British town', *Social History*, 24 (1999).

Croll, A., *Civilizing the Urban: Popular Culture and Public Space in Merthyr, c.1870–1914* (Cardiff, 2000).

Cronin, J. E., *The Politics of State Expansion: War, State and Society in Twentieth-Century Britain* (London, 1991).

Crosby, A. G., ed., *The Family Records of Benjamin Shaw, Mechanic of Dent, Dolphinholme and Preston, 1772–1841* (Lancashire and Cheshire, 1991).

Crotty, R., *Irish Agricultural Production: Its Volume and Structure* (Cork, 1966).

Crouzet, F., *The First Industrialists: The Problem of Origins* (Cambridge, 1985).

Crouzet, F., *Britain Ascendant: Comparative Studies in Franco-British Economic History* (Cambridge, 1990).

Crowther, M. A., *The Workhouse System, 1834–1929* (London, 1981).

Crozier, M., ed., *Cultural Traditions in Northern Ireland: Varieties of Irishness* (Belfast, 1989).

Cullen, L., 'The Irish diaspora of the seventeenth and eighteenth centuries', in N. Canny, ed., *Europeans on the Move: Studies in European Migration 1500–1800* (Oxford, 1994).

Cunningham, H., *Leisure in the Industrial Revolution, c.1780–c.1880* (London, 1980).

Cunningham, H., 'The language of patriotism, 1750–1914', *History Workshop Journal*, 12 (1981).

Cunningham, H., 'Leisure and culture', in F. M. L. Thompson, ed., *The Cambridge Social History of Britain 1750–1950*, vol. 2, *People and their Environment* (Cambridge, 1990).

Cunningham, H., *The Challenge of Democracy: Britain 1832–1918* (Harlow, 2001).

Cunningham, V., ed., *The Victorians: An Anthology of Poetry and Poetics* (Oxford, 2000).

Curran, J. and Seaton, J., *Power Without Responsibility: The Press and Broadcasting in Britain* (London, 1981).

Curtin, N., *The United Irishmen: Popular Politics in Ulster and Dublin, 1791–1798* (Oxford, 1994).

Curtin, P., 'The British Empire and Commonwealth in recent historiography', *American Historical Review*, 65 (1959).

Curtis, L., *The Cause of Ireland: From the United Irishmen to Partition* (Belfast, 1994).

Dakers, C., *The Holland Park Circle: Artists and Victorian Society* (New Haven, CT, 1999).

Daly, M. E., *The Famine in Ireland* (Dundalk, Scotland, 1986).

Dasgupta, P. and Weale, M., 'On measuring the quality of life', *World Development*, 20 (1992).

Daunton, M. J., *Coal Metropolis: Cardiff 1870–1914* (Leicester, 1977).

Daunton, M. J., ' "Gentlemanly capitalism" and British industry 1820–1914', *Past and Present*, 122 (1989).

Daunton, M. J., *Progress and Poverty: An Economic and Social History of Britain 1700–1850* (Oxford, 1995).

Daunton, M. J., ed., *The Cambridge Urban History of Britain*, vol. 3, *1840–1950* (Cambridge, 2000).

David, D., *Rule Britannia: Women, Empire and Victorian Writing* (Ithaca, NY, 1995).

David, D., ed., *The Cambridge Companion to the Victorian Novel* (Cambridge, 2001).

Davidoff, L., *Worlds Between: Historical Perspectives on Gender and Class* (Cambridge, 1995).

Davidoff, L. and Hall, C., *Family Fortunes: Men and Women of the English Middle Class 1780–1850* (London, 2002).

Davidoff, L., Doolittle, M., Fink, J. and Holden, K., *The Family Story: Blood, Contract and Intimacy, 1830–1960* (London, 1999).

Davidson, C., *A Woman's Work is Never Done: A History of Housework in the British Isles 1650–1950* (London, 1982).

Davies, E. T., *Religion and Society in Nineteenth Century Wales* (Llandybie, 1981).

Davies, J., *Cardiff and the Marquesses of Bute* (Cardiff, 1981).

Davies, J., *A History of Wales* (London, 1993).

Davies, N., *The Isles: A History* (London, 1999).

Davies, P., 'Nineteenth-century ocean trade and transport', in P. Mathias and J. Davis, eds, *International Trade and British Economic Growth* (Oxford, 1996).

Davies, R., *Secret Sins: Sex, Violence and Society in Carmarthenshire, 1870–1920* (Cardiff, 1996).

Davin, A., 'Imperialism and motherhood', *History Workshop Journal*, 5 (1978).

Davis, G., *The Irish in Britain 1815–1914* (London, 1991).

Davis, J., 'The London garrotting panic of 1862: a moral panic and the creation of a criminal class in mid-Victorian England', in V. A. C. Gatrell, B. Lenham and G. Parker, eds, *Crime and the Law: A Social History of Crime in Western Europe since 1500* (London, 1980).

Davis, L. and Huttenback, R. A., *Mammon and the Pursuit of Empire: The Economics of British Imperialism* (Cambridge, 1988).

Davis, R[alph], *The Industrial Revolution and British Overseas Trade* (Leicester, 1979).

Davis, R[ichard], *Revolutionary Imperialist: William Smith O'Brien 1803–1864* (Dublin, 1998).

Davis, R. W., 'Toryism to Tamworth: the triumph of reform, 1827–35', *Albion*, 12 (1980).

Davison, G., 'The city as a natural system: theories of urban society in early nineteenth-century Britain', in D. Fraser and A. Sutcliffe, eds, *The Pursuit of Urban History* (London, 1983).

D'Cruze, S., *Crimes of Outrage: Sex, Violence and Victorian Working Women* (London, 1998).

D'Cruze, S., ed., *Everyday Violence in Britain, 1850–1950: Gender and Class* (Harlow, 2000).

D'Cruze, S., 'Unguarded passions: violence, history and the everyday', in S. D'Cruze, ed., *Everyday Violence in Britain, 1850–1950: Gender and Class* (Harlow, 2000).

Deane, P. and Cole, W. A., *British Economic Growth, 1688–1959* (Cambridge, 1962).

Delamont, S., 'The contradictions in ladies' education', in S. Delamont and L. Duffin, eds, *Nineteenth Century Woman: Her Cultural and Physical World* (London, 1978).

de Larrabeiti, M., 'Conspicuous before the world: the political rhetoric of Chartist women', in E. Yeo, ed., *Radical Femininity: Women's Self-Representation in the Public Sphere* (Manchester, 1998).

de Marchi, N., 'John Stuart Mill, interpretations since Schumpeter', in W. Thweatt, ed., *Classical Political Economy: A Survey of Recent Literature* (Boston, 1988).

den Otter, S., *British Idealism and Social Explanation: A Study in Late Victorian Thought* (Oxford, 1996).

Denvir, B., *The Late Victorians: Art, Design and Society 1852–1910* (London, 1986).

Desmond, A., *The Politics of Evolution: Morphology, Medicine, and Reform in Radical London* (Chicago, 1989).

Desmond, A. and Moore, J. R., *Darwin* (London, 1991).

Devine, T. M., ed., *Farm Servants and Labour in Lowland Scotland, 1770–1914* (Edinburgh, 1984).

Devine, T. M., *The Great Highland Famine: Famine, Hunger and Emigration and the Scottish Highlands* (Edinburgh, 1988).

Devine, T. M., ed., *Irish Immigrants and Scottish Society in the Nineteenth and Twentieth Centuries* (Edinburgh, 1991).

Devine, T. M., *Clanship to Crofters' War: The Social Transformation of the Scottish Highlands* (Manchester, 1994).

Devine, T. M., ed., *Scottish Elites* (Edinburgh, 1994).

Devine, T. M., *The Transformation of Rural Scotland: Social Change and the Agrarian Economy, 1660–1815* (Edinburgh, 1994).

Devine, T. M., *The Scottish Nation 1707–2000* (Harmondsworth, 1999).

DeVries, J., 'Between purchasing power and the world of goods: understanding the household economy in early modern Europe', in R. Porter and J. Brewer, eds, *Consumption and the World of Goods* (London, 1993).

Dickinson, H. T., ed., *A Companion to Eighteenth-Century Britain* (Oxford, 2002).

Digby, A., *Pauper Palaces* (London, 1978).

Digby, A., *The Evolution of British General Practice 1850–1948* (Oxford, 1999).

Dodd, P., 'Englishness and the national culture', in R. Colls and P. Dodd, eds, *Englishness: Politics and Culture 1880–1920* (Beckenham, Kent, 1986).

Donnelly, J. S., 'Mass eviction and the great famine', in C. Póirtéir, *The Great Irish Famine* (Cork, 1995).

Donnelly, J. S., *The Great Irish Potato Famine* (Stroud, 2001).

Doolittle, M., 'Close relations? Bringing together gender and family in English history', *Gender and History*, 11 (1999).

Drescher, S., *Capitalism and Antislavery: British Mobilization in Comparative Perspective* (New York, 1987).

Dudley Edwards, R., *The Faithful Tribe: An Intimate Portrait of the Loyal Institutions* (London, 1999).

Dugan, S. and Dugan, D., *The Day the World Took Off: The Roots of the Industrial Revolution* (London, 2000).

Dunbabin, J. P. D.. *Rural Discontent in Nineteenth Century Britain* (London, 1974).

Dyck, I., *William Cobbett and Rural Popular Culture* (Cambridge, 1992).

Dyhouse, C., *Girls Growing Up in Late Victorian and Edwardian England* (London, 1981).

Dyos, H. J., *Victorian Suburb: A Study of the Growth of Camberwell* (Leicester, 1961).

Dyos, H. J. and Wolff, M., eds, *The Victorian City: Images and Realities* (London, 1973).

Eagles, R., *Francophilia in English Society 1748–1815* (Basingstoke, 2000).

Eagleton, T., *Scholars and Rebels in Nineteenth-Century Ireland* (Oxford, 1999).

Eastwood, D., 'Peel: a reassessment', *History Today*, 42 (1992).

Eastwood, D., 'Contesting the politics of deference: the rural electorate, 1820–60', in J. Lawrence and M. Taylor, eds, *Party, State and Society: Electoral Behaviour in Britain since 1820* (Aldershot, 1997).

Eastwood, D., 'History, politics and reputation: E. P. Thompson reconsidered', *History*, 85 (2000).

Eastwood, D., Brockliss, L. and John, M., 'Conclusion: from dynastic union to unitary state: the European experience', in L. Brockliss and D. Eastwood, eds, *A Union of Multiple Identities: The British Isles, c.1750–c.1850* (Manchester, 1997).

Eatwell, J., Milgate, M. and Newman, P., eds, *The New Palgrave: A Dictionary of Economic Thought* (3 vols, London, 1987).

Edelstein, M., 'Foreign investment and accumulation, 1860–1914', in R. C. Floud and D. McCloskey, eds, *The Economic History of Britain since 1700*, vol. 2, *1860–1939* (Cambridge, 1994).

Edelstein, M., 'Imperialism: cost and benefit', in R. C. Floud and D. McCloskey, eds, *The Economic History of Britain since 1700*, vol. 2, *1860–1939* (Cambridge, 1994).

Edwards, R. D. and Williams, T. D., eds, *The Great Famine: Studies in Irish History, 1845–52* (Dublin, 1995).

Elliott, M., *The Catholics of Ulster: A History* (London, 2000).

Emsley, C., *Crime and Society in England, 1750–1900* (Harlow, 1996).

Emsley, C., *The English Police: A Political and Social History* (Harlow, 1996).

Engerman, S., 'Reflections on "the standard of living debate": new arguments and new evidence', in J. A. James and M. Thomas, eds, *Capitalism in Context: Essays in Economic Development and Cultural Change in Honour of R. M. Hartwell* (Chicago, 1995).

English, B., 'Debate: the Kanpur massacres in India in the revolt of 1857', *Past and Present*, 142 (1994).

Ensor, R. C. K., *England 1870–1914* (Oxford, 1936).

Epstein, J., *Radical Expression: Political Language, Ritual and Symbol in England, 1790–1850* (Oxford, 1994).

Erickson C., *Leaving England: Essays on British Emigration in the Nineteenth Century* (London, 1994).

Ernle, Lord, *English Farming Past and Present* (London, 1961).

Evans, C., *'The Labyrinth of Flames': Work and Social Conflict in Early Industrial Merthyr Tydfil* (Cardiff, 1993).

Evans, E. J., *The Forging of the Modern State: Early Industrial Britain 1783–1870* (Harlow, 1996).

Evans, T., *The Background to Modern Welsh Politics, 1789–1846* (Cardiff, 1936).

Feinstein, C. H., 'Capital formation in Great Britain', in P. Mathias and M. M. Postan, eds, *The Cambridge Economic History of Europe*, vol. 7 (Cambridge, 1978).

Feinstein, C. H., 'Pessimism perpetuated: real wages and the standard of living in Britain during and after the industrial revolution', *Journal of Economic History*, 58 (1998).

Feldman, D. and Stedman Jones, G., eds, *Metropolis London: Histories and Representations since 1800* (London, 1989).

Fetter, F. W., 'Economic articles in the *Quarterly Review*', *Journal of Political Economy*, 66 (1958).

Fetter, F. W., *The Economist in Parliament: 1780–1860* (Durham, NC, 1980).

Ffinch, M., *Gilbert and Sullivan* (London, 1993).

Fforde, M., *Conservatism and Collectivism 1886–1914* (Edinburgh, 1990).

Fieldhouse, D., 'Can Humpty Dumpty be put together again? Imperial history in the 1980s', *Journal of Imperial and Commonwealth History*, 12 (1984).

Finer, S. E., *The Life and Times of Sir Edwin Chadwick* (London, 1952).

Finlay, R., 'The rise and fall of popular imperialism in Scotland, 1850–1950', *Scottish Geographical Magazine*, 113 (1997).

Finn, M. C., *After Chartism: Class and Nation in English Radical Politics, 1848–1874* (Cambridge, 1993).

Finnegan, F., *Poverty and Prostitution: A Study of Victorian Prostitutes in York* (Cambridge, 1979).

Fitzpatrick, D., 'The disappearance of the Irish agricultural labourer, 1841–1912', *Irish Economic and Social History*, 7 (1980).

Fletcher, T. W., 'The great depression of English agriculture, 1873–1896', *Economic History Review*, 13 (1960–1).

Floud, R., Wachter, K. and Gregory, A., *Height, Health and History: Nutritional Status in the United Kingdom, 1750–1980* (Cambridge, 1990).

Fortescue, J. W., *A History of the British Army* (London, 1897–1930).

Foster, R., 'We are all revisionists now', *Irish Review*, 1 (1986).

Foster, R., *Modern Ireland, 1600–1972* (London, 1988).

Foster, R., ed., *The Oxford Illustrated History of Ireland* (Oxford, 1989).

Foster, R., *The Irish Story: Telling Tales and Making it up in Ireland* (London, 2001).

Foucault, M., *Madness and Civilization: A History of Insanity in the Age of Reason* (London, 1967).

Foucault, M., *Birth of the Clinic: An Archaeology of Medical Perception* (London, 1973).

Foucault, M., *Discipline and Punish: The Birth of the Prison* (London, 1977).

Fox, A. W., 'Agricultural wages in England and Wales during the last fifty years', in W. E. Minchinton, ed., *Essays in Agrarian History* (Newton Abbot, 1968).

Francis, M. and Morrow, J., *A History of English Political Thought in the Nineteenth Century* (London, 1995).

Frank, A. G., *ReOrient: Global Economy in the Asian Age* (Berkeley, 1998).

Fraser, D., *The Evolution of the British Welfare State* (London, 1973).

Fraser, D., *Urban Politics in Victorian England* (Leicester, 1976).

Fraser, W. H., *Scottish Popular Politics: From Chartism to Labour* (Edinburgh, 2000).

Fraser, W. H. and Lee, C. H., eds, *Aberdeen 1800–2000: A New History* (E. Linton, Scotland, 2000).

Fraser, W. H. and Morris, R. J., eds, *People and Society in Scotland*, vol. 2, *1830–1914* (Edinburgh, 1990).

Freeden, M., *The New Liberalism: An Ideology of Social Reform* (Oxford, 1978).

Frost, G., *Promises Broken: Courtship, Class and Gender in Victorian England* (Charlottesville, 1995).

Frost, G., 'Bigamy and cohabitation in Victorian England', *Journal of Family History*, 22 (1997).

Fry, M., 'The Whig interpretation of Scottish history,' in I. Donnachie and C. Whatley, eds, *The Manufacture of Scottish History* (Edinburgh, 1992).

Fry, M., *The Scottish Empire* (E. Linton, Scotland, 2001).

Fuchs, C. J., *The Trade Policy of Great Britain and Her Colonies since 1860* (London, 1905).

Gahan, D., *The People's Rising: Wexford, 1798* (Dublin, 1995).

Gallagher, T., *Glasgow: The Uneasy Peace* (Manchester, 1987).

Gambles, A., 'Rethinking the politics of protection: Conservatism and the Corn Laws, 1830–52', *English Historical Review*, 113 (1998).

Gandy, G. N., 'Illegitimacy in a handloom weaving community: fertility patterns in Culceth, Lancaster, 1781–1860', D. Phil. diss., University of Oxford, 1978.

Garrard, J., *Leadership and Power in Victorian Industrial Towns 1830–1880* (Manchester, 1983).

Garrard, J., 'Urban elites, 1850–1914: the rule and decline of a new squirearchy?', *Albion*, 27 (1995).

Gash, N., *Reaction and Reconstruction in English Politics, 1832–52* (Oxford, 1965).

Gash, N., *Peel* (London, 1976).

Gash, N., *Aristocracy and People: Britain 1815–1865* (London, 1979).

Gates, D., *The Napoleonic Wars, 1803–1815* (London, 1997).

Gatrell, V. A. C., 'Crime, authority and the policeman-state', in F. M. L. Thompson, ed., *The Cambridge Social History of Britain 1750–1950*, vol. 3, *Social Agencies and Institutions* (Cambridge, 1990).

Gatrell, V. A. C., *The Hanging Tree: Execution and the English People 1770–1868* (Oxford, 1994).

Gay, P., *The Bourgeois Experience – Victoria to Freud*, vol. 1, *Education of the Senses* (London, 1983).

Geary, L. M., ed., *Rebellion and Remembrance in Modern Ireland* (Dublin, 2001).

Geertz, C., *The Interpretation of Cultures* (New York, 1973).

Geertz, C., *The Interpretation of Cultures: Selected Essays* (London, 1993).

Geison, G., *Michael Foster and the Cambridge School of Physiology* (Princeton, NJ, 1978).

Geoghegan, P. M., *The Irish Act of Union: A Study of High Politics 1798–1801* (Dublin, 1999).

Gerard, D. E., *David Elwyn, John Ruskin and William Morris: The Energies of Order and Love* (London, 1988).

Giedion, S., *Mechanization Takes Command: A Contribution to Anonymous History* (New York, 1969).

Gilbert, A. D., *Religion and Society in Industrial England: Church, Chapel, and Social Change 1740–1914* (London, 1976).

Gilbert, A. D., *The Making of Post-Christian Britain* (London, 1980).

Gilbert, S. M. and Gubar, S., *The Madwoman in the Attic: The Woman Writer and the Nineteenth-Century Literary Imagination* (New Haven, CT, 1979).

Gill, S., *Women and the Church of England from the Eighteenth Century to the Present* (London, 1994).

Gilley, S., *Newman and his Age* (London, 1990).

Gilley, S. and Sheils, W. J., *A History of Religion in Britain* (Oxford, 1994).

Gillis, J., *For Better, For Worse: British Marriages, 1600 to the Present* (Oxford, 1985).

Gillis, J., *A World of Their Own Making: Myth, Ritual, and the Quest for Family Values* (New York, 1996).

Girouard, M., *The English Town* (New Haven, 1990).

Glazier, M., ed., *Encyclopaedia of the Irish in America* (Chicago, 2000).

Gleadle, K., *The Early Feminists: Radical Unitarians and the Emergence of the Women's Rights Movement, 1831–51* (Basingstoke, 1995).

Gleadle, K., ' "Our several spheres": middle-class women and the feminisms of early Victorian radical politics', in K. Gleadle and S. Richardson, eds, *Women in British Politics, 1760–1860: The Power of the Petticoat* (Basingstoke, 2000).

Gleadle, K. and Richardson, S., eds, *Women in British Politics, 1760–1860: The Power of the Petticoat* (Basingstoke, 2000).

Golby, J. M. and Purdue, A. W., *The Civilisation of the Crowd: Popular Culture in England 1750–1900* (Stroud, 1999).

Goodman, J. and Harrop, S., eds, *Women, Educational Policy-Making and Administration in England* (London, 2000).

Gordon, B., *Political Economy in Parliament, 1819–1823* (London, 1976).

Gordon, E. and Breitenbach, E., eds, *The World is Ill Divided: Women's Work in Scotland in the Nineteenth and early Twentieth Centuries* (Edinburgh, 1990).

Gordon, E. and Nair, G., 'Middle class family structure in nineteenth century Glasgow', *Journal of Family History*, 24 (1999).

Gourvish, T. R., *Railways and the British Economy* (London, 1980).

Granshaw, L., ' "Fame and fortune by means of bricks and mortar": the medical profession and specialist hospitals in Britain 1800–1948', in L. Granshaw and R. Porter, eds, *The Hospital in History* (London, 1989).

Grant, A. and Stringer, K., eds, *Uniting the Kingdom? The Making of British History* (London, 1995).

Graves, P., *Labour Women: Women in British Working-Class Politics, 1918–1939* (Cambridge, 1994).

Gray, R. and Loftus, D., 'Industrial regulation, urban space and the boundaries of the workplace: mid-Victorian Nottingham', *Urban History*, 26 (1999).

Green, A., *Education and State Formation: The Rise of Education Systems in England, France and the USA* (London, 1990).

Green, S. J. D., *Religion in the Age of Decline: Organisation and Experience in Industrial Yorkshire, 1870–1920* (Cambridge, 1996).

Greenleaf, W. H., *The British Political Tradition*, vol. 2, *The Ideological Heritage* (London, 1983).

Griffiths, D., ed., *The Encyclopedia of the British Press 1422–1992* (London, 1992).

Grigg, D., 'E. G. Ravenstein and the "laws of migration" ', *Journal of Historical Geography*, 9 (1977).

Grigg, D., 'Farm size in England and Wales, from Victorian times to the present', *Agricultural History Review*, 35 (1987).

Grigg, D., *English Agriculture: An Historical Perspective* (Oxford, 1989).

Guha, R., *An Indian Historiography of India: A Nineteenth Century Agenda and its Implications* (Calcutta, 1987).

Guinnane, T. W., *The Vanishing Irish: Households, Migration and the Rural Economy in Ireland, 1850–1914* (Princeton, NJ, 1997).

Gullette, M. M., 'Male midlife sexuality in a gerontocratic economy: the privileged state of the long midlife in nineteenth-century age-ideology', *Journal of the History of Sexuality*, 5 (1994).

Gunn, S., *The Public Culture of the Victorian Middle Class: Ritual and Authority in the English Industrial City, 1840–1914* (Manchester, 2000).

Gunn, S. and Bell, R., *Middle Classes: Their Rise and Sprawl* (London, 2002).

Gurney, S., *British Poetry of the Nineteenth Century* (New York, 1993).

Gutzke, D. W., 'Gentrifying the British public house, 1896–1914', *International Labor and Working-Class History*, 45 (1994).

Habermas, J., *The Structural Transformation of the Public Sphere* (Cambridge, 1989).

Halévy, E., *A History of the English People in 1815* (London, 1938).

Halévy, E., *A History of the English People in the Nineteenth Century*, [vol. 2] *The Liberal Awakening (1815–1830)* (London, 1949).

Halévy, E., *The Growth of Philosophic Radicalism* (London, 1952).

Hall, C., *White, Male and Middle Class: Explorations in Feminism and History* (London, 1992).

Hall, C., 'White visions, black lives: the free villages of Jamaica', *History Workshop Journal*, 36 (1993).

Hall, C., 'The rule of difference: gender, class and empire in the making of the 1832 Reform Act', in I. Blom, K. Hagemann and C. Hall, eds, *Gendered Nations: Nationalisms and Gender Order in the Long Nineteenth Century* (Oxford, 2000).

Hall, C., McClelland, K. and Rendall, J., *Defining the Victorian Nation: Class, Race, Gender and the Reform Act of 1867* (Cambridge, 2000).

Hamer, D. A., *Liberal Politics in the Age of Gladstone and Rosebery* (Oxford, 1972).

Hamer, W. S., *British Army: Civil–Military Relations, 1885–1905* (Oxford, 1970).

Hamilton, C. I., *Anglo-French Naval Rivalry 1840–1870* (Oxford, 1993).

Hamlin, C., 'Muddling in bumbledom: on the economy of large sanitary improvements in four British towns, 1855–1885', *Victorian Studies*, 32 (1988).

Hamlin, C., *Public Health and Social Justice in the Age of Chadwick: Britain, 1800–1854* (Cambridge, 1998).

Hammerton, A. J., *Cruelty and Companionship: Conflict in Nineteenth Century Married Life* (London, 1992).

Hammond, J. L., *Gladstone and the Irish Nation* (London, 1964).

Hammond, J. L. and Hammond, B., *The Village Labourer* (London, 1978).

Hampton, M., ' "Understanding media": theories of the press in Britain, 1850–1914', *Media, Culture and Society*, 23 (2001).

Handley, J. E., *The Irish in Modern Scotland* (Cork, 1947).

Hanham, H. J., *Elections and Party Management: Politics in the Time of Disraeli and Gladstone* (Longman, 1959).

Hannam, J., ' "In the comradeship of the sexes lies the hope of progress and social regeneration": women in the West Riding Independent Labour Party, c.1890–1914', in J. Rendall, ed., *Equal or Different: Women's Politics, 1800–1914* (Oxford, 1987).

Hardy, A., *Epidemic Streets: Infectious Disease and the Rise of Preventive Medicine, 1856–1900* (Oxford, 1993).

Harley, C. K., 'British industrialization before 1841: evidence of slower growth during the industrial revolution', *Journal of Economic History*, 42 (1982).

Harley, C. K., 'Foreign trade: comparative advantage and performance', in R. C. Floud and D. McCloskey, eds, *The Economic History of Britain since 1700*, vol. 1, *1700–1860* (Cambridge, 1994).

Harley, C. K., 'Harley on British economic growth, 1688–1959', EH.Net Review, September 2001.

Harling, P., *The Waning of 'Old Corruption': The Politics of Economical Reform in Britain, 1779–1846* (Oxford, 1996).

Harling, P. and Mandler, P., 'From "fiscal-military" state to *laissez-faire* state, 1760–1850', *Journal of British Studies*, 32 (1993).

Harries-Jenkins, G., *The Army in Victorian Society* (London, 1977).

Harris, J., *Private Lives, Public Spirit: Britain 1870–1914* (London, 1993).

Harris, J. R., *The British Iron Industry 1700–1850* (Basingstoke, 1988).

Harris, J. R., *Industrial Espionage and Technology Transfer: Britain and France in the Eighteenth Century* (Aldershot, 1998).

Harrison, B., *Drink and the Victorians: The Temperance Question in England* (London, 1971).

Harrison, B., *The Transformation of British Politics, 1860–1995* (Oxford, 1996).

Harrison, F., *Order and Progress*, ed. M. Vogeler (Brighton, 1975).

Harrison, J. F. C., *Early Victorian Britain 1832–51* (London, 1988).

Harrison, J. F. C., *Late Victorian Britain 1875–1901* (London, 1991).

Hart, J., 'Nineteenth-century social reform: a Tory interpretation of history', *Past and Present*, 31 (1965).

Harvey, J., *The Art of Piety: The Visual Culture of Welsh Nonconformity* (Cardiff, 1995).

Harvie, C., *The Lights of Liberalism: University Liberals and the Challenge of Democracy, 1860–86* (London, 1976).

Hastings, A., *The Construction of Nationhood: Ethnicity, Religion and Nationalism* (Cambridge, 1997).

Hay, D., Linebaugh, P. and Thompson, E. P., *Albion's Fatal Tree: Crime and Society in Eighteenth Century England* (London, 1975).

Hayes, W. A., *The Background and Passage of the Third Reform Act* (New York, 1982).

Headrick, D. R., *The Tools of Empire: Technology and European Imperialism in the Nineteenth Century* (Oxford, 1981).

Hearnshaw, F. J. C., *The Social and Political Ideas of Some Representative Thinkers of the Victorian Age* (London, 1933).

Heimann, M., *Catholic Devotion in Victorian England* (Oxford, 1995).

Helmstadter, R., 'The Nonconformist conscience', in P. Marsh, ed., *The Conscience of the Victorian State* (New York, 1979).

Hempton, D., *Methodism and Politics in British Society 1750–1850* (London, 1984).

Hempton, D., *The Religion of the People: Methodism and Popular Religion c.1750–1900* (London, 1996).

Hempton, D., *Religion and Political Culture in Britain and Ireland: From the Glorious Revolution to the Decline of the Empire* (Cambridge, 1996).

Hempton, D. and Hill, M., *Evangelical Protestantism in Ulster Society, 1740–1890* (London, 1992).

Henderson, J., *Early Mathematical Economics: William Whewell and the British Case* (London, 1996).

Hendrick, H., *Child Welfare: England 1872–1989* (London, 1994).

Henriques, U. R. Q., *Before the Welfare State: Social Administration in Early Industrial Britain* (London, 1979).

Henry, J., *The Making of Neoclassical Economics* (London, 1990).

Heuman, G., 'The Killing Time': The Morant Bay Rebellion in Jamaica* (Knoxville, 1994).

Heyck, T. W., *The Peoples of the British Isles: A New History*, vol. 2, *From 1688 to 1870* (Belmont, 1992).

Heyck, T. W., *The Peoples of the British Isles: A New History*, vol. 3, *From 1870 to the Present* (Belmont, 1992).

Hickman, M., 'Alternative historiographies of the Irish in Britain: a critique of the segregation/assimilation model', in R. Swift and S. Gilley, eds, *The Irish in Victorian Britain: The Local Dimension* (Dublin, 1999).

Hicks, J. and Hollander, S., 'Mr Ricardo and the moderns', *Quarterly Journal of Economics*, 91 (1977).

Higgs, E., 'Occupational censuses and the agricultural workforce in Victorian England and Wales', *Economic History Review*, 48 (1995).

Hill, B., 'The marriage age of women and the demographers', *History Workshop Journal*, 28 (1989).

Hill, B., 'Women, work and the census – a problem for historians of women', *History Workshop Journal*, 35 (1993).

Hill, J., 'British sports history: a postmodern future?', *Journal of Sport History*, 23 (1996).

Hill, J., 'The legend of Denis Compton', *The Sports Historian*, 18 (1998).

Hill, J. R., ed., *The Oxford Illustrated History of the Royal Navy* (Oxford, 1995).

Hill, K., ' "Thoroughly embued with the spirit of ancient Greece": symbolism and space in Victorian civic culture', in A. Kidd and D. Nicholls, eds, *Gender, Civic Culture and Consumerism: Middle-Class Identity in Britain 1800–1940* (Manchester, 1999).

Hillis, P., 'Education and evangelisation: Presbyterian missions in mid-nineteenth century Glasgow', *Scottish Historical Review*, 66 (1988).

Hilton, B., *Cash, Corn and Commerce: The Economic Policies of the Tory Governments, 1815–30* (Oxford, 1977).

Hilton, B., *The Age of Atonement: The Influence of Evangelicalism on Social and Economic Thought, 1795–1865* (Oxford, 1988).

Hirshfield, C., 'Liberal women's organisations and the war against the Boers, 1899–1902', *Albion*, 14 (1982).

Hirshfield, C., 'Fractured faith: Liberal Party women and the suffrage issue in Britain, 1892–1914', *Gender and History*, 2 (1990).

Hobsbawm, E. J., *Worlds of Labour: Further Studies in the History of Labour* (London, 1984).

Hobsbawm, E. J., *Nations and Nationalism since 1780: Programme, Myth, Reality* (Cambridge, 1990).

Hobsbawm, E. J. and Ranger, T., eds, *The Invention of Tradition* (Cambridge, 1983).

Hobsbawm, E. J. and Rudé, G., *Captain Swing* (London, 1970).

Hobson, J. A., *Imperialism: A Study* (London, 1948).

Hoff, J., 'Gender as a postmodern category of paralysis', *Women's History Review*, 3 (1994).

Hollander, S., *The Economics of David Ricardo* (London, 1979).

Hollander, S., 'The wage path in classical growth models: Ricardo, Malthus and Mill', *Oxford Economic Papers*, 36 (1984).

Hollander, S., *The Economics of John Stuart Mill* (Toronto, 1997).

Hollis, P., *The Pauper Press: A Study in Working-Class Radicalism of the 1830s* (Oxford, 1970).

Hollis, P., *Ladies Elect: Women in English Local Government, 1865–1918* (Oxford, 1987).

Holmes, C., *John Bull's Island: Immigration and British Society, 1871–1971* (Basingstoke, 1988).

Holmes, F., *The Presbyterian Church in Ireland: A Popular History* (Dublin, 2000).

Holt, R., *Sport and the British: A Modern History* (Oxford, 1989).

Holt, T. C., *The Problem of Freedom: Race, Labor, and Politics in Jamaica and Britain, 1832–1938* (Baltimore, 1991).

Holton, S. S., *Feminism and Democracy: Women's Suffrage and Reform Politics in Britain, 1900–1918* (Cambridge, 1986).

Homans, M., *Royal Representations: Queen Victoria and British Culture, 1837–1876* (Chicago, 1998).

Hoppen, K. T., 'The franchise and electoral politics in England and Ireland 1832–1885', *History*, 70 (1985).

Hoppen, K. T., *The Mid-Victorian Generation, 1846–1886* (Oxford, 1998).

Hoppitt, J., 'Counting the industrial revolution', *Economic History Review*, 43 (1990).

Horn, P., *Education in Rural England 1800–1914* (Dublin, 1978).

Horrell, S., 'Home demand and British industrialization', *Journal of Economic History*, 56 (1996).

Horrell, S. and Humphries, J., 'Old questions, new data and alternative perspectives: families' living standards in the industrial revolution', *Journal of Economic History*, 52 (1992).

Horrell, S. and Humphries, J., 'Women's labour force participation and the transition to the male-breadwinner family, 1790–1865', *Economic History Review*, 48 (1995).

Horrell, S. and Humphries, J., *Household Budgets and the Standard of Living in the Industrial Revolution* (Cambridge, forthcoming).

Horrell, S., Humphries, J. and Voth, H.-J., 'Stature and relative deprivation: fatherless children in early industrial Britain', *Continuity and Change*, 13 (1998).

Houston, R. A., 'Geographical mobility in Scotland 1652–1811: the evidence of testimonials', *Journal of Historical Geography*, 11 (1985).

Howard, M. and King, J., *A History of Marxian Economics, 1883–1929* (London, 1989).

Howe, A., *Free Trade and Liberal England, 1846–1946* (Oxford, 1997).

Howe, S., *Ireland and Empire: Colonial Legacies in Irish History and Culture* (Oxford, 2000).

Howell, D. W., *Land and People in Nineteenth-Century Wales* (London, 1977).

Howkins, A., 'The discovery of rural England', in R. Colls and P. Dodd, eds, *Englishness: Politics and Culture 1880–1920* (Beckenham, 1986).

Howkins, A., *Reshaping Rural England: A Social History 1850–1925* (London, 1991).

Howkins, A., 'The English farm labourer in the nineteenth century: farm, family and community', in B. Short, ed., *The English Rural Community: Image and Analysis* (Cambridge, 1992).

Howkins, A., 'Peasants, servants and labourers: the marginal workforce in British agriculture, c.1870–1914', *Agricultural History Review*, 42 (1994).

Huck, P., 'Infant mortality and living standards of English workers during the industrial revolution', *Journal of Economic History*, 55 (1995).

Hudson, P., ed., *Regions and Industries: A Perspective on the Industrial Revolution in Britain* (Cambridge, 1989).

Hudson, P., *The Industrial Revolution* (London, 1992).

Hudston, S., *Victorian Theatricals: From Menageries to Melodrama* (London, 2000).

Huggins, M., 'Second-class citizens? English middle-class culture and sport, 1850–1910: a reconsideration', *International Journal of the History of Sport*, 17 (2000).

Humphries, J., 'Women and paid work', in J. Purvis, ed., *Women's History: Britain, 1850–1945* (London, 1995).

Hunt, B., *The Maxwellians* (Ithaca, NY, 1991).

Hunter, J., *The Making of the Crofting Community* (Edinburgh, 1976).

Hurt, J., *Elementary Schooling and the Working Classes 1860–1918* (London, 1979).

Hurt, J., *Outside the Mainstream: A History of Special Education* (London, 1988).

Hutchison, I. G. C., *A Political History of Scotland, 1832–1924: Parties, Elections and Issues* (Edinburgh, 1986).

Hutchison, T. W., 'The "marginal revolution" and the decline of English classical political economy', in R. D. C. Black, A. W. Coats and C. D. W. Goodwin, eds, *The Marginal Revolution in Economics: Interpretation and Evaluation* (Durham, NC, 1973).

Hyam, R., *Britain's Imperial Century: A Study of Empire and Expansion* (London, 1993).

Hylson-Smith, K., *The Churches in England from Elizabeth I to Elizabeth II* (London, 1996–8).

Ignatieff, M., *A Just Measure of Pain: The Penitentiary in the Industrial Revolution, 1750–1850* (London, 1978).

Illich, I., *Medical Nemesis: The Expropriation of Health* (London, 1975).

Imlah, A. H., *Economic Elements in the Pax Britannica: Studies in British Foreign Trade in the Nineteenth Century* (Cambridge, MA, 1958).

Inglis, K. S., *Churches and the Working Classes in Victorian England* (London, 1963).

Inkster, I. and Morrell, J., eds, *Metropolis and Province: Science and British Culture, 1780–1850* (London, 1983).

Jackson, A., *The Ulster Party: Irish Unionists in the House of Commons 1885–1911* (Oxford, 1989).

Jackson, A., *Ireland, 1798–1998: Politics and War* (Oxford, 1999).

Jackson, L. A., *Child Sexual Abuse in Victorian England* (London, 2000).

Jalland, P., *Women, Marriage and Politics, 1860–1914* (Oxford, 1986).

James, L., ed., *Print and the People 1819–1851* (London, 1976).

Jarvis, D., '"Behind every great party": women and Conservatism in twentieth century Britain', in A. Vickery, ed., *Women, Privilege and Power: British Politics, 1750 to the Present* (Stanford, 2001).

Jeffrey, K., ed., *'An Irish Empire'? Aspects of Ireland and the British Empire* (Manchester, 1996).

Jenkins, A., *The Making of Victorian Drama* (Cambridge, 1991).

Jenkins, D., *The Agricultural Community in South-West Wales at the Turn of the Twentieth Century* (Cardiff, 1971).

Jenkins, G. H., ed., *Language and Community in the Nineteenth Century* (Cardiff, 1998).

Jenkins, G. H., ed., *The Welsh Language and its Social Domains, 1801–1911* (Cardiff, 2000).

Jenkins, R. T., 'The development of nationalism in Wales', *Sociological Review*, 27 (1935).

Jenkins, T. A., *The Liberal Ascendancy, 1830–1886* (Basingstoke, 1994).

Jenks, L. H., *The Migration of British Capital to 1875* (London, 1971).

Jewson, N., 'Medical knowledge and the patronage system in eighteenth century England', *Sociology*, 8 (1974).

Joannou, M. and Purvis, J., eds, *The Women's Suffrage Movement: New Feminist Perspectives* (Manchester, 1998).

John, A. V., ed., *Our Mothers' Land: Chapters in Welsh Women's History, 1830–1939* (Cardiff, 1991).

John, A. V. and Eustance, C., eds, *The Men's Share? Masculinities, Male Support and Women's Suffrage in Britain* (London, 1997).

Johnson, D. A., *The Changing Shape of English Nonconformity 1825–1925* (New York, 1999).

Johnson, P. and Nicholas, S., 'Male and female living standards in England and Wales, 1812–1857: evidence from criminal height records', *Economic History Review*, 48 (1995).

Johnson, R., 'Education policy and social control in early Victorian England', *Past and Present*, 49 (1979).

Johnston, R., *Clydeside Capital, 1870–1920: A Social History of Employers* (E. Linton, Scotland, 2000).

Joll, J., ed., *Britain and Europe: Pitt to Churchill 1793–1940* (London, 1950).

Jones, A., *The Politics of Reform 1884* (Cambridge, 1972).

Jones, A. G., *Press, Politics and Society: A History of Journalism in Wales* (Cardiff, 1993).

Jones, C. A., *International Business in the Nineteenth Century: The Rise and Fall of a Cosmopolitan Bourgeoisie* (Brighton, 1987).

Jones, D. J. V., *Before Rebecca: Popular Protests in Wales 1793–1835* (London, 1973).

Jones, D. J. V., *Crime, Protest, Community and Police in Nineteenth-Century Britain* (London, 1982).

Jones, D. J. V., *The Last Rising: The Newport Insurrection of 1839* (Oxford, 1985).

Jones, D. J. V., *Rebecca's Children: A Study of Rural Society, Crime, and Protest* (Oxford, 1989).

Jones, D. J. V., *Crime in Nineteenth Century Wales* (Cardiff, 1992).

Jones, G., *Social Darwinism and English Thought: The Interaction between Biological and Social Theory* (Brighton, 1980).

Jones, G. E., *Controls and Conflicts in Welsh Secondary Education, 1889–1944* (Cardiff, 1982).

Jones, H. S., *Victorian Political Thought* (Basingstoke, 2000).

Jones, I. G., *Explorations and Explanations: Essays in the Social History of Victorian Wales* (Llandysul, 1981).

Jones, I. G., *Communities: Essays in the Social History of Victorian Wales* (Llandysul, 1987).

Jones, I. G., *Mid Victorian Wales: The Observers and the Observed* (Cardiff, 1992).

Jones, I. G. and Williams, D., eds, *The Religious Census of 1851: A Calendar of the Returns Relating to Wales* (Cardiff, 1976 & 1981).

Jones, R. M., *The North Wales Quarrymen, 1874–1922* (Cardiff, 1981).

Jones, R. T., 'The Church and the Welsh language in the nineteenth century', in G. H. Jenkins, ed., *The Welsh Language and its Social Domains, 1801–1911* (Cardiff, 2000).

Joyce, P., *Visions of the People: Industrial England and the Question of Class, 1848–1914* (Cambridge, 1991).

Joyce, P., ed., *Class* (Oxford, 1995).

Joyce, P., *The Rule of Freedom* (London, 2003).

Jupp, P. J., 'The landed elite and political authority in Britain, 1760–1850', *Journal of British Studies*, 29 (1990).

Kadish, A., *The Oxford Economists in the Late Nineteenth Century* (Oxford, 1982).

Kapur, D. and Raychaudhuri, T., eds, *The Cambridge Economic History of India* (Cambridge, 1982–3).

Kargon, R., *Science in Victorian Manchester: Enterprise and Expertise* (Baltimore, 1977).

Kearney, H., *The British Isles: A History of Four Nations* (Cambridge, 1989).

Kebbel, T. E., *Selected Speeches of the Late Right Honourable the Earl of Beaconsfield* (London, 1882).

Kelleher, M., *The Feminization of Famine: Expressions of the Inexpressible?* (Cork, 1997).

Kennedy, D., 'Imperial history and post-colonial theory', *Journal of Imperial and Commonwealth History*, 24 (1996).

Kennedy, L. and Ollerenshaw, P., *An Economic History of Ulster, 1820–1939* (Manchester, 1985).

Kennedy, P. M., *The Rise and Fall of British Naval Mastery* (London, 1976).

Kennedy, P. M., *The Rise of the Anglo-German Antagonism 1860–1914* (London, 1980).

Kent, C., *Brains and Numbers: Elitism, Comtism, and Democracy in Mid-Victorian England* (Toronto, 1978).

Kenwood, A. G. and Lougheed, A. L., *The Growth of the International Economy, 1820–2000* (London, 1999).

Keogh, D. and Furlong, N., eds, *The Mighty Wave: The 1798 Rebellion in Wexford* (Dublin, 1996).

Keogh, D. and Furlong, N., *The Women of 1798* (Dublin, 1998).

Ker, I., *John Henry Newman: A Biography* (Oxford, 1990).

Kerber, L., 'Separate spheres, female worlds, woman's place: the rhetoric of women's history', *Journal of American History*, 75 (1988).

Kettle, A., *The Nineteenth-Century Novel* (London, 1981).

Keynes, J. M., *Essays in Biography*, in D. Moggridge, ed., *The Collected Writings of John Maynard Keynes* (London, 1972).

Keynes, J. N., *The Scope and Method of Political Economy* (London, 1890).

Kidd, C., *British Identities Before Nationalism: Ethnicity and Nationhood in the Atlantic World, 1600–1800* (Cambridge, 1999).

Kift, D., *The Victorian Music Hall: Culture, Class and Conflict* (Cambridge, 1996).

Kinealy, C., *This Great Calamity: The Irish Famine 1845–52* (Dublin, 1994).

Kinealy, C., *The Great Famine: Impact, Ideology and Rebellion* (Basingstoke, 2002).

Kinealy, C. and MacAtasney, G., *The Hidden Famine: Hunger, Poverty and Sectarianism in Belfast 1840–50* (London, 2000).

King, P., 'Punishing assault: the transformation of attitudes in the English courts', *Journal of Interdisciplinary History*, 27 (1996).

King, P., 'Pauper inventories and the material lives of the poor in the eighteenth and early nineteenth centuries', in T. Hitchcock, P. King and P. Sharpe, eds, *Chronicling Poverty: The Voices and Strategies of the English Poor* (Basingstoke, 1997).

King, P., 'The rise of juvenile delinquency in England, 1780–1840: changing patterns of perception and prosecution', *Past and Present*, 160 (1998).

Kirk, N., ed., *Social Class and Marxism: Defences and Challenges* (London, 1996).

Knight, A., 'Britain and Latin America', in A. Porter, ed., *The Oxford History of the British Empire*, vol. 3, *The Nineteenth Century* (Oxford, 1999).

Knight, F., *The Nineteenth-Century Church and English Society* (Cambridge, 1995).

Knights, B., *The Idea of the Clerisy in the Nineteenth Century* (Cambridge, 1978).

Knox, W. W., *Industrial Nation: Work, Culture and Society in Scotland, 1800–Present* (Edinburgh, 1999).

Komlos, J., 'The secular trend in the biological standard of living in the UK, 1730–1860', *Economic History Review*, 46 (1993).

Koning, N., *The Failure of Agrarian Capitalism: Agrarian Politics in the United Kingdom, Germany, the Netherlands and the USA, 1846–1919* (London, 1994).

Koot, G., *English Historical Economics, 1870–1926: The Rise of Economic History and Neo-Mercantilism* (Cambridge, 1987).

Koss, S. E., *The Rise and Fall of the Political Press in Britain*, vol. 1, *The Nineteenth Century* (London, 1981).

Kuhn, W. M., *Democratic Royalism: The Transformation of the British Monarchy, 1861–1914* (Basingstoke, 1996).

Kuhn, W. M., *Henry and Mary Ponsonby: Life at the Court of Queen Victoria* (London, 2002).

Lambert, A. D., *The Crimean War: British Grand Strategy, 1853–56* (Manchester, 1990).

Lambert, W. R., *Drink and Sobriety in Victorian Wales c.1820–1895* (Cardiff, 1983).

Landau, N., 'Who was subject to the Laws of Settlement? Procedure under the Settlement Laws in eighteenth-century England', *Agricultural History Review*, 49 (1995).

Lane, J., *The Social History of Medicine: Health, Healing and Disease in England, 1750–1950* (London, 2001).

Langford, P., *A Polite and Commercial People: England 1727–1783* (Oxford, 1983).

Langford, P., *Englishness Identified: Manners and Character 1650–1850* (Oxford, 2000).

Langhorne, R., *The Collapse of the Concert of Europe: International Politics 1830–1914* (Basingstoke, 1981).

Langton, J., 'The Industrial Revolution and the regional geography of England', *Transactions of the Institute of British Geographers*, new ser., 9 (1984).

Larkin, E., *The Historical Dimensions of Irish Catholicism* (New York, 1981).

Larsen, T., *Friends of Religious Equality: Nonconformist Politics in Mid-Victorian England* (Woodbridge, 1999).

Laslett, P., *The World We Have Lost: Further Explored* (London, 1983).

Lauder, J., 'Partnerships in preservation: the experience of the NEWSPLAN 2000 project', International Federation of Library Associations and Institutions (IFLA) 2002 Conference proceedings, online at www.ifla.org.

Lawrence, C., 'Incommunicable knowledge: science, technology and clinical art in Britain 1850–1914', *Journal of Contemporary History*, 20 (1985).

Lawrence, C., *Medicine in the Making of Modern Britain, 1700–1920* (London, 1994).

Lawrence, J., *Speaking for the People: Party, Language and Popular Politics in England, 1867–1914* (Cambridge, 1998).

Lawrence, J. and Taylor, M., eds, *Party, State and Society: Electoral Behaviour in Britain since 1820* (Aldershot, 1997).

Lecky, W. E., *The Empire: Its Value and Its Growth: An Inaugural Address* (London, 1893).

Lee, A. J., *The Origins of the Popular Press in England, 1855–1914* (London, 1976).

Lee, A. J., 'The structure, ownership and control of the press, 1855–1914', in G. Boyce, J. Curran and P. Wingate, eds, *Newspaper History: From the Seventeenth Century to the Present Day* (London, 1978).

Lees, L. H., *Exiles of Erin: Irish migrants in Victorian London* (Manchester, 1979).

Lees, L. H., *The Solidarities of Strangers: The English Poor Laws and the People, 1700–1948* (Cambridge, 1998).

Leighton, A., ed., *Victorian Women Poets: A Critical Reader* (Oxford, 1996).

Leighton, C. D. A., *Catholicism in a Protestant Kingdom: A Study of the Irish Ancien Régime* (London, 1994).

Levine, P., *Feminist Lives in Victorian England: Private Roles and Public Commitment* (Oxford, 1990).

Levine-Clarke, D., 'Dysfunctional domesticity: female insanity and family relationships among the West Riding poor in the mid-nineteenth century', *Journal of Family History*, 26 (2000).

Levitt, I. and Smout, C., *The State of the Scottish Working Class in 1843* (Edinburgh, 1979).

Lewis, J., *Women in England 1870–1950: Sexual Divisions and Social Change* (Brighton, 1984).

Lewis, M., *The Navy in Transition 1814–1864: A Social History* (London, 1965).

Liddington, J. and Norris, J., *One Hand Tied Behind Us: The Rise of the Women's Suffrage Movement* (London, 1978).

Lieven, D., *The Aristocracy in Europe, 1815–1914* (Basingstoke, 1992).

Lightman, B., ed., *Victorian Science in Context* (Chicago, 1997).

Lindert, P. H., 'English occupations, 1670–1811', *Journal of Economic History*, 40 (1980).

Lindert, P. H. and Williamson, J. G., 'English workers' living standards during the industrial revolution: a new look', *Economic History Review*, 36 (1983).

Linton, D. and Roston, R., eds, *The Newspaper Press in Britain: An Annotated Bibliography* (London, 1987).

Long, J., *Conversations in Cold Rooms: Women, Work and Poverty in Nineteenth Century Northumberland* (Woodbridge, 1999).

Longford, E., *Queen Victoria* (New York, 1965).

Lorimer, D., *Colour, Class and the Victorians* (Leicester, 1978).

Loudon, I., *Medical Care and the General Practitioner 1750–1850* (Oxford, 1986).

Loughlin, J., *Ulster Unionism and British National Identity since 1885* (Leicester, 1995).

Louis, W. R., ed., *Imperialism: The Robinson and Gallagher Controversy* (New York, 1975).

Lowe, C. J., *Salisbury and the Mediterranean, 1886–1896* (London, 1965).

Lowe, J., *The Great Powers, Imperialism and the German Problem 1865–1895* (London, 1994).

Lowe, J., *Britain and Foreign Affairs, 1815–1885: Europe and Overseas* (London, 1998).

Lowe, R., ed., *History of Education: Major Themes* (London, 2000).

Lowerson, J., *Sport and the English Middle Classes, 1870–1914* (Manchester, 1993).

Lowndes, G. A. N., *The Silent Social Revolution* (Oxford, 1937).

Luddy, M. and Murphy, C., *Women Surviving: Studies in Irish Women's History in the Nineteenth and Twentieth Centuries* (Dublin, 1990).

Lynch, M., *Scotland: A New History* (London, 1991).

Lynch, M., ed., *The Oxford Companion to Scottish History* (Oxford, 2001).

Lynn, M., 'British policy, trade, and informal empire in the mid-nineteenth century', in A. Porter, ed., *The Oxford History of the British Empire*, vol. 3, *The Nineteenth Century* (Oxford, 1999).

Lyons, F. S. L., *Culture and Anarchy in Ireland 1890–1939* (Oxford, 1979).

MacAtasney, G., *'This Dreadful Visitation': The Famine in Lurgan and Portadown* (Belfast, 1997).

MacBriar, A. M., *Fabian Socialism and English Politics, 1884–1918* (Cambridge, 1962).

McCaffrey, J. F., *Scotland in the Nineteenth Century* (Basingstoke, 1999).

McCalman, I. D., *Radical Underworld: Prophets, Revolutionaries and Pornographers in London, 1795–1840* (Cambridge, 1988).

McClelland, K., 'Masculinity and the "representative artisan" in Britain, 1850–80', in M. Roper and J. Tosh, eds, *Manful Assertions: Masculinities in Britain since 1800* (London, 1991).

McCloskey, D., *Enterprise and Trade in Victorian Britain: Essays in Historical Economics* (London, 1981).

McConville, S., *A History of English Prison Administration*, vol. 1, *1750–1877* (London, 1981).

McConville, S., *English Local Prisons 1860–1900: Next Only to Death* (London, 1995).

McCord, N., 'Some difficulties of parliamentary reform', *Historical Journal*, 10 (1967).

McCulloch, G. and Richardson, W., *Historical Research in Educational Settings* (Buckingham, 2000).

MacDonagh, O., 'The nineteenth-century revolution in government: a reappraisal', *Historical Journal*, 1 (1958).

MacDonagh, O., *The Emancipist: Daniel O'Connell 1830–1847* (London, 1989).

Macdonald C. M. M., *The Radical Thread: Political Change in Scotland, Paisley Politics 1885–1924* (E. Linton, Scotland, 2000).

McGowen, R., 'Civilising punishment: the end of the public execution in England', *Journal of British Studies*, 33 (1994).

Machin, I., *Disraeli* (London, 1995).

Macintyre, A. D., 'Lord George Bentinck and the Protectionists: a lost cause?', *Transactions of the Royal Historical Society*, 5th ser., 39 (1989).

Mackay, J. and Thane, P., 'The Englishwoman', in R. Colls and P. Dodd, eds, *Englishness: Politics and Culture 1880–1920* (Beckenham, 1986).

MacKenzie, J. M., *Propaganda and Empire: The Manipulation of British Public Opinion, 1880–1960* (Manchester, 1984).

MacKenzie, J. M., ed., *Imperialism and Popular Culture* (Manchester, 1986).

MacKenzie, J. M., ed., *Imperialism and the Natural World* (Manchester, 1990).

MacKenzie, J. M., 'Empire and metropolitan cultures', in A. Porter, ed., *The Oxford History of the British Empire*, vol. 3, *The Nineteenth Century* (Oxford, 1999).

McKeown, T., *The Modern Rise of Population* (London, 1976).

McKibbin, R., *The Ideologies of Class: Social Relations in Britain, 1880–1950* (Oxford, 1990).

MacKinnon, W., *On the Rise, Progress, and Present State of Public Opinion* (London, 1828).

Macleod, D. S., *Art and the Victorian Middle Class: Money and the Making of a Cultural Identity* (Cambridge, 1996).

McLeod, H. M., *Class and Religion in the Late Victorian City* (London, 1974).

MacLeod, R., ed., *Nature and Empire: Science and the Colonial Enterprise* (Chicago, 2001).

MacRaild, D. M., ed., *The Great Famine and Beyond: Irish Migrants in Britain in the Nineteenth and Twentieth Centuries* (Dublin, 2000).

MacRaild, D. M. and Martin, D. E., *Labour in British Society, 1830–1914* (Basingstoke, 2000).

Magarey, S., 'The invention of juvenile delinquency in early nineteenth century England', *Labour History*, 34 (1978).

Magnus, P., *Gladstone* (London, 1954).

Maguire, G. E., *Conservative Women: A History of Women and the Conservative Party, 1874–1997* (Basingstoke, 1998).

Mahood, L., *The Magdalenes: Prostitution in the Nineteenth Century* (London, 1990).

Mahood, L., *Policing Gender, Class and Family: Britain, 1850–1940* (London, 1995).

Malchow, H. L., *Gentlemen Capitalists: The Social and Political World of the Victorian Businessman* (London, 1991).

Malcolmson, R. W., *Popular Recreations in English Society, 1700–1850* (Cambridge, 1973).

Maloney, J., *Marshall, Orthodoxy and the Professionalisation of Economics* (Cambridge, 1985).

Mandler, P., *Aristocratic Government in the Age of Reform* (Oxford, 1990).

Mandler, P., ' "Race" and "nation" in mid-Victorian thought', in S. Collini, R. Whatmore and B. Young, eds, *History, Religion and Culture: British Intellectual History 1750–1950* (Cambridge, 2000).

Mangan, J. A., ed., *The Imperial Curriculum: Racial Images and Education in the British Colonial Experience* (London, 1993).

Manning, P. J., 'Wordsworth in the *Keepsake* 1829', in J. O. Jordan and R. L. Patten, eds, *Literature in the Marketplace: Nineteenth-Century British Publishing and Reading Practices* (Cambridge, 1995).

Marcus, S., *The Other Victorians: A Study of Sexuality and Pornography in Mid-Nineteenth Century England* (New York, 1966).

Marder, A. J., *The Anatomy of British Sea Power: A History of British Naval Policy in the Pre-Dreadnought Era, 1880–1905* (Hamden, CT, 1964).

Marsden, W. E., *Unequal Educational Provision in England and Wales: The Nineteenth-Century Roots* (London, 1987).

Marshall, P. J., ed., *The Cambridge Illustrated History of the British Empire* (Cambridge, 1996).

Marshall, P. J., 'Presidential address: Britain and the world in the eighteenth century: IV, The turning outwards of Britain', *Transactions of the Royal Historical Society*, 6th ser., 11 (2001).

Martin, T., *The Life of His Royal Highness the Prince Consort* (5 vols, New York, 1875).

Mason, M., *The Making of Victorian Sexual Attitudes* (Oxford, 1994).

Mason, M., *The Making of Victorian Sexuality* (Oxford, 1994).

Mather, F. C., *High Church Prophet: Bishop Samuel Horsley and the Caroline Tradition in the Later Georgian Church* (Oxford, 1992).

Mathias, P., *The First Industrial Nation* (London, 1969).

Matthew, C., ed., *The Nineteenth Century: The British Isles: 1815–1901* (Oxford, 2000).

Matthew, H. C. G., *Gladstone: 1809–1874* (Oxford, 1986).

Matthew, H. C. G., *Gladstone: 1875–1898* (Oxford, 1995).

Matthew, H. C. G., *Gladstone: 1809–1898* (Oxford, 1997).

Matthews, I., 'Debate: conscience or coercion? Clerical influence at the general election of 1868 in Wales', *Past and Present*, 169 (2000).

Matthews, R. C. O., Feinstein, C. H. and Odling-Smee, J. C., *British Economic Growth, 1856–1914* (Oxford, 1982).

Maver, I., *Glasgow* (Edinburgh, 2000).

Maynard, J., *Victorian Discourses on Sexuality and Religion* (Cambridge, 1993).

Mayne, A., *The Imagined Slum: Newspaper Representation in Three Cities, 1870–1914* (Leicester, 1993).

Meadowcroft, J., *Conceptualizing the State: Innovation and Dispute in British Political Thought, 1880–1914* (Oxford, 1995).

Medlicott, W. N., *Bismarck, Gladstone, and the Concert of Europe* (New York, 1969).

Mehta, U. S., *Liberalism and Empire: A Study in Nineteenth Century British Liberal Thought* (Chicago, 2000).

Meier, P., *William Morris: The Marxist Dreamer* (Hassocks, Sussex, 1978).

Meisel, M., *Realizations: Narrative, Pictorial, and Theatrical Arts in Nineteenth-Century England* (Princeton, NJ, 1983).

Mendilow, J., *The Romantic Tradition in British Political Thought* (London, 1986).

Mermin, D., 'The damsel, the knight, and the Victorian woman poet', *Critical Inquiry*, 13 (1986).

Metcalf, T. R., *An Imperial Vision: Indian Architecture and Britain's Raj* (Berkeley, CA, 1989).

Midgley, C., *Women Against Slavery: The British Campaigns, 1780–1870* (London, 1992).

Midgley, C., ed., *Gender and Imperialism* (Manchester, 1995).

Miles, A., *Social Mobility in Nineteenth- and Early Twentieth-Century England* (Basingstoke, 1999).

Miller, K., *Emigrants and Exiles: Ireland and the Irish Exodus to North America* (Oxford, 1985).

Milward, R. and Bell, F., 'Infant mortality in Victorian Britain: the mother as medium', *Economic History Review*, 4 (2001).

Mingay, G. E., ed., *The Victorian Countryside* (London, 1981).

Mingay, G. E., ed., *The Agrarian History of England and Wales*, vol. 6, *1750–1850* (Cambridge, 1989).

Miskell, L., Whately, C. and Harris, B., eds, *Victorian Dundee: Images and Realities* (E. Linton, Scotland, 2000).

Mitch, D., *The Rise of Popular Literacy in Victorian England* (Philadelphia, 1992).

Mitch, D., 'The role of human capital in the first industrial revolution', in J. Mokyr, ed., *The British Industrial Revolution* (Boulder, CO, 1993).

Mitchell, B. R., *Economic Development of the British Coal Industry* (Cambridge, 1984).

Mitchell, B. R., *British Historical Statistics* (Cambridge, 1988).

Mitchell, B. R. and Deane, P., *Abstract of British Historical Statistics* (Cambridge, 1962).

Mitchell, L. G., 'Foxite politics and the Great Reform Bill', *English Historical Review*, 108 (1993).

Mokyr, J., 'Malthusian models and Irish history', *Journal of Economic History*, 40 (1980).

Mokyr, J., *Why Ireland Starved: A Quantitative and Analytical Analysis of the Irish Economy, 1800–1859* (London, 1983).

Mokyr, J., 'Is there still life in the pessimist case? Consumption during the industrial revolution, 1790–1850', *Journal of Economic History*, 48 (1988).

Moore, D. C., 'Concession or cure: the sociological premises of the First Reform Act', *Historical Journal*, 9 (1966).

Moore, D. C., *The Politics of Deference* (Hassocks, Sussex, 1976).

Moore, J. R., *The Post Darwinian Controversies: A Study of the Protestant Struggle to Come to Terms with Darwin in Great Britain and America 1870–1900* (Cambridge, 1979).

Moore-Gilbert, B., *Postcolonial Theory: Context, Practices, Politics* (London, 1997).

More, C., *The Industrial Age: Economy and Society in Britain 1750–1995* (London, 1997).

Morgan, K., *The Birth of Industrial Britain: Economic Change 1750–1850* (London, 1999).

Morgan, K. O., *Wales in British Politics, 1868–1922* (Cardiff, 1963).

Morgan, K. O., *Rebirth of a Nation: Wales, 1880–1980* (Oxford, 1981).

Morgan, M., *National Identities and Travel in Victorian Britain* (Basingstoke, 2001).

Morgan, P., 'The hunt for the Welsh past in the golden age', in E. Hobsbawm and T. Ranger, eds, *The Invention of Tradition* (Cambridge, 1983).

Morgan, P., 'Early Victorian Wales and its crisis of identity', in L. Brockliss and D. Eastwood, eds, *A Union of Multiple Identities: The British Isles, c.1750–c.1850* (Manchester, 1997).

Morgan, S., 'Domestic economy and political agitation: women and the Anti-Corn Law League, 1839–46', in K. Gleadle and S. Richardson, eds, *Women in British Politics, 1760–1860: The Power of the Petticoat* (Basingstoke, 2000).

Morrell, J. and Thackray, A., *Gentlemen of Science: The Early Years of the British Association for the Advancement of Science* (Oxford, 1981).

Morris, J. N., *Religion and Urban Change: Croydon, 1840–1914* (Woodbridge, Suffolk, 1992).

Morris, R. J., *Class and Class Consciousness in the Industrial Revolution 1780–1850* (Basingstoke, 1976).

Morris, R. J., *Class, Sect and Party: The Making of the British Middle Class, Leeds 1820–1850* (Manchester, 1990).

Morris, R. J. and Trainor, R. H., eds, *Urban Governance: Britain and Beyond since 1750* (Aldershot, 2000).

Morton, G., *Unionist Nationalism: Governing Urban Scotland, 1830–60* (E. Linton, Scotland, 2000).

Morus, I. R., *Frankenstein's Children: Electricity, Exhibition and Experiment in Early-Nineteenth-Century London* (Princeton, NJ, 1998).

Moss, L., *Mountifort Longfield: Ireland's First Professor of Political Economy* (Ottawa, 1976).

Muir, R., *Britain and the Defeat of Napoleon 1807–1815* (New Haven, CT, and London, 1996).

Mukherjee, R., 'Reply', *Past and Present*, 142 (1994).

Mukherjee, R., *Spectre of Violence: The 1857 Kanpur Massacres* (Delhi, 1998).

Müller, F. L., *Britain and the German Question: Perceptions of Nationalism and Political Reform, 1830–63* (Basingstoke, 2002).

Mumm, S., *Stolen Daughters, Virgin Mothers: Anglican Sisterhoods in Victorian Britain* (London, 1999).

Munich, A., *Queen Victoria's Secrets* (New York, 1996).

Murray, R. H., *Studies in the English Social and Political Thinkers of the Nineteenth Century* (Cambridge, 1929).

Musson, A. E., 'James Nasymyth and the early growth of mechanical engineering', *Economic History Review*, 10 (1957).

Nairn, T., *The Break Up of Britain: Crisis and Neonationalism* (London, 1977).

Nairn, T., *The Enchanted Glass: Britain and its Monarchy* (London, 1988).

Neale, R. S., *Writing Marxist History: British Society, Economy and Culture since 1700* (Oxford, 1985).

Needham, G., *Nineteenth-Century Realist Art* (New York, 1988).

Neeson, J. M., *Commoners: Common Right, Enclosure and Social Change in England 1700–1820* (Cambridge, 1993).

Newbould, I., 'Peel and the Conservative party 1832–41: a study in failure', *English Historical Review*, 98 (1983).

Newbould, I., *Whiggery and Reform: The Politics of Government, 1830–41* (Stanford, 1990).

Newman, G., *The Rise of English Nationalism: A Cultural History, 1740–1830* (London, 1987).

Nicholas, S. and Steckel, R. H., 'Heights and living standards of English workers during the early years of industrialization', *Journal of Economic History*, 51 (1991).

Nicholson, P., *The Political Philosophy of the British Idealists: Selected Studies* (Cambridge, 1990).

Nockles, P. B., *The Oxford Movement in Context* (Cambridge, 1994).

Nord, D. E., *Walking the Victorian Streets: Women, Representation and the City* (Ithaca, NY, 1995).

Norman, E., *The English Catholic Church in the Nineteenth Century* (Oxford, 1984).

Northedge, F. S., *The Foreign Policies of the Powers* (London, 1968).

Nunn, P. G., *Problem Pictures: Women and Men in Victorian Painting* (Aldershot, 1995).

Nussbaum, M. C. and Glover, J., eds, *Women, Culture and Development: A Study of Human Capabilities* (Oxford, 1995).

O'Brien, D. P., *J. R. McCulloch: A Study in Classical Economics* (London, 1970).

O'Brien, G., *The Economic History of Ireland in the Eighteenth Century* (Dublin, 1918).

O'Brien, P. K., 'The costs and benefits of British imperialism, 1846–1914', *Past and Present*, 120 (1988).

O'Brien, P. K., 'Imperialism and the rise and decline of the British economy, 1688–1989', *New Left Review*, 238 (1999).

Ó Ceallaigh, D., ed., *Reconsiderations of Irish History and Culture* (Dublin, 1994).

O'Dowd, A., *Spalpeens and Tattie Hokers: History and Folklore of the Irish Migratory Worker in Ireland and Britain* (Dublin, 1991).

Odubena, S. A., 'The idea of "concert" in diplomatic practice between 1878 and 1906', PhD diss., University of London, 1995.

Offer, A., 'Costs and benefits, prosperity and security, 1870–1914', in A. Porter, ed., *The Oxford History of the British Empire*, vol. 3, *The Nineteenth Century* (Oxford, 1999).

O'Gorman, F., 'Electoral deference in unreformed England, 1760–1832', *Journal of Modern History*, 56 (1984).

O'Gorman, F., *Voters, Patrons, and Parties: The Unreformed Electoral System of Hanoverian England, 1734–1832* (Oxford, 1989).

O'Gorman, F., 'The electorate before and after 1832', *Parliamentary History*, 12 (1993).

O'Gorman, F., 'Campaign rituals and ceremonies: the social meaning of elections in England 1780–1860', *Past and Present*, 135 (1994).

Ó Gráda, C., *Ireland Before and After the Famine: Explorations in Economic History, 1808–1925* (Manchester, 1993).

Ó Gráda, C., 'British agriculture, 1860–1914', in R. C. Floud and D. McCloskey, eds, *The Economic History of Britain since 1700*, vol. 2, *1860–1939* (Cambridge, 1994).

Ó Gráda, C., *Ireland: A New Economic History 1780–1939* (Oxford, 1994).

Ó Gráda, C., *Black '47 and Beyond: The Great Irish Famine in History, Economy, and Memory* (Princeton, NJ, 1999).

Oldfield, J. R., *Popular Politics and British Anti-Slavery: The Mobilisation of Public Opinion against the Slave Trade, 1787–1807* (Manchester, 1995).

O'Leary, P., *Immigration and Integration: The Irish in Wales, 1798–1922* (Cardiff, 2000).

O'Rourke, K. H. and Williamson, J. G., *Globalization and History: The Evolution of a Nineteenth-Century Atlantic Economy* (Cambridge, MA, 1999).

Otter, C., 'Making liberalism durable: vision and civility in the late Victorian city', *Social History*, 27 (2002).

Overton, M., *Agricultural Revolution in England: The Transformation of the Agrarian Economy, 1500–1850* (Cambridge, 1996).

Owens, A., 'Property, gender and the life course: inheritance and family welfare provision in early nineteenth-century England', *Social History*, 26 (2001).

Pakenham, T., *The Boer War* (London, 1979).

Paley, R., ' "An imperfect, inadequate and wretched system?": policing London before Peel', *Criminal Justice History*, 10 (1989).

Palmer, S. H., *Police and Protest in England and Ireland, 1780–1850* (Cambridge, 1988).

Parratt, C. M., *'More Than Mere Amusement': Working-Class Women's Leisure in England, 1750–1914* (Boston, MA, 2001).

Parry, J., *The Rise and Fall of Liberal Government in Victorian Britain* (New Haven, CT, 1993).

Parsons, G., 'From dissenters to free churchmen', in G. Parsons, ed., *Religion in Victorian Britain*, vol. 1, *Traditions* (Manchester, 1988).

Parsons, G., ed., *Religion in Victorian Britain*, vol. 2, *Controversies* (Manchester, 1988).

Parsons, G., ed., *Religion in Victorian Britain*, vol. 4, *Interpretations* (Manchester, 1988).

Partridge, M. S., *Military Planning for the Defense of the United Kingdom, 1814–1870* (Westport, CT, 1989).

Paz, D. G., *Popular Anti-Catholicism in Mid-Victorian England* (Stanford, 1992).

Peach, T., 'David Ricardo: a review of some interpretative issues', in W. Thweatt, ed., *Classical Political Economy: A Survey of Recent Literature* (Boston, 1988).

Pearsall, R., *Victorian Popular Music* (Newton Abbot, 1973).

Pearson, G., *Hooligan: A History of Respectable Fears* (London, 1983).

Pearson, R. and Williams, G., *Political Thought and Public Policy in the Nineteenth Century: An Introduction* (London, 1984).

Peart, S., *The Economics of W. S. Jevons* (London, 1996).

Peers, D. M., ' "Those noble exemplars of the true military tradition": constructions of the Indian Army in the mid-Victorian press', *Modern Asian Studies*, 31 (1997).

Pelling, M., *Cholera, Fever and English Medicine, 1825–1865* (Oxford, 1978).

Perkin, H., *Origins of Modern English Society* (London, 1968).

Perkin, H., 'Individualism versus collectivism in nineteenth-century Britain: a false dichotomy', *Journal of British Studies*, 17 (1977).

Perren, R., *Agriculture in Depression, 1870–1940* (Cambridge, 1995).

Perry, P. J., 'Working class isolation and mobility in rural Dorset, 1837–1936: a study of marriage distances', *Transactions of the Institute of British Geographers*, 46 (1969).

Perry, P. J., *British Farming in the Great Depression 1870–1914: An Historical Geography* (Newton Abbot, 1974).

Petrow, S., *Policing Morals: The Metropolitan Police and the Home Office, 1870–1914* (Oxford, 1994).

Phoenix, E., *Northern Nationalism: Nationalist Politics, Partition and the Catholic Minority in Northern Ireland 1890–1940* (Belfast, 1994).

Philips, D., *Crime and Authority in Victorian England: The Black Country, 1835–60* (London, 1977).

Philips, D. and Storch, R., *Policing Provincial England, 1829–1856: The Politics of Reform* (London, 1999).

Phillips, J., 'Popular politics in unreformed England', *Journal of Modern History*, 52 (1980).

Phillips, J., *Electoral Behavior in Unreformed England: Plumpers, Splitters, and Straights* (Princeton, NJ, 1982).

Phillips, J., *The Great Reform Bill in the Boroughs: English Electoral Behaviour 1818–1841* (Oxford, 1992).

Phillips, J., 'Unintended consequences: parliamentary blueprints in the hands of provincial builders', in D. Dean and C. Jones, eds, *Parliament and Locality 1660–1939* (Edinburgh, 1998).

Pierson, S., *Marxism and the Origins of British Socialism: The Struggle for a New Consciousness* (Ithaca, NY, 1973).

Platt, D. C. M., *Finance, Trade and Politics in British Foreign Policy 1815–1914* (Oxford, 1968).

Platt, D. C. M., 'The imperialism of free trade: some reservations', *Economic History Review*, 21 (1968).

Platt, D. C. M., 'Further objections to an "imperialism of free trade", 1830–1860', *Economic History Review*, 22 (1973).

Platt, D. C. M., *Mickey Mouse Numbers in World History* (Basingstoke, 1989).

Pocock, J. G. A., 'British history: a plea for a new subject', *Journal of Modern History*, 47 (1975).

Pocock, J. G. A., 'The limits and divisions of British history: in search of the unknown subject', *American Historical Review*, 87 (1982).

Polanyi, K., *The Great Transformation: The Political and Economic Origins of Our Time* (New York, 1944).

Pollard, S., 'Sheffield and sweet auburn – amenities and living standards in the British industrial revolution: a comment', *Journal of Economic History*, 41 (1981).

Pollard, S., 'Capital exports, 1870–1914: harmful or beneficial?', *Economic History Review*, 38 (1985).

Pooley, C. G. and D'Cruze, S., 'Migration and urbanization in North-West England c.1760–1830', *Social History*, 19 (1994).

Pooley, C. G. and Turnbull, J., *Migration and Mobility in Britain since the Eighteenth Century* (London, 1998).

Pooley, C. G. and Whyte, I. D., eds, *Migrants, Emigrants and Immigrants: A Social History of Migration* (London, 1991).

Poovey, M., *Making a Social Body: British Cultural Formation 1830–1864* (Chicago, 1995).

Porter, A., ed., *The Oxford History of the British Empire*, vol. 3, *The Nineteenth Century* (Oxford, 1999).

Porter, A., 'Trusteeship, anti-slavery, and humanitarianism', in A. Porter, ed., *The Oxford History of the British Empire*, vol. 3, *The Nineteenth Century* (Oxford, 1999).

Porter, B., *The Lion's Share: A Short History of British Imperialism, 1850–1995* (London, 1996).

Porter, R., *Quacks: Fakers and Charlatans in English Medicine* (Stroud, 2000).

Preston, A. and Major, J., *Send a Gunboat! A Study of the Gunboat and its Role in British Policy, 1854–1904* (London, 1967).

Prettejohn, E., ed., *After the Pre-Raphaelites: Art and Aestheticism in Victorian England* (Manchester, 1999).

Price, R., *An Imperial War and the British Working Class: Working-Class Attitudes and Reactions to the Boer War, 1899–1902* (London, 1977).

Price, R., *Labour in British Society: An Interpretative History* (London, 1986).

Price, R., *British Society, 1680–1880: Dynamism, Containment and Change* (Cambridge, 1999).

Prochaska, F. K., *Women and Philanthropy in Nineteenth-Century England* (Oxford, 1980).

Prochaska, F. K., *Royal Bounty: The Making of a Welfare Monarchy* (New Haven, CT, 1995).

Prochaska, F. K., *The Republic of Britain, 1760–2000* (London, 2000).

Pugh, M., *The Making of Modern British Politics 1867–1945* (Oxford, 2002).

Purvis, J., *A History of Women's Education in England* (Milton Keynes, 1991).

Quinault, R., 'Westminster and the Victorian constitution', *Transactions of the Royal Historical Society*, 6th ser., 2 (1992).

Radzinowicz, L. and Hood, R., *A History of English Criminal Law and its Administration from 1750*, vol. 5, *The Emergence of Penal Policy in Victorian and Edwardian England* (London, 1986).

Rafferty, A. M., *The Politics of Nursing Knowledge* (London, 1996).

Rafferty, O. P., *Catholicism in Ulster 1603–1983: An Interpretative History* (Dublin, 1995).

Randall, A., *Before the Luddites: Custom, Community and Machinery in the English Woollen Industry, 1776–1809* (Cambridge, 1991).

Ranft, B., ed., *Technical Change and British Naval Policy 1860–1939* (London, 1977).

Ranlett, J., '"Checking nature's desecration": late-Victorian environmental organisation', *Victorian Studies*, 26 (1983).

Rashid, S., 'Recent literature on Malthus', in W. Thweatt, ed., *Classical Political Economy: A Survey of Recent Literature* (Boston, 1988).

Read, B., *Victorian Sculpture* (New Haven, CT, 1982).

Read, D., *England 1868–1914: The Age of Urban Democracy* (London, 1979).

Reed, M. and Wells, R. A. E., eds, *Class, Conflict and Protest in the English Countryside, 1700–1880* (London, 1990).

Reeder, D., ed., *Educating Our Masters* (Leicester, 1980).

Reid, A. J., *Social Classes and Social Relations in Britain, 1850–1914* (Basingstoke, 1992).

Reiner, R., *The Politics of the Police* (London, 1992).

Reisman, D., *Alfred Marshall's Mission* (Basingstoke, 1990).

Rendall, J., *The Origins of Modern Feminism: Women in Britain, France and the United States, 1780–1860* (Basingstoke, 1985).

Rendall, J., ed., *Equal or Different: Women's Politics, 1800–1914* (Oxford, 1987).

Reynolds, K. D., *Aristocratic Women and Political Society in Victorian Britain* (Oxford, 1998).

Richards, E., *A History of the Highland Clearances* (2 vols, London, 1982 & 1985).

Richards, E., 'Voices of British and Irish migrants in nineteenth-century Australia', in C. G. Pooley and I. D. Whyte, eds, *Migrants, Emigrants and Immigrants: A Social History of Migration* (London, 1991).

Richards, E., *The Highland Clearances* (Edinburgh, 2000).

Richards, T., *The Commodity Culture of Victorian England: Advertising and Spectacle, 1851–1914* (London, 1991).

Richardson, S., ' "Well-neighboured houses": the political networks of elite women, 1780–1860', in K. Gleadle and S. Richardson, eds, *Women in British Politics, 1760–1860: The Power of the Petticoat* (Basingstoke, 2000).

Richardson, W., 'Historians and educationists: the history of education as a field of study in post-war England', *History of Education*, 28 (1999).

Richter, M., *The Politics of Conscience: T. H. Green and His Age* (London, 1964).

Riley, J. C., *Sick not Dead: The Health of British Workingmen during the Mortality Decline* (Baltimore, 1997).

Robb, J., *The Primrose League, 1883–1906* (New York, 1942).

Robbins, K., *Nineteenth-Century Britain: England, Scotland and Wales: The Making of a Nation* (Oxford, 1989).

Robbins, K., *The Eclipse of a Great Power: Modern Britain 1870–1975* (London, 1994).

Robbins, R. and Wolfreys, J., eds, *Victorian Identities: Social and Cultural Formations in Nineteenth-Century Literature* (London, 1996).

Roberts, D., *Victorian Origins of the British Welfare State* (New Haven, CT, 1960).

Roberts, E., *Working Class Barrow and Lancaster 1890–1930* (Lancaster, 1976).

Roberts, R., *The Classic Slum: Salford Life in the First Quarter of the Century* (Manchester, 1971).

Robinson, R. and Gallagher, J., *Africa and the Victorians: The Official Mind of Imperialism* (London, 1961).

Robson, J., *The Improvement of Mankind: The Social and Political Thought of John Stuart Mill* (Toronto, 1968).

Robson, W., ed., *The Collected Works of John Stuart Mill* (Toronto, 1963).

Rodger, R., *Housing in Urban Britain, 1780–1914: Class, Capitalism and Construction* (Cambridge, 1995).

Rodney, W., *How Europe Underdeveloped Africa* (Washington, 1981).

Rogers, H., ' "The prayer, the passion, and the reason" of Eliza Sharples: free-thought, women's rights and republicanism, 1832–52', in E. Yeo, ed., *Radical Femininity: Women's Self-Representation in the Public Sphere* (Manchester, 1998).

Rogers, H., *Women and the People: Authority, Authorship and the Radical Tradition in Nineteenth Century England* (Aldershot, 2000).

Roper, J., *Democracy and Its Critics: Anglo-American Democratic Thought in the Nineteenth Century* (London, 1989).

Roper, M. and Tosh, J., eds, *Manful Assertions: Masculinities in Britain since 1800* (London, 1991).

Rose, J., *The Intellectual Life of the British Working Classes* (New Haven, CT, 2001).

Rose, J. H. et al., eds, *The Cambridge History of the British Empire* (9 vols, Cambridge, 1929–59).

Rose, S., *Limited Livelihoods: Gender and Class in Nineteenth-Century England* (Berkeley, 1991).

Ross, E., ' "Fierce questions and taunts": married life in working-class London, 1870–1914', *Feminist Studies*, 8 (1982).

Ross, E., *Love and Toil: Motherhood in Outcast London, 1870–1918* (Oxford, 1993).

Ross, E., 'Survival networks: women's neighbourhood sharing in London before World War 1', *History Workshop Journal*, 15 (1993).

Rothblatt, S., *The Modern University and its Discontents* (Cambridge, 1997).

Rowbotham, S., *Hidden from History* (London, 1973).

Rubinstein, W. D., *Men of Property: The Very Wealthy in Britain since the Industrial Revolution* (London, 1981).

Rubinstein, W. D., *Britain's Century: A Political and Social History 1815–1905* (London, 1998).

Rudwick, M., *The Great Devonian Controversy: The Shaping of Scientific Knowledge amongst Gentlemanly Specialists* (Chicago, 1985).

Rule, J., 'The property of skill in the period of manufacture', in P. Joyce, ed., *The Historical Meanings of Work* (Cambridge, 1987).

Russell, D., *Popular Music in England, 1815–1914: A Social History* (Manchester, 1987).

Russett, C. E., *Sexual Science: The Victorian Construction of Womanhood* (Cambridge MA, 1989).

Sabel, C. F. and Zeitlin, J., 'Stories, strategies, structures: rethinking historical alternatives to mass production', in C. F. Sabel and J. Zeitlin, eds, *World of Possibilities: Flexibility and Mass Production in Western Industrialization* (Cambridge, 1997).

Said, E., *Orientalism* (London, 1978).

Said, E., *Culture and Imperialism* (London, 1993).

Samuel, R., 'The workshop of the world: steam-power and hand technology in mid-Victorian Britain', *History Workshop Journal*, 3 (1977).

Samuel, R., ed., *Patriotism: The Making and Unmaking of British National Identity* (London, 1989).

Sanderson, M., *The Universities and British Industry, 1850–1970* (London, 1972).

Sanderson, M., *Education, Economic Change and Society in England 1780–1870* (Cambridge, 1995).

Saul, S. B., *Studies in British Overseas Trade, 1870–1914* (Liverpool, 1960).

Saul, S. B., *The Myth of the Great Depression, 1873–1896* (Basingstoke, 1985).

Schaffer, S., 'Late Victorian metrology and its instrumentation: a manufactory of ohms', in R. Bud and S. Cozzens, eds, *Invisible Connections: Instruments, Institutions and Science* (Bellingham, 1992).

Schaffer, S., 'Babbage's intelligence: calculating engines and the factory system', *Critical Inquiry*, 21 (1994).

Schellekens, J., 'Wages, secondary workers, and fertility: a working-class perspective of the fertility transition in England and Wales', *Journal of Family History*, 18 (1993).

Schivelbusch, W., *The Railway Journey: The Industrialization of Time and Space in the Nineteenth Century* (Leamington Spa, 1986).

Schlör, J., *Nights in the Big City: Paris, Berlin, London 1840–1930* (London, 1998).

Schlote, W., *British Overseas Trade from 1700 to the 1930s* (Oxford, 1939).

Schroeder, P. W., *The Transformation of European Politics 1763–1848* (Oxford, 1994).

Schumpeter, J. A., *Imperialism and Social Classes* (Oxford, 1951).

Schumpeter, J. A., *A History of Economic Analysis* (Oxford, 1954).

Schwarzkopf, J., *Women in the Chartist Movement* (Basingstoke, 1991).

Scott, J. W., 'Gender: a useful category of historical analysis', *American Historical Review*, 91 (1986).

Scott, J. W., *Gender and the Politics of History* (New York, 1988).

Searle, G. R., *Entrepreneurial Politics in Mid-Victorian Britain* (Oxford, 1993).

Seccombe, W., 'Patriarchy stabilised: the construction of the male breadwinner model in nine-teenth-century Britain', *Social History*, 11 (1986).

Seccombe, W., *Weathering the Storm: Working-Class Families from the Industrial Revolution to the Fertility Decline* (London, 1993).

Secord, J. A., *Controversy in Victorian Geology: The Cambrian–Silurian Debate* (Princeton, NJ, 1986).

Secord, J. A., *Victorian Sensation: The Extraordinary Publication, Reception, and Secret Authorship of* Vestiges of the Natural History of Creation (Chicago, 2000).

Seligman, E., 'On some neglected economists', *Economic Journal*, 13 (1903).

Sen, A., *The Standard of Living* (Cambridge, 1987).

Sen, A., *Development as Freedom* (New York, 2000).

Senior, H., *Orangeism in Ireland and Britain 1795–1836* (London, 1966).

Sennett, R., *Flesh and Stone: The Body and the City in Western Civilization* (London, 1994).

Seton-Watson, R. W., *Britain in Europe 1789–1914* (Cambridge, 1937).

Seymour, C., *Electoral Reform in England and Wales* (New Haven, 1915).

Shannon, R., *The Crisis of Imperialism 1865–1915* (London, 1976).

Shannon, R., *The Age of Disraeli, 1868–81: The Rise of Tory Democracy* (London, 1992).

Shannon, R., *The Age of Salisbury, 1881–1902: Unionism and Empire* (London, 1996).

Shannon, R., *Gladstone: Heroic Minister, 1865–98* (London, 1999).

Sharpe, J. A., *Crime in Early Modern England, 1550–1750* (Harlow, 1999).

Shattock, J. and Wolff, M., *The Victorian Periodical Press: Samplings and Soundings* (Leicester, 1982).

Shoemaker, R. B., *Gender in English Society 1650–1850* (London, 1998).

Shore, H., *Artful Dodgers: Youth and Crime in Early Nineteenth Century London* (Woodbridge, 1999).

Showalter, E., *The Female Malady: Women, Madness and English Culture, 1830–1980* (London, 1987).

Silver, H., *Education as History: Interpreting Nineteenth- and Twentieth-Century Education* (London, 1983).

Simon, B., *Education and the Labour Movement, 1870–1920* (London, 1965).

Simon, B., *The State and Educational Change: Essays in the History of Education and Pedagogy* (London, 1994).

Simonton, D., *A History of European Women's Work: 1700 to the Present* (London, 1998).

Sinha, M., *Colonial Masculinity: The 'Englishman' and the 'Effeminate Bengali' in the Late Nineteenth-Century* (Manchester, 1995).

Skelley, A. R., *The Victorian Army at Home: The Recruitment and Terms and Conditions of the British Regular, 1859–1899* (London, 1977).

Skilton, D., ed., *The Early and Mid-Victorian Novel* (London, 1993).

Slaven, A., *The Development of the West of Scotland, 1750–1960* (London, 1975).

Sloan, R., *William Smith O'Brien and the Young Ireland Rebellion of 1848* (Dublin, 2000).

Smith, A. D., *Nationalism and Modernism: A Critical Survey of Recent Theories of Nations and Nationalism* (London, 1998).

Smith, C., *The Science of Energy: A Cultural History of Energy Physics in Victorian Britain* (London, 1998).

Smith, C. and Wise, M. N., *Energy and Empire: A Biographical Study of Lord Kelvin* (Cambridge, 1989).

Smith, D., *Aneurin Bevan and the World of South Wales* (Cardiff, 1993).

Smith, E. A., *George IV* (New Haven, CT, 1999).

Smith, F. B., *The Making of the Second Reform Bill* (Cambridge, 1966).

Smith, L., *Victorian Photography, Painting and Poetry: The Enigma of Visibility in Ruskin, Morris and the Pre-Raphaelites* (Cambridge, 1995).

Smith, M. A., *Religion in Industrial Society: Oldham and Saddleworth, 1740–1865* (Oxford, 1994).

Smith, P., *Disraelian Conservatism and Social Reform* (London, 1967).

Smith, P., ed., *Bagehot: The English Constitution* (Cambridge, 2001).

Smith, R., *Schools, Politics and Society: Elementary Education in Wales, 1870–1902* (Cardiff, 1999).

Smout, T. C., *A Century of the Scottish People, 1830–1950* (London, 1987).

Smout, T. C., *Nature Contested: Environmental History in Scotland and Northern England since 1600* (Edinburgh, 2000).

Smyth, J., *Labour in Glasgow 1896–1936* (E. Linton, Scotland, 2000).

Snell, K. D. M., 'Settlement, Poor Law and the rural historian: new approaches and opportunities', *Rural History*, 3 (1992).

Snell, K. D. M. and Ell, P. S., *Rival Jerusalems: The Geography of Victorian Religion* (Cambridge, 2000).

Solow, B. L., *The Land Question and the Irish Economy, 1870–1903* (Cambridge, MA, 1971).

Somervell, D. C., *English Thought in the Nineteenth Century* (London, 1929).

Sparks, C., 'Goodbye, Hildy Johnson: the vanishing "serious press"', in P. Dahlgren and C. Sparks, eds, *Communication and Citizenship: Journalism and the Public Sphere* (London, 1991).

Spiers, E. M., *The Army and Society, 1815–1914* (London, 1980).

Spiers, E. M., *The Late Victorian Army 1868–1902* (Manchester, 1992).

Sraffa, P., ed., *The Works and Correspondence of David Ricardo* (Cambridge, 1951–2).

Stamp, G., *Victorian Buildings of London 1837–1887: An Illustrated Guide* (London, 1980).

Starkey, D., 'The modern monarchy: rituals of privacy and their subversion', in R. Smith and J. S. Moore, eds, *The Monarchy: Fifteen Hundred Years of British Tradition* (London, 1998).

Stedman Jones, G., *Languages of Class: Studies in English Working Class History, 1832–1982* (Cambridge, 1983).

Steedman, C., *Policing the Victorian Community: The Formation of English Provincial Police Forces, 1856–80* (London, 1984).

Steedman, I., 'Introduction', to P. Wicksteed, *An Essay on the Co-ordination of the Laws of Distribution* (London, 1987).

Steedman, I., *Socialism and Marginalism in Economics, 1870–1930* (London, 1990).

Steegman, J., *Victorian Taste: A Study of the Arts and Architecture from 1830–1870* (Cambridge, MA, 1970).

Steele, E. D., *Palmerston and Liberalism, 1856–65* (Cambridge, 1991).

Steiner, Z. S., *Britain and the Origins of the First World War* (Basingstoke, 1977).

Stenberg, K. Y., 'Working-class women in London local politics, 1894–1914', *Twentieth Century British History*, 9 (1998).

Stephen, L., *The English Utilitarians* (London, 1900).

Stephens, W. B., *Education, Literacy and Society: The Geography of Diversity in Provincial England* (Manchester, 1987).

Stephens, W. B., *Education in Britain 1750–1914* (London, 1998).

Stokes, E., *The Peasant Armed: The Indian Revolt of 1857* (Oxford, 1986).

Stoler, A. L., *Carnal Knowledge and Imperial Power: Race and the Intimate in Colonial Rule* (Berkeley, 2002).

Stone, I., *The Global Export of Capital from Great Britain, 1865–1914* (Basingstoke, 1999).

Storch, R. D., 'The plague of blue locusts: police reform and popular resistance in northern England, 1840–1857', *International Review of Social History*, 20 (1975).

Storch, R. D., 'The policeman as domestic missionary: urban discipline and popular culture in northern England, 1850–80', *Journal of Social History*, 9 (1976).

Strachan, H., 'The early Victorian army and the nineteenth-century revolution in government', *English Historical Review*, 85 (1980).

Strachan, H., *Wellington's Legacy: The Reform of the British Army 1830–54* (Manchester, 1984).

Sturt, M., *The Education of the People: A History of Primary Education in England and Wlaes in the Nineteenth Century* (London, 1967).

Sutherland, G., *Policy Making in Elementary Education 1870–1895* (Oxford, 1973).

Sutherland, G., 'Education', in F. M. L. Thompson, ed., *The Cambridge Social History of Britain 1750–1950*, vol. 3, *Social Agencies and Institutions* (Cambridge, 1990).

Sutherland, K., 'Hannah More's counter-revolutionary feminism', in K. Everest, ed., *Revolution in Writing: British Literary Responses to the French Revolution* (Milton Keynes, 1991).

Swift, R. and Gilley, S., eds, *The Irish in the Victorian City* (London, 1985).

Swift, R. and Gilley, S., eds, *The Irish in Britain 1815–1939* (London, 1989).

Sykes, A., *The Rise and Fall of British Liberalism, 1776–1988* (London, 1997).

Szasz, T., *The Manufacture of Madness: A Comparative Study of the Inquisition and the Mental Health Movement* (New York, 1970).

Szostak, R., *The Role of Transportation in the Industrial Revolution: A Comparison of England and France* (Montreal, 1991).

Szreter, S., 'The importance of social intervention in Britain's mortality decline c.1850–1914: a reinterpretation of the role of public health', *Social History of Medicine*, 1 (1988).

Szreter, S., *Fertility, Class and Gender in Britain, 1860–1940* (Cambridge, 1996).

Taylor, A. J., ed., *The Standard of Living in Britain in the Industrial Revolution* (London, 1975).

Taylor, A. J. P., *The Struggle for Mastery in Europe, 1848–1918* (Oxford, 1954).

Taylor, B., *Eve and the New Jerusalem: Socialism and Feminism in the Nineteenth Century* (London, 1983).

Taylor, H[arvey], *A Claim on the Countryside: A History of the British Outdoor Movement* (Edinburgh, 1997).

Taylor, H[oward], 'Rationing crime: the political economy of criminal statistics since the 1850s', *Economic History Review*, 51 (1998).

Taylor, M., 'John Bull and the iconography of public opinion in England c.1712–1929', *Past and Present*, 134 (1992).

Taylor, M., *The Decline of British Radicalism 1847–1860* (Oxford, 1995).

Taylor, M., 'Interests, parties and the state: the urban electorate in England, 1820–72', in J. Lawrence and M. Taylor, eds, *Party, State and Society: Electoral Behaviour in Britain since 1820* (Aldershot, 1997).

Taylor, M., 'Introduction', to W. Bagehot, *The English Constitution* (Oxford, 2001).

Taylor, M. W., *Men versus the State: Herbert Spencer and Late Victorian Individualism* (Oxford, 1992).

Taylor, R., 'Manning the Royal Navy: the reform of the recruiting system, 1852–1862', *Mariner's Mirror*, 44 (1958) and 45 (1959).

Tebbutt, M., *Women's Talk? A Social History of 'Gossip' in Working-Class Neighbourhoods, 1880–1960* (Aldershot, 1995).

Temperley, H. and Penson, L. M., *Foundations of British Foreign Policy: From Pitt (1792) to Salisbury (1902)* (Cambridge, 1938).

Tennyson, A., 'The Palace of Art', *The Poems of Tennyson*, ed. C. Ricks (Harlow, 1969), vol. 1.

Thane, P., 'Women and the Poor Law in Victorian and Edwardian England', *History Workshop Journal*, 6 (1978).

Thane, P., *Foundations of the Welfare State* (London, 1982).

Thane, P., 'Women in the British Labour Party and the construction of state welfare, 1906–1939', in S. Koven and S. Michel, eds, *Mothers of a New World: Maternalist Politics and the Origins of Welfare States* (London, 1993).

Thomas, W., *The Philosophic Radicals: Nine Studies in Theory and Practice, 1817–1841* (Oxford, 1979).

Thompson, A. S., *Imperial Britain: The Empire in British Politics c.1880–1932* (Harlow, 2000).

Thompson, D., *Queen Victoria: Gender and Power* (New York, 1990).

Thompson, D. F., *John Stuart Mill and Representative Government* (Princeton, NJ, 1976).

Thompson, E. P., *The Making of the English Working Class* (London, 1963).

Thompson, E. P., 'Time, work-discipline, and industrial capitalism', *Past and Present*, 38 (1967).

Thompson, E. P., *William Morris: Romantic to Revolutionary* (London, 1977).

Thompson, F. M. L., *English Landed Society in the Nineteenth Century* (London, 1963).

Thompson, F. M. L., ed., *The Rise of Suburbia* (Leicester, 1982).

Thompson, F. M. L., *The Rise of Respectable Society: A Social History of Victorian Britain, 1830–1900* (London, 1988)

Thompson, F. M. L., ed., *The Cambridge Social History of Britain 1750–1950*, vol. 1, *Regions and Communities* (Cambridge, 1990).

Thompson, F. M. L., ed., *The Cambridge Social History of Britain 1750–1950*, vol. 2, *People and their Environment* (Cambridge, 1990).

Thompson, F. M. L., ed., *The Cambridge Social History of Britain 1750–1950*, vol. 3, *Social Agencies and Institutions* (Cambridge, 1990).

Thompson, F. M. L., 'Town and city', in F. M. L. Thompson, ed., *The Cambridge Social History of Britain 1750–1950*, vol. 1, *Regions and Communities* (Cambridge, 1990).

Thompson, F. M. L., 'An anatomy of English agriculture, 1870–1914', in B. A. Holderness and M. E. Turner, eds, *Land, Labour and Agriculture, 1700–1920: Essays for Gordon Mingay* (London, 1991).

Thompson, F. M. L., 'Presidential address: English landed society in the twentieth century' [I–IV], *Transactions of the Royal Historical Society* (1990–3): 'I, prosperity, collapse and survival', 5th ser., 40 (1990); 'II, new poor, new rich', 6th ser., 1 (1991); 'III, self-help and outdoor relief', 6th ser., 2 (1992); 'IV, prestige without power?', 6th ser., 3 (1993).

Thompson, K. A., *Bureaucracy and Church Reform: The Organizational Response of the Church of England to Social Change, 1800–1965* (Oxford, 1970).

Thompson, N., *The Real Rights of Man: Political Economies for the Working Class, 1750–1850* (London, 1998).

Thompson, T., *Edwardian Childhoods* (London, 1981).

Thomson, D., *England in the Nineteenth Century (1815–1914)* (Harmondsworth, 1950).

Thornton, A. P., *The Imperial Idea and Its Enemies: A Study in British Power* (London, 1959).

Thweatt, W., ed., *Classical Political Economy: A Survey of Recent Literature* (Boston, 1988).

Tilly, L. A. and Scott, J. W., *Women, Work and Family* (New York, 1978).

Tobias, J. J., *Crime and Industrial Society in the Nineteenth Century* (London, 1967).

Tomlinson, B. R., 'Empire of the dandelion: ecological imperialism and economic expansion, 1860–1914', *Journal of Imperial and Commonwealth History*, 26 (1998).

Tosh, J., *A Man's Place: Masculinity and the Middle-Class Home in Victorian England* (London, 1999).

Trainor, R. H., *Black Country Elites: The Exercise of Authority in an Industrialized Area, 1830–1900* (Oxford, 1993).

Tranter, N., *Sport, Economy and Society in Britain, 1750–1914* (Cambridge, 1998).

Treuherz, J., *Victorian Painting* (London, 1993).

Trevelyan, G. M., *British History in the Nineteenth Century (1782–1901)* (London, 1927).

Tropp, A., *The Schoolteachers* (London, 1957).

Turnbull, J. and Pooley, C. G., 'Leaving home: the experience of migration from the parental home in Britain since c.1770', *Journal of Family History*, 22 (1997).

Turner, C. B., 'Revivalism and Welsh society in the nineteenth century', in J. Obelkevich, L. Roper and R. Samuel, eds, *Disciplines of Faith: Studies in Religion, Politics and Patriarchy* (London, 1987).

Turner, F., 'The Victorian conflict between science and religion: a professional dimension', in G. Parsons, ed., *Religion in Victorian Britain*, vol. 4, *Interpretations* (Manchester, 1988).

Turner, M. E., *After the Famine: Irish Agriculture 1850–1914* (Cambridge, 1996).

Turner, M. E., 'Agricultural output, income and productivity', in E. J. T. Collins, ed., *The Agrarian History of England and Wales*, vol. 7, *1850–1914* (Cambridge, 2000).

Tuttle, C., 'A revival of the pessimist view: child labour and the industrial revolution', *Research in Economic History*, 18 (1998).

Tyrrell, A., '"Woman's mission" and pressure group politics (1825–1860)', *Bulletin of the John Rylands Library*, 63 (1980).

Valenze, D. M., *Prophetic Sons and Daughters: Female Preaching and Popular Religion in Industrial England* (Princeton, NJ, 1985).

Vallone, L., *Becoming Victoria* (New Haven, CT, 2001).

Van Zanden, J., 'The first "green revolution": the growth of production and productivity in European agriculture, 1870–1914', *Economic History Review*, 44 (1991).

Vaughan, W. E., *Landlords and Tenants in Ireland 1848–1904* (Dublin, 1984).

Vaughan, W. E., *Landlords and Tenants in Mid-Victorian Ireland* (Oxford, 1994).

Vernon, J., *Politics and the People: A Study in English Political Culture c.1815–1867* (Cambridge, 1993).

Vernon, J., ed., *Re-Reading the Constitution: New Narratives in the Political History of England's Long Nineteenth Century* (Cambridge, 1996).

Vickery, A., 'Golden age to separate spheres? A review of the categories and chronology of English women's history', *Historical Journal*, 36 (1993).

Vickery, A., ed., *Women, Privilege and Power: British Politics, 1750 to the Present* (Stanford, 2001).

Victoria, Queen of Great Britain and Ireland, *Leaves from the Journal of Our Life in the Highlands, from 1848 to 1861*, ed. A. Helps (New York, 1868).

Victoria, Queen of Great Britain and Ireland, *More Leaves from the Journal of a Life in the Highlands, from 1862 to 1882* (New York, 1884).

Victoria, Queen of Great Britain and Ireland, *The Letters of Queen Victoria, 1837–61*, ed. A. C. Benson and Viscount Esher (3 vols, London, 1907); *1862–85*, ed. G. E. Buckle (3 vols, London, 1926–8); *1886–1901*, ed. G. E. Buckle (3 vols, London, 1930–2).

Vincent, A. and Plant, R., *Philosophy, Politics and Citizenship: The Life and Thought of British Idealists* (Oxford, 1984).

Vincent, D., *Literacy and Popular Culture: England 1750–1914* (Cambridge, 1989).

Vincent, J., *The Formation of the Liberal Party* (Cambridge, 1965).

Vincent, J., *Pollbooks: How Victorians Voted* (Cambridge, 1967).

Vlaeminke, M., *The English Higher Grade Schools: A Lost Opportunity* (London, 2000).

Vlock, D., *Dickens, Novel Reading and the Victorian Family Magazine* (Basingstoke, 2001).

Von Tunzelmann, G. N., *Steam Power and British Industrialization to 1860* (Oxford, 1978).

Von Tunzelmann, G. N., 'The standard of living debate and optimal economic growth', in J. Mokyr, ed., *The Economics of the Industrial Revolution* (London, 1985).

Voth, H.-J., *Time and Work in England, 1750–1830* (Oxford, 2000).

Voth, H.-J., 'Living standards and the urban environment', in R. C. Floud and P. Johnson, eds, *The Cambridge Economic History of Modern Britain*, vol. 1, *Industrialisation, 1700–1860* (Cambridge, 2003).

Waddams, S. M., *Sexual Slander in Nineteenth-Century England: Defamation in the Ecclesiastical Courts, 1815–1855* (Toronto, 2000).

Waddington, I., *Medical Profession in the Industrial Revolution* (Dublin, 1984).

Waddington, K., *Charity and the London Hospitals 1850–1898* (Woodbridge, Suffolk, 2000).

Wahrman, D., *Imagining the Middle Class: The Political Representation of Class in Britain, c.1780–1840* (Cambridge, 1995).

Walker, B., *Ulster Politics: The Formative Years 1868–86* (Belfast, 1989).

Walker, B., *Dancing to History's Tune: History, Myth and Politics in Ireland* (Belfast, 1996).

Walkowitz, J. R., *Prostitution and Victorian Society: Women, Class and the State* (Cambridge, 1980).

Walkowitz, J. R., *City of Dreadful Delight: Narratives of Sexual Danger in Late-Victorian London* (London, 1992).

Waller, P. J., *Town, City, and Nation: England 1850–1914* (Oxford, 1983).

Waller, P. J., ed., *The English Urban Landscape* (Oxford, 2000).

Walsh, J. D., Haydon, C. and Taylor, S., eds, *The Church of England c.1689–c.1833* (Cambridge, 1993).

Walton, J. K., *The English Seaside Resort: A Social History, 1750–1914* (Leicester, 1983).

Walvin, J., 'Sport, social history and the historian', *British Journal of Sports History*, 1 (1984).

Ward, A. and Gooch, G. P., *The Cambridge History of British Foreign Policy* (Cambridge, 1923).

Ward, D., 'Environs and neighbours in the "two nations": residential differentiation in mid nineteenth-century Leeds', *Journal of Historical Geography*, 6 (1980).

Ward, J. T., *The Conservative Leadership* (London, 1974).

Ward, M., *The Missing Sex: Putting Women into Irish History* (Dublin, 1991).

Ward, P., *Red Flag and Union Jack: Englishness, Patriotism and the British Left* (Woodbridge, 1998).

Ward, W. R., *Religion and Society in England 1790–1850* (London, 1972).

Ware, V., *Beyond the Pale: White Women, Racism and History* (London, 1992).

Warner, J. H., 'The history of science and the sciences of medicine', *Osiris*, 10 (1995).

Warwick, A. C., *Masters of Theory: Cambridge and the Rise of Mathematical Physics* (Chicago, 2003).

Waterman, A., *Revolution, Economics and Religion: Christian Political Economy, 1798–1833* (Cambridge, 1992).

Watson, G., *The English Ideology: Studies in the Language of Victorian Politics* (London, 1973).

Watt, I., *The Rise of the Novel* (London, 1987).

Webb, R. K., *The British Working Class Reader* (London, 1955).

Webb, R. K., *Modern England: From the Eighteenth Century to the Present* (London, 1980)

Webster, C. K., *The Foreign Policy of Lord Castlereagh* (2 vols, London, 1931–4).

Webster, C. K., *The Congress of Vienna, 1814–1815* (London, 1934).

Weeks, J., *Sex, Politics and Society: The Regulation of Sexuality since 1800* (London, 1981).

West, E. G., *Education and the Industrial Revolution* (London, 1975).

West, S., ed., *The Victorians and Race* (London, 1997).

Weston, C. C., *The House of Lords and Ideological Politics: Lord Salisbury's Referendal Theory and the Conservative Party, 1846–1922* (Philadephia, 1995).

Whatley, C. A., *Scottish Society, 1707–1830: Beyond Jacobitism towards Industrialisation* (Manchester, 2000).

Whitaker, J., 'Alfred Marshall', in J. Eatwell, M. Milgate and P. Newman, eds, *The New Palgrave: A Dictionary of Economic Thought*, vol. 3 (London, 1987).

Whyte, I. D., *Migration and Society in Britain 1550–1830* (Basingstoke, 2000).

Wickham, E. R., *Church and People in an Industrial City* (London, 1957).

Wiener, J. H., *The War of the Unstamped: A History of the Movement to Repeal the British Newspaper Tax, 1830–1836* (Ithaca, NY, 1969).

Wiener, J. H., *A Descriptive Finding List of Unstamped British Periodicals, 1830–1836* (London, 1970).

Wiener, J. H., ed., *Papers for the Millions: The New Journalism in Britain, 1850s to 1914* (New York, 1988).

Wiener, M. J., *English Culture and the Decline of the Industrial Spirit, 1850–1980* (Cambridge, 1981).

Wiener, M. J., *Reconstructing the Criminal: Culture, Law and Policy in England, 1830–1914* (Cambridge, 1990).

Wiener, M. J., 'The Victorian criminalisation of men', in P. Spierenburg, ed., *Men and Violence: Gender, Honor, and Rituals in Modern Europe and America* (Columbus, OH, 1998).

Williams, C., *Democratic Rhondda: Politics and Society, 1885–1951* (Cardiff, 1996).

Williams, D., *John Frost: A Study in Chartism* (Cardiff, 1939).

Williams, D., *The Rebecca Riots: A Study in Agrarian Discontent* (Cardiff, 1955).

Williams, E., *Capitalism and Slavery* (Chapel Hill, 1944).

Williams, G. A., 'The Merthyr of Dic Penderyn', in G. Williams, ed., *Merthyr Politics: The Making of a Working-Class Tradition* (Cardiff, 1966).

Williams, G. A., *When Was Wales? A History of the Welsh* (London, 1985).

Williams, R[aymond], *The Long Revolution* (London, 1961).

Williams, R[aymond], *Keywords* (London, 1983).

Williams, R[ichard], *The Contentious Crown: Public Discussion of the British Monarchy in the Reign of Queen Victoria* (Aldershot, 1997).

Williams, S. C., *Religious Belief and Popular Culture in Southwark c.1880–1939* (Oxford, 1999).

Williamson, J. G., 'Urban disamenities, dark satanic mills, and the British standard of living debate', *Journal of Economic History*, 41 (1981).

Williamson, J. G., *Did British Capitalism Breed Inequality?* (London, 1985).

Winch, D., *Riches and Poverty: An Intellectual History of Political Economy, 1750–1834* (Cambridge, 1996).

Winch, D. and O'Brien, P. K., eds, *The Political Economy of British Historical Experience, 1688–1914* (Oxford, 2002).

Winks, R. W., ed., *The Historiography of the British Empire–Commonwealth: Trends, Interpretations and Resources* (Durham, NC, 1966).

Winks, R. W., ed., *The Oxford History of the British Empire*, vol. 5, *Historiography* (Oxford, 1999).

Winter, A., *Mesmerized: Powers of Mind in Victorian Britain* (Chicago, 1998).

Winton, J., *Hurrah for the Life of a Sailor! Life on the Lower-deck of the Victorian Navy* (London, 1977).

Withers, C. W., 'Highland migration to Dundee, Perth and Stirling 1783–1891', *Journal of Historical Geography*, 11 (1985).

Witz, A., *Professions and Patriarchy* (London, 1992).

Wohl, A., *Endangered Lives: Public Health in Victorian Britain* (London, 1983).

Wolfe, P., 'Imperialism and history: a century of theory, from Marx to postcolonialism', *American Historical Review*, 102 (1997).

Wolffe, J., *The Protestant Crusade in Great Britain 1829–1860* (Oxford, 1991).

Wolffe, J., *God and Greater Britain: Religion and National Life in Britain and Ireland 1843–1945* (London, 1994).

Wolffe, J., ed., *Religion in Victorian Britain*, vol. 5, *Culture and Empire* (Manchester, 1997).

Wolffe, J., *Great Deaths: Grieving, Religion, and Nationhood in Victorian and Edwardian Britain* (Oxford, 2000).

Woodham-Smith, C., *The Great Hunger: Ireland 1845–1849* (London, 1962).

Woodward, L., *The Age of Reform 1815–1870* (Oxford, 1962).

Worboys, M., *Spreading Germs: Disease Theories and Medical Practice in Britain, 1865–1900* (Cambridge, 2000).

Wright, D., 'Family strategies and the institutional confinement of "idiot" children in Victorian England', *Journal of Family History*, 23 (1998).

Wright, F., *Two Lands on One Soil: Ulster Politics before Home Rule* (Dublin, 1996).

Wright, T. W., *The Religion of Humanity: The Impact of Comtean Positivism on Victorian Britain* (Cambridge, 1986).

Wrigley, C., ed., *A Companion to Early Twentieth-Century Britain* (Oxford, 2003).

Wrigley, E. A., *Continuity, Chance and Change: The Character of the Industrial Revolution in England* (Cambridge, 1990).

Wrigley, E. A. and Schofield, R. S., *The Population History of England, 1541–1871: A Reconstruction* (London, 1981).

Yates, N., *Anglican Ritualism in Victorian Britain 1830–1910* (Oxford, 1999).

Yeo, E., ed., *Radical Femininity: Women's Self-Representation in the Public Sphere* (Manchester, 1998).

Young, L., *Middle-Class Culture in the Nineteenth Century: America, Australia and Britain* (Basingstoke, 2002).

Young, R. J. C., *Postcolonialism: An Historical Introduction* (Oxford, 2001).

Yuval-Davis, N., *Gender and Nation* (London, 1997).

Zedner, L., *Women, Crime, and Custody in Victorian England* (Oxford, 1991).

Zeitlin, J., 'Between flexibility and mass production: strategic ambiguity and selective adaptation in the British engineering industry, 1830–1914', in C. F. Sabel and J. Zeitlin, eds, *World of Possibilities: Flexibility and Mass Production in Western Industrialization* (Cambridge, 1997).

Zelinsky, W., 'The hypothesis of the mobility transition', *Geographical Review*, 61 (1971).

Ziegler, P., *King William IV* (London, 1971).

Zon, B., ed., *Nineteenth-Century British Music Studies* (2 vols, Aldershot, 1999 & 2001).

Index